FOUNDATIONS OF GENETIC ALGORITHMS • 6

THE MORGAN KAUFMANN SERIES IN EVOLUTIONARY COMPUTATION

Series Editor David B. Fogel

Swarm Intelligence
James Kennedy and Russell C. Eberhart, with Yuhui Shi

Illustrating Evolutionary Computation with Mathematica
Christian Jacob

Evolutionary Design by Computers
Edited by Peter J. Bentley

Genetic Programming III: Darwinian Invention and Problem Solving
John R. Koza, Forrest H. Bennett III, David Andre, and Martin A. Keane

Genetic Programming: An Introduction
Wolfgang Banzhaf, Peter Nordin, Robert E. Keller, and Frank D. Francone

FOGA Foundations of Genetic Algorithms Volume 5
Edited by Wolfgang Banzhaf and Colin Reeves

FOGA Foundations of Genetic Algorithms Volume 4
Edited by Richard K. Belew and Michael D. Vose

FOGA Foundations of Genetic Algorithms Volume 3
Edited by L. Darrell Whitley and Michael D. Vose

FOGA Foundations of Genetic Algorithms Volume 2
Edited by L. Darrell Whitley

FOGA Foundations of Genetic Algorithms Volume 1
Edited by Gregory J. E. Rawlins

Proceedings

GECCO Proceedings of the Genetic and Evolutionary Computation Conference (GECCO), the Joint Meeting of the International Conference on Genetic Algorithms (ICGA) and the Annual Genetic Programming Conference (GP)
GECCO 2000
GECCO 1999

GP International Conference on Genetic Programming
GP 4, 1999
GP 3, 1998
GP 2, 1997

ICGA International Conference on Genetic Algorithms
ICGA 7, 1997
ICGA 6, 1995
ICGA 5, 1993
ICGA 4, 1991
ICGA 3, 1989

Forthcoming

Blondie24: The Fascinating Story of How a Computer Taught Herself to Win at Checkers
David B. Fogel

FOGA Foundations of Genetic Algorithms Volume 6
Edited by Worthy N. Martin and William M. Spears

Creative Evolutionary Systems
Edited by Peter J. Bentley and David W. Corne

Evolutionary Computation in Bioinformatics
Edited by Gary Fogel and David W. Corne

FOUNDATIONS OF GENETIC ALGORITHMS•6

EDITED BY

WORTHY N. MARTIN

AND

WILLIAM M. SPEARS

MORGAN KAUFMANN PUBLISHERS

AN IMPRINT OF ACADEMIC PRESS

A Harcourt Science and Technology Company

SAN FRANCISCO SAN DIEGO NEW YORK BOSTON

LONDON SYDNEY TOKYO

Senior Acquisitions Editor Denise E. M. Penrose
Assistant Developmental Editor Marilyn Alan
Publishing Services Manager Scott Norton
Associate Production Editor Marnie Boyd
Editorial Coordinator Emilia Thiuri
Cover Design Susan M. Sheldrake
Printer Edwards Brothers, Inc.

Morgan Kaufmann Publishers, Inc.
340 Pine Street, Sixth Floor
San Francisco, CA 94104-3205, USA
http://www.mkp.com

ACADEMIC PRESS
A Harcourt Science and Technology Company
525 B Street, Suite 1900
San Diego, CA 92101-4495, USA
http://www.academicpress.com

Academic Press
Harcourt Place, 32 Jamestown Road,
London, NW1 7BY, United Kingdom
http://www.academicpress.com

Printed in the United States of America

06 05 04 03 02 5 4 3 2 1

ISSN 1081-6593
ISBN 1-55860-734-x

This book is printed on acid-free paper.

FOGA–2000

THE PROGRAM COMMITTEE

Emile Aarts, *Philips Research Laboratories, Netherlands*
Lee Altenberg, *Maui High Performance Computing Center, USA*
Thomas Bäck, *University of Dortmund, Germany*
Wolfgang Banzhaf, *University of Dortmund, Germany*
Hans-Georg Beyer, *University of Dortmund, Germany*
Lashon Booker, *MITRE Corporation, USA*
Joseph Culberson, *University of Alberta, Canada*
Robert Daley, *University of Pittsburgh, USA*
Kenneth De Jong, *George Mason University, USA*
Kalyan Deb, *Indian Institute of Technology, India*
Marco Dorigo, *Université Libre de Bruxelles, Belgium*
Larry Eshelman, *Philips Research Laboratories, USA*
David Fogel, *Natural Selection Inc., USA*
Attilio Giordana, *University of Torino, Italy*
David Goldberg, *University of Illinois, USA*
John Grefenstette, *George Mason University, USA*
William Hart, *Sandia National Laboratory, USA*
Jeffrey Horn, *Northern Michigan University, USA*
Gary Koehler, *University of Florida, USA*
William Langdon, *Centrum voor Wiskunde en Informatica, Netherlands*
Bernard Manderick, *Free University of Brussels, Belgium*
Zbigniew Michalewicz, *University of North Carolina, USA*
Heinz Mühlenbein, *GMD National Research Center, Germany*
Una-May O'Reilly, *MIT AI Laboratory, USA*
Riccardo Poli, *University of Birmingham, UK*
Adam Prügel-Bennett, *University of Southampton, UK*
Soraya Rana-Stevens, *BBN Technologies, USA*
Colin Reeves, *Coventry University, UK*
Jonathan Rowe, *De Montfort University, UK*
Lorenza Saitta, *University of Torino, Italy*
David Schaffer, *Philips Research Laboratories, USA*
Marc Schoenauer, *École Polytechnique, France*
Hans-Paul Schwefel, *University of Dortmund, Germany*
Jonathan Shapiro, *University of Manchester, UK*
Robert Smith, *University of the West, England, UK*
Stephen Smith, *Carnegie-Mellon University, USA*
Michael Vose, *Colorado State University, USA*
Karsten Weicker, *University of Stuttgart, Germany*
Nicole Weicker, *University of Stuttgart, Germany*
Darrell Whitley, *Colorado State University, USA*
Alden Wright, *University of Montana, USA*

Contents

$$\oint_{90}^{00} g(a)$$

FOGA 2000

Introduction

The 2000 Foundations of Genetic Algorithms (FOGA-6) workshop was the sixth biennial meeting in this series of workshops. From the beginning, FOGA was conceived as a way of exploring and focusing on theoretical issues related to genetic algorithms (GAs). It has hence expanded to include the general field of evolutionary computation (EC), including evolution strategies (ES), evolutionary programming (EP), genetic programming (GP), and other population-based search techniques or evolutionary algorithms (EAs). FOGA now especially encourages submissions from members of other communities, such as mathematicians, physicists, population geneticists, and evolutionary biologists, in the hope of providing radically novel theoretical approaches to the analysis of evolutionary computation.

One of the strengths of the FOGA format is the emphasis on having a small relaxed workshop with very high quality presentations. To provide a pleasant and relaxing atmosphere, FOGA-6 was held in the charming city of Charlottesville, VA. To provide the quality, submissions went through a double-review process, conducted by highly qualified reviewers. Of the 30 submissions, 17 were accepted for presentation and are presented in this volume. Hence, the quality of the papers in this volume is considerably higher than the quality of papers generally encountered in workshops. FOGA-6 also had two invited talks. The first was given by David H. Wood of the University of Delaware. Entitled, *Can You Use a Population Size of a Million Million Million*, David's excellent talk concentrated on the connections between DNA and evolutionary computation, providing a provocative way to start the workshop. Later in the workshop, Kenneth A. De Jong of George Mason University gave an extremely useful outline of where we are with respect to evolutionary computation theory and where we need to go, in his talk entitled, *Future Research Directions*.

One common problem with the empirical methodology often used in the EA community occurs when the EA is carefully tuned to outperform some other algorithm on a few ad hoc problems. Unfortunately, the results of such studies typically have only weak predictive value regarding the performance of EAs on new problems. A better methodology is to identify characteristics of problems (e.g., epistasis, deception, multimodality) that affect

EA performance, and to then use *test-problem generators* to produce random instances of such problems, with those characteristics.

We are pleased to present a FOGA volume containing a large number of papers that focus on the issue of problem characteristics and how they affect EA performance. D.V. Arnold and H.-G. Beyer (*Local Performance of the $(\mu/\mu_I, \lambda)$-ES in a Noisy Environment*) examine the characteristic of noise and show how this affects the performance of multi-parent evolution strategies. R.A. Watson (*Analysis of Recombinative Algorithms on a Non-Separable Building-Block Problem*) examines an interesting class (even if somewhat restricted) of problems which have non-separable building blocks and compares the performance of GAs with a recombinative hill-climber. K.D. Mathias, L.J. Eshelman, and J.D. Schaffer (*Niches in NK-Landscapes*) provide an in-depth comparison of GAs to other algorithms on NK-Landscape problems showing areas of superior GA performance. R.E. Smith and J.E. Smith (*New Methods for Tunable, Random Landscapes*) further generalize the class of NK-Landscape problems by introducing new parameters – the number of epistatic partitions P, a relative scale S of lower- and higher-order effects in the partitions, and the correlation R between lower- and higher-order effects in the partitions.

Some papers address issues pertaining to more arbitrary landscapes. D. Whitley, L. Barbulescu, and J.-P. Watson (*Local Search and High Precision Gray Codes: Convergence Results and Neighborhoods*) show how the neighborhood structure of landscapes is affected by the use of different coding mechanisms, such as Gray and Binary codes. C.R. Reeves (*Direct Statistical Estimation of GA Landscape Properties*) gives techniques for providing direct statistical estimates of the number of attractors that exist for the GA population, in the hopes that this will provide a measure of GA difficulty. M.J. Oates and D. Corne (*Overcoming Fitness Barriers in Multi-Modal Search Spaces*) show that EAs have certain performance features that appear over a range of different problems. Finally, D. Naudts and I. Landrieu (*Comparing Population Mean Curves*) point out that it is often difficult to compare EA performance over different problems, since different problems have different fitness ranges. In response they provide a renormalization that allows one to compare population mean curves across very different problems.

Other papers in this volume concentrate more on the dynamics of the algorithms per se, or on components of those algorithms. For example, A.H. Wright and J.E. Rowe (*Continuous Dynamical System Models of Steady-State Genetic Algorithms*) construct discrete-time and continuous-time models of steady-state evolutionary algorithms, examining their fixed points and their asymptotic stability. R. Poli (*Recursive Conditional Schema Theorem, Convergence and Population Sizing in Genetic Algorithms*) extends traditional schema analyses in order to predict with a known probability whether the number of instances of a schema at the next generation will be above a given threshold. P. Albuquerque and C. Mazza (*Mutation-Selection Algorithm: A Large Deviation Approach*) provide a mathematical analysis of the convergence of an EA-like algorithm composed of Boltzmann selection and mutation, based on the probabilistic theory of large deviations. S. Droste, T. Jansen, and I. Wegener (*Dynamic Parameter Control in Simple Evolutionary Algorithms*) examine methods of dynamic parameter control and rigorously prove that such methods can greatly speed up optimization for simple (1+1) evolutionary algorithms. W.M. Spears (*The Equilibrium and Transient Behavior of Mutation and Recombination*) analyzes the transient behavior of mutation and recombination in the absence of selection, tying the more conventional schema analyses with the theory of recombination distributions.

Finally, in a related paper, A. Prügel-Bennett (*The Mixing Rate of Different Crossover Operators*) also examines recombination in the absence of selection, showing how different recombination operators affect the rate of mixing in a population

This volume is fortunate to have papers that address issues and concepts not commonly found in FOGA proceedings. The first, by K. Weicker and N. Weicker (*Burden and Benefits of Redundancy*), explores how different techniques for introducing redundancy into a representation affects schema processing, mutation, recombination, and performance. F.J. Burbowski (*Evolutionary Optimization Through PAC Learning*) introduces a novel population-based algorithm referred to as the 'Rising Tide Algorithm,' which is then analyzed using techniques from the PAC learning community. The goal here is to show that evolutionary optimization techniques can fall under the analytically rich environment of PAC learning. Finally, T. Kovacs (*Towards a Theory of Strong Overgeneral Classifiers*) discusses the issues of overgeneralization in traditional learning classifier systems – these issues also affect traditional EAs that attempt to learn rule sets, Lisp expressions, and finite-state automata. The only other classifier system paper in a FOGA proceedings was in the first FOGA workshop in 1990.

All in all, we believe the papers in this volume exemplify the strengths of FOGA – the exploitation of previous techniques and ideas, merged with the exploration of novel views and methods of analysis. We hope to see FOGA continue for many further generations!

Worthy N. Martin
University of Virginia

William M. Spears
Naval Research Laboratory

Ode
Beethoven

Overcoming Fitness Barriers in Multi-Modal Search Spaces

Martin J Oates
BT Labs, Adastral Park, Martlesham Heath, Suffolk, England, IP5 3RE

David Corne
Dept of Computer Science, University of Reading, Reading, RG6 6AY

Abstract

In order to test the suitability of an evolutionary algorithm designed for real-world application, thorough parameter testing is needed to establish parameter sensitivity, solution quality reliability, and associated issues. One approach is to produce 'performance profiles', which display performance measures against a variety of parameter settings. Interesting and robust features have recently been observed in performance profiles of an evolutionary algorithm applied to a real world problem, which have also been observed in the performance profiles of several other problems, under a wide variety of conditions. These features are essentially the existence of several peaks and troughs, indicating a range of locally optimal mutation rates in terms of (a measure of) convergence time. An explanation of these features is proposed, which involves the identification of three phases of search behaviour, where each phase is identified with an interval of mutation rates for non-adaptive evolutionary algorithms. These phases repeat cyclically as mutation rate is increased, and the onsets of certain phases seem to coincide with the availability of certain types of mutation event. We briefly discuss future directions and possible implications for these observations.

1 INTRODUCTION

The demands of real-world optimization problems provide the evolutionary algorithm researcher with several challenges. One of the key challenges is that industry needs to feel confident about the speed, reliability, and robustness of EA-based methods [1,4,5,8]. In particular, these issues must be addressed on a case by case basis in respect of tailored

EA-based approaches to specific problems. A standard way to address these issues is, of course, to empirically test the performance of a chosen tailored EA against a suite of realistic problems and over a wide range of parameter and /or strategy settings.

Certainly, there are several applications where such a thorough analysis is not strictly necessary. However, where the EA is designed for use in near-real time applications and/or is expected to perform within a given 'quality of service' constraint, substantial testing and validation of the algorithm is certainly required. An example of a problem of this type, called the Adaptive Distributed Database Management Problem (ADDMP), is reported in [13,14,16].

In order to provide suitably thorough evaluation of the performance of EAs on the ADDMP, substantial experiments have been run to generate *performance profiles*. A performance profile is a plot of 'mean evaluations exploited' (the z axis) over a grid defining combinations of population size and mutation rate (the x and y axes). See Figure 1 for an example, with several others in [13,14,16]. 'Mean evaluations exploited' is essentially a measure of convergence time – that is, the time taken (in terms of number of evaluations) for the EA to first find the best solution it happens to find in a single trial run. However we do not call it 'convergence time', since it does not correspond, for example, to fixation of the entire population at a particular fitness value. It is recognised that this measure is only of real significance if its variation is low. The choice of mean evaluations exploited as a performance measure is guided by the industrial need for speed. The alternative measure would of course be 'best-fitness found', but we also need to carefully consider the speed of finding the solution. With reference also to the standard mean-fitness plot, an evaluations-exploited performance profile indicates not only whether adequate fitness can be delivered within the time limit at certain parameter settings, but whether or not we can often expect good solutions well before the time limit – this is of course important and exploitable in near real-time applications.

A single (x,y,z) point in a performance profile corresponds to the mean evaluations exploited (z) over 50 (unless otherwise stated) trial runs with mutation rate set to x and population size set to y. An entire performance profile typically contains several hundred such points, An important feature associated with a performance profile is the time-limit (again, in terms of number of evaluations) given to individual trial runs. A performance profile with a time limit of 20,000 evaluations, for example, consumes in total around half a billion evaluations.

Although a very time consuming enterprise, plotting performance profiles for the ADDMP has yielded some interesting features which has prompted further investigation. As discussed in [13], the original aim has been served in that performance profiles of the ADDMP reveal suitably wide regions of parameter space in which the EA delivers solutions with reliable speed and quality. This initial finding has been sufficiently convincing, for example, to enable maintained funding for further study towards adoption of this EA for live applications (this work is currently at the demonstrator stage). Beyond these basic issues, however, performance profiles on the ADDMP have yielded robust and unexpected features, which have consistently appeared in other problems which have now been explored. The original naïve expectation was that the profile would essentially reveal a 'well' with its lowest points (corresponding to fast convergence to good solutions) corresponding to ideal parameter choices. What was unexpected was that beyond this well (towards the right – higher mutation rates) there seemed to be an additional well, corresponding to locally good but higher mutation rates yielding fast convergence. Essentially, we expected profiles to be similar in structure to the area between mutation rate = 0 and the second peak to the right in Figure 1; however, instead we tended to find further local structure beyond this second peak.

Hence, the performance profile of the ADDMP seemed to reveal two locally optimal mutation rates in terms of fast and reliable convergence to good solutions. Concerned that this may simply have been an artefact of the chosen EA and the chosen test problems, several further performance profiles were generated which used different time limits, quite different EA designs, and different test problems. These studies revealed that the multimodality of the performance profile seemed to be a general feature of evolutionary search [16–19].

Recently, we have looked further into the multimodal features in the performance profiles of a range of standard test problems, and looked into the positions of the features with respect to the variation in the evaluations exploited measure, and also mean fitness. This has yielded the suggestion that there are identifiable *phases* of search behaviour which change and repeat as we increase the mutation rate, and that an understanding of these phases could underlay an understanding of the multimodality in performance profiles. Note that these phases are not associated with intervals of time in a single trial run, but with intervals of parameter space. Hence a single run of a particular (non-adaptive) EA operates in a particular phase.

In this article, we describe these observations of phase-based behaviour in association with multimodal performance profiles, considering a range of test problems. In particular, we explore a possible explanation of the phase behaviour in terms of the frequencies of particular mutation events available as we change the mutation rate. In section 2 we describe some background and preliminary studies in more detail, setting the stage for the explorations in this article. Section 3 then describes the main test problem we focus on, Watson et al's H-IFF problem [21], and describes the phase-based behaviour exhibited by H-IFF performance profiles. In section 4 we set out a simple model to explain phase onsets in terms of the frequencies with which certain specific types of mutation event become available as we increase the mutation rate. The model is investigated with respect to the H-IFF performance profile and found to have some explanatory power, whilst actual fitness distributions are explored in section 5. Section 6 then investigates whether similar effects occur on other problems, namely Kauffman NK landscapes [6] and the tuneable Royal Staircase problem [11,12], and explores the explanatory power of the 'mutation-event' based explanation on these problems. A discussion and conclusions appear in sections 7 and 8 respectively.

2 PRELIMINARY OBSERVATION OF CYCLIC PHASE BEHAVIOUR IN PERFORMANCE PROFILES

In recent studies of the performance profile of the ADDMP [13,14], Watson et al's H-IFF problem [21], Kauffman NK landscapes [6] and the tuneable Royal Staircase problem [11], as well as simple MAX-ONES, a cyclic tri-phase behaviour has been observed [18,19], where phases correspond to intervals on the mutation rate axis. The phases were characterised in terms of three key features: evaluations exploited, its variation, and mean fitness. In what has been called Phase A, evaluations exploited rises as its variation decreases, while mean fitness gradually rises. This seems to be a 'discovery' phase, within which, as mutation rate rises, the EA is able to increasingly exploit a greater frequency of useful mutations becoming available to it. In Phase B, evaluations exploited falls, while its variation stays low, and mean fitness remains steady. This seems to be a tuning phase, wherein the increasing frequency with which useful mutations are becoming available serves to enable the EA to converge more quickly. This is followed, however, by Phase C, where evaluations exploited starts to rise again, and its variation becomes quite high. In this phase, it seems that the EA has broken through a 'fitness barrier', aided by the sudden availability of mutation events (eg: a significant number of two-gene mutations) which were unavailable in previous phases. The end of Phase C corresponds with the onset of a new Phase A in which the newly available mutation events are beginning to deliver an improved of a new Phase A, during which the EA makes increasing use of the mutations newly available to (over the previous Phase A) fitness more and more reliably. Depending strongly on the problem at hand, these phases can be seen to repeat cyclically.

Figure 2, described later in more detail, provides an example of this behaviour, which was reported on for H-IFF in [18] and for other uni- and multi-modal search spaces in [19]. Whilst these publications voiced some tentative ideas to explain the phase onsets and their positions, no analysis nor detailed explanation was offered. Our current hypothesis is essentially that these phases demonstrate that the number of '*k*-gene' mutations that can be usefully exploited *remains constant* over certain bands of mutation rate. Hence, as the mutation rate is increased within Phase B, for example, search simply needs to proceed until a certain number of *k*-gene mutations have occurred (k=1 for the first Phase B, 2 for the second Phase B, and so on). So, the total number of evaluations used will fall as the mutation rate increases. According to this hypothesis, the onset of Phase C represents a mutation rate at which k+1-gene mutations are becoming available in numbers significant enough to be exploited towards, at first unreliably, delivering a better final fitness value. The next Phase A begins when the new best fitness begins to be found with a significant reliability, and becomes increasingly so as mutation rate is further increased.

In this paper, we analyse the data from the experiments reported in [18, 19] in closer detail, and consider the expected and used numbers of specific types of mutation event. Next, we begin by looking more closely at the H-IFF performance profile.

3 THE H-IFF PERFORMANCE PROFILE

Watson et al's Hierarchical If and only If problem (H-IFF) [21,22] was devised to explore the performance of search strategies employing crossover operators to find and combine 'building blocks' of a decomposable, but potentially contradictory nature. The fitness of a potential solution to this problem is defined to be the sum of weighted, aligned blocks of either contiguous 1's or 0's and can be described by :

$$f(B) = \begin{cases} 1, & \text{if } |B| = 1 \\ |B| + f(B_L) + f(B_R), & \text{if } (|B| > 1) \text{ and } (\forall i \{b_i = 0\} \text{ or } \forall i \{b_i = 1\}), \\ f(B_L) + f(B_R), & \text{otherwise} \end{cases}$$

where B is a block of bits, $\{b_1, b_2, \ldots b_n\}$, $|B|$ is the size of the block=n, b_i is the *i*th element of B, and B_L and B_R are the left and right halves of B (i.e. $B_L = \{b_1, \ldots b_{n/2}\}$, $B_R = \{b_{n/2+1}, \ldots b_n\}$. n must be an integer power of 2.

This produces a search landscape in which 2 global optima exist, one as a string of all 1s, the other of all 0's. However a single mutation from either of these positions produces a much lower fitness. Secondary optima exist at strings of 32 contiguous 0's followed by 32 contiguous 1's (for a binary string of length 64) and vice versa. Again, further sub-optima occur at 16 contiguous 0's followed by 48 contiguous 1's etc. Watson showed that hillclimbing performs extremely badly on this problem [22].

To establish a performance profile for a simple evolutionary search technique on this problem, a set of tests were run using a simple EA (described shortly) over a range of population sizes (20 through 500) and mutation rates (1e-7 rising exponentially through to 0.83), noting the fitness of the best solution found, and the number of evaluations taken to first find it out of a limit of 1 million evaluations. Each trial was repeated 50 times and the mean number of evaluations used is shown in Figure 1. This clearly shows a multi-modal performance profile, particularly at lower population sizes, and is an extension of the number of features of the profile first seen in [17] in which a clear tri-modal profile was first published on the H-IFF problem with an evaluation limit of only 20,000 evaluations. Previous studies of various instances of the ADDMP and One Max problem [15,16] (also limited to only 20,000 evaluations) had shown only bi-modal profiles.

Unless otherwise stated, all EAs used within this paper are steady state; employing one point crossover [5] at a probability of 1.0; single, three-way tournament selection [4] (where the resulting child automatically replaces the poorest member of the tournament); and 'per gene' New Random Allele (NRA) mutation at a fixed rate throughout the run of 1 million evaluations (NRA mutation is used for consistency with earlier studies on the ADDMP, where a symbolic k-ary representation is used rather than a binary one). Mutation rates varied from 1 E-7 through to 0.83 usually doubling every 4 points creating up to 93 sampled rates over 7 orders of magnitude. All experiments are repeated 50 times with the same parameter values but with different, randomly generated initial populations. Further experiments with Generational, Elitist, Breeder strategies [9] and Uniform crossover [20] are also yielding similar results.

Figure 2, shows detailed results on the H-IFF problem at a population size of 20, superimposing plots of mean evaluations used and its co-efficient of variation (standard deviation over the 50 runs divided by the mean). Figure 3 plots the 'total mutations used' (being the product of the mutation rate, the mean number of evaluations used and the chromosome length) and mean fitness, the mutation axis here being a factor of 4 times more detailed than in Figure 1. These clearly show a multi-peaked performance profile with peaks in the number of evaluations used occurring at mutation rates of around 1.6 E-6, 1.6 E-3, 5.2 E-2 and 2.1 E-1. These results seemed to indicate that the dynamics of the performance profile yield a repeating three-phase structure, with the phases characterised in terms of the combined behaviour of mean number of evaluations exploited, its variation, and mean fitness of best solution found, as the mutation rate increases.

In Phase A, evaluations exploited rises with decreasing variation, while mean fitness also rises. This seems to be a 'Delivery' phase, in which the rise in mutation rate is gradually

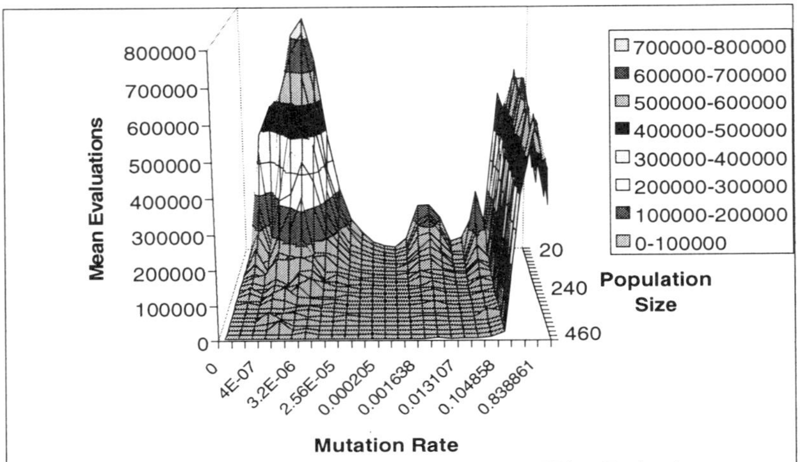

Figure 1 - Mean Evaluations on H-IFF 64 at 1 Million Evaluations

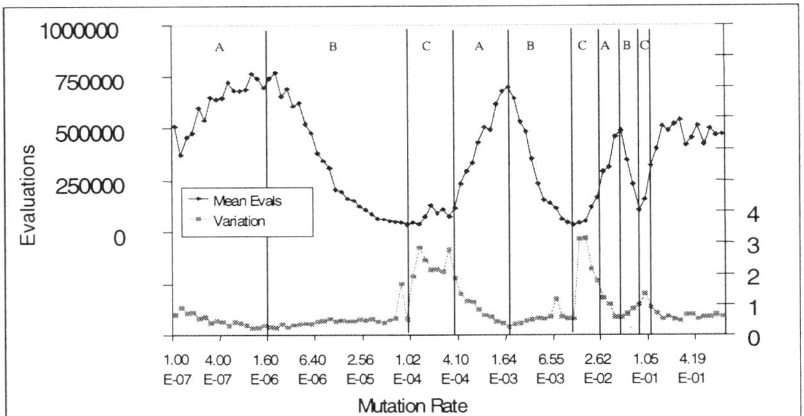

Figure 2 – Mean Evaluations and Variation at 1 Million evaluations for pop size = 20

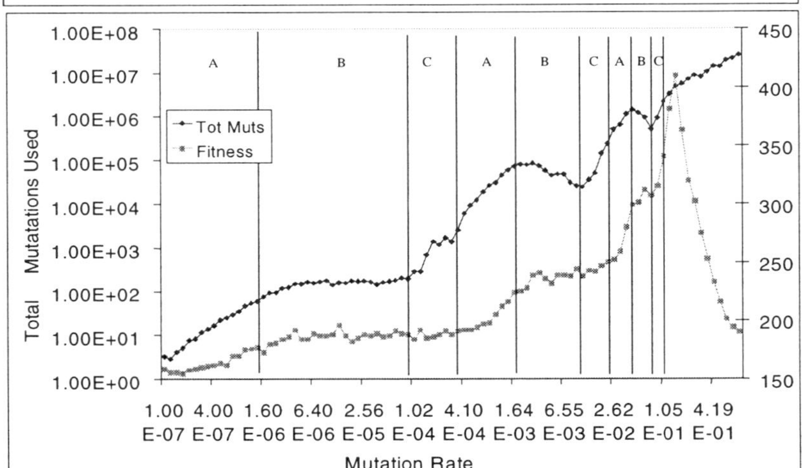

Figure 3 – Mutations used and Fitness at 1 Million evaluations at pop size = 20

delivering more and more of the material needed for the EA to reliably deliver a certain level of mean fitness. In Phase B, mean fitness stays level and evaluations exploited starts to fall, with little change in variation. This seems to be a 'Tuning' phase, in which the needed material is being delivered more and more quickly, but the level of mutation is not yet high enough to provide the EA with the opportunity of reliably reaching better optima. In Phase C, we start to see a slight improvement in mean fitness, together with an increase in evaluations exploited with a very marked increase in its variation. This seems to be a 'Transition' phase, in which the mutation rate has just become high enough to start to deliver a certain kind of neighbourhood move which the EA is able to exploit towards finding better solutions than in the previous phases. The frequency of these newly available moves is quite low, so more evaluations are needed to attempt to exploit them, and their successful exploitation is unreliable, but as we proceed into a new Phase A, we are gradually able to improve the rate at which they are exploited successfully and hence mean fitness begins to rise. We then move into a new Phase B, in which the newly available mutations are being delivered more and more quickly, and so forth, repeating the cycle.

The mutation rate inducing the start of the first 'Transition' Phase (C) is around 8.7 E-5 and has been calculated to be that which first produces an 'expected number' of around four 2-bit mutations in 1 million evaluations. In repeated experiments with evaluation limits of 200,000 and 50,000, these transition mutation rates were seen to be at higher rates [18], and were also calculated to be the rates required to first produce roughly the same number of expected 2 bit mutations in their respective number of evaluations allowed.

4 PHASES AND MUTATION EVENTS

Whilst Figures 2 and 3 show plots of the 'total mutations used' by the EA by calculating the product of the mean number of evaluations used, the 'per gene' mutation rate applied and the chromosome length, this estimation does not distinguish between the different 'types' of mutation affecting each chromosome. For example, at low rates of 'per gene' mutation, the likelihood of 1 bit mutation per chromosome will be far higher than the likelihood of 2 bit mutation etc. At very high rates of 'per gene' mutation, multi-bit mutation within a chromosome will be more likely than single bit mutation. We can model the frequencies of particular mutation events as follows :

For a 'new random binary allele' mutation rate of p, there is a $p/2$ chance of returning the original allele, hence the chance of no change is $(1-p/2)$. Let $p(k)$ be the chance of k genes changing their alleles in a single mutation event. For a string of length 64, the probability of performing no change on the entire chromosome is therefore :

$$p(0) = (1 - p / 2)^{64}$$

and for higher order mutation, of the general form as in Garnier et al [3]:

$$p(k) = {}^{L}\mathrm{C}_{k} \cdot (1 - p/2)^{L-k} \cdot (p/2)^{k}$$

where k is the number of mutations in the string, L is the length of the string and ${}^{L}\mathrm{C}_{k}$ is the number of combinations of k in L given by :

$$^{L}C_k = L! / (k! \cdot (L-k)!)$$

These 'k-bit' type mutation probabilities are plotted for $k = 0$ through 4 in Figure 4. This shows that for mutation rates below 0.001 per gene, the most probable outcome is no change to the chromosome. However above this rate, the probability of 1 bit mutation rises rapidly, peaking at a 'per gene' new random allele mutation rate of around 0.03 (approx 2/64). It can also be seen that before the probability of 1 bit mutations peaks, the probability of 2 bit mutations has already become significant, and this peaks at a slightly higher 'per gene' mutation rate, and with a lower peak probability. This trend continues for higher order bit mutations.

If these 'per chromosome' profiles are multiplied by the total number of evaluations allowed in the run, then one obtains the value of the 'expected' number of occurrences of each type of mutation in the run. For a run of 1 million evaluations this is shown on the log-log plot of Figure 5. It is important to remember however, that given that these 'per chromosome' events are being applied across a population of chromosomes, the expected change to any individual will be significantly reduced by an amount related to both population size and selection pressure.

So far this simple model has only given us an estimate of the expected number of 'n-bit' mutations that will have occurred by the end of the run. However, if we multiply the 'per chromosome' profiles by the mean number of evaluations taken to first find the best solution found in the run, taken from our earlier experiments, we get the profiles shown in Figure 6. This gives an estimate of the number of each type of mutation (1 through 4 bit) that have occurred at the point in the run at which the algorithm, on average, first finds the best solution it is going to find in the run. As we have seen, over key ranges of mutation rates the variation around this mean can be surprisingly low, especially given in most cases, at least an order of magnitude more evaluations allowed in the run. Given moderate selection pressure, it can be shown that the rest of the population will soon become clones of this solution within relatively few further evaluations, and thus this point is seen as a useful indicator of the onset of convergence. Where there are multiple solutions of equal fitness present in the population, this process will take more time, as selection pressure cannot distinguish between these points and one must wait for the effects of genetic drift [7] to take place, given the limited population size.

Figure 6 clearly shows a plateau of the estimated number of 1 bit mutations (flips) between 'per gene' mutation rates of 5 E-6 and 1 E-4, wherein the number of 1 bit flips remains constant at around 85 (= the 170 new random allele mutations reported on in [18]). Figure 5 shows us that below a 'per gene' mutation rate of 1 E-4, the expected number of 2 bit mutations in the entire run of 1 million evaluations is less than 1 and therefore unlikely and unable to play any significant part in the evolutionary search. Given that we have seen from Figure 3 that over the same range of mutation rates, no increase in mean fitness was observed, we conclude that this shows that the algorithm has indeed exhausted the usefulness of 1 bit mutation, and that the population is stuck in local optima from which it cannot escape by means of single bit mutation or crossover.

However from Figure 5 we can see that just above 'per gene' mutation rates of 1 E-4, the expected number of 2 bit mutations that occur in the entire run of 1 million evaluations

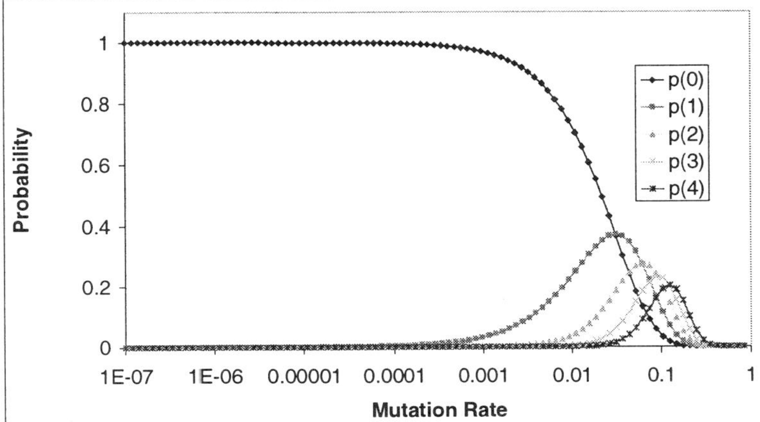

Figure 4 - Probabilities of 'n' bit flips on a 64 bit string

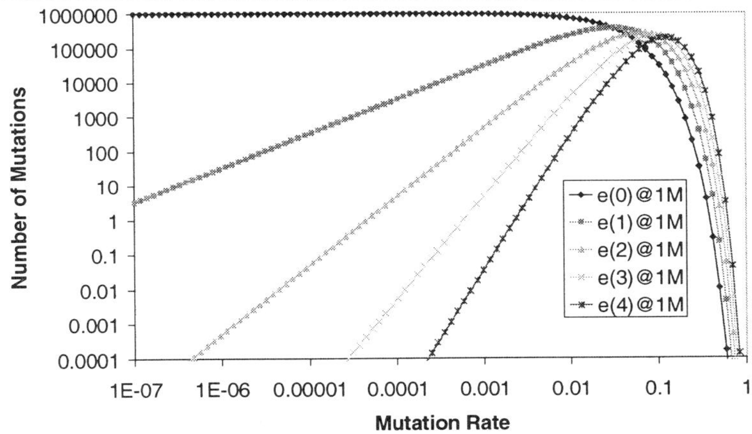

Figure 5 - Expected number of 'n' bit flips at end of 1M Evals

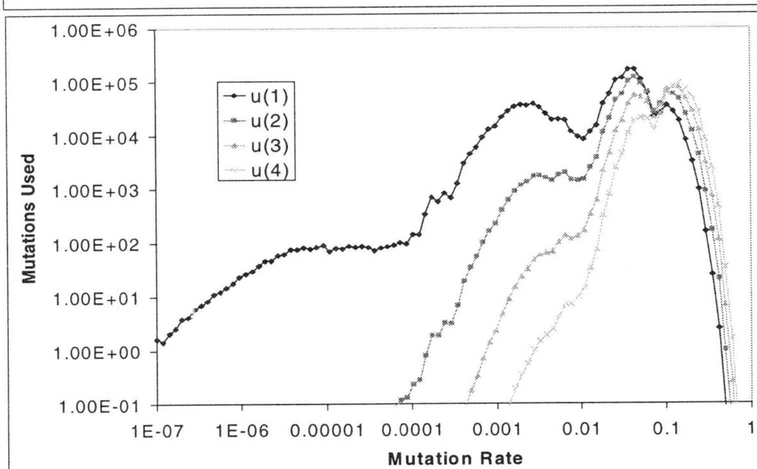

Figure 6 - Estimated number of 'n' bit flips used in 1M Evals

starts to become significant, and indeed Figure 2 shows us that around this rate of mutation a large increase occurs in the variation of number of evaluations used to first find the best solution found in the run. However this is initially accompanied by only a slight rise in the mean number of evaluations used and no increase in the mean fitness of the best solution found over the 50 runs.

As the 'per gene' mutation rate is increased beyond 1 E-4, the number of 2 bit mutations used is seen (in Figure 6) to rise until at around 2 E-3 a plateau is seen in the number of 2 bit mutations used extending to rates up to around 1 E-2. This again corresponds to a plateau of mean fitness (Figure 3) and a region of low evaluation variation (Figure 2) and occurs whilst the expected number of 3 bit mutations is also very low (Figure 5).

This plateau in the number of 2 bit mutations is of particular importance as it corresponds to the second 'B' Phase of Figure 3 in which the 'total mutations used' was seen to fall. What Figure 6 shows us is that whilst the total number of mutations does fall, this is because the total is dominated by the expected number of (now ineffective) 1 bit mutations. Thus by separating out the expected number of different types of mutation (1 bit, 2 bit etc), we can indeed see that the number of 2 bit mutations remains roughly constant within this second Phase B region, strongly supporting the hypothesis put forward in [18 and 19].

As the expected number of 3 bit mutations occurring in the whole run start to become significant (at around 1 E-2), Fig 2 shows the expected large increase in evaluation variation, followed again at slightly higher 'per gene' mutation rates, by a rise in the mean fitness and mean number of evaluations used.

A subsequent plateau in the number of 3 bit mutations used is not apparent in Figure 6, however there is evidence to suggest a plateau in the number of 4 bit mutations between rates of 4.41 E-2 and 6.23 E-2. These are the same rates that characterised the third Phase B region in Figure 3. On reflection, this is perhaps not surprising as the hierarchical block nature of H-IFF suggests that 3 bit mutations are unlikely to prove particularly useful (especially coming after 1 and 2 bit optimisation exhaustion). The H-IFF structure is however likely to be particularly responsive to 1, 2 and 4 bit mutations.

Figure 7 shows results from experiments where the runs are only allowed a total of 50,000 evaluations. Here, as might be expected, the features seen in Figure 6 occur at higher mutations rates. This is because the 'transitions' caused by the sudden introduction of significant expected numbers of higher order 'n-bit' mutations occur at higher mutation rates than with 1 Million evaluations. In particular, the introduction of 3 bit mutations is seen to occur before the exhaustion of useful 2 bit mutations in the second Phase B region, and hence towards the right hand edge of the this region the significant number of 3 bit mutations 'interfere' with the 2 bit mutations, causing a drop in the number of 2 bit mutations before deterioration occurs into the erratic Phase C.

As was pointed out earlier, because these mutations are applied to a population affected by selection pressure, no specific indication of the length of useful random walks induced by 'n-bit' mutation can easily be drawn. What can be seen in Figure 1, is that higher population sizes attenuate the height of the peaks in the plot of mean evaluations used, both diluting the effects of mutation on individuals and increasing the effectiveness of the one-point crossover operator.

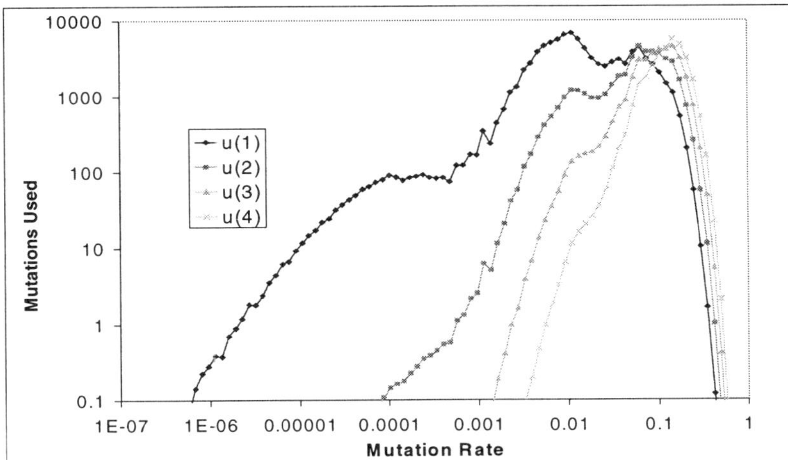

Figure 7 - Estimated number of 'n' bit flips used in 50k Evals

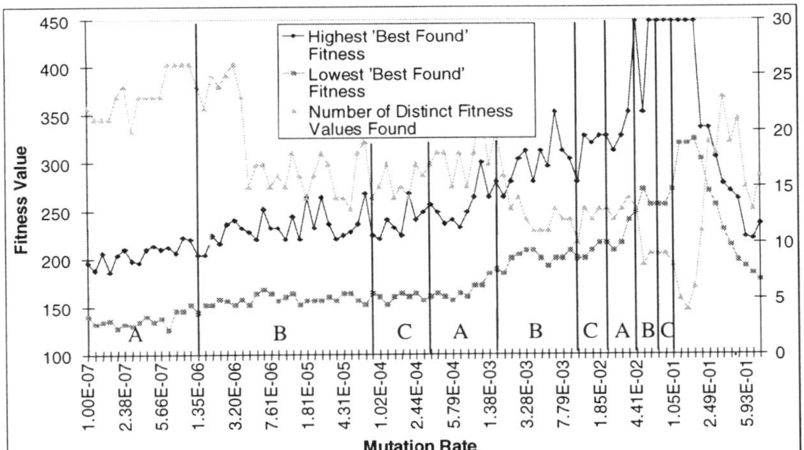

Figure 8 - Number of Distinct Fitness Values with Ranges

5 'BEST FOUND' FITNESS DISTRIBUTIONS

Whilst Figure 3 shows the mean value of the 'best found' fitness over each of the 50 runs (with the same mutation rate and population size), Figure 8 shows the highest and lowest fitness values of these 50 'best found' fitnesses, together with the number of distinct fitness values found over the 50 values. The A, B and C Phases are superimposed on these plots clearly showing that within each B Phase, the number of distinct fitness values found drops dramatically. It is also noticable that once reduced, the level is roughly maintained until the next A Phase, during which it rises, before falling significantly in the subsequent B Phase. The 'highest' and 'lowest' 'best found' fitness values can be seen to rise during the latter part of A Phases and early part of B Phases, remaining roughly level at other times.

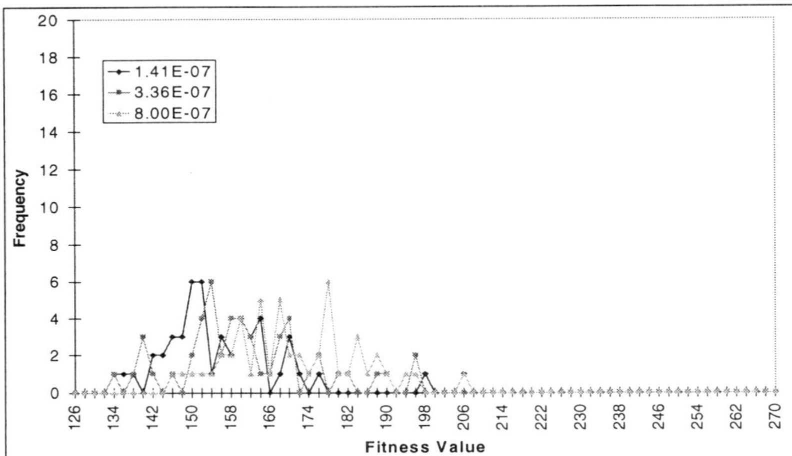

Figure 9 - Fitness Value Distribution in Region A1

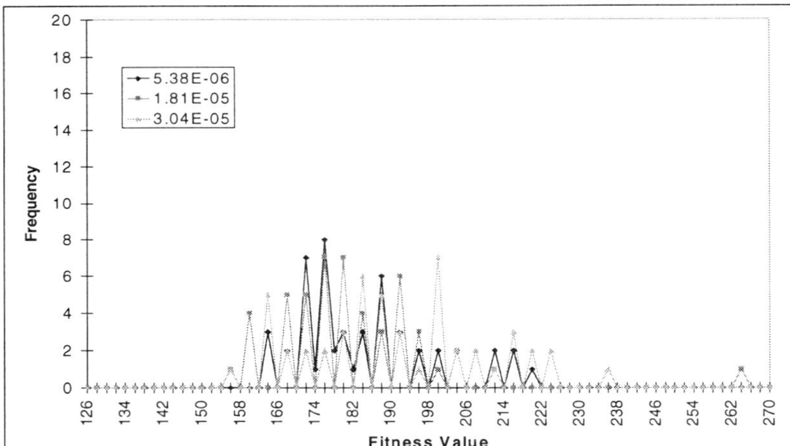

Figure 10 - Fitness Value Distribution in Region B1

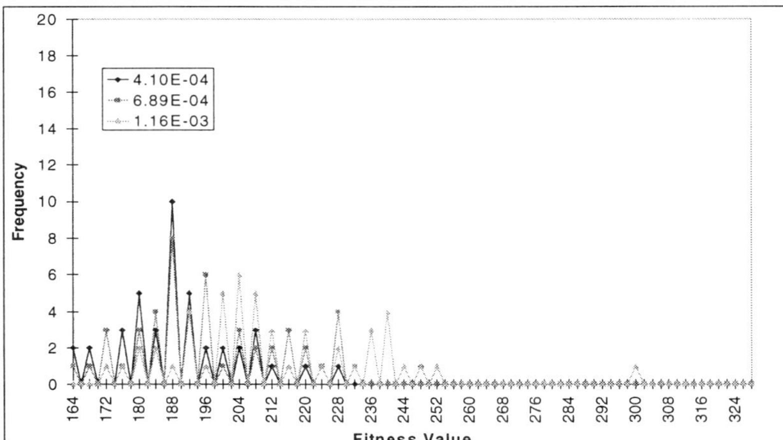

Figure 11 - Fitness Value Distribution in Region A2

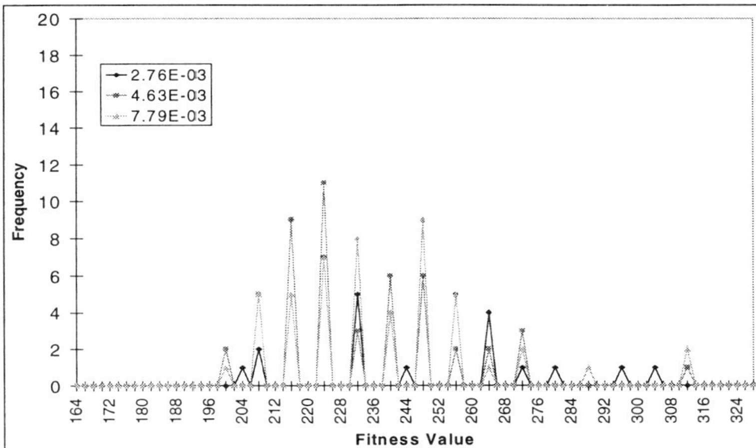

Figure 12 - Fitness Value Distribution in Region B2

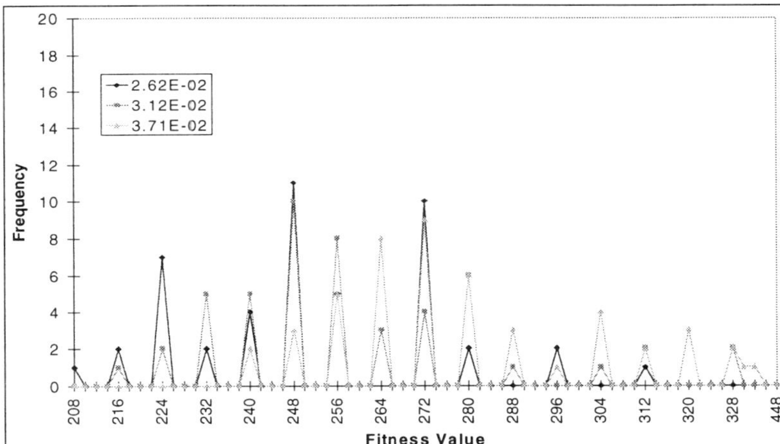

Figure 13 - Fitness Value Distribution in Region A3

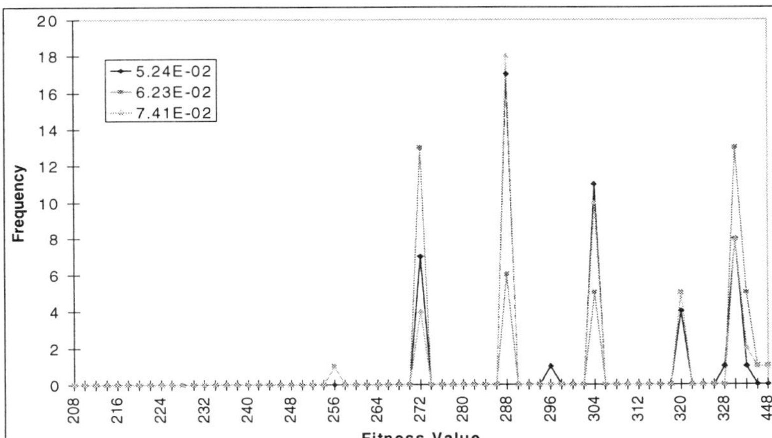

Figure 14 - Fitness Value Distribution in Region B3

To investigate this further, in each phase and each cycle, 3 mutation rates were selected (evenly spaced within each phase's exponential scale), and the distribution of their 50 'best found' fitness values was plotted. Figure 9 shows these distributions for the 3 mutation rates selected from the leftmost A Phase in Figure 8. It can clearly be seen that no specific value is returned more that 6 times out of the 50 runs, and that most fitness values are 'found' in at least 1 run, over the fitness range 132 through 200 (It should be noted that the nature of the H-IFF fitness functions allows only even numbered fitness values). It can also be seen that in general, as mutation rate increases, so the distribution moves to the right, also shown by increasing mean 'best found' fitness in Figure 3. By stark contrast, Figure 10 shows the distribution for 3 mutation rates in the leftmost B Phase. Here it can be seen that in general, only every other fitness value is settled upon, clearly indicating that intermediate fitness values can easily be improved upon by mutation rates in this Phase. It can also be seen that the distribution occupies a higher range than the distributions in the corresponding Phase A. The distributions for the C Phases are very similar to those for the B Phase and are not presented for space reasons.

Figure 11 shows the distribution for 3 mutation rates in the second A Phase. Once again, only every other fitness value is represented, and the range of values is seen to occur at higher values than for the preceding B Phase. Again by contrast, Figure 12 shows the distribution of 'best found' fitness values in the second B Phase. Note here that in general only every fourth fitness value is settled upon, and that the frequency of selection of any specific value has increased to peak at 11. Clearly over this range of mutation rates, the search process is able to break through a different class of fitness barrier. Figure 13 shows the distribution for 3 mutation values in the rightmost Phase A. Again, the range of values is higher, but still only every fourth fitness value is favoured. For the rightmost B Phase (Figure 14), this has changed yet again to show only every eighth fitness value being selected (Note – up to Fitness Value 328, all even Fitness Values are categorised, beyond this value only Fitness Values 336, 352, 384 and 448 are deliverable by the H-IFF 64 function. Between 64 and 324, all even fitness values are deliverable).

6 FURTHER EXPERIMENTS: KAUFFMAN NK, ROYAL STAIRCASE AND MAX-ONES

To investigate these phenomena further, a series of experiments was conducted over a range of other multi- and uni-modal search spaces looking at two distinct types of problem with significantly different search space characteristics. For rugged, multi-modal search spaces, the Kauffman NK model [6] was used, generated by defining a table of random numbers of dimension 50 by 512. For a binary chromosome of length N = 50 with K set to 8, starting at each of the 50 gene positions, K+1 exponentially weighted consecutive genes are used to generate an index (in the range 0-511), and the 50 values so indexed from the table are summed to give a fitness value. For NK landscapes with a K value of 0, each gene position contributes individually to fitness, hence producing a uni-modal landscape to single point mutation hillclimbers. However as K is increased, any single point mutation will affect K+1 indexes, rapidly introducing linkage into the problem and producing a rugged and increasingly unstructured landscape. Experiments were run with K values of 0, 1, 2, 4 and 8.

To investigate the effect of neutral fitness regions in uni-modal search spaces, another set of experiments was run on versions of the tuneable Royal Staircase [11,12] problem, in

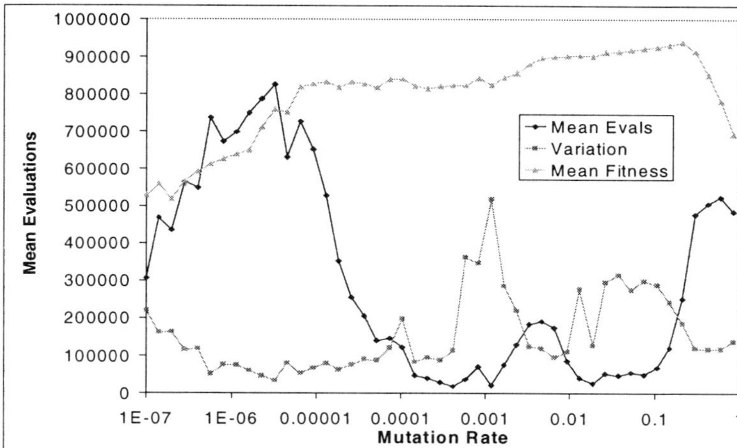

Figure 15 - Profile for NK 50-2 pop size 20

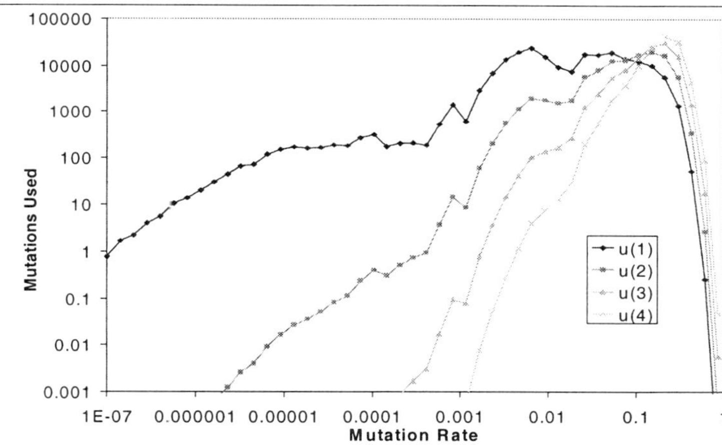

Figure 16 - Estimated number of 'n' bit flips in NK50-2

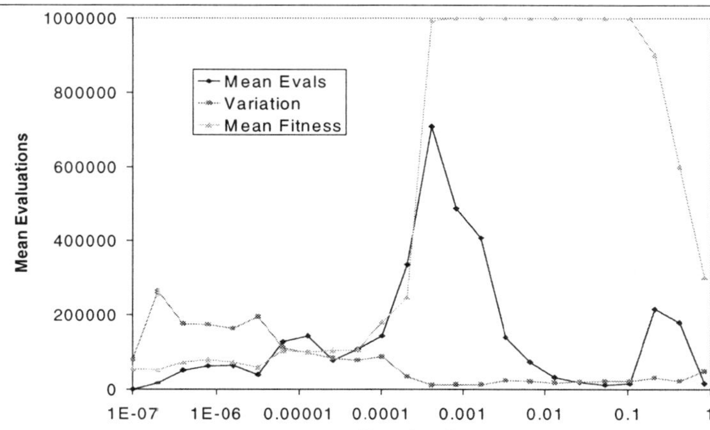

Figure 17 - Profile for RS 10-5 pop size 20

which fitness is measured as the number of complete, consecutive blocks of contiguous 1's in the chromosome starting from the first gene. Again, for a chromosome of length 50, block sizes of 1, 5 and 10 were tried giving search spaces with respectively 50, 10 and 5 distinct neutral fitness regions. Results from some of these experiments are reported on in [19], with additional results given here in Figures 15 and 17.

Figure 15 shows the performance profile for our simple EA on a Kauffman NK landscape, where the length of the string was set to 50, the K value set to 2, population size set at 20 and each run allowed 1 million evaluations. Again 50 runs at each fixed mutation rate have been averaged. The superimposed plots of mean evaluations used, evaluation number variation and mean fitness, clearly show at least 2 repeating cycles of 3 phases before optimal fitness is achieved, again implying the exhaustion of useful 1 bit and 2 bit mutations. This is emphasised in Figure 16, showing the estimated number of each type of mutation used up to the mean point of first finding the best solution found in the run. Mutation type probabilities have been recalculated based on a string length of 50. Once again, the first B Phase in Figure 15 is seen to correspond to a plateau in the number of 1 bit mutations ending only once 2 bit mutations become significant. Also, a plateau in 2-bit mutations is seen (in Figure 16) at rates corresponding to the second B Phase in Figure 15. Similar results were also seen at K values of 1,4 and 8. As was observed in [19], these features are attenuated as population size is increased but with the peaks and troughs persistent at the same rates of mutation.

By contrast, Figure 17 shows the performance profile for the instance of the uni-modal Royal Staircase problem, where a 50 bit string is evaluated as 10 blocks each of length 5. Here there is no repeating, multi-phase behaviour. At low mutation rates, mean number of evaluations is low and rising, mean fitness is low and rising, but evaluation number variation is high but falling. This is typical of Phase A behaviour. At a mutation rate of around 2 E-4 fitness improves dramatically, leading to a region of high fitness, falling mean evaluations and low evaluation number variation, typical of Phase B behaviour. However there is no significant later rise in variation (which would typify the start of a 'transitional' C Phase), and as mutation rate is increased, the search degenerates into random search.

Figure 18 shows the estimated number of each type of mutation used showing no plateau at any particular mutation rate. The number of 1 bit mutations used is seen to peak around the mutation rate which first induces reliable finding of the globally optimum solution (1.6 E-3 in Figure 17) whilst the numbers of all other mutation types used are seen to increase (as mean number of evaluations falls) converging on a point at which a minimum of evaluations is needed by the algorithm at a rate of 5.2 E-2 which is approximately 2 / 50 (NRA). A slightly higher rate induces roughly the same number of each type of mutation plotted. This is not surprising because, as was seen in Figure 4, a mutation rate of 2 / 50 induces the peak in 1 bit mutations, shortly followed by the peak in 2 bit mutations etc. Around this mutation rate, low order mutation type probabilities are all of the same order of magnitude, with the peaks of higher order mutation types getting closer together and of lower peak probability. In contrast to the multi-modal search spaces, it was clearly shown in [19] that the peak and trough features in the performance profile of the uni-modal problems was not significantly attenuated by increasing population size. The height of the peaks in mean evaluations used was still considerable in population sizes up to the limit of 500 members investigated.

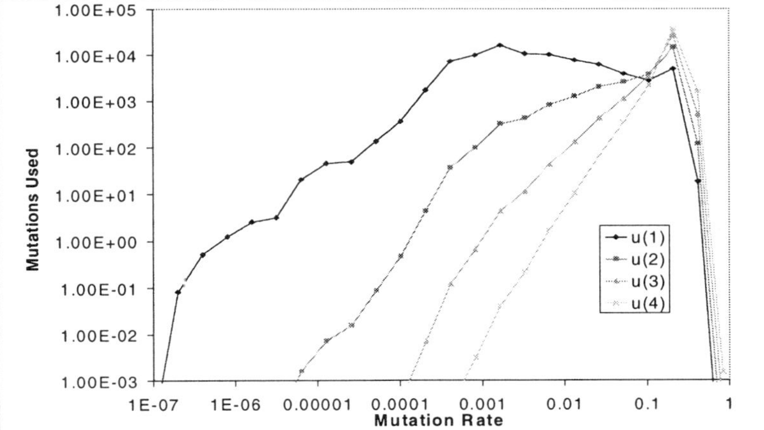

Figure 18 - Estimated number of 'n' bit flips in RS10-5

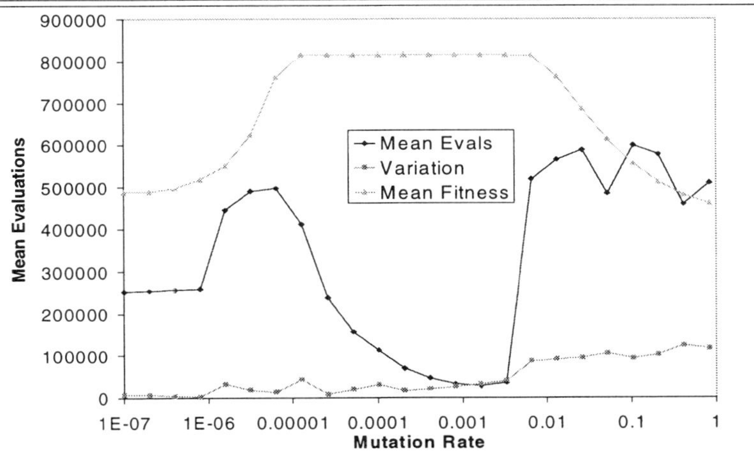

Figure 19 - Profile for One Max 1630 pop size 20

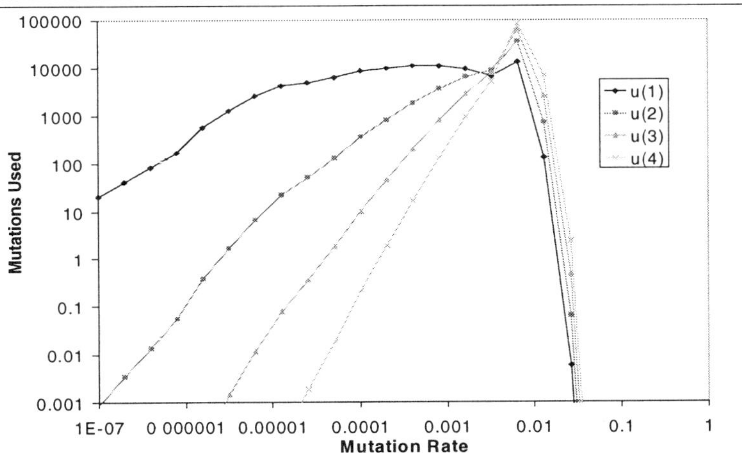

Figure 20 - Estimated number of 'n' bit flips in One Max 1630

Figure 19 shows a performance profile for a steady state, 3 way single tournament EA, this time using uniform crossover [21] on an instance of the One Max problem, for a binary string length of 1630 (similar trials have also been run at string lengths of 50 and 300). As with the uni-modal Royal Staircase search space, this profile can very clearly be seen to exhibit only one Phase A and Phase B before too high a mutation rate causes degeneration towards random search. Figure 20 shows the estimated number of each of 1 through 4 bit mutation, based on n-bit mutation probabilities on a binary string of length 1630. Once again, 1 bit mutation is seen to rise rapidly until reaching mutation rates which reliably find the global optimum. The number of used mutations of all other types is seen to rise, converging on a rate at which the number used of all types is roughly the same, which again corresponds to a mutation rate just above that which reliably finds the global optimum in the lowest number of evaluations (1.6 E-3 which equals approximately 2 / 1630 NRA), prior to degeneration into random search.

7 DISCUSSION

At low population sizes, the opportunities for progress by the crossover operator are severely limited due to lack of initial (or ongoing) diversity. Indeed it can be argued that a population size of only 20 is barely sufficient to claim that the algorithm is a true EA. However, as was clearly shown in [16-18], the 'multi–modal' profile was clearly apparent in the ADDMP performance profile at population sizes at least as high as 500, and Figure 1 shows it to be a significant feature in H-IFF up to at least 200. In general it is seen that the magnitude of the features are attenuated by larger population size together with a general increase in the 'floor' level of mean number of evaluations used in the intervening troughs. Thus a population size of 20 was chosen to give a good opportunity of distinguishing the features of the profile. Further, whilst the results on the multi-modal problems all show significant attenuation with increased population size, studies reported on in [18] clearly showed that on the uni-modal problems this was not the case. At trials with population sizes of 20, 100 and 500 members, the performance features were shown to be robust, with attenuation values of between only 0 and 50% being seen between the tested extremes of 20 and 500 member runs.

Earlier studies [14,15] at lower evaluation limits (typically 5,000 to 20,000) on the ADDMP and other problems had implied that a mutation rate close to the reciprocal of the chromosome length yielded highest fitness solutions in a locally minimum number of evaluations. This was particularly true for search spaces which had been deemed 'easy' to search. However it can now be seen that allowing the search process more time (ie increasing the number of evaluations) shows that these results are in general only finding local optima with specific characteristics, particularly where the search spaces contain a wide range of optima, where the fitter optima have small basins of attraction. On multi-modal search spaces, at sufficiently high evaluation limits, the bi-modal performance profile is shown to transform into a multi-modal profile, with each peak and trough corresponding to the availabilty and exploitation of higher order multi-bit mutations. This becomes particularly true for mutation rates around the reciprocal of the chromosome length and higher.

'Optimal' performance with mutation rates close to the reciprocal of the chromosome length is a result seen in many other empirical and theoretical studies, for example [1, 2, 3, 9, 10] particularly by Bäck, and Mühlenbein. Indeed Mühlenbein has shown in [9] that for uni-modal problems a value of 1 / chromosome length (1 / L) is predicted to be the rate that finds the optimum in a minimum of evaluations. This result is clearly seen in this and related studies [16,18]. Interestingly, this study also shows that for multi-modal problems, such as H-IFF and Kauffman NK (K > 0), a rate greater than 1 / chromosome length is needed to achieve optimal fitness however, for the problems investigated and evaluation limits imposed here, this may not represent reliable finding of the global optimum. Indeed contradictory evidence is seen between the H-IFF profile (Figure 2) and the NK profile (Figure 15). In the former, optimal fitness occurs in a region of relatively high levels of numbers of evaluations, with low variation, whilst for the latter, optimal fitness is found at mutation rates inducing a low mean number of evaluations but with high variation. Given the resolution of the mutation rate axis, and the dependency of performance on evaluation limit (over this range of high mutation rates) seen in [17], no specific conclusions can be drawn from this other than general support for Mühlenbein's prediction that mutation rates higher than 1 / chromosome length (approaching k / L where k is the number of deceptive optima) should perform better than 1 / L on multi-modal search spaces.

8 CONCLUSIONS

This paper has shown that evolutionary search performance profiles for the H-IFF problem and a range of other problems show certain consistent features. In particular, certain distinct 'phases' of search behaviour can be identified corresponding to specific ranges of mutation rates. For a multi-modal search space, a fixed choice of mutation rate seems to condemn the search process to a particular phase. If this is Phase A, the mutation rate is such that certain mutation events (single-gene mutations in the first Phase A, two-gene mutations in the second Phase A, etc.) are starting to become available, which occasionally enable the search process to find certain local optima. A higher mutation rate would have enabled these optima to be found more reliably, though at the cost of more time. If instead a search process operates in Phase B, these mutation events occur with sufficient regularity to reliably achieve the aforementioned optima. Higher mutation rates simply deliver the needed material in fewer evaluations. However, if the search process is operating in Phase C, the situation is essentially chaotic: the mutation rate being such that a certain type of new mutation event may become available only in a very small percentage of runs, occasionally enabling the search process to break through a 'fitness barrier'. This barrier being related to the size of the basin of attraction of particular local optima. However as such an event occurs unreliably, the variation in number of evaluations used is high, though the mean remains low. A search process with an even higher mutation rate could be within the next Phase A, which occurs when the likelihood of breaking through a particular barrier starts to become significant, hence the mean number of evaluations used rises to higher levels, but with reduced variation.

These studies of the expected numbers of *k*-bit mutations for different mutation rates, and the estimations of the numbers of each type of mutation exploited in regions of the performance profiles studied, appear to confirm the notion that 'mutation events' and their frequencies provide an explanation of this phase-oriented behaviour. Notably, as apparent in Figures 6 and 16, we see that there are intervals of mutation rate at which the numbers of certain mutation events used stay approximately constant. This indicates that, at the onset of the constant interval, the usefulness of that mutation event has been exhausted. Higher mutation rates therefore lead to lower total evaluations exploited, as this constant number of mutations of this type are delivered more quickly.

According to our hypothesis, we would only expect to see cyclic phase behaviour when the problem has several increasingly fit optima, and as we have seen, only the performance profiles of multi-modal problems exhibit this cyclic feature. On uni-modal problems, the phase behaviour still seems apparent, but without cycles. That is, Phase B represents the optimal region, while Phase C incorporates the deterioration into random search.

Confirmation of Mühlenbein's 1 / L rule is clearly seen for the uni-modal search spaces reported on here and in [18], giving highest fitness in the lowest number of evaluations with low variation. A mutation rate above this is seen to cause deterioration in best fitness found, an increase in the mean number of evaluations found and increase in its variation. For the multi-modal search spaces, the mutation rate finding optimum fitness is seen to occur at rates significantly higher than 1 / chromosome length, but at the expense of greater process instability and unreliability. Although previous studies at lower evaluation limits have shown that a rate close to 1 / L can often find 'reasonable' local optima in a local minimum of evaluation limits, at higher evaluation limits, the performance of the search is seen to be highly dependent on the characteristics of the search space and the relative usefulness of the increased availability of higher order mutation types. Thus any particular mutation rate greater than 1 / L will dictate, given the chromosome length and evaluation limit, the relative distribution of a range of high order mutation types, and thus determine in which predominant phase of behaviour the search will operate.

Phase behaviour appears to be a consistent feature of evolutionary search, given the wide range of problem landscapes and EA designs over which it has now been observed. The authors believe it may be of particular use in the future, subject to much further exploration, in generally understanding EA behaviour on difficult multi-modal problems. In the shorter term however, two potential avenues present themselves which may prove useful. Firstly, it may be possible in general to detect the phase within which a particular evolutionary search is operating. This would offer guidance as regards whether better fitness levels may be available at higher mutation rates, or perhaps whether similar fitness levels may be available with increased speed at higher rates. If phase behaviour turns out to be consistent across a wider range of applications, and phase-detection is possible, then this could yield control algorithms for self-adaptive EAs. Secondly, since it appears that evolutionary search behaviour seems tied to the availabilities of certain types of mutation event, future studies might be well employed to investigate mutation operators which exploit this. In particular, instead of a single 'per gene' mutation rate, the operator could offer a tailored distribution of mutation events, essentially delivering 'n' gene mutations according to pre-specified probabilities, which could be made to vary during the lifetime of the search.

Acknowledgements

The authors wish to thank Richard Watson of Brandeis University for invaluable technical input and British Telecommunications Plc for ongoing support for this research.

References

[1] T Bäck, *Evolutionary Algorithms in Theory and Practice*, Oxford University Press, 1996

[2] K Deb and S Agrawal : *Understanding Interactions among Genetic Algorithm Parameters*. in Foundations of Genetic Algorithms 5, Morgan Kaufmann, pp.265-286.

[3] J Garnier, L Kallel and M Schoenauer, *Rigorous hitting times for binary mutations*, Evolutionary Computing Vol 7 No 2, pp.167-203, 1999.

[4] D Goldberg (1989), *Genetic Algorithms in Search Optimisation and Machine Learning*, Addison Wesley.

[5] J Holland, *Adaptation in Natural and Artificial Systems*, MIT press, Cambridge, MA, 1993

[6] Kauffman, S.A., *The Origins of Order: Self-Organization and Selection in Evolution*, Oxford University Press, 1993

[7] J Maynard Smith, *Evolutionary Genetics*, Oxford University Press,1989, pp24-27

[8] Z Michalewicz, *Genetic Algorithms + Data Structures = Evolution Programs*, Springer, 1996.

[9] H Mühlenbein and D Schlierkamp-Voosen (1994), *The Science of Breeding and its application to the Breeder Genetic Algorithm*, Evolutionary Computation 1, pp. 335-360.

[10] H Mühlenbein, *How genetic algorithms really work: I. Mutation and hillclimbing*, in R.Manner, B. Manderick (eds), Proc. of PPSN 2, Elsevier, pp 15-25.

[11] E van Nimwegen and J Crutchfield : *Optmizing Epochal Evolutionary Search: Population-Size Independent Theory*, in Computer Methods in Applied Mechanics and Engineering, special issue on Evolutionary and Genetic Algorithms in Computational Mechanics and Engineering, D Goldberg and K Deb, editors, 1998.

[12] E van Nimwegen and J Crutchfield : *Optmizing Epochal Evolutionary Search: Population-Size Dependent Theory*, Santa Fe Institute Working Paper 98-10-090, also submitted to Machine Learning, 1998.

[13] M Oates, D Corne and R Loader, *Investigating Evolutionary Approaches for Self-Adaption in Large Distributed Databases*, in Proceedings of the 1998 IEEE ICEC, pp. 452-457.

[14] M Oates and D Corne, *Investigating Evolutionary Approaches to Adaptive Database Management against various Quality of Service Metrics*, LNCS, Procs of 5th Intl Conf on Parallel Problem Solving from Nature, PPSN-V (1998), pp. 775-784.

[15] M Oates, D Corne and R Loader , *Investigation of a Characteristic Bimodal Convergence-time/Mutation-rate Feature in Evolutionary Search*, in Procs of Congress on Evolutionary Computation 99 Vol 3, IEEE, pp. 2175-2182.

[16] Oates M, Corne D and Loader R, *Variation in Evolutionary Algorithm Performance Characteristics on the Adaptive Distributed Database Management Problem*, in Procs of Genetic and Evolutionary Computation Conference 99, Morgan Kaufmann, pp.480-487.

[17] Oates M, Corne D and Loader R, *Multimodal Performance Profiles on the Adaptive Distributed Database Management Problem*, in Real World Applications of Evolutionary Computing, Cagnoni et al (Eds), Springer LNCS 1803, pp. 224-234.

[18] Oates M, Corne D and Loader R, *A Tri-Phase Multimodal Evolutionary Search Performance Profile on the 'Hierarchical If and Only If' Problem*, in Procs of the Genetic and Evolutionary Computation Conference 2000, Morgan Kaufmann, pp. 339-346.

[19] M.Oates, D Corne and R Loader, *Tri-Phase Performance Profile of Evolutionary Search on Uni- and Multi- Modal Search Spaces*, in Procs of the Congress on Evolutionary Computation 2000, La Jolla, CA, July 2000 (in press).

[20] G Syswerda (1989), *Uniform Crossover in Genetic Algorithms*, in Schaffer J. (ed), Procs of the Third Int. Conf. on Genetic Algorithms. Morgan Kaufmann, pp. 2 – 9

[21] Watson RA, Hornby GS, and Pollack JB, *Modelling Building-Block Interdependency*, LNCS, Procs of 5th Intl Conf on Parallel Problem Solving from Nature, PPSN-V (1998), pp. 97-106.

[22] Watson RA, Pollack JB, *Hierarchically Consistent Test Problems for Genetic Algorithms*, in Procs of Congress on Evolution 99, Vol 2, IEEE, pp. 1406-1413

Niches in NK-Landscapes

Keith E. Mathias, Larry J. Eshelman and J. David Schaffer
Philips Research
345 Scarborough Road
Briarcliff Manor, NY 10510
Keith.Mathias/Larry.Eshelman/Dave.Schaffer@philips.com (914) 945-6430/6491/6168

Abstract

Introduced by Kauffman in 1989, NK-landscapes have been the focus of numerous theoretical and empirical studies in the field of evolutionary computation. Despite all that has been learned from these studies, there are still many open questions concerning NK-landscapes. Most of these studies have been performed using very small problems and have neglected to benchmark the performances of genetic algorithms (GA) with those of hill-climbers, leaving us to wonder if a GA would be the best tool for solving any size NK-landscape problem. Heckendorn, Rana, and Whitley [7] performed initial investigations addressing these questions for NK-landscapes where $N = 100$, concluding that an enhanced random bit-climber was best for solving NK-landscapes. Replicating and extending their work, we conclude that a niche exists for GAs like CHC in the NK-landscape functions and describe the bounds of this niche. We also offer some explanations for these bounds and speculate about how the bounds might change as the NK-landscape functions become larger.

1 INTRODUCTION

Introduced by Kauffman in 1989 NK-landscapes [10] are functions that allow the degree of epistasis to be tuned and are defined in terms of N, the length of the bit string and K, the number of bits that contribute to the evaluation of each of the N loci in the string (i.e., the degree of epistasis). The objective function for NK-landscapes is computed as the sum of the evaluation values from N subproblems, normalized (i.e., divided) by N. The subproblem at each locus, i, is given by a value in a lookup table that corresponds to the substring formed by the bit values present at the locus, i, and its K interactors. The lookup table for each locus contains 2^{K+1} elements randomly selected in the range [0.0...1.0]. Thus, the lookup table for the entire problem is an N by 2^{K+1} matrix.[1] When $K = 0$ the landscape is unimodal and the optimum can easily be found by a simple hill-climber such as RBC (random bit climber) in $N + 1$ evaluations. When $K = N - 1$ (the maximum possible value for K), the landscape is random and completely uncorrelated (i.e., knowing the value at any point provides no information about other points in the space, even those that differ from the known point by only a single bit).

NK-landscapes have been the focus of numerous theoretical and empirical studies in the field of evolutionary computation [11, 9, 8, 7, 12]. Yet, in spite of numerous studies and all that has been learned about NK-landscapes, there are still many open questions with regard to the ruggedness that is induced on the landscape as K is increased. Particularly, is there enough regularity (i.e., structure) in the landscape for a genetic algorithm (GA) to exploit? Since a hill-climber is the preferred search algorithm at $K = 0$ and nothing will be better than random search at $K = N - 1$, the question remains: is there any niche for GAs in NK-landscapes at any value of K?

Heckendorn, Rana, and Whitley's [7] study, comparing GAs with random bit-climbers, suggested answers to some of these questions for NK-landscapes where $N = 100$. Figure 1 is replicated here using data supplied by Heckendorn, et al., and shows the performance for three search algorithms on randomly generated NK-landscape problems where $N = 100$. Figure 1 differs from the figure presented by Heckendorn, et al., in that we present error bars that are ± 2 standard errors of the mean (SEM), roughly the 95% confidence interval for the mean. Figure 1 also provides an inset to magnify the performance values in the interval $3 \leq K \leq 12$. Heckendorn, et al. observed:

- The enhanced hill-climber, RBC+ [7], performed the best of the algorithms they tested.
- A niche for more robust GAs, like CHC [3], may not exist at all since CHC generally performed worse than a robust hill-climber and the performance of CHC becomes very poor when $K \geq 12$.
- The performance of the simple genetic algorithm (SGA) is never competitive with that of other algorithms.

Their work raises several questions: Why are the average best values found by the algorithms decreasing when $0 \leq K \leq 5$, and why are the average best values found by the algorithms increasing for $K > 6$? Can we determine if and when any of these algorithms are capable of locating the global optima in NK-landscapes? What does the dramatic worsening in the average best values found by CHC, relative to the hill-climbers, for $K > 10$ tell us about the structure of the NK-landscape functions as K increases. What is the significance of CHC's remarkably stable performance for $K > 20$? And perhaps most interesting, is there a niche where a GA is demonstrably better than other algorithms in NK-landscapes?

---

[1] NK-landscapes can be treated as minimization or maximization functions, and the K interactors for each locus, i, can be randomly chosen from any of the $N - 1$ remaining string positions or from the loci in the neighborhood adjacent to i. For this work the problems have been treated as minimization problems, and the K interactors have been randomly chosen from any of the $N - 1$ remaining string positions.

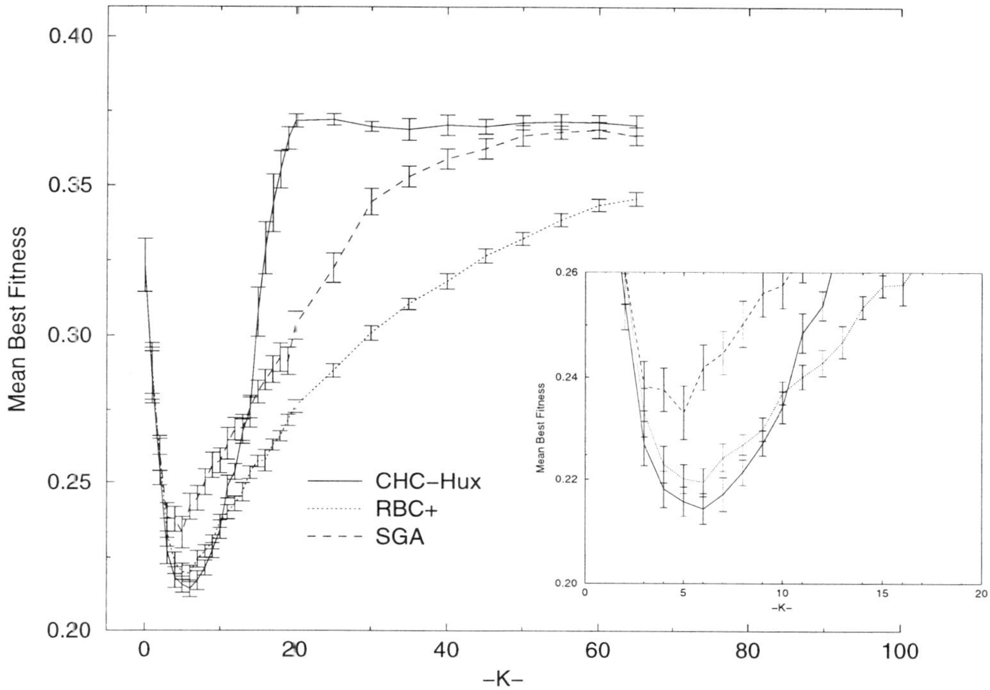

Figure 1 Performances for CHC, RBC+, and SGA on NK-landscape problems, treated as minimization problems, where $N = 100$. This graph is reproduced using the data given in Heckendorn, et al. [7]. We have added error bars representing $2 * SEM$.

2 THE ALGORITHMS

In this work we have begun to characterize the performance niches for random search, CHC using the HUX [3] and two-point reduced surrogate recombination (2X) [1] operators, a random bit-climber, RBC [2], and an enhanced random bit-climber, RBC+ [7]. The random search algorithm we tested here kept the string with the best fitness observed (i.e., minimum value) from T randomly generated strings, where T represents the total allotted trials. The strings were generated randomly with replacement (i.e., a memoryless algorithm).

CHC is a generational style GA which prevents parents from mating if their genetic material is too similar (i.e., incest prevention). Controlling the production of offspring in this way maintains diversity and slows population convergence. Selection is elitist: only the best M individuals, where M is the population size, survive from the pool of both the offspring and parents. CHC also uses a "soft restart" mechanism. When convergence has been detected, or the search stops making progress, the best individual found so far in the search is preserved. The rest of the population is reinitialized: using the best string as a template, some percentage of the template's bits are flipped (i.e., the divergence rate) to form the remaining members of the population. This introduces new genetic diversity into the population in order to continue search but without losing the progress that has already been made. CHC uses no other form of mutation.

The CHC algorithm is typically implemented using the HUX recombination operator for binary representations, but any recombination operator may be used with the algorithm. HUX recombination produces two offspring which are maximally distant from their two parent strings by exchanging exactly half of the bits that differ in the two parents. While using HUX results in the most robust performance across a wide variety of problems, other operators such as 2X [1] and uniform crossover [13] have been used with varying degrees of success [5, 4]. Here, we use HUX and 2X and a population size of 50.

RBC, a random bit climber defined by Davis [2], begins search with a random string. Bits are complemented (i.e., flipped) one at a time and the string is re-evaluated. All changes that result in equally good or improved solutions are kept. The order that bit flips are tested is random, and a new random testing order is established for each cycle. A cycle is defined as N complements, where N is the length of the string, and each position is tested exactly once during the cycle. A local optimum is found if no improvements are found in a complete test cycle. After a local optimum has been discovered, testing may continue until some number of total trials are expended by choosing a new random start string.

RBC+ [7] is a variant of RBC that performs a "soft restart" when a local optimum is reached. In RBC+, the testing of bit flips is carried out exactly as described for RBC. However, when a local optimum is reached, a random bit is complemented and the change is accepted regardless of the resulting fitness. A new testing order is determined and testing continues as described for RBC. These soft restarts are repeated until $5 * N$ changes are accepted (including the bit changes that constituted the soft restarts), at which point a new random bit string is generated (i.e., a "hard restart"). This process continues until the total trials have been expended.

3 THE NK OPTIMA

One striking characteristic of the performance curves in Figure 1 is the dramatic decrease in the average best objective values found by all of the search algorithms when $0 \leq K \leq 6$ and the increase in the average best values found by all of the search algorithms when $K > 6$. One may reasonably ask whether these trends represent improvement in the performance of the algorithms followed by worsening performances or whether they indicate something about the NK-landscapes involved.

A hint at the answer may be seen by looking ahead to Figure 4 where a plot of the performance of a random search algorithm shows the same behavior (i.e., decreasing objective values) when $K \leq 6$ but levels off for higher K. The basic reason for this can be explained in terms of expected variance in increasing sample sizes. The fitness for an NK-landscape where $N = 100$ and $K = 0$ is simply the average of 100 values, where the search algorithm chooses the better of the two values available at each locus. When $K = 1$ the fitness is determined by taking one of four randomly assigned values; the four values come from the combinations of possible bit values for the locus in question and its single interactor (i.e., 00, 01, 10, and 11). In general, averages of more random numbers will have more variance, leading to more extreme values. However, this ignores the constraints

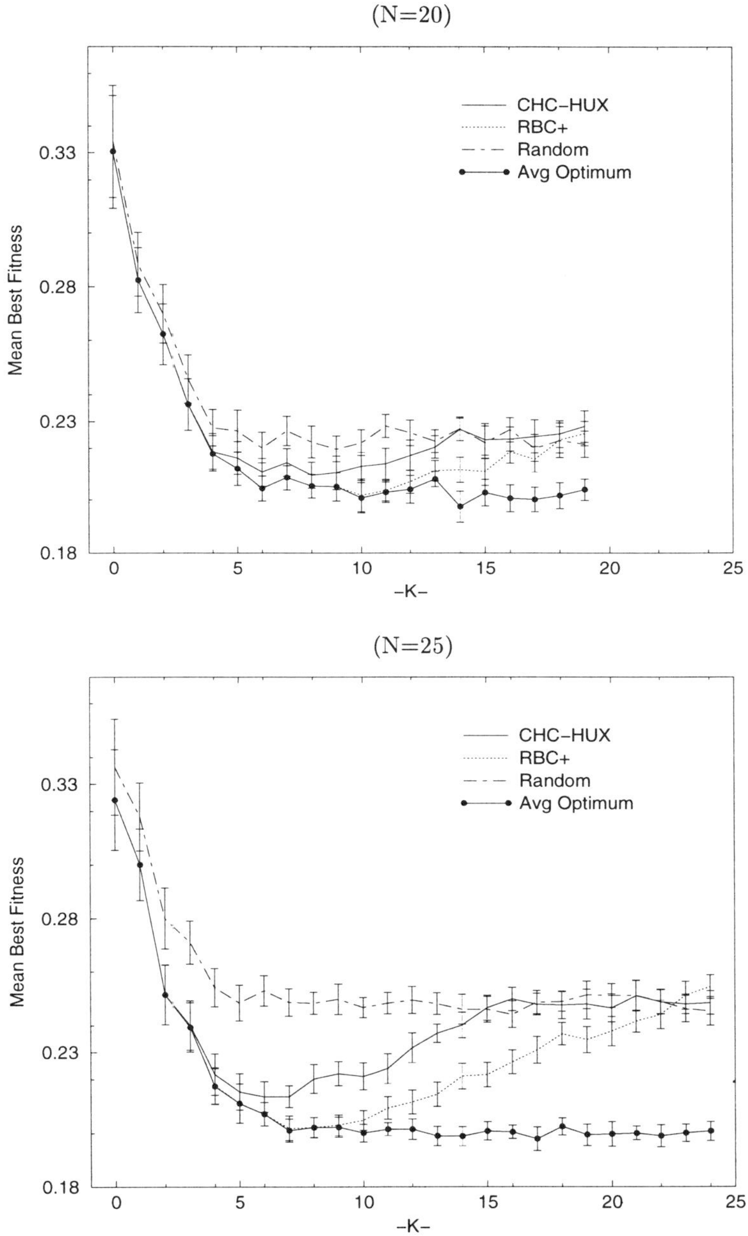

Figure 2 Average optimal solution for 30 random problems on NK-landscapes where $N = 20$ and $N = 25$. Performances for CHC-HUX, RBC+, and random search are also shown. Error bars represent $2 * SEM$.

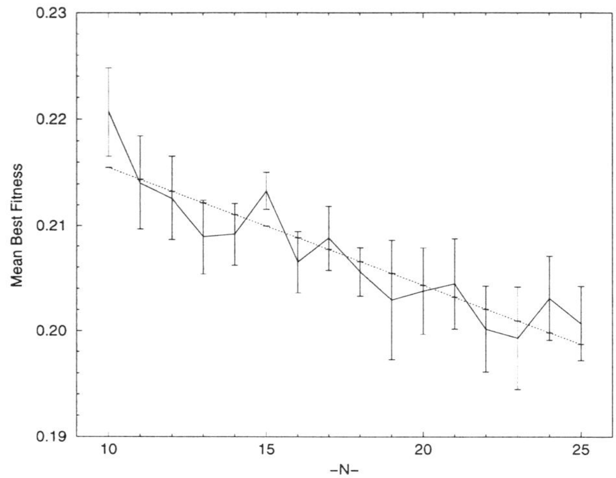

Figure 3 Average global optima for 30 random NK-landscapes when $K = N - 1$ for $10 \leq N \leq 25$. Error bars represent $2 * SEM$.

imposed by making a choice at a particular locus and how that affects the choices at other loci. We expect that this would at least cause the downward slope of the curve to level off at some point, if not rise, as K increases. This is consistent with the findings of Smith and Smith [12] who found a slight but significant correlation between K and the minimum fitness.

We performed exhaustive search on 30 random problems, at every K, for $10 \leq N \leq 25$. Figure 2 shows the average global optima (Avg Optimum) and the performance (average best found) for CHC-HUX, RBC+, and random search allowing 200,000 trials for $N = 20$ and $N = 25$. We see that the average of the global optima decreases as K increases from 0 to 6 and then it remains essentially constant for both $N = 20$ and $N = 25$.[2] We conjecture that this pattern also holds for larger values of N. Also in Figure 2, we see the answer to our second question concerning the values of the optimal solutions in an NK-landscape where $K > 6$. The increasing best values found by the algorithms when $K > 6$ indicates that search performance is in fact worsening, and not that the values of the optima in the NK-landscapes are increasing.

If we accept that the optima for these NK-landscapes have essentially reached a minimum when $K > 6$, then we can examine how this minimum varies with N by examining only the optima at $K = N - 1$. Figure 3 presents the average global optima for 30 random problems at $K = N - 1$ for the range $10 \leq N \leq 25$. The values of N are shown on the X-axis. And a linear regression line, with a general downward trend[3] and a correlation coefficient of 0.91, has been inserted. This observation is consistent with the Smith and Smith [12] finding of a correlation between N and best average fitnesses in NK-landscapes.

[2] These same trends hold for the entire range $10 \leq N \leq 25$.

[3] We conjecture that the average of the optima shown at $N = 15$ is an experimental anomaly given the narrow range for the standard error of the mean.

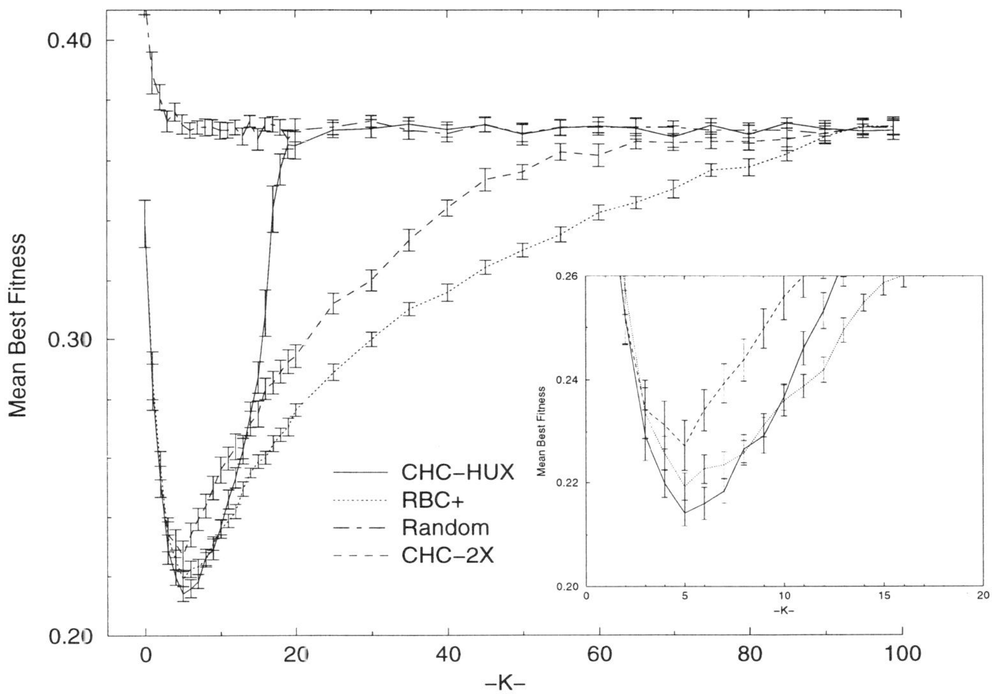

Figure 4 Average best performances of CHC-HUX, RBC+, random search, and CHC-2X on 30 random NK-landscape problems where $N = 100$. Error bars represent $2 * SEM$.

4 NK NICHES

Comparing algorithm performances on NK-landscape functions where the optima are known, although useful, limits us to small N problems where exhaustive search is still practical. One of the contributions of Heckendorn, et al. [7] was that they made their comparisons for $N = 100$, a much larger value of N than used in most other studies. As a starting point for extending the comparisons made by Heckendorn, et al. for larger N problems, we performed independent verification experiments. We tested CHC using the HUX and 2X recombination operators, as well as RBC, RBC+ and random search on NK-landscapes where $N = 100$, generating thirty random problems for each value of K tested.[4] We tested all values for K in the range $0 \leq K \leq 20$, values in increments of 5 for the range $25 \leq K \leq 95$, and $K = 99$. The total number of trials allowed for each experiment was 200,000. Figure 4 shows the results of our verification experiments and the behavior of random search. Figure 4 exhibits the same properties as those observed by Heckendorn, et al., and shown in Figure 1.

[4] Since the performance of the SGA is never better than all other algorithms for any value of K, we have omitted the SGA here for simplicity.

Figure 4 shows that when $N = 100$, the performance of each of the algorithms becomes indistinguishable from random search at some point. CHC-HUX is the first to do so (at $K = 20$). Figure 4 also shows that CHC-HUX performs better than RBC+ in the region $1 \leq K \leq 7$ but the performance of CHC-HUX is better than RBC+ by more than two standard errors only in the region $4 \leq K \leq 7$.[5] Furthermore, it is interesting to note that the $N = 100$ problems are surprisingly difficult even for low values of K. For example, none of the algorithms tested can consistently locate the same best solution in 30 repetitions of the same problem for most of the $K = 2$ problems generated.

CHC-2X never performs as well as CHC-HUX in the range $3 \leq K \leq 13$, but the performance of CHC-2X does not degrade as rapidly as CHC-HUX when $K \geq 15$, and the performance of CHC-2X does not regress to random search until $K \geq 70$. 2X produces offspring that are much more like their parents than HUX. This results in much less vigorous search than when using HUX. Thus, the performance of CHC-2X is more like that of the hill-climbers. Furthermore, by comparing Figure 1 with Figure 4 it can be seen that CHC-2X performs at least as well as the SGA (using one-point crossover) over all $K's$ and usually much better.

RBC+ exhibits the most robust performance over all $K's$ when $N = 100$, as observed by Heckendorn, et al., and performs significantly better than CHC-HUX when $K \geq 11$. When $N = 100$, RBC performs better then RBC+ for $K = 1$ and is statistically indistinguishable from RBC+ when $K \geq 20$.[6] The performance of both hill-climbers becomes indistinguishable from random search when $K \geq 90$.

Comparing the performances of all of these algorithms on NK-landscapes where $N = 100$ indicates that no algorithm performs better than all of the others for all values of K (i.e., dominates). Rather, we see niches where the advantage of an algorithm over the others persists for some range of values of K. These observations are consistent with what we saw for low N in the previous section. For example, re-examination of Figure 2 shows that the performance of CHC-HUX becomes indistinguishable from that of random search at lower values of K than does the performance of the hill-climbers, which is consistent with the behavior of CHC-HUX when $N = 100$ (Figure 4). However, there does not appear to be any niche in which CHC-HUX performs better than RBC+ when $N = 20$ or $N = 25$, as shown in Figure 2. In fact, CHC-HUX is unable to consistently find the optimum solution even when K is quite small (i.e., $K \geq 3$ for $N = 20$ and $K \geq 1$ for $N = 25$) as indicated by the divergence of the lines for CHC-HUX performance and the average optimum. RBC+, on the other hand, consistently finds the optimum for much larger values of K.

[5] The inset in Figure 4 is provided to magnify the performance values of the algorithms in the interval $3 \leq K \leq 12$.

[6] The RBC runs have not been included on the graphs to avoid confusion and clutter.

Table 1 Highest value of K at which CHC-HUX, CHC-2X, RBC and RBC+ consistently locate the optimum solution.

N	19	20	21	22	23	24	25
CHC-HUX	1	3	1	1	1	1	1
CHC-2X	8	5	6	5	3	3	4
RBC+	9	9	7	6	7	6	6
RBC	11	9	9	8	9	7	6

Table 1 shows the highest value of K at which CHC-HUX, CHC-2X, RBC+, and RBC are able to consistently locate the optimal solution for all 30 problems in the range $19 \leq N \leq 25$. CHC-2X, RBC, and RBC+ are all able to consistently locate the optimum at higher values of K than CHC-HUX when $19 \leq N \leq 25$. And RBC is better at locating the optimum consistently than any of the other algorithms for this region. This is critical in that most work testing GA performance on NK-landscapes has been done using small values for N and often do not include hill-climbers as benchmarks. The performance information in Table 1 makes it clear that there is not a niche for even a robust GA like CHC in NK-landscapes where N is small. This indicates that if niches exist for different algorithms in the NK-landscapes they will have to be characterized in both the N and K dimensions.

Figure 5 shows the performances for CHC-HUX, RBC+, and random search on NK-landscapes where $N = 50$ and $N = 80$, for all values of K where $K \leq 20$, in increments of 5 for $25 \leq K \leq N - 5$, and for $K = N - 1$. Thirty random problems were generated for each (N, K) combination tested.[7] At $N = 50$, RBC+ still performs better than CHC-HUX for all $K's$ tested. But at $N = 80$, $K = 4$ and $K = 5$ we see the first hint of a niche for CHC-HUX in NK-landscapes (i.e., CHC-HUX performs significantly better than RBC+). Figure 4 showed that the niche where CHC-HUX performs best extended to $K = 7$ and Figure 6 shows that the niche for CHC-HUX also includes up to $K = 9$ when $N = 150$ and $K = 10$ when $N = 200$.

Figures 7(a-d) indicate those NK-landscapes where one algorithm performs better than another, based on the average best values found after 200,000 trials for all of the values of N and K that we have tested (i.e., $19 \leq N \leq 25$ in increments of 1, $30 \leq N \leq 100$ in increments of 10; K was tested in increments of 1 for $0 \leq K \leq 20$, and in increments of 5 for $20 \leq K \leq N - 5$, and $K = N - 1$). Unfilled circles represent NK-landscapes where one algorithm performs better than another, while filled circles indicate *significantly* (i.e., $> (2 * SEM)$) better performance by one algorithm over another. The points that were tested at which no circle is present indicates that the algorithms being compared were able to locate the same local optima (i.e., tied). These points occur occasionally and only when $K \leq 9$ and $N \leq 30$. Figure 7-a shows those NK-landscapes where RBC+ performs better/significantly better than RBC while Figure 7-b shows those NK-landscapes where RBC performs better/significantly better than RBC+. Figure 7-c shows the NK-landscapes where RBC+ performs better than CHC-HUX, and Figure 7-d

[7] We tested values for N in the range $10 \leq N \leq 25$ and N = 30, 40, 50, 60, 70, 80, 90, 100, 150, and 200.

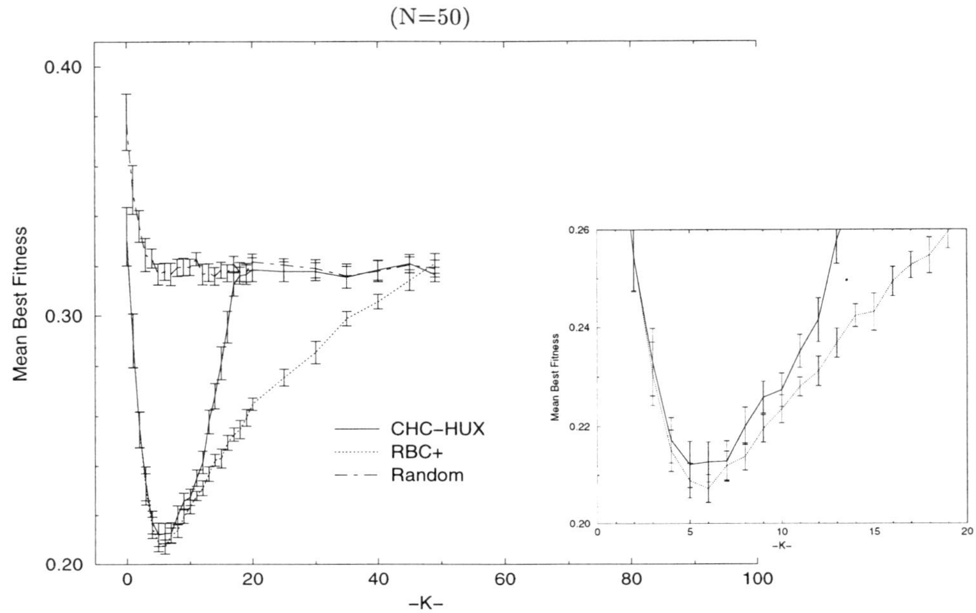

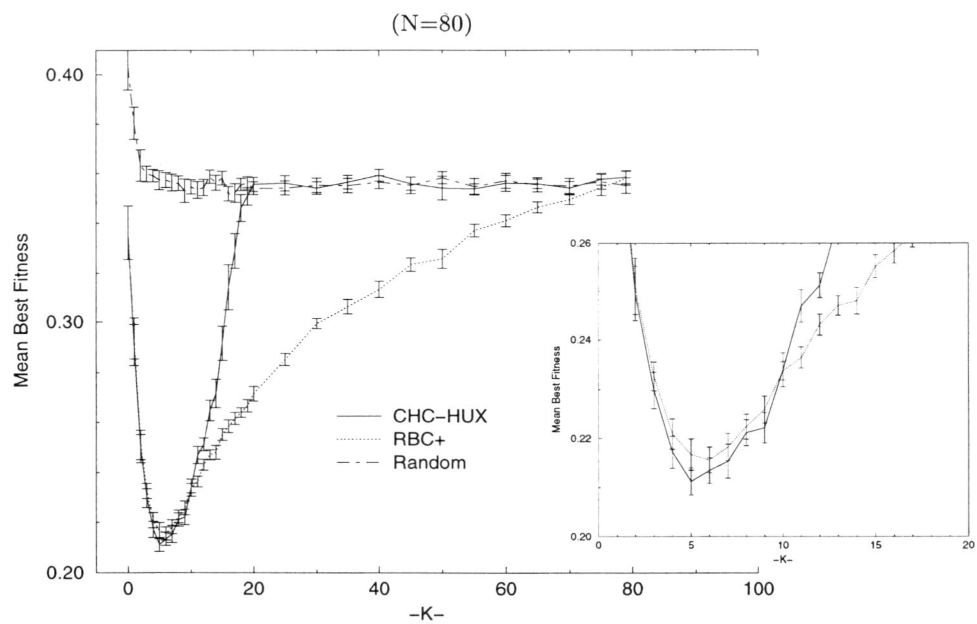

Figure 5 Average best performance for CHC-HUX, RBC+, and random search on 30 random NK-landscapes where $N = 50$ and $N = 80$. Error bars represent $2 * SEM$.

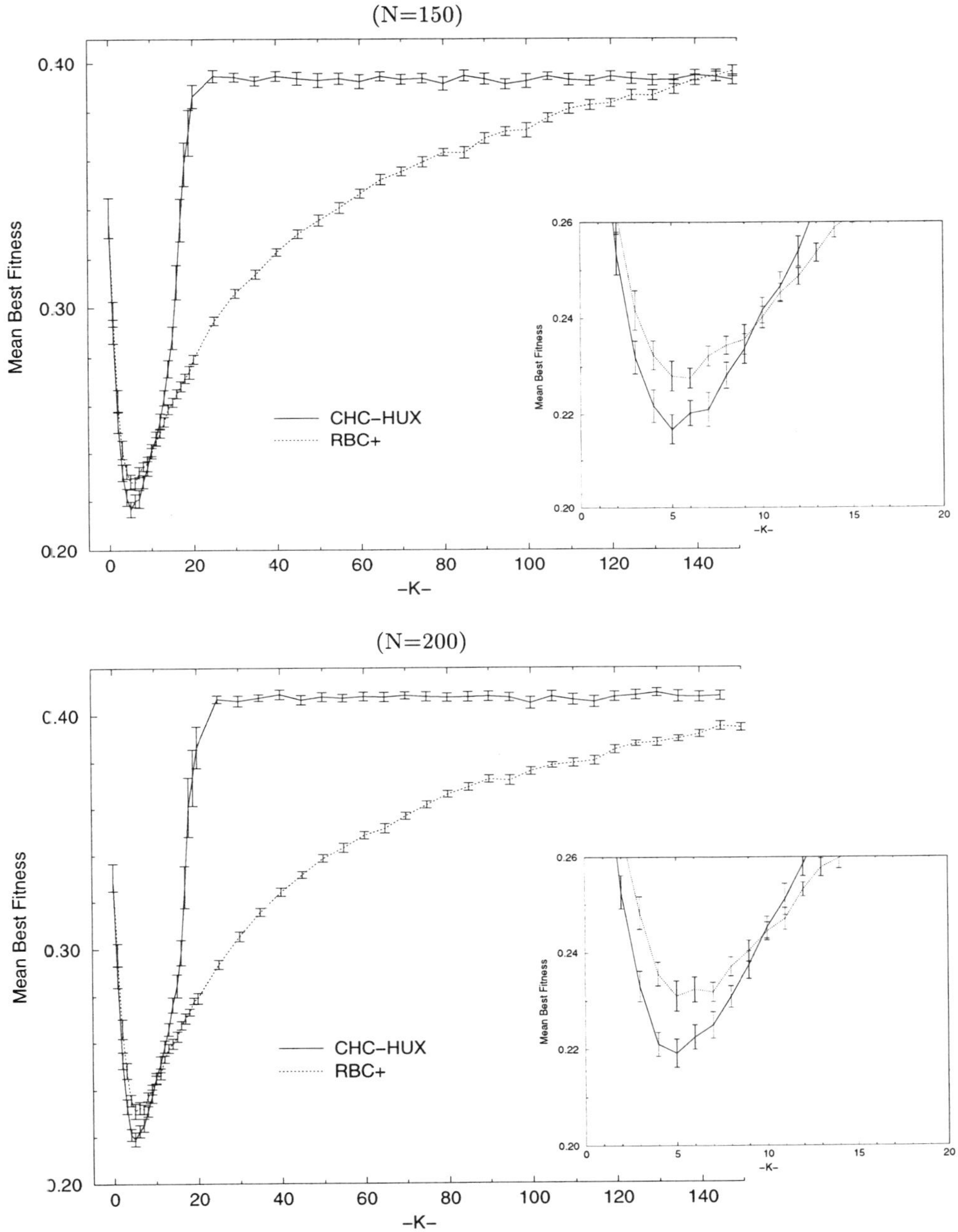

Figure 6 Average best performance for CHC-HUX and RBC+ on 30 random NK-landscapes where $N = 150$ and $N = 200$. Error bars represent $2 * SEM$.

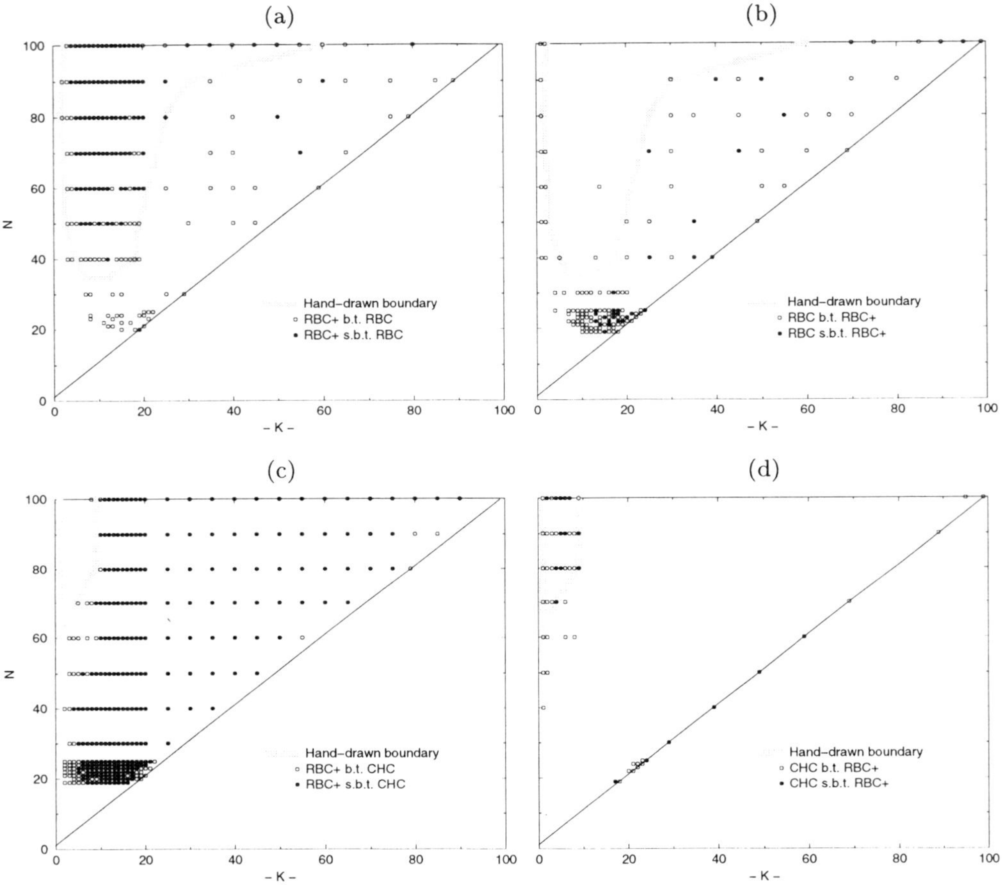

Figure 7 Scatter plots showing the points (K, N) at which one algorithm performs better than and significantly better (i.e., $2 * SEM$) than another.

indicates the NK-landscapes where CHC-HUX performs better/significantly better than RBC+.

The information presented in Figures 7(a-d) gives a coarse pairwise comparison of the NK-landscapes where various algorithms might be useful. While there are regions where no algorithm seems to be the best, there are certainly regions where one algorithm is a better choice than the others and some regions where one algorithm is much worse than the other two. Figure 8 summarizes those regions where each algorithm is observed to exhibit an advantage over the others. Additional analysis information (i.e., trials to find the best local minima when the local minima found are the same for the algorithms) was sometimes necessary to make this determination, as explained in the next section.

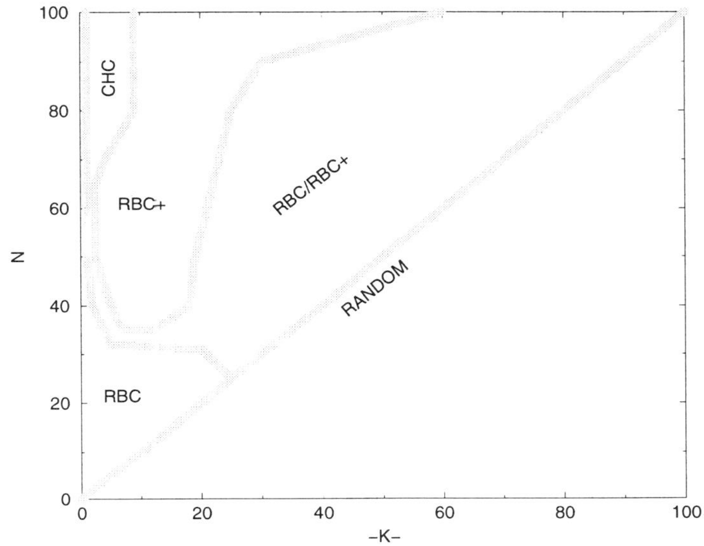

Figure 8 Algorithmic Niches.

5 DISCUSSION

As Figures 7(c-d) indicate, the GAs niche in the universe of NK-landscapes is quite small. And not all GAs even have a niche: as we have seen, the SGA, as well as CHC-2X, are completely dominated by RBC+. On the other hand, CHC-HUX does dominate RBC+ for a small region, but its performance quickly deteriorates to no better than random search for $K \geq 20$. What does this tell us about CHC-HUX and about the structure of NK-landscapes?

There are at least two types of landscapes where a hill-climber like RBC should have an advantage over a GA: when the landscape is very simple or when it is very complex. By a simple landscape we mean one that has two properties. First, the landscape is such that the catchment basin of the global optimum (or some other very good point) is large enough that there is a good chance that a randomly chosen point will fall in this basin, and thus it will not take too many random restarts before the hill-climber lands in the right basin. Second, the paths to the bottoms of the catchment basins are not too long. Of course, there can be some tradeoff between these two conditions. The expected cost of finding the global optimum is a product of how many iterations it takes before the hill-climber is likely to fall in the right basin, and how many cycles the average climb will take before no more improvements can be found.

If the hill-climber allows for soft restarts, like RBC+, then an additional condition needs to be added: many of the local optima which are good are very near (in Hamming distance) to the global optimum.[8] This means that if the hill-climber gets stuck in one of these

[8] This is analogous to the exploration of correlation length by Manderick et al., [11].

regions, exploring other local optima in this region (via soft restarts) will be useful. Again there will be tradeoffs. If there are not that many local optima relative to the total number of trials the hill-climber is allowed, then the overhead of exploring nearby local optima may penalize a hill-climber with soft restarts (like RBC+).

Of course, the easiest problem for a hill-climber is a bitwise linear problem like the One-max problem. The $K = 0$ problems fall in this category, and, as expected, RBC and RBC+ can solve these problems in one cycle. For other problems, a hill-climber may get trapped in a local minimum, but for low N (e.g., 20) and low K (e.g., $K = 1$ or $K = 2$) we would expect that RBC and RBC+ will do fairly well. In fact, RBC should have a competitive advantage over a GA in these types of problems because it does not waste evaluations exploring neighboring local optima. However, as N is increased, the number of local optima will increase, so that even for $K = 1$, RBC and RBC+ will lose their advantage over CHC.

The break even point for $K = 1$ problems is at about $N = 30$. At $N = 30$ RBC, RBC+ and CHC-HUX all find the same best solutions for all 30 problems. RBC and CHC take about the same number of trials to find these solutions, whereas RBC+ takes about three times as many. At $N = 40$ and $K = 1$, RBC and CHC find the same set of solutions, but RBC takes about two and half as many trials, whereas RBC+ sometimes fails to find solutions as good as RBC and CHC and takes about three times as many trials as RBC. As N increases this trend continues for $K = 1$ and $K = 2$, with CHC dominating RBC, and RBC dominating RBC+. The reason RBC+ does relatively poorly in this region is that it is paying a price for the overhead of its soft restarts with very little gain. The local minima are in large attraction basins so that soft restarts tend to repeatedly find the same solutions, thus wasting evaluations. RBC, on the other hand, is able to explore many more local minima than RBC+ in the same number of evaluations. Although CHC-HUX suffers from the same problem as RBC+ (its soft restarts tend to bring it back to the same solution) this problem does not arise for low K, since CHC-HUX is usually able to find the good solutions for these problems without any restarts. So on these problems two very different strategies work fairly well: quickly exploring many local minima (RBC) or slowly exploring the global structure, gradually focusing in on the good local minima (CHC-HUX). As N increases, the probability of exploring all the local minima decreases, and the second strategy gains an advantage.

A more detailed look at the RBC runs on the $N = 30$, $K = 1$ problems (i.e., 30 different problems) shows that in 200,000 trials, constituting about 2200 restarts, RBC finds, on average, about 33 different local optima, although this varies across problems from a low of 8 to a high of 145. However, RBC is better at finding the best solution than this might indicate: RBC finds the best solution, on average, in about 11% of its restarts, although, again, this varies across problems from a low of 1% to a high of 27%.

The second type of landscape that will give a hill-climber a competitive advantage over a GA is a complex landscape. The particular type of complex landscape we have in mind here is one where there are many local optima of varying depths, but a good local optimum does not indicate that neighboring local optima are any good. In other words, there is structure at the fine grain level but not at a more coarse grain level, so finding good solutions at the local level tells one nothing about good solutions at the regional level. Such a problem will be very difficult for a GA since crossing over two good, but unrelated solutions, will very likely produce poor solutions. This tendency will be exacerbated by HUX and incest

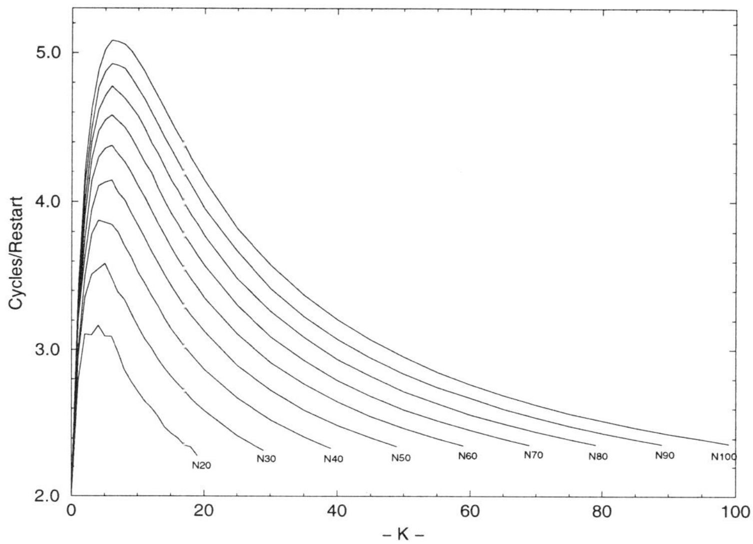

Figure 9 Average number of cycles per restart for RBC.

prevention. When presented with a surface characterized by rampant multi-modality with little or no regional structure, CHC-HUX is reduced to random search. A hill-climber, on the other hand, will do much better because of its ability to search many more attraction basins. Of course, it will not be able to find the global optimum, unless it is a very small search space, but it will, simply by brute force, search many more basins, and thus do better. Furthermore, the ability of RBC+ to search neighboring basins will give it an advantage over RBC for larger N. Since RBC will only be able to search a small fraction of all the local minima, the ability to search deeper in each region explored will give RBC+ an advantage. However, as K increases and the regional structure disappears, RBC+ starts to lose its advantage over RBC and the performance of the two algorithms become indistinguishable.

Finally, for very high K, e g., $K = N - 1$, CHC-HUX has an advantage again. This can be seen in Figures 7(d) where CHC-HUX has many "wins" along the diagonal. The reason for this is that for these NK-landscapes, CHC-HUX is better at random search than the hill-climbers. Both RBC and RBC+ must waste evaluations each cycle ascertaining that there are no more improvements possible by a single bit-flip. CHC-HUX, on the other hand, will rarely generate solutions for such high K that are identical to previously generated solutions.

In summary, perhaps the reason that CHC-HUX's niche in the universe of NK-landscapes is small is because the region of "effective complexity" is small. Information theory would call bit strings of all zeros/ones the most simple, and completely random strings the most complex. Gell-Mann [6] has proposed the notion of "effective complexity" that would reach its maximum somewhere between these extremes and would more accurately reflect our intuitions about complexity. Figures 9-11 illustrate in various ways how this critical region

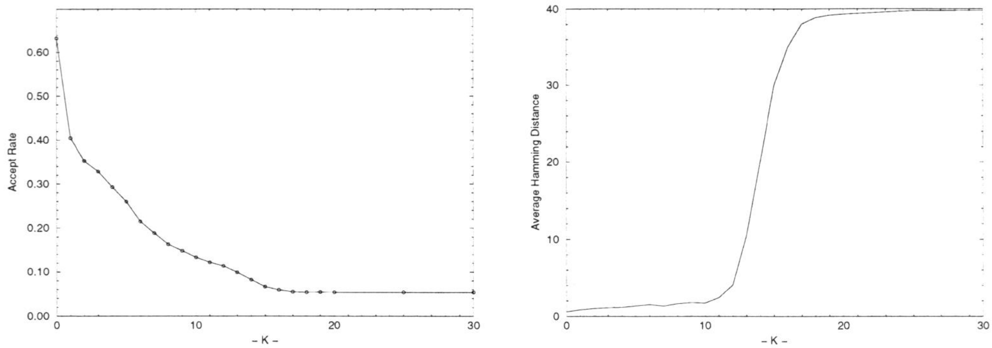

(a) (b)

Figure 10 Average acceptance rates (a) and average convergence at restarts (b) for CHC-HUX.

affects the algorithms differently. Figure 9 shows the number of cycles in RBC per restart over K for a set of representative N's. Note that all the N curves peak between K of 3 and 6, with 6 being the peak value for $N = 100$. The minimum number of cycles is two, a second pass being required to verify that there are no more changes that lead to an improvement. As expected, all N with $K = 0$ require only two cycles. Furthermore, the number of cycles per restart for all N approaches two as K approaches $N - 1$. As the number of local optima increase, the average attraction basin gets smaller and shallower. The intriguing point is that the measure of cycles per restart peak in the same region where CHC-HUX has a competitive advantage, possibly indicating effective complexity.

Figure 10-a shows the acceptance rates for CHC-HUX on $N = 100$ NK-landscapes for various K. The acceptance rate is the fraction of offspring generated that are fit enough to replace some worse individual in the population. As a rule of thumb, CHC-HUX does best on problems where its acceptance rate is around 0.2. If the acceptance rate is very high, the problem may be better suited for a hill-climber like RBC. For example, on the One-max problem the acceptance rate is around 0.6. On the other hand, if the acceptance rate is below 0.1, then this usually indicates that the problem will be difficult for CHC. Sometimes this can be remedied by either using a less disruptive crossover operator or a different representation. As can be seen in Figure 10-a, the acceptance rates deteriorate to about 0.055 by $K = 18$. An acceptance rate this low indicates that the members of the population have very little common information that CHC-HUX can exploit, and that crossover is, in effect, reduced to random search. In fact, most of the accepts come in the first few generations after either a soft restart or creation of the initial population, where a population of mostly randomly generated solutions is being replaced. Interestingly, the acceptance rates fall much more slowly when CHC uses 2X instead of HUX as its crossover operator. As we noted earlier 2X does much better than HUX in the range where $K \geq 15$, although not as well as HUX in the range where $3 \leq K \leq 13$.

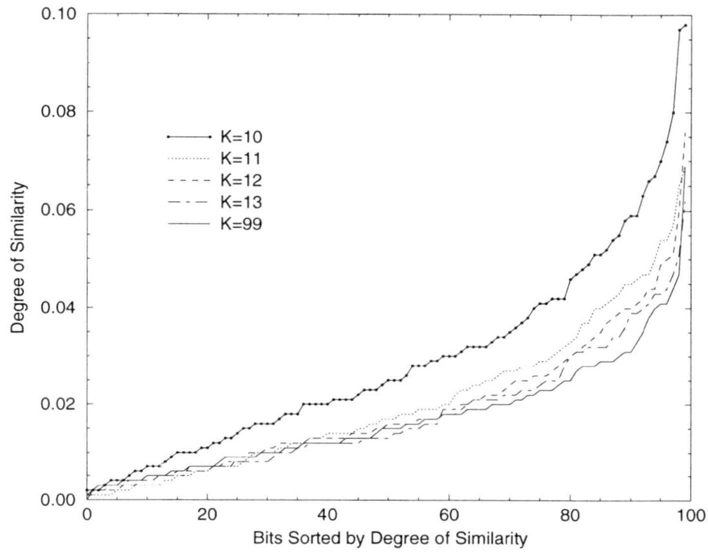

Figure 11 Hamming Similarity of local minima.

An even more dramatic illustration of this phenomenon can be seen in Figure 10-b, which shows the degree to which CHC-HUX's population is converged immediately before it restarts. CHC has two criteria for doing a soft restart: (1) All the members of the population have the same fitness value. (2) The incest threshold has dropped below zero.[9] If CHC is having difficulty generating new offspring that are fit enough to be accepted into the population, then the incest threshold will drop to zero before the population has converged. Figure 10-b shows the average Hamming distance over K between randomly paired individuals in the population at the point of a restart, averaged over all restarts for all experiments for the $N = 100$ problems where $0 \leq K \leq 30$. After $K \geq 12$ the amount of convergence rapidly deteriorates, leveling off at about 40. Note that this is only slightly less than 50, the expected Hamming distance between two random strings of length 100.

Figure 11 shows the degree of similarity of the local optima found by RBC over K for the $N = 100$ problems. For each K the solutions for 2000 hill-climbs are pooled and the degree of similarity is determined for each locus. These loci are sorted according to the degree of similarity, with the most similar loci on the right. Note that by about $K = 13$, the results are indistinguishable from the amount of similarity expected in random strings, represented here by $K = 99$. This, as we have seen, is the point where CHC-HUX rapidly deteriorates, although CHC does somewhat better than random search until $K \geq 20$. In effect, this is showing that there is very little in the way of schemata for CHC to exploit after $K = 12$, the point where it is over taken by RBC+.

[9]The incest threshold is decremented each generation that no offspring are better than the worst member of the parent population.

Table 2 Average trials to find best local minima discovered (not necessarily the optimum) and the standard error of the mean (SEM).

	Trials (SEM)	Trials (SEM)	Trials (SEM)
N=30			
	RBC	RBC+	CHC-HUX
K=1	1702 (308)	5204 (862)	1609 (962)
K=2	4165 (815)	11309 (3400)	14225 (1062)
K=3	24747 (7487)	14204 (2793)	5701 (1880)
K=4	12935 (3465)	18818 (4930)	17510 (1570)
N=40			
	RBC	RBC+	CHC-HUX
K=1	10100 (3078)	37554 (8052)	4094 (1190)
K=2	26009 (6904)	24445 (4740)	12476 (1516)
K=3	33269 (6957)	33157 (4801)	22034 (8739)
K=4	63735 (10828	62600 (9016)	33881 (9659)
N=50			
	RBC	RBC+	CHC-HUX
K=1	26797 (7834)	35959 (6714)	2843 (1438)
K=2	48725 (8180)	82634 (9965)	22337 (8713)
K=3	87742 (9389)	93575 (10014)	28352 (7930)
K=4	98147 (11166)	80636 (9698)	30571 (6348)

Finally, Table 2 shows the mean number of trials to the best solution found and the standard error of the mean for CHC-HUX, RBC, and RBC+ in the region where their three niches meet. Note that CHC usually requires fewer trials before it stops making progress. While we have not yet performed the tests needed to support conclusions for other values, we speculate that if fewer trials were allotted for search than the 200,000 used for the experiments presented in this paper, the niche for CHC-HUX will expand at the expense of the hill-climbers. This results from the hill-climber's reliance on numerous restarts. Conversely, increasing the number of trials allowed for search should benefit the hill-climbers while providing little benefit for CHC-HUX. CHC-HUX's biases are so strong that they achieve their good effects (when they do) very quickly. Allowing large numbers of "soft-restarts" for CHC-HUX (beyond the minimum needed for the problem) usually does not help.

6 CONCLUSIONS

We have presented results of extensive empirical examinations of the behaviors of hill-climbers and GAs on NK-landscapes over the range $19 \leq N \leq 100$. These provide the evidence for the following:

- While the quality of local minima found by both GAs and hill-climbers deteriorates as both N and K increase, there is evidence that the values of the global optima decrease as N increases.
- There is a niche in the landscape of NK-landscapes where a powerful GA gives the best performance of the algorithms tested; it is in the region of $N > 30$ for $K = 1$ and $N > 60$ for $1 \leq K < 12$.
- NK-landscapes are uncorrelated when $K = N - 1$, but our evidence shows that the structure in NK-landscapes deteriorates rapidly as K increases, becoming such that none of the studied algorithms can effectively exploit it when $K > 12$ for N up to 200. This K-region is remarkably similar for a wide range of N's.
- Finally, the advantage that random bit-climbers enjoy over CHC-HUX depends on three things: the number of random restarts executed (a function of the total number of trials allotted and the depth of attraction basins in the landscape), the number of attraction basins in the space, and the size of the attraction basin containing the global optimum relative to the other basins in the space. If the total trials allowed is held constant, then as N increases CHC-HUX becomes dominant for higher and higher K.

Acknowledgments

We would like to thank Robert Heckendorn and Soraya Rana for their help and cooperation throughout our investigation. They willingly provided data, clarifications and even ran validation tests in support of this work.

References

[1] Lashon Booker. Improving Search in Genetic Algorithms. In Lawrence Davis, editor, *Genetic Algorithms and Simulated Annealing*, chapter 5, pages 61–73. Morgan Kaufmann, 1987.

[2] Lawrence Davis. Bit-Climbing, Representational Bias, and Test Suite Design. In L. Booker and R. Belew, editors, *Proceedings of the Fourth International Conference on Genetic Algorithms*, pages 18–23. Morgan Kauffman, 1991.

[3] Larry Eshelman. The CHC Adaptive Search Algorithm. How to Have Safe Search When Engaging in Nontraditional Genetic Recombination. In G. Rawlins, editor, *Foundations of Genetic Algorithms*, pages 265–283. Morgan Kaufmann, 1991.

[4] Larry Eshelman and J. David Schaffer. Productive Recombination and Propagating and Preserving Schemata. In D. Whitley and M. Vose, editors, *Foundations of Genetic Algorithms - 3*, pages 299–313. Morgan Kaufmann, 1995.

[5] Larry J. Eshelman and J. David Schaffer. Crossover's Niche. In Stephanie Forrest, editor, *Proceedings of the Fifth International Conference on Genetic Algorithms*, pages 9–14. Morgan Kauffman, 1993.

[6] Murray Gell-Mann. *The Quark and the Jaguar: Adventures in the Simple and the Complex.* W.H. Freeman Company, San Francisco, 1994.

[7] Robert Heckendorn, Soraya Rana, and Darrell Whitley. Test Function Generators as Embedded Landscapes. In Wolfgang Banzhof and Colin Reeves, editors, *Foundations of Genetic Algorithms - 5*, pages 183–198. Morgan Kaufmann, 1999.

[8] Robert Heckendorn and Darrell Whitley. A Walsh Analysis of NK-Landscapes. In Thomas Bäck, editor, *Proceedings of the Seventh International Conference on Genetic Algorithms*, pages 41–48. Morgan Kaufmann, 1997.

[9] Terry Jones. *Evolutionary Algorithms, Fitness Landscapes and Search.* PhD thesis, University of New Mexico, Department of Computer Science Fort Collins, Colorado, 1994.

[10] S.A. Kauffman. Adaptation on Rugged Fitness Landscapes. In D.L. Stein, editor, *Lectures in the Science of Complexity*, pages 527–618. Addison-Wesley, 1989.

[11] Bernard Manderick, Mark de Weger, and Piet Spiessens. The Genetic Algorithm and the Structure of the Fitness Landscape. In L. Booker and R. Belew, editors, *Proceedings of the Fourth International Conference on Genetic Algorithms*, pages 143–150. Morgan Kauffman, 1991.

[12] R. Smith and J. Smith. An Examination of Tunable, Random Search Landscapes. In Wolfgang Banzhaf and Colin Reeves, editors, *Foundations of Genetic Algorithms - 5*, pages 165–181. Morgan Kaufmann, 1998.

[13] Gilbert Syswerda. Uniform Crossover in Genetic Algorithms. In J. D. Schaffer, editor, *Proceedings of the Third International Conference on Genetic Algorithms.* Morgan Kaufmann, 1989.

New Methods for Tunable, Random Landscapes

R. E. Smith and J. E. Smith
The Intelligent Computer Systems Centre
The University of The West of England
Bristol, UK

Abstract

To understand the behaviour of search methods (including GAs), it is useful to understand the nature of the landscapes they search. What makes a landscape complex to search? Since there are an infinite number of landscapes, with an infinite number of characteristics, this is a difficult question. Therefore, it is interesting to consider parameterised landscape generators, if the parameters they employ have direct and identifiable effects on landscape complexity. A prototypical examination of this sort is the generator provided by NK landscapes. However, previous work by the authors and others has shown that NK models are limited in the landscapes they generate, and in the complexity control provided by their two parameters (N, the size of the landscape, and K, the degree of *epistasis*). Previous work suggested an added parameter, which the authors called P, which affects the number of epistatic interactions. Although this provided generation of all possible search landscapes (with given epistasis K), previous work indicated that control over certain aspects of complexity was limited in the NKP generator. This paper builds on previous work, suggesting that two additional parameters are helpful in controlling complexity: the relative scale of higher order and lower order epistatic effects, and the correlation of higher order and lower order effects. A generator based on these principles is presented, and it is examined, both analytically, and through actual GA runs on landscapes from this generator. In some cases, the GA's performance is as analysis would suggest. However, for particular cases of K and P, the results run counter to analytical intuition. The paper presents the results of these examinations, discusses their implications, and suggests areas for further examination.

1 Introduction

There are a number of advantages to generating random landscapes as GA test problems, and as exemplars for studies of search problem complexity. Specifically, it would be advantageous to have a few "knobs" that allow direct adjustment of landscape complexity, while retaining the ability to generate a large number of landscapes at a given complexity "setting". The NK landscape procedure, suggested by Kauffman [5], is often employed for this purpose. However, as has been discussed in previous papers [4, 10], the prime parameter in this generation procedure (K) fails to reflect and adequately control landscape complexity in several ways. In addition, NK landscapes have been shown to be incapable of generating all possible landscapes of size N and (given) epistasis K. Previous work [4, 10] considers a generator with an additional parameter, called the NKP generation procedure, that can cover the space of possible landscapes. However, previous work also indicates that K and P are not particularly good controls over some important forms of landscape complexity.

This paper suggests new sets of controls over complexity in random landscape generators, and examines a particular generator based on these controls. The paper presents theoretical examination of landscapes generated with this procedure, as well as GA results that show how the new controls affect GA performance.

2 NK and NKP Landscapes

By way of introduction, this section overviews NK and NKP landscapes, and past results. In this discussion we will assume all genes are binary, for convenience. However, the results are extensible to problems with larger gene alphabets.

2.1 NK Landscapes

Specifying an NK landscape requires the following parameters:

N - the total number of bits (genes).

K - the amount of epistasis. Each bit depends on K other bits to determine that its fitness contribution. We will call the K+1 bits involved in each contribution a *subfunction.*

b_i - N (possibly random) bit masks ($i = 1, 2, 3 \ldots, N$). Each bit mask is of length N, and contains K+1 ones. The 1s in a bit mask indicate the bits in an individual that are used to determine the value of the ith subfunction.

Given these parameters, one can construct a random NK landscapes as follows:

A. Construct an N by 2^{K+1} table, $\mathbf{X}$.

B. Fill $\mathbf{X}$ with random numbers, typically from a standard uniform distribution.

Given the table $\mathbf{X}$, and the bit masks, one determines the fitness of an individual as follows:

C. For each bit mask b_i, select out the substring of the individual that correspond with the K+1 one-valued bits in that bit mask.

D. Decode these bits into their decimal integer equivalent j.

E. Add the entry $X(i, j)$ to the overall fitness function value for this individual.

Note that the fitness values are typically normalized by dividing by N.

A typical set of bit masks for this type of problem consists of all N bit masks that have K+1 consecutive ones. In this case the string is treated as a circle, so that the consecutive 1 bits wrap around. This set of bit masks outlines a function where any given bit depends on the K preceding bits to determine its contribution to fitness. However, bit masks are sometimes used such that b_i has the ith bit set to one, but the remaining K one-valued bits are selected at random. Some other possibilities are discussed in [2].

2.2 NKP Landscapes

Altenberg [1, 2], and later Heckendorn and Whitley [4], allude to a set of landscapes that we will call the NKP landscapes. If one uses an analogy to the NK landscapes, specifying an NKP landscape requires the same parameters as the NK landscapes, with one addition:

P - the number of subfunctions (each assumed to be of epistasis K, for this discussion) that contribute to the overall fitness function. This discussion also assumes that the P subfunctions are simply summed to determine overall fitness. Each subfunction is associated with a bit mask (also called a *partition*) b_i. Note that, for coverage of the space of all K epistatic functions

$$0 \leq P \leq \binom{N}{(K+1)}.$$

Moreover, this means that one must specify P bit masks, rather than only N. This means that table **X** must be extended to be P by 2^{K+1}. Otherwise, the construction and decoding procedure is the same as that for NK landscapes.

3 Past Results

In his examination of NK landscapes, Kauffman only considers aspects of the landscapes that pertain to hill climbing search. In this paper, these will be called *peak distribution characteristics*. Previous investigations [10] have considered these aspects, and aspects of the landscapes that pertain to juxtapositional search operators, like crossover. In this paper, these will be called *juxtapositional characteristics*.

3.1 Juxtapositional Complexity Considerations

A previous paper [10] defined a yardstick for juxtapositional complexity, called *misleadingness*. Specifically, it defined **the probability of nth order misleadingness, to be the probability that, when one considers all building blocks of n bits or less, the compliment of the optimum appears as fit or more fit than the optimum itself.** Although misleadingness is a less strict phenomenon than deception [3], it is related, and it yields a calculable measure of juxtapostional complexity in the randomly generated landscapes we consider here.

3.2 Observations

Examinations of NKP landscapes [10] (of which NK landscapes are a subset, with P=N), revealed the following with regard to peak distribution characteristics:

- The parameter P has little effect on the most critical of these characteristics.
- However, P acts as a "gain factor" on the landscape's expected range of fitness values.
- Moreover, P seems more responsible than K for the so-called *complexity catastrophe* in these landscapes.

A more general observation is that K is an overly sensitive control on peak distribution complexity. That is, for values of K much larger than 3, landscapes become intractable. It is worth considering that since this analysis was based on exhaustive searches, landscapes with $N > 20$ were not considered, and it is possible that the critical value of K is related to N, perhaps in a logarithmic fashion

With regard to juxtapositional characteristics, the following is observed:

- The expected juxtapositional complexity (that is, the complexity of the building block structure) of landscapes generated by the NKP procedure is limited.
- P seems to have little effect on changing the juxtapositional characteristics of landscapes generated by the NKP procedure.

Finally, [10] suggests that it may be possible to directly manipulate Walsh coefficient statistics, and thus develop random landscapes with more desirable and controllable juxtapositional characteristics. Previous work [10] did not speculate about the effects of such manipulation on peak distribution characteristics. The following section introduces the general notion of Walsh-based landscapes, in a form analogous to NKP landscapes, and later sections introduce a particular form of generator based on this idea.

4 Walsh-based Landscapes

Consider a search space defined over length L binary strings. In terms of the Walsh coefficients, define the fitness of an individual as

$$f(x) = \sum_{j=0}^{2^L} w_j \prod_{i=1}^{L} \Psi(x_i, J_i)$$

where x is the bit string representing the individual, x_i is the ith bit in that string, w_j is the Walsh coefficient corresponding to the *partition* (bit mask) numbered j, J is the bit mask (which is the N-bit binary integer representation of j), J_i is the ith bit in the bit mask, and Ψ is the function described in Table 1.

Let us call the *order* of a Walsh coefficient the number of ones in the partition (bit mask) associated with that coefficient. If a function has a non-zero Walsh coefficient of a given order (say, K+1), that means that there is a fitness contribution that depends on all K+1 bits in the associated partition.

Table 1 Walsh Transform Function Ψ

x_i	J_i	$\Psi(x_i\ J_i)$
0	0	1
0	1	1
1	0	1
1	1	−1

If one uses an analogy to the NKP landscapes, specifying a similar type of Walsh-based landscape is straightforward. It requires the same set of parameters as the NKP landscapes. Given these parameters, one can construct a random Walsh-based function of length N and epistasis K as follows:

A. Construct a P by 2^{K+1} table **W**.

B. Fill the table **W** with random numbers, taken from some distribution, possibly a normal distribution.

One determines the fitness of an individual as follows:

C. For each bit mask b_i, select out the bits in the individual that correspond with the K+1 1-valued bits in the bit mask. Call this length K+1 bit string S_i.

D. For each partition order m, $m = 0, \ldots, (K+1)$, determine the parity of all the order m partitions of S_i. That is, determine the parity of each subset of m bits that can be taken from string S_i. Note that there are a total of 2^{K+1} partitions that must be examined for parity. Each of these corresponds to a column in the random table **W** described above.

E. If the parity of the jth partition of S_i is even, add table entry **W**(i, j) to the overall fitness. If the parity of the jth partition of S_i is odd, subtract table entry **W**(i,j) from the overall fitness.

Note that if the bit masks b_i are non-overlapping, the values in the random table correspond directly to the Walsh coefficients for various, associate partitions in the overall fitness function. However, if the bit masks overlap, the direct correspondence to the overall Walsh coefficients is less clear. However, as Heckendorn and Whitley [4] point out, the overlap in the bit masks affects only the Walsh coefficients associated with partitions in the overlapping region. The Walsh coefficients in these overlapping regions must have an order less than K+1.

5 More on Juxtapositional Complexity

Previous work [10] has shown that, for the landscape generation procedures introduced above, one can often calculate the probability of misleadingness, by assuming that the order k Walsh coefficients are drawn from a normal distribution with mean μ_k and variance σ_k^2.

Let A be the random variable given by the sum of the odd-ordered Walsh coefficients of order κ or less, and B be the random variable given by the sum of the odd-ordered

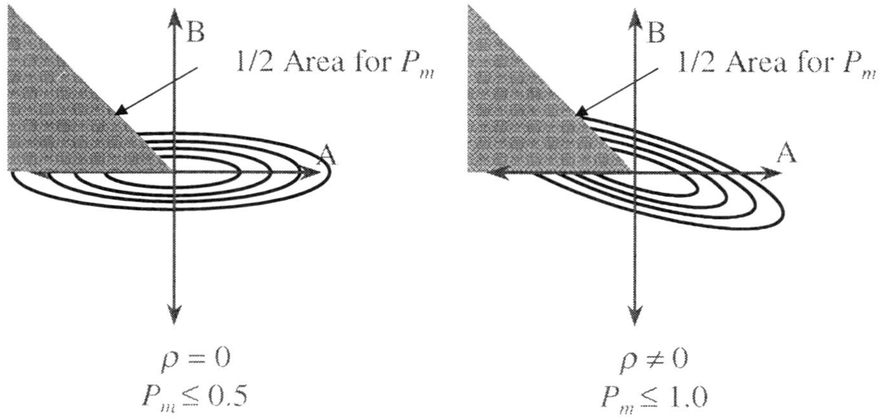

Figure 1 Visualization of the probability of misleadingness. The ellipsoid is a bivariate normal distribution. The volume under the shaded octant is half the probability. The figure on the left shows the distribution with no correlation between high and lower order Walsh coefficients. The figure on the right shows the situation where there is negative correlation.

Walsh coefficients with order greater than κ. Under the assumptions given above, these random variables follow a bivariate normal distribution, with correlation coefficient ρ, and variances as follows:

$$\sigma_A^2 = \sum_{\kappa=n/2}^{(L-1)/2} \binom{L}{2\kappa+1} \sigma^2_{(2\kappa+1)}, \; \sigma_B^2 = \sum_{\kappa=0}^{(n-1)/2} \binom{L}{2\kappa+1} \sigma^2_{(2\kappa+1)}.,$$

This gives the probability of misleadingness as

$$P_m = \frac{1}{\pi}\left[\tan^{-1}\left(\sqrt{\frac{\lambda_1}{\lambda_2}}\left(\frac{\rho\sigma_A\sigma_B}{(\lambda_1-\sigma_A^2)}\right)\right) - \tan^{-1}\left(\sqrt{\frac{\lambda_1}{\lambda_2}}\left(\frac{\rho\sigma_A\sigma_B-(\lambda_1-\sigma_A^2)}{\rho\sigma_A\sigma_B+(\lambda_1-\sigma_A^2)}\right)\right)\right]$$

where λ_1, λ_2 are the eigenvalues of the covariance matrix for A and B, given by:

$$\lambda_1, \lambda_2 = \frac{1}{2}\left[\left(\sigma_A^2+\sigma_B^2\right) \pm \sqrt{\sigma_A^4 + 2\left(2\rho^2-1\right)\sigma_A^2\sigma_B^2 + \sigma_B^4}\right].$$

One can visualize this calculation as twice the volume under a generally oriented ellipsoid, under the fourth octant of the plane, as shown in Figure 1.

The ellipsoid represents a bivariate normal distribution, and the octant is the area where the effects of higher-order Walsh coefficients contradict and overrule those of lower order.

The rotation of the ellipsoid in the plane is caused by ρ, and "length" of the ellipsoid is caused by the ratio of σ_a to σ_b, coupled with ρ. For $\rho = 0$, the major and minor axes of the ellipsoid align with the axes of the plane. Note that in this uncorrelated case, the maximum value of P_m is 0.5, since (for large σ_a/σ_b), at most 1/4 of the ellipsoid is in the octant. Previous investigations [10] empirically demonstrated that this was the case for NKP landscapes, and thus their juxtapositional complexity was limited. Note that in the correlated case, P_m can approach 1.0, since up to 1/2 of the ellipsoid can fall beneath the octant.

6 New Generation Methods

Figure 1 illustrates that to manipulate juxtapositional complexity, one must stretch and rotate the "tongue" of the ellipsoid into the fourth octant. This involves two factors: the relative scale of the sums of higher and lower (odd) ordered Walsh coefficients, and the correlation of these sums. This suggests a class of methods can be developed that use the Walsh generation procedure suggestion in Section 4, and direct manipulation of the relative scale of correlation of normally generated Walsh coefficients.

7 One Such Generator

There are quite a number of ways to develop generators based on these principles, given that there are several values of K for which one can consider the relative scales and correlations. Moreover, these scales and correlations are interrelated, given that they involve progressive sums of Walsh coefficients.

Also, note that there are a number of ways to correlate random variables, such that they yield the desired marginal distributions and correlation in the sample of landscapes [8]. Some methods are less appropriate to our goal of constructing a landscape generator than others. For instance, one could use a mixture of maximally correlated pairs and uncorrelated pairs.

With this structure, one number x_A could be randomly generated from a standard normal distribution. Then, with a preselected probability p, another number x_B could be taken as a linear function of x_A, and with probability $1 - p$, x_B could be set as an independent random variable.

Such a procedure could give a generator that had the desired correlation characteristics over the space of x_A, x_B pairs. However, if these numbers were used in the generation of landscapes, it would not yield a situation where any one landscape had some desired complexity characteristic.

A more desirable procedure is to generate x_A randomly from a standard normal distribution, and generate x_B as follows:

$$x_B = \left[(R x_A) + (1 - |R|) \left[\sigma \left(0, 1 \right) \right] \right],$$

where $\sigma(0,1)$ is another standard normal, and R is a parameter, $-1 \leq R \leq 1$. This method produces the correlated standard normal random variables, and the correlation will have the same sign as R. However, note that the correlation will not necessarily have the same magnitude as R.

Using this correlation procedure, we have implemented the following generator:

Given an even value of K, set all Walsh coefficients to zero:

A Set $i = 1$, and identify all the Walsh coefficients w_j (subpartition coefficients belonging to the first partition) of order K or less indicated in the (randomly generated) set of P partitions.

B Set a counter $count_j$ to equal the number of partitions within which each w_j has an effect.

C To each w_j add a random number x_j, taken from a standard normal distribution with mean zero and variance $\frac{1}{count_j}$. If w_j is of odd order, add x_j to the running sum sum_i, and x_j^2 to var_i.

D Repeat for each partition $i = 2, \ldots, P$.

E Set the P order K+1 Walsh coefficients indicated by the set of P partitions, using the following formula:

$$w_i = \frac{1}{PS}\left[(R\, sum_j) + (1 - |R|)\left[\sigma\left(0, \sqrt{var_i}\right)\right]\right],$$

where the sum is taken over odd ordered subpartitions, the S is a scale parameter, and R is a correlation parameter, which ranges from -1 to 1. One determines the fitness of an individual as in steps C through E in Section 4. Note that the complexity of step **A** is to limit unintentional cross-correlation between overlapping subpartitions.

Note that R controls correlation between higher and lower order coefficients, and small S yields higher order coefficients that are much larger than those of lower order, within the same partition. Thus, one would expect more juxtapositional complexity with lower S, and more highly negative R.

This landscape procedure involves 5 parameters: N, K, P, S, and R, and are thus referred to as NKPSR landscapes. Although the additional parameters may seem to complicate manipulating these landscapes, previous work [10] shows that one must be able to manipulate each of these aspects of a landscape to manipulate peak distribution and juxtapositional complexity.

In summary, the landscape has the following parameters:

(1) N - size of the landscape,

(2) K - the size of largest epistatic partitions,

(3) P - number of epistatic partitions,

(4) S - the relative scale of lower and higher order effects in the partitions,

(5) R - correlation between lower and higher order effects in the partitions.

8 Observations About the New Generator

Given our previous work we wish to consider three aspects of the generator; peak distribution characteristics, juxtaposition characteristics, and, finally, performance on the landscapes using a real GA. Each of these is considered in the following sections.

8.1 Peak Distribution Characteristics

In order to evaluate the properties of NKPSR landscapes, a number of landscapes were created for each of a set of combinations of parameter values. For landscapes of size N = 12,14,16,18 and 20, 10 landscapes were created for each of the valid combinations of the following parameters:

K = {2,4,6,8,}

P = {4,8,16,32,64}

R = (-0.81, -0.2, 0.0, 0.2, 0.81}

S = {0.01, 0.1, 1.0}

Each landscape was exhaustively probed in order to discover the location and value of all the optima (both local and global), and the following values were then calculated for each landscape:

- Maximum, minimum, mean and standard deviation of fitness,
- Mean and standard deviation of optima fitness,
- Number of optima, mean and standard deviation of distance of optima from the global optimum,
- Correlation between relative fitness of local optima and distance from the global optimum.

The results were subjected to a one-way *analysis of variance* (ANOVA) for the factors N, K, P, R and S, and to tests for linearity. The results are summarized in Table 2. Where the ANOVA tests indicate statistical significance at the 1% level, the ε^2 value (a measure of the proportion of the variance in the measured value that can be attributed to the factor) is given where the factor accounts for more than 1% of the observed variance. Particularly meaningful values are shown in bold, and a hyphen indicates that the ε^2value is less than 5% although the ANOVA results show that the factor is significant. In all cases, NSS indicates no statistical significance. Where a factor appears to be a major determinant in the value of the variable, and tests suggest a significant linearity between the values of the factor and the observations, the correlation co-efficient is shown in braces.

The analysis shows that the factor R is not statistically significant for the distance related measures, and never accounts for more than 2% of the observed variance in the fitness related measures, and so this column is omitted for clarity.

From these results we can observe that as with the NKP landscapes, the dominant factors affecting these coarse peak distribution statistics are N, K and P.

Previously reported analysis on NKP landscapes [10] showed that the major effect of P was as a kind of "gain control", altering the spread of fitness values present in the landscape

Table 2 Statistical factors indicating the effects of N, K, Pand S on peak distribution characteristics of landscapes. The Optima Correlation row pertains to the correlation between local optima fitness, and distance from the global optimum.

Measure	N	K	P	S
Landscape Max. Fitness	-	**0.4979 (0.6982)**	**0.2909 (-0.4518)**	-
Landscape Min. Fitness	-	**0.4972 (-0.6979)**	**0.2926 (0.4528)**	-
Land Std. Dev. Fitness	-	**0.4051 (0.6309)**	**0.4669 (-0.5329)**	-
Mean Fitness Local Optima	-	**0.4221 (0.6459)**	**0.4281 (-0.5416)**	-
Std Dev Opt. Fitness	NSS	**0.3807 (0.6086)**	0.1547	0.1180
Number of Local Optima	**0.1821 (0.3671)**	0.05177	0.1087	-
Mean Distance	NSS	**0.1210 (0.3156)**	-	0.1385
Std. Dev. Distance	**0.4384 (-0.6567)**	0.1585	-	0.0913
Optima Correlation	-	**0.3134 (0.5444)**	0.0606	**0.1588 (-0.3945)**

but not affecting the location of peaks. This is a secondary effect arising from the fact that if partitions overlap it is not possible to simultaneously optimise them all, and as the number of partitions increases so do the number of partitions with sub optimal values in optima. This effect can be seen again in these results, and there is an additional affect that P now accounts for over 10% in the observed variance in the number of peaks, the number reducing as P is increased.

Unlike the NKP landscapes, the value of K now has a significant effect on the range of fitness values present, with both the range of fitness value, and the mean fitness of local optima increasing with K. This can be explained by the fact that as K increases, so the number of low order Walsh coefficients within each partition increases, with a corresponding increase in the variance of the normal distribution from which the high order coefficient is drawn.

As K increases, the mean distance of local optima from the global optimum, the mean and standard deviation of their fitnesses (relative to that of the global optimum), and the positive correlation between fitness and distance from the global optimum all increase, reflecting the pattern observed by Kauffman of a "massif central" present at low K but disappearing as the K increases.

The significant (i.e. $\varepsilon^2 > 1\%$) effects of S as it increases from 0.01 to 1.0, (i.e the high order co-efficients become less important) are:

- the mean distance of local optima from the global decreases
- the correlation between their fitness and that distance becomes more negative
- the standard deviations of both fitness and distances increases.

The first two observations can be understood when it is considered that the scale factor S stochastically affects whether the high order co-efficient outweighs the effect of the low order values in determining the location of the global optimum: S approaches 1.0 there is less chance of creating a misleading landscape.

The effects of S on the peak distribution characteristics are more clear when a single set of values are considered for N,K and P, for example the correlation values for N = P = 16, K = 2 with R = -0.81 are -0.2278 for S = 0.01 and -0.5520 for S = 1.0.

However when N,K,P and S are fixed, the effects of changing R are not statistically significant, suggesting that these peak distribution characteristics are perhaps too coarse to detect the effects of a single deceptive global optimum

In conclusion it would appear that in terms of the peak distribution metrics, the characteristics of the NKPRS landscapes are broadly similar to those of the NKP landscapes, and are largely determined by K, with secondary effects due to S as noted. These metrics are based on measuring distance in Hamming space, which more closely reflects search conducted by "bit-flipping" hill climbers and mutational operators.

8.2 Juxtapositional Characteristics

To evaluate the effects of the various parameters of NKPSR landscapes on juxtapositional complexity, 40 landscapes were generated for a number of combinations of these parameters, and the results were used to calculate the probability of misleadingness, as discussed in Section 5. Typical results of this exploration are shown in Figure 2 through Figure 5.

Note that, as one would expect, the complexity of the landscape increases with negative R. P also has a noticeable effect. Complexity also increases with decreasing S, as one would expect.

8.3 GA Performance

The previous sections show that over the space of possible landscapes of a given size N, one would expect K and S to have the most effect of peak distribution, while K, S, and R should have effects on juxtapositional complexity. Whether these effects result in actual complexity for the GA remains to be established. To examine this issue, we applied a relatively simple GA to a selection of problems constructed with this generator.

The GA used a population of 100 binary individuals, with uniform crossover, applied with probability one, point mutation applied with probability 0.05, and tournament selection. This GA was in no way optimised for these problems, since we simply wished to illustrate variations in GA performance over the space of landscapes generated. For each set of generator settings the GA was run 100 times: 10 random restarts on 10 separate landscapes.

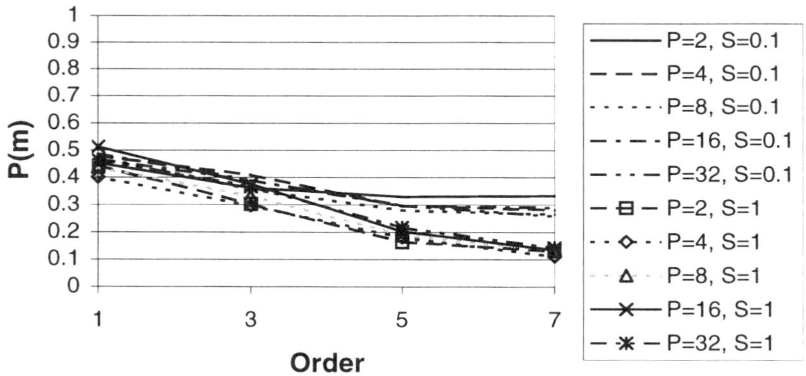

Figure 4 Probability of misleadingness as a function of building block order in NKPSR landscapes. In this figure, N = 16, K =8, R=+0.5. Although such a large value of K is not recommended, it helps to illustrate the general shape of the graphs for all K values. P(m) is 0 for all orders greater than or equal to K.

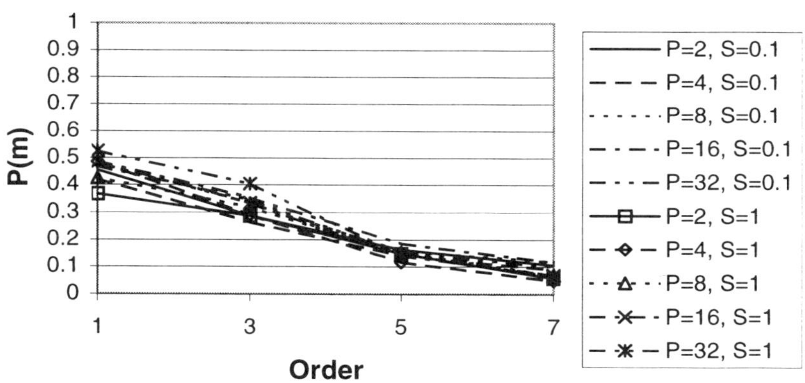

Figure 5 Probability of misleadingness as a function of building block order in NKPSR landscapes. In this figure, N = 16, K =8, R=+0.5. Although such a large value of K is not recommended, it helps to illustrate the general shape of the graphs for all K values. P(m) is 0 for all orders greater than or equal to K.

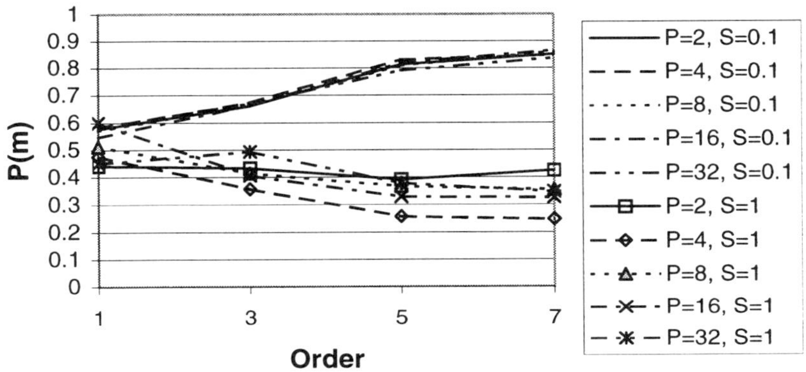

Figure 2 Probability of misleadingness as a function of building block order in NKPSR landscapes. In this figure, N = 16, K =8, R=-0.8. Although such a large value of K is not recommended, it helps to illustrate the general shape of the graphs for all K values. P(m) is 0 for all orders greater than or equal to K.

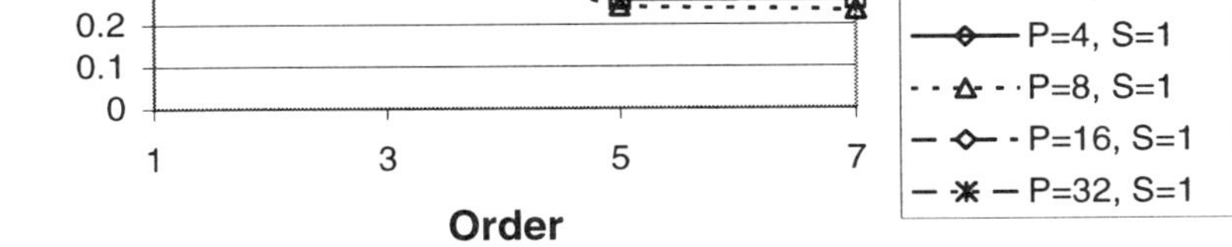

Figure 3 Probability of misleadingness as a function of building block order in NKPSR landscapes. In this figure, N = 16, K =8, R=-0.5. Although such a large value of K is not recommended, it helps to illustrate the general shape of the graphs for all K values. P(m) is 0 for all orders greater than or equal to K.

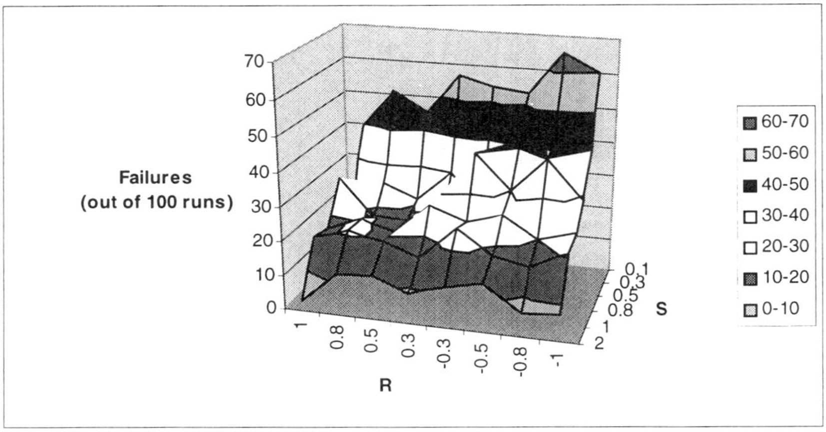

Figure 6 Failures to find the optimum out of 100 runs for a GA applied to landscapes using the specified generator, N=15, K=2, P=15, and indicated values of S and R.

In each landscape, we exhaustively located the optimum, and ran the GA until it either found this point, or completed 300 generations. We recorded the number of GA runs that located the optimum, and the number of generations to find the optimum in those cases.

Figure 6 shows the results of the GA for N=15, K=2, and P=15. Note that this yields 3-bit interactions, and the number of partitions typical in NK landscapes. As expected, this figure shows increasing difficulty for the GA as S becomes smaller and R becomes more negative. However, note that for large values of S (where problems are relatively easy for the GA), distinctions in R become less important.

Similar results are seen by observing the number of generations needed to locate the optimum, for the runs where the optimum is found (see Figure 7).

However, it is interesting to note that the pattern shifts for higher levels of epistasis. Consider the results for K=4 and P=15, shown in Figure 8 and Figure 9. Note that in Figure 8 the S axis is shown in reverse order (relative to previous plots) for clarity. As one would expect, these problems, which have higher order Walsh coefficients, become more difficult for the GA to solve. However, at this level of epistasis, it seems that the effect of S (scale) is reversed. High S yields problems that are more difficult for the GA, in terms of actually finding the optimum. This runs counter to the intuition of our previous analysis. However, note that Figure 9 generally shows the familiar pattern predicted by our analysis. Apparently, the effects of Walsh coefficient scale change, in some way that is unexplained by our current analysis. For such landscapes, the optimum becomes more difficult for the GA to discover with higher S. The effects of R are less clear, although the seem to follow the pattern predicted by analysis for intermediate values of R, shown in Figure 8. However, when the optimum is found by the GA, the number of generations increases with lower S, as our analysis would suggest.

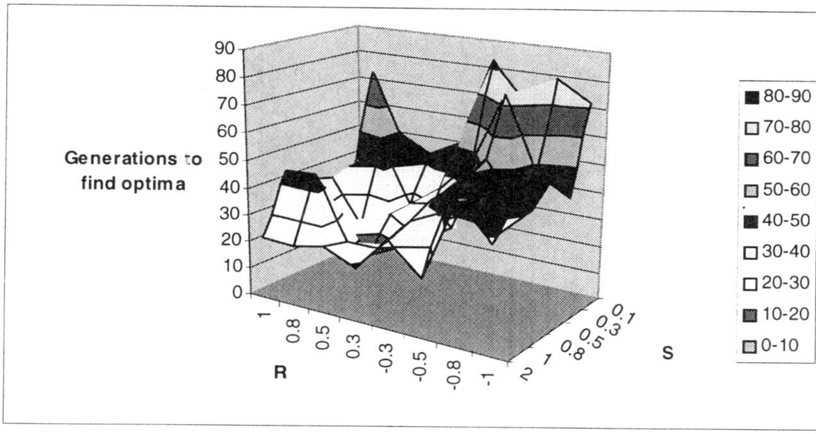

Figure 7 Generations to find the optimum (when it is found). Results averaged over 100 runs of a GA applied to landscapes using the specified generator, N=15, K=2, P=15, and indicated values of S and R.

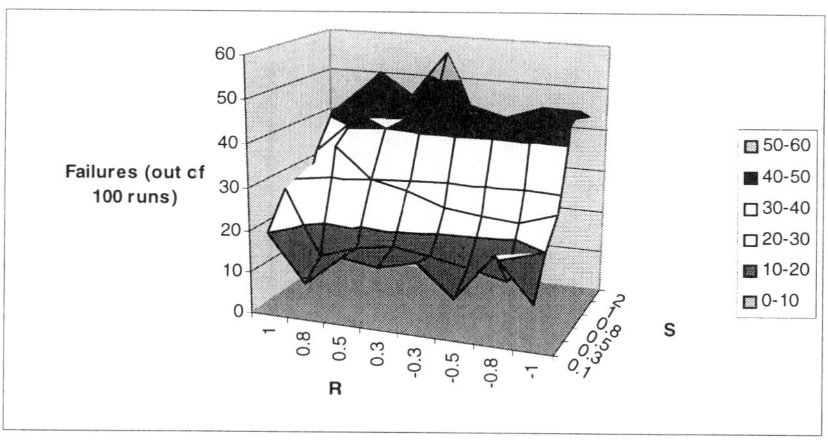

Figure 8 Failures to find the optimum out of 100 runs for a GA applied to landscapes using the specified generator, N=15, K=4, P=15, and indicated values of S and R. Note that in this figure the S axis is in reversed order, relative to previous plots, for clarity.

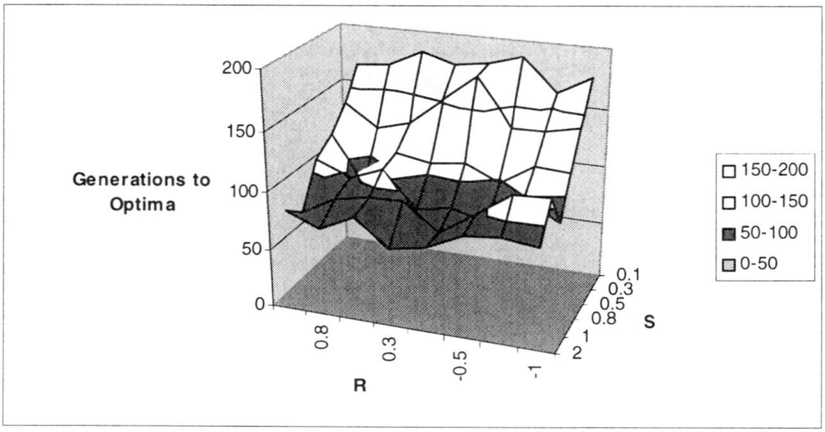

Figure 9 Generations to find the optimum (when it is found). Results averaged over 100 runs of a GA applied to landscapes using the specified generator, N=15, K=4, P=15, and indicated values of S and R.

It is also interesting to examine patterns of performance with respect to S and R for low values of P. These problems are generally easy for the GA. For instance, consider results for K=4 and P=5 shown in Figure 10 and Figure 11. There is still some pattern of declining difficulty with increasing S and more negative R, particularly in the generations-to-optimum results, shown in Figure 11.

It is also useful to observe landscape behaviour for levels of P greater than N. Figure 12 and Figure 13 show results for K=2 and P=20. In this case, the pattern of increasing difficulty with decreasing S is shown in both success in finding the optimum, and the number of generations required. A general pattern of increasing numbers of generations to find the optimum with more negative R is generally observed as well (Figure 13). However, the effects of R on success of the GA in finding the optima (Figure 12) are less clear, and seem to sometimes reflect the opposite of the expected, giving decreasing difficulty with lower and more negative R, particularly for the intermediate values of S.

Finally, we consider results for K=4 and P=20, shown in Figure 14 and Figure 15. As in previous plots with K=4, note that Figure 14, has the S axis reversed, since the effects of S on the GAs ability to find the optimum are generally the opposite of our intuition. Moreover, in this case (and in other higher K and P scenarios), the effects of R seem reversed, as well. However, in the generations-to-optima results (Figure 15), the results stay relatively consistent with our analytical intuitions, as they have in our other experiments.

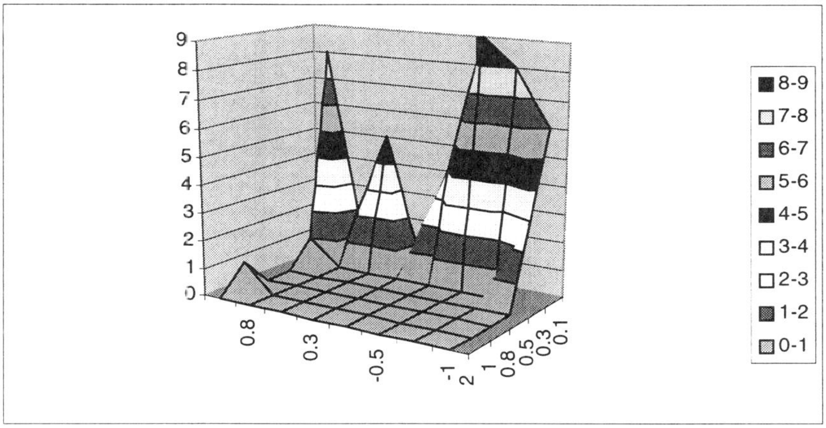

Figure 10 Failures to find the optimum out of 100 runs for a GA applied to landscapes using the specified generator, N=15, K=4, P=5, and indicated values of S and R.

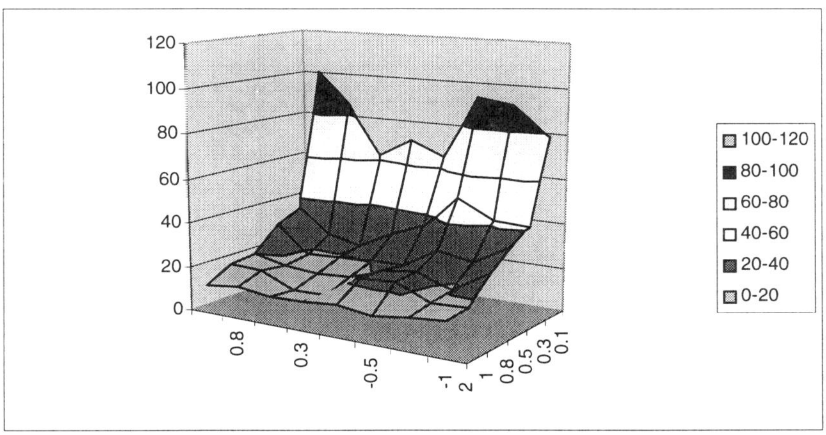

Figure 11 Generations to find the optimum (when it is found). Results averaged over 100 runs of a GA applied to landscapes using the specified generator, N=15, K=4, P=5, and indicated values of S and R.

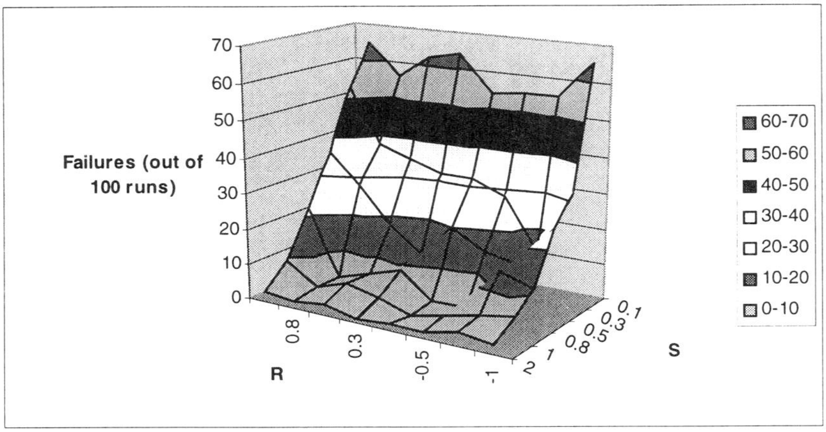

Figure 12 Failures to find the optimum out of 100 runs for a GA applied to landscapes using the specified generator, N=15, K=2, P=20, and indicated values of S and R.

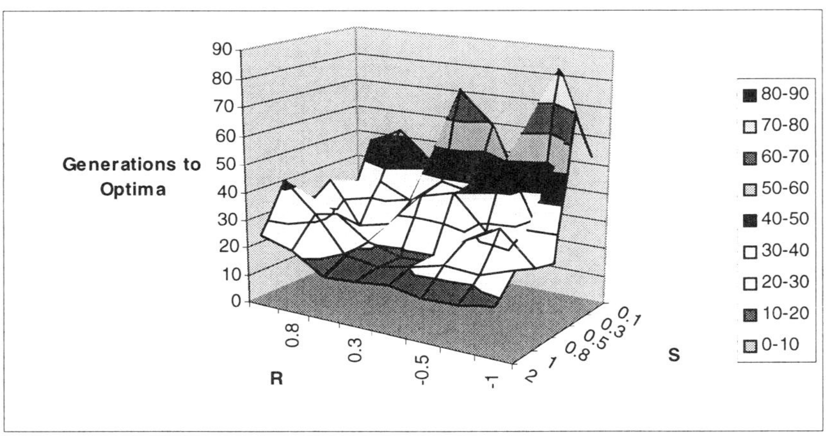

Figure 13 Generations to find the optimum (when it is found). Results averaged over 100 runs of a GA applied to landscapes using the specified generator, N=15, K=2, P=20, and indicated values of S and R.

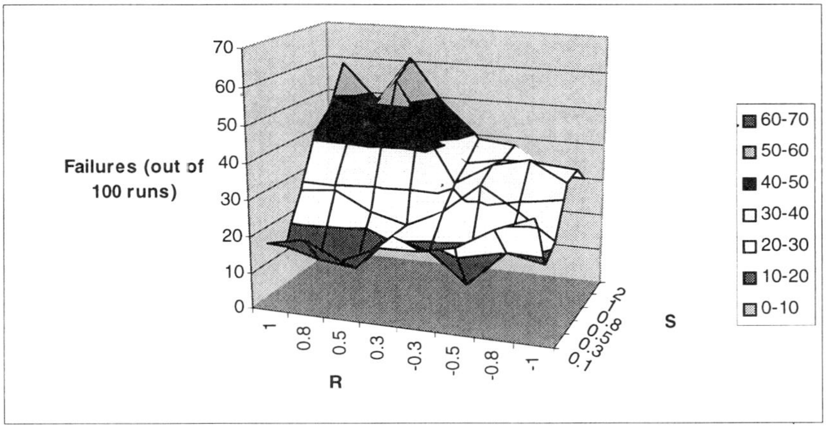

Figure 14 Failures to find the optimum out of 100 runs for a GA applied to landscapes using the specified generator, N=15, K=4, P=20, and indicated values of S and R. Note that in this figure the S axis is in reversed order, relative to previous plots, for clarity

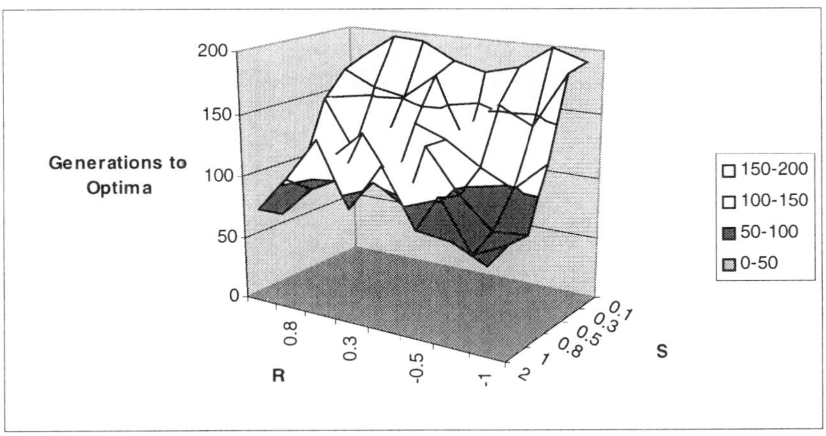

Figure 15 Generations to find the optimum (when it is found). Results averaged over 100 runs of a GA applied to landscapes using the specified generator, N=15, K=4, P=20, and indicated values of S and R.

9 Final Comments

We believe that the addition of a correlation (R) and scale (S) parameter to the landscape size (N), epistatic partition size (K), and number of partitions (P) parameters, yields more adequate controls over the complexity in randomly generated landscapes.

The results presented from a series of runs with a "vanilla" GA show patterns which indicate that an important factor is the degree of overlap between partitions, which governed by the combination of K and P. For low overlap, the behaviour is much as predicted, with the values of S and R providing a useful extra method for controlling "GA difficulty". As the amount of ovelap between partitions increases however, the behaviour of the GA changes (with respect to S) so that although the time taken to locate the optimum still behaves as predicted, the frequency with which the optimum is found decreases as S approaches 1.0. A likely explanation is that the increased overlap is introducing spurious low order effects, which are outweighing the effects of the high order co-efficients unless the scale factor is high enough. Development of new generators which attempt to avoid this problem remains a topic for future research.

We believe random landscapes with appropriate controls will allow for more general exploration of performance and robustness of a variety of GA configurations, and of other search algorithms. The exploration may also yield deeper insights into the general nature of search landscape complexity itself.

References

[1] Altenberg, L. (1994). Evolving better representations through selective genome growth. *In Proceedings of the 1st IEEE Conference on Evolutionary Computation.* pp. 182-187.

[2] Altenberg, L. 1997. NK fitness landscapes. In Back, T., Fogel, D., and Michalewicz, Z. (eds.) *The Handbook of Evolutionary Computation.* Oxford University Press. pp. B2.7:5-B2.7:10.

[3] Deb, K. 1997. Deceptive landscapes. In Back, T., Fogel, D., and Michalewicz, Z. (eds.) *The Handbook of Evolutionary Computation.* Oxford University Press. pp. B2.7:1-B2.7:5.

[4] Heckendorn, R. B., and Whitley, D. (1997). A Walsh analysis of NK-landscapes. In Baek, T. (ed.) *Proceedings of the Seventh International Conference on Genetic Algorithms.* pp. 41-48. Morgan Kauffman.

[5] Kauffman, S. A. (1993). The Origins of Order: Self-Organization and Selection in Evolution. New York: Oxford University Press.

[6] Looney, S. W (1996). Sample size determination for correlation coefficient inference: Practical problems and practical solutions. Paper presented at 1996 Joint Statistical Meeting, August 4-8, Chicago, Illinois.

[7] Maghsoodloo, S. and Huang, C. L. (1995). Computing probability integrals of a bivariate normal distribution. Interstat. (http://interstat.stat.vt.edu/interstat/ARTICLES/1995/abstracts/S95001.html-ssi).

[8] Miller, J. O. (1998). Bivar: A program for generating correlated random numbers. Behavior Research Methods, Instruments, and Computers, 30, 720-723.

[9] Weinberger, E.D. (1991). Local properties of Kauffman's N-K model, a tuneably rugged energy landscape. *Physical Review A,* 44(10). pp. 6399-6413.

[10] Smith, R. E., and Smith, J. E. (1999) An Examination of Tunable, Random Search Landscapes. In *Foundations of Genetic Algorithms 5.* Morgan Kaufmann. pp. 165-182.

Analysis of recombinative algorithms on a non-separable building-block problem

Richard A. Watson
Dynamical & Evolutionary Machine Organization,
Volen Center for Complex Systems,
Brandeis University, Waltham, MA, USA
richardw@cs.brandeis.edu

Abstract

Our analysis seeks to exemplify the utility of crossover by studying a non-separable building-block problem that is as easy as possible under recombination but very hard for any kind of mutation-based algorithm. The interdependent fitness contributions of blocks in this problem produce a search space that has an exponential number of local optima for a mutation-only algorithm. In contrast, the problem has no local optima for a recombinative algorithm - that is, there is always a path of monotonically increasing fitness leading to the global optimum. We give an upper bound on the expected time for a recombinative algorithm to solve this problem by proving the existence of a path to the solution and calculating the time for each step on this path. Ordinarily, such a straightforward approach would be defeated because both the existence of a path, and the time for a step, are dependent on the state of the population when using recombination. However, to calculate an upper bound on the expected time it is sufficient to know certain properties, or invariants, of the population rather than its exact state. Our initial proofs utilise a 'recombinative hill-climber', which applies crossover repeatedly to just two strings, for this purpose. Though our analysis does not transfer directly to a GA with a full population, a solution time based on the assumption that the population has the necessary invariant properties agrees with empirical results.

1 INTRODUCTION

A fitness landscape is a surface defined by a space of candidate solutions, a fitness function acting on these solutions giving the height of the surface at that point, and a neighbourhood metric that determines the proximity of solutions in the space (Jones 1995). We understand certain properties of this landscape to indicate critical features of problem difficulty – for example, a rugged surface, with many local optima, is taken to indicate a difficult problem (Kauffman 1993). Despite the common usage of fitness landscapes in attempting to gain intuition about problems, we are aware that they have their limitations. Jones cautions us that the proximity of points in the space should be determined by the variation operators provided by the algorithm. For example, two points that are distant under mutation may be close under recombination and so these two different neighbourhood metrics produce very different fitness landscapes. From this point of view, properties like ruggedness do not indicate the difficulty of a problem, *per se*, but rather the difficulty of a problem *for some algorithm*. The task of a successful algorithm can therefore be seen as the task of re-organizing the space of candidate solutions such that the resulting landscape is favourable: for example, to reorganize the space such that there are fewer local optima. Characterising the different features of a fitness landscape under different operators can assist us in understanding the problem class for which those operators are well suited.

Unfortunately, it is very difficult to imagine exactly what kind of structure a fitness landscape has when it is transformed by recombination, and worse, since the reachable-points from any given point are dependent on the current state of the population, the shape of the landscape must change as search progresses. Although this may limit the intuition we can gain from imagining landscapes, we may nonetheless retain the notion that under a successful variation operator a problem may be 'easy', whereas under another operator, say mutation, the problem may appear difficult.

It can be quite straightforward to calculate an expected time to solution when there are no local optima in a problem – that is, when there is a path of monotonically increasing fitness from any point in the search space to the solution. In this case, the expected time is simply the product of the length of this path and the expected time for each step on the path. This is the approach that we will take in the following analyses. The interesting part will be to prove the existence of such a path under recombination despite the fact that there is no such path for a mutation based algorithm. Ordinarily, such a straightforward approach would be defeated because both the existence of a path, and the time for a step, are dependent on the state of the population when using recombination. However, to calculate an upper bound on the expected time it is sufficient to know certain properties, or invariants, of the population rather than its exact state. For example, Wright and Zhao (1999) provide an analysis of a recombinative algorithm on a separable building-block problem by using the property of the algorithm that prevents alleles from being lost. Under these conditions (that we will detail shortly) there is always some recombination operation that will improve the fitness of the best individual in the population.

Here we extend this idea to a non-separable, hierarchical building-block problem. First, we analyse a 'recombinative hill-climber' that applies crossover repeatedly to just two strings. This simplification provides appropriate invariants that enable us to prove that there is always some choice of crossover points that will improve fitness, and to give an expected time to find such an improvement. Accordingly, we are able to give an analytical time to solution on this problem, and this is far faster than could be expected from a mutation-based hill-climber.

These analyses are possible because of particular regularities in the standard form of the problem; when these regularities are removed the recombinative hill-climber fails. Nevertheless, the principle of an algorithm that follows the recombination landscape is useful to us in less restricted cases. We show that a variant of the problem that is not solvable by the recombinative hill-climber is solvable by a true GA – that is, a GA using a population. Though our analysis does not transfer directly to the true GA, a solution time based on the assumption that the GA is exploiting the recombination landscape agrees with empirical results.

1.1 A TEST PROBLEM APPROPRIATE FOR RECOMBINATION

The building-block hypothesis (Holland 1975, Goldberg 1989) states that the GA will perform well when it is possible to combine low-order schemata of above-average fitness to find higher-order schemata of higher-fitness. The simplest kind of problem for us to imagine where this property of schemata is true is a separable building-block function. That is, a problem where the fitness of a string can be described as the sum of fitness contributions from a number of non-overlapping partitions. When such a problem has tight-linkage, (i.e. when the bits of a partition are adjacent on the genome), then it is quite possible for recombination to combine above average fitness schemata corresponding to these blocks to find higher-order schemata of higher-fitness. Accordingly, much of the GA literature uses building-block problems that are separable. However, the unfortunate characteristic of tight-linkage separable building-block problems is that they can be solved by mutation-based hill-climbers much faster than by GAs (Forrest and Mitchell 1993, and Mitchell et al, 1995). Even when each building-block corresponds to a deceptive trap function, a particular hill-climber, the macro-mutation hill-climber (MMHC), can out-perform the GA by using the assumption of tight-linkage to cluster mutations on one sub-function at a time (Jones, 1995 pp. 57-58). So we must look to a different kind of problem to exemplify the utility of the GA.

There are at least two ways to break these hill-climbing algorithms that perform so well on separable problems. One is make the problems non-separable, and the other is to remove the assumption that the bits of a block are adjacent on the genome. These two alternatives correspond to unfavourable *epistatic linkage* and unfavourable *genetic linkage*, respectively. Genetic linkage refers to the proximity of genes on the genome and their corresponding tendency to travel together during crossover. Epistatic linkage refers to the interdependency of gene contributions (without regard for gene position).[1] The trouble with problems that have poor genetic linkage is that, although they defeat all kinds of hill-climber, including the MMHC, they also defeat the GA - when the bits of a block are non-adjacent, crossover cannot combine building-blocks effectively. There has been considerable effort directed at overcoming difficult genetic linkage (e.g. Harik & Goldberg 1996, Kargupta 1997) and the resultant algorithms use recombination operators that are more intelligent than standard crossover. But, our intent in this paper is to address ordinary crossover on building-block problems of tight genetic linkage – the subject of the building-block hypothesis. So, let us return to the other alternative – epistatic linkage. In these problems the fitness of a string cannot be decomposed into the sum of fitness contributions from non-overlapping sub-blocks because the value of one block depends on the setting of bits in another block. The trouble with problems that have epistatic linkage is that its difficult to understand how *any* algorithm

---

[1] The unqualified term linkage, as in "tight-linkage", usually refers to *genetic* linkage but the concepts are often conflated in the literature.

could possibly identify such blocks if their fitnesses are interdependent in this manner. It seems to be a contradiction that a problem can have identifiable sub-parts when these sub-parts are strongly and non-linearly dependent on one another.

This is likely the reason why issues of epistatic linkage have largely been overshadowed in the GA literature by problems of difficult genetic linkage.[2] However, previous work (Watson et al 1998, Watson & Pollack 1999a) identified the class of hierarchically decomposable problems which show that it is possible to define a problem with strong epistatic linkage, (i.e. where the building-blocks are not separable), and yet the blocks can still be discovered and recombined. The canonical example of this problem class, which we call Hierarchical-if-and-only-if (H-IFF), defeats the mutation-based hill-climbing algorithms that solve separable problems. But the GA is able to solve this problem with ordinary two-point crossover. Since this problem is designed to be hard in mutation space but easy in recombination space it provides an appropriate problem for our analyses.

A non-separable building-block problem such as H-IFF is not amenable to analytic approaches usually adopted in the literature. Firstly, it is not possible to apply any analysis that assumes that the population as a whole converges incrementally on particular hyperplanes. In H-IFF the operation of recombination may be defeated if the population is allowed to converge at even one locus. Secondly, most analyses assume separable problems, and, surprisingly often, focus on the extreme case where every bit is separable – the max-ones problem. However, Wright and Zhao (1999) provide an approach to analysis that, although directed at separable building-block problems, can be adapted for our purposes. Their approach is to prove that there is always a way to improve fitness, and then to give a solution time based on the product of the length of the path to the solution, and the time for each step on the path. Here we extend this work to use the same approach for a non-separable problem.

The remainder of this paper is organized as follows: Section 2 describes the analysis of Wright & Zhao. We provide a variation of their model that will be easy to adapt to our needs, and describe the Gene Invariant GA (GIGA) on which both their and our analyses are based. Section 3 describes the problem, H-IFF, that we will analyse, and discusses some of its properties. Section 4.1 proves several theorems for the expected time to find a global optimum in H-IFF using a 'recombinative hill-climber' based on GIGA with a population of two. Our analyses are possible because of particular symmetries in the problem that match properties of GIGA, but the principle behind the operation of recombination is more general. In Section 4.2, we then discuss a variant of H-IFF that is not solvable by the recombinative hill-climber but is solvable by a GA using a real population. Our proofs for solution time cannot be transferred to the population case directly, but we can give an estimate of solution time based on assumptions about the state of the population. These assumptions are somewhat heavy-handed but experimental results in Section 5 support our analytic results, and suggest that the GA is using the recombinative landscape effectively. Section 6 concludes.

---

[2] The exception here is Kauffman's 'N-K landscapes' which explicitly model epistatic linkage. However this class of problem does not exhibit a building-block structure, has not been demonstrated to be GA-easy, and is difficult to analyse.

2 ANALYSIS ON SEPARABLE PROBLEMS

The analysis provided by Wright & Zhao (1999), and the analyses that follow, feature the Gene Invariant GA (GIGA) (Culberson 1992). The variant of GIGA that best suits our purposes is described in Figure 1.

- Choose an initial population (see text)
- Repeat until satisfied:
    - Pick two parents at random from the population.
    - Produce a pair of offspring from these parents using crossover only.
    - If the fittest offspring is fitter than the fittest parent then replace the two parents with the pair of offspring.

Figure 1: A simple form of the Gene Invariant GA.

There are several features to note about this algorithm. Competition is restricted to parents versus their offspring. The two offspring are created from the parents using the same crossover point(s) and so each gene donated by the parents will be acquired by exactly one of the offspring. Given this and the fact that either both offspring are retained or both parents are retained (and there is no mutation) it follows that alleles are never lost from the population – hence, 'Gene Invariant' GA. Finally, note that the algorithm is elitist – the fittest member of the population cannot be replaced by an inferior individual.

Wright & Zhao add several other assumptions to this model: the problem is separable; a set of crossover masks is used that restrict crossover to operations that move exactly one block from one parent to the other; finally, the population is systematically initialised such that every possible bit combination within each block is present. This initialisation gives a population size of c^k, where c is the size of the alphabet and k is the number of bits in a block.

These simplifying assumptions enable a useful property to follow: given the gene invariance property of the algorithm and that crossover points are not permitted to move partial blocks, it is guaranteed that building-blocks are never lost from the population; since all possible candidates for a block are present in the initial population and they can never be lost, there will always be some individual in the population that has any block that should be required. Thus, if the best individual in the population is not yet optimal then it must have some sub-optimal block, and this block can be obtained from some member of the population using some crossover mask. This is the invariant property of the population that is required for the analysis. Although the exact structure of the population is not known, this property ensures that there is always some way to improve fitness using recombination.

To calculate an upper bound on the expected time, T, required for the population to find an individual that has reached the global optimum[3] Wright & Zhao focus attention on the fittest individual in the population. Their version of the algorithm asserts that one of the parents is the fittest individual (and the other parent is selected at random). The possible states that the algorithm may pass through in the course of search, i.e. the possible populations, are then categorized into equivalence sets based on the fitness of the fittest individual. T is then given by the maximum possible number of fitness increases of this fittest individual, and the time expected for each increase. This yields $T=Br(D/d)$, where B is the number of blocks in the problem (equals the number of crossover masks), r is the size of the population, D is the

[3] In Wright & Zhao (1999), time, T, is measured in steps of the algorithm in Figure 1, but each step requires two evaluations.

difference in fitness between the global optimum and the worst possible string, and d is the difference in fitness between the global optimum and the next best string (i.e. the minimum fitness increase for finding a correct block).

In Theorem 1 below we modify the proof provided by Wright & Zhao and use the same assumptions about the problem, crossover masks, and initialisation. However, Wright & Zhao categorize the state of the algorithm using the fitness of the fittest individual in the population and always use this individual as one of the parents. But, we will categorize the state of the algorithm using the number of fully optimised blocks in a particular individual, which we will always use as one of the parents. But, this individual may not be the fittest individual in the population. Indeed, although the fittest individual possible (the global optimum) must have all blocks fully optimised, the fittest individual in the population at a given time does not necessarily have any blocks fully optimised.

In order to transform the theorem to work on the number of optimised blocks we need to be sure that we never reduce the number of optimised blocks when we accept an offspring. We cannot directly measure the number of fully optimised blocks in an individual; neither can we infer the number of fully optimised blocks from a fitness measure. However, we can use the following observation: a fitness increase created by changing one block in an individual cannot reduce the number of fully optimised blocks in that individual. Figure 2 describes a modified algorithm that ensures this condition is applied.

- Choose an initial population (as before)
- Pick one parent at random from the population, $p1$.
- Repeat until satisfied:
    - Pick one parent at random from the population, $p2$.
    - Produce a pair of offspring from $p1$ & $p2$ using crossover only. Let $c1$ be the offspring that results from $p1$ plus one block from $p2$; let $c2$ result from $p2$ plus one block from $p1$.
    - If $c1$ is fitter than $p1$ then replace $p1$ with $c1$, and $p2$ with $c2$.

Figure 2: A modified Gene Invariant GA.

This algorithm is almost the same as the algorithm in Figure 1, but the replacement is more specific about which offspring is compared to which parent. Note that the algorithm only selects one new parent in each iteration, and only evaluates one of the new offspring. This means that maybe the second offspring, $c2$, was fitter than the one evaluated – and maybe we missed an opportunity to increase fitness. But for our purposes, it is more important that we know that $p1$ does not decrease in the number of optimised blocks. Although, the algorithm in Figure 2 explicitly makes reference to the fact that the partitions of blocks are known, and that the crossover masks only swap one block at a time, we are not adding any new assumptions to those used by Wright and Zhao. Importantly, note that the modified algorithm maintains the gene invariant property, and the property that building-blocks are never lost from the population.

Theorem 1: An upper bound on the expected time for some individual in the population to find the globally optimal string, using the algorithm in Figure 2, is given by $T \leq B^2 r$, where B is the number of blocks in the separable problem and, r is the size of the population ($r=c^k$, where c is the alphabet size and k is the number of symbols in a block).

Proof:[4] Partition the set of possible algorithm states into categories based on the number of optimal blocks in $p1$. Category, j, for j=0,1,...,B, is the set of states where $p1$ has exactly j blocks fully optimised. Let Sj be the random variable which denotes the number of evaluations that the algorithm spends in category j. If the GA is in category j with $j<B$, then $p1$ has some block which is not at optimum, and there is a crossover operation that will swap in the optimal configuration of bits for that block from some other member of the population. This operation moves the algorithm state to a new category and has a probability of at least $1/(Br)$ since there are B crossover masks and r possible choices for the second parent. An upper bound for the expected time to leave any state is the inverse of a lower bound on the probability of leaving that state. Thus, the expected value of Sj, at $j<B$, is at most Br. The expected time to reach a population that contains the globally optimum string is at most the time it takes for the algorithm to reach category B, i.e.

$$T \leq \sum_{j=1}^{B} S_j \leq B^2 r \qquad \text{[end].}$$

The intuition behind this analysis is now very simple. T is given by the product of the number of blocks to be found, and the time to find a block in another individual and move it in by crossover. The number of blocks is B, and getting a block into the best individual requires finding the right crossover mask (of which there are B), and picking the right donor individual (of which there are r) – hence B^2r, or $B^2(c^k)$.

This expected time has the desirable property that it is not dependent on any measurement of fitness values in the problem. And the resultant upper bound for T is lower than that which Wright & Zhao provide, at least whenever $B<(D/d)$. Both analytic times assume that each crossover mask corresponds to exactly one block. However, Wright and Zhao's analysis could be modified to a more general set of masks, giving $T \leq Mr(D/d)$, where M is the number of crossover masks used. This set of masks may include masks that match with more than one block so long as they only match with whole blocks, and it must include the set of masks that correspond to the single fitness blocks, as before. In any case, an approach based on counting optimised blocks, rather than fitness improvements, is better suited to our needs in the following sections.

So we have an upper bound on the expected time to solution for a recombinative algorithm on a separable building-block problem. However, we have to ask whether the simplified problems and algorithms involved in these analyses have captured the interesting properties of a GA. We have permitted modifications to the algorithm that do not violate the assumptions made about the problem – but we notice that we are getting gradually closer to something much simpler than a GA. In fact, notice that using only the same assumptions about a problem as those used above (i.e. that the partitions of building-blocks are known), a simple systematic hill-climbing technique would suffice. That is, in a separable problem with known partitions, each subset of interdependent parameters may be searched exhaustively – i.e. each block may be processed systematically by testing every possible bit combination within that block and selecting the highest fitness configuration. Whilst one block is being processed, we hold the setting of bits in other blocks constant to some arbitrary configuration. The particular configuration of bits used in other blocks does not matter since we know that the blocks are separable. Since systematic search within a block requires testing c^k bit configurations, and there are B blocks to be processed, this simple systematic search takes only $T \leq Bc^k$.

[4] This proof is a direct adaptation of that provided by Wright & Zhao (1999).

Further, for their analysis using GIGA, Wright & Zhao suggest that if the partitioning of blocks is not known then their analytic time can be multiplied by the number of possible partitionings. Since this can be applied to our simple systematic hill-climber too, by this analysis, the simple method is still superior even if the partitioning is not known. We make this observation not to criticize the approach of Wright and Zhao, rather we present it as an illustration that separable problems simply do not justify the use of a population-based recombinative technique. Nonetheless, the above version of Wright & Zhao's analysis provides a good starting point for an analysis of GIGA on H-IFF which is not separable and, we shall argue, does require a recombinative algorithm.

3 HIERARCHICAL-IF-AND-ONLY-IF

In previous work we provided a test problem with sub-blocks that are strongly and non-linearly dependent on one another yet the problem is GA-friendly (Watson et al 1998, Watson & Pollack 1999a). H-IFF is a hierarchically decomposable building-block problem where the blocks are non-separable in a sense which is a little stronger than usual. We define a *non-separable* building-block problem as one where the optimal setting of bits in one block is dependent on the setting of bits in some other block (or blocks). In this case, we may also say that the blocks are *interdependent.*

This definition excludes some building-block problems in the literature that are non-separable in a degenerate sense. For example, the second version of the Royal Road problem, RR2, has non-linear interactions between blocks such that the fitness of certain combinations of blocks is not equal to the sum of their independent fitness contributions. However, the 'bonus' fitness contributions never contradict the setting of blocks that are rewarded at the individual block level, and this kind of problem is still solvable by simple mutation-based hill-climbing algorithms.

In H-IFF the interdependency of blocks is implemented in the following manner. At any given level in the hierarchical structure there are two equally valuable schemata for each block. These competing schemata within each block are maximally distinct – specifically, all-ones and all-zeros. From the perspective of this level, it does not matter which solution is found – the blocks are, as far as this level goes, separable. However, higher-order schemata, from the next level up in the hierarchy, are then used to reward particular configurations of schemata from the previous level. For a given block, which of the two schemata should be used depends on which has been used in a neighbouring block – if the neighbouring block is based on ones then so should the block in question, if zeros then zeros. This compatibility of blocks is rewarded by fitness contributions from the next level of the hierarchical structure. Each correct pair of blocks creates a new single block for the next level in the hierarchy. This means that the blocks at the original level were not, in fact, separable, and it creates an interdependency between blocks which is strongly non-linear, but it is highly structured.

We define the fitness of a string using H-IFF with the recursive function given below, Equation 1, (Watson & Pollack 1999a). This function interprets a string as a binary tree and recursively decomposes the string into left and right halves. Each resultant sub-string constitutes a building-block and confers a fitness contribution equal to its size if all the bits in the block have the same value - either all ones or all zeros. The fitness of the whole string is the sum of these fitness contributions for all blocks at all levels. Figure 3 evaluates an example string using H-IFF.

$$f(A)=\begin{cases} 1, & \text{if } |A|=1, \\ |A| + f(A_L) + f(A_R), & \text{if } (|A|>1) \text{ and } (\forall i\{a_i=0\} \text{ or } \forall i\{a_i=1\}), \\ f(A_L) + f(A_R), & \text{otherwise.} \end{cases} \qquad \textbf{Eq. 1}$$

where A is a block of bits, $\{a_1,a_2,...a_n\}$, $|A|$ is the size of the block=n, a_i is the ith element of A, and A_L and A_R are the left and right halves of A (i.e. $A_L=\{a_1,...a_{n/2}\}$, $A_R=\{a_{n/2+1},...a_n\}$). The length of the string evaluated, must equal 2^p where p is an integer (the number of hierarchical levels).

00001011	|A|=8, # correct blocks=0, fitness from level 3=	0
0000, 1011	|A|=4, # correct blocks=1, fitness from level 2=	4
00, 00, 10, 11	|A|=2, # correct blocks=3, fitness from level 1=	6
0, 0, 0, 0, 1, 0, 1, 1	|A|=1, # correct blocks=8, fitness from level 0=	8
	Total fitness =	18

Figure 3: Evaluating an example string, "00001011", using H-IFF. At the top level, level 3, one string of size 8 is presented, it is not correct and no fitness contribution is conferred. At the next level, level 2, the two halves of the original string are presented, one is correct (all zeros) and confers a fitness contribution of 4. Each size-4 block from level 2 is decomposed into two size-2 blocks at level 1, three of these are correct (two based on zeros, one based on ones), each of these three confers a fitness contribution of 2. At level 0, all bits are 'correct' and this level effectively adds a constant to the fitness total.

Some features of this apparently simple function should be highlighted. Each block, either ones or zeros, represents a schema that contains one of the two global optima at all-ones or all-zeros. Local optima in H-IFF occur when incompatible building-blocks are brought together. For example, consider "11110000"; when viewed as two blocks from the previous level (i.e. "1111..." and "...0000") both blocks are good - but when these incompatible blocks are put together they create a sub-optimal string that is maximally distant from the next best strings i.e. "11111111" and "00000000". However, although local optima and global optima are distant in Hamming space, they may be close in recombination space (Jones 1995); for example, consider a population containing both "11110000" and "00001111" individuals. Thus H-IFF exemplifies a class of problems for which recombinative algorithms are well suited. Watson et al (1998), showed that H-IFF is easy for a GA to solve given that diversity in the population is maintained and genetic linkage is tight. But, since the local optima in H-IFF are numerous and evenly distributed, H-IFF is very hard for any kind of mutation-based hill-climber.

The first proviso for success of the GA, appropriate population diversity, is discussed in (Watson & Pollack 1999a), and superior alternative methods have since been used in (Watson & Pollack 2000a), and (Watson & Pollack 2000b), as will be employed later in this paper. Algorithms to address the second proviso, poor linkage, are addressed in (Watson & Pollack 1999b) and (Watson & Pollack 2000a). The latter work shows that a new form of recombinative algorithm, the "Symbiogenic Evolutionary Adaptation Model" (SEAM), can solve the *shuffled H-IFF* problem, which has the same epistatic linkage structure as H-IFF but the position of bits is randomly re-ordered giving it difficult genetic linkage also. However, we will not address the poor linkage problem or this new algorithm in this paper. Our focus here is to demonstrate the utility of standard crossover on a building-block problem with tight genetic linkage, as described by the Building-Block Hypothesis.

Tight linkage permits the crossover masks provided by two-point crossover to include a mask for every building-block in H-IFF. And later we will show that one-point is similarly appropriate for H-IFF. The success of the algorithms we analyse depends on this, and the match of the building-blocks to the crossover operators certainly gives crossover an advantage over mutation. Indeed, this is the intent behind the design of the problem. Nonetheless, a successful algorithm must still resolve the strong epistatic linkage in H-IFF. The fact that removing problems of genetic linkage does not make H-IFF easy is evidenced by the fact that non-population based hill-climbers based on the assumption of tight linkage, i.e. macro-mutation hill climbing, MMHC, cannot solve H-IFF (Watson et al 1998). (Note that MMHC can solve the Royal Road problems, or tight-linkage concatenated trap functions often used in GA testing (Goldberg 1989), much faster than the GA (Jones 1995)).

Variations and more general forms of H-IFF that allow different alphabets (instead of binary), different numbers of sub-blocks per block (instead of pairs), unequal fitness contributions of blocks, and the construction of other hierarchically-consistent building-block functions, are defined in (Watson & Pollack 1999a). For the purposes of this paper, the canonical form given above, and one new variant described later, will be sufficient for illustration.

3.1 DIMENSIONAL REDUCTION

How is it that the GA is able to solve H-IFF easily despite the strong interdependency of blocks? From a bottom-up point of view, we can see H-IFF as defining a hierarchy of building-blocks which may be assembled together in pairs, doubling in size and reward at each level. Accordingly, an algorithm that exploits this structure will be seen to progress from searching combinations of bits at the bottom level, to searching combinations of schemata of successively higher order, at all subsequent levels. At each transition in levels, the dimensionality of the problem is reduced. For example, at the first level in a H-IFF of just 4 bits there are two size two blocks to be processed. Each block has four possible combinations of bits two of which are solutions. At the next level there is one size-four block to be processed, but rather than searching all 16 combinations of bits we need only search the four combinations of "00" and "11" solutions from the previous level. This dimensional reduction enables a recombinative algorithm to take advantage of the problem structure.

Notice that this view is in contrast to the discovery of blocks in a separable problem. In a separable problem the blocks at the first level are discovered unambiguously – there is only one best solution to each block – thus there is no need to search combinations of blocks at the next level (if there is a next level). Similarly, the kind of recombination that is required to put separable blocks together is degenerate – consider the number of block combinations to be searched given by C^B, where C is the number of solutions to each block, and B is the number of blocks. In a separable problem C=1. This is why a hill-climber is able to solve separable problems – there is no need to maintain competing sub-solutions because there are no interdependencies between blocks, and thus the sub-problems can be processed sequentially. In contrast, the structure of H-IFF requires that competing sub-solutions are maintained by the population for at least as long as is required to resolve their interdependencies at the next level in the hierarchy. Section 4 will formalize these intuitive concepts.

3.2 THE H-IFF LANDSCAPE FOR MUTATION HILL-CLIMBERS

Using the notion of a path to solution and the expected time for steps on this path, we may reasonably say that an algorithm is not reliably successful on a problem if there is no guaranteed path to solution, if the path may be exponentially long, or if any step on the path takes exponential time. For a single-bit mutation hill-climber there is no guaranteed path on H-IFF. H-IFF has $2^{N/2}$ local optima under single-bit mutation (where N is the size of the problem in bits), only two of which are globally optimal. More generally, a k-bit mutation hill-climber will be faced with $2^{(N/h)}$ local optima, where h is the smallest integer power of 2 which is greater than k, i.e. $h=2^p>k$.[5] A random mutation hill climber (RMHC) (Forrest and Mitchell 1993) mutates every bit with a given probability *Pmut*. In principle no problem can have local optima under this operator since the probability of moving from any point to any other point is non-zero. However, consider the case where the current string is $N/2$ zeros followed by $N/2$ ones. The next best string is the global optima at all ones or all zeros. To achieve this jump, mutation must flip $N/2$ bits whilst keeping $N/2$ undisrupted. The best mutation rate to achieve this is $Pmut$=0.5 and this gives an expected time for the step which is 2^N – and search is equivalent to random guessing. A macro-mutation hill-climber, MMHC (Jones 1995), has the best chance of success. MMHC chooses two points and randomises the loci between them, thus concentrating mutations on a particular sub-string whilst leaving the remainder untouched. But still, to escape from the next-best optima it must choose the right points which has probability $1/N(N-1)$ (this allows macro-mutations both 'inside' and 'outside' the chosen points), and assign all ones (or all zeros) to $N/2$ bits – this occurs in expected time $O(N^2 2^{(N/2)})$. Thus we see that by these criteria, all these mutation-based hill-climbers either have no guaranteed path to the optimum, or cannot be guaranteed to take a step on the path in time less than exponential in N.

4 ANALYSES ON H-IFF

The approach of Wright and Zhao is quite intuitive: their algorithm and assumptions guarantee that there is always some choice of parents for which some crossover operation can produce an offspring that is the next step in a progression of individuals which increase in fitness. In other words, their approach is to prove that separable building-block problems have no local optima using their algorithm. We follow the same approach but for non-separable building-block problems, and whereas the proof of Wright and Zhao is based on the fitness of an individual, our approach, as used in Theorem 1, is based on the number of blocks that are fully optimised in an individual.

Condition 1: There is always some choice of parents for which some crossover operation can produce an offspring that is the next step in a progression of individuals which increase in the number of fully-optimised building-blocks. (Except when the progression has already arrived at a global optimum.)

This condition is central to our approach in this paper. It refers to the ability of an algorithm to utilize the building-block structure of a problem. Or alternatively, to an invariant property of a population that enables an algorithm to utilize the building-block structure. Any algorithm that satisfies Condition 1 and follows such a progression will take time $T \leq BS$, where B is the number of blocks to be found in a globally optimal string (equals the maximum number of

---

[5] Any string made by concatenating h-sized correct blocks cannot be improved by a k-bit mutation algorithm where $h>k$. There are $2^{(N/h)}$ possible strings of such concatenations.

steps in the progression), and S is the expected time for each step in the progression. For a recombinative algorithm where Condition 1 holds, $S \leq PM$, where P is the number of different ways of choosing parents, and M is the number of crossover masks, thus

$$T \leq BPM. \qquad \textbf{Eq.2.}$$

Equation 2 will hold for any problem that can be described in terms of blocks in some way such that Condition 1 holds. Proving that Condition 1 holds (and that an algorithm follows this progression) will be more or less difficult depending on the assumptions made about the algorithm and the problem. In the separable problem addressed in Theorem 1, Condition 1 holds because all possible configurations for each block are given by initialisation and cannot be lost by the variation operators that the algorithm uses. In Theorem 1, $M=B$, and $P=r$, the size of the population. We cannot expect to prove Condition 1 for a standard recombinative algorithm on a general non-separable problem. However, H-IFF is specifically designed to be easy for a recombinative algorithm and, GIGA is ideally suited for adaptation to our purposes.

4.1 A RECOMBINATIVE HILL-CLIMBER

For Theorems 2 and 3 we will reduce the GIGA to a form of hill-climber – by which we mean that we will not use a population to speak of – just two strings. However, this will be a recombinative hill-climber not a mutation-based hill-climber, Figure 4.

- Initialise a population of two random, but complementary, strings.
- Repeat until satisfied:
  - Using the two strings as parents create a pair of offspring by crossover only.
  - If the fittest offspring is fitter than the fittest parent then replace the parents with the pair of offspring.

Figure 4: Recombinative hill-climber based on GIGA.

Hoehn and Reeves (1996) call recombination like that above "complementary crossover". Alternatively, one might call it a macro-mutation hill-climber (MMHC) from (Jones 95) that uses bit-flip mutation (instead of assignment of a new random value). Arguably, this is a degenerate form of recombination. Hoehn and Reeves point out that a second parent is redundant. And we concede that the choice of complementary parents is ideally suited to the complementary schemata rewarded in H-IFF. Nonetheless, we maintain that it is more informative to regard the above algorithm as recombining two strings (that happen to be complementary) rather than bit-flipping. Hoehn and Reeves agree that there is a close relation between this operator and crossover, and suggest that the fitness landscape under this operator "reasonably approximates the crossover landscape". The purpose of using this algorithm here is to illustrate the concept of the crossover landscape as it is found in H-IFF, and to provide a basis for understanding how a true GA might operate on this class of problems by avoiding the local optima inherent in the mutation landscape.

The following theorems do *not* assume that the algorithm is provided with a set of crossover masks corresponding to blocks in the problem. Ordinary crossover may be used with no restriction on where crossover points may fall. Theorem 2 is based on two-point crossover, Theorem 3 is based on one-point crossover - in the latter case it is a little more difficult to show that Condition 1 holds. Note that these analyses are not restricted to just the one problem instance defined in Equation 1. H-IFF has regular block sizes within a level, regular fitness contributions for blocks within a level, exactly two sub-blocks per block, and global optima that happen to be all-ones and all-zeros. The analyses hold for the class of problems with any of these particulars relaxed, but for these analyses, the global optima must be complementary, and the fitness contribution of competing schemata in the same block partition must be the same. We will discuss in Section 4.2 an extension to the class where building-blocks are not necessarily complementary.

Theorem 2: $T \leq \frac{1}{2}N^3$, where T is an upper bound on expected time to find a global optimum in H-IFF using the algorithm in Figure 4 with 2-point crossover, and N is the problem size in bits.

Proof: From Equation 2, $T \leq BPM$ if Condition 1 holds. For H-IFF, B, the maximum number of blocks that need to be discovered in a globally optimum string is $\sum_{p=0}^{(\lg N)-1} 2^p = N-1$, thus $B<N$ (Here, and henceforth, we use "lg" to mean logarithm base 2). For two-point crossover, M, the number of possible pairs of crossover points is $\frac{1}{2}N(N-1) < \frac{1}{2}N^2$. And for the algorithm given in Figure 4, the number of different ways to choose parents, P, is just 1. Thus, $T \leq \frac{1}{2}N^3$ if Condition 1 holds. Now prove that Condition 1 holds: The two strings are complementary at initialisation and since the gene invariance property of the algorithm holds the strings must always be complementary. This means that if a block is discovered in one individual the complementary block must necessarily be discovered in the other individual. Therefore any block not present in one individual can be swapped in from the other individual given the right crossover mask. Two-point crossover is a superset of the crossover masks required for this crossover to occur. The algorithm will detect such a successful crossover and follow this progression since it will always result in a fitter individual. So Condition 1 holds. [end]

Theorem 3: $T \leq N^2$, where T is an upper bound on expected time to find a global optimum in H-IFF using the algorithm in Figure 4 with 1-point crossover, and N is the problem size.

Proof: Following the proof of Theorem 2, the number of crossover masks for one-point crossover $<N$, and thus, $T \leq N^2$ if Condition 1 holds under one-point crossover. Now prove that Condition 1 holds: If an individual is non-optimal then it contains some block that either has both of its sub-blocks correct (but not matching) or has some sub-block incorrect. This applies recursively. Consider the smallest incorrect block that has both of its sub-blocks correct (possibly just a pair of bits) and consider the crossover point between them. Since no fitness contribution can occur for a block that spans the crossover point (because it would include mismatched sub-blocks), the fitness of this individual is the sum of fitnesses of the sub-strings to the left and right of this point. The other individual used in the algorithm has the same fitness as the first, and its fitness is the same sum of fitnesses from the left and right sub-strings defined by the crossover point. Thus, if this crossover point is used the fitness of the resulting offspring will have at least the same contributions from the two sub-strings and in addition, since the two individuals are complementary, the crossover will necessarily introduce matching sub-blocks that create a new correct block spanning the crossover point. Thus there is always some one-point crossover operation that will increase the number of correct blocks in the best individual, i.e. Condition 1 holds. [end]

Figure 5 illustrates the reasoning for Condition 1 under one point crossover.

11010001	Consider an arbitrary string as an example. This size-8 string is sub-optimal. It is composed of two incorrect size-4 blocks. So we recurse on either of the two incorrect size-4 blocks, for example, the left block.
1101----	This size 4 block is composed of a correct size-2 block (left), and an incorrect size-2 block (right). So we recurse on the incorrect block i.e. right.
--01----	This size 2 block is sub-optimal. But, it is composed of two correct size-1 blocks, that are incompatible.
110|10001	So, we place the crossover point between the two size-1 blocks (bits) at this point. The fitness of the entire string can be expressed as the sum of F_left=f(110------) on the left hand side of the crossover point, and F_right=f(---10001) on the right of the point.
001|01110	The other string used in the algorithm is the exact compliment. And the left and right sides of the crossover point have the same fitnesses, i.e. F_left and F_right.
110|01110	The string created by combining the left of the first string and the right of the second string, still has at least the fitness of F_left + F_right.
--0|0----	But in addition, it now has an additional correct block here, created across the crossover point.

Figure 5: Illustrating that Condition 1 holds using recombinative hill-climber on H-IFF with one-point crossover. Since there is always some crossover point that comes between correct but incompatible blocks, it is always possible to use this point to create a string that has higher fitness by using one-point crossover.

Thus far we have proved that Condition 1 holds on H-IFF for the algorithm in Figure 4 using both 1-point and 2-point crossover. This shows that although a mutation hill-climber finds a number of local optima that is exponential in *N*, H-IFF has no local optima at all under recombination – there is always some way to increase the number of correct blocks, as Condition 1 states. In this sense, H-IFF exemplifies the transformation of a fitness landscape under different operators from a problem that is very hard under mutation into a problem that is as easy as it could be under crossover. Having shown that there is always a path to an optimum, we now focus on improving our estimate of the time to traverse this path.

We may improve on the upper bounds given in theorems 2 and 3 by returning to our original reasoning, $T \leq BS$, where B is the number of blocks to be found (i.e. steps on the path to the optimum) and S is the expected time to find a block (i.e. time to take a step). In the above theorems we prove Condition 1 to assert that there is at least one crossover operation that will find a block given some choice of parents. So we have used $S \leq PM$, and accordingly, $T \leq BPM$. But it should be clear that for this algorithm on H-IFF there will be many opportunities to increase the number of correct blocks. For example, at the beginning of search there are many size-two blocks to be found and many possible crossovers that may find one.

So, we can use an estimate of time to progress along the path to the optimum that takes account of the fact that the expected time for a step changes with each step, as the number of possible ways to find a block changes. The time to find one of q available blocks is PM/q, thus;

$$T \leq \sum_{b=1}^{B} \frac{PM}{q_b} \qquad \textbf{Eq. 3.}$$

where B is the maximum number of steps in the path to the optimum, P is the number of choices of parents, M is the number of possible crossovers, and q_b is the number of ways that an additional block can be swapped-in at the bth step.

Thus, we may write $T \leq PMu$, where u is the sum of $1/q$ for all steps in the path to the optimum. Theorem 4 uses an upper bound on u to give an improved time to solution on H-IFF.

Theorem 4: $T \leq \frac{1}{2} M \lg^2 N$, where T is an upper bound on the expected time to find a global optimum in H-IFF using the algorithm in Figure 4, M is the number of crossover masks ($M=N-1<N$ for 1-point crossover, $M=\frac{1}{2}N(N-1)$ for two-point), and N is the problem size in bits (for $N>20$).

Proof: To use $T \leq PMu$ we must find u which is the sum of $1/q$ over all steps in the path, where q is the number of blocks that may be discovered at that step. At the first hierarchical level in H-IFF there are $N/2$ size-2 blocks to be discovered (in the worst case, we may assume that the initial strings have none of their size-2 blocks correct). By the reasoning of Theorems 2 or 3, any one of these blocks may be discovered by one or two-point crossover. Thus $q_1=(N/2)$. There are now $N/2-1$ blocks remaining to be found at the first level, so $q_2=(N/2-1)$. For the entire first level we require the sum of $1/q_1$ through $1/q_{(N/2)}=1+1/2+1/3+\ldots+1/(N/2) \leq \ln(N/2)+1$. The sum of $1/q$ for the pth level is $\leq \ln(N/2^p)+1$. The overall sum of $1/q$ for all levels, u, is

$$\begin{aligned} u &= \sum_{p=1}^{\lg N} \sum_{k=1}^{N/2^p} \left(\tfrac{1}{k}\right) \\ &\leq \sum_{p=1}^{\lg N} \left(\ln\left(\tfrac{N}{2^p}\right)+1\right) \\ &= \sum_{p=1}^{\lg N} (\ln N - p \ln 2 + 1) \\ &= \lg N\left(\tfrac{\lg N}{\lg e}+1\right) - \tfrac{\ln 2}{2}\left(\lg N(\lg N+1)\right) \\ &= \tfrac{\ln 2}{2} \lg^2 N + \left(1-\tfrac{\ln 2}{2}\right)\lg N. \end{aligned}$$

For the algorithm in Figure 4, $P=1$. So,

$$T \leq Mu = M\left(\tfrac{\ln 2}{2}\lg^2 N + \left(1-\tfrac{\ln 2}{2}\right)\lg N\right)$$

Thus T is $O(M\lg^2 N)$, and numerically, $T \leq \frac{1}{2}M\lg^2 N$, for $N>20$. [end]

4.2 FROM A RECOMBINATIVE HILL-CLIMBER TO A RECOMBINATIVE POPULATION

Theorems 2 through 4 use the recombinative hill-climber of Figure 4, and in fact, demonstrate that a population greater than this degenerate case of two is not strictly necessary to solve the canonical form of H-IFF. However, this is only the case because of biases in the algorithm that match particular properties of H-IFF. Specifically, GIGA is biased toward finding complementary individuals (a bias which becomes 'the rule' when the population is of size 2), and H-IFF has competing schemata that are exactly complementary. It is quite easy to break this non-population based version of GIGA by making the global optima in H-IFF non-complementary. We can do this by choosing two random strings as the global optima and rewarding left and right sub-strings recursively. Alternatively, and without loss of generality, we can keep one of the optima at all ones and randomise the other. Either way, the bits in the two global optima will agree in some loci and be complementary in others. This prevents the algorithm given in Figure 4 from succeeding since the complement of a good block is no longer (necessarily) a good block. Equation 4 defines a variant of H-IFF based on this idea, that we will refer to as H-IFF2. $\boldsymbol{F}(A)$ runs through the string twice using f and sums results; before the first pass the string is XORed with one global optimum, and before the second it is XORed with the second global optimum. $f(A)$ now simply checks for blocks of all zeros. The fitness of a string, A, under H-IFF2 is given by:

$$\boldsymbol{F}(A)=f(A\otimes \mathrm{g1})+f(A\otimes \mathrm{g2}),$$

$$f(A)=\begin{cases} 1, & \text{if } |A|=1, \\ |A|+f(A_L)+f(A_R), & \text{if } (|A|>1) \text{ and } \forall i\{a_i=0\}, \\ f(A_L)+f(A_R), & \text{otherwise.} \end{cases} \qquad \textbf{Eq. 4.}$$

where A, A_L and A_R are as per Equation 1, and $p\otimes q$ is the bit-wise exclusive OR of p with q, and $g1$ and $g2$ are the two global optima.

In the experiments that follow we will use the all-ones string as $g1$, and $g2$= "010101..." (i.e. loci with an odd index take the value 0, and the even loci take the value 1). Thus the two optima have exactly 50% of bits in agreement and 50% complementary. The proofs of Theorems 2 through 4 are not valid for the function in Equation 4 – it should be clear that the recombinative hill-climber cannot succeed on this problem. However, if we re-introduce an adequate population we can recover a successful algorithm. Unfortunately, we are not able to prove a time to solution on this problem using a population. However, we will see that an estimate based on *assumed* invariants of the population gives reasonable times. Specifically, we use the rather heavy-handed assumption below. This assumption states explicitly that diversity is being maintained appropriately for recombination to work effectively. It supposes a level-wise discovery of blocks and that all members of the population progress together.

Assumption 1: When looking for a block at level p, all individuals in the population consist of complete blocks from level p-1, and these blocks will be a sub-string of either global optimum, $g1$ or $g2$, with equal probability.

Theorem 5: $T\leq\frac{1}{2}N^2\lg^2 N$, where T is an upper bound on expected time to find a global optimum in H-IFF or H-IFF2 using a GA with two-point crossover, where Assumption 1 holds, and N>20 is the problem size.

Proof: Using $T\leq PMu$. Without the condition that every pair of parents are the exact compliment of one another we cannot apply the reasoning of one-point crossover from Theorem 3. But the reasoning for two-point crossover from Theorem 2 applies with a slight modification. Since we do not assume that the parents are necessarily complementary but rather they consist of correct sub-blocks of either type with equal probability, half of the blocks swapped-in will make no improvement. The sum of $1/q$, where q is the number of ways to make an improvement at each step, is therefore twice the value of u calculated in Theorem 4. Given that Assumption 1 refers to all individuals in the population, the same opportunity for improvement is available for any choice of parents, so P=1. The expected time to solution is therefore twice that of Theorem 4, with $M=\frac{1}{2}N(N-1)<\frac{1}{2}N^2$ for two-point crossover. [end]

This estimate of the expected time for a GA on H-IFF takes no account of the population size, selection pressure, or any other aspect of the algorithm – all of these are embedded in Assumption 1. Nonetheless, our empirical results given in the next section give times to solution that are under this upper bound on expected time and accordingly, support the validity of the assumption for our experimental set-up.

5 EXPERIMENTAL RESULTS

5.1 VERIFYING THEOREM 4: RECOMBINATIVE HILL-CLIMBER WITH ONE-POINT CROSSOVER APPLIED TO H-IFF.

To validate Theorem 4 we implemented the algorithm of Figure 4 with one-point crossover. Figure 6a) shows the results of 30 runs on each problem size N=32 doubling to N=4096. All 30 runs were successful at every size. We show the fastest, the slowest and the mean time to find the solution from each N. The analytical time, $T\leq\frac{1}{2}N\lg^2N$, provides a good upper bound. It appears to be too high by a factor less than $\lg N$ (see $\frac{1}{2}N\lg N$ curve for comparison). Figure 6b) shows the same data on a log log plot.

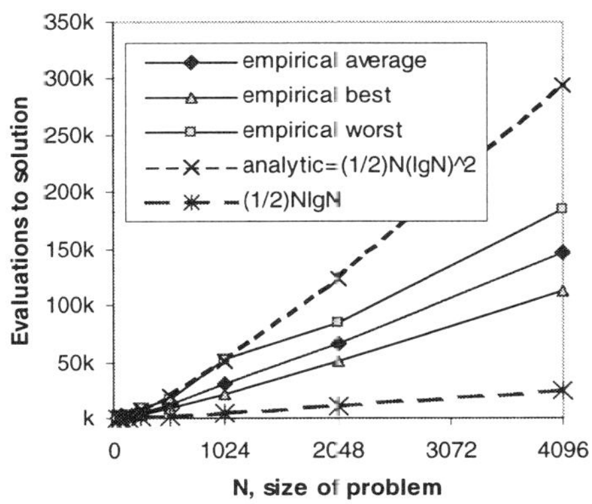

Figure 6a) Performance of recombinative hill-climber on H-IFF.

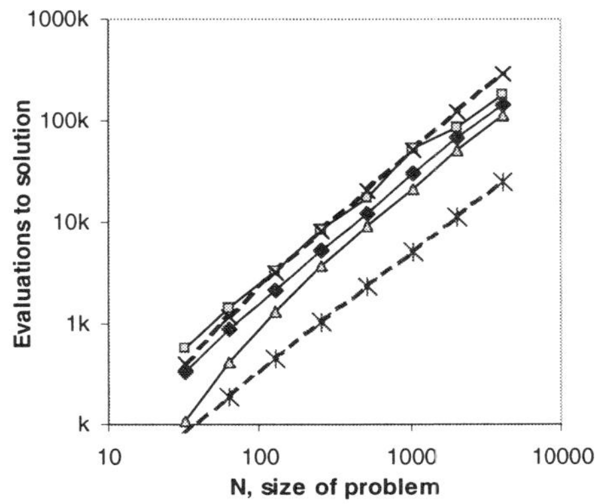

Figure 6b) Data as per Figure 6a, on log log plot.

5.2 VERIFYING THEOREM 5: GA WITH TWO-POINT CROSSOVER APPLIED TO H-IFF2

Theorem 5 is not based on any particular GA and empirically, we find that the algorithm in Figure 7, deterministic crowding, works faster and more reliably than GIGA on this problem. This is possibly because deterministic crowding (Mahfoud 1995) allows some convergence whilst also segregating competition and thereby maintaining diversity.

- Initialise population to random strings.
- Repeat until satisfied:
  - Pick two parents at random from the population, *p*1 & *p*2.
  - Produce a pair of offspring from these parents using crossover only, *c*1 & *c*2.
  - Pair-up each offspring with one parent according to the pairing rule below.
  - For each parent/offspring pair, if the offspring is fitter than the parent then replace the parent with the offspring.

Pairing rule: if **H**(*p*1,*c*1)+**H**(*p*2,*c*2) <**H**(*p*1,*c*2)+**H**(*p*2,*c*1) then pair *p*1 with *c*1, and *p*2 with *c*2, else pair *p*1 with *c*2, and *p*2 with *c*1, where **H** gives the genotypic Hamming distance between two individuals.

Figure 7: A simple form of a GA using deterministic crowding.

Figure 8a) shows the solution times for the algorithm in Figure 4 for N=32 doubling to N=256 and for population sizes from 32 doubling to 4096. Average solution times over 30 runs are shown only for those population sizes that succeeded on at least 90% of runs (in an evaluation limit of 200 times the population size). For example, only the population size 4096 succeeded reliably on N=256. We see that the time to solution is approximately linear with population size for those sizes that succeed. We also note that for each doubling of N, the minimum population size that succeeds reliably quadruples (See log log plot in Figure 8b).

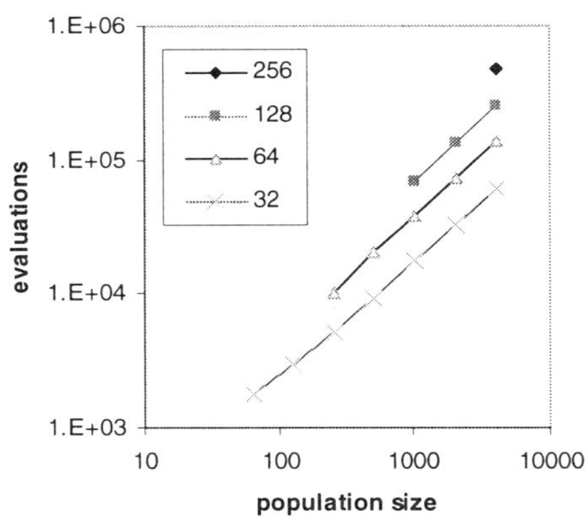

Figure 8a) Performance of GA on H-IFF2, various problem sizes, & population sizes.

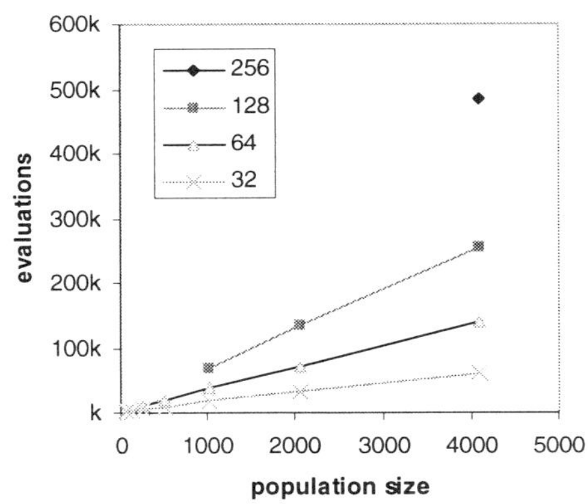

Figure 8b) Data as per Figure 8a, on log log plot.

Since we are interested in whether there is any configuration for the GA such that time to solution is reliably better than our upper bound, we now focus on the smallest population size that succeeds reliably. We extract the average time to solution for each N using this population size, i.e. the first point on each curve. These points are compared with analytic time, from Theorem 5 in Figure 9a). This expected time, $T \le \frac{1}{2}N^2 \lg^2 N$, provides an overestimate of the experimental time. Figure 9b), shows the same data as 9a) on a log log plot.

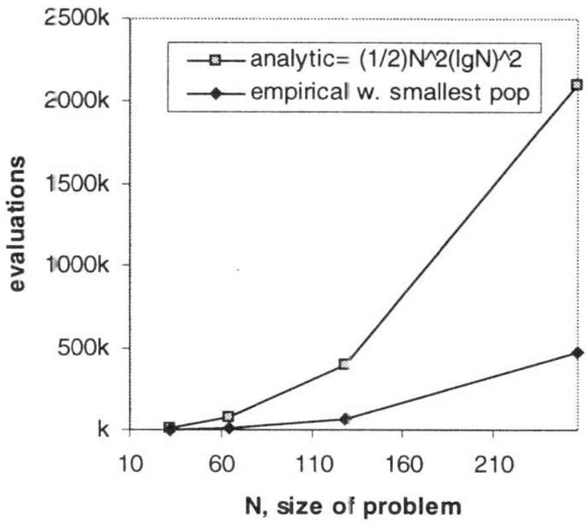

Figure 9a) Performance of GA on H-IFF2 using smallest reliable population.

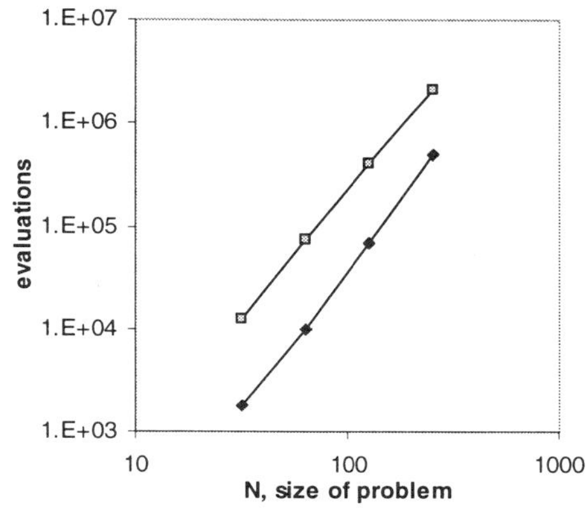

Figure 9b) Data as per Figure 9a, on log log plot.

The fact that the empirical time is better than our analytic time does not necessarily mean that Assumption 1 was correct. However, we can make some statements about the operation of the algorithm from this result. Note that the algorithm uses elitist replacement; an individual can only be replaced by a new offspring if the new individual is fitter. An algorithm incorporating such a replacement strategy cannot succeed unless its variation operators successfully manipulate the search space so as to ensure that there is always at least one way in which a fitter individual can be created from the current population. Note also, that in H-IFF, since all blocks within a level are the same fitness, and higher level blocks must contain correct lower-level blocks, superior fitness can only arise from a greater number of correct blocks. Thus we know that since this algorithm succeeds then there must be a progression of individuals with monotonically increasing number of correct blocks, i.e. Condition 1 must be true. Further, we may say that an algorithm that performs better than our analytic time, as this algorithm does, either has more opportunities to find a next step on a path to the optimum, or has a shorter path than we than we thought. These observations suggest that the GA is able to properly exploit the decomposable structure of H-IFF by following the crossover landscape.

6 CONCLUSIONS

We have provided an analytic time to solution for a recombinative algorithm on a non-separable building-block problem. The upper bound on expected time is based on proving a path to the optimum and the time for each step on the path. In the limited case of a population of two we have proved that the expected time to solution is at most $O(N\lg^2 N)$, where N is the size of the problem in bits. This is verified empirically. For the more general population case we provide a time $O(N^2\lg^2 N)$ based on the assumption that, at any time, the state of the population is such that the algorithm is able to provide recombination steps that follow the path we have described.

This time estimate does not take account of population size (though we know empirically that time increases approximately linearly with population size for a given N). Instead, factors such as this are embedded into the assumption that the population is sufficient to provide recombinative steps. The empirical times therefore use the smallest population size (for each

N) that succeeds reliably. In these cases it seems that there is a population size for which the GA succeeds reliably and our analytic time to solution is an overestimate.

These expected times are in contrast to the performance of mutation-based hill-climbers which either fail, or are not guaranteed to find solution in less than time exponential in N.

Our test problem does not involve difficult genetic linkage and the algorithm does not involve non-standard crossover operators – we use building-blocks with tight genetic linkage, and ordinary two-point crossover, as the Building-Block Hypothesis suggests. It is the epistatic linkage between building-blocks that makes the problem difficult for mutation, whereas an algorithm that is able to search combinations of building-blocks finds this problem easy. More specifically, the problem has a landscape with an exponential number of local optima for mutation, but in contrast, under the adaptive reorganisation of the landscape afforded by a population-based recombinative algorithm there are no local optima. Finally, our experimental results verify that the GA with crossover is able to properly exploit the hierarchically decomposable structure of this problem class and illustrate the potential value of recombination in more general non-separable problems.

Acknowledgements

Many thanks to Alden Wright for suggesting that H-IFF may yield to an adaptation of his analysis, and assisting with my preliminary analyses. Thanks also to the anonymous reviewers, and the members of DEMO at Brandeis especially Ofer Melnik, Anthony Bucci, and Jordan Pollack.

References

Culberson, J, 1992, "*Genetic Invariance: A New Paradigm for Genetic Algorithm Design*", technical report TR92-02, University of Alberta.

Forrest, S & Mitchell, M, 1993 "Relative Building-block fitness and the Building-block Hypothesis", in *FOGA 2*, Morgan Kaufmann, San Mateo, CA.

Goldberg, DE, 1989 "*Genetic Algorithms in Search, Optimization and Machine Learning*", Reading Massachusetts, Addison-Wesley.

Harik, GR, & Goldberg, DE, 1996, "Learning Linkage" in *FOGA 4*, Morgan Kaufmann, San Mateo, CA.

Hoehn, C, & Reeves, C, 1996, "Are long path problems hard for genetic algorithms?", in *PPSN IV*, Voigt, Ebeling, Rechenberg, Schwefel, eds. Springer.

Holland, JH, 1975 "*Adaptation in Natural and Artificial Systems*", Ann Arbor, MI: The Uni. of Michigan Press.

Jones, T, 1995, *Evolutionary Algorithms, Fitness Landscapes and Search*, PhD dissertation, 95-05-048, University of New Mexico, Albuquerque.

Kargupta, H, 1997, "Gene Expression: The Missing Link In Evolutionary Computation" *Genetic Algorithms in Engineering and Computer Science*, Eds. Quagliarella, Q Periaux, J, and Winter, G.: John Wiley and Sons.

Kauffman, S, 1993, *The Origins of Order*, Oxford University Press.

Mahfoud, S, 1995, *"Niching Methods for Genetic Algorithms"*, PhD thesis University of Illinois, also IlliGAl Report No. 95001.

Mitchell, M, Holland, JH, & Forrest, S, 1995 "When will a Genetic Algorithm Outperform Hill-climbing?" *Advances in NIPS 6*, Morgan Kaufmann, San Mateo, CA.

Watson, RA, Hornby, GS, & Pollack, JB, 1998, "Modeling Building-Block Interdependency", *PPSN V*, Eds. Eiben, Back, Schoenauer, Schweffel: Springer. pp. 97-106.

Watson, RA, & Pollack, JB, 1999a, "Hierarchically-Consistent Test Problems for Genetic Algorithms", *Procs. of 1999 CEC.* Angeline, et al. eds. IEEE Press, pp.1406-1413.

Watson, RA, & Pollack, JB, 1999b, "Incremental Commitment in Genetic Algorithms", *Proceedings of GECCO 1999.* Banzhaf, et al. eds., Morgan Kaufmann, pp.710-717.

Watson, RA, & Pollack, JB, 2000a, "Symbiotic Combination as an Alternative to Sexual Recombination in Genetic Algorithms", *PPSN VI*, Schoenauer et al. eds., Springer.

Watson, RA & Pollack, JB, 2000b, "Recombination Without Respect: Schema Combination and Disruption in Genetic Algorithm Crossover", *Procs. of GECCO 2000*, Whitley, D, et al (eds.), Morgan Kaufmann. pp. 112-119

Wright, AH, & Zhao, Y, 1999, "Markov Chain Models of Genetic Algorithms", *Procs. of GECCO'99*, Banzhaf, et al. eds., Morgan Kaufmann, pp. 734-741.

Direct Statistical Estimation of GA Landscape Properties

Colin R. Reeves
School of Mathematical and Information Sciences
Coventry University
UK
Email: C.Reeves@coventry.ac.uk

Abstract

A variety of predictive measures have been suggested for assessing how difficult it might be to solve a particular problem instance using a particular algorithm. However, most of these measures have been indirect. For neighbourhood search methods, one direct indicator of problem difficulty is the number of local optima that exist in the problem landscape. In the case of evolutionary algorithms, the concept of a local optimum is not easy to define, but it is known that GA populations, for example, commonly converge to fixed points or 'attractors'. Whether we speak of local optima or attractors, however, estimating the number of them is not an easy problem. In this paper some probability distributions are derived for quantities that can be measured in repeated application of heuristic search methods. It is then shown how this can be used to provide direct statistical estimates of the number of attractors using maximum likelihood methods. We discuss practical questions of numerical estimation, provide some illustrations of how the method works in the case of a GA, and discuss some implications of the assumptions made in deriving the estimates.

1 INTRODUCTION

Many attempts have been made in the last 10 years to answer a question that recurs in using evolutionary algorithms such as GAs to solve optimization problems: which algorithm is best suited to optimize this particular function? It is a natural corollary of the 'No-Free-Lunch' (NFL) theorem (Wolpert and Macready, 1997) that there will be differences among algorithms in any specific case, but finding ways of distinguishing between algorithms seems to be problematic.

Some have focused on measures of problem difficulty that we can compute by sampling the Universe of all potential solutions (Davidor, 1990; Davidor, 1991; Aizawa, 1997). These use measures that rely simply on the function itself, which is of uncertain utility if we wish to compare algorithms. The underlying factor in these approaches is the Walsh decomposition of the function, which is captured in a single value known as the 'epistasis variance'. Reeves provides a recent survey and critique (Reeves, 1999a) of some of these ideas, and shows that there are considerable practical and interpretative problems in using such measures.

Others have tried to take account heuristically of the way that the proposed algorithm works (Jones and Forrest, 1995). More recently Stadler and Wagner have put in place a more rigorous mathematical foundation (Stadler and Wagner, 1997) whereby the 'amplitude spectrum' of the landscape induced by a particular operator can be estimated. Interestingly, this measure again depends in a fundamental way on the Walsh decomposition.

However, all of these methods can really only compute a proxy for the properties that make a problem instance difficult. These include the number of local optima, their depth and width, and the size of their basins of attraction. Such concepts can be defined quite straightforwardly in the case of a deterministic neighbourhood search (NS). However, the concept of a local optimum is rather harder to pin down in the case of GAs, since the landscape in any specific generation depends not merely on the operators used (as is solely the case for NS), but also on the nature of the current population, and on the particular pairs of parents selected for mating. Nevertheless, the work of (Vose, 1999) has shown that GAs commonly converge towards fixed points in the sense of stable populations of strings, and that these tend to be near the corner of the population simplex—i.e., where the population is a set of identical strings.

In this paper we shall be interested in estimating the number of these fixed points or 'attractors' for a given instance. An important point to realize is that while at least one of the local optima in NS is sure to be the global optimum, we cannot of course be certain that any attractor of a GA is actually the global optimum. Nevertheless, many successful practical applications of GAs are fairly convincing evidence that the set of such attractors has a high probability of including the global optima or at least other very high-quality points.

Clearly, while not the only characteristic of interest, and not the only determinant of solution quality, the number of attractors is one property of the 'landscape' that is likely to influence how difficult the problem is. Methods based on Walsh decomposition cannot be certain of measuring this well. As is shown by (Reeves, 2000), it is possible to generate large numbers of functions that have identical epistasis variance measures, or amplitude spectra, and yet the number of NS local optima can vary widely. To have a direct measure of the number of attractors would therefore be very useful.

In this paper we describe a methodology for computing an estimate of the number of attractors using data obtained from repeated sampling. Although we shall couch the argument in terms of attractors for an evolutionary algorithm, it also obviously applies *mutatis mutandis* to any search algorithm. For example, in the case of deterministic neighbourhood search, for 'attractors' we simply read 'local optima'; for simulated annealing (say) we might be interested in the number of 'high-quality' local optima, since it would be assumed that the chance of being trapped in low-quality ones is reduced almost to zero.

Previous work in this direction has been hinted at in (Schaffer *et al.*, 1989), and the technique used there has been reported recently by (Caruana and Mullins, 1999). Ideas similar to those which we consider in the current paper have also been presented by (Kallel and Garnier, 2000), but with a different focus.

In the next section of this paper, the probability model that we shall use is introduced. Questions of estimation, approximations and numerical methods are considered, along with some details on the statistical properties of the estimators derived. A parameter of importance is κ, the proportion of distinct attractors found in repeated sampling. Sections 3 and 4 consider specifically the cases where κ is large (close to 1), and small (below 0.5) respectively. Finally, in section 5 some applications are presented in the context of a GA solving some relatively simple optimization problems.

2 A PROBABILITY MODEL

Suppose there are ν attractors, and that when using a GA from an initial random population the chance of encountering each attractor is the same. This may be interpreted as an assumption that all attractors have the same size basin of attraction—a first approximation that is probably not valid, but it is a reasonable starting point for the development of a model. We shall return to this point later.

Suppose the GA is run to convergence—i.e., an attractor is discovered. The process is then repeated many times. When there are many attractors, many repetitions may take place and very few attractors are found more than once. On the other hand, if the number of attractors is few, we will soon encounter previously discovered attractors. We can devise a probability model that describes this behaviour as follows:

Suppose that the GA is repeated r times, and that the trials are independent. The random variable K describes the number of *distinct* attractors that are found.

Proposition 1 *The probability distribution of K is given by*

$$P[K = k] = \frac{\nu(\nu-1)\dots(\nu-k+1)S(r,k)}{\nu^r} \qquad 1 \leq k \leq \min(r,\nu),$$

or

$$P[K = k] = \frac{\nu!}{(\nu-k)!}\frac{S(r,k)}{\nu^r},$$

where $S(r,k)$ is the Stirling number of the second kind.

The proof of this proposition follows a straightforward application of the inclusion-exclusion principle of combinatorics—see (Johnson and Kotz, 1969) , who call this the Arfwedson distribution. □

Johnson and Kotz further give the mean as

$$E[K] = \nu\{1-(1-1/\nu)^r\}. \tag{1}$$

However, in our position, ν is an unknown parameter which we wish to estimate. The well-known principle of maximum likelihood (Beaumont, 1980) provides a well-tested pathway to obtain an estimate $\hat{\nu}$. Maximum likelihood (ML) estimators have certain useful properties, such as asymptotic consistency, that make them generally better to use than simple moment estimators, for example. The first step is to write the log-likelihood as

$$l(\nu) = \log P = \log \nu! - \log(\nu - k)! + \log S(r, k) - r \log \nu,$$

and then find its maximum by solving

$$\Delta l = l(\nu) - l(\nu - 1) = 0$$

since ν is a discrete quantity. This is straightforward in principle, since $\Delta \log \nu! = \log \nu$, and we find that the equation reduces to

$$r \log(1 - 1/\nu) - \log(1 - k/\nu) = 0 \tag{2}$$

which can be solved by numerical methods. In fact this equation can also be derived from the relationship for the mean above. In other words, the ML estimator and the moment estimator here coincide.

2.1 Approximations

In the case of large ν, we can expand the logarithms in Eq. 2 in powers of $1/\nu$, truncate and equate the two sides of the equation in order to provide approximate values for $\hat{\nu}$. Suppressing—temporarily—the ^ symbols for clarity, we obtain the equation

$$\frac{k}{\nu} + \frac{k^2}{2\nu^2} + \frac{k^3}{3\nu^3} + \ldots = \frac{r}{\nu} + \frac{r}{2\nu^2} + \frac{r}{3\nu^3} + \ldots$$

Truncating after 2 terms reduces to

$$\frac{k}{\nu} + \frac{k^2}{2\nu^2} = \frac{r}{\nu} + \frac{r}{2\nu^2}$$

which implies that

$$2\nu(r - k) = k^2 - r \qquad \text{or } \hat{\nu} \approx \frac{k^2 - r}{2(r - k)}.$$

Adding a 3rd term gives

$$6\nu^2 k + 3\nu k^2 + 2k^3 = 6\nu^2 r + 3\nu r + 2r$$

collecting terms

$$6\nu^2(r - k) + \nu(r - 3k^2) + 2(r - k^3) = 0$$

so that finally

$$\hat{\nu} \approx \frac{(3k^2 - r) \pm \sqrt{(r - 3k^2)^2 + 48(r - k)(k^3 - r)}}{12(r - k)}. \tag{3}$$

2.2 Bias, variance and confidence intervals

In fact the procedure we have described is formally identical to the so-called 'Schnabel census' used by ecologists to estimate the number of animals in a closed population (Seber, 1982). Thus results from that field—first obtained by (Darroch, 1958)—may be adapted for the case we are considering. In (Darroch, 1958) it is shown that the ML estimate has a bias given by

$$b \approx \frac{\theta^2}{2}(e^\theta - 1 - \theta)^{-2},$$

where

$$\theta = r/\nu.$$

In most cases of interest here, θ will be small, and $\hat{\nu}$ will overestimate ν by about 1, which is hardly important when we expect ν to be several orders of magnitude higher! The variance of $\hat{\nu}$ is shown to be

$$V[\hat{\nu}] = \nu(e^\theta - 1 - \theta).$$

In order to obtain numerical estimates for these quantities, the value ν must be replaced by $\hat{\nu}$—the estimate obtained as in Eq. 2. In (Darroch, 1958) an upper bound is derived for $\hat{\nu}$:

$$\nu^* = r/\theta^* \tag{4}$$

where θ^* is the solution of

$$\frac{1 - e^{-\theta}}{\theta} = \frac{k}{r}.$$

In many cases, this is also a good approximation to $\hat{\nu}$.

The expression for variance could be used directly to find a confidence interval for $\hat{\nu}$. We can estimate its first two moments, as above, but the distribution of $\hat{\nu}$ is hardly Normal, and Darroch recommends that confidence limits should be found indirectly from the distribution of K, whose distribution is much closer to Normal. This entails solving the equations

$$k \pm z_{\alpha/2}s(\nu) = m(\nu) \tag{5}$$

where $m(\nu)$ is Eq. 1, considered as a function of ν, $z_{\alpha/2}$ is the appropriate Normal distribution ordinate for a $100(1-\alpha)\%$ confidence interval, and

$$s(\nu) = (\nu - m(\nu))(m(\nu) - m(\nu - 1)).$$

Of course, a closed form solution is impossible, and the equations have to be solved numerically.

2.3 Numerical methods

Eq. 2 can be rewritten as

$$g(\nu) = r\log(1 - 1/\nu) - \log(1 - k/\nu) = 0$$

and then an iterative scheme such as binary search or Newton-Raphson can be used to find a numerical solution. Approximations such as those given above can be used to provide an initial estimate of ν for this iteration. In experimenting with several approaches, the author found the most reliable method was to use the upper bound of Eq. 4 for the initial estimate, with the discrete version of Newton-Raphson

$$\nu^{(i+1)} = \nu^{(i)} - \frac{g(\nu^{(i)})}{g(\nu^{(i)}) - g(\nu^{(i)} - 1)}$$

as suggested by (Robson and Regier, 1968). Tables 1 (respectively 2) display point (respectively 95% confidence interval) estimates of ν for a representative range of values of $\kappa = k/r$ and r.

Table 1 Estimates of ν (expected values) at some values of $\kappa = k/r$ and r.

	$\kappa = k/r$				
r	0.5	0.6	0.7	0.8	0.9
100	62	88	130	214	462
200	125	177	262	429	928
500	313	443	656	1075	2326
1000	627	887	1312	2152	4656
2000	1255	1775	2626	4307	9317
5000	3137	4439	6566	10769	23300
10000	6275	8878	13132	21540	46604
20000	12550	17757	26265	43082	93212
50000	31375	44394	65665	107707	233035
100000	62750	88789	131330	215417	466075
200000	125500	177578	262661	430835	932154
500000	313750	443946	656655	1077091	2330392

Regression using a varying-coefficients model for the expected values results in a fitted equation

$$\hat{\nu} = 0.0277r(324)^{\kappa}$$

which shows a (not unexpected) linear dependence on r, but an exponential relationship with κ. This demonstrates that as κ increases (i.e., as the proportion of distinct attractors in the sample increases) the expected number of attractors in the search space increases dramatically. The results for confidence intervals in Table 2 show that there will be considerable uncertainty for small samples ($r < 10000$, say, at least for relatively large κ), but of course, with larger samples, the estimate becomes more precise. The other noteworthy feature is the asymmetric nature of the intervals, reflecting a highly-skewed distribution for $\hat{\nu}$. Finally, for large values of κ (> 0.95, say), it is not possible to use Eq. 5 at all, since the implied value of k when the + sign of Eq. 5 is taken exceeds r.

On the other hand, in cases where r is large relative to ν, the ratio k/r may be very small, and care is needed in attempting to solve Eq. 2 numerically. In such cases, the best estimate of ν is often simply k or $k+1$. Likewise, the approximation in Eq. 3 is not suitable for small values of κ—in fact, simple numerical calculations show that unless $\kappa > 0.55$, Eq. 3 yields a value for ν that is actually smaller than k, which is clearly impossible.

Table 2 95% confidence intervals for ν at some values of k/r and r. For example, if $\kappa = 0.7$ and $r = 500$, we are 95% confident that ν lies between 581 and 745.

	$\kappa = k/r$				
r	0.5	0.6	0.7	0.8	0.9
100	53-73	72-110	101-176	153-331	288-1040
200	112-140	153-206	217-322	336-576	653-1539
500	292-337	404-488	581-745	917-1286	1842-3116
1000	596-660	830-950	1204-1436	1920-2437	3930-5680
2000	1210-1301	1693-1862	2470-2797	3969-4696	8244-10684
5000	3066-3210	4308-4575	6315-6831	10222-11368	21532-25357
10000	6174-6377	8692-9070	12775-13504	20756-22375	44051-49445
20000	12407-12694	17493-18027	25758-26788	41964-44252	89547-97165
50000	31148-31603	43975-44819	64857-66487	105925-109542	227163-239197
100000	62429-63072	88195-89388	130185-132490	212885-218000	457712-474726
200000	125046-125956	176737-178425	261039-264299	427244-434478	920270-944328
500000	313031-314470	442614-445283	654086-659240	1071398-1082835	2311519-2349554

In practice this is likely to be irrelevant for most optimization problems—the interesting cases are those where we expect that $\kappa > 0.7$, say, and ν will be much larger than r. Nevertheless, we now consider both issues—the cases of large and small κ.

3 FIRST REPETITION WAITING TIME DISTRIBUTION

As remarked above, in many cases ν will be a very large number, as will be k—so it might be that every one of the attractors found is distinct unless r itself is quite large. Of course, if we find that $k = r$ there will be no solution to Eq. 2, and all that we can say for certain is that there are at least k attractors. This outcome would be most unlikely, of course. One possibility is to keep sampling the set of all attractors until the *first* re-occurrence of a previously encountered attractor. Suppose this occurs on iteration T. We will call this the waiting time to the first repetition.

Proposition 2 *The probability distribution of* T *is given by*

$$P[T = t] = \frac{\nu!(t-1)}{(\nu - t + 1)!\nu^t} \qquad 2 \leq t \leq \nu + 1$$

or

$$P[T = t] = \frac{\nu(\nu - 1)\dots(\nu - t + 2)(t - 1)}{\nu^t}.$$

The proof of this proposition again follows a straightforward combinatorial argument: the number of ways of choosing $(t-1)$ distinct objects from ν (in any order) is $\binom{\nu}{t-1}(t-1)!$, while the total number of possible arrangements of ν objects in $(t-1)$ trials is ν^{t-1}. The ratio of these quantities gives the probability that $(t-1)$ *distinct* attractors are encountered in $(t-1)$ trials. The probability that the tth trial encounters one of those attractors previously seen is $(t-1)/\nu$. Hence the result. □

The mean of T is

$$E[T] = \frac{2}{\nu} + \sum_{t=3}^{\nu+1} \frac{t(t-1)\nu!}{(\nu-t+1)!\nu^t},$$

which seems to have no obvious closed-form solution. However, this and other statistics can in principle be computed for a given value of N using the obvious recurrence formulae

$$P[T=t+1] = \frac{t}{t-1}\frac{\nu-t+1}{\nu}P[T=t]$$

(with $P[T=2] = 1/\nu$) to calculate the probabilities. For large values of ν this may take some time, and it is quicker to evaluate the median. Figure 1 shows the results of computations of median waiting time, and associated upper and lower quartiles, for a range of values of ν.

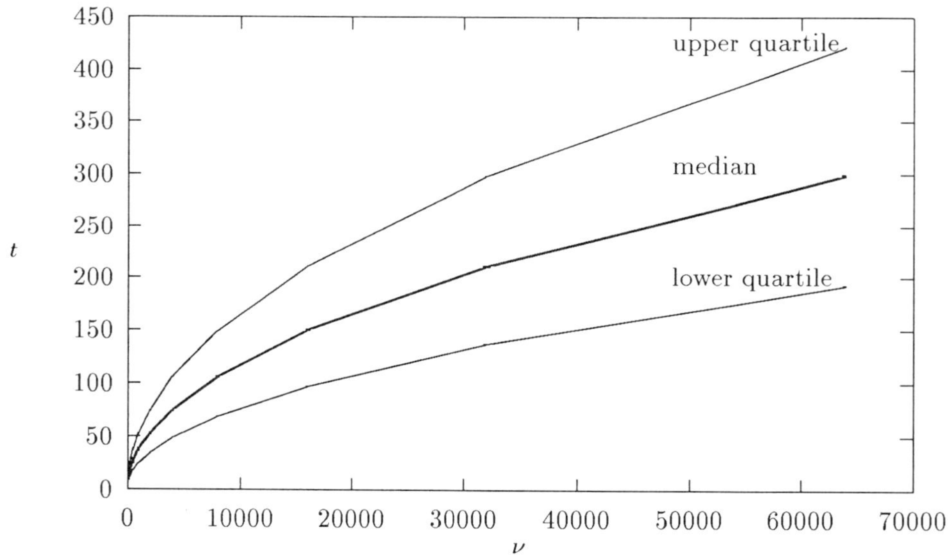

Figure 1 Waiting times for first repetition of an attractor for a range of values of ν, the total number of attractors.

From this diagram it appears that the average waiting time is increasing as something like $\nu^{0.5}$. A linear regression analysis confirmed that this is a plausible model, the actual relationship estimated over the range of values in the diagram being

$$t_{med} = 0.673 + 1.25\sqrt{\nu}$$

with a coefficient of determination (R^2) of almost 100%.

3.1 Maximum likelihood estimation

For a single determination $T = t$ the log-likelihood is

$$l(\nu) = \log \nu! + \log(t-1) - \log(\nu - t + 1)! - t \log \nu \tag{6}$$

and the first difference is

$$\Delta l = \log \nu - \log(\nu - t + 1) - t(\log \nu - \log(\nu - 1))$$

which gives an equation that is clearly a special case of Eq. 2

$$\log(1 - \frac{t-1}{\nu}) = t \log(1 - 1/\nu).$$

Thus the numerical methods described in section 2.3 can also be used for this case. If we carry out multiple runs of the algorithm, so that we have m determinations $(t_1, \ldots, t_m)$, the generalization of the above is simply

$$\sum_{i=1}^{m} \log\left(1 - \frac{t_i - 1}{\nu}\right) = \log(1 - 1/\nu) \sum_{i=1}^{m} t_i.$$

This can be simplified to

$$l(\nu) = \sum_{i=1}^{m} \left(\sum_{k=\nu - t_i + 2}^{\nu} \log k - t_i \log \nu \right) + \text{ terms not involving } \nu \tag{7}$$

From this a direct line search algorithm can be devised for finding the maximum of $l(\nu)$ and hence the maximum likelihood estimator of ν. (Note that further algorithmic simplifications can be made by realising that many of the terms in the sum over k are repeated for all values of i—in fact all of them after $k = \nu - t_{min} + 1$ where t_{min} is the smallest value among the t_i.) The author found that a golden section search based on this approach worked almost as well as the Newton-Raphson method used in section 2.3.

We can also find what appears to be a fairly good approximation, using natural logarithms in Eq. 6, and Stirling's approximation

$$\ln \nu! \approx \frac{\ln 2\pi}{2} + (\nu + \frac{1}{2}) \ln \nu - \nu$$

Setting $\frac{dl(\nu)}{d\nu} = 0$ gives the following, after some algebra:

$$\nu = -\frac{\frac{x}{2(1-x)} + t}{\ln(1-x)} \tag{8}$$

where $x = (t-1)/\nu$. This can easily be iterated to a solution. (It is very easily handled in a spreadsheet, for example.) Again, if we have multiple determinations of T, the generalization is easy to obtain:

$$\nu = -\frac{\sum_{i=1}^{m} \left[\frac{x_i}{2(1-x_i)} + t_i\right]}{\sum_{i=1}^{m} \ln(1 - x_i)}.$$

Note that even when we exhaust our resources, and still we have $k = r$, we could use the techniques described above on the assumption that iteration $r + 1$ will provide the first re-occurrence. In this way, we could calculate a conservative estimate of ν.

3.2 Further Approximations

Since we can expect $x \ll 1$ in most interesting instances of optimization problems, it is possible to expand the right-hand side of Eq. 8 in powers of x, truncate, and solve the resulting equation for ν. This produces

$$\nu(x + \frac{x^2}{2} + \frac{x^3}{3} + \ldots) = \frac{x}{2} + \frac{x^2}{2} + \frac{x^3}{2} + \ldots + t$$

Truncating after the 1st term clearly fails to provide a sensible estimate, but truncating after the second-order term gives the following:

$$\nu\left(x + \frac{x^2}{2}\right) = \frac{x}{2} + \frac{x^2}{2} + t.$$

On substituting for x, and after some algebra, we find

$$2\nu^2 - (t-1)(t-2)\nu + (t-1)^2 = 0,$$

and solving the quadratic for ν (and taking the positive square root) leads to

$$\nu^* \approx \frac{(t-1)(t-2)}{2},$$

which confirms the empirical observation in Fig. 1. In the case of multiple runs the quadratic is

$$a\nu^2 + b\nu + c = 0$$

with coefficients

$$a = 2m, \; b = -(U_2 - 3U_1 + 2m), \; c = U_2 - 2U_1 + m$$

where

$$U_k = \sum_{i=1}^{m} (t_i)^k.$$

4 ESTIMATING THE NUMBER OF SAMPLES

We might expect that most of the time we will be faced with problems having large values of ν (and thus of κ). However, some problem instances may have relatively small values, in which case we have a different but still interesting question: how long should we sample before we can reasonably be sure that all attractors have been found? We can model this situation as follows.

Suppose there are ν attractors, and that we have already found k of them. The waiting time W_k for the $(k+1)$st attractor will have a geometric distribution

$$f(t|k) = \frac{\nu - k}{\nu}\left(\frac{k}{\nu}\right)^{t-1}$$

with expectation $\nu/(\nu-k)$ and variance $k\nu/(\nu-k)^2$. The overall waiting time will be

$$W = 1 + \sum_{k=1}^{\nu-1} W_k$$

and since these waiting times are independent, we can approximate the expectation and variance as follows:

$$\begin{aligned} E[W] &= 1 + \sum_{k=1}^{\nu-1} \frac{\nu}{\nu-k} \\ &= \nu \sum_{k=1}^{\nu} \frac{1}{k} \\ &\approx \nu(\ln \nu + \gamma) \end{aligned}$$

where $\gamma = 0.57721..$ is Euler's constant; and

$$\begin{aligned} V[W] &= 0 + \sum_{k=1}^{\nu-1} \frac{k\nu}{(\nu-k)^2} \\ &= \nu^2 \sum_{k=1}^{\nu-1} \frac{1}{k^2} - \nu \sum_{k=1}^{\nu-1} \frac{1}{k} \\ &\approx \nu^2 \zeta(2) - \nu(\ln \nu + \gamma - 1/\nu) \end{aligned}$$

where $\zeta(s) = \sum_1^\infty k^{-s}$ is Riemann's zeta function. The case $s = 2$ is a special case, for which $\zeta(2) = \pi^2/6$, so finally

$$V[W] \approx \frac{(\nu\pi)^2}{6} + 1 - \nu(\ln \nu + \gamma).$$

Although both expressions are approximations, the errors are fairly small. The error in using Euler's constant is already below 1% for $\nu = 15$, and while larger and slower to fall, the error in the infinite sum approximation drops below 2.5% for $\nu = 25$. Further, the errors are in opposite directions—one is a lower and the other an upper bound, so the net effect is likely to be unimportant.

We can use these estimates together with a Normal approximation to establish with probability α that the waiting time will exceed a given value:

$$W > \nu(\ln \nu + \gamma) + z_\alpha \sqrt{\frac{(\nu\pi)^2}{6} + 1 - \nu(\ln \nu + \gamma)}.$$

where z_α is the appropriate standard Normal value. Finally, the right-hand side of the above expression can be inverted (numerically) to find a confidence limit on ν. Table 3 gives some representative values, obtained very simply by using a spreadsheet equation solver.

If the actual number of distinct local optima found in r samples is no more than the value given by such calculations, we can be confident (to approximately the degree specified)

Table 3 Table giving upper confidence limits for ν at some representative values of r. For example, if we sample 2000 times and find 210 local optima, we can be 99% (but not 99.9%) confident that we have found them all.

No. samples (r)	upper limit on ν 99%	99.9%
100	16	14
200	29	26
500	65	59
1000	120	109
2000	223	204
5000	511	468
10000	959	884
20000	1808	1673

that we have found all the local optima. As already remarked, while the estimates of both mean and variance have small errors, they are unlikely to have a large influence on the degree of confidence. However, while the assumption of Normality is convenient, it is probably not well-founded: there is clearly a lower bound on the value of W, since it cannot be less than ν, while the upper tail of the distribution may be very long. Thus, we should perhaps make do with Chebyshev's inequality

$$Pr\left[\left|\frac{W - E[W]}{V[W]}\right| \geq c\right] \leq \frac{1}{c^2}$$

which gives a less sharp, but still useful, confidence limit.

5 AN APPLICATION

In principle, this approach could be useful in providing some assurance of the quality of solutions obtained in the course of a heuristic search. Not only does it tell us something (although not everything) about the landscape, but at least tentatively, we now have a statistical way of assessing the amount of search that we need in order to find the global optimum with a reasonable probability.

It also gives us a means of comparing different representations and operators. For example, in the case of a GA, we could estimate the number of attractors resulting from the application of a GA, and compare this with what happens using a deterministic neighbourhood search using a bit flip operator, as a way of measuring the 'improvement' resulting from using a GA. (Of course, just looking at the numbers is not the only criterion—the quality of the respective solutions should also be taken into account.)

In (Reeves, 2000) it is shown that it is possible to generate sets of equivalent NK-landscapes—as introduced by (Kauffman, 1993); equivalent in the sense that all have the same epistasis variance, while having widely differing numbers of local optima with respect to a bit flip neighbourhood search. (The use of this operator implies that the underlying the landscape is based on the Hamming metric. Thus we shall call it the Hamming landscape.) However, how these landscapes compare with respect to a GA is not clear. Two NK-functions with $N = 10, 12$ and $K = 4$ were chosen, representing those furthest apart in terms of numbers of Hamming landscape local optima. These are labelled 'hard' and 'easy' below. Each problem was solved repeatedly using a steady-state GA having the following parameters: population size 32, linear rank-based selection of parents, crossover was always performed (either one or two point), followed by mutation at a rate of either 0.05 or 0.10 per bit. One new offspring was produced at each iteration, and it replaced one of the worst 50% of the existing population. The run was terminated at convergence to an attractor.

At this point, we should explain what is meant by 'convergence'. In the sense of (Vose, 1999), an attractor is a *population*, which does not necessarily coincide with a corner point of the simplex—i.e., it may not consist of multiple copies of a single string. Whenever mutation is involved, there is always the possibility of some variation, so detecting that an attractor (in the Vose sense) has been found is somewhat imprecise. As a reasonable heuristic, in these experiments it was defined as the situation when 90% of the population agreed about the allele at each locus. In order to guard against very long convergence times in the computer experiments, a termination criterion was also included in the code: that the run should be ended after 512 strings (a large fraction of the entire search space for these problems) had been evaluated. As a matter of fact, however, this criterion was never needed for the parameters tested, although with higher mutation rates and a softer selection pressure such a criterion might become necessary.

The numbers of attractors found on this basis in a sample of 100 replicate runs were counted and an estimate made using the methodology developed above. The results were as shown in Table 4. The numbers of local optima with respect to the neighbourhood search were obtained by exact counting using a version of Jones's 'reverse hill-climbing' approach (Jones, 1995). However, it is not possible to compute the numbers of attractors exactly for a GA, even when the parameters are fixed, since there is so much randomization involved. What we estimate therefore is in some sense the number of the 'most common' attractors, ignoring possible pathological behaviour.

This is merely a small example, but even this demonstrates some interesting differences in the performances of the GAs. The number of GA attractors for the 'easy' landscapes is generally smaller (with a notable exception for the $N = 12$ case with mutation at 0.05) than for the 'hard' ones, and there does appear to be a difference between the 1-point and 2-point crossovers. We might also intuit that high mutation rates would imply fewer attractors, and this is evident in most cases (with the $N = 12$ case again an exception). It is also clear that just examining the NS landscape may not be adequate in predicting the performance of a GA. The number of attractors is clearly more than the number of NS-local optima in the 'easy' case, and seems likely to be fewer in the 'hard' case.

In some further experiments, a set of 35 equivalent NK-functions (with $N = 15, K = 4$) was investigated; for each case a GA was run (as described above, with 1-point crossover and 0.10/bit mutation rate) for 100 independent trials. The number of attractors was estimated and compared with the (known) number of bit-flip local optima for each of the related landscapes. The correlation between the number of GA attractors and the number of Hamming local optima was 0.72, a statistically significant value. When the actual strings

Table 4 A comparison of two equally 'epistatic' NK-landscapes with respect to NS and GAs for two different mutation rates and for 1-point and 2-point crossover.

Landscape	# NS-local optima	# GA attractors		
			Mut rate	
$N = 10, K = 4$		xover	0.10	0.05
'easy'	9	1	15	17
		2	12	14
'hard'	35	1	16	23
		2	18	18
$N = 12, K = 4$				
'easy'	16	1	14	25
		2	14	18
'hard'	52	1	23	24
		2	16	22

were compared, the set of GA attractors was almost always a subset of the Hamming local optima. Thus, although the landscapes are different in general, it seems that their fixed points tend to coincide, and despite the conceptual difference between deterministic point-based NS methods and stochastic population-based GAs, their respective landscapes seem to have similar properties.

Finally, the numbers of GA attractors was re-estimated using 500 independent runs instead of 100. In every case, the initial estimated number of attractors was exceeded, and although the numbers of attractors using 500 runs was well predicted by the numbers estimated using 100 runs (all fell within the initial 95% confidence interval), the correlation with the numbers of Hamming local optima was less strong (0.51 instead of 0.72). Now the set of attractors included points that were not Hamming local optima, so this reduction in correlation was not altogether a surprise. However, the 'new' attractors tended to be less fit than those found in the first 100 runs, and obviously they had a smaller attractive basin. This has some implications for the usefulness of the methodology that will be discussed in the next, final, section.

6 CONCLUSIONS AND FURTHER WORK

Several procedures have been presented for an empirical investigation of one aspect of a GA landscape. Previous approaches have not been able directly to answer the question of how many attractors there are, but the approach described here is able to estimate this quantity. Several practical questions of implementation have been reviewed, and an application has been made in order to demonstrate the methodology. The techniques described are not limited to GAs, but can in principle be applied to any heuristic search method.

There are some caveats that we should mention. Firstly, there is clearly a substantial computational burden in such investigations, and the size of the problem instance is clearly a factor in the feasibility of this approach. The number of samples needed may become infeasibly large as the size of the problem space increases.

Secondly, any estimate is useful only as long as the assumptions upon which it is based are valid. The fundamental assumption made above is that the attractors are *isotropically* distributed in the landscape, which implies that their basins of attraction are of more or less equal size. In fact, this is almost certainly not the case for many instances of NS landscapes. Such landscapes have been investigated empirically for such problems as the TSP, graph bisection and flowshop scheduling (Kauffman, 1993; Boese *et al.*, 1994; Reeves, 1999b), and in many cases it is found that the local optima tend to be clustered in a 'big valley'—closer to each other (and to the global optima) than a pair of randomly chosen points would be. Furthermore, the better optima tend to be closer to the global optima, and to have larger basins of attraction, than the poorer ones. Thus, optima found by repeated local searches are disproportionately likely to be these 'more attractive' (and hopefully fitter) ones. The number of local optima found by assuming an isotropic distribution is therefore likely to be an under-estimate of the true value. Nevertheless, we might hope that the statistical estimates would still be useful, as many of the local optima that we failed to find in a non-isotropic landscape would not (if the big valley conjecture holds) be very important anyway.

We do not know if similar patterns affect GA landscapes and attractors, but we have to recognize the possibility. Certainly, this is suggested by the analysis of the 35 equivalent NK-functions in the previous section. When the number of runs was extended from 100 to 500, several more attractors were found, more than had been estimated by the methods of the previous sections. These attractors seemed to have small basins, and to be less fit, so the remarks above relating to local optima seem to be echoed for the case of GA landscapes too.

In the applications above the effect of a non-isotropic distribution of attractors is probably not acute. When we compare the *relative* performance of different operators, for example, the effects of a non-isotropic distribution may apply in the same way to all of them. Also, on the empirical evidence of many fairly large studies of NS landscapes, and on the (admittedly much smaller) examples of GA landscapes investigated above, the attractors in the 'tail' of the distribution of basin sizes may be relatively unimportant. The assumption of approximate uniformity among the ones that we do care about is much more reasonable, and might mean that the estimates we obtain are fairly accurate, as long as we interpret them as referring to these 'good' attractors.

Nevertheless, if we wish to find still better estimates of the number of attractors, the effects of a non-uniform spread of attractors should be taken into account. A second paper that is currently in preparation will both examine the extent of the effect of the assumptions in the above analysis, and also explore stochastic models of non-isotropic landscapes.

References

A.Aizawa (1997) Fitness landscape characterization by variance of decompositions. In R.K.Belew and M.D.Vose (Eds.) (1997) *Foundations of Genetic Algorithms 4*, Morgan Kaufmann, San Francisco, CA, 225-245.

G.P.Beaumont (1980) *Intermediate Mathematical Statistics*, Chapman & Hall, London.

K.D.Boese, A.B.Kahng and S.Muddu (1994) A new adaptive multi-start technique for combinatorial global optimizations. *Operations Research Letters*, **16**, 101-113.

R.Caruana and M.Mullins (1999) Estimating the number of local minima in complex search spaces. *Proc. International Conference on Artificial Intelligence: Workshop on Optimization.*

J.N.Darroch (1958) The multiple-recapture census. I: estimation of a closed population. *Biometrika*, **45**, 343-359.

Y.Davidor (1990) Epistasis variance: suitability of a representation to genetic algorithms. *Complex Systems*, **4**, 369-383.

Y.Davidor (1991) Epistasis variance: a viewpoint on GA-hardness. In G.J.E.Rawlins (Ed.) (1991) *Foundations of Genetic Algorithms*, Morgan Kaufmann, San Mateo, CA.

T.Jones and S.Forrest (1995) Fitness distance correlation as a measure of problem difficulty for genetic algorithms. In L.J.Eshelman (Ed.) *Proceedings of the* 6th *International Conference on Genetic Algorithms*, Morgan Kaufmann, San Mateo, CA, 184-192.

N.L.Johnson and S.Kotz (1969) *Discrete distributions*, Wiley, New York.

T.C.Jones (1995) *Evolutionary Algorithms, Fitness Landscapes and Search*, Doctoral dissertation, University of New Mexico, Albuquerque, NM.

L.Kallel and J.Garnier (2000) How to detect all maxima of a function. Talk given at Seminar 00071 on the Theory of Evolutionary Algorithms, Schloss Dagstuhl, Germany, February 2000.

S.Kauffman (1993) *The Origins of Order: Self-Organization and Selection in Evolution.* Oxford University Press.

C.R.Reeves (1999a) Predictive measures for problem difficulty. In *Proceedings of 1999 Congress on Evolutionary Computation*, IEEE Press, 736-743.

C.R.Reeves (1999b) Landscapes, operators and heuristic search. *Annals of Operational Research*, **86**, 473-490.

C.R.Reeves (2000) Experiments with tunable landscapes. In M.Schoenauer, K.Deb, G.Rudolph, X.Yao, E.Lutton, J.J.Merelo and H-P.Schwefel (Eds.) (2000) *Parallel Problem-Solving from Nature—PPSN VI*, Springer-Verlag, Berlin, 139-148.

D.S.Robson and H.A.Regier (1968) Estimation of population number and mortality rates. In W.E.Ricker (Ed.) (1968) *Methods for Assessment of Fish Production in Fresh Waters*, Blackwell Scientific Publications, Oxford, 124-158.

J.D.Schaffer, R.A.Caruana, L.J.Eshelman and R.Das (1989) A study of control parameters affecting online performance of genetic algorithms for function optimization. In J.D.Schaffer (Ed.) (1989) *Proceedings of 3rd International Conference on Genetic Algorithms*, Morgan Kaufmann, Los Altos, CA, 51-60.

G.A.F.Seber (1982) *The Estimation of Animal Abundance*, Charles Griffin, London.

P.F.Stadler and G.P.Wagner (1998) Algebraic theory of recombination spaces. *Evolutionary Computation*, **5**, 241-275.

M.D.Vose (1999) What are genetic algorithms? A mathematical perspective. In L.D.Davis, K.DeJong, M.D.Vose and L.D.Whitley (Eds.) (1999) *Evolutionary Algorithms*: IMA Volumes in Mathematics and its Applications, Vol 111, Springer-Verlag, New York, 251-276.

D.H.Wolpert and W.G.Macready (1997) No free lunch theorems for optimization. *IEEE Trans.Ev.Comp*, **1**, 67-82.

Comparing population mean curves

B. Naudts and **I. Landrieu**
Department of Mathematics and Computer Science
University of Antwerpen (RUCA)
Groenenborgerlaan 171, B-2020 Antwerpen, Belgium
e-mail: {*bnaudts,landrieu*}*@ruca.ua.ac.be*

Abstract

One approach to the *a posteriori* classification of problem/algorithm combinations in the context of evolutionary algorithms (EAs), is to record and analyse a number of summary statistics of the evolution of the population. This paper discusses a necessary normalization of the population mean curve, i.e., the curve of the average fitness of the individuals in the population, plotted per generation. The normalization is based on a transformation w.r.t. the *density of states* (DoS) of the problem, the distribution of all fitness values. Experiments are carried out on the onemax problem and on randomly sampled MAX-3-SAT problem instances, for a whole array of different EA-settings. The expected DoS of MAX-3-SAT instances is approximated using probabilistic and computational techniques. As a side-product of the transformation, the paper proposes a definition for the *velocity* of the algorithm, which can be used as a performance measure for EAs.

1 Introduction

A classification of search problems according to their difficulty for evolutionary algorithms (EAs) has been pursued by many researchers since the beginning of the 1980s. Two rather different approaches exist: *a priori* classification, i.e. classification before running the algorithm itself, and *a posteriori* classification, classification based on information gathered during one or more runs of the algorithm on the problem in question. The former is also referred to as problem difficulty prediction.

Search problem classification serves two goals. Firstly, it is an approach to studying EAs. As such, it is tightly linked to the construction of typical problems or functions, like Royal Road functions, deceptive functions, etc., to gain a better insight in the behavior of the algorithm on different types of problems. Secondly, it is meant to guide a person optimizing a particular problem in their choice of algorithm, representation, parameter settings. Such an activity could also be automated and ideally occur *on-line*.

The most famous of the *a priori* classification attempts are probably *epistasis variance* [2] and *fitness distance correlation* [8], which each summarize a different property of the fitness landscape into one number or graph. There was hope that this summary information could be somehow related to the problem difficulty of this landscape for GAs. However, the last five years revealed the many deficiencies of these summary statistics, the main problem being that the landscape as seen by the GA is very different from the Hamming or bit-flip landscape. On the positive side, better – yet much more complex – tools to study fitness landscapes were developed. Techniques to study landscapes induced by recombination operators are available now, and a complete description of the landscape as one particular GA sees it, may be achieved in the near future.

Not much attention has gone to *a posteriori* classification up to now. The methodology is simple: statistics of the population are recorded during the run of the algorithm, and then compared to reference material. Kallel [9], for example, defines two such statistics, and uses them to classify functions by comparing with the onemax problem. The clear advantage of this approach is that algorithm and search problem are dealt with together. Given that small changes in an algorithm's parameter, like the mutation rate or population size, may have a significant impact on the dynamics of the algorithm, it is important that the algorithm itself is involved in the classification process if high reliability is required.

With this paper we hope to give the *a posteriori* approach a new impetus by discussing a first step towards a fully automated system for classifying algorithm/problem combinations. We discuss a means of normalizing the *population mean curves* with respect to the *density of states* (DoS) of the search problem.

The first cumulant κ_1 of the fitness distribution of a population P is defined as

$$\kappa_1 = \frac{1}{|P|} \sum_{s \in P} f(s).$$

It is the mean or average of the fitness values in the population. As a function of the time or generation counter t, $\kappa_1(t)$ is interpreted as a curve. To keep the names short, we call it the population mean curve. It is the most obvious starting point for classification attempts. Higher cumulants will also be required, but this paper does not deal with them.

The DoS is the term used by Rosé et al. [15] to denote the distribution of the fitness values of all strings: for each value r in the range of the fitness function, it gives the proportion of strings which map to this value. Examples follow.

As detailed in section 3, the transformation turns a fitness value into a dimensionless number related to the proportion of strings with an equal or better fitness value. The derivative of the transformed population mean curve is called the *velocity* of the algorithm.

Motivation Before the population mean curve can be used in *a posteriori* classification, it has to be normalized or rescaled in some way: different problems tend to have different fitness ranges. A linear rescaling of the fitness values to some standard interval seems appropriate, but is in general insufficient. To see this, consider the following minimization problems, defined on the space of length ℓ binary strings, $\Omega = \{0,1\}^\ell$, where the b_i are constants drawn from a normal distribution:

$$f_1(s) = \sum_i |b_i| s_i \qquad f_2(s) = \sum_i \sqrt{|b_i|} s_i$$

$$f_3(s) = \sum_i b_i^2 s_i \qquad f_4(s) = \sqrt{\sum_i b_i^2 s_i}.$$

Figure 1(a) shows the population mean curves after a linear rescaling to an identical fitness range. Clearly, f_3 and f_4 are identical for a GA, but their population mean curves cannot be mapped

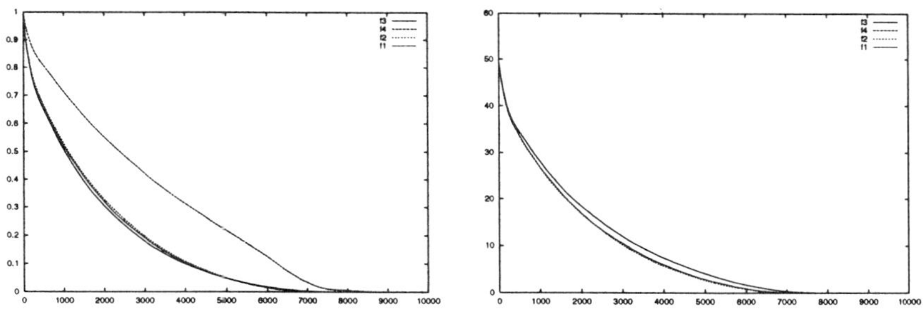

(a) (b)

Figure 1 (a) Linearly rescaled population mean curves of a steady state GA (population size 100, binary tournament selection with worst replacement, uniform crossover with rate 0.5 and per bit mutation with rate $1/\ell$) run on the problems $f_1, \ldots, f_4$, defined in section 1. The string length is 100; the curves are averages over 100 independent runs. Problems f_3 and f_4 are identical for a GA, but the square root in the fitness function cannot disappear with a linear transformation. Problems f_1 and f_2 differ componentwise by a square root, but this effect is cancelled out by the linear transformation, as explained in section 3.2. (b) The 'average proportion of zeros in the population' statistic for the same algorithm/problem combinations. It shows that for the GA, there is little difference between f_1 and f_2. Only one line is visible for f_3 and f_4.

to each other by a linear transformation. The problems f_1 and f_2 differ slightly from each other from a GA point of view, as can be seen from the 'average proportion of zeros in the population' statistic which is plotted in figure 1(b). Despite the presence of the square roots, however, the linear transformation brings the population mean curves close together. This is explained in section 3.2.

While the previous example was a motivation for a more complex transformation, the following one indicates why a transformation with respect to the DoS makes sense. Consider the following three minimization problems on Ω, defined by associating a penalty function per consecutive group of 2 bits:

$$f_{\text{left}} = \begin{cases} 00 & \mapsto 0 \\ 01 & \mapsto 0 \\ 10 & \mapsto 0 \\ 11 & \mapsto 1 \end{cases} \qquad f_{\text{onemin}} = \begin{cases} 00 & \mapsto 0 \\ 01 & \mapsto 1 \\ 10 & \mapsto 1 \\ 11 & \mapsto 2 \end{cases} \qquad f_{\text{right}} = \begin{cases} 00 & \mapsto 0 \\ 01 & \mapsto 1 \\ 10 & \mapsto 1 \\ 11 & \mapsto 1 \end{cases}$$

Problem f_{left} has a DoS which is highly skewed towards the optimum $00\ldots0$ (binomial distribution with success probability 1/4), and f_{right} one that is skewed away from the optimum (binomial distribution with success probability 3/4). The three DoSs are shown in figure 2(a). Figures 2(b)–(d) show the population mean curves for a GA, unmodified, linearly rescaled, and transformed with respect to their DoS. One observes in the unmodified version that f_{left} converges faster than f_{onemin} and f_{right} slower than f_{onemin}. But what can we learn from the curves about our choice of operators and parameter settings? Not much, unless the huge DoS advantage of f_{left} and the serious DoS disadvantage of f_{right} are taken into account. The transformed curves are initially very close to each other and do allow an interpretation (see section 3.3).

Outline of the paper Section 2 discusses the density of states in more detail. The DoS of a number of classical problems is computed, and a method is discussed to approximate the DoS of any search problem. In section 3, the transformation of κ_1 is defined, as is the velocity of the algorithm. In section 4, it is time for experiments: we show the transformed curves of a GA running on the onemin problem (which is identical to the onemax problem) and on the MAX-3-SAT problem.

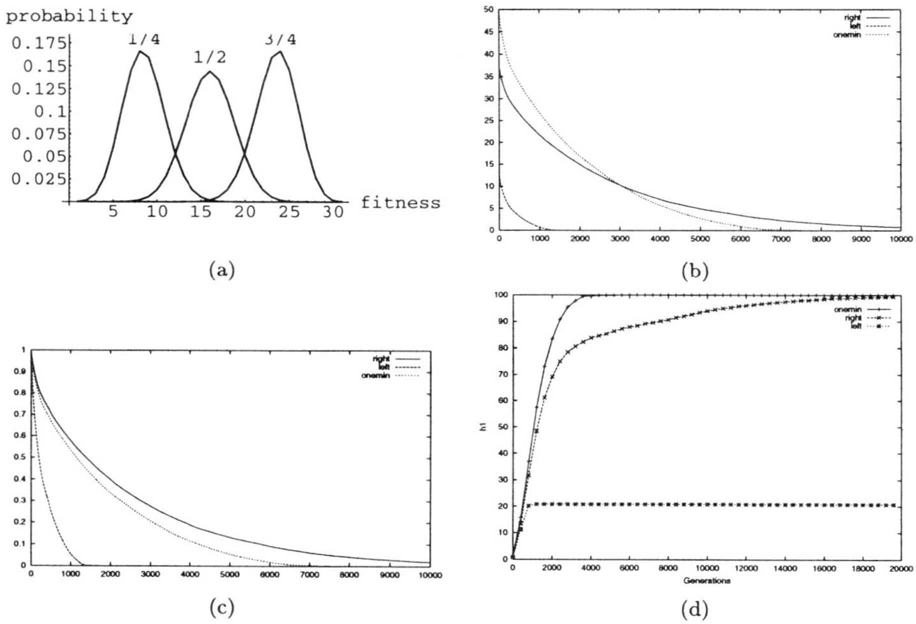

Figure 2 (a) gives a graphical impression of the bionomial distribution with $n = 30$ and success probabilities 1/4, 1/2 and 3/4. (b) gives the κ_1 or population mean curves for the functions f_{left}, f_{onemin} and f_{right}. The GA used is the one described in figure 1; again the string length is 100 and the curves are averages over 100 independent runs. In (c), the curves are rescaled to have identical begin points. In (d), they are transformed with respect to their DoS.

Section 5 discusses the properties of the velocity of the algorithm as a performance measure. The paper is concluded in section 6 with a brief summary and an outline of further work.

2 Density of states issues

Unless otherwise specified in this section, problems are defined on the search space $\Omega = \{0,1\}^\ell$ of binary strings of length ℓ.

2.1 Direct calculation for toy problems

The famous *onemax* problem consists of maximizing the number of ones in a binary string. For the sake of clarity, we consider the onemin version, where the number of ones is to be minimized, and 0 is the optimum. Formally, for $s \in \Omega$,

$$f_{\text{onemin}}(s) = \sum_{i=1}^{\ell} s_i. \tag{1}$$

It is well known that the fitness values of f_{onemin} are binomially distributed with $n = \ell$ and succes probability 1/2, i.e., there are $\binom{\ell}{i}$ strings with fitness value i.

The *leading ones* problem is defined by maximizing the function

$$\begin{aligned}
&f_{\text{leading}}(0\#\ldots\#) = 0\\
&f_{\text{leading}}(10\#\ldots\#) = 1\\
&f_{\text{leading}}(110\#\ldots\#) = 2\\
&\ldots\\
&f_{\text{leading}}(11\ldots10) = \ell - 1\\
&f_{\text{leading}}(11\ldots11) = \ell.
\end{aligned}$$

The DoS of this problem is given by the amount of wildcard symbols at a fitness level. There are $2^{\ell-i-1}$ strings at fitness level i, for $0 \le i < \ell$, and there is one string at fitness level ℓ.

2.2 Approximations for more realistic problems

Computing the DoS of more realistic problems is not that trivial, however. When no obvious analytical form is available, three alternatives are available: a simple approximation using probabilistic arguments, a more correct mathematical approximation using complicated techniques from statistical mechanics, and a straightforward computational approximation, making use of the foundations of statistical mechanics. Additionally, *extreme value theory* (e.g., [7]) may help to study the tails of fitness distributions, where approximations are typically worse.

We use the NP-hard MAX-3-SAT optimization problem as a case study of approximating the DoS. Random instances of the NP-complete 3-SAT problem (e.g., [4]) play an important role in the study of difficulty of search problems. In the context of EAs, which require a fitness function, it is more natural to study MAX-3-SAT, where the number of satisfied clauses is maximized, instead of 3-SAT, where there is a boolean function returning whether all clauses are satisfied, or not. As it is both easy and instructive to compute a reasonable approximation of the expected DoS of random MAX-3-SAT instances using probabilistic arguments, we present the calculation in detail in section 2.4.

Around a proportion $\alpha \approx 4.3$ of clauses per variable, randomly generated MAX-3-SAT instances undergo a phase transition from solvable (underconstrained, many solutions) to unsolvable (overconstrained, no solutions) [6]. For specialized deterministic algorithms, only problem instances close to this phase transition are hard to solve (ignoring for a moment, each algorithm's set of exceptionally hard problems [16]).

Monasson and Zecchina [11, 12] use statistical mechanics techniques to study the phase transition in K-SAT and compute the number of solutions near the phase transition. The complexity of the techniques they use to do better than the approximation of section 2.4 is overwhelming and impractical for frequent DoS analysis. Section 2.5 therefore presents the computational approach.

It is no surprise that statistical mechanics comes in to compute DoSs. The probability π_T that a large system of interacting particles, in thermal equilibrium, is in a particular state s depends on the energy of the state, and follows the Boltzmann distribution

$$\pi_T(s) = \frac{1}{Z_T} \exp(-E(s)/kT), \quad Z_T = \sum_{w \in S} \exp(-E(w)/kT). \tag{2}$$

Here, E is the energy functional, and Z_T the normalizing constant of the distribution, also known as the partition sum. The analogy with MAX-3-SAT is clear: the particles are the variables, the states are strings or assignments to all variables, the interactions are defined by the clauses, and the energy functional is the penalty function.

The Boltzmann distribution is the stationary distribution of the Metropolis algorithm [10]. Run at a given temperature T, it can therefore be used to obtain a fitness histogram of states (or strings) that are "typical" for that temperature. In the limit of $T \to \infty$, all states are equally likely, and a histogram of uniformly randomly sampled strings is obtained. In the limit of $T \to 0$, the ground states (solutions of the problem) are recovered.

There are two immediate problems with the Metropolis method to compute DoSs. Firstly, the Metropolis algorithm may take too much time to get to the low energy states (this is the problem of simulated annealing). Secondly, the normalizing constants Z_T cannot be computed easily (see [5] for statistical techniques). Even if one succeeds, the fitnesses worse than the average fitness are typically not investigated, and the global normalizing constant of the distribution cannot be recovered.

2.3 Why DoSs are often close to normal

Many energy functionals in physics are quadratic, not because nature behaves exactly in this way, but because it is a good approximation and higher order terms make the calculations too complex. Clearly, when E is a quadratic function on a contiuous state space, the Boltzmann distribution is a normal distribution. Many NP-complete problems, like graph coloring, feature a binary interaction between the variables. The penalty function (energy functional) becomes the discrete analogue of a quadratic function.

Another reason that DoSs of complex optimization problems are often close to normal is the central limit theorem. Consider the TSP problem where each city has to be visited exactly once. If we assume that the distances $d(i, j)$ between cities i and j are i.i.d.[1], then the fitness of a tour $\sigma = \sigma_1 \sigma_2 \ldots \sigma_\ell$, $\ell \gg 0$, given by

$$f(\sigma) = d(\sigma_\ell, \sigma_1) + \sum_{i=1}^{\ell-1} d(\sigma_i, \sigma_{i+1}), \tag{3}$$

is approximately normally distributed.

[1] independent and identically distributed

2.4 Case study MAX-3-SAT: infinite temperature approximation

Let α be the proportion of clauses versus variables of the MAX-3-SAT problem. Then there are $\alpha\ell$ clauses in total; we assume $\alpha\ell$ to be an integer value. A clause is a disjunction of 3 variables, each variable possibly negated. An example is $c = \overline{s_i} \vee s_j \vee s_k$. The set of clauses $C = \{c_1, \ldots, c_{\alpha\ell}\}$ defines a problem instance. Using the shorthands $V = \{1, \ldots, \ell\}$ and $B = \{0, 1\}$, let

$$\mathcal{C}_{\alpha,\ell} = (B \times V \times B \times V \times B \times V)^{\alpha\ell} \tag{4}$$

denote the set of all possible problem instances. To draw random instances, we put the counting measure on this set. The value 0 in the set B corresponds to a negation sign, the value 1 to the absence of a negation sign. The (standard) penalty or fitness function is defined as

$$f_{\text{MAX-3-SAT}}(s) = \sum_{j=1}^{\alpha\ell} c_j(s), \tag{5}$$

where $c_j(s)$ returns 1 if the three bits of s relevant to clause c_j are set such that the clause is not satisfied. The optimization goal is to minimize the penalty function. A string with a fitness value of 0 is called a solution.

We start by computing the probability distribution

$$\mathbb{E}_{\mathcal{C}_{\alpha,\ell}}\left[f_{\text{MAX-3-SAT}}(0)\right] = \mathbb{E}_{\mathcal{C}_{\alpha,\ell}}\left[\sum_{j=1}^{\alpha\ell} c_j(0)\right] \tag{6}$$

of the fitness values of the string $0 = 00\ldots0$ of arbitrary problem instances. Note that

$$\mathbb{E}_{\mathcal{C}_{\alpha,\ell}} = \mathbb{E}_{V^{\alpha\ell}\times V^{\alpha\ell}\times V^{\alpha\ell}} \times \mathbb{E}_{B^{\alpha\ell}\times B^{\alpha\ell}\times B^{\alpha\ell}} \tag{7}$$

due to the use of the counting measure. Also note that the variable specifications in a clause are unimportant because we compute the fitness value of the string with all zeros. It therefore suffices to find the distribution of

$$\mathbb{E}_{B^{\alpha\ell}\times B^{\alpha\ell}\times B^{\alpha\ell}}\left[\sum_{j=1}^{\alpha\ell} c_j(0)\right]. \tag{8}$$

Now $c_j(0) = 1$ if and only if none of the variables of clause j has a negation sign associated with it. It follows that $\mathbb{E}_{B\times B\times B}[c_j(0)]$ is Bernoulli distributed with success probability 1/8. Due to the independence of clauses, (8), and therefore also (6), is binomially distributed with $n = \alpha\ell$ and success probability 1/8.

Observing that the meaning of 0 and 1 can be exchanged for every bit position (true becomes false, and false becomes true), we find that the fitness distribution for one string is independent of the choice of this string. It is, however, not correct to conclude that the expected DoS of all strings together is equal to the distribution of all individual strings. It is an infinite temperature or random string approximation, which will be shown to be fairly good in the next section. It is easy to show that it is not exact: the expected number of solutions for $\alpha = 5$ should be zero, because 5 is beyond the phase transition. Yet the binomial distribution for $\ell = 30$ predicts 2.15 – obviously wrong.

Figure 3 shows the expected DoSs for $\ell = 30$ and $\alpha = 3, 4, 5$, with the DoS of the onemin problem of 30 bits as a reference.

2.5 Case study MAX-3-SAT: computational verification

We chose to verify the infinite temperature prediction for $\ell = 100$ and $\alpha = 2.2, 4.2$, and 5.2. We ran the Metropolis at 6 different values of $\beta = 1/T$: 0, 0.5, 1, 1.5, 2 and 3. We filled a histogram by

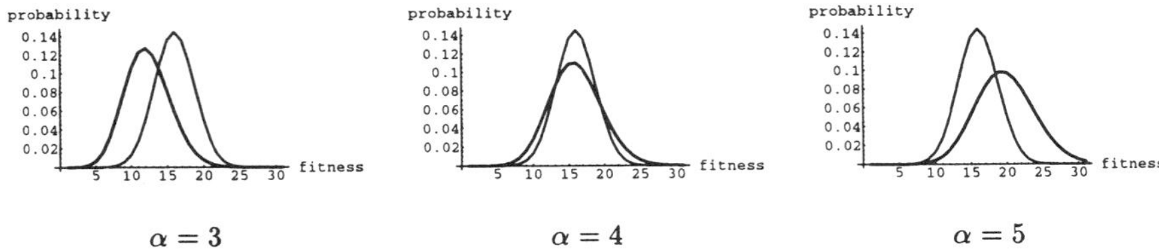

Figure 3 Infinite temperature approximation of the expected DoS of MAX-3-SAT instances on $\ell = 30$ bits for three values of α. The DoS of a 30 bit onemin problem is shown as a reference. All four distributions are binomial.

first dropping 10^5 accepted strings (to reach the temperature), and then inserting the fitness value of every 10th of 5.10^6 accepted strings (to avoid local correlations).

This histogram was computed for 20 independent problem instances and then averaged. The equilibrium distribution for inverse temperature β was obtained by scaling the average histogram by $\exp(\beta f)$, and normalizing it. All computer simulations together took less than 3 hours on a modern PC.

The final step to obtain a global picture of the expected DoS is to (manually) scale the equilibrium distributions of the different βs. This is easily done after taking logarithms: the scaling becomes a translation. The results are in the figures 4(a–f). For comparison, the predicted binomial distribution is also shown. We find that the approximation is worst for $\alpha = 5.2$, and relatively good for $\alpha = 2.2$.

3 The transformation

In this section, we define the transformation of $\kappa_1(t)$ into $h_1(t)$, and give a definition for the velocity of an algorithm. We discuss possible interpretations of the velocity, and discuss a first set of experiments.

3.1 Definition

Throughout this section, we assume, without loss of generality, minimization towards zero on the space $\Omega = \{0,1\}^\ell$ of binary strings of length ℓ, and the existence of at least one string with fitness value 0.

For any fitness value $x \geq 0$, we define $T(x)$ as minus the base-two logarithm of the proportion of states (or strings) with a fitness value equal to or less than x. In the continuous case, this is written as

$$T(x) = -\log_2 \int_0^x p(y)\,dy, \tag{9}$$

with $p(x)$ the DoS of the search problem. When the fitness range is discrete, the definition can be written as

$$T(x) = \ell - \log_2 |\{s \in \Omega; f(s) \leq x\}| \tag{10}$$

for all x in the range of f. Linear interpolation is used to define T for all positive real values:

$$T(x) = T(x_2) + \frac{x_2 - x}{x_2 - x_1}\,(T(x_1) - T(x_2)) \tag{11}$$

for $x_1 < x < x_2$, with x_1 and x_2 the elements closest surrounding x in the range of f.

The transformed curve $h_1(t)$ is defined as $T(\kappa_1(t))$, for all generations or time steps t. We call the derivative to the time $\dot{h}_1(t)$ the *velocity of the algorithm.*

Often the DoS is only known up to a scaling factor z. This is necessarily the case when the Metropolis algorithm is used to obtain an approximation $\hat{p}(x)$ of the DoS on the better half of the fitness range, say from 0 to x_0. In such a situation, we have $p(x) \approx z\hat{p}(x)$ for all $0 \leq x \leq x_0$. The scaling factor translates $h_1(t)$ and leaves the velocity unaffected:

$$\begin{aligned}\dot{h}_1(t) &= \frac{d}{dt}\left(-\log_2 \int_0^{\kappa_1(t)} p(x)dx\right)\\ &\approx \frac{d}{dt}\left(-\log_2(z) - \log_2 \int_0^{\kappa_1(t)} \hat{p}(x)dx\right) = \dot{\hat{h}}_1(t),\end{aligned}$$

for $\kappa_1(t) \leq x_0$.

No normalization of the h_1 curve with respect to the problem size is done: i.e., transformations w.r.t. a DoS with a larger support can return higher h_1 values (see also figure 5). Motivations for this decision are given in section 3.3.

3.2 Normal DoS

The cumulative distribution functions of normal DoSs can be linearly mapped onto each other:

$$F_X(\frac{x-\mu}{\sigma}) = F_Z(x), \quad \text{for } X \sim N(\mu, \sigma^2),\ Z \sim (0,1).$$

This explains what happens with the functions f_1 and f_2 defined in section 1. The result of summing up 100 values of which, on average, 50 are non-zero and i.i.d. drawn, automatically results in a normal distribution, regardless of the distribution of the individual terms. The presence of the square roots is unimportant: both f_1 and f_2 have a close-to-normal fitness distribution. Linear rescaling is in this case sufficient.

One could argue that the binomial distribution can always be approximated by a normal one, and that we therefore do not present any problem with a non-normal distribution. Only the logarithm in the transformation T would remain – and that is not necessarily needed to *compare* curves.

There are at least three arguments against applying only linear transformations: (a) the approximation by a normal is not always possible (for bimodal distributions, e.g.), so you need a general theory, (b) it will frequently be bad in the near-optimal fitness regions, especially when the continuous normal distribution is used to approximate a discrete distribution such as the binomial, and (c) the transformed curve allows a useful interpretation, as explained in the next section.

3.3 Interpretation

Rather than indicating the fitness difference, $h_1(t)$ gives a measure of the part of the search space that still needs to be searched. As such, $h_1(t)$ is a fitness independent, dimensionless value. An increment of 1 means that the size of the remaining search space is halved.

One can interpret $h_1(t)$ as *the number of bits already fixed.* The velocity can then be expressed in *number of bits fixed per generation.* This interpretation is literally true for the leading ones problem, where $T_{\text{leading}}(x) = x$, and fixing the correct bit actually halves the part of the search space that needs to be searched. Note that when the function value decreases because a bit is flipped from 1 to 0 in the onemin problem, the search space is not necessarily halved, because the order of flipping the bits to 0 is unimportant.

In the case of evolution strategies on spherical functions, the velocity corresponds, up to constant factor, to the normalized progress rate φ^*. This can be seen as follows. First, note that when $f(y) = g(\|\hat{y} - y\|) = g(r)$, for all $y \in \mathbb{R}^n$, with $\hat{y} \in \mathbb{R}^n$ the optimum and g monotonously increasing, the cumulative distribution function $V(r)$ is proportional to r^n, say $V(r) = k(n)r^n$. Second, let $R(t)$ denote the expected distance to the optimum at time t. The dynamics of the ES is given by (see, e.g., [1], Sect. 2.4)

$$R(t) = R(0) \exp\left(-\frac{1}{n}\int_0^t \varphi^*(u)du\right).$$

Clearly,

$$\begin{aligned} h_1(t) &= -\log_2(V(R(t))) = -\log_2(k(n)R(t)^n) \\ &= -\log_2(k(n)R(0)^n) - \log_2(e)\int_0^t \varphi^*(u)du. \end{aligned}$$

It follows that $\dot{h}_1(t) = \log_2(e)\varphi^*(t)$.

The interpretation of fixed and free bits is related to the concept of *free variables* in a physical model. In problems with a complex interaction structure, like 3-SAT, the idea of fixing a bit is not as wild as it may appear. Recent statistical physics research about the phase transition in K-SAT speculates about a *backbone* [13], a set of variables that are frozen into one value for all states better than a given fitness value.

Independent of this interpretation, one observes in figure 2(d) that the h_1 curve of a very standard GA (population size 100, binary tournament selection, uniform crossover with rate 0.5 and per bit mutation with rate $1/\ell$) running on a onemin problem, is *very close to a straight line*, i.e., its velocity is almost constant. Problem f_{right}, defined in section 1, yields an h_1 curve which first follows the onemin curve closely (generations 1–1300 of a steady state algorithm), and then slowly deviates from the onemin curve: halving the search space becomes increasingly more difficult for the GA.

The constant velocity of this GA on the onemin problem forms an excellent baseline for comparisons, as we will see in section 4.1.

4 Experiments

We have already shown the transformed curves for onemin (f_{onemin}), f_{left}, and f_{right} in figure 2(d). We present an in-depth treatment of the onemin problem, and one set of experiments on MAX-3-SAT problem instances.

4.1 Onemin

In figure 5 we see that the speed at which the search space is halved is constant for onemin problems with different string lengths. The values at which the curves level off are determined by the string length.

In figure 9 one sees the GA on the onemin problem without crossover. The initial slope seems to be a function of the selection pressure, while the mutation rate influences the point when this initial slope is left. For the lowest mutation rate of $0.5/\ell$ the detrimental effects of mutation at the end of the run do not occur. For this mutation rate it is clear however that the GA is slower initially than when using higher mutation rates. This effect has not been seen when reintroducing crossover however, e.g. figure 6. From figures 7 and 8 we deduce that the initial slope is also influenced by the crossover rate, as expected on a unitation problem as onemin where crossover is effective, and the population size, which is also expected as we don't use any normalization to remove the steady state effects.

4.2 MAX-3-SAT

The MAX-3-SAT experiments were performed with the same simple GA used to produce figures 1 and 2. The curves are averages of 10 independent instances, with 100 GA runs per instance. We used the binomial distribution instead of the more correct Metropolis results, because of the relatively small errors and the known normalizing constant. As a consequence, we also used the same expected distribution for each individual problem instance, being well aware that the individual distributions can deviate from the expected one.

Applying the transformation on κ_1 curves of MAX-3-SAT problems with different values for α, we find a strong independence of α (figure 10) and dependence on the selection pressure (figure 11). This could have been predicted from results of Rana and Whitley [14] which show that the relative importance of 1st, 2nd and 3rd order Walsh coefficients is practically independent of α. We conclude that for a GA, the easiness of MAX-3-SAT instances before the phase transition is entirely due to their favorable DoS, since the GA's velocity to the optimal region is practically independent of α.

5 The velocity as a hardness measure

In [15], the DoS is presented as an algorithm-independent difficulty measure for search problems. Figure 3 shows that the DoS cannot play this role in a general way. Following their definition, the onemin problem would be a little harder than the $\alpha = 4.2$ MAX-3-SAT problem instances, which is proven to be incorrect in figure 10.

The DoS does not determine the problem difficulty for an EA entirely, the best example indeed being the onemin problem. It has a very disadvantageous DoS, but the *path to the optimum* is simple for the standard genetic operators. It is the proper balance between the DoS and a path to the optimum that determines the speed. Taking the DoS into account reveals how the genetic operators cope with the interaction structure of the problem. In the case of onemin, there are no interactions and the genetic operators are ideal. In the case of MAX-3-SAT, the interaction structure is complicated and the genetic operators are not taylored to the second and third order interactions.

The curve $\dot{h}_1$, or the average speed to the best value found, can serve as a performance measure and withstand the comparison with other *a posteriori* measures presented in the literature ([9] gives an overview). It easily satisfies the requirements for a performance measure set in [3]:

1. It is *normalized* to allow for a comparison of different combinations of algorithm and problem. No normalization is done with respect to search space size, but this is not a problem.
2. It does reflect problem difficulty for the given algorithm if *difficult* and *slow* are related.
3. When the density of states is known or approximated over the whole search space, h_1 indicates how far the optimizer got in the best possible way, namely the number of states with an equal or better fitness value. When the density of states is approximated from some starting point to the optimum, the absolute number of states left to search is not known but the relative number is.

The onemin problem can be used as a basis for comparison. Note that because the density of states is involved, this comparison is different from Kallel's [9]. Of course the normalization can also be applied to best-so-far and other statistics of the population expressed in fitness values.

6 Conclusions and further work

We present a normalization technique for population mean curves produced by EAs which is based on a transformation with respect to the density of states of the problem. We motivate this choice by a number of examples. Computing the DoS to a reasonable degree of accuracy is a feasible task for many problems and should not be an obstacle. We describe a large number of experiments on randomly generated MAX-3-SAT problem instances and on the onemin problem. We show that a classification of GA-instances based on the transformed curves is achievable for the onemin problem. Finally, we compare the properties of the transformed curve with a set of requirements for a performance measure and find that it satisfies all of them.

Of course, one statistic is likely to be insufficient to classify more general search problems. Additional statistics that we will include can be divided into three groups:

1. fitness based statistics, such as the higher cumulants κ_2, κ_3, and κ_4, which correspond to the variance, skewness, and curtosis of the fitness distribution;
2. string based statistics, like the linear correlation between the bits in the population, or the 'average number of zeros' statistic used in section 1;
3. generation based statistics, such as the mean time between improvements.

We plan to obtain a reliable classification on the onemin domain for different GA instances shortly. The most useful tool in our *a posteriori classification* project is a database in which the outcome of every run is stored. The summary statistics are to be stored in a compact way using B-splines. Statistical techniques are used to do the actual classification.

Acknowledgments

The first author is a Post-doctoral Fellow and the second author a Research Assistant of the Fund for Scientific Research (FWO-Flanders, Belgium). They gratefully acknowledge the efforts of the three referees who brought up many of the shortcomings of the initial abstract, and wish to thank H.-G. Beyer for additional comments and the connection with the normalized progress rate in ES.

References

[1] H.-G. Beyer. *The Theory of Evolution Strategies.* Natural Computing Series. Springer-Verlag, 2000.

[2] Y. Davidor. Epistasis variance: a viewpoint on GA-hardness. In G. J. E. Rawlins, editor, *Foundations of Genetic Algorithms*, pages 23–35, San Francisco, 1991. Morgan Kaufmann.

[3] S. Forrest and M. Mitchell. The performance of genetic algorithms on walsh polynomials: Some anomalous results and their explanation. In R. K. Belew and L. B. Booker, editors, *Proceedings of the 4th International Conference on Genetic Algorithms*, pages 182–189, San Francisco, 1991. Morgan Kaufmann.

[4] M. R. Garey and D. S. Johnson. *Computers and Intractability – A Guide to the Theory of NP-Completeness.* W. H. Freeman, San Francisco, 1979.

[5] A. Gelman and X.-L. Meng. Simulating normalizing constants: From importance sampling to bridge sampling to path sampling. To appear in: Statistical Science.

[6] T. Hogg, B. A. Huberman, and C. P. Williams. Editorial: Phase transitions and the search problem. *Artificial Intelligence*, 81:1–15, 1996.

[7] J. Hüsler and R.-D. Reiss, editors. *Extreme Value Theory*, volume 51 of *Lecture Notes in Statistics.* Springer-Verlag, 1987.

[8] T. Jones and S. Forrest. Fitness distance correlation as a measure of problem difficulty for genetic algorithms. In L. J. Eshelman, editor, *Proceedings of the 6th International Conference on Genetic Algorithms*, pages 184–192. Morgan Kaufmann, 1995.

[9] L. Kallel. Inside GA-dynamics: ground basis for comparison. In A. E. Eiben, Th. Bäck, M. Schoenauer, and H.-P. Schwefel, editors, *Proceedings of the 5th Conference on Parallel Problem Solving from Nature*, volume 1498 of *LNCS*, pages 57–66, Berlin Heidelberg New York, 1998. Springer-Verlag.

[10] N. Metropolis, A. Rosenbluth, M. Rosenbluth, A. Teller, and E. Teller. Equations of state calculations by fast computing machines. *Journal of Chemical Physics*, 21:1087–1091, 1953.

[11] R. Monasson and R. Zecchina. The entropy of the K-satisfiability problem. *Phys. Rev. Lett.*, 76:3881, 1996.

[12] R. Monasson and R. Zecchina. Statistical mechanics of the random K-SAT model. *Phys. Rev. E*, 56:1357, 1997.

[13] R. Monasson, R. Zecchina, S. Kirkpatrick, B. Selman, and L. Troyansky. $2 + p$-sat: relation of typical-case complexity to the nature of the phase transition. *Random structures and algorithms*, 15:414–435, 1999.

[14] S. Rana and D. Whitley. Genetic algorithm behavior in the MAXSAT domain. In A. E. Eiben, Th. Bäck, M. Schoenauer, and H.-P. Schwefel, editors, *Proceedings of the 5th Conference on Parallel Problem Solving from Nature*, volume 1498 of *LNCS*, pages 785–794, Berlin Heidelberg New York, 1998. Springer-Verlag.

[15] H. Rosé, W. Ebeling, and T. Asselmeyer. The density of states – a measure of the difficulty of optimization problems. In H.-M. Voigt, W. Ebeling, I. Rechenberg, and H.-P. Schwefel, editors, *Proceedings of the 4th Conference on Parallel Problem Solving from Nature*, volume 1141 of *LNCS*. Springer-Verlag, 1996.

[16] B. M. Smith and S. A. Grant. Modelling exceptionally hard constraint satisfaction problems. In G. Smolka, editor, *Principles and Practice of Constraint Programming, CP97*, pages 192–195. Springer-Verlag, LNCS 1330, 1997.

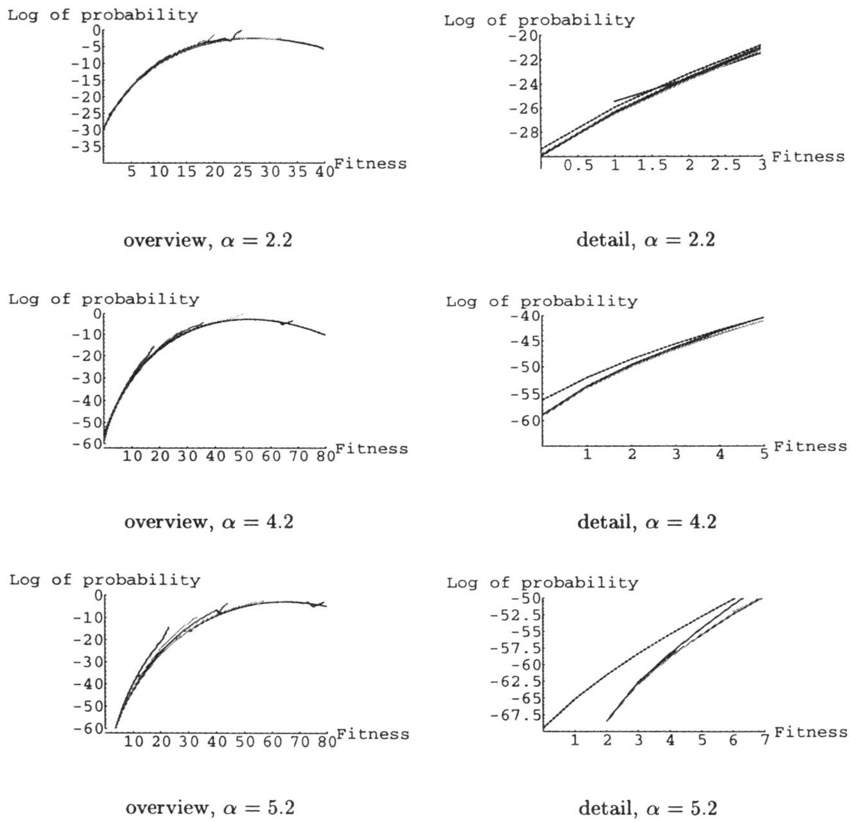

Figure 4 The expected DoS of randomly sampled MAX-3-SAT problem instances, approximated by the Metropolis algorithm at 6 different temperatures, as detailed in section 2.5. The dotted line, representing the infinite temperature approximation, is only shown in the right-hand plots. The approximation is worse for higher values of α. For $\alpha = 5.2$, the binomial distribution predicts a (low) number of solutions, whereas the Metropolis algorithm is confident that there are none. The Metropolis runs conform with the phase transition being around $\alpha \approx 4.3$.

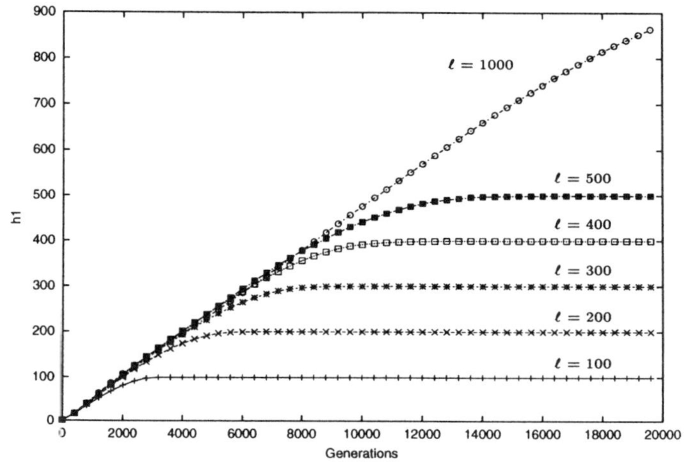

Figure 5 h_1 curves of a steady state GA (population size 100, binary tournament selection with worst replacement, uniform crossover with rate 0.5 and per bit mutation with rate $1/\ell$) run on onemin problems. The string lengths are 100, 200, 300, 400, 500, 1000; the curves are averages over 100 independent runs. The initial speed of the GA on these problems is clearly identical, as indicated by the identical initial slopes of the curves.

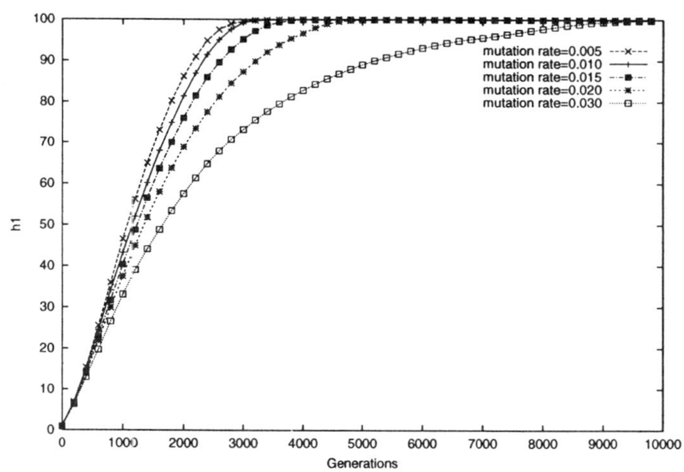

Figure 6 h_1 curves using the same GA as in figure 5 on the onemin problem but with variable mutation rate. The string length is 100; the curves are averages over 100 independent runs. The per bit mutation rates used are $0.5/\ell$, $1/\ell$, $1.5/\ell$, $2/\ell$, $3/\ell$. The speed decreases in the end (curves leveling off) as crossover becomes less effective and improvements have to come from mutation only. Higher mutation rates slow down the progress of the GA as they become disruptive.

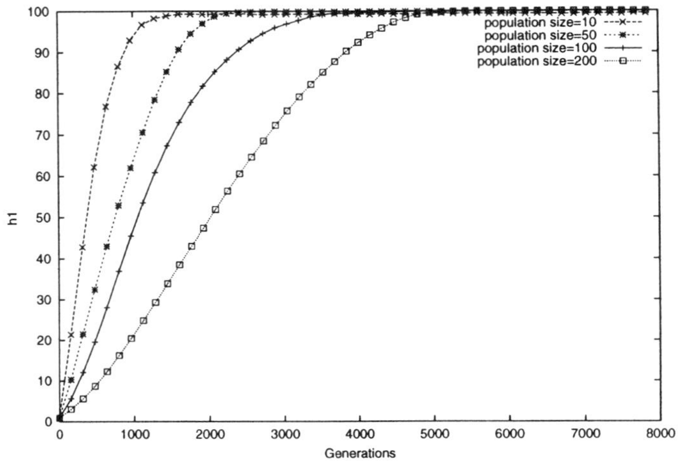

Figure 7 h_1 curves of a steady state GA (binary tournament selection with worst replacement, uniform crossover with rate 0.5 and per bit mutation with rate $1/\ell$) run on onemin problems. The string length is 100; the curves are averages over 100 independent runs. Population sizes used are 10, 50, 100, 200.

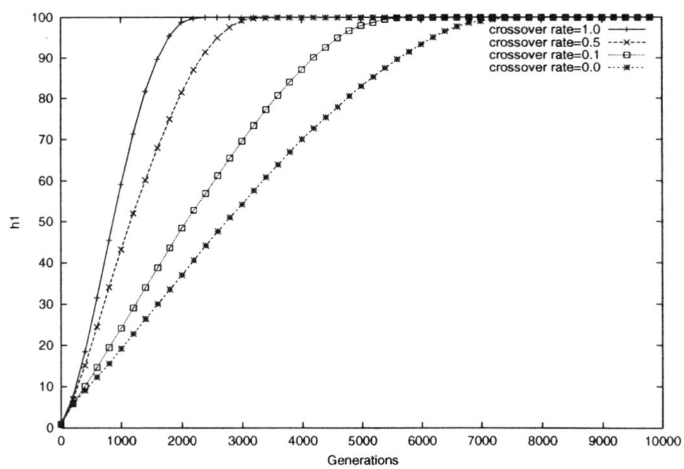

Figure 8 h_1 curves of a steady state GA (population size 100, binary tournament selection with worst replacement, per bit mutation rate of 1/l and uniform crossover) run on onemin problems. The string length is 100; the curves are averages over 100 independent runs. The crossover rates used are 0, 0.1, 0.5, 0.9, 1.0.

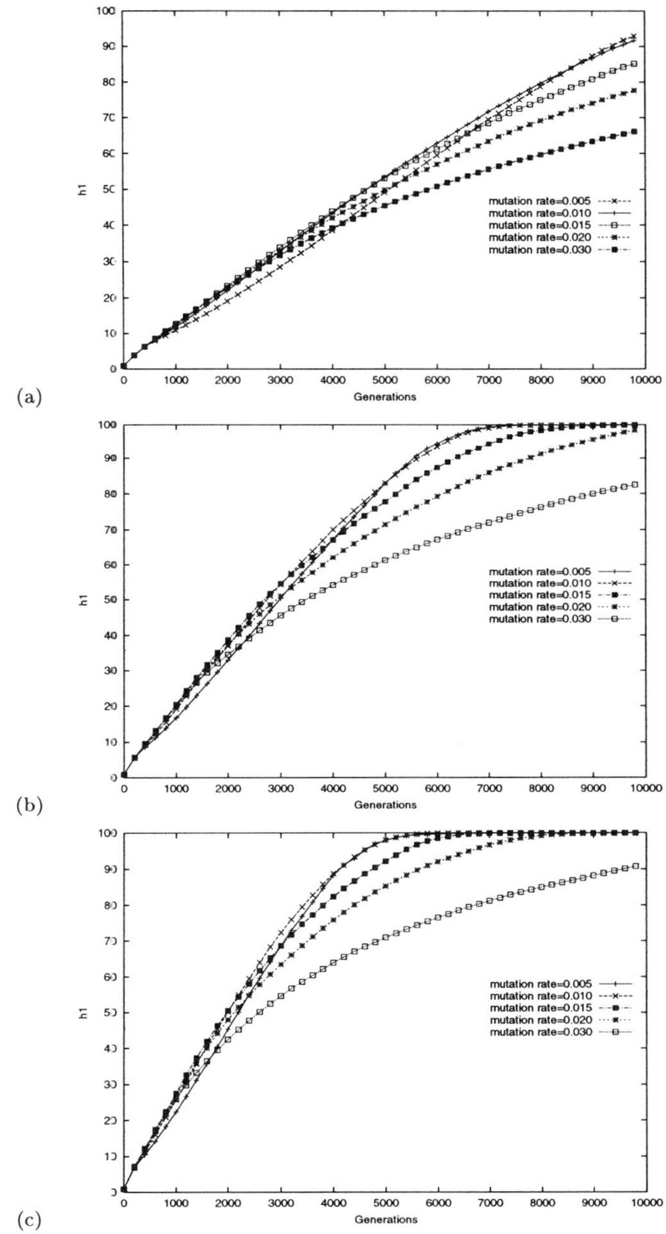

Figure 9 (a) h_1 Plots of a steady state GA (population size 100, *no* crossover and per bit mutation rate) run on onemin problems with problem size $l = 100$. The GA in plot (a) uses fitness proportional selection, the one in (b) uses binary tournament selection and (c) uses ternary tournament selection. The curves are averages over 100 independent runs. Selection pressure influences the initial slope of the curves, mutation rate influences the deviation point.

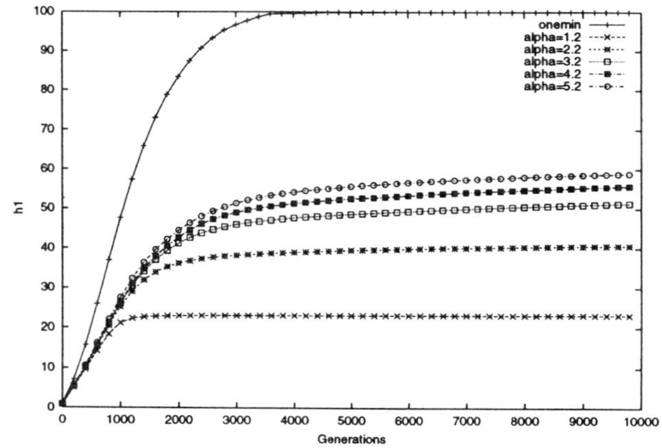

Figure 10 h_1 curves of randomly generated 100-bit MAX-3-SAT problem instances, for 5 different α values. The GA is the one described in figure 1; the onemin (f_{onemin}) curve is shown as a baseline; the curves are averages of 100 independent runs for each of the 10 independently sampled problem instances. The GA processes the search space initially equally fast for different α values. The curves level off at different heights because the number of solutions differs for different α values.

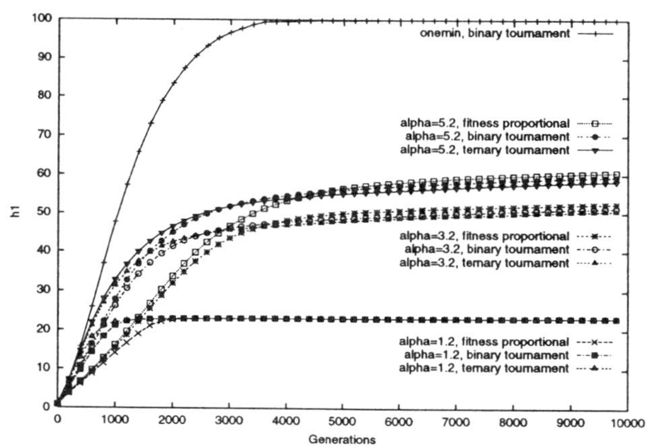

Figure 11 h_1 curves of randomly generated 100-bit MAX-3-SAT problem instances, for 3 different selection pressures and 3 different α values. The other parameters are the same as in the GA described in figure 1; the curves are averages of 100 independent runs for each of the 10 independently sampled problem instances. The different selection operators are fitness proportional selection, binary and ternary tournament selection. The initial slope is steeper as the selection pressure grows, the curves level off at values defined by the α parameter.

Local Performance of the $(\mu/\mu_I, \lambda)$-ES in a Noisy Environment

Dirk V. Arnold and Hans-Georg Beyer
Department of Computer Science XI
University of Dortmund
44221 Dortmund, Germany
{arnold,beyer}@ls11.cs.uni-dortmund.de

Abstract

While noise is a phenomenon present in many real-world optimization problems, the understanding of its potential effects on the performance of evolutionary algorithms is still incomplete. In the realm of evolution strategies in particular, it can frequently be observed that one-parent strategies are outperformed by multi-parent strategies in noisy environments. However, mathematical analyses of the performance of evolution strategies in noisy environments have so far been restricted to the simpler one-parent strategies.

This paper investigates the local performance of a multi-parent evolution strategy employing intermediate multi-recombination on a noisy sphere in the limit of infinite parameter space dimension. The performance law that is derived neatly generalizes a number of previously obtained results. Genetic repair is shown to be present and unaffected by the noise. In contrast to previous findings in a noise-free environment, the efficiency of the simple (1+1)-ES can be exceeded by multi-parent strategies in the presence of noise. It is demonstrated that a much improved performance as compared to one-parent strategies can be achieved. For large population sizes the effects of noise all but vanish.

1 INTRODUCTION

Noise is a common phenomenon in many real-world optimization problems. It can stem from sources as different as errors of measurement in experiments, from the use of stochastic sampling or simulation procedures, or from interactions with users, to name but a few. Reduced convergence velocity or even inability to approach the optimum are commonly observed consequences of the presence of noise on optimization strategies.

It can frequently be observed in experiments that evolutionary algorithms (EAs) are comparatively robust with regard to the effects of noise. In fact, noisy environments are considered to be a prime area for the application of EAs. For genetic algorithms (GA), optimization in noisy environments has been investigated, among others, by Fitzpatrick and Grefenstette [10], Miller and Goldberg [12], and Rattray and Shapiro [15]. Their work has led to recommendations regarding population sizing and the use of resampling, and it has been shown that in the limit of an infinitely large population the effects of noise on the performance of a GA employing Boltzmann selection are entirely removed.

In the realm of evolution strategies (ESs), theoretical studies of the effects of noise date back to early work of Rechenberg [16] who analyzed the performance of a $(1 + 1)$-ES in a noisy corridor. An analysis of the performance of the $(1 \stackrel{+}{,} \lambda)$-ES on a noisy sphere by Beyer [3] sparked empirical research by Hammel and Bäck [11] who concluded that the findings made for GAs do not always easily translate to ES. Arnold and Beyer [2] address the effects of overvaluation of the parental fitness using a $(1 + 1)$-ES on a noisy sphere. Both Rechenberg [17] and Beyer [7, 8] give results regarding rescaled mutations in $(1, \lambda)$-ES. For an overview of the status quo of ES research concerned with noisy environments and for additional references see [1, 8].

Empirical evidence presented by Rechenberg [17] and by Nissen and Propach [13] as well as by a number of others suggests that population-based optimization methods are generally superior to point-based methods in noisy environments. However, analytically obtained results in the field of ES have been published only for single-parent strategies. The present paper attempts to close part of this gap between theory and empirical observations by presenting a formal analysis of the local performance of a $(\mu/\mu_I, \lambda)$-ES on a noisy sphere in the limit of infinite parameter space dimensionality. The results of the analysis can serve as an approximation for large but finite parameter space dimensionality provided that population sizes are chosen not too large.

Much of the theoretically-oriented research on ES relies on the examination of the local behavior of the strategies in very simple fitness environments. While such environments bear only little resemblance to real-world problems, they have the advantage of mathematical tractability. Frequently, consideration of simple fitness environments, such as the sphere or the ridge, leads to an understanding of working mechanisms of ES that can explain phenomena observable or be of practical use in more complex fitness environments. The discovery of the genetic repair principle [5] and the recommendation regarding the sizing of the learning parameter in self-adaptive strategies in [19] are but two examples. The present paper continues this line of research by analyzing the behavior of the $(\mu/\mu_I, \lambda)$-ES on a sphere with fitness measurements disturbed by Gaussian noise. The results derived are accurate in the limit of an infinite-dimensional parameter space and can serve as approximations for large but finite-dimensional parameter spaces.

This paper is organized as follows. Section 2 outlines the $(\mu/\mu_I, \lambda)$-ES algorithm and the fitness environment for which its performance will be analyzed. The notion of fitness noise is introduced. In Section 3, a local performance measure – the expected fitness gain from one generation to the next – is computed. It is argued that for the spherically symmetric environment that is investigated, in the limit of an infinite-dimensional parameter space the expected fitness gain formally agrees with the progress rate. Section 4 discusses the results. It is demonstrated that the performance gain as compared with one-parent strategies is present for small population sizes already. It is shown that in contrast to the noise-free situation, the efficiency of the (1+1)-ES can be exceeded by that of a $(\mu/\mu_I, \lambda)$-ES if noise is present. Section 5 concludes with a brief summary and suggestions for future research.

2 ALGORITHM AND FITNESS ENVIRONMENT

Section 2.1 describes the $(\mu/\mu_I, \lambda)$-ES with isotropic normal mutations applied to optimization problems with a fitness function of the form $f : I\!R^N \rightarrow I\!R$. Without loss of generality, it can be assumed that the task at hand is minimization, i.e. that high values of f correspond to low fitness and vice versa. Section 2.2 outlines the fitness environment for which the performance of the algorithm is analyzed in the succeeding sections.

2.1 THE $(\mu/\mu_I, \lambda)$-ES

As an evolutionary algorithm, the $(\mu/\mu_I, \lambda)$-ES strives to drive a population of candidate solutions to an optimization problem towards increasingly better regions of the search space by means of variation and selection. The parameters λ and μ refer to the number of candidate solutions generated per time step and the number of those retained after selection, respectively. Obviously, λ is also the number of fitness function evaluations required per time step.

Selection simply consists in retaining the μ best of the candidate solutions and discarding the remaining ones. The comma in $(\mu/\mu, \lambda)$ indicates that the set of candidate solutions to choose from consists only of the λ offspring, whereas a plus would indicate that selection is from the union of the set of offspring and the parental population. As shown in [2], plus-selection in noisy environments introduces overvaluation as an additional factor to consider, thus rendering the analysis considerably more complicated. Moreover, as detailed by Schwefel [19], comma-selection is known to be preferable if the strategy employs mutative self-adaptation of the mutation strength, making it the more interesting variant to consider.

Variation is accomplished by means of recombination and mutation. As indicated by the second μ and the subscript I in $(\mu/\mu_I, \lambda)$, recombination is "global intermediate". More specifically, let $\mathbf{x}^{(i)} \in I\!R^N$, $i = 1, \ldots, \mu$, be the parameter space locations of the parent individuals. Recombination consists in computing the centroid

$$\langle \mathbf{x} \rangle = \frac{1}{\mu} \sum_{i=1}^{\mu} \mathbf{x}^{(i)}$$

of the parental population. Mutations are isotropically normal. For every descendant $\mathbf{y}^{(j)} \in I\!R^N$, $j = 1, \ldots, \lambda$, a mutation vector $\mathbf{z}^{(j)}$, $j = 1, \ldots, \lambda$, which consists of N independent, normally distributed components with mean 0 and variance σ^2, is generated and added to the centroid of the parental population. That is,

$$\mathbf{y}^{(j)} = \langle \mathbf{x} \rangle + \mathbf{z}^{(j)}.$$

The standard deviation σ of the components of the mutation vectors is referred to as the *mutation strength*.

The *fitness advantage* associated with a mutation $\mathbf{z}$ applied to search space location $\mathbf{x}$ is defined as

$$q_{\mathbf{x}}(\mathbf{z}) = f(\mathbf{x}) - f(\mathbf{x}+\mathbf{z}). \tag{1}$$

For a fixed location $\mathbf{x}$ in parameter space, $q_{\mathbf{x}}$ is a scalar random variate with a distribution that depends both on the fitness function and on the mutation strength.

The local performance of the algorithm can be measured either in parameter space or in terms of fitness. The corresponding performance measures are the *progress rate* φ and the *expected fitness gain* q, respectively. The expected fitness gain is the expected difference in fitness between the centroids of the population at consecutive time steps. That is, letting $\langle\mathbf{x}\rangle^{(g)}$ denote the centroid of the parental population at generation g, the expected fitness gain is the expected value of $f(\langle\mathbf{x}\rangle^{(g)}) - f(\langle\mathbf{x}\rangle^{(g+1)})$. The progress rate is the expected distance in parameter space in direction of the location of the optimum covered by the population's centroid from one generation to the next. That is, letting $R^{(g)}$ denote the Euclidean distance between the centroid of the parental population and the optimum of the fitness function, the progress rate is the expected value of $R^{(g)} - R^{(g+1)}$. For the fitness environment outlined in Section 2.2 the two performance measures coincide in the limit $N \to \infty$ if appropriately normalized as will be seen in Section 3.

2.2 THE FITNESS ENVIRONMENT

Computing the expected fitness gain is a hopeless task for all but the most simple fitness functions. In ES theory, a repertoire of fitness functions simple enough to be amenable to mathematical analysis while at the same time interesting enough to yield non-trivial results and insights has been established [4, 14]. The most commonplace of these fitness functions is the quadratic sphere

$$f(\mathbf{x}) = \sum_{i=1}^{N} (\hat{x}_i - x_i)^2 ,$$

where $\mathbf{x} = (x_1, \ldots, x_N)^{\mathrm{T}}$ is the location in parameter space of the optimal fitness value. This fitness function simply maps points in $I\!R^N$ to the square of their Euclidean distance to the optimum at $\hat{\mathbf{x}}$. By formally letting the parameter space dimension N tend to infinity and introducing appropriate normalizations as defined below, a number of simplifying conditions hold true. Note that often results that have been obtained for the sphere can be extended to more general situations. Rudolph [18] derives bounds for the performance of ES for arbitrary convex fitness functions. Beyer [4] presents a differential geometric approach that locally approximates arbitrary fitness functions and presents a fitness gain theory that applies to general quadratic fitness functions.

In what follows it is assumed that there is noise involved in the process of evaluating the fitness function. This form of noise has therefore been termed *fitness noise*. Loosely speaking, it deceives the selection mechanism. An individual at parameter space location $\mathbf{x}$ has an *ideal fitness* $f(\mathbf{x})$ and a *perceived fitness* that may differ from its ideal fitness. Fitness noise is commonly modeled by means of an additive, normally distributed random

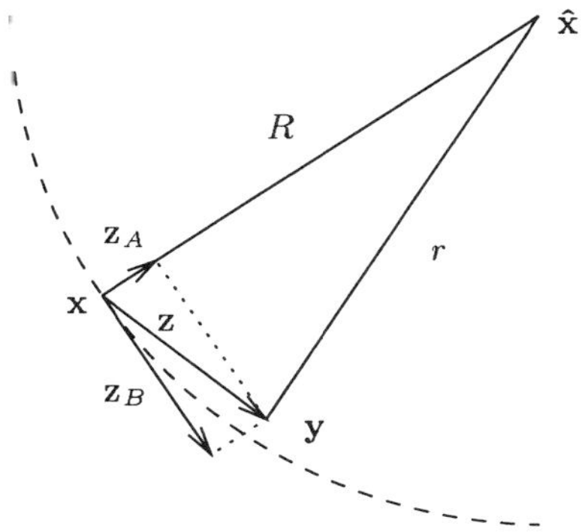

Figure 1 *Decomposition of a mutation vector* $\mathbf{z}$ *into two components* $\mathbf{z}_A$ *and* $\mathbf{z}_B$*. Vector* $\mathbf{z}_A$ *is parallel to* $\hat{\mathbf{x}} - \mathbf{x}$*, vector* $\mathbf{z}_B$ *is in the hyper-plane perpendicular to that. The starting and end points,* $\mathbf{x}$ *and* $\mathbf{y}$*, of the mutation are at distances* R *and* r*, respectively, from the location of the optimum.*

term with mean zero. That is, in a noisy environment, evaluation of the fitness function at parameter space location $\mathbf{x}$ yields perceived fitness $f(\mathbf{x}) + \sigma_\epsilon \delta$, where δ is a standard normally distributed random variate. Quite naturally, σ_ϵ is referred to as the *noise strength* and may depend on the parameter space location $\mathbf{x}$.

3 PERFORMANCE

This section computes the expected fitness gain, or, equivalently, the progress rate, for the $(\mu/\mu_I, \lambda)$-ES in the environment outlined in Section 2.2. It relies on a decomposition of mutation vectors suggested in both [3] and in [17] and is illustrated in Figure 1. A mutation vector $\mathbf{z}$ originating at parameter space location $\mathbf{x}$ can be written as the sum of two vectors $\mathbf{z}_A$ and $\mathbf{z}_B$, where $\mathbf{z}_A$ is parallel to $\hat{\mathbf{x}} - \mathbf{x}$ and $\mathbf{z}_B$ is in the hyper-plane perpendicular to that. Due to the isotropy of mutations, it can without loss of generality be assumed that $\mathbf{z}_A = \sigma(z_1, 0, \ldots, 0)^{\mathrm{T}}$ and $\mathbf{z}_B = \sigma(0, z_2, \ldots, z_N)^{\mathrm{T}}$, where the z_i, $i = 1, \ldots, N$, are independent, standard normally distributed random variates and σ is the mutation strength. Using elementary geometry and denoting the respective distances of $\mathbf{x}$ and of $\mathbf{y} = \mathbf{x} + \mathbf{z}$ to the location of the optimum by R and r, respectively, it can be seen from Figure 1 that

$$\begin{aligned} r^2 &= (R - \sigma z_1)^2 + \|\mathbf{z}_B\|^2 \\ &= R^2 - 2R\sigma z_1 + \sigma^2 z_1^2 + \sigma^2 \sum_{i=2}^{N} z_i^2 . \end{aligned} \tag{2}$$

Introducing normalized quantities

$$\sigma^* = \sigma \frac{N}{R} \quad , \quad \sigma_\epsilon^* = \sigma_\epsilon \frac{N}{2R^2} \quad \text{and} \quad q_{\mathbf{x}}^*(\mathbf{z}) = q_{\mathbf{x}}(\mathbf{z}) \frac{N}{2R^2},$$

the normalized fitness advantage associated with mutation vector $\mathbf{z}$ from Equation (1) is thus

$$q^*(\mathbf{z}) = \frac{N}{2R^2}\left(R^2 - r^2\right)$$
$$= \sigma^* z_1 - \frac{\sigma^{*2}}{2N} z_1^2 - \frac{\sigma^{*2}}{2N} \sum_{i=2}^{N} z_i^2. \tag{3}$$

Note that the index $\mathbf{x}$ of the normalized fitness advantage has been dropped as the normalized fitness advantage is independent of the location in parameter space due to the choice of normalizations.

The second summand on the right hand side of Equation (3) can for large N with overwhelming probability be neglected compared to the third summand. The term $\sum_{i=2}^{N} z_i^2/N$ contained in the third summand on the right hand side of Equation (3) is according to the Central Limit Theorem of Statistics asymptotically normal with mean $(N-1)/N \approx 1$ and variance $2(N-1)/N^2 \approx 2/N$. In the limit $N \to \infty$, the third summand and therefore the contribution of the $\mathbf{z}_B$ component to the fitness advantage is thus simply $-\sigma^{*2}/2$. Note that the components z_i, $i = 2, \ldots, N$ of the mutation vector do not influence the fitness advantage associated with a mutation as for large enough N they statistically average out. Thus, the z_i, $i = 2, \ldots, N$, are selectively neutral and for large N the fitness advantage associated with mutation vector $\mathbf{z}$ can be approximated as

$$q^*(\mathbf{z}) \approx \sigma^* z_1 - \frac{\sigma^{*2}}{2}. \tag{4}$$

As shown in Appendix A this relation is exact in the limit $N \to \infty$.

Selection is performed on the basis of perceived fitness rather than ideal fitness. With the definition of fitness noise from Section 2.2, the perceived normalized fitness advantage associated with mutation vector $\mathbf{z}$ in the limit $N \to \infty$ is

$$q^*(\mathbf{z}) + \sigma_\epsilon^* \delta = \sigma^*(z_1 + \vartheta\delta) - \frac{\sigma^{*2}}{2}, \tag{5}$$

where δ is a standard normal random variate and $\vartheta = \sigma_\epsilon^*/\sigma^*$ is the noise-to-signal ratio. Those μ offspring individuals with the highest perceived fitness are selected to form the parental population of the succeeding time step. Let $(k;\lambda)$, $k = 1, \ldots, \lambda$, be the index of the offspring individual with the kth highest perceived fitness. The difference between the parameter space location of the centroid of the selected offspring and the centroid of the parental population of the present time step is the *progress vector*

$$\langle \mathbf{z} \rangle = \frac{1}{\mu} \sum_{k=1}^{\mu} \mathbf{z}^{(k;\lambda)},$$

which consists of components $\langle z_i \rangle = \sum_{k=1}^{\mu} z_i^{(k;\lambda)}/\mu$. The expected fitness gain of the strategy is the expected value of the fitness advantage

$$q^*(\langle \mathbf{z} \rangle) = \sigma^* \langle z_1 \rangle - \frac{\sigma^{*2}}{2N} \langle z_1 \rangle^2 - \frac{\sigma^{*2}}{2N} \sum_{i=2}^{N} \langle z_i \rangle^2 \tag{6}$$

associated with this vector.

The vector $\langle \mathbf{z} \rangle$ can be decomposed into two components $\langle \mathbf{z}_A \rangle$ and $\langle \mathbf{z}_B \rangle$ in very much the same manner as shown above and as illustrated in Figure 1 for mutation vectors. As the $\mathbf{z}_B$ components of mutation vectors are selectively neutral, the $\mathbf{z}_B$ components of the mutation vectors that are averaged are independent. Therefore, each of the $\langle z_i \rangle$, $i = 2, \ldots, N$, is normal with mean 0 and variance $1/\mu$. Following the line of argument outlined in the derivation leading to Equation (4), the contribution of the $\mathbf{z}_B$ components to the expected fitness gain is thus $-\sigma^{*2}/2\mu$. Note the occurence of the factor μ in the denominator that reflects the presence of genetic repair, the influence that has in [5] been found to be responsible for the improved performance of the $(\mu/\mu_I, \lambda)$-ES as compared with the $(1, \lambda)$-ES.

We now argue that the second summand on the right hand side of Equation (6) can be neglected compared with the third provided that N is large enough. This is the case if $\mu \langle z_1 \rangle^2 \ll N$. Assume that λ is fixed and finite. The value of $\langle z_1 \rangle^2$ is independent of N. Its mean is not greater than the square of the average of the first μ order statistics of λ independent, standard normally distributed random variables. Therefore, for any $\epsilon > 0$ an N can be given such that the probability that $\mu \langle z_1 \rangle^2 \ll N$ does not hold is less than ϵ. As a consequence, the second summand can be neglected.

Computing the expected value of the first summand on the right hand side of Equation (6) is technically involved but straightforward. The calculations are referred to Appendix B. Denoting the cumulative distribution function of the standard normal distribution by Φ and following [5] in defining the $(\mu/\mu, \lambda)$-progress coefficient as

$$c_{\mu/\mu,\lambda} = \frac{\lambda - \mu}{2\pi} \binom{\lambda}{\mu} \int_{-\infty}^{\infty} \mathrm{e}^{-x^2} \left[\Phi(x)\right]^{\lambda-\mu-1} \left[1 - \Phi(x)\right]^{\mu-1} \mathrm{d}x, \tag{7}$$

the result arrived at in Equation (13) reads

$$\overline{\langle z_1 \rangle} = \frac{c_{\mu/\mu,\lambda}}{\sqrt{1 + \vartheta^2}}.$$

Therefore, the expected fitness gain of the $(\mu/\mu_I, \lambda)$-ES on the noisy, infinite-dimensional quadratic sphere is

$$\overline{q}^* = \frac{c_{\mu/\mu,\lambda} \sigma^*}{\sqrt{1 + \vartheta^2}} - \frac{\sigma^{*2}}{2\mu}. \tag{8}$$

The relevance of this result is discussed in Section 4.

We now make plausible that this result formally agrees with the result for the normalized progress rate, i.e. that in the limit $N \to \infty$ the progress rate law

$$\varphi^* = \frac{c_{\mu/\mu,\lambda} \sigma^*}{\sqrt{1 + \vartheta^2}} - \frac{\sigma^{*2}}{2\mu}, \tag{9}$$

where φ^* is the expected value of $N(R - r)/R$, holds. For finite normalized mutation strength the normalized fitness gain is finite. Therefore, with increasing N the expected value of the difference between the distance R of the parental centroid from the location

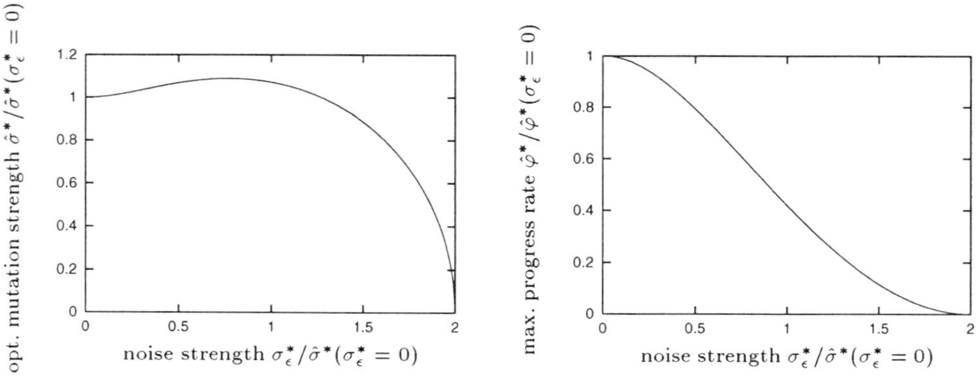

Figure 2 *Optimal normalized mutation strength $\hat{\sigma}^*$ and maximal progress rate $\hat{\varphi}^*$ as functions of normalized noise strength σ^*_ϵ. Note the scaling of the axes: normalized mutation strength and normalized progress rate are scaled by their respective optimal values in the absence of noise; the normalized noise strength is scaled by the optimal normalized mutation strength in the absence of noise.*

of the optimum and the distance r of the centroid of the selected offspring to the location of the optimum tends to zero. As

$$N\frac{R^2 - r^2}{2R^2} = N\frac{R-r}{R} \cdot \frac{R+r}{2R},$$

and as $(R+r)/2R$ tends to one, it follows that Equation (9) holds.

4 DISCUSSION

Equation (9) generalizes several previously obtained results and confirms a number of previously made hypotheses and observations. In particular, for $\sigma^*_\epsilon = 0$, Equation (9) agrees formally with the result of the progress rate analysis of the $(\mu/\mu_I, \lambda)$-ES on the noise-free sphere published in [5]. For $\mu = 1$, results of the analysis of the $(1, \lambda)$-ES on the noisy sphere that have been derived in [3] and [17] appear as special cases. Moreover, solving Equation (9) for the distance to the optimum R proves the validity of a hypothesis regarding the residual location error made in [8]. Finally, Equation (9) confirms empirical findings regarding the performance of the $(\mu/\mu_I, \lambda)$-ES made by Herdy that are quoted in [17].

Figure 2 is obtained by numerically solving Equation (9) for the normalized mutation strength $\hat{\sigma}^*$ that maximizes the normalized progress rate. Throughout this section, this mutation strength is considered optimal. Both the optimal normalized mutation strength and the resulting normalized progress rate are shown as functions of the normalized noise strength. Note that the axes are scaled by dividing by the optimal normalized mutation strength $\hat{\sigma}^*(\sigma^*_\epsilon = 0) = \mu c_{\mu/\mu,\lambda}$ in the absence of noise for normalized noise strength and normalized mutation strength and by the maximal normalized progress rate $\hat{\varphi}^*(\sigma^*_\epsilon = 0) = \mu c^2_{\mu/\mu/\lambda}/2$ in the absence of noise for the normalized progress rate. Using the scaled quantities the resulting graphs are independent of the population size parameters. For the noisy $(1, \lambda)$-ES the figure can already be found in [17].

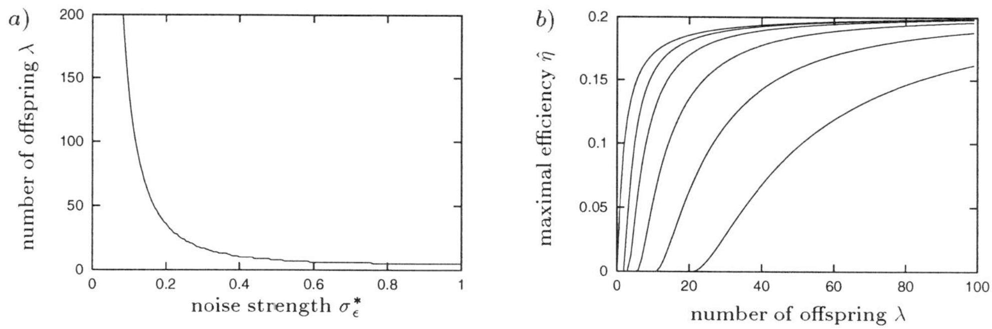

Figure 3 *a) The number of offspring per generation λ above which an optimally adjusted $(\mu/\mu_I, \lambda)$-ES outperforms an optimally adjusted $(1+1)$-ES as a function of normalized noise strength. b) Efficiency $\hat{\eta}$ of the $(\mu/\mu_I, \lambda)$-ES with optimally chosen number of parents μ as a function of the number of offspring λ. The lines correspond to, from top to bottom, normalized noise strengths $\sigma_\epsilon^* = 0.0$, 1.0, 2.0, 4.0, 8.0, and 16.0.*

It can be seen from Figure 2 that a $(1, \lambda)$-ES is capable of progress up to a normalized noise strength of $\sigma_\epsilon^* = 2c_{1,\lambda}$, while a $(\mu/\mu_I, \lambda)$-ES is capable of progress up to a normalized noise strength of $2\mu c_{\mu/\mu,\lambda}$. That is, a positive progress rate can be achieved for any noise strength by increasing the population size. The reason for this improved performance is – as in the absence of noise – the genetic repair effect. Genetic repair acts in the noisy environment as it does in the noise-free one: the components of the mutation vectors that do not lead towards the optimum but away from it are reduced by the averaging effect of recombination as signified by the presence of the factor μ in the denominator of the loss term in Equation (9). As a consequence, it is possible to explore the search space at higher mutation strengths. In a noisy environment, these increased mutation strengths have the additional benefit of leading to a reduced noise-to-signal ratio ϑ that in limit of very large population sizes tends to zero. Note however that care is in place here as finite population sizes had to be assumed in the limiting process $N \to \infty$. Therefore, no statements regarding the limiting case $\mu \to \infty$ can be made. A performance analysis of the $(\mu/\mu_I, \lambda)$-ES in finite-dimensional search spaces will be necessary to arrive at conclusive statements regarding the behavior of strategies employing very large populations or to obtain conclusive results in rather low dimensional search spaces.

The benefit of increased mutation strengths in noisy environments has been recognized before and has led to the formulation of $(1, \lambda)$-ES using rescaled mutations in [17, 7, 8]. The present analysis shows that the positive effect of an increased mutation strength can naturally be achieved in $(\mu/\mu_I, \lambda)$-ES, and that no rescaling is required. However, this does not solve the problems related to mutation strength adaptation of $(1, \lambda)$-ES using rescaled mutations pointed out in [8] as the self-adaptation of mutation strengths in $(\mu/\mu_I, \lambda)$-ES does not work optimally either.

Defining the *efficiency* η of an ES as the expected normalized fitness gain, or equivalently the normalized progress rate, per fitness function evaluation for optimally chosen mutation strength, Beyer [6] has shown that on the sphere in the absence of noise, the efficiency of the $(1+1)$-ES cannot be exceeded by any $(\mu/\mu_I, \lambda)$-ES but only asymptotically be reached for very large population sizes. This is not so in noisy environments. Figure 3*a*) shows the number of offspring per generation λ above which an optimally adjusted $(\mu/\mu_I, \lambda)$-ES outperforms an optimally adjusted $(1+1)$-ES on the infinite-dimensional noisy sphere. It has been obtained by numerically comparing the efficiency of the $(\mu/\mu_I, \lambda)$-ES that follows from dividing the normalized progress rate φ^* in Equation (9) by λ with the normalized progress rate of the $(1+1)$-ES computed in [2]. It can be seen that the efficiency of the $(1+1)$-ES can be exceeded even for moderate population sizes if there is noise present. For example, for normalized noise strengths above about 0.59, a $(2/2_I, 6)$-ES can be more efficient than a $(1+1)$-ES. Only for relatively small normalized noise strengths below 0.2 are large population sizes required to outperform the $(1+1)$-ES. This is a strong point in favor of the use of multi-parent rather than single-parent optimization strategies in noisy environments.

Figure 3*b*) shows the efficiency of $(\mu/\mu_I, \lambda)$-ES with optimally chosen parameter μ as a function of the number of offspring per generation λ for a number of noise levels. It has been obtained by numerically optimizing the efficiency while considering μ as a real valued parameter in order to smoothen the curves. It can be seen from the asymptotic behavior of each line in the figure that by sufficiently increasing the population size the efficiency can be increased up to its maximal value of 0.202 in the absence of noise. However, it is once more stressed that the relevance of this result for finite-dimensional parameter spaces is rather limited.

5 CONCLUSION

To conclude, the local performance of the $(\mu/\mu_I, \lambda)$-ES on the noisy, infinite-dimensional quadratic sphere has been analyzed. It has been shown that by increasing the population size the effects of noise can be entirely removed. This theoretical result seems to support the validity for ES of empirical observations made by Fitzpatrick and Grefenstette [10] for GAs. For $(\mu/\mu_I, \lambda)$-ES the improved performance is due to genetic repair which makes it possible to use increased mutation strengths and thereby to decrease the noise-to-signal ratio. It has also been demonstrated that, in contrast to the noise-free case, the efficiency of the $(1+1)$-ES can be exceeded by a multi-parent strategy employing recombination, and that even for relatively moderate noise strengths rather small population sizes are sufficient to achieve this.

Future work includes analyzing the performance of the $(\mu/\mu_I, \lambda)$-ES in other fitness environments and extending the analysis to strategies employing dominant rather than intermediate recombination by means of surrogate mutations as exemplified for noise-free environments in [17, 5]. Of particular interest is the extension of the analysis presented here to finite-dimensional parameter spaces. Furthermore, the analysis of the performance of ES employing no recombination or recombination with fewer than μ parents remains as a challenge for the future. The results of such an analysis may prove to be of particular interest as empirical results quoted in [17] indicate that performance improvements not accounted for by the present theory can be observed. Finally, an investigation of the effects of noise on the behavior of mutation strength adaptation schemes such as mutative self-adaptation is of great interest as such schemes are an essential ingredient of ES.

APPENDIX A: SHOWING THE ASYMPTOTIC NORMALITY OF THE FITNESS ADVANTAGE ASSOCIATED WITH A MUTATION VECTOR

The goal of this appendix is to formally show that in the limit $N \to \infty$ the distribution of the normalized fitness advantage is normal with mean $-\sigma^{*2}/2$ and variance σ^{*2}. Let

$$f_1(z_1) = \sigma^* z_1 - \frac{\sigma^{*2}}{2N} z_1^2$$

and

$$f_2(z_2, \ldots, z_N) = -\frac{\sigma^{*2}}{2N} \sum_{i=2}^{N} z_i^2.$$

Then $q^*(\mathbf{z}) = f_1(z_1) + f_2(z_2, \ldots, z_N)$ and the characteristic function of $q^*(\mathbf{z})$ is the product of the characteristic functions of $f_1(z_1)$ and $f_2(z_2, \ldots, z_N)$ due to the independence of the summands.

The characteristic function of $f_2(z_2, \ldots, z_N)$ is easily determined. As the sum $\sum_{i=2}^{N} z_i^2$ is χ_{N-1}^2-distributed, the charateristic function of $f_2(z_2, \ldots, z_N)$ is

$$\phi_2(t) = \left(1 + \frac{\sigma^{*2}}{N} \imath t\right)^{-\frac{1}{2}(N-1)},$$

where $\imath$ denotes the imaginary unit.

The characteristic function of $f_1(z_1)$ is not as easily obtained. It can be verified that for $y \leq N/2$

$$f_1(z_1) < y \quad \Leftrightarrow \quad z_1 < \frac{N}{\sigma^*}\left[1 - \sqrt{1 - \frac{2y}{N}}\right] \quad \text{or} \quad z_1 > \frac{N}{\sigma^*}\left[1 + \sqrt{1 - \frac{2y}{N}}\right]$$

and that $f_1(z_1) < y$ with probability 1.0 if $y > N/2$. Recall that z_1 is standard normally distributed. Let

$$\Phi(x) = \frac{1}{\sqrt{2\pi}} \int_{-\infty}^{x} \mathrm{e}^{-\frac{1}{2}t^2} \mathrm{d}t$$

denote the cumulative distribution function of the standard normal distribution. The cumulative distribution function of $f_1(z_1)$ is then

$$P_1(y) = \begin{cases} 1 & \text{if } y \geq N/2 \\ \Phi\left(\frac{N}{\sigma^*}\left(1 - \sqrt{1 - \frac{2y}{N}}\right)\right) + 1 - \Phi\left(\frac{N}{\sigma^*}\left(1 + \sqrt{1 - \frac{2y}{N}}\right)\right) & \text{if } y < N/2 \end{cases}.$$

The corresponding probability density function

$$p_1(y) = \begin{cases} 0 & \text{if } y \geq N/2 \\ \frac{1}{\sqrt{2\pi}\sigma^* \sqrt{1 - 2y/N}} \left[\exp\left(-\frac{N^2}{2\sigma^{*2}}\left(1 - \sqrt{1 - \frac{2y}{N}}\right)^2\right) \right. & \\ \qquad \left. + \exp\left(-\frac{N^2}{2\sigma^{*2}}\left(1 + \sqrt{1 - \frac{2y}{N}}\right)^2\right)\right] & \text{if } y < N/2 \end{cases}.$$

is obtained by differentiation. Using substitution $z = \sqrt{1 - 2y/N}$ it follows

$$\begin{aligned}\phi_1(t) &= \int_{-\infty}^{\infty} p_1(y) e^{\imath t y} \mathrm{d}y \\ &= \frac{N}{\sqrt{2\pi}\sigma^*} \int_0^{\infty} \left[\exp\left(-\frac{N^2(1-z)^2}{2\sigma^{*2}}\right) + \exp\left(-\frac{N^2(1+z)^2}{2\sigma^{*2}}\right)\right] \exp\left(\imath t \frac{N}{2}(1-z^2)\right) \mathrm{d}z \\ &= \frac{1}{\sqrt{1+\sigma^{*2}\imath t/N}} \exp\left(-\frac{1}{2}\frac{\sigma^{*2}t^2}{1+\sigma^{*2}\imath t/N}\right).\end{aligned}$$

for the characteristic function of $f_1(z_1)$, where the final step can be verified using an algebraic manipulation system.

Thus, overall the characteristic function of $q^*(\mathbf{z})$ is

$$\begin{aligned}\phi(t) &= \phi_1(t)\phi_2(t) \\ &= \frac{1}{(1+\sigma^{*2}\imath t/N)^{N/2}} \exp\left(-\frac{1}{2}\frac{\sigma^{*2}t^2}{1+\sigma^{*2}\imath t/N}\right). \end{aligned} \tag{10}$$

We now use a property that Stuart and Ord [20] refer to as *The Converse of the First Limit Theorem* on characteristic functions: If a sequence of characteristic functions converges to some characteristic function everywhere in its parameter space, then the corresponding sequence of distribution functions tends to a distribution function that corresponds to that characteristic function. Due to the relationship

$$\lim_{N\to\infty} \frac{1}{(1+x/N)^{N/2}} = \exp\left(-\frac{x}{2}\right),$$

the first factor on the right hand side of Equation (10) tends to $\exp(-\sigma^{*2}\imath t/2)$. The second factor tends to $\exp(-\sigma^{*2}t^2/2)$. Therefore, it follows that for any t

$$\lim_{N\to\infty} \phi(t) = \exp\left(-\frac{\sigma^{*2}}{2}\left(t^2 + \imath t\right)\right).$$

As this is the characteristic function of a normal distribution with mean $-\sigma^{*2}/2$ and variance σ^{*2} the asymptotic normality of the fitness advantage has been shown.

APPENDIX B: COMPUTING THE MEAN OF $\langle z_1 \rangle$

Let $z_1^{(i)}$ and $\delta^{(i)}$, $i = 1, \ldots, \lambda$, be independent standard normally distributed random variables. Let $(k;\lambda)$ denote the index with the kth largest value of $z_1^{(i)} + \vartheta\delta^{(i)}$. The goal of this appendix is to compute the expected value of the average

$$\langle z_1 \rangle = \frac{1}{\mu}\sum_{k=1}^{\mu} z_1^{(k;\lambda)},$$

of those μ of the $z_1^{(i)}$ that have the largest values of $z_1^{(i)} + \vartheta\delta^{(i)}$.

Denoting the probability density function of $z_1^{(k;\lambda)}$ as $p_{k;\lambda}$, the expected value can be written as

$$\overline{\langle z_1 \rangle} = \frac{1}{\mu} \sum_{k=1}^{\mu} \int_{-\infty}^{\infty} x p_{k;\lambda}(x) \mathrm{d}x. \tag{11}$$

Determining the density $p_{k;\lambda}$ requires the use of order statistics. The $z_1^{(i)}$ have standard normal density. The terms $z_1^{(i)} + \vartheta\delta^{(i)}$ are independently normally distributed with mean 0 and variance $1 + \vartheta^2$. The value of $z_1^{(i)} + \vartheta\delta^{(i)}$ is for given $z_1^{(i)} = x$ normally distributed with mean x and variance ϑ^2. For an index to have the kth largest value of $z_1^{(i)} + \vartheta\delta^{(i)}$, $k - 1$ of the indices must have larger values of $z_1^{(i)} + \vartheta\delta^{(i)}$, and $\lambda - k$ must have smaller values of $z_1^{(i)} + \vartheta\delta^{(i)}$. As there are λ times $k - 1$ out of $\lambda - 1$ different such cases, it follows

$$p_{k;\lambda}(x) = \frac{1}{2\pi\vartheta} \frac{\lambda!}{(\lambda - k)!(k-1)!} \mathrm{e}^{-\frac{1}{2}x^2} \int_{-\infty}^{\infty} \exp\left(-\frac{1}{2}\left(\frac{y-x}{\vartheta}\right)^2\right) \left[\Phi\left(\frac{y}{\sqrt{1+\vartheta^2}}\right)\right]^{\lambda-k} \left[1 - \Phi\left(\frac{y}{\sqrt{1+\vartheta^2}}\right)\right]^{k-1} \mathrm{d}y \tag{12}$$

for the density of $z_{k;\lambda}$.

Inserting Equation (12) into Equation (11) and swapping the order of integration and summation it follows

$$\overline{\langle z_1 \rangle} = \frac{1}{2\pi\mu\vartheta} \int_{-\infty}^{\infty} x\mathrm{e}^{-\frac{1}{2}x^2} \int_{-\infty}^{\infty} \exp\left(-\frac{1}{2}\left(\frac{y-x}{\vartheta}\right)^2\right) \sum_{k=1}^{\mu} \frac{\lambda!}{(\lambda-k)!(k-1)!} \left[\Phi\left(\frac{y}{\sqrt{1+\vartheta^2}}\right)\right]^{\lambda-k} \left[1 - \Phi\left(\frac{y}{\sqrt{1+\vartheta^2}}\right)\right]^{k-1} \mathrm{d}y\mathrm{d}x.$$

Using the identity (compare [6], Equation (5.14))

$$\sum_{k=1}^{\mu} \frac{\lambda!}{(\lambda-k)!(k-1)!} P^{\lambda-k} [1 - P]^{k-1} = \frac{\lambda!}{(\lambda-\mu-1)!(\mu-1)!} \int_0^P z^{\lambda-\mu-1}[1-z]^{\mu-1}\mathrm{d}z$$

it follows

$$\overline{\langle z_1 \rangle} = \frac{\lambda-\mu}{2\pi\vartheta} \binom{\lambda}{\mu} \int_{-\infty}^{\infty} x\mathrm{e}^{-\frac{1}{2}x^2} \int_{-\infty}^{\infty} \exp\left(-\frac{1}{2}\left(\frac{y-x}{\vartheta}\right)^2\right) \int_0^{\Phi\left(y/\sqrt{1+\vartheta^2}\right)} z^{\lambda-\mu-1}[1-z]^{\mu-1}\mathrm{d}z\mathrm{d}y\mathrm{d}x.$$

Substituting $z = \Phi(u/\sqrt{1+\vartheta^2})$ yields

$$\overline{\langle z_1 \rangle} = \frac{\lambda-\mu}{\sqrt{2\pi}^3\vartheta\sqrt{1+\vartheta^2}} \binom{\lambda}{\mu} \int_{-\infty}^{\infty} x\mathrm{e}^{-\frac{1}{2}x^2} \int_{-\infty}^{\infty} \exp\left(-\frac{1}{2}\left(\frac{y-x}{\vartheta}\right)^2\right) \int_{-\infty}^{y} \exp\left(-\frac{1}{2}\frac{u^2}{1+\vartheta^2}\right) \left[\Phi\left(\frac{u}{\sqrt{1+\vartheta^2}}\right)\right]^{\lambda-\mu-1} \left[1 - \Phi\left(\frac{u}{\sqrt{1+\vartheta^2}}\right)\right]^{\mu-1} \mathrm{d}u\mathrm{d}y\mathrm{d}x,$$

and changing the order of the integrations results in

$$\overline{\langle z_1 \rangle} = \frac{\lambda-\mu}{\sqrt{2\pi}^3\,\vartheta\sqrt{1+\vartheta^2}}\binom{\lambda}{\mu}\int_{-\infty}^{\infty}\exp\left(-\frac{1}{2}\frac{u^2}{1+\vartheta^2}\right)\left[\Phi\left(\frac{u}{\sqrt{1+\vartheta^2}}\right)\right]^{\lambda-\mu-1}$$
$$\left[1-\Phi\left(\frac{u}{\sqrt{1+\vartheta^2}}\right)\right]^{\mu-1}\int_{-\infty}^{\infty} x\mathrm{e}^{-\frac{1}{2}x^2}\int_{u}^{\infty}\exp\left(-\frac{1}{2}\left(\frac{y-x}{\vartheta}\right)^2\right)\mathrm{d}y\mathrm{d}x\mathrm{d}u.$$

The inner integrals can easily be solved. It is readily verified that

$$\frac{1}{\sqrt{2\pi}\vartheta}\int_{-\infty}^{\infty} x\mathrm{e}^{-\frac{1}{2}x^2}\int_{u}^{\infty}\exp\left(-\frac{1}{2}\left(\frac{y-x}{\vartheta}\right)^2\right)\mathrm{d}y\mathrm{d}x = \frac{1}{\sqrt{1+\vartheta^2}}\exp\left(-\frac{1}{2}\left(\frac{u}{\sqrt{1+\vartheta^2}}\right)^2\right).$$

Therefore,

$$\overline{\langle z_1 \rangle} = \frac{\lambda-\mu}{2\pi(1+\vartheta^2)}\binom{\lambda}{\mu}\int_{-\infty}^{\infty}\exp\left(-\frac{u^2}{1+\vartheta^2}\right)$$
$$\left[\Phi\left(\frac{u}{\sqrt{1+\vartheta^2}}\right)\right]^{\lambda-\mu-1}\left[1-\Phi\left(\frac{u}{\sqrt{1+\vartheta^2}}\right)\right]^{\mu-1}\mathrm{d}u.$$

Using substitution $x = u/\sqrt{1+\vartheta^2}$ it follows

$$\begin{aligned}\overline{\langle z_1 \rangle} &= \frac{\lambda-\mu}{2\pi\sqrt{1+\vartheta^2}}\binom{\lambda}{\mu}\int_{-\infty}^{\infty}\mathrm{e}^{-x^2}\left[\Phi(x)\right]^{\lambda-\mu-1}\left[1-\Phi(x)\right]^{\mu-1}\mathrm{d}x \\ &= \frac{c_{\mu/\mu,\lambda}}{\sqrt{1+\vartheta^2}},\end{aligned} \quad (13)$$

where $c_{\mu/\mu,\lambda}$ denotes the $(\mu/\mu,\lambda)$-progress coefficient defined in Equation (7).

Acknowledgements

Support by the Deutsche Forschungsgemeinschaft (DFG) under grants Be 1578/4-1 and Be 1578/6-1 is gratefully acknowledged. The second author is a Heisenberg fellow of the DFG.

References

[1] D. V. Arnold, "Evolution Strategies in Noisy Environments – A Survey of Existing Work", in L. Kallel, B. Naudts, and A. Rogers, editors, *Theoretical Aspects of Evolutionary Computing*, pages 241-252, (Springer, Berlin, 2000).

[2] D. V. Arnold and H.-G. Beyer, "Local Performance of the (1 + 1)-ES in a Noisy Environment", Technical Report CI-80/00, SFB 531, Universität Dortmund, (2000).

[3] H.-G. Beyer, "Toward a Theory of Evolution Strategies: Some Asymptotical Results from the $(1 \overset{+}{,} \lambda)$-Theory, *Evolutionary Computation*, 1(2), pages 165-188, (1993).

[4] H.-G. Beyer, "Towards a Theory of 'Evolution Strategies': Progress Rates and Quality Gain for $(1 \overset{+}{,} \lambda)$-Strategies on (Nearly) Arbitrary Fitness Functions", in Y. Davidor, R. Männer, and H.-P. Schwefel, editors, *Parallel Problem Solving from Nature*, 3, pages 58-67, (Springer, Heidelberg, 1994).

[5] H.-G. Beyer, "Toward a Theory of Evolution Strategies: On the Benefit of Sex – the $(\mu/\mu, \lambda)$-Theory", *Evolutionary Computation*, 3(1), pages 81-111, (1995).

[6] H.-G. Beyer, *Zur Analyse der Evolutionsstrategien*, Habilitationsschrift, Universität Dortmund, (1996). (see also [9])

[7] H.-G. Beyer, "Mutate Large, but Inherit Small! On the Analysis of Rescaled Mutations in $(\tilde{1}, \tilde{\lambda})$-ES with Noisy Fitness Data", in A. E. Eiben, T. Bäck, M. Schoenauer, and H.-P. Schwefel, editors, *Parallel Problem Solving from Nature*, 5, pages 159-168, (Springer, Berlin, 1998).

[8] H.-G. Beyer, "Evolutionary Algorithms in Noisy Environments: Theoretical Issues and Guidelines for Practice", in *Computer Methods in Mechanics and Applied Engineering*, 186, pages 239-267, (2000).

[9] H.-G. Beyer, *The Theory of Evolution Strategies*, (Springer, Heidelberg, 2000).

[10] J. M. Fitzpatrick and J. J. Grefenstette, "Genetic Algorithms in Noisy Environments", in P. Langley, editor, *Machine Learning*, pages 101-120, (Kluwer, Dordrecht, 1988).

[11] U. Hammel and T. Bäck, "Evolution Strategies on Noisy Functions. How to Improve Convergence Properties", in Y. Davidor, R. Männer, and H.-P. Schwefel, editors, *Parallel Problem Solving from Nature*, 3, pages 159-168, (Springer, Heidelberg, 1994).

[12] B. L. Miller and D. E. Goldberg, "Genetic Algorithms, Selection Schemes, and the Varying Effects of Noise", *Evolutionary Computation*, 4(2), pages 113-131, (1997).

[13] V. Nissen and J. Propach, "Optimization with Noisy Function Evaluations", in A. E. Eiben, T. Bäck, M. Schoenauer, and H.-P. Schwefel, editors, *Parallel Problem Solving from Nature*, 5, pages 34-43, (Springer, Heidelberg, 1998).

[14] A. I. Oyman, H.-G. Beyer, and H.-P. Schwefel, "Where Elitists Start Limping: Evolution Strategies at Ridge Functions", in A. E. Eiben, T. Bäck, M. Schoenauer, and H.-P. Schwefel, editors, *Parallel Problem Solving from Nature*, 5, pages 34-43, (Springer, Heidelberg, 1998).

[15] M. Rattray and J. Shapiro, "Noisy Fitness Evaluation in Genetic Algorithms and the Dynamics of Learning", in R. K. Belew and M. D. Vose, editors, *Foundations of Genetic Algorithms*, 4, (Morgan Kaufmann, San Mateo, CA, 1997).

[16] I. Rechenberg, *Evolutionsstrategie: Optimierung Technischer Systeme nach den Prinzipien der biologischen Evolution*, (Frommann-Holzboog, Stuttgart, 1973).

[17] I. Rechenberg, *Evolutionsstrategie '94*, (Frommann-Holzboog, Stuttgart, 1994).

[18] G. Rudolph, *Convergence Properties of Evolutionary Algorithms*, (Kovac, Hamburg, 1997).

[19] H.-P. Schwefel, *Numerische Optimierung von Computer-Modellen mittels der Evolutionsstrategie*, (Birkhäuser, Basel, 1977).

[20] A. Stuart and J. K. Ord, *Kendall's Advanced Theory of Statistics*, Volume 1: Distribution Theory, Sixth edition, (Arnold, London, 1994).

Recursive Conditional Schema Theorem, Convergence and Population Sizing in Genetic Algorithms

Riccardo Poli
School of Computer Science
The University of Birmingham
Birmingham, B15 2TT, UK
R.Poli@cs.bham.ac.uk

Abstract

In this paper we start by presenting two forms of schema theorem in which expectations are not present. These theorems allow one to predict with a known probability whether the number of instances of a schema at the next generation will be above a given threshold. Then we clarify that in the presence of stochasticity schema theorems should be interpreted as conditional statements and we use a conditional version of schema theorem backwards to predict the past from the future. Assuming that at least x instances of a schema are present in one generation, this allows us to find the conditions (at the previous generation) under which such x instances will indeed be present with a given probability. This suggests a possible strategy to study GA convergence based on schemata. We use this strategy to obtain a recursive version of the schema theorem. Among other uses, this schema theorem allows one to find under which conditions on the initial generation a GA will converge to a solution on the hypothesis that building block and population fitnesses are known. We use these conditions to propose a strategy to attack the population sizing problem. This allows us to make explicit the relation between population size, schema fitness and probability of convergence over multiple generations.

1 INTRODUCTION

Schema theories can be seen as *macroscopic* models of genetic algorithms. What this means is that they state something about the properties of a population at the next generation in terms of macroscopic quantities (like schema fitness, population fitness, number of individuals in a schema, etc.) measured at the current generation. These kinds of models tend to hide the huge number of degrees of freedom of a GA behind their macroscopic quantities (which are typically averages over the population or subsets of it). This typically leads to relatively simple equations which are easy to study and understand. A macroscopic model does not have to be an approximate or worst-case-scenario model, although many schema theorems proposed in the past were so. These properties are in sharp contrast to those shown by *microscopic* models, such as Vose's model [Nix and Vose, 1992, Vose, 1999] (see also [Davis and Principe, 1993, Rudolph, 1997c, Rudolph, 1997a, Rudolph, 1994, Rudolph, 1997b], which are always exact (at least in predicting the expected behaviour of a GA) but tend to produce equations with enormous numbers of degrees of freedom.

The usefulness of schemata and the schema theorem has been widely criticised (see for example [Chung and Perez, 1994, Altenberg, 1995, Fogel and Ghozeil, 1997, Fogel and Ghozeil, 1998]). While some criticisms are really not justified as discussed in [Radcliffe, 1997, Poli, 2000c] others are reasonable and apply to many schema theories.

One of the criticisms is that schema theorems only give *lower bounds* on the *expected value* of the number of individuals sampling a given schema at the next generation. Therefore, they cannot be used to make predictions over multiple generations.[1] Clearly, there is some truth in this. For these reasons, many researchers nowadays believe that schema theorems are nothing more than trivial tautologies of no use whatsoever (see for example [Vose, 1999, preface]). However, this does not mean that the situation cannot be changed and that all schema theories are useless. As shown by recent work [Stephens and Waelbroeck, 1997, Stephens and Waelbroeck, 1999, Poli, 1999b, Poli, 2000b, Poli, 2000a] schema theories have not been fully exploited nor fully developed. For example, recently Stephens and Waelbroeck [Stephens and Waelbroeck, 1997, Stephens and Waelbroeck, 1999] have produced a new schema theorem which gives an exact formulation (rather than a lower bound) for the expected number of instances of a schema at the next generation in terms of macroscopic quantities.[2] Stephens and Waelbroeck used this result as a starting point

[1]If the population is assumed to be infinite, then the expectation operator can be removed from schema theorems. So, the theorems can be used to make long-term predictions on schema propagation. However, these predictions may become easily very inaccurate due to the fact that typically schema theorems provide only lower bounds.

[2]The novelty of this result is not that it can predict exactly how many individuals a schema will contain on average in the future. This could be calculated easily with microscopic models, e.g. using Vose's model by explicitly monitoring the number of instances of a given schema in the expected trajectory of the GA using an approach such as the one in [De Jong et al., 1995]. The novelty of Stephens and Waelbroeck's result, which will be presented in a simplified form in the next section, is that it makes explicit how and with which probability higher order schemata can be assembled from lower order ones, and it does this by using only a small number of macroscopic quantities.

for a number of other results on the behaviour of a GA over multiple generations on the assumption of infinite populations.

Encouraged by these recent developments, we decided to investigate the possibility of studying GA convergence using schema theorems and information on schema variance. This paper presents the results of this effort.

The paper is organised as follows. After describing the assumptions on which the work is based (Section 2), two forms of schema theorem in which expectations are not present are introduced, in Section 3. These theorems allow one to predict *with a known probability* whether the number of instances of a schema at the next generation will be above a given threshold. Then (Section 4), we clarify that in the presence of stochasticity schema theorems should be interpreted as conditional statements and we use a conditional version of schema theorem backwards to predict the past from the future. Assuming that at least x instances of a schema are present in one generation, this allows us to find the conditions (at the previous generation) under which such x instances will indeed be present with a given probability. As discussed in Section 5, this suggests a possible strategy to study GA convergence based on schemata. Using this strategy a conditional recursive version of the schema theorem is obtained (Section 6). Among other uses, this schema theorem allows one to find under which conditions on the initial generation the GA will converge to a solution in constant time with a known probability on the hypothesis that building block and population fitnesses are known, as illustrated in Section 7. In Section 8 we use these conditions to propose a strategy to attack the population sizing problem which makes explicit the relation between population size, schema fitness and probability of convergence over multiple generations. We draw some conclusions and identify interesting directions for future work in Section 9.

2 SOME ASSUMPTIONS AND DEFINITIONS

In this work we consider a simple generational binary GA with fitness proportionate selection, one-point crossover and no mutation with a population of M bit strings of length N. The crossover operator produces one child (the one whose left-hand side comes from the first parent).

One of the objectives of this work is to find conditions which guarantee that a GA will find at least one solution with a given probability (perhaps in multiple runs). This is what is meant by *GA convergence* in this paper. Let us denote such a solution with $S = b_1 b_2 \cdots b_N$.

We define the *total transmission probability* for a schema H, $\alpha(H,t)$, as the probability that, at generation t, every time we create (through selection, crossover and mutation) a new individual to be inserted in the next generation such an individual will sample H [Poli et al., 1998]. This quantity is important because it allows to write an exact schema theorem of the following form:

$$E[m(H,t+1)] = M\alpha(H,t), \tag{1}$$

where $m(H,t+1)$ is the number of copies of the schema H at generation $t+1$ and $E[\cdot]$ is the expectation operator.

In a binary GA in the absence of mutation the total transmission probability is given by the following equation (which can be obtained by simplifying the results in

[Stephens and Waelbroeck, 1997, Stephens and Waelbroeck, 1999] or, perhaps more simply, as described in the following paragraph):

$$\alpha(H,t) = (1-p_{xo})p(H,t) + \frac{p_{xo}}{N-1}\sum_{i=1}^{N-1} p(L(H,i),t)p(R(H,i),t) \tag{2}$$

where p_{xo} is the crossover probability, $p(K,t)$ is the selection probability of a schema K at generation t, $L(H,i)$ is the schema obtained by replacing all the elements of H from position $i+1$ to position N with "don't care" symbols, $R(H,i)$ is the schema obtained by replacing all the elements of H from position 1 to position i with "don't care" symbols, and i varies over the valid crossover points.[3] For example, if $H =$**1111, then $L(H,1) =$******, $R(H,1) =$**1111, $L(H,3) =$**1***, and $R(H,3) =$***111. If one, for example, wanted to calculate the total transmission probability of the schema *11, the previous equation would give:

$$\begin{aligned}\alpha(*11,t) &= (1-p_{xo})p(*11,t) + \frac{p_{xo}}{2}\Big(p(***,t)p(*11,t) + p(*1*,t)p(**1,t)\Big)\\ &= \left(1-\frac{p_{xo}}{2}\right)p(*11,t) + \frac{p_{xo}}{2}p(*1*,t)p(**1,t).\end{aligned}$$

It should be noted that Equation 2 is in a considerably different form with respect to the equivalent results in [Stephens and Waelbroeck, 1997, Stephens and Waelbroeck, 1999]. This is because we developed it using our own notation and following the simpler approach described below. Let us assume that while producing each individual for a new generation one flips a biased coin to decide whether to apply selection only (probability $1-p_{xo}$) or selection followed by crossover (probability p_{xo}). If selection only is applied, then there is a probability $p(H,t)$ that the new individual created sample H (hence the first term in Equation 2). If instead selection followed by crossover is selected, let us imagine that we first choose the crossover point and then the parents (which is entirely equivalent to choosing first the parents and then the crossover point). When selecting the crossover point, one has to choose randomly one of the $N-1$ crossover points each of which has a probability $1/(N-1)$ of being selected. Once this decision has been made, one has to select two parents. Then crossover is executed. This will result in an individual that samples H only if the first parent has the correct left-hand side (with respect to the crossover point) *and* the second parent has the correct right-hand side. These two events are independent because each parent is selected with an independent Bernoulli trial. So, the probability of the joint event is the product of the probabilities of the two events. Assuming that crossover point i has been selected, the first parent has the correct left-hand side if it belongs to $L(H,i)$ while the second parent has the correct right-hand side if it belongs to $R(H,i)$. The probabilities of these events are $p(L(H,i),t)$ and $p(R(H,i),t)$, respectively (whereby the terms in the summation in Equation 2, the summation being there because there are $N-1$ possible crossover points). Combining the probabilities all these events one obtains Equation 2.

[3]The symbol L stands for "left part of", while R stands for "right part of".

3 PROBABILISTIC SCHEMA THEOREMS WITHOUT EXPECTED VALUES

In previous work [Poli et al., 1998, Poli, 1999b] we emphasised that the process of propagation of a schema from generation t to generation $t+1$ can be seen as a Bernoulli trial with success probability $\alpha(H,t)$ (this is why Equation 1 is so simple). Therefore, the number of successes (i.e. the number of strings matching the schema H at generation $t+1$, $m(H,t+1)$) is binomially distributed, i.e.

$$\Pr\{m(H,t+1)=k\} = \binom{M}{k} [\alpha(H,t)]^k [1-\alpha(H,t)]^{M-k}.$$

This is really not surprising. In fact it is a simple extension of the ideas, originally formulated mathematically in [Wright, 1931], at the basis of the well-known Wright-Fisher model of reproduction for a gene in a finite population with non-overlapping generations.

So, if we know the value of α, we can calculate exactly the probability that the schema H will have at least x instances at generation $t+1$:

Theorem 1 Probabilistic Schema Theorem (Strong Form). *For a schema H under fitness proportionate selection, one-point crossover applied with probability p_{xo} and no mutation,*

$$\Pr\{m(H,t+1) \geq x\} = \sum_{k=x}^{M} \binom{M}{k} [\alpha(H,t)]^k [1-\alpha(H,t)]^{M-k},$$

where, $\alpha(\cdot)$ is defined in Equation 2 and the probability of selection of a generic schema K is $p(K,t) = \frac{m(K,t)}{M}\frac{f(K,t)}{\bar{f}(t)}$ where $f(K,t)$ is the average fitness of the individuals sampling K in the population at generation t, while $\bar{f}(t)$ is the average fitness of the individuals in the population at generation t.

In theory this theorem could be used to find conditions on α under which, for some prefixed value of x, the r.h.s. of the previous equation takes a value y. This is very important since it is the first step to find sufficient conditions for the conditional convergence of a GA, as shown later. Unfortunately, there is one problem with this idea: although the equation $\sum_{k=x}^{M} \binom{M}{k} \alpha(H,t)]^k [1-\alpha(H,t)]^{M-k} = y$ can be solved for α, as reported in [Poli, 1999a], its solution is expressed in terms of Γ functions and the hypergeometric probability distribution. So, it is really not easy to handle.

As briefly discussed in [Poli, 1999b], one way to remove this problem is *not* to fully exploit our knowledge that the probability distribution of $m(H,t+1)$ is binomial when computing $\Pr\{m(H,t+1) \geq x\}$. Instead we could use Chebyshev's inequality [Spiegel, 1975],

$$\Pr\{|X-\mu| < k\sigma\} \geq 1 - \frac{1}{k^2},$$

where X is a stochastic variable (with *any* probability distribution), $\mu = E[X]$ is the mean of X and $\sigma = \sqrt{E[(X-\mu)^2]}$ is its standard deviation.

Since $m(H,t+1)$ is binomially distributed, $\mu = E[m(H,t+1)] = M\alpha(H,t)$ and $\sigma = \sqrt{M\alpha(H,t)\,[1-\alpha(H,t)]}$. By substituting these equations into Chebyshev's inequality we obtain:

Theorem 2 Probabilistic Schema Theorem (Weak Form). *For a schema H under fitness proportionate selection, one-point crossover applied with probability p_{xo} and no mutation,*

$$\Pr\{m(H,t+1) > M\alpha(H,t) - k\sqrt{M\alpha(H,t)(1-\alpha(H,t))}\} \geq 1 - \frac{1}{k^2} \tag{3}$$

for any fixed $k > 0$, with the same meaning of the symbols as in Theorem 1.

Unlike Theorem 1, this theorem provides an easy way to compute a value for α such that $m(H,t+1) > x$ with a probability not smaller than a prefixed constant y, by first solving the equation

$$M\alpha - k\sqrt{M\alpha(1-\alpha)} = x \tag{4}$$

for α (as described in the following section) and then substituting $k = \frac{1}{\sqrt{1-y}}$ into the result.

It is well-known that for most probability distributions Chebychev inequality tends to provide overly large bounds, particularly for large values of k. Other inequalities exist which provide tighter bounds. Examples of these are the one-sided Chebychev inequality, and the Chernoff–Hoeffding bounds [Chernoff, 1952, Hoeffding, 1963, Schmidt et al., 1992] which provide bounds for the probability tails of sums of binary random variables. These inequalities can all lead to interesting new schema theorems. Unfortunately, the left-hand sides of these inequalities (i.e. the bound for the probability) are not constant, but depend on the expected value of the variable for which we want to estimate the probability tail. This seems to suggest that the calculations necessary to compute the probability of convergence of a GA might become quite complicated when using such inequalities. We intend to investigate this issue in future research.

Finally, it is important to stress that both Theorem 1 and Theorem 2 could be modified to provide upper bounds and confidence intervals. (An extension of Theorem 2 in this direction is described in [Poli, 1999b].) Since in this paper we are interested in the probability of finding solutions (rather than the probability of failing to find solutions), we deemed more important to concentrate our attention on lower bounds for such a probability. Nonetheless, it seems possible to extend some of the results in this paper to the case of upper bounds.

4 CONDITIONAL SCHEMA THEOREMS

The schema theorems described in the previous sections and in other work are valid on the assumption that the value of $\alpha(H,t)$ is a constant. If instead α is a random variable, the theorems need appropriate modifications.

For example, Equation 1 needs to be interpreted as:

$$E[m(H,t+1)|\alpha(H,t)=a] = Ma, \tag{5}$$

a being an arbitrary constant in [0,1], which provides information on the conditional expected value of the number of instances of a schema at the next generation. So, if one wanted to know the true expected value of $m(H, t+1)$ the following integration would have to be performed:

$$E[m(H, t+1)] = \int E[m(H, t+1)|\alpha(H, t) = a]\text{pdf}(a)da,$$

where pdf(a) is the probability density function of $\alpha(H, t)$. (A more extensive discussion on the validity of schema theorems in the presence of stochastic effects is presented in [Poli, 2000c].)

Likewise, the weak form of the schema theorem becomes:

Theorem 3 Conditional Probabilistic Schema Theorem (Weak Form).
For a schema H under fitness proportionate selection, one-point crossover applied with probability p_{xo} and no mutation, and for any fixed $k > 0$

$$\Pr\{m(H, t+1) > Ma - k\sqrt{Ma(1-a)}|\alpha(H, t) = a\} \geq 1 - \frac{1}{k^2} \tag{6}$$

where a is an arbitrary number in [0,1] and the other symbols have the same meaning as in Theorem 1.

This theorem provides a probabilistic lower bond for $m(H, t+1)$ valid on the assumption that $\alpha(H, t) = a$. This can be transformed into:

Theorem 4 Conditional Probabilistic Schema Theorem (Expanded Weak Form).
For a schema H under fitness proportionate selection, one-point crossover applied with p_{xo} probability and no mutation,

$$\Pr\left\{m(H, t+1) > x\middle|(1-p_{xo})\frac{m(H, t)f(H, t)}{M\bar{f}(t)} + \frac{p_{xo}}{(N-1)M^2\bar{f}^2(t)}\cdot \right. \tag{7}$$
$$\left.\cdot\sum_{i=1}^{N-1}[m(L(H, i), t)f(L(H, i), t)m(R(H, i), t)f(R(H, i), t)] \geq \tilde{\alpha}(k, x, M)\right\} \geq 1 - \frac{1}{k^2}$$

where

$$\tilde{\alpha}(k, x, M) = \frac{1}{2}\frac{M(k^2 + 2x) + k\sqrt{M^2k^2 + 4\,Mx(M - x)}}{M(k^2 + M)}. \tag{8}$$

Proof. The l.h.s. of Equation 4 is continuous, differentiable, has always a positive second derivative w.r.t. α and is zero for $\alpha = 0$ and $\alpha = k^2/(M + k^2)$. So, its minimum is between these two values, and it is therefore an increasing function of α for $\alpha \geq k^2/(M + k^2)$.

We are really interested only in the case in which $\alpha \geq k^2/(M + k^2)$ since $m(H, t+1) \in \{0, 1, \ldots, M\}\, \forall H, \forall t$ whereby only non-negative values of x make sense in Equation 4. Therefore, the l.h.s. of the equation is invertible (i.e. Equation 4 can be solved for x) and its inverse (w.r.t. x), $\tilde{\alpha}(k, x, M)$ (see Equation 8), is a continuous increasing function of x. This allows one to transform Equation 6 into

$$\Pr\{m(H, t+1) > x|\alpha(H, t) = \tilde{\alpha}(k, x, M)\} \geq 1 - \frac{1}{k^2}. \tag{9}$$

From the properties of $\tilde{\alpha}(k,x,M)$ it follows that $\forall\epsilon \in [0, 1-\tilde{\alpha}(k,x,M)]\,\exists\delta$ such that $\tilde{\alpha}(k,x,M)+\epsilon = \tilde{\alpha}(k,x+\delta,M)$. Therefore,

$$\begin{aligned}
&\Pr\{m(H,t+1) > x | \alpha(H,t) = \tilde{\alpha}(k,x,M)+\epsilon\} \\
&\quad \geq \Pr\{m(H,t+1) > x+\delta | \alpha(H,t) = \tilde{\alpha}(k,x,M)+\epsilon\} \\
&\quad = \Pr\{m(H,t+1) > x+\delta | \alpha(H,t) = \tilde{\alpha}(k,x+\delta,M)\} \\
&\quad \geq 1-\frac{1}{k^2}
\end{aligned}$$

Since this is true for all valid values of ϵ, it follows that

$$\Pr\{m(H,t+1) > x | 1 \geq \alpha(H,t) \geq \tilde{\alpha}(k,x,M)\} \geq 1-\frac{1}{k^2}.$$

In this equation the condition $1 \geq \alpha(H,t)$ may be omitted since $\alpha(H,t)$ represents a probability, and so it cannot be meaningfully bigger than 1.

The proof is completed by substituting Equation 2 into the previous equation and considering that in fitness proportionate selection $p(K,t) = \frac{m(K,t)}{M}\frac{f(K,t)}{\bar{f}(t)}$. □

For simplicity *in the rest of the paper it will be assumed that* $p_{xo} = 1$ in which case the theorem becomes

$$\Pr\left\{ m(H,t+1) > x \left| \frac{1}{(N-1)M^2\bar{f}^2(t)} \cdot \sum_{i=1}^{N-1} [m(L(H,i),t)f(L(H,i),t)m(R(H,i),t)f(R(H,i),t)] \geq \tilde{\alpha}(k,x,M) \right. \right\} \geq 1-\frac{1}{k^2} \tag{10}$$

5 A POSSIBLE ROUTE TO PROVING GA CONVERGENCE

Equation 10 is valid for any generation t, for any schema H and for any value of x, including $H = S$ (a solution) and $x = 0$. For these assignments, $m(S,t) > 0$ (i.e. the GA will find a solution at generation t) with probability $1 - 1/k^2$ (or higher), *if the conditioning event in Equation 10 is true at generation* $t-1$. So, the equation indicates a condition that the potential building blocks of S need to satisfy at the penultimate generation in order for the GA to converge with a given probability.

Since a GA is a stochastic algorithm, in general it is impossible to guarantee that the condition in Equation 10 be satisfied. It is only possible to ensure that the probability of it being satisfied be say P (or at least P). This does not change the situation too much: it only means that $m(S,t) > 0$ with a probability of at least $P \cdot (1-1/k^2)$. If P and/or k are small this probability will be small. However, if one can perform multiple runs, the probability of finding at least a solution in R runs, $1-[1-P\cdot(1-1/k^2)]^R$, can be made arbitrarily large by increasing R.

So, if we knew P we would have a proof of convergence for GAs. The question is how to compute P. The following is a possible route to doing this (other alternatives exist, but we will not consider them in this paper).

Suppose we could transform the condition expressed by Equation 10 into a set of simpler but sufficient conditions of the form $m(L(H,i),t) > \mathcal{M}_{L(H,i),t}$ and $m(R(H,i),t) > \mathcal{M}_{R(H,i),t}$ (for $i = 1, \ldots, N-1$) where $\mathcal{M}_{L(H,i),t}$ and $\mathcal{M}_{R(H,i),t}$ are appropriate constants so that if all these simpler conditions are satisfied then also the conditioning event in Equation 10 is satisfied. Then we could apply Equation 10 recursively to each of the schemata $L(H,i)$ and $R(H,i)$, obtaining $2 \times (N-1)$ conditions like the one in Equation 10 but for generation $t-1$.[4] Assuming that each is satisfied with a probability of at least P' and that all these events are independent (which may not be the case, see below) then $P \geq (P')^{2(N-1)}$. Now the problem would be to compute P'. However, exactly the same procedure just used for P could be used to compute P'. So, the condition in Equation 10 at generation t would become $[2 \times (N-1)]^2$ conditions at generation $t-2$. Assuming that each is satisfied with a probability of at least P'' then, $P' \geq (P'')^{2(N-1)}$, whereby $P' \geq \left((P'')^{2(N-1)}\right)^{2(N-1)} = (P'')^{[2(N-1)]^2}$. Now the problem would be to compute P''.

This process could continue until quantities at generations 1 were involved. These are normally easily computable, thus allowing the completion of a GA convergence proof. Potentially this would involve a huge number of simple conditions to be satisfied at generation 1. However, this would not be the only complication. In order to compute a correct lower bound for P it would be necessary to compute the probabilities of being true of complex events which are the intersection of many non-independent events. This would not be easy to do.

Despite these difficulties all this might work, *if* we could transform the condition in Equation 10 into a set of simpler but sufficient conditions of the form mentioned above. Unfortunately, as one had to expect, this is not an easy thing to do either, because schema fitnesses and population fitness are present in Equation 10. These make the problem of computing P in its general form even harder to tackle mathematically.

A number of strategies are possible to find bounds for these fitnesses. For example one could use the ideas in the discussion on variance adjustments to the schema theorem in [Goldberg and Rudnick, 1991a, Goldberg and Rudnick, 1991b]. Another possibility would be to exploit something like Theorem 5 in [Altenberg, 1995] which gives the expected fitness distribution at the next generation. Similarly, perhaps one could use a statistical mechanics approach [Prügel-Bennett and Shapiro, 1994] to predict schema and population fitnesses. We have started to explore these ideas in extensions to the work presented in this paper. However, in the following we will not attempt to get rid of the population and schema fitnesses from our results. Instead we will use a variant of the strategy described in this section (which does not require assumptions on the independence of the events mentioned above) to find fitness-dependent convergence results. That is, we will find a lower bound for the *conditional probability of convergence* given a set of schema fitnesses. To do that we will use a different formulation of Equation 10.

In Equation 10 the quantities $\bar{f}(t)$, $m(L(H,i),t)$, $f(L(H,i),t)$, $m(R(H,i),t)$, $f(R(H,i),t)$ (for $i = 1, \ldots, N-1$) are stochastic variables. However, this equation can be specialised to the case in which we restrict ourselves to considering specific values for some (or all) such variables. When this is done, some additional conditioning events need to be added to the equation. For example, if we assume that the values of all the fitness-related variables

[4]Some of these conditions would actually coincide, leading to a smaller number of conditions.

$\bar{f}(t)$, $f(L(H,i),t)$, $f(R(H,i),t)$ (for $i = 1, \ldots, N-1$) are known, Equation 10 should be transformed into:

$$
\begin{aligned}
\Pr\Big\{ m(H,t+1) > x \Big| & \qquad\qquad (11) \\
& \frac{\sum_{i=1}^{N-1} [m(L(H,i),t)\langle f(L(H,i),t)\rangle m(R(H,i),t)\langle f(R(H,i),t)\rangle]}{(N-1)M^2\langle \bar{f}(t)\rangle^2} \geq \tilde{\alpha}(k,x,M), \\
& \bar{f}(t) = \langle \bar{f}(t)\rangle, f(L(H,1),t) = \langle f(L(H,1),t)\rangle, f(R(H,1),t) = \langle f(R(H,1),t)\rangle, \ldots, \\
& f(L(H,N-1),t) = \langle f(L(H,N-1),t)\rangle, f(R(H,N-1),t) = \langle f(R(H,N-1),t)\rangle \Big\} \\
\geq \; & 1 - \frac{1}{k^2},
\end{aligned}
$$

where we used the following *notation*: if X is any random variable then $\langle X\rangle$ is taken to be a particular explicit value of X.[5]

It is easy to convince oneself of the correctness of this kind of specialisations of Equation 10, by noticing that Chebychev inequality guarantees that $Pr\{m(H,t+1) > x\} \geq 1 - \frac{1}{k^2}$ in any world in which $\alpha(H,t) \geq \tilde{\alpha}(k,x,M)$ independently of the value of the variables on which α depends.

6 RECURSIVE CONDITIONAL SCHEMA THEOREM

By using the strategy described in the previous section and a specialisation of Equation 10 we obtain the following

Theorem 5 Conditional Recursive Schema Theorem. *For a schema H under fitness proportionate selection, one-point crossover applied with 100% probability and no mutation,*

$$
\Pr\{m(H,t+1) > \mathcal{M}_{H,t+1} | \mu_\iota, \phi_\iota\} \geq
$$
$$
\left(1 - \frac{1}{k^2}\right)\left(\Pr\{m(L(H,\iota),t) > \mathcal{M}_{L(H,\iota),t} | \mu_\iota, \phi_\iota\} + \Pr\{m(R(H,\iota),t) > \mathcal{M}_{R(H,\iota),t} | \mu_\iota, \phi_\iota\} - 1\right)
$$

where

$$
\mu_\iota = \left\{ \mathcal{M}_{L(H,\iota),t}\mathcal{M}_{R(H,\iota),t} > \frac{\tilde{\alpha}(k, \mathcal{M}_{H,t+1}, M)(N-1)M^2\langle \bar{f}(t)\rangle^2}{\langle f(L(H,\iota),t)\rangle\langle f(R(H,\iota),t)\rangle} \right\}
$$

and

$$
\phi_\iota = \{\bar{f}(t) = \langle \bar{f}(t)\rangle, f(L(H,\iota),t) = \langle f(L(H,\iota),t)\rangle, f(R(H,\iota),t) = \langle f(R(H,\iota),t)\rangle\},
$$

for any choice of the constants $\iota \in \{1, \ldots, N-1\}$, $\mathcal{M}_{H,t+1} \in [0,M]$, $\mathcal{M}_{L(H,\iota),t} \in [0,M]$ and $\mathcal{M}_{R(H,\iota),t} \in [0,M]$.

---

[5] If the value of a random variable $\langle X\rangle$ appears more than once in an equation, all the instances are assumed to represent the same number.

Proof. For brevity in this proof we will use the definition

$$\sigma_\iota = \frac{1}{(N-1)M^2\langle\bar{f}(t)\rangle^2} \cdot \Big(m(L(H,\iota),t)\langle f(L(H,\iota),t)\rangle m(R(H,\iota),t)\langle f(R(H,\iota),t)\rangle + \sum_{i=1, i\neq\iota}^{N-1} m(L(H,i),t)f(L(H,i),t)m(R(H,i),t)f(R(H,i),t)\Big).$$

When the joint event $\phi_\iota = \{\bar{f}(t) = \langle\bar{f}(t)\rangle, f(L(H,\iota),t) = \langle f(L(H,\iota),t)\rangle, f(R(H,\iota),t) = \langle f(R(H,\iota),t)\rangle\}$ happens the event $\{m(H,t+1) > \mathcal{M}_{H,t+1}\}$ can only happen in two mutually exclusive situations: either when $\{\sigma_\iota \geq \tilde{\alpha}(k,\mathcal{M}_{H,t+1},M)\}$ or when $\{\sigma_\iota < \tilde{\alpha}(k,\mathcal{M}_{H,t+1},M)\}$. As a consequence,

$$\begin{aligned}
\Pr\{m(H,t+1) > \mathcal{M}_{H,t+1}|\phi_\iota\} &= \Pr\{m(H,t+1) > \mathcal{M}_{H,t+1}, \sigma_\iota \geq \tilde{\alpha}(k,\mathcal{M}_{H,t+1},M)|\phi_\iota\} + \\
&\quad \Pr\{m(H,t+1) > \mathcal{M}_{H,t+1}, \sigma_\iota < \tilde{\alpha}(k,\mathcal{M}_{H,t+1},M)|\phi_\iota\} \\
&\geq \Pr\{m(H,t+1) > \mathcal{M}_{H,t+1}, \sigma_\iota \geq \tilde{\alpha}(k,\mathcal{M}_{H,t+1},M)|\phi_\iota\} \\
&= \Pr\{m(H,t+1) > \mathcal{M}_{H,t+1}|\sigma_\iota \geq \tilde{\alpha}(k,\mathcal{M}_{H,t+1},M),\phi_\iota\} \cdot \\
&\quad \Pr\{\sigma_\iota \geq \tilde{\alpha}(k,\mathcal{M}_{H,t+1},M)|\phi_\iota\} \\
&\geq \left(1-\frac{1}{k^2}\right) \cdot \Pr\{\sigma_\iota \geq \tilde{\alpha}(k,\mathcal{M}_{H,t+1},M)|\phi_\iota\},
\end{aligned}$$

where in the last inequality we used a specialisation of Equation 10, i.e. a version of schema theorem, in which the values of $\bar{f}(t)$, $f(L(H,\iota),t)$ and $f(R(H,\iota),t)$ are assumed to be known.

Under any conditioning events the probability of the event $\{\sigma_\iota \geq \tilde{\alpha}(k,\mathcal{M}_{H,t+1},M)\}$ is necessarily greater than or equal to the probability of the event $\{\frac{1}{(N-1)M^2\langle\bar{f}(t)\rangle^2}[m(L(H,\iota),t)\langle f(L(H,\iota),t)\rangle m(R(H,\iota),t)\langle f(R(H,\iota),t)\rangle] \geq \tilde{\alpha}(k,\mathcal{M}_{H,t+1},M)\}$ for any choice of the constant $\iota \in \{1,\ldots,N-1\}$, provided that the fitness function is non-negative.[6] Therefore, from the previous equations we obtain:

$$\Pr\{m(H,t+1) > \mathcal{M}_{H,t+1}|\phi_\iota\} \geq \left(1-\frac{1}{k^2}\right)\Pr\left\{\frac{m(L(H,\iota),t)\langle f(L(H,\iota),t)\rangle m(R(H,\iota),t)\langle f(R(H,\iota),t)\rangle}{(N-1)M^2\langle\bar{f}(t)\rangle^2} \geq \tilde{\alpha}(k,\mathcal{M}_{H,t+1},M)\Big|\phi_\iota\right\}.$$

This can be rewritten as

$$\Pr\{m(H,t+1) > \mathcal{M}_{H,t+1}|\phi_\iota\} \geq \left(1-\frac{1}{k^2}\right)\Pr\left\{m(L(H,\iota),t)m(R(H,\iota),t) \geq \frac{\tilde{\alpha}(k,\mathcal{M}_{H,t+1},M)(N-1)M^2\langle\bar{f}(t)\rangle^2}{\langle f(L(H,\iota),t)\rangle\langle f(R(H,\iota),t)}\Big|\phi_\iota\right\}.$$

The event on the right-hand side of this equation is not of the same form as the event on the left-hand side. So, it is not possible to use this result recursively. However, further simplifications can be obtained by noticing that if $m(L(H,\iota),t)$ and $m(R(H,\iota),t)$

[6] The difference between the probabilities of these two events may be very large, particularly if N is large. This means that the bounds provided by the theorem may be very pessimistic. However, at this stage we are not interested in the accuracy of our bounds.

are both greater than two suitably large constants, $\mathcal{M}_{L(H,\iota),t}$ and $\mathcal{M}_{R(H,\iota),t}$, the product $m(L(H,\iota),t)m(R(H,\iota),t)$ will always be greater than $\frac{\tilde{\alpha}(k,\mathcal{M}_{H,t+1},M)(N-1)M^2\langle \bar{f}(t)\rangle^2}{\langle f(L(H,\iota),t)\rangle\langle f(R(H,\iota),t)}$ (although obviously this can happen also when either $m(L(H,\iota),t)$ or $m(R(H,\iota),t)$ are not greater than $\mathcal{M}_{L(H,\iota),t}$ and $\mathcal{M}_{R(H,\iota),t}$). In order for this to happen the two constants need to be chosen such that the event $\mu_\iota = \left\{\mathcal{M}_{L(H,\iota),t}\mathcal{M}_{R(H,\iota),t} > \frac{\tilde{\alpha}(k,\mathcal{M}_{H,t+1},M)(N-1)M^2\langle \bar{f}(t)\rangle^2}{\langle f(L(H,\iota),t)\rangle\langle f(R(H,\iota),t)}\right\}$ is the case. Therefore,

$$\Pr\left\{m(L(H,\iota),t)m(R(H,\iota),t) \geq \frac{\tilde{\alpha}(k,\mathcal{M}_{H,t+1},M)(N-1)M^2\langle \bar{f}(t)\rangle^2}{\langle f(L(H,\iota),t)\rangle\langle f(R(H,\iota),t)}\middle|\mu_\iota,\phi_\iota\right\} \geq \Pr\left\{m(L(H,\iota),t) > \mathcal{M}_{L(H,\iota),t}, m(R(H,\iota),t) > \mathcal{M}_{R(H,\iota),t}\middle|\mu_\iota,\phi_\iota\right\}$$

where the extra conditioning event μ_ι has been introduced to guarantee that the choice of two constants $\mathcal{M}_{L(H,\iota),t}$ and $\mathcal{M}_{R(H,\iota),t}$ is appropriate. So, by repeating the calculations presented in this proof with this extra conditioning event, we obtain:

$$\begin{aligned}&\Pr\{m(H,t+1) > \mathcal{M}_{H,t+1}|\mu_\iota,\phi_\iota\}\\ &\geq \left(1-\frac{1}{k^2}\right)\Pr\{m(L(H,\iota),t) > \mathcal{M}_{L(H,\iota),t}, m(R(H,\iota),t) > \mathcal{M}_{R(H,\iota),t}|\mu_\iota,\phi_\iota\}. \quad (12)\end{aligned}$$

In order to obtain a recursive form of schema theorem we now need to simplify (or find a lower bound for) the conditional probability of the joint event $\{m(L(H,\iota),t) > \mathcal{M}_{L(H,\iota),t}, m(R(H,\iota),t) > \mathcal{M}_{R(H,\iota),t}\}$.

If the events $\{m(L(H,\iota),t) > \mathcal{M}_{L(H,\iota),t}\}$ and $\{m(R(H,\iota),t) > \mathcal{M}_{R(H,\iota),t}\}$ were independent we could write $\Pr\{m(L(H,\iota),t) > \mathcal{M}_{L(H,\iota),t}, m(R(H,\iota),t) > \mathcal{M}_{R(H,\iota),t}\} = \Pr\{m(L(H,\iota),t) > \mathcal{M}_{L(H,\iota),t}\} \cdot \Pr\{m(R(H,\iota),t) > \mathcal{M}_{R(H,\iota),t}\}$. However, in this paper we prefer to make no assumption on the independence of these events (more on this later). Fortunately, there is a way to compute a lower bound for their joint conditional probability: to use the Bonferroni inequality [Sobel and Uppuluri, 1972]. This states that $\Pr\{A,B\} \geq \Pr\{A\} + \Pr\{B\} - 1$ where A and B are two arbitrary (dependent or independent) events, which can trivially be extended to conditional probabilities obtaining: $\Pr\{A,B|C\} \geq \Pr\{A|C\} + \Pr\{B|C\} - 1$ where C is another arbitrary event. This leads to the following inequality:

$$\begin{aligned}&\Pr\{m(L(H,\iota),t) > \mathcal{M}_{L(H,\iota),t}, m(R(H,\iota),t) > \mathcal{M}_{R(H,\iota),t}|\mu_\iota,\phi_\iota\} \geq\\ &\quad \Pr\{m(L(H,\iota),t) > \mathcal{M}_{L(H,\iota),t}|\mu_\iota,\phi_\iota\} + \Pr\{m(R(H,\iota),t) > \mathcal{M}_{R(H,\iota),t}|\mu_\iota,\phi_\iota\} - 1,\end{aligned}$$

which, substituted into Equation 12, completes the proof of the theorem. □

This theorem is recursive in the sense that with appropriate additional conditioning events similar to μ_ι and ϕ_ι (necessary to restrict the fitness of the building blocks of the building blocks of the schema H and to make sure appropriate constants are used) the theorem can be applied again to the events in its right-hand side, and then again the right-hand side of the resulting expressions and so on. So, this theorem provides information on the long term behaviour of a GA with respect to schema propagation in the same spirit as the well-known argument on the exponential increase/decrease of the number of instances of a schema [Goldberg, 1989][page 30]. However, unlike such argument, Theorem 5 does not make any assumptions on the fitness of the schema or its building blocks.

It is obvious that this result is useful only when the probabilities on the right-hand side are all bigger than 0.5 (at least on average). If this is not the case the bound would be less than 0, whereby the theorem would simply state an obvious property of all probabilities.

It would be possible to obtain a much stronger result if the events $\{m(L(H,\iota),t) > \mathcal{M}_{L(H,\iota),t}\}$ and $\{m(R(H,\iota),t) > \mathcal{M}_{R(H,\iota),t}\}$ could be shown to be independent. This would allow to replace the Bonferroni inequality with a much tighter bound.[7] However, at present the author is unable to prove or disprove whether $\{m(L(H,\iota),t) > \mathcal{M}_{L(H,\iota),t}\}$ and $\{m(R(H,\iota),t) > \mathcal{M}_{R(H,\iota),t}\}$ are indeed independent in all cases. So, Bonferroni inequality is the safest choice.

It is perhaps important to discuss why $\{m(L(H,\iota),t) > \mathcal{M}_{L(H,\iota),t}\}$ and $\{m(R(H,\iota),t) > \mathcal{M}_{R(H,\iota),t}\}$ might be independent. As two of the reviewers of this paper suggested, one might think that there is dependence between the two events due to any linkage disequilibrium that exists between the schemata $L(H,\iota)$ and $R(H,\iota)$ (interpreted as bit patterns), i.e. to the fact that $L(H,\iota)$ and $R(H,\iota)$ may tend to occur together among individuals in the population (positive linkage disequilibrium) or may be not found in the same individuals (negative linkage disequilibrium). This would be correct if in order to decide whether $\{m(L(H,\iota),t) > \mathcal{M}_{L(H,\iota),t}, m(R(H,\iota),t) > \mathcal{M}_{R(H,\iota),t}\}$ is the case one sampled the population M times counting how many of the individuals selected belong to $L(H,\iota)$ and/or $R(H,\iota)$. However, this is not the correct way of interpreting $\{m(L(H,\iota),t) > \mathcal{M}_{L(H,\iota),t}, m(R(H,\iota),t) > \mathcal{M}_{R(H,\iota),t}\}$. This is because the first event in such a joint event refers to a property of the first parents selected for crossover, while the second event refers to a property of the second parents. So, the correct way to check whether $\{m(L(H,\iota),t) > \mathcal{M}_{L(H,\iota),t}, m(R(H,\iota),t) > \mathcal{M}_{R(H,\iota),t}\}$ is the case is to: a) sample the population $2M$ times to produce M first parents and M second parents, b) count how many first parents are in $L(H,\iota)$, c) count how many second parents are in $R(H,\iota)$, and finally d) ask whether $\{m(L(H,\iota),t) > \mathcal{M}_{L(H,\iota),t}\}$ and $\{m(R(H,\iota),t) > \mathcal{M}_{R(H,\iota),t}\}$ are both the case.

If the population at generation t was fixed, these two events would seem to be independent for the simple reason that the first and the second parents in each crossover operation are selected with independent Bernoulli trials (e.g. with independent sweeps of the roulette). However, in this work we do not assume that the population is fixed, rather we see it as stochastic (i.e. we consider α as a stochastic variable). So, if the population instances were generated according to some particular distribution, surely the probability distributions of the stochastic variables $m(L(H,\iota),t)$ and $m(R(H,\iota),t)$ would be functions of the probability distribution of the population. So, some form of dependence between the events $\{m(L(H,\iota),t) > \mathcal{M}_{L(H,\iota),t}\}$ and $\{m(R(H,\iota),t) > \mathcal{M}_{R(H,\iota),t}\}$ would seem possible. However, one might reason, these events are independent for any particular instantiation of the population (and therefore for any particular value of α). So, it is possible that the events $\{m(L(H,\iota),t) > \mathcal{M}_{L(H,\iota),t}\}$ and $\{m(R(H,\iota),t) > \mathcal{M}_{R(H,\iota),t}\}$ remain independent when the population is treated as a stochastic quantity. We intend to study this hypothesis further in future work.

[7] In the case of independence, the r.h.s. of the theorem would become $\left(1-\frac{1}{k^2}\right)\Pr\{m(L(H,\iota),t) > \mathcal{M}_{L(H,\iota),t}|\mu_\iota,\phi_\iota\}\Pr\{m(R(H,\iota),t) > \mathcal{M}_{R(H,\iota),t}|\mu_\iota,\phi_\iota\}$.

7 CONDITIONAL CONVERGENCE PROBABILITY

Despite its weakness, the previous theorem is important because it can be used to built equations which predict a property of a schema more than one generation in the future on the basis of properties of the building blocks of such a schema at an earlier generation. In particular the theorem can be used to find a lower bound for the conditional probability that the GA will converge to a particular solution S with a known effort. Here, instead of introducing a general but complicated conditional convergence theorem to show this, we prefer to illustrate the basic idea by using an example.

Suppose $N = 4$ and we want to know a lower bound for the probability that there will be at least one instance of the schema $H = S = b_1b_2b_3b_4$ in the population by generation 3, on the assumption that the fitnesses of the building blocks of H and of the population at previous generations are known. A lower bound for this can be obtained using the theorem with $t = 2$ and $\mathcal{M}_{H,t+1} = \mathcal{M}_{b_1b_2b_3b_4,3} = 0$.

If we set $k = 2$, we obtain $\tilde{\alpha}(k, \mathcal{M}_{H,t+1}, M)(N-1)M^2 = 3M^2\tilde{\alpha}(2,0,M)$. So, if we choose $\iota = 2$, in order for the theorem to be applicable we need to make sure that the event $\mu_2 = \left\{\mathcal{M}_{\mathtt{b_1b_2**},2}\mathcal{M}_{\mathtt{**b_3b_4},2} > \frac{3M^2\tilde{\alpha}(2,0,M)\langle\bar{f}(2)\rangle^2}{\langle f(\mathtt{b_1b_2**},2)\rangle\langle f(\mathtt{**b_3b_4},2)\rangle}\right\}$ is the case. There are many ways to do this. A very simple one is to set $\mathcal{M}_{\mathtt{b_1b_2**},2} = \frac{\sqrt{3M^2\tilde{\alpha}(2,0,M)+1}\langle\bar{f}(2)\rangle}{\langle f(\mathtt{b_1b_2**},2)\rangle}$ and $\mathcal{M}_{\mathtt{**b_3b_4},2} = \frac{\sqrt{3M^2\tilde{\alpha}(2,0,M)+1}\langle\bar{f}(2)\rangle}{\langle f(\mathtt{**b_3b_4},2)\rangle}$, which, substituted into the theorem, lead to the following result:

$$\begin{aligned}
&\Pr\{m(\mathtt{b_1b_2b_3b_4},3) > 0|\phi_2\} \geq \\
&0.75 \cdot \left(\Pr\left\{m(\mathtt{b_1b_2**},2) > \frac{\sqrt{3M^2\tilde{\alpha}(2,0,M)+1}\langle\bar{f}(2)\rangle}{\langle f(\mathtt{b_1b_2**},2)\rangle}\middle|\phi_2\right\} + \right. \\
&\qquad \left. \Pr\left\{m(\mathtt{**b_3b_4},2) > \frac{\sqrt{3M^2\tilde{\alpha}(2,0,M)+1}\langle\bar{f}(2)\rangle}{\langle f(\mathtt{**b_3b_4},2)\rangle}\middle|\phi_2\right\} - 1\right),
\end{aligned}$$

where $\phi_2 = \{\bar{f}(2) = \langle\bar{f}(2)\rangle, f(\mathtt{b_1b_2**},2) = \langle f(\mathtt{b_1b_2**},2)\rangle, f(\mathtt{**b_3b_4},2) = \langle f(\mathtt{**b_3b_4},2)\rangle\}$. It should be noted that we have omitted the conditioning event μ_2 from the previous equation because we have chosen the constants $\mathcal{M}_{\mathtt{b_1b_2**},2}$ and $\mathcal{M}_{\mathtt{**b_3b_4},2}$ in such a way that μ_2 is always the case (effectively considering a special case of the recursive schema theorem given in the previous section).

The previous equation shows quite clearly how pessimistic our bound is. In fact, unless the schema fitnesses are sufficiently bigger than the average fitness of the population, the probabilities of the events on the right-hand side will be 0.

The recursive schema theorem can be applied again to such probabilities. For example let us calculate a lower bound for the probability that there will be at least $\frac{\sqrt{3M^2\tilde{\alpha}(2,0,M)+1}\langle\bar{f}(2)\rangle}{\langle f(\mathtt{b_1b_2**},2)\rangle}$ instances of the schema $H = \mathtt{b_1b_2**}$ in the population at generation 2, on the assumption that the fitnesses of the building blocks of H and of the population at previous generations are known. A lower bound for this can be obtained using the recursive schema theorem with $t = 1$ and $\mathcal{M}_{H,t+1} = \frac{\sqrt{3M^2\tilde{\alpha}(2,0,M)+1}\langle\bar{f}(2)\rangle}{\langle f(\mathtt{b_1b_2**},2)\rangle}$. If we set $k = 2$ again, we obtain $\tilde{\alpha}(k, \mathcal{M}_{H,t+1,M})(N-1)M = 3M^2\tilde{\alpha}(2, \frac{\sqrt{3M^2\tilde{\alpha}(2,0,M)+1}\langle\bar{f}(2)\rangle}{\langle f(\mathtt{b_1b_2**},2)\rangle}, M)$.

So, if we choose $\iota = 1$, $\mathcal{M}_{b_1***,2} = \sqrt{3M^2\tilde{\alpha}\left(2, \frac{\sqrt{3M^2\tilde{\alpha}(2,0,M)+1}\langle\bar{f}(2)\rangle}{\langle f(\mathrm{b_1 b_2}**,2)\rangle}, M\right) + 1}\frac{\langle\bar{f}(1)\rangle}{\langle f(b_1***,1)\rangle}$ and $\mathcal{M}_{*b_2**,2} = \sqrt{3M^2\tilde{\alpha}\left(2, \frac{\sqrt{3M^2\tilde{\alpha}(2,0,M)+1}\langle\bar{f}(2)\rangle}{\langle f(\mathrm{b_1 b_2}**,2)\rangle}, M\right) + 1}\frac{\langle\bar{f}(1)\rangle}{\langle f(*b_2**,1)\rangle}$, and we substitute these values into the conditional recursive schema theorem, we obtain:

$$
\begin{aligned}
&\Pr\left\{m(\mathrm{b_1 b_2}**,2) > \frac{\sqrt{3M^2\tilde{\alpha}(2,0,M)+1}\langle\bar{f}(2)\rangle}{\langle f(\mathrm{b_1 b_2}**,2)\rangle}\middle|\phi_1,\phi_2\right\} \geq \\
&0.75\cdot\left(\Pr\left\{m(\mathrm{b_1}***,1) > \sqrt{3M^2\tilde{\alpha}\left(2, \frac{\sqrt{3M^2\tilde{\alpha}(2,0,M)+1}\langle\bar{f}(2)\rangle}{\langle f(\mathrm{b_1 b_2}**,2)\rangle}, M\right) + 1}\frac{\langle\bar{f}(1)\rangle}{\langle f(b_1***,1)\rangle}\middle|\phi_1,\phi_2\right\} + \right. \\
&\quad\left.\Pr\left\{m(*\mathrm{b_2}**,1) > \sqrt{3M^2\tilde{\alpha}\left(2, \frac{\sqrt{3M^2\tilde{\alpha}(2,0,M)+1}\langle\bar{f}(2)\rangle}{\langle f(\mathrm{b_1 b_2}**,2)\rangle}, M\right) + 1}\frac{\langle\bar{f}(1)\rangle}{\langle f(*b_2**,1)\rangle}\middle|\phi_1,\phi_2\right\} - 1\right)
\end{aligned}
$$

where $\phi_1 = \{\bar{f}(1) = \langle\bar{f}(1)\rangle, f(\mathrm{b_1}***,1) = \langle f(\mathrm{b_1}***,1)\rangle, f(*\mathrm{b_2}**,1) = \langle f(*\mathrm{b_2}**,1)\rangle\}$. A similar equation holds for the schema $H = **b_3b_4$, for which we will assume to use $\iota = 3$. By making use of these inequalities and representing the conditioning events on schema and population fitnesses with the symbol $\mathcal{F}$ for brevity, we obtain:

$$
\begin{aligned}
&\Pr\{m(\mathrm{b_1 b_2 b_3 b_4},3) > 0|\mathcal{F}\} \geq \qquad (13)\\
&0.5625\cdot\left(\Pr\left\{m(\mathrm{b_1}***,1) > \sqrt{3M^2\tilde{\alpha}\left(2, \frac{\sqrt{3M^2\tilde{\alpha}(2,0,M)+1}\langle\bar{f}(2)\rangle}{\langle f(\mathrm{b_1 b_2}**,2)\rangle}, M\right) + 1}\frac{\langle\bar{f}(1)\rangle}{\langle f(b_1***,1)\rangle}\middle|\mathcal{F}\right\} + \right. \\
&\quad\Pr\left\{m(*\mathrm{b_2}**,1) > \sqrt{3M^2\tilde{\alpha}\left(2, \frac{\sqrt{3M^2\tilde{\alpha}(2,0,M)+1}\langle\bar{f}(2)\rangle}{\langle f(\mathrm{b_1 b_2}**,2)\rangle}, M\right) + 1}\frac{\langle\bar{f}(1)\rangle}{\langle f(*b_2**,1)\rangle}\middle|\mathcal{F}\right\} + \\
&\quad\Pr\left\{m(**\mathrm{b_3}*,1) > \sqrt{3M^2\tilde{\alpha}\left(2, \frac{\sqrt{3M^2\tilde{\alpha}(2,0,M)+1}\langle\bar{f}(2)\rangle}{\langle f(**\mathrm{b_3 b_4},2)\rangle}, M\right) + 1}\frac{\langle\bar{f}(1)\rangle}{\langle f(**\mathrm{b_3}*,1)\rangle}\middle|\mathcal{F}\right\} + \\
&\quad\left.\Pr\left\{m(***\mathrm{b_4},1) > \sqrt{3M^2\tilde{\alpha}\left(2, \frac{\sqrt{3M^2\tilde{\alpha}(2,0,M)+1}\langle\bar{f}(2)\rangle}{\langle f(**\mathrm{b_3 b_4},2)\rangle}, M\right) + 1}\frac{\langle\bar{f}(1)\rangle}{\langle f(***b_4,1)\rangle}\middle|\mathcal{F}\right\}\right) \\
&\quad -1.875
\end{aligned}
$$

So, *the lower bound for the probability of convergence at a given generation is a linear combination of the probabilities of having a sufficiently large number of building blocks of order 1 at the initial generation.*

The weakness of this result is quite obvious. When all the probabilities on the right-hand side of the equation are 1, the lower bound we obtain is 0.375.[8] In all other cases we get

[8]In case the events $\{m(L(H,\iota),t) > \mathcal{M}_{L(H,\iota),t}\}$ and $\{m(R(H,\iota),t) > \mathcal{M}_{R(H,\iota),t}\}$ could be shown to be independent, the bound in Equation 13 would be proportional to the product of the probabilities of having a sufficiently large number of building blocks of order 1 at the initial generation. In the example considered in this section, the bound would be 0.5625, with a 50% improvement with respect to the linear bound 0.375.

smaller bounds. In any case it should be noted that some of the quantities present in this equation are under our control since they depend on the initialisation strategy adopted. Therefore, it is not impossible for the events in the right-hand side of the equation to be all the case.

8 POPULATION SIZING

The recursive conditional schema theorem can be used to study the effect of the population size M on the conditional probability of convergence. We will show this continuing the example in the previous section.

For the sake of simplicity, let us assume that we initialise the population making sure that all the building blocks of order 1 have exactly the same number of instances, i.e. $m(0*\cdots*,1) = m(1*\cdots*,1) = m(*0*\cdots*,1) = m(*1*\cdots*,1) = \ldots = m(*\cdots*0,1) = m(*\cdots*1,1) = M/2$.

A reasonable way to size the population in the previous example would be to choose M so as to maximise the lower bound in Equation 13.[9] To achieve this one would have to make sure that each of the four events in the r.h.s. of the equation happen. Let us start from the first one: $\left\{m(\mathtt{b}_1***,1) > \sqrt{3M^2\tilde{\alpha}\left(2, \frac{\sqrt{3M^2\tilde{\alpha}(2,0,M)+1}\langle\bar{f}(2)\rangle}{\langle f(\mathtt{b}_1\mathtt{b}_2**,2)\rangle}, M\right) + 1\frac{\langle\bar{f}(1)\rangle}{\langle f(\mathtt{b}_1***,1)\rangle}}\middle|\mathcal{F}\right\}$.

Since $m(\mathtt{b}_1***,1) = M/2$, the event happens with probability 1 if

$$\frac{M}{2} > \sqrt{3M^2\tilde{\alpha}(2, \frac{\sqrt{3M^2\tilde{\alpha}(2,0,M)+1}\langle\bar{f}(2)\rangle}{\langle f(\mathtt{b}_1\mathtt{b}_2**,2)\rangle}, M) + 1\frac{\langle\bar{f}(1)\rangle}{\langle f(\mathtt{b}_1***,1)\rangle}}.$$

Clearly, we are interested in the smallest value of M for which this inequality is satisfied. Since it is assumed that $\langle\bar{f}(1)\rangle$, $\langle f(\mathtt{b}_1***,1)\rangle$, $\langle\bar{f}(2)\rangle$ and $\langle f(\mathtt{b}_1\mathtt{b}_2**,2)\rangle$ are known, such a value of M, let us call it M_1, can easily be obtained numerically.

The same procedure can be repeated for the other events in Equation 13, obtaining the lower bounds M_2, M_3 and M_4. Therefore, the minimum population size that maximises the right-hand side of Equation 13 is

$$M_{min} = \lceil \max(M_1, M_2, M_3, M_4) \rceil.$$

Of course, given the known weaknesses of the bounds used to derive the recursive schema theorem, it has to be expected that M_{min} will be much larger than necessary. To give a feel for the values suggested by the equation, let us imagine that the ratios between building block fitness and population fitness ($\langle f(\mathtt{b}_1***,1)\rangle/\langle\bar{f}(1)\rangle$, $\langle f(*\mathtt{b}_2**,1)\rangle/\langle\bar{f}(1)\rangle$, $\langle f(\mathtt{b}_1\mathtt{b}_2**,2)\rangle/\langle\bar{f}(2)\rangle$, $\langle f(**\mathtt{b}_3\mathtt{b}_4,2)\rangle/\langle\bar{f}(2)\rangle$, etc.) be all equal to r. When the fitness ratio $r = 1$ (for example because the fitness landscape is flat) the population size suggested by the previous equation ($M_{min} = 2,322$) is huge considering that the length of the bit-strings in the population is only 4. The situation is even worse if $r < 1$. However, if the building blocks of the solution have well above average fitness, more realistic population sizes are suggested (e.g. if $r = 3$ one obtains $M_{min} = 6$).

[9]This is by no means neither the only nor the best way to size the population, but it is probably one of the simplest.

Table 1 Population sizes obtained for different fitness ratios for order-1 (r_1) and order-2 (r_2) building blocks.

	r_2						
r_1	0.5	0.75	1	2	3	4	5
0.5	119,896	55,416	32,394	9,378	4,778	3,054	2,204
0.75	24,590	11,566	6,874	2,112	1,130	754	564
1	8,056	3,848	2,322	750	418	288	222
2	556	276	172	62	38	28	24
3	106	52	32	10	6	6	4
4	42	16	6	2	2	2	2
5	42	16	6	2	2	2	2

It is interesting to compare how order-1 and order-2 building block fitnesses influence the population size. Let us imagine that the ratios between order-1 building block fitnesses and population fitness at generation 1 ($\langle f(\mathtt{b}_1 * **, 1)\rangle / \langle \bar{f}(1)\rangle$, $\langle f(*\mathtt{b}_2 * *, 1)\rangle / \langle \bar{f}(1)\rangle$, etc.) be constant and equal to r_1 and that the ratios between order-2 building block fitnesses and population fitness at generation 2 ($\langle f(\mathtt{b}_1\mathtt{b}_2 * *, 2)\rangle / \langle \bar{f}(2)\rangle$ and $\langle f(* * \mathtt{b}_3\mathtt{b}_4, 2)\rangle / \langle \bar{f}(2)\rangle$) be constant and equal to r_2. Table 1 shows the values of M_{min} resulting from different values of r_1 and r_2. The population sizes in the table are all even because of the particular initialisation strategy adopted.

Clearly, the recursive schema theorem presented in this paper will need to be strengthened if we want to use it to size the population in practical applications. However, the procedure indicated in this section demonstrates that in principle this is a viable approach and that useful insights can be obtained already. For example, it is interesting to notice that the population sizes in the table depend significantly more on the order-1/generation-1 building-block fitness ratio r_1 than on the order-2/generation-2 building-block fitness ratio r_2. This seems to suggest that problems with deceptive attractors for low-order building-blocks may be harder to solve for a GA than problems where deception is present when higher-order building-blocks are assembled. This conjecture will be checked in future work. In the future it would also be very interesting to compare the population sizing equations derived from this approach with those obtained by others (e.g. see [Goldberg et al., 1992]).

9 CONCLUSIONS AND FUTURE WORK

In this paper we have used a form of schema theorem in which expectations are not present in an unusual way, i.e. to predict the past from the future. This has allowed the derivation of a recursive version of the schema theorem which is applicable to the case of finite populations. This schema theorem allows one to find under which conditions on the initial generation the GA will converge to a solution in constant time. As an example, in the paper we have shown how such conditions can be derived for a generic 4-bit problem.

All the results in this paper are based on the assumption that the fitness of the building blocks involved in the process of finding a solution and the population fitness are known at each generation. Therefore, our results do not represent a full schema-theorem-based proof of convergence for GAs. In future research we intend to explore the possibility of getting rid of schema and population fitnesses by replacing them with appropriate bounds based on the "true" characteristics of the schemata involved such as their static fitness. As indicated in Section 5, several approaches to tackle this problem are possible. If this step is successful, it will allow to identify rigorous strategies to size the population and therefore to calculate the computational effort required to solve a given problem using a GA. This in turn will open the way to a precise definition of "GA-friendly" ("GA-easy") fitness functions. Such functions would simply be those for which the number of fitness evaluations necessary to find a solution with say 99% probability in multiple runs is smaller (much smaller) than 99% of the effort required by exhaustive search or random search without resampling.

Since the results in this paper are based on Chebychev inequality and Bonferroni bound, they are quite conservative. As a result they tend to considerably overestimate the population size necessary to solve a problem with a known level of performance. This does not mean that they will be useless in predicting on which functions a GA can do well. It simply means that they will over-restrict the set of GA-friendly functions. A lot can be done to improve the tightness of the lower bounds obtained in the paper. When less conservative results became available, more functions could be included in the GA-friendly set.

Not many people nowadays use fixed-size binary GAs with one-point crossover in practical applications. So, the theory presented in this paper, as often happens to all theory, could be thought as being ten or twenty years or so behind practice. However, there is really a considerable scope for extension to more recent operators and representations. For example, by using the crossover-mask-based approach presented in [Altenberg, 1995][Section 3 and Appendix] one could write an equation similar to Equation 2 valid for *any* type of homologous crossover on binary strings. The theory presented in this paper could then be extended for many crossover operators of practical interest. Also, in the exact schema theorem presented in [Stephens and Waelbroeck, 1997, Stephens and Waelbroeck, 1999] point mutation was present. So, it seems possible to extend the results presented in this paper to the case of point mutation (either alone or with some form of crossover). Finally, Stephens and Waelbroeck's theory has been recently generalised in [Poli, 2000b, Poli, 2000a] where an exact expression of $\alpha(H, t)$ for genetic programming with one-point crossover was reported. This is valid for variable-length and non-binary GAs as well as GP and standard GAs. As a result, it seems possible to extend the results presented in this paper to such representations and operators, too. So, although in its current form the theory presented in this paper is somehow behind practice, it is arguable that it might not remain so for long.

Despite their current limitations, we believe that the results reported in this paper are important because, unlike previous results, they make explicit the relation between population size, schema fitness and probability of convergence over multiple generations. These and other recent results show that schema theories are potentially very useful in analysing and designing GAs and that the scepticism with which they are dismissed in the evolutionary computation community is becoming less and less justifiable.

Acknowledgements

The author wishes to thank the members of the Evolutionary and Emergent Behaviour Intelligence and Computation (EEBIC) group at Birmingham, Bill Spears, Ken De Jong and Jonathan Rowe for useful comments and discussion. The reviewers of this paper are also thanked warmly for their thorough analysis and helpful comments. Finally, many thanks to Günter Rudolf for pointing out to us the existence of the Chernoff–Hoeffding bounds.

References

[Altenberg, 1995] Altenberg, L. (1995). The Schema Theorem and Price's Theorem. In Whitley, L. D. and Vose, M. D., editors, *Foundations of Genetic Algorithms 3*, pages 23–49, Estes Park, Colorado, USA. Morgan Kaufmann.

[Chernoff, 1952] Chernoff, H. (1952). a measure of asymptotic efficiency for tests of a hypothesis based on the sum of observations. *annals of mathematical statistics*, 23(4):493–507.

[Chung and Perez, 1994] Chung, S. W. and Perez, R. A. (1994). The schema theorem considered insufficient. In *Proceedings of the Sixth IEEE International Conference on Tools with Artificial Intelligence*, pages 748–751, New Orleans.

[Davis and Principe, 1993] Davis, T. E. and Principe, J. C. (1993). A Markov chain framework for the simple genetic algorithm. *Evolutionary Computation*, 1(3):269–288.

[De Jong et al., 1995] De Jong, K. A., Spears, W. M., and Gordon, D. F. (1995). Using Markov chains to analyze GAFOs. In Whitley, L. D. and Vose, M. D., editors, *Foundations of Genetic Algorithms 3*, pages 115–137. Morgan Kaufmann, San Francisco, CA.

[Fogel and Ghozeil, 1997] Fogel, D. B. and Ghozeil, A. (1997). Schema processing under proportional selection in the presence of random effects. *IEEE Transactions on Evolutionary Computation*, 1(4):290–293.

[Fogel and Ghozeil, 1998] Fogel, D. B. and Ghozeil, A. (1998). The schema theorem and the misallocation of trials in the presence of stochastic effects. In Porto, V. W., Saravanan, N., Waagen, D., and Eiben, A. E., editors, *Evolutionary Programming VII: Proc. of the 7th Ann. Conf. on Evolutionary Programming*, pages 313–321, Berlin. Springer.

[Goldberg, 1989] Goldberg, D. E. (1989). *Genetic Algorithms in Search, Optimization, and Machine Learning*. Addison-Wesley, Reading, Massachusetts.

[Goldberg et al., 1992] Goldberg, D. E., Deb, K., and Clark, J. H. (1992). Accounting for noise in the sizing of populations. In Whitley, D., editor, *Foundations of Genetic Algorithms Workshop (FOGA-92)*, Vail, Colorado.

[Goldberg and Rudnick, 1991a] Goldberg, D. E. and Rudnick, M. (1991a). Genetic algorithms and the variance of fitness. Technical Report IlliGAL Report No 91001, Department of General Engineering, University of Illinois at Urbana-Champaign.

[Goldberg and Rudnick, 1991b] Goldberg, D. E. and Rudnick, M. (1991b). Genetic algorithms and the variance of fitness. *Complex systems*, 5:265–278.

[Hoeffding, 1963] Hoeffding, W. (1963). Probability inequalities for sums of bonded random variables. *Journal of the American Statistical Association*, 58(301):13–30.

[Nix and Vose, 1992] Nix, A. E. and Vose, M. D. (1992). Modeling genetic algorithms with Markov chains. *Annals of Mathematics and Artificial Intelligence*, 5:79–88.

[Poli, 1999a] Poli, R. (1999a). Probabilistic schema theorems without expectation, recursive conditional schema theorem, convergence and population sizing in genetic algorithms. Technical Report CSRP-99-3, University of Birmingham, School of Computer Science.

[Poli, 1999b] Poli, R. (1999b). Schema theorems without expectations. In Banzhaf, W., Daida, J., Eiben, A. E., Garzon, M. H., Honavar, V., Jakiela, M., and Smith, R. E., editors, *Proceedings of the Genetic and Evolutionary Computation Conference*, volume 1, page 806, Orlando, Florida, USA. Morgan Kaufmann.

[Poli, 2000a] Poli, R. (2000a). Exact schema theorem and effective fitness for GP with one-point crossover. In Whitley, D., Goldberg, D., Cantu-Paz, E., Spector, L., Parmee, I., and Beyer, H.-G., editors, *Proceedings of the Genetic and Evolutionary Computation Conference*, pages 469–476, Las Vegas. Morgan Kaufmann.

[Poli, 2000b] Poli, R. (2000b). Hyperschema theory for GP with one-point crossover, building blocks, and some new results in GA theory. In Poli, R., Banzhaf, W., Langdon, W. B., Miller, J. F., Nordin, P., and Fogarty, T. C., editors, *Genetic Programming, Proceedings of EuroGP'2000*, volume 1802 of *LNCS*, pages 163–180, Edinburgh. Springer-Verlag.

[Poli, 2000c] Poli, R. (2000c). Why the schema theorem is correct also in the presence of stochastic effects. In *Proceedings of the Congress on Evolutionary Computation (CEC 2000)*, pages 487–492, San Diego, USA.

[Poli et al., 1998] Poli, R., Langdon, W. B., and O'Reilly, U.-M. (1998). Analysis of schema variance and short term extinction likelihoods. In Koza, J. R., Banzhaf, W., Chellapilla, K., Deb, K., Dorigo, M., Fogel, D. B., Garzon, M. H., Goldberg, D. E., Iba, H., and Riolo, R., editors, *Genetic Programming 1998: Proceedings of the Third Annual Conference*, pages 284–292, University of Wisconsin, Madison, Wisconsin, USA. Morgan Kaufmann.

[Prügel-Bennett and Shapiro, 1994] Prügel-Bennett, A. and Shapiro, J. L. (1994). An analysis of genetic algorithms using statistical mechanics. *Physical Review Letters*, 72:1305–1309.

[Radcliffe, 1997] Radcliffe, N. J. (1997). Schema processing. In Baeck, T., Fogel, D. B., and Michalewicz, Z., editors, *Handbook of Evolutionary Computation*, pages B2.5–1–10. Oxford University Press.

[Rudolph, 1994] Rudolph, G. (1994). Convergence analysis of canonical genetic algorithm. *IEEE Transactions on Neural Networks*, 5(1):96–101.

[Rudolph, 1997a] Rudolph, G. (1997a). Genetic algorithms. In Baeck, T., Fogel, D. B., and Michalewicz, Z., editors, *Handbook of Evolutionary Computation*, pages B2.4–20–27. Oxford University Press.

[Rudolph, 1997b] Rudolph, G. (1997b). Models of stochastic convergence. In Baeck, T., Fogel, D. B., and Michalewicz, Z., editors, *Handbook of Evolutionary Computation*, pages B2.3–1–3. Oxford University Press.

[Rudolph, 1997c] Rudolph, G. (1997c). Stochastic processes. In Baeck, T., Fogel, D. B., and Michalewicz, Z., editors, *Handbook of Evolutionary Computation*, pages B2.2–1–8. Oxford University Press.

[Schmidt et al., 1992] Schmidt, J. P., Siegel, A., and Srinivasan, A. (1992). Chernoff-Hoeffding bounds for applications with limited independence. Technical Report 92-1305, Department of Computer Science, Cornell University.

[Sobel and Uppuluri, 1972] Sobel, M. and Uppuluri, V. R. R. (1972). On Bonferroni-type inequalities of the same degree for the probability of unions and intersections. *Annals of Mathematical Statistics*, 43(5):1549–1558.

[Spiegel, 1975] Spiegel, M. R. (1975). *Probability and Statistics.* McGraw-Hill, New York.

[Stephens and Waelbroeck, 1997] Stephens, C. R. and Waelbroeck, H. (1997). Effective degrees of freedom in genetic algorithms and the block hypothesis. In Bäck, T., editor, *Proceedings of the Seventh International Conference on Genetic Algorithms (ICGA97)*, pages 34–40, East Lansing. Morgan Kaufmann.

[Stephens and Waelbroeck, 1999] Stephens, C. R. and Waelbroeck, H. (1999). Schemata evolution and building blocks. *Evolutionary Computation*, 7(2):109–124.

[Vose, 1999] Vose, M. D. (1999). *The simple genetic algorithm: Foundations and theory.* MIT Press, Cambridge, MA.

[Wright, 1931] Wright, S. (1931). Evolution in mendelian populations. *Genetics*, 16:97–159.

Towards a Theory of Strong Overgeneral Classifiers

Tim Kovacs
School of Computer Science
University of Birmingham
Birmingham B15 2TT United Kingdom
Email: T.Kovacs@cs.bham.ac.uk

Abstract

We analyse the concept of strong overgeneral rules, the Achilles' heel of traditional Michigan-style learning classifier systems, using both the traditional strength-based and newer accuracy-based approaches to rule fitness. We argue that different definitions of overgenerality are needed to match the goals of the two approaches, present minimal conditions and environments which will support strong overgeneral rules, demonstrate their dependence on the reward function, and give some indication of what kind of reward functions will avoid them. Finally, we distinguish fit overgeneral rules, show how strength and accuracy-based fitness differ in their response to fit overgenerals and conclude by considering possible extensions to this work.

1 INTRODUCTION

Learning Classifier Systems (LCS) typically use a Genetic Algorithm (GA) to evolve sets of if-then rules called *classifiers* to determine their behaviour in a problem environment. In *Pittsburgh*-style LCS the GA operates on chromosomes which are complete solutions (entire sets of rules), whereas in the more common *Michigan*-style LCS chromosomes are partial solutions (individual rules). In either case chromosome fitness is somehow determined by the performance of the LCS in a problem environment. We'll consider LCS for reinforcement learning tasks, in which performance is measured by the amount of reward (a scalar) the environment gives the LCS. Precisely how to relate LCS performance to chromosome fitness has been the subject of much research, and is of great significance because adaptation of rules and LCS alike depends on it.

We undertake an analysis of the causes and effects of certain rule pathologies in Michigan LCS and trace them ultimately to the relation between LCS performance and rule fitness. We examine situations in which less desirable rules can achieve higher fitness than more desirable rules, which results in a mismatch between the goal of the LCS as a whole and the goal of the GA, since the goal of the GA is to find high-fitness rules.

We assume some familiarity with genetic algorithms, LCS, and Wilson's XCS (Wilson, 1995), a new direction in LCS research. The most interesting feature of XCS is that it bases the fitness of rules on the accuracy with which they predict rewards, rather than the magnitude of rewards, as traditional LCS do. We call XCS an *accuracy-based LCS* to contrast it with traditional LCS, which we call *strength-based LCS*.

1.1 OVERGENERAL AND STRONG OVERGENERAL RULES

Dealing with *overgeneral rules* – rules which are simply too general – is a fundamental problem for LCS. Such rules may specify the desired action in a subset of the states they match, but, by definition, not in all states, so relying on them harms performance.

Another problem faced by some LCS is *greedy classifier creation* (Cliff and Ross, 1995; Wilson, 1994). To obtain better rules, an LCS's GA allocates reproductive events preferentially to rules with higher fitness. Greedy classifier creation occurs in LCS in which the fitness of a rule depends on the magnitude of the reward it receives from the problem environment. In such systems rules which match in higher-rewarding parts of the environment will reproduce more than others. If the bias in reproduction of rules is strong enough there may be too few rules, or even no rules, matching low-rewarding states. (In the latter case, we say there's a gap in the rules' covering map of the input/action space.)

Cliff and Ross (1995) recognised that overgeneral rules can interact with greedy classifier creation, an effect Kovacs (2000) referred to as the problem of *strong overgenerals*. The interaction occurs when an overgeneral rule acts correctly in a high reward state and incorrectly in a low reward state. The rule is overgeneral because it acts incorrectly in one state, but at the same time it prospers because of greedy classifier creation and the high reward it receives in the other state. The proliferation of strong overgenerals can be disastrous for the performance of an LCS: such rules are unreliable, but outweigh more reliable rules when it comes to action selection. Worse, they may prosper under the influence of the GA, and may even reproduce more than reliable but low-rewarding rules, possibly driving them out of the population.

This work extends the analysis of strong overgenerals in (Kovacs, 2000) to show exactly what requirements must be met for them to arise in both strength and accuracy-based LCS. In order to compare the two approaches we begin by defining Goliath, a strength-based LCS which differs as little as possible from accuracy-based XCS, which allows us to isolate the effects of the fitness calculation on performance. We then argue that different definitions of overgenerality and strong overgenerality are appropriate for the two types of LCS. We later make a further, novel, distinction between strong and fit overgeneral rules. We present minimal environments which will support strong overgenerals, demonstrate the dependence of strong overgenerals on the reward function, and prove certain theorems regarding their prevalence under simplifying assumptions. We show that strength and accuracy-based fitness have different kinds of tolerance for biases (see section 3.5) in reward functions, and (within the context of various simplifying assumptions) to what extent we can bias them without producing strong overgenerals. We show what kinds of problems will not produce strong overgenerals even without our simplifying assumptions. We present results of experiments which show how XCS and Goliath differ in their response to fit overgenerals. Finally, we consider the value of the approach taken here and directions for further study.

2 BACKGROUND AND METHODOLOGY

2.1 LCS FOR REINFORCEMENT LEARNING

Reinforcement learning consists of cycles in which a learning agent is presented with an input describing the current environmental state, responds with an action and receives some reward as an indication of the value of its action. The reward received is defined by the *reward function*, which maps state/action pairs to the real number line, and which is part of the problem definition (Sutton and Barto, 1998). For simplicity we consider only *single-step* tasks, meaning the agent's actions do not affect which states it visits in the future. The goal of the agent is to maximise the rewards it receives, and, in single-step tasks, it can do so in each state independently. In other words, it need not consider sequences of actions in order to maximise reward.

When an LCS receives an input it forms the *match set* [M] of rules whose conditions match the environmental input.[1] The LCS then selects an action from among those advocated by the rules in [M]. The subset of [M] which advocates the selected action is called the *action set* [A]. Occasionally the LCS will trigger a reproductive event, in which it calls upon the GA to modify the population of rules.

We will consider LCS in which, on each cycle, only the rules in [A] are updated based on the reward received – rules not in [A] are not updated.

2.2 THE STANDARD TERNARY LCS LANGUAGE

A number of representations have been used with LCS, in particular a number of variations based on binary and ternary strings. Using what we'll call the *standard ternary LCS language* each rule has a single condition and a single action. Conditions are fixed length strings from $\{0,1,\#\}^l$, while rule actions and environmental inputs are fixed length strings from $\{0,1\}^l$. In all problems considered here $l = 1$.

A rule's condition c matches an environmental input m if for each character m_i the character in the corresponding position c_i is identical or the wildcard (#). The wildcard is the means by which rules generalise over environmental states; the more #s a rule contains the more general it is. Since actions do not contain wildcards the system cannot generalise over them.

2.3 STRENGTH-BASED AND ACCURACY-BASED FITNESS

Although the fitness of a rule is determined by the rewards the LCS receives when it is used, LCS differ in how they calculate rule fitness. In traditional strength-based systems (see, e.g., Goldberg, 1989; Wilson, 1994), the fitness of a rule is called its *strength*. This value is used in both action selection and reproduction. In contrast, the more recent accuracy-based XCS (Wilson, 1995) maintains separate estimates of rule utility for action selection and reproduction.

One of the goals of this work is to compare the way strength and accuracy-based systems handle overgeneral and strong overgeneral rules. To do so, we'll compare accuracy-based XCS with a strength-based LCS called Goliath which differs as little as possible from XCS, and which closely resembles Wilson's ZCS (Wilson, 1994). To be more specific, Goliath (in single-step tasks) uses the delta rule to update rule strengths:

[1] Since we deal only with single-step tasks, we consider only stimulus-response LCS, that is, LCS lacking an internal message list.

Strength (a.k.a. prediction):

$$s_j \leftarrow s_j + \beta(R - s_j)$$

where s_j is the strength of rule j, $0 < \beta \leq 1$ is a constant controlling the learning rate and R is the reward from the environment. Goliath uses the same strength value for both action selection and reproduction. That is, the fitness of a rule in the GA is simply its strength.

XCS uses this same update to calculate rule strength,[2] and uses strength in action selection, but goes on to derive other statistics from it. In particular, from strength it derives the accuracy of a rule, which it uses as the basis of its fitness in the GA. This is achieved by updating a number of parameters as follows (see Wilson, 1995, for more). Following the update of a rule's strength s_j, we update its prediction error ε_j:

Prediction error:

$$\varepsilon_j \leftarrow \varepsilon_j + \beta\left(\frac{|R - s_j|}{R_{max} - R_{min}} - \varepsilon_j\right)$$

where R_{max} and R_{min} are the highest and lowest rewards possible in any state. Next we calculate the rule's accuracy κ_j:

Accuracy:

$$\kappa_j = \begin{cases} 1 & \text{if } \varepsilon_j < \varepsilon_o \\ \alpha(\varepsilon_j/\varepsilon_o)^{-v} & \text{otherwise} \end{cases}$$

where $0 < \varepsilon_o$ is a constant controlling the tolerance for prediction error and $0 < \alpha < 1$ and $0 < v$ are constants controlling the rate of decline in accuracy when ε_o is exceeded. Once the accuracy of all rules in [A] has been updated we update each rule's relative accuracy κ'_j :

Relative accuracy:

$$\kappa'_j \leftarrow \frac{\kappa_j}{\sum_{x \in [A]} \kappa_x}$$

Finally, each rule's fitness is updated:

Fitness:

$$F_j \leftarrow F_j + \beta(\kappa'_j - F_j)$$

To summarise, the XCS updates treat the strength of a rule as a prediction of the reward to be received, and maintain an estimate of the error ε_j in each rule's prediction. An accuracy score κ_j is calculated based on the error as follows. If error is below some threshold ε_o the rule is fully accurate (has an accuracy of 1), otherwise its accuracy drops off quickly. The accuracy values in the action set [A] are then converted to relative accuracies (the κ'_j update), and finally each rule's fitness F_j is updated towards its relative accuracy.

To simplify, in XCS fitness is an inverse function of the error in reward prediction, with errors below ε_o being ignored entirely.

---

[2] Wilson (1995) refers to strength as *prediction* because he treats it as a prediction of the reward the system will receive when the rule is used.

2.3.1 XCS, Goliath and other LCS

Goliath is not simply a straw man for XCS to outperform. It is a functional LCS, and is capable of solving some problems as well as any other LCS, including XCS. Goliath's value is that we can study when and why it fails, and we can attribute any difference between its performance and that of XCS to the difference in fitness calculation.

Goliath differs from many other strength-based Michigan LCS in that it (following XCS) does not use any form of tax, and does not deduct rule "bids" from their strengths (see, e.g., Goldberg, 1989). See (Kovacs, 2001) for full details of both XCS and Goliath.

2.4 METHOD

LCS are complicated systems and analysis of their behaviour is often quite difficult. To make our analysis more tractable we'll make a number of simplifications, perhaps the greatest of which is to study very small problems. Although very small, these problems illustrate different types of rules and the effects of different fitness definitions on them – indeed, they illustrate them better for their simplicity.

Another great simplification is to consider the much simpler case of single-step problems rather than multi-step ones. Multi-step problems present their own difficulties, but those present in the single-step case persist in the more complex multi-step case. We feel study of single-step problems can uncover fundamental features of the systems under consideration while limiting the complexity which needs to be dealt with.

To further simplify matters we'll remove the GA from the picture and enumerate all possible classifiers for each problem, which is trivial given the small problems we'll consider. Simplifying further still, we'll consider only the expected values of rules, and not deviations from expectation. Similarly, we'll consider steady state values, and not worry about how steady state values are reached (at least not until section 7). We'll consider deterministic reward functions, although it would be easy to generalise to stochastic reward functions simply by referring to expected values. We'll restrict our considerations to the standard ternary LCS language of section 2.2 because it is the most commonly used and because we are interested in fitness calculations and the ontology of rules, not in their representation. Finally, to simplify our calculations we'll assume that, in all problem environments, states and actions are chosen equiprobably.

Removing the GA and choosing actions at random does not leave us with much of a classifier system. In fact, our simplifications mean that any quantitative results we obtain do not apply to any realistic applications of an LCS. Our results will, however, give us a qualitative sense of the behaviour of two types of LCS. In particular, this approach seems well suited to the qualitative study of rule ontology. Section 3 contains examples of this approach.

2.4.1 Default Hierarchies

Default Hierarchies (DHs) (see, e.g., Riolo, 1988; Goldberg, 1989; Smith, 1991) have traditionally been considered an important feature of strength-based LCS. XCS, however, does not support them because they involve inherently inaccurate rules. Although Goliath does not have this restriction, it does not encourage DHs, as some other LCS do, by, e.g., factoring rule specificity into action selection.

Table 1 Reward Function for a Simple Test Problem.

State	Action	Reward	State	Action	Reward
0	0	1000	0	1	500
1	0	500	1	1	500

Table 2 All Possible Classifiers for the Simple Test Problem in Table 1 and their Classifications using Strength-Based and Accuracy-Based Fitness.

Classifier	Condition	Action	E[Strength]	Strength Classification	Accuracy Classification
A	0	0	1000	Correct	Accurate
B	0	1	500	Incorrect	Accurate
C	1	0	500	Correct	Accurate
D	1	1	500	Correct	Accurate
E	#	0	750	Correct	Overgeneral
F	#	1	500	Overgeneral	Accurate

Consequently, default hierarchies have not been included in the analysis presented here, and their incorporation has been left for future work. DHs are potentially significant in that they may allow strength LCS to overcome some of the difficulties with strong overgeneral rules we will show them to have. If so, this would increase both the significance of DHs and the significance of the well-known difficulty of finding and maintaining them.

3 DEFINITIONS

3.1 CORRECT AND INCORRECT ACTIONS

Since the goal of our reinforcement learning agents is to maximise the rewards they receive, it's useful to have terminology which distinguishes actions which do so from those which do not:

Correct action: In any given state the learner must choose from a set of available actions. A correct action is one which results in the maximum reward possible for the given state and set of available actions.

Incorrect action: One which does not maximise reward.

Table 1 defines a simple single-step test problem, in which for state 0 the correct action is 0, while in state 1 both actions 0 and 1 are correct. Note that an action is correct or incorrect only in the context of a given state, and the context of the rewards available in that state.

3.2 OVERGENERAL RULES

Table 2 shows all possible rules for the environment in table 1 using the standard ternary language of section 2.3. Each rule's expected strength is also shown, using the simplifying assumption of equiprobable states and actions from section 2.4. The classification shown for each rule will eventually be explained in sections 3.2.2 and 3.2.3.

We're interested in distinguishing overgeneral from non-overgeneral rules. Rules A,B,C and D are clearly not overgeneral, since they each match only one input. What about E and F? So far we haven't explicitly defined overgenerality, so let's make our implicit notion of overgenerality clear:

Overgeneral rule: A rule O from which a superior rule can be derived by reducing the generality of O's condition.

This definition seems clear, but relies on our ability to evaluate the superiority of rules. That is, to know whether a rule X is overgeneral, we need to know whether there is any possible Y, some more specific version of X, which is superior to X. How should we define superiority?

3.2.1 Are Stronger Rules Superior Rules?

Can we simply use fitness itself to determine the superiority of rules? After all, this is the role of fitness in the GA. In other words, let's say X is overgeneral if some more specific version Y is fitter than X.

In Goliath, our strength-based system, fitter rules are those which receive higher rewards, and so have higher strength. Let's see if E and F are overgeneral using strength to define the superiority of rules.

Rule E. The condition of E can be specialised to produce A and C. C is inferior to E (it has lower strength) while A is superior (it has greater strength). Because A is superior, E is overgeneral.

This doesn't seem right – intuitively E should *not* be overgeneral, since it is correct in both states it matches. In fact all three rules (A, C and E) advocate only correct actions, and yet A is supposedly superior to the other two. This seems wrong since E subsumes A and C, which suggests that, if any of the three is more valuable, it should be E.

Rule F. The condition of F can be specialised to produce B and D. Using strength as our value metric all three rules are are equally valuable, since they have the same expected strength, so F is not overgeneral.

This doesn't seem right either – surely F *is* overgeneral since it is incorrect in state 0. Surely D should be superior to F since it is always correct.

Clearly using strength as our value metric doesn't capture our intuitions about what the system should be doing.

To define the value of rules let's return to the goal of the LCS, which, as mentioned earlier, is to maximise the reward it receives. Maximising reward means taking the correct action in each state. It is the correctness of its actions which determines a rule's value, rather than how much reward it receives (its strength).

Recall from section 2.3 that strength is derived from environmental reward. Strength is a measure of how good – *on average* – a rule is at obtaining reward. Using strength as fitness in the GA, we will evolve rules which are – *on average* – good at obtaining reward. However, many of these rules will actually perform poorly in some states, and only achieve good average performance by doing particularly well in other states. Such rules are overgeneral; superior rules can be obtained by restricting their conditions to match only the states in which they do well.

To maximise rewards, we do not want to evolve rules which obtain the highest rewards possible *in any state*, but to evolve rules which obtain the highest rewards possible *in the states in which they act*. That is, rather than rules which are *globally* good at obtaining reward, we want rules which are *locally* good at obtaining reward. In other words, we want rules whose actions are correct in all states they match. What's more, each state must be covered by a correct rule because an LCS must know how to act in each state. (In reinforcement learning terminology, we say it must have a *policy*.)

To encourage the evolution of consistently correct rules, rather than rules which are good on average, we can use techniques like fitness sharing. But, while such techniques may help, there remains a fundamental mismatch between using strength as fitness and the goal of evolving rules with consistently correct actions. See (Kovacs, 2000) for more.

3.2.2 Strength and Best Action Only Maps

To maximise rewards, a strength-based LCS needs a population of rules which advocates the correct action in each state. If, in each state, only the best action is advocated, the population constitutes a *best action only map* (Kovacs, 2000). While a best action only map is an ideal representation, it is still possible to maximise rewards when incorrect actions are also advocated, as long as they are not selected. This is what we hope for in practise.

Now let's return to the question of how to define overgenerality in a strength-based system. Instead of saying X is overgeneral if some Y is fitter (stronger), let's say it is overgeneral if some Y is more consistent with the goal of forming a best action only map; that is, if Y is correct in more cases than X.

Notice that we're now speaking of the correctness of rules (not just the correctness of actions), and of their relative correctness at that. Let's emphasise these ideas:

Fully Correct Rule: One which advocates a correct action in every state it matches.

Fully Incorrect Rule: One which advocates an incorrect action in every state it matches.

Overgeneral Rule: One which advocates a correct action in some states and an incorrect action in others (i.e. a rule which is neither fully correct nor fully incorrect).

Correctness of a Rule: The correctness of a rule is the proportion of states in which it advocates the correct action.[3]

The notion of the relative correctness of a rule allows us to say a rule Y is *more* correct (and hence *less* overgeneral) than a rule X, even if neither is fully correct.

Now let's reevaluate E and F from table 2 to see how consistent they are with the goal of forming a best action only map. Rule E matches two states and advocates a correct action in both. This is compatible with forming a best action only map, so E is not overgeneral. Rule F also matches both states, but advocates an incorrect action in state 0, making F incompatible with the goal of forming a best action only map. Because a superior rule (D) can be obtain by specialising F, F is overgeneral.

Notice that we've now defined overgeneral rules twice: once in section 3.2 and once in this section. For the problems we're considering here the two definitions coincide, although they do not always. For example, in the presence of perceptual aliasing (where an input to the LCS does not always describe a unique environmental state) a rule may be overgeneral by one definition but not by the

[3] The correctness of a rule corresponds to classification accuracy in pattern classification.

other. That is, it may be neither fully correct nor fully incorrect, and yet it may be impossible to generate a more correct rule because a finer distinction of states cannot be expressed.

The above assumes the states referred to in the definition of overgenerality are environmental states. If we consider perceptual states rather than environmental states the rule is sometimes correct and sometimes incorrect *in the same state* (which is not possible in the basic environments studied here). We could take this to mean the rule is not fully correct, and thus overgeneral, or we might choose to do otherwise.

3.2.3 Accuracy and Complete Maps

While all reinforcement learners seek to maximise rewards, the approach of XCS differs from that of strength-based LCS. Where strength LCS seek to form best action only maps, XCS seeks to form a *complete map*: a set of rules such that each action in each state is advocated by at least one rule (Wilson, 1995; Kovacs, 2000). This set of rules allows XCS to approximate the entire reward function and (hopefully) accurately predict the reward for any action in any state. XCS's fitness metric *is* consistent with this goal, and we'll use it to define the superiority of rules for XCS.

The different approaches to fitness mean that while in strength-based systems we contrast fully correct, fully incorrect and overgeneral rules, with accuracy-based fitness we contrast accurate and inaccurate rules.

In XCS, fitter rules are those with lower prediction errors – at least up to a point: small errors in prediction are ignored, and rules with small enough errors are considered fully accurate (see the accuracy update in section 2.3). In other words, XCS has some tolerance for prediction error, or, put another way, some tolerance for changes in a rule's strength, since changes in strength are what produce prediction error. We'll use this tolerance for prediction error as our definition of overgenerality in XCS, and say that a rule is overgeneral if its prediction error exceeds the tolerance threshold, i.e. if $\varepsilon_j \geq \varepsilon_o$. In XCS 'overgeneral' is synonymous with 'not-fully-accurate'.

Although this work uses XCS as a model, we hope it will apply to other future accuracy-based LCS. To keep the discussion more general, instead of focusing on XCS and its error threshold, we'll refer to a somewhat abstract notion of tolerance called τ. Let $\tau \geq 0$ be an accuracy-based LCS's tolerance for oscillations in strength, above which a rule is judged overgeneral.

Like XCS's error threshold, τ is an adjustable parameter of the system. This means that in an accuracy-based system, whether a rule is overgeneral or not depends on how we set τ. If τ is set very high, then both E and F from table 2 will fall within the tolerance for error and neither will be overgeneral. If we gradually decrease τ, however, we will reach a point where E is overgeneral while F is not. Notice that this last case is the reverse of the situation we had in section 3.2.2 when using strength-based fitness. So which rule is overgeneral depends on our fitness metric.

3.2.4 Defining Overgenerality

To match the different goals of the two systems we need different definitions of overgenerality:

Strength-based overgeneral: For strength-based fitness, an overgeneral rule is one which matches multiple states and acts incorrectly in some.[4]

[4] This restatement of strength-based overgenerality matches the definition given in section 3.2.2.

Accuracy-based overgeneral: For accuracy-based fitness, an overgeneral rule is one which matches multiple states, some of which return (sufficiently) different rewards, and hence has (sufficiently) oscillating strength. Here a rule is overgeneral if its oscillations exceed τ.

Note that the strength definition requires action on the part of the classifiers while the accuracy definition does not. Thus we can have overgenerals in a problem which allows 0 actions (or, equivalently, 1 action) using accuracy (see, e.g., table 3), but not using strength.

3.3 STRONG OVERGENERAL RULES

Now that we've finally defined overgenerality satisfactorily let's turn to the subject of strong overgenerality. Strength is used to determine a rule's influence in action selection, and action selection is a competition between alternatives. Consequently it makes no sense to speak of the strength of a rule in isolation. Put another way, strength is a way of ordering rules. With a single rule there are no alternative orderings, and hence no need for strength.

In other words, strength is a relation between rules; a rule can only be stronger or weaker than other rules – there is no such thing as a rule which is strong in isolation. Therefore, for a rule to be a strong overgeneral, it must be stronger than another rule. In particular, a rule's strength is relevant when compared to another rule with which it competes for action selection.

Now we can define strong overgeneral rules, although to do so we need two definitions to match our two definitions of overgenerality:

Strength-based strong overgeneral: A rule which sometimes advocates an incorrect action, and yet whose expected strength is greater than that of some correct (i.e. not-overgeneral) competitor for action selection.

Accuracy-based strong overgeneral: A rule whose strength oscillates unacceptably, and yet whose expected strength is greater than that of some accurate (i.e. not-overgeneral) competitor for action selection.

The intention is that competitors be possible, not that they need actually exist in a given population.

The strength-based definition refers to competition with *correct* rules because strength-based systems are not interested in maintaining incorrect rules (see section 3.2.2). This definition suits the analysis in this work. However, situations in which more overgeneral rules have higher fitness than less overgeneral – but still overgeneral – competitors are also pathological. Parallel scenarios exist for accuracy-based fitness. Such cases resemble the well-known idea of *deception* in GAs, in which search is lead away from desired solutions (see, e.g., Goldberg, 1989).

3.4 FIT OVERGENERAL RULES

In our definitions of strong overgenerals we refer to competition for action selection, but rules also compete for reproduction. To deal with the latter case we introduce the concept of *fit overgenerals* as a parallel to that of strong overgenerals. A rule can be both, or either. The definitions for strength and accuracy-based fit overgenerals are identical to those for strong overgenerals, except that we refer to fitness (not expected strength) and competition for reproduction (not action selection):

Strength-based fit overgeneral: A rule which sometimes advocates an incorrect action, and yet whose expected *fitness* is greater than that of some correct (i.e. not-overgeneral) competitor *for reproduction*.

Accuracy-based fit overgeneral: A rule whose strength oscillates unacceptably, and yet whose expected *fitness* is greater than that of some accurate (i.e. not-overgeneral) competitor *for reproduction*.

We won't consider fit overgenerals as a separate case in our initial analysis since in Goliath any fit overgeneral is also a strong overgeneral.[5] Later, in section 7, we'll see how XCS handles both fit and strong overgenerals.

3.5 OTHER DEFINITIONS

For reference we include a number of other definitions:

Reward function: A function which maps state/action pairs to a numeric reward.

Constant function: A function which returns the same value regardless of its arguments. A function may be said to be constant over a range of arguments.

Unbiased reward function: One in which all correct actions receive the same reward.

Biased reward function: One which is not unbiased.

Best action only map: A population of rules which advocates only the correct action for each state.

Complete map: A population of rules such that each action in each state is advocated by at least one rule.

4 WHEN ARE STRONG OVERGENERALS POSSIBLE?

We've seen definitions for strong and fit overgeneral rules, but what are the exact conditions under which an environment can be expected to produce them? If such rules are a serious problem for LCS, knowing when to expect them should be a major concern: if we know what kinds of environment are likely to produce them (and how many) we'll know something about what kinds of environment should be difficult for LCS (and how difficult).

Not surprisingly, the requirements for the production of strong and fit overgenerals depend on which definition we adopt. Looking at the accuracy-based definition of strong overgenerality we can see that we need two rules (a strong overgeneral and a not-overgeneral rule), that the two rules must compete for action selection, and that the overgeneral rule must be stronger than the not-overgeneral rule. The environmental conditions which make this situation possible are as follows:

1. The environment must contain at least two states, in order that we can have a rule which generalises (incorrectly).[6]

---

[5] Nonetheless, there is still a difference between strong and fit overgenerals in strength-based systems, since the two forms of competition may take place between different sets of rules.

[6] We assume the use of the standard LCS language in which generalisation over actions does not occur. Otherwise, it would be possible to produce an overgeneral in an environment with only a single state (and multiple actions) by generalising over actions instead of states.

Table 3 A Minimal (2x1) Strong Overgeneral Environment for Accuracy and all its Classifiers.

State	Action	Reward
0	0	$a = 1000$
1	0	$c = 0$

Classifier	Condition	Action	E[Strength]
A	0	0	$a = 1000$
C	1	0	$c = 0$
E	#	0	$(a+c)/2 = 500$

2. The environment may allow any number of actions in the two states, including 0 (or, equivalently, 1) action. (We'll see later that strength-based systems differ in this respect.)
3. In order to be a strong overgeneral, the overgeneral must have higher expected strength than the not-overgeneral rule. For this to be the case the reward function must return different values for the two rules. More specifically, it must return more reward to the overgeneral rule.
4. The overgeneral and not-overgeneral rules must compete for action selection. This constrains which environments will support strong overgenerals.

The conditions which will support fit overgenerals are clearly very similar: 1) and 2) are the same, while for 3) the overgeneral must have greater fitness (rather than strength) than the not-overgeneral, and for 4) they must compete for reproduction rather than action selection.

4.1 THE REWARD FUNCTION IS RELEVANT

Let's look at the last two requirements for strong overgenerals in more detail. First, in order to have differences in the expectations of the strengths of rules there must be differences in the rewards returned from the environment. So the values in the reward function are relevant to the formation of strong overgenerals. More specifically, it must be the rewards returned to competing classifiers which differ. So subsets of the reward function are relevant to the formation of individual strong or fit overgenerals.

In (Kovacs, 2000), having different rewards for different correct actions is called a *bias* in the reward function (see section 3.5). For strong or fit overgenerals to occur, there must be a bias in the reward function at state/action pairs which map to competing classifiers.

5 ACCURACY-BASED SYSTEMS

In section 4 we saw that, using the accuracy definition, strong overgenerals require an environment with at least two states, and that each state can have any number of actions. We also saw that the reward function was relevant but did not see exactly how. Now let's look at a minimal strong overgeneral supporting environment for accuracy and see exactly what is required of the reward function to produce strong overgenerals. Table 3 shows a reward function for an environment with two states and one action and all possible classifiers for it. As always, the expected strengths shown are due to the simplifying assumption that states and actions occur equiprobably (section 2.4).

Table 4 A Binary State Binary Action (2x2) Environment.

State	Action	Reward	State	Action	Reward
0	0	w	0	1	y
1	0	x	1	1	z

Classifier	Condition	Action	E[Strength]	Overgeneral unless
A	0	0	w	never
B	0	1	y	never
C	1	0	x	never
D	1	1	z	never
E	#	0	$(w+x)/2$	$\|w-x\| \leq \tau$
F	#	1	$(y+z)/2$	$\|y-z\| \leq \tau$

In section 2.4 we made a number of simplifying assumptions, and for now let's make a further one: that there is no tolerance for oscillating strengths ($\tau = 0$), so that any rule whose strength oscillates at all is overgeneral. This means rule E in table 3 is an overgeneral because it is updated towards different rewards. It is also a strong overgeneral because it is stronger than some not-overgeneral rule with which it competes, namely rule C. In section 4 we saw that strong overgenerals depend on the reward function returning more strength to the strong overgeneral than its not-overgeneral competitor. Are there reward functions under which E will not be a strong overgeneral? Since the strength of E is an average of the two rewards returned (labelled a and c in table 3 to correspond to the names of the fully specific rules which obtain them), and the strength of C is c, then as long as $a > c$, rule E will be a strong overgeneral. Symmetrically, if $c > a$ then E will still be a strong overgeneral, in this case stronger than not-overgeneral rule A. The only reward functions which do not cause strong overgenerals are those in which $a = c$. So in this case *any* bias in the reward function makes the formation of a strong overgeneral possible.

If we allow some tolerance for oscillations in strength without judging a rule overgeneral, then rule E is not overgeneral only if $a - c \leq \tau$ where τ is the tolerance for oscillations. In this case only reward functions in which $a - c > \tau$ will produce strong overgeneral rules.

5.1 A 2x2 ENVIRONMENT

We've just seen an example where any bias in the reward function will produce strong overgenerals. However, this is not the case when we have more than one action available, as in table 4. The strengths of the two fully generalised rules, E & F, are dependent only on the values associated with the actions they advocate. Differences in the rewards returned for different actions do not result in strong overgenerals – as long as we don't generalise over actions, which was one of our assumptions from section 2.4.

5.2 SOME PROPERTIES OF ACCURACY-BASED FITNESS

At this point it seems natural to ask how common strong overgenerals are and, given that the structure of the reward function is related to their occurrence, to ask what reward functions make them impossible. In this section we'll prove some simple, but perhaps surprising, theorems concerning overgeneral rules and accuracy-based fitness. However, we won't go too deeply into the subject for reasons which will become clear later.

Let's begin with a first approximation to when overgeneral rules are impossible:

Theorem 1 *Using accuracy-based fitness, overgeneral rules are impossible when the reward function is constant over each action.*

Proof. The strength of a rule is a function of the values towards which it is updated, and these values are a subset of the rewards for the action it advocates. If all such rewards are equivalent there can be no oscillations in a rule's strength, so it cannot be overgeneral. □

More generally, strong overgenerals are impossible when the reward function is sufficiently close to constancy over each action that oscillations in any rule's strength are less than τ. Now we can see when strong overgenerals are possible:

Theorem 2 *Using accuracy-based fitness, if the environmental structure meets requirements 1 and 4 of section 4 at least one overgeneral rule will be possible for each action for which the reward function is not within τ of being constant.*

Proof. A fully generalised rule matches all inputs and its strength is updated towards all possible rewards for the action it advocates. Unless all such rewards are within τ of equivalence it will be overgeneral. □

In other words, if the rewards for the same action differ by more than τ the fully generalised rule for that action will be overgeneral. To avoid overgeneral rules completely, we'd have to constrain the reward function to be within τ of constancy for each action. That overgeneral rules are widely possible should not be surprising. But it turns out that with accuracy-based fitness there is no distinction between overgeneral and strong overgeneral rules:

Theorem 3 *Using accuracy-based fitness, all overgeneral rules are strong overgenerals.*

Proof. Let's consider the reward function as a vector $R = [r_1\ r_2\ r_3\ \ldots\ r_n]$, and, for simplicity, assume $\tau = 0$. An overgeneral matches at least two states, and so is updated towards two or more distinct values from the vector, whereas accurate rules are updated towards only one value (since $\tau = 0$) no matter how many states they match. For each r_i in the vector there is some fully specific (and so not overgeneral) rule which is only updated towards it. Consequently, any overgeneral rule competes with at least two accurate rules.

Now consider the vector $X = [x_1\ x_2\ x_3\ \ldots\ x_n]$ which is composed of the subset of vector R towards which the overgeneral in question is updated. Because we've assumed states and actions occur equiprobably, the strength of a rule is just the mean of the values it is updated towards. So the strength of the overgeneral is $\bar{X}$, the mean of X.

The overgeneral will be a strong overgeneral if it is stronger than some accurate rule with which it competes. The weakest such rule's strength is $\min x_i$. The inequality $\min x_i < \bar{X}$ is true for all reward vectors except those which are constant functions, so all overgenerals are strong overgenerals. □

Taking theorems 2 and 3 together yields:

Theorem 4 *Using accuracy-based fitness, if the environmental structure meets requirements 1 and 4 of section 4 at least one* **strong** *overgeneral rule will be possible for each action for which the reward function is not within τ of being constant.*

Table 5 A 2x2 Unbiased Reward Function and all its Classifiers.

State	Action	Reward	State	Action	Reward
0	0	1000	0	1	0
1	0	0	1	1	1000

Classifier	Condition	Action	E[Strength]	Status
A	0	0	1000	Correct
B	0	1	0	Incorrect
C	1	0	0	Incorrect
D	1	1	1000	Correct
E	#	0	500	Overgeneral
F	#	1	500	Overgeneral

In short, using accuracy-based fitness and reasonably small τ only a highly restricted class of reward functions and environments do not support strong overgeneral rules. These theorems hold for environments with more than 2 actions.

Note that the 'for each action' part of the theorems we've just seen depends on the inability of rules to generalise over actions, a syntactic limitation of the standard LCS language. If we remove this arbitrary limitation then we further restrict the class of reward functions which will not support strong overgenerals.

6 STRENGTH-BASED SYSTEMS

We've seen how the reward function determines when strong overgeneral classifiers are possible in accuracy-based systems. Now let's look at the effect of the reward function using Goliath, our strength-based system. Recall from the strength-based definition of strong overgenerals that we need two rules (a strong overgeneral and a not-overgeneral correct rule), that the two rules must compete for action selection, and that the overgeneral rule must be stronger than the correct rule. The conditions which make this situation possible are the same as those for accuracy-based systems, except for a change to condition 2: there needs to be at least one state in which at least two actions are possible, so that the overgeneral rule can act incorrectly. (It doesn't make sense to speak of overgeneral rules in a strength-based system unless there is more than one action available.)

A second difference is that in strength-based systems there is no tolerance for oscillations in a rule's strength built into the update rules. This tolerance is simply not needed in Goliath where all that matters is that a rule advocate the correct action, not that its strength be consistent.

A complication to the analysis done earlier for accuracy-based systems is that strength-based systems tend towards best action only maps (see section 3 and Kovacs, 2000). Simply put, Goliath is not interested in maintaining incorrect rules, so we are interested in overgenerals only when they are stronger than some correct rule. For example, consider the binary state binary action environment of table 5. Using this unbiased reward function, rules E & F are overgenerals (since they are sometimes incorrect), but not strong overgenerals because the rules they are stronger than (B & C) are incorrect. (Recall from the definition of a strong overgeneral in a strength LCS in section 3.3 that the strong

Table 6 A 2x2 Biased Reward Function which is a Minimal Strong Overgeneral Environment for Strength-Based LCS, and all its Classifiers.

State	Action	Reward	State	Action	Reward
0	0	$w = 1000$	0	1	$y = 0$
1	0	$x = 0$	1	1	$z = 200$

Classifier	Condition	Action	E[Strength]	Strong overgeneral if
A	0	0	$w = 1000$	never
B	0	1	$y = 0$	never
C	1	0	$x = 0$	never
D	1	1	$z = 200$	never
E	#	0	$(w+x)/2 = 500$	$(w+x)/2 > z$
F	#	1	$(y+z)/2 = 100$	$(y+z)/2 > z$

overgeneral must be stronger than a *correct* rule.) This demonstrates that in strength-based systems (unlike accuracy-based systems) not all overgeneral rules are strong overgenerals.

What consequence does this disinterest in incorrect rules have on the dependence of strong overgenerals on the reward function? The reward function in this example is not constant over either action, and the accuracy-based concept of tolerance does not apply. In an accuracy-based system there must be strong overgenerals under such conditions, and yet there are none in this example.

6.1 WHEN ARE STRONG OVERGENERALS IMPOSSIBLE IN A STRENGTH LCS?

Let's begin with a first approximation to when strong overgenerals are impossible:

Theorem 5 *Using strength-based fitness, strong overgenerals are impossible when the reward function is unbiased (i.e. constant over correct actions).*

Proof. A correct action is one which receives the highest reward possible in its state. If all correct actions receive the same reward, this reward is higher than that for acting incorrectly in *any* state. Consequently no overgeneral rule can have higher strength than a correct rule, so no overgeneral can be a strong overgeneral. □

To make theorem 5 more concrete, reconsider the reward values in table 4. By definition, a correct action in a state is one which returns the highest reward for that state, so if we want w and z to be the only correct actions then $w > y, z > x$. If the reward function returns the same value for all correct actions then $w = z$. Then the strengths of the overgeneral rules are less than those of the correct accurate rules: E's expected strength is $(w+x)/2$ which is less than A's expected strength of w and F's expected strength is $(y+z)/2$ which is less than D's z, so the overgenerals cannot be strong overgenerals. (If $w < y$ and $z < x$ then we have a symmetrical situation in which the correct action is different, but strong overgenerals are still impossible.)

6.2 WHAT MAKES STRONG OVERGENERALS POSSIBLE IN STRENGTH LCS?

It is possible to obtain strong overgenerals in a strength-based system by defining a reward function which returns different values for correct actions. An example of a minimal strong overgeneral supporting environment for Goliath is given in table 6. Using this reward function, E *is* a strong overgeneral, as it is stronger than the correct rule D with which it competes for action selection (and for reproduction if the GA runs in the match set or panmictically (see Wilson, 1995)).

However, not all differences in rewards are sufficient to produce strong overgenerals. How much tolerance does Goliath have before biases in the reward function produce strong overgenerals? Suppose the rewards are such that w and z are correct (i.e. $w > y, z > x$) and the reward function is biased such that $w > z$. How much of a bias is needed to produce a strong overgeneral? I.e. how much greater than z must w be? Rule E competes with D for action selection, and will be a strong overgeneral if its expected strength exceeds D's, i.e. if $(w+x)/2 > z$, which is equivalent to $w > 2z - x$. So a bias of $w > 2z - x$ means E will be a strong overgeneral with respect to D, while a lesser bias means it will not.

E also competes with A for reproduction, and will be fitter than A if $(w+x)/2 > w$, which is equivalent to $x > w$. So a bias of $x > w$ means E will be a fit overgeneral with respect to A, while a lesser bias means it will not. (Symmetrical competitions occur between F & A and F & D.)

We'll take the last two examples as proof of the following theorem:

Theorem 6 *Using strength-based fitness, if the environmental structure meets requirements 1 and 4 of section 4 and the modified requirement 2 from section 6, a strong overgeneral is possible whenever the reward function is biased such that* $(w+x)/2 > z$ *for some* w, x *&* z.

The examples in this section show there is a certain tolerance for differences in rewards within which overgenerals are not strong enough to outcompete correct rules. Knowing what tolerance there is is important as it allows us to design single-step reward functions which will not produce strong overgenerals. Unfortunately, because of the simplifying assumptions we've made (see section 2.4) these results do not apply to more realistic problems. However, they do tell us how biases in the reward function affect the formation of strong overgenerals, and give us a sense of the magnitudes involved. An extension of this work would be to find limits to tolerable reward function bias empirically. Two results which do transfer to more realistic cases are theorems 1 and 5, which tell us under what conditions strong overgenerals are impossible for the two types of LCS. These results hold even when our simplifying assumptions do not.

7 THE SURVIVAL OF RULES UNDER THE GA

We've examined the conditions under which strong overgenerals are possible under both types of fitness. The whole notion of a strong overgeneral is that of an overgeneral rule which can outcompete other, preferable, rules. But, as noted earlier, there are two forms of competition between rules: action selection and reproduction. Our two systems handle the first in the same way, but handle reproduction differently. In this section we examine the effect of the fitness metric on the survival of strong overgenerals.

XCS and Goliath were compared empirically on the environment in table 5. For these tests the GA was disabled and all possible rules inserted into the LCS at the outset. The following settings were used: $\beta = 0.2$, $\varepsilon_o = 0.01$ (see section 2.3). The number of cycles shown on the x-axes of the following

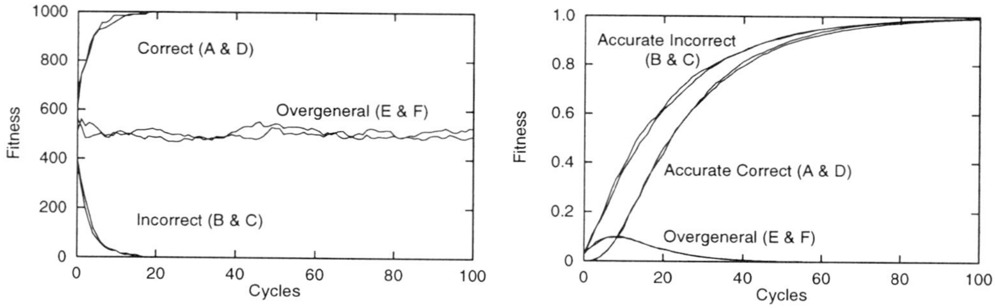

Figure 1 Rule Fitness using Strength-Based Goliath (Left) and Accuracy-Based XCS (Right) on the Unbiased Function from Table 5.

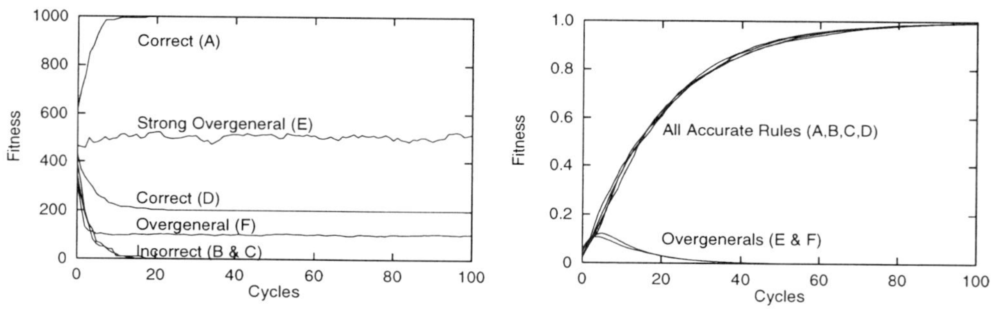

Figure 2 Goliath (Left) and XCS (Right) on the Biased Function from Table 6.

figures indicates the number of explore cycles using Wilson's pure explore/exploit scheme (Wilson, 1995), which is effectively the number of environmental inputs seen by the LCS.[7]

Figure 1 shows the fitness of each rule using strength (left) and accuracy (right), with results averaged over 100 runs. The first thing to note is that we are now considering the development of a rule's strength and fitness over time (admittedly with the GA turned off), whereas until this section we had only considered steady state strengths (as pointed out in section 2.4). We can see that the actual strengths indeed converge towards the expected strengths shown in table 5. We can also see that the strengths of the overgeneral rules (E & F) oscillate as they are updated towards different values.

Using strength (figure 1, left), the correct rules A & D have highest fitness, so if the GA was operating we'd expect Goliath to reproduce them preferentially and learn to act correctly in this environment.

Using accuracy (figure 1, right), all accurate rules (A, B, C & D) have high fitness, while the overgenerals (E & F) have low fitness. Note that even though the incorrect rules (B & C) have high fitness and will survive with the GA operational, they have low strength, so they will not have much influence in action selection. Consequently we can expect XCS to learn to act correctly in this environment.

---

[7] Wilson chooses explore and exploit cycles at random while we simply alternate between them.

While both systems seem to be able to handle the unbiased reward function, compare them on the same problem when the reward function is biased as in table 6. Consider the results shown in figure 2 (again, averaged over 100 runs). Although XCS (right) treats the rules in the same way now that the reward function is biased. Goliath (left) treats them differently. In particular, rule E, which is overgeneral, has higher expected strength than rule D, which is correct, and with which it competes for action selection. Consequently E is a strong overgeneral (and a fit overgeneral if E and D also compete for reproduction).

These trivial environments demonstrate that accuracy-based fitness is effective at penalising overgeneral, strong overgeneral, and fit overgeneral rules. This shouldn't be surprising: for accuracy, we've defined overgeneral rules precisely as those which are less than fully accurate. With fitness based on accuracy these are precisely the rules which fare poorly.

With Goliath's use of strength as fitness, strong overgenerals are fit overgenerals. But with XCS's accuracy-based fitness, strong overgenerals – at least those encountered so far – have low fitness and can be expected to fare poorly. It is unknown whether XCS can suffer from fit overgenerals, but it may be possible if we suitably bias the variance in the reward function.

8 DISCUSSION

We've analysed and extended the concept of overgeneral rules under different fitness schemes. We consider dealing with such rules a major issue for Michigan-style evolutionary rule-based systems in general, not just for the two classifier systems we have considered here. For example, the use of alternative representations (e.g. fuzzy classifiers), rule discovery systems (e.g. evolution strategies) or the addition of internal memory should not alter the fundamental types of rules which are possible. In all these cases, the system would still be confronted with the problems of greedy classifier creation, overgeneral, strong overgeneral, and fit overgeneral rules. Only by modifying the way in which rule fitness is calculated, or by restricting ourselves to benign reward functions, can we influence which types of rules are possible.

Although we haven't described it as such, this work has examined the fitness landscapes defined by the reward function and the fitness scheme used. We can try to avoid pathological fitness landscapes by choosing suitable fitness schemes, which is clearly essential if we are to give evolutionary search the best chance of success. This approach of altering the LCS to fit the problem seems more sensible than trying to alter the problem to fit the LCS by using only reward functions which strength LCS can handle.

8.1 EXTENSIONS AND QUANTITATIVE ANALYSIS

We could extend the approach taken in this work by removing some of the simplifying assumptions we made in section 2.4 and dealing with the resultant additional complexity. For example, we could put aside the assumption of equiprobable states and actions, and extend the inequalities showing the requirements of the reward function for the emergence of strong overgenerals to include the frequencies with which states and actions occur. Taken far enough such extensions might allow quantitative analysis of non-trivial problems. Unfortunately, while some extensions would be fairly simple, others would be rather more difficult.

At the same time, we feel the most significant results from this approach are qualitative, and some such results have already been obtained: we have refined the concept of overgenerality (section 3.2), argued that strength and accuracy-based LCS have different goals (section 3.2), and introduced the concept of fit overgenerals (section 3.4).

We've seen that, qualitatively, strong and fit overgenerals depend essentially on the reward function, and that they are very common. We've also seen that the newer accuracy-based fitness has, so far, dealt with them much better than Goliath's more traditional strength-based fitness (although we have not yet considered default hierarchies). This is in keeping with the analysis in section 3.2.1 which suggests that using strength as fitness results in a mismatch between the goals of the LCS and its GA.

Rather than pursue quantitative results we would prefer to extend this qualitative approach to consider the effects of default hierarchies and mechanisms to promote them, and the question of whether persistent strong and fit overgenerals can be produced under accuracy-based fitness. Also of interest are multi-step problems and hybrid strength/accuracy-based fitness schemes, as opposed to the purely strength-based fitness of Goliath and purely accuracy-based fitness of XCS.

Acknowledgements

Thank you to Manfred Kerber and the anonymous reviewers for comments, and to the organisers for their interest in classifier systems. This work was funded by the School of Computer Science at the University of Birmingham.

References

Dave Cliff and Susi Ross (1995). Adding Temporary Memory to ZCS. *Adaptive Behavior*, 3(2): 101–150.

David E. Goldberg (1989). *Genetic Algorithms in Search, Optimization, and Machine Learning*. Addison-Wesley.

Tim Kovacs (2000). Strength or Accuracy? Fitness Calculation in Learning Classifier Systems. In P. L. Lanzi, W. Stolzmann, and S. W. Wilson, editors, *Learning Classifier Systems: An Introduction to Contemporary Research*, pages 143–160. Springer–Verlag.

Tim Kovacs (2001). Forthcoming PhD Thesis, University of Birmingham.

Rick L. Riolo (1988). Empirical Studies of Default Hierarchies and Sequences of Rules in Learning Classifier Systems. PhD Thesis, University of Michigan.

Robert E. Smith (1991). Default Hierarchy Formation and Memory Exploitation in Learning Classifier Systems. PhD Thesis, University of Alabama.

Richard S. Sutton and Andrew G. Barto (1998). *Reinforcement Learning: An Introduction*. MIT Press.

Stewart W. Wilson (1994). ZCS: A Zeroth Level Classifier System. *Evolutionary Computation*, 2 (1):1–18.

Stewart W. Wilson (1995). Classifier Fitness Based on Accuracy. *Evolutionary Computation*, 3(2): 149–175.

Evolutionary Optimization Through PAC Learning

Forbes J. Burkowski
Department of Computer Science
University of Waterloo
Canada

Abstract

Strategies for evolutionary optimization (EO) typically experience a convergence phenomenon that involves a steady increase in the frequency of particular allelic combinations. When some allele is consistent throughout the population we essentially have a reduction in the dimension of the binary string space that is the objective function domain of feasible solutions. In this paper we consider dimension reduction to be the most salient feature of evolutionary optimization and present the theoretical setting for a novel algorithm that manages this reduction in a very controlled albeit stochastic manner. The "Rising Tide Algorithm" facilitates dimension reductions through the discovery of bit interdependencies that are expressible as ring-sum-expansions (linear combinations in GF2). When suitable constraints are placed on the objective function these interdependencies are generated by algorithms involving approximations to the discrete Fourier transform (or Walsh Transform). Based on analytic techniques that are now used by researchers in PAC learning, the Rising Tide Algorithm attempts to capitalize on the intrinsic binary nature of the fitness function deriving from it a representation that is highly amenable to a theoretical analysis. Our overall objective is to describe certain algorithms for evolutionary optimization as heuristic techniques that work within the analytically rich environment of PAC learning. We also contend that formulation of these algorithms and empirical demonstrations of their success should give EO practitioners new insights into the current traditional strategies.

1 Introduction

The publication of L. Valiant's "A Theory of the Learnable" (Valiant, 1984) established a solid foundation for computational learning theory because it provided a rigorous framework within which formal questions could be posed. Subsequently, computational learning has spread to other areas of research, for example, (Baum, 1991), and (Anthony, 1997) discuss the application of Valiant's PAC (Probably Approximately Correct) model to learnability using neural nets.

The focus of this paper will be to provide an extension of the PAC model that we consider beneficial for the study of Evolutionary Algorithms (EAs). Learning is not new to EAs, see (Belew, 1989) and (Sebag and Schoenauer, 1994). Other research has addressed related issues such as discovery of gene linkage in the representation (Harik, 1997) and adaptation of crossover operators (Smith and Fogarty, 1996) and (Davis, 1989). See (Kargupta and Goldberg, 1997) for another very interesting study. The work of (Ros, 1993) uses genetic algorithms to do PAC learning. In this paper we are essentially going in the opposite direction: using PAC learning to do evolutionary computation.

The benefits of placing evolutionary computation, and particularly genetic algorithms, in a more theoretical framework have been a recurrent research objective for more than a decade. Various researchers have striven to get more theoretical insights into representation of feasible solutions especially with regard to interdependencies among the bits in a feasible solution, hereafter referred to as a genome. While many papers have dealt with these concerns, the following references should give the reader a reasonable perspective on those issues that are relevant to this paper:

(Liepins and Vose, 1990) discusses various representational issues in genetic optimization. The paper elaborates the failure modes of a GA and eventually discusses the existence of an affine transformation that would convert a deceptive objective function to an easily optimizable objective function. Later work (Vose and Liepins, 1991) furthers their examination of schema analysis by examining how the crossover operator interacts with schemata. A notable result here: "Every function has a representation in which it is essentially the counting 1's problem". Explicit derivation of the representation is not discussed.

(Manela and Campbell, 1992) considers schema analysis from the broader viewpoint provided by abstract harmonic analysis. Their approach starts with group theoretic ideas and concepts elaborated by (Lechner, 1971) and ends with a discussion about epistasis and its relation to GA difficulty.

(Radcliffe, 1992) argues that for many problems conventional linear chromosomes and recombination operators are inadequate for effective genetic search. His critique of intrinsic parallelism is especially noteworthy.

(Heckendorn and Whitley, 1999) do extensive analysis of epistasis using the Walsh transform.

Another promising line of research considers optimization heuristics that learn in the sense of estimating probability distributions that guide further exploration of the search space. These EDA's (Estimation of Distribution Algorithms) have been studied in (Mühlenbein and Mahnig, 1999) and (Pelikan, Goldberg, and Lobo, 1999).

1.1 Overview

The outline of this paper is as follows: Section 2 gives a short motivational "sermon" on the guiding principles of our research and essentially extends some of the concerns discussed in the papers just cited. The remainder of the paper is best understood if the reader is familiar with certain results in PAC learning and so, trusting the patience of the reader, we quickly present in Section 3 some required PAC definitions and results. Section 4 presents our motivation for using the PAC model and Section 5 introduces the main theme of the paper: the link between PAC and EO. Sections 6 and 7 discuss some novel EO operators that rely on an approximation to the discrete Fourier transform while Section 8 presents some ideas on how these approximations can be calculated. Section 9 presents more EO technique, specifically dimension reduction and Section 10 summarizes the RTA, an evolutionary optimization algorithm that is the focal point of the paper. Some empirical results are reviewed in Section 11 while Section 12 considers some theory that indicates limitations of our algorithm. Some speculative ideas are also presented. Finally, Section 13 presents conclusions.

2 Motivation

As noted by (Vose, 1999), the "schema theorem" explains virtually nothing about SGA behaviour. With that issue put aside, we can go on to three other issues that may also need some "mathematical tightening" namely: positional bias and crossover, deception, and notions of locality. In attempting to adopt a more mathematically grounded stance, this paper will adhere to certain views and methodologies specified as follows:

2.1 Opinions and Methods

Positional Bias and Crossover

Evolutionary operators such as one-point crossover are inherently sensitive to bit order. For example, adjacent bits in a parent are very likely to end up as adjacent bits in a child genome. Consequently, navigation of the search space, while stochastic, will nonetheless manifest a predisposition for restricted movement through various hyper-planes of the domain, an unpredictable phenomenon that may provide unexpected advantages but may also hamper the success of an optimization algorithm. These are the effects of positional bias, a term described in (Eshelman, Caruana, and Schaffer, 1989). The usual description of a Genetic Algorithm is somewhat ill posed in the sense that there is no recommendation and no restriction on the bit order of a representation. With this "anything goes" acceptance in the setup of a problem, we might suspect that choice of bit representation involves more art than science. More significant from an analytic view point is that it is difficult to predict the extent to which the success of the GA is dependent on a given bit representation.

Methodology 1: Symmetry of bit processing The position taken in this paper is that an evolutionary operator should be "an equal opportunity bit processor". Although there may be practical advantages to moving adjacent bits from a parent to a child during crossover we do not depend on such adjacency unless it can be explicitly characterized by the definition of the objective function.

With this approach, uniform crossover is considered acceptable while single point crossover is avoided. Later, we introduce other operators that exhibit a lack of positional bias.

The main concern is to establish a "level playing field" when evaluating the ability of EO algorithms. If bit adjacency helps in a practical application then this is fine. If its effects cannot be adequately characterized in an empirical study that is comparing two competing algorithms, then it is best avoided.

Deception

Considering the many definitions of deception, the notion of deception is somewhat murky but is nonetheless promoted by a certain point of view that seems to accuse the wrong party, as if to say: "The algorithm is fine, it's just that the problem is deceptive". As noted by (Forrest and Mitchell, 1993) there is no generally accepted definition of the term "deception". They go on to state that: "strictly speaking, deception is a property of a particular representation of a problem rather than of the problem itself. In principle, a deceptive representation could be transformed into a non-deceptive one, but in practice it is usually an intractable problem to find the appropriate transformation."

Methodology 2: Reversible Transformations We adopt the approach that a given bit representation for a problem should be used primarily for evaluation of the objective function. More to the point, it may be best to apply evolutionary operators to various transformations of these bits. While recognizing the intractability of a computation designed to secure a transformation that would eliminate deception, it should also be recognized that many of the problems given to a GA are themselves intractable. Accordingly, one should at least be open to algorithms that may reduce the complexity of a problem if an easy opportunity to do so arises through the application of a reversible transformation.

Notions of Locality

In this paper we try to avoid any explicit use or mention of a *landscape structure* imposed by evolutionary operators. We regard the $\{0,1\}^n$ search space as the ultimate in symmetry: all possible binary strings in a finite n-dimensional space. As such, it lacks any intrinsic neighbourhood structure. Furthermore, we contend that it is beneficial to avoid an ad hoc neighbourhood structure *unless such a neighbourhood is defined by a metric that is somehow imposed by the objective function itself.* To express this more succinctly: Given an arbitrary function $F(x)$ defined on $\{0,1\}^n$ there is, from the perspective of mathematical analysis, absolutely no justification for a neighbourhood-defining distance measure in the domain of $F(x)$ unless one has extra knowledge about the structure of $F(x)$ leading to a proper definition of such a metric.

This is in contrast to the case when $F(x)$ is a *continuous* function mapping some subset of the real line to another subset of the real line. This is such a powerful and concise description of the organizational structure of a mapping between two infinite sets that we gladly accept the usual underlying Euclidean metric for the domain of $F(x)$. Now, although this indispensable metric facilitates a concise description of the continuous mapping, it also causes us to see the fluctuations in $F(x)$ as possibly going through various local optima, a characteristic of F that may later plague us during a search activity for a *global* optimum.

Perhaps due to this on-going familiarity with neighbourhood structures associated with continuous functions, many researchers still strive to describe a mapping from points in a $\{0,1\}^n$ search space to the real line as somehow holding local and global distinctions. This is typically done by visualizing a "landscape" over a search domain that is given a neighbourhood structure consistent with the evolutionary operators. For example, neighbourhood distance may be defined using a Hamming metric or by essentially counting the number of applications of an operator in going from point x to point y in the search domain. But the crucial question then arises: Why should we carry over to functions defined on the finite domain $\{0,1\}^n$ *any* notion of a metric and its imposed, possibly restrictive, neighborhood structure unless that structure is provably beneficial?

Methodology 3: Recognition of Structure Progress of an iterative search algorithm will require the ability to define subsets in the search space. As described below, we do this by using algorithms that strive to learn certain structural properties of the objective function. Moreover, these algorithms are *not* influenced by any preordained notion of an intrinsic metric that is independent of the objective function.

An approach that is consistent with Methodology 3 would be to deploy the usual population of bit strings each with a calculated fitness value obtained via the objective function. The population is then sorted and evolutionary operators are invoked to generate new offspring by essentially *recognizing patterns* in the bit strings that correspond to high fitness individuals, contrasting these with the bit patterns that are associated with low fitness individuals. If this approach is successful then multi-modality essentially disappears but of course one does have to contend with a possibly very difficult pattern recognition problem.

It should be stated that these methodologies are not proposed to boost the speed of computation but rather to provide a kind of "base line" set of mathematical assumptions that are not dependent on ill-defined but fortuitous advantages of bit adjacency and its relationship to a crossover operator.

3 PAC Learning Preliminaries

Our main objective is to develop algorithms that do evolutionary optimization of an objective function $F(x)$ by learning certain properties of various Boolean functions that are derived from $F(x)$. The formulation of these learning strategies is derived from PAC learning principles. The reader may consult (Kearns and Vazirani, 1994) or (Mitchell, 1997) for excellent introductions to PAC learning theory. Discussing evolutionary optimization in the setting of PAC learning will require a merging of terminology used in two somewhat separate research cultures. Terms and definitions from both research communities have been borrowed and modified to suit the anticipated needs of our research (with apologies to readers from both communities).

Our learning strategy assumes that we are in possession of a learning algorithm that has access to a Boolean function $f(x)$ mapping $X=\{0,1\}^n$ to $\{-1,+1\}$. The algorithm can evaluate $f(x)$ for any value $x \in X$ but it has no additional knowledge about the structure of this function. After performing a certain number of function evaluations the algorithm will output an hypothesis function $h(x)$ that acts as an ϵ-approximation of $f(x)$.

Definition: ϵ-approximation
Given a pre-specified accuracy value ϵ in the open interval $(0,1)$, and a probability distribution $D(x)$ defined over X, we will say that $h(x)$ is an ϵ-approximation for $f(x)$ if

$f(x)$ and $h(x)$ seldom differ when x is sampled from X using the distribution D. That is:

$$\Pr_D [h(x) = f(x)] \geq 1 - \epsilon. \tag{1}$$

Definition: PAC learnable
We say that a class $\mathcal{F}$ of representations of functions (for example, the class DNF) is PAC learnable if there is an algorithm $\mathcal{A}$ such that for any ϵ, δ in the interval $(0, 1)$, and any f in $\mathcal{F}$ we will be guaranteed that with a probability at least $1 - \delta$, algorithm $\mathcal{A}$ (f, ϵ, δ) produces an ϵ-approximation $h(x)$ for $f(x)$. Furthermore, this computation must produce $h(x)$ in time polynomial in $n, 1/\epsilon, 1/\delta$, and s the size of f. For a DNF function f, size s would be the number of disjunctive terms in f.

Theory in PAC learning is very precise about the mechanisms that may be used to obtain information about the function being learned.

Definition: Example Oracle
An example oracle for f with respect to D is a source that on request draws an instance x at random according to the probability distribution D and returns the example <x, $f(x)$>.

Definition: Membership Oracle
A membership oracle for f is an oracle that simply provides the value $f(x)$ when given the input value x.

The Discrete Fourier Transform
The multidimensional discrete Fourier transform (or Walsh transform) is a very useful tool in learning theory. Given any $x \in X$, with x represented using the column vector: $(x_1, x_2, ..., x_n)$, and a function $f : X \rightarrow R$, we define the Fourier transform of f as:

$$\widehat{f}(u) = \frac{1}{2^n} \sum_{x \in X} f(x) \, t_u(x). \tag{2}$$

where the parity functions $t_u : X \rightarrow \{-1, +1\}$ are defined for $u \in X$ as:

$$t_u(x) = (-1)^{u^T x} \qquad \text{where} \qquad u^T x = \sum_{i=1}^{n} u_i x_i. \tag{3}$$

So, $t_u(x)$ has value -1 if the number of indices i at which $u_i = x_i = 1$ is odd, and 1 otherwise.

The set $\{t_u(x)\}_{x \in X}$ is an orthonormal basis for the vector space of real-valued functions on X. We can recover f from its transform by using:

$$f(x) = \sum_{u \in X} \widehat{f}(u) \, t_u(x). \tag{4}$$

This unique expansion of $f(x)$ in terms of the parity basis $t_u(x)$ is its Fourier series and the sequence of Fourier coefficients is called the spectrum of $f(x)$.

Definition: Large Fourier Coefficient Property
Consider Z a subset of X. For a given $f(x)$ and $\theta > 0$, we will say that Z has the large Fourier coefficient property (Jackson, 1995, pg. 47) if:

1. For all v such that $\left|\widehat{f}(v)\right| \geq \theta$, we have $v \in Z$ and
2. for all $v \in Z$, we have $\left|\widehat{f}(v)\right| \geq \frac{\theta}{\sqrt{2}}$.

Now the Fourier transform $\widehat{f}(u)$ is a sum across all $x \in X$. This involves an amount of computation that is exponential in n. To be of practical use we need a lemma from (Jackson, 1995) that is an extension of earlier work done in (Kushilevitz and Mansour, 1993).

Lemma 1:
There is an algorithm KM such that, for any function $f : X \rightarrow R$, threshold $\theta > 0$, and confidence δ with $0 < \delta < 1$, KM returns, with probability at least $1 - \delta$, a set with the large Fourier coefficient property. KM uses membership queries and runs in time polynomial in $n, 1/\theta, log(1/\delta)$ and $\max_{x \in X} |f(x)|$.

The large Fourier coefficient property provides a vital step in the practical use of the discrete Fourier transform. We can take a given function f and approximate it with a function $f_Z(x)$ defined as:

$$f_Z(x) = \sum_{v \in Z} \widehat{f}(v)\, t_v(x). \tag{5}$$

with a set size $|Z|$ that is not exponential in size.

Using the results of Lemma 1 Jackson proved that there is an algorithm that finds an ϵ–approximation to a DNF function with $\epsilon = \frac{1}{2} - \frac{1}{poly(n,s)}$. Since ϵ is close to 1/2 instead of close to 1, it is necessary to employ a boosting algorithm (Freund, 1990) so as to increase the accuracy of the ϵ-approximator.

Jackson's algorithm, called the Harmonic Sieve, expresses the ϵ–approximation $h(x)$ as a threshold of parity (TOP) function. In general, a TOP representation of a multi-dimensional Boolean function f is a majority vote over a collection of (possibly negated) parity functions, where each parity function is a ring-sum-expansion (RSE) over some subset of f's input bits. We will assume RSE's reflect operations in GF2 and are Boolean functions over the base $\{\wedge, \oplus, 1\}$ restricted to monomials (for example, $x_1 \oplus x_5 \oplus x_{31}$) (Fischer and Simon, 1992). The main idea behind Jackson's Harmonic Sieve is that the RSE's required by the $h(x)$ TOP function are derived by calculating locations of the large Fourier coefficients. The algorithm ensures that the accurate determination of these locations has a probability of success that is above a prespecified threshold of $1 - \mathcal{E}$. The algorithm uses a recursive strategy that determines a sequence of successive partitions of the domain space of the Fourier coefficients. When a partition is defined, the algorithm applies Parseval's Theorem in conjunction with Hoeffding's inequality to determine whether or not it is highly likely that a subpartition contains a large Fourier coefficient. If so, the algorithm will recursively continue the partitioning of this subpartition. The important result in Jackson's thesis is that finding these large coefficients can be done in polynomial time with a sample size (for our purposes, population size) that is also polynomial in n, s, and $1/\epsilon$. Unfortunately, the degrees of the polynomials are rather high for practical purposes. However, recent work by (Bshouty, Jackson, and Tamon, 1999) gives a more efficient algorithm, thus showing that Jackson's Harmonic

Sieve can find the large Fourier coefficients in time $O(ns^4/\epsilon^4)$ working with a sample size of $O(ns^2/\epsilon^4)$.

Before going any further, we introduce some additional terminology. Each $u \in X$ is a bit sequence that we will refer to as a parity string. Corresponding to each parity string we have a parity function $t_u(x)$. Note that for Boolean f we have $\widehat{f}(u) = E[f \cdot t_u]$ where E denotes the expectation operator and so the expression represents the correlation of f and t_u with respect to the uniform distribution. We will then regard $\widehat{f}(u)$ as representing the *correlation* of the parity string u.

4 Why We Should Work in a PAC Setting

Our motivation for adopting a PAC learning paradigm as a setting for evolutionary optimization involves the following perceived benefits:

1. **A Necessary Compromise**
   A PAC setting *deliberately* weakens the objectives of a learning activity:
   i) In a certain sense the final answer may be approximate, and
   ii) the algorithm itself has only a certain (hopefully high) probability of finding this answer.
   Although life in a PAC setting seems to be very uncertain, there is an advantage to be obtained by this compromise. We benefit through the opportunity to derive an analysis that specifies, in probabilistic terms, algorithmic results that can be achieved in polynomial time using a population size that also has polynomial bounds.
2. **Learning the Structure of the Objective Function**
   Most evolutionary algorithms simply evaluate the objective function $F(x)$ at various points in the search space and then subject these values to further operations that serve to distinguish high fitness genomes from low fitness genomes, for example, by building a roulette wheel for parent selection. The central idea of our research is that by applying a learning algorithm to the binary function $f(x) = \text{sgn}(F(x))$ we will derive certain information that is useful in an evolutionary optimization of $F(x)$. In particular, the derivation of a RSE can point the way to transformations of the domain space that hopefully allow dimension reduction with little or no loss of genomes having high fitness.
3. **In Praise of Symmetry**
   The tools now present in the PAC learning community hold the promise of defining evolutionary operators that are free of bit position bias since learning algorithms typically work with values of Boolean variables and there is no reliance on bit string formats.
4. **Algorithmic Analysis Related to Complexity**
   Learning theory has an excellent mathematical foundation that is strongly related to computational complexity. Many of the theorems work within some hypothetical setting that is characterized by making assumptions about the complexity of a function class, for example, the maximum depth and width of a circuit that would implement a function in the class under discussion.

5 PAC Learning Applied to Evolutionary Optimization

The main goal of this paper is to demonstrate that there is a beneficial interplay between Evolutionary Optimization and PAC learning. We hope to use PAC learning as a basis for analytical studies and also as a toolkit that would supply practical techniques for the design of algorithms. The key idea is that a learning exercise applied to the objective function provides an EO algorithm with valuable information that can be used in the search for a global optimum.

There is an obvious connection between an example oracle used in PAC learning and the population of genomes used in genetic algorithms. However, in using PAC learning, it may be necessary to maintain a population in ways that are different from the techniques used in "traditional" EO. In our approach to optimization we will need values of the objective function that provide examples of both high fitness and low fitness, or expressed in terms of an *adjusted* objective function, we will need to maintain two subpopulations, one for positive fitness genomes and another for negative fitness genomes. Learning techniques would then aid an optimization algorithm that attempts to generate ever-higher fitness values while avoiding low (negative) fitness.

The adjustment of the fitness function $F(x)$, shifted so that $E\left[F \cdot t_{\overline{0}}\right] = E\left[F\right] = 0$, is done to provide a sign function $f(x)$ that is reasonably balanced in its distribution of positive and negative values. This does not change the location of the global optimum and it increases the correlation between the signum function $f(x)$ and the parity functions $t_u(x)$ which are also balanced in this way. The deliberate strategy to provide both positive and negative examples of the objective function is motivated by the idea that these examples are needed since dimension reduction should attempt to isolate high fitness and at the same time avoid low (i.e. negative) fitness. This approach is also consistent with (Fischer and Simon, 1992) which reports that learning RSE's can be done, with reasonable restrictions on $f(x)$, but one must use both positive and negative examples to guide the learning process.

We next present an informal description of such an optimization algorithm.

5.1 The Rising Tide Algorithm

To appreciate the main strategy of our algorithm in action the reader may visualize the following scenario: In place of hill-climbing imagery, with its explicit or implicit notions of locality, we adopt the mindset of using an algorithm that is analogous to a rising tide. The reader may imagine a flood plane with various rocky outcroppings. As the tide water floods in, the various outcroppings, each in turn, become submerged and, most important for our discussion, the last one to disappear is the highest outcropping.

Before continuing, it is important not to be led astray by the pleasant continuity of this simple scene, which is only used to provide an initial visual aid. In particular it is to be stressed that the justification of the algorithm involves no *a priori* notion of locality in the search space. In fact, any specification of selected points in the domain $\{0,1\}^n$ is done using a set theoretic approach that will define a sub-domain through the use of constraints that are expressed in terms of ring-sum-expansions, these in turn being derived from computations done on $F(x)$.

From an algorithmic perspective, our task is to provide some type of computational test that will serve to separate the sub-domain that supports positive fitness values from the sub-domain that support negative fitness values. In a dimension reduction step, we then alter the objective function by restricting it to the sub-domain with higher fitness values. An obvious strategy is to then repeat the process to find a sequence of nested sub-domains each supporting progressively higher fitness genomes while avoiding an increasing number of lower fitness genomes.

In summary, the intention of the Rising Tide Algorithm (RTA) is to isolate successive subsets of the search space that are *most likely* to contain the global maximum by essentially recognizing patterns in the domain made evident through a judicious use of an approximation to the discrete Fourier transform. Of particular note: If a sub-domain that supports positive values can be approximately specified by using a TOP function, then the RSE's of that function can be used to apply a linear transform to the input variables of $F(x)$. The goal of the transformation would be to give a dimension reduction that is designed to close off the portion of the space that, with high probability, supports negative values of the fitness function. With this dimension reduction we have essentially "raised the tide". We have derived a new fitness function with a domain that represents a "hyper-slice" through the domain of the previous objective function. The new fitness function is related to the given objective function in that both have the same global optimum unless, with hopefully very low probability, we have been unfortunate enough to close off a subset of the domain that actually contains the global maximum. If the function is not unduly complex, repeated application of the technique would lead to a sub-domain that is small enough for an exhaustive search.

5.2 The RTA in a PAC Setting

In what follows we will consider the objective function $F(x)$ to be a product of its signum function $f(x)$ and its absolute value:

$$F(x) = f(x) \cdot |F(x)| . \tag{6}$$

This is done to underscore two important connections with learning theory. The signum function $f(x)$ is a binary function that will be subjected to our learning algorithm and when properly normalized, the function $|F(x)|$ essentially provides the probability distribution $D(x)$ defined in section 3. More precisely:

$$D(x) = \frac{|F(x)|}{\sum_{x \in X} |F(x)|}. \tag{7}$$

Apart from the obvious connection with the familiar roulette wheel construction used in genetic algorithms we see the employment of $D(x)$ as a natural mechanism for an algorithm that seeks to characterize $f(x)$ with the goal of aiding an optimization activity.

It is reasonable to assume that we would want the learning of $f(x)$ to be most accurately achieved for genomes x having extreme fitness values. This directly corresponds to the larger values of the distribution $D(x)$. So, when learning $f(x)$ via an approximation to the discrete Fourier transform of $F(x)$, it will be as if the population has high replication for the genomes with extreme values of fitness.

More to the point, the definition of ϵ−approximation (1) works with $f(x)$ in a way that is consistent with our goals. The heuristic strategy here is that we do *not* want an ϵ−approximation of $f(x)$ that is uniform across all x in the search space. The intermediate "close to zero" values of $F(x)$ should be essentially neglected in that they contribute little to the stated containment-avoidance objectives of the algorithm and only add to the perceived complexity of the function $f(x)$.

5.3 Learnability Issues

We start with the reaffirmation that the learning of $f(x)$ is important because $f(x)$ is a two valued function that partitions the X domain into two subspaces corresponding to positive and negative values of $F(x)$. The heuristic behind RTA is to attempt a characterization of *both* of these subspaces so that we can try to contain the extreme positive $F(x)$ values while avoiding the extreme negative $F(x)$ values. Of even more importance is the attempt to characterize $F(x)$ through the succession of different $f(x)$ functions that appear as the algorithm progresses, (more picturesquely: as the tide rises).

The re-mapping of f values from the set $\{-1,+1\}$ to $\{1,0\}$, done by replacing f with $(1-f)/2$, allows us to see the sign function as a regular binary function. In some cases the learnability of $f(x)$, at least in a theoretical sense, can be guaranteed if $f(x)$ belongs to a class that is known to be learnable. Research in learning theory gives several descriptions of such classes. Three examples may be cited:

1-RSE*
: If $f(x)$ is equivalent to a ring-sum-expansion such that each monomial contains at most one variable but does not contain the monomial 1, then $f(x)$ is learnable (Fischer and Simon, 1992).

DNF
: If $f(x)$ is equivalent to a disjunctive normal form then $f(x)$ is PAC learnable assuming the distribution D(x) is uniform (Jackson, 1995) and (Bshouty, Jackson, and Tamon, 1999).

AC^0 Circuits
: An AC^0 circuit consists of AND and OR gates, with inputs $x_1, x_2, ..., x_n$ and $\overline{x}_1, \overline{x}_2, ..., \overline{x}_n$. Fanin to the gates is unbounded and the number of gates is bounded by a polynomial in n. Depth is bounded by a constant. Learnability of AC^0 circuits is discussed in (Linial, Mansour, and Nisan, 1993).

As noted in (Jackson, 1995), the learnability of DNF is not guaranteed by currently known theory if $D(x)$ is arbitrary. Jackson's thesis does investigate learnability, getting positive results, when $D(x)$ is a product distribution. For our purposes, we adopt the positive attitude that when there is no clear guarantee of learnability, we at least have some notion about the characterization of an objective function that may cause trouble for our optimization algorithm.

6 Transformation of a Representation

Before presenting the main features of our algorithm we discuss a strategy that allows us to change the representation of a genome by essentially performing an n-dimensional rotation of its representation. The main idea here is that a suitable rotation may allow us to "dump" the low fitness genomes into a hyper-plane that is subsequently sealed off from further investigation. A compelling visualization of this strategy would be to think of the puzzle known as Rubik's cube[1]. By using various rotation operations we can separate or combine corners of the cube in myriad ways placing any four of them in either the same face or in different faces of the cube. Considering the possibilities in 3-space, the transformations in n-space tend to boggle the mind but we need this operational complexity if a rotation is to accomplish the genome separation described earlier.

Transformation of a representation is initiated by collecting a set Z of the parity strings corresponding to the large Fourier coefficients. We then extract from Z a set W of linearly independent w that are at most n in number. These will be used as the rows of a rotation matrix A. If the number of these w is less than n, then we can fill out remaining rows by setting $a_{ii} = 1$ and $a_{ij} = 0$ for off-diagonal elements. The motivation for generating A in this way rests on the following simple observation:

Starting with $f(x) = \sum_{u \in X} \widehat{f}(u)\, t_u(x)$ we replace x with $A^{-1}y$ to get:

$$f(x) = f\left(A^{-1}y\right) = g(y) = \sum_{u \in X} (-1)^{u^T A^{-1} y} \widehat{f}(u) = \sum_{u \in X} (-1)^{\left[\left(A^T\right)^{-1} u\right]^T y} \widehat{f}(u). \qquad (8)$$

Now, since A^T is nonsingular it possesses a nonsingular inverse, or more noteworthy, it provides a bijective mapping of X onto X. Since u in the last summation will go through all possible n bit strings in X we can replace u with $A^T u$ and the equation is still valid. Consequently:

$$g(y) = \sum_{u \in X} (-1)^{u^T y} \widehat{f}\left(A^T u\right) = \sum_{e \in E} (-1)^{e^T y} \widehat{f}\left(A^T e\right) + \sum_{\substack{u \in X \\ u \notin E}} (-1)^{u^T y} \widehat{f}\left(A^T u\right). \qquad (9)$$

where E is the collection of all n bit strings that have all entries 0 with a single 1 bit. Note that when a particular e vector is multiplied by A^T we simply get one of the w in the set W and so $\widehat{f}\left(A^T e\right)$ is a large Fourier coefficient. Consequently, *if* there are only a few large Fourier coefficients[2], we might expect the first sum in the last equation to have a significant influence on the value of the objective function. When this is the case, a y value producing a highly fit value for $g(y)$ might be easily determined. In fact, the signs of the large Fourier coefficients essentially spell out the y bit string that will maximize the first sum. We will refer to this particular bit string as the *signature* of A. For example, if *all* the large Fourier coefficients in this sum are negative then the value of y will be all 1's and we have the "ones counting" situation similar to that described in (Vose and Liepins, 1991).

---

[1] Rubik's Cube^{TM} is a trademark of Seven Towns Limited.

[2] Can we usually assume that there are few large Fourier coefficients? Surprisingly, the answer is often in the affirmative. In an important paper by (Linial, Mansour and Nisan, 1993) it is shown that for an AC^0 Boolean function, almost all of its "power spectrum" (the sum of the squares of the Fourier coefficients) resides in the low-order coefficients and this gives us an algorithm that can learn such functions in time of order $n^{poly \log(n)}$. While this may be disappointing for practical purposes it does show that exponential time is not needed to accomplish learning of certain functions.

So, our main strategy is to generate a non-singular matrix A that will map the typical genome x to a different representation $y = Ax$. The objective function $F(x)$ then becomes $F(A^{-1}y) = g(y)$ and we hope to isolate the positive values of $g(y)$ by a judicious setting of bits in the y string.

Note that matrix transforms have been discussed earlier by (Battle and Vose, 1991) who consider the notion of an invertible matrix to transform a genome x into a genome y that resides in a population considered to be isomorphic to the population holding genome x. They also note that converting a standard binary encoding of a genome to a Gray encoding is a special case of such a transformation.

Our techniques may be seen as attempts to derive an explicit form for a matrix transformation that is used with the goal of reducing simple epistasis describable as a ring-sum dependency among the bits of a genome. To nullify any *a priori* advantage or disadvantage that may be present due to the format of the initial representation, knowledge used to construct matrix A is derived only through evaluations of the fitness function $F(x)$. By using $F(x)$ as a "black box" we are not allowed to prescribe a Gray encoding, for example, on the hunch that it will aid our optimization activity. Instead, we let the algorithm derive the new encoding which, of course, may or may not be a Gray encoding. With these "rules of engagement" we forego any attempt to characterize those fitness functions that would benefit from the use of a Gray encoding. Instead, we seek to develop algorithms that lead to a theoretical analysis of the more general transformation, for example, the characterization of a fitness function that would provide the derivation of a matrix A that serves to reduce epistasis.

Recalling "Methodology 2" in Section 2.1, we emphasize some important aspects of our approach: The given genome representation is considered to be only useful for fitness evaluation. Evolutionary operators leading to dimension reduction are usually applied to a transformation of the genome not the genome itself. Although we start with a genome that is the given linear bit string, our initial operations on that string will be symmetric with respect to all bits. Any future asymmetry in bit processing will arise in due course as a natural consequence of the algorithm interacting with $F(x)$. To enforce this approach, operators with positional-bias, such as single point crossover, will be avoided. For similar reasons, we avoid any analysis that deals with bit-order related concepts such as "length of schemata".

7 Evolutionary Operators

Equation (9) becomes the starting point for many heuristics dealing with the construction of an evolutionary operator. First some observations and terminology are needed. We will say that a parity string with a large Fourier coefficient (large in absolute value) has a *high correlation*. This correlation may be very positive or very negative, but in either case, it helps us characterize $f(x)$. Considering equation (9), we will refer to the sum $\sum (-1)^{e^T y} \widehat{f}\left(A^T e\right)$ as the unit vector sum and the last sum $\sum (-1)^{u^T y} \widehat{f}\left(A^T u\right)$ will be the high order sum. As noted in the previous section, for a given non-singular matrix A there is an easily derived particular binary vector y, called the signature of A, that will maximize the unit vector sum.

Before going further, we should note that if A is the identity matrix, then x is not rotated (i.e. $y = x$), and more importantly, we then see the first sum in equation (9) as holding Fourier coefficients corresponding to simple unit vectors in the given non-rotated space. So, if we retain the original given representation, mutational changes made to a genome by any genetic algorithm essentially involves working with first sum terms that do not necessarily correspond to the large Fourier coefficients. In this light, we see a properly constructed rotational transformation as hopefully providing an edge, namely the ability to directly manipulate terms that are more influential in the first sum of equation (9). Of course, we should note that this heuristic may be overly optimistic in that maximization of the first sum will have "down-stream" effects on the second sum of equation (9). For example, it is easy to imagine that the signature vector, while maximizing the unit vector sum may cause the high order sum to overwhelm this gain with a large negative value. This is especially likely when the power spectrum corresponding to the Fourier transform is more uniform and not concentrated on a small number of large Fourier coefficients. Our approach is to accept this possible limitation and proceed with the heuristic motivation that the first sum is easily maximized and so represents a good starting point for further exploration of the search space, an exploration that may involve further rotations as deemed necessary as the population evolves.

Keeping these motivational ideas in mind, we seek to design an effective evolutionary operator that depends on the use of a rotation matrix A. We have experimented with several heuristics but will discuss only two of them:

Genome creation from a signature
For this heuristic, we generate A by selecting high correlation parity strings using a roulette strategy. We then form the signature y and compute a new positive fitness genome as $A^{-1}y$. In a similar fashion, the complement of y can be used to generate a new negative fitness genome as $A^{-1}\overline{y}$.

Uniform crossover in the rotated space
We start with a matrix A that is created using a greedy approach, selecting the first n high correlation parity strings that will form a singular matrix. We use roulette to select a high fitness parent genome and rotate it so that we calculate its corresponding representation as a y vector. We are essentially investigating how this high fitness genome has tackled the problem of attempting to maximize the unit vector sum while tolerating the downstream effects of the high order sum. The same rotation is performed on another parent and a child is generated using uniform crossover. Naturally, the child is brought back into the original space using the inverse rotation supplied by A^{-1}. Once this is done, we evaluate fitness and do the subtraction to get its adjusted fitness. A similar procedure involving negative fitness parents is done to get negative children.

Figure 1 presents these strategies in diagram form. Note that genome creation from a signature does not use the matrix A directly, but rather its inverse.

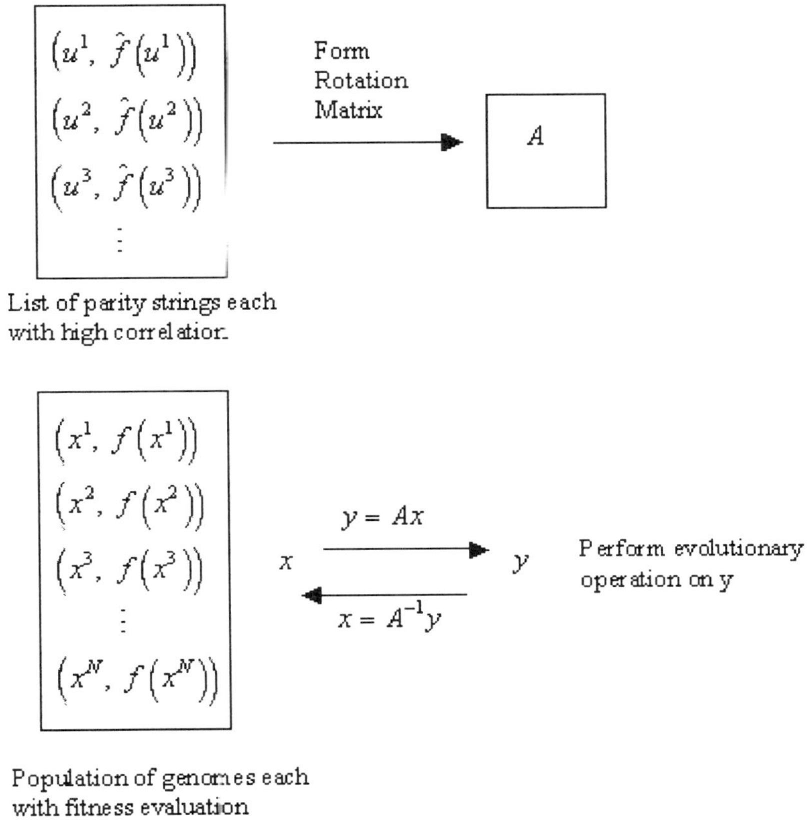

Figure 1 Using the High Correlation Parity Strings

8 Finding High Correlation Parity Strings

An implementation that derives the large Fourier coefficients using Jackson's algorithm involves very extensive calculations and so we have adopted other strategies that attempt to find high correlation parity strings. The main idea here is that the beautiful symmetry of the equations defining the transform and its inverse, leads to the compelling notion that if we can evolve genomes using a parity string population then the same evolutionary operators should allow us to generate parity strings using a genome population.

In going along with this strategy, we have done various experiments that work with *two* coevolving populations, one for the genomes, and another for the parity strings. The key observation is that the parity strings also have a type of "fitness" namely the estimation of the correlation value, or Fourier coefficient, associated with the string.

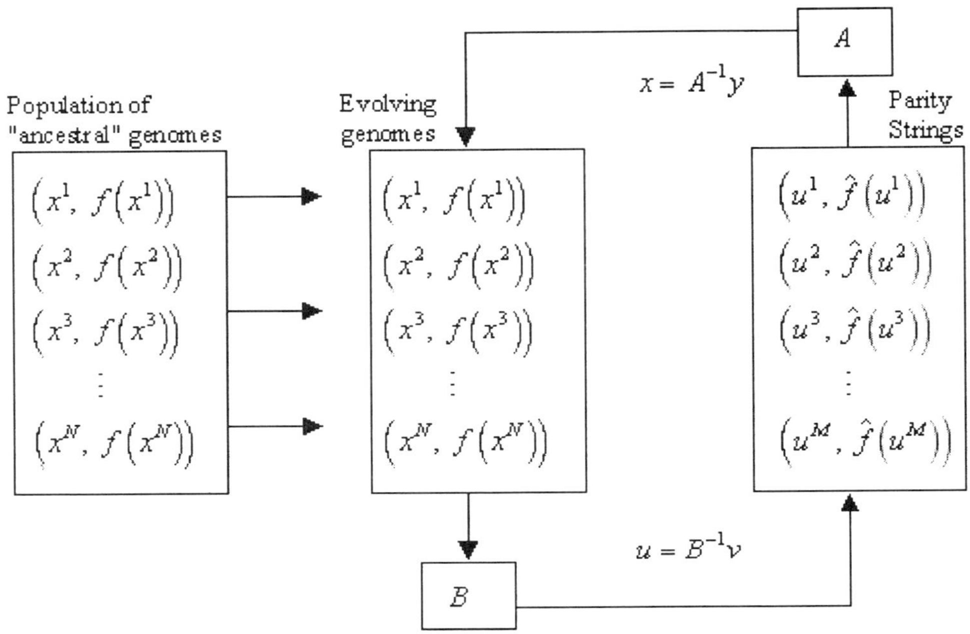

Figure 2 Generation of Parity Strings

Our initial experiments attempted to implement this in a straightforward manner: the parity string population provided a rotation matrix A used to evolve members of the genome population while the genome population provided a rotation matrix B used to evolve members of the parity string population. Results were disappointing because there is a trap involved in this line of thinking. The estimation of a correlation value is based on a *uniform* distribution of strings in the genome population. If the two populations are allowed to undergo a concurrent evolution then the genome population becomes skewed with genomes of extreme fitness and eventually the estimation of correlation becomes more and more in error. To remedy this situation we use instead a strategy described by Figure 2. We start with a randomly initialized genome population referred to as the "ancestral" population. It is used for calculations of correlation estimation and will remain fixed until there is a dimension reduction. The population of evolving genomes is randomly initialized and concurrent evolution proceeds just as described except that all correlation calculations work with the ancestral population. Going back to our definitions in the PAC introduction, the ancestral population essentially makes use of an example oracle while the evolving population continually makes use of a membership oracle. This is illustrated in Figure 2.

A reasonable question is whether we can evaluate the correlation of a parity string using a genome population of reasonable size or will we definitely require an exponential number of genomes to do this properly? To answer this we appeal to a lemma by (Hoeffding, 1963):

Lemma 2:
Let $X_1, X_2, ..., X_m$ be independent random variables all with mean μ such that for all i, $a \leq X_i \leq b$. Then for any $\lambda > 0$,

$$\Pr\left[\left|\mu - \frac{1}{m}\sum_{i=1}^{m} X_i\right| \geq \lambda\right] \leq 2e^{-2\lambda^2 m/(b-a)^2}. \tag{10}$$

To apply this we reason as follows: Suppose we have guessed that v is a high correlation parity string with correlation $\widehat{f}(v)$ and we wish to verify this guess. We would draw a sample X, in our case a population X of $x \in \{0,1\}^n$ uniformly at random and compute $\frac{1}{|X|}\sum_{x\in X} F(x)t_v(x)$ where $|X|$ represents the size of the genome population. For this discussion the values of a and b delimit the interval containing the range of values for the function $F(x)$. In Hoeffding's inequality μ represents the true value of the correlation and the sum is our estimate. Following (Jackson, 1995) we can make this probability arbitrarily small, say less than δ by ensuring that m is large enough. It is easily demonstrated that the absolute value of the difference will only exceed the tolerance value λ with some low probability δ if we insist that:

$$m \geq \frac{(b-a)^2 \ln\left(\frac{2}{\delta}\right)}{2\lambda^2} \tag{11}$$

This gives us a theoretical guarantee that the population has a size that is at most quadratic in the given parameter values.

9 Dimension Reduction

As described in Section 7, application of the evolutionary operators is done with the hope that the evolving populations will produce ever more extreme values. The populations evolve and eventually we obtain the high fitness genomes that we desire. An additional strategy is to recognize exceptionally high correlation parity strings and use them to provide a rotation of the space followed by a "freezing" of a particular bit in the y representation that essentially closes off half of the search space. This will essentially reduce the complexity of the problem and will present us with a new fitness function working on $n-1$ bits instead of n bits. Within this new space we carry on as we did prior to the reduction, doing rotations, fostering mutual evolution, and waiting for the opportunity to do the next dimension reduction. In our implementation of this scheme, the rotation transformation is followed by a permutation transformation that puts the frozen bit into the last bit position of the new representation. While this amounts to some extra computation it certainly makes it easier to follow the progress of the algorithm.

Whenever a rotation and permutation are done we also compute the inverse of this matrix product R to maintain a recovery matrix R^{-1} that can bring us back to the original representation so that the fitness of the genome can be evaluated. Figure 3 illustrates the data flow involved.

10 The Rising Tide Algorithm

We now summarize the content of the previous sections by describing the sequence of steps in a generic description of the Rising Tide Algorithm.

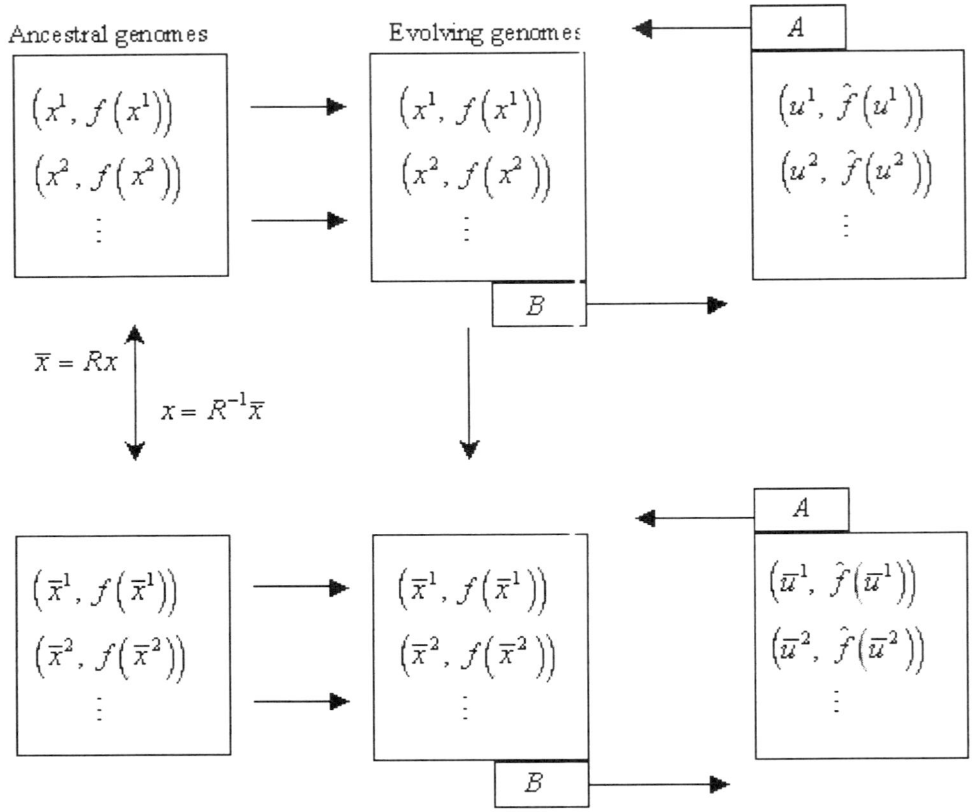

Figure 3 Dimension Reduction

The Rising Tide Algorithm:

1. Randomly generate two populations of binary strings each a member of $\{0, 1\}^n$.
2. Use the objective function to evaluate the fitness of each string in the genome population.
3. Adjust each fitness value by subtracting from it the average fitness of all members in the population. These adjusted values define the fitness function $F(x)$ and we further assume that $f(x) = \text{sgn}(F(x))$.
4. Using the genome population as a sample space, calculate an approximation to the correlation value for each parity string in the parity population.
5. Designate the genome population as the ancestral population and duplicate it to form the evolving genome population.

6. Perform evolutionary computations on the parity population. These are facilitated through the construction of a matrix B that is built from a linearly independent set of extreme fitness genome extracted from the evolving genome population. Computation of correlation for a new child parity string is done by working with the ancestral population.
7. Perform evolutionary computations on the genome population. These are facilitated through the construction of a matrix A that is built from a linearly independent set of extreme correlation parity strings extracted from the evolving parity string population.
8. Repeat steps 6 and 7 until a parity string has a correlation that exceeds some pre-specified threshold value.
9. Use the high correlation parity string to perform a rotation of the ancestral genome population followed by a bit freeze that will constrain the population to that half of the search space containing the highest fitness genomes. We then generate new genomes to replace those that do not meet the constraints specified by the frozen bits.
10. Repetition of steps 6, 7, 8, and 9 is done until either the evolving genome population converges with no further dimension reduction, or the dimension reduction is carried on to the extent that most of the bits freeze to particular values leaving a few unfrozen bits that may be processed using a straightforward exhaustive search.

11 Empirical Results

Experimental results are still being collected for a variety of problems. At the present time, results are mixed and, it would seem, heavily dependent on the ability of the RTA to generate parity strings with a high level of consistency. Here we consider consistency as the ability to meet the requirements of step (9): providing a separating plane that distinguishes as much as possible, the two subpopulations of high and low fitness. In simple cases such as the DeJong Test Function #1, optimizing $F(x, y, z) = x^2 + y^2 + z^2$ over the domain $-5.12 < x, y, z < 5.12$ with x, y, and z represented by 10 bit values, we get very compelling results. Of particular note is the manner in which the global optimum is attained. In Table 1 we present a snapshot of the top ranking genomes at the end of the program's execution. The first column shows the bit patterns of the genomes that were produced by the final evolving population while the second column shows the same genomes with the recovery transformation applied to produce the original bit representation used for the fitness evaluation which is presented in column 3.

Column 1 tells us that their rotated representations are very similar, having identical bit patterns in the frozen subsequence at the end of each string. More significantly, an inspection of the results reveals that even though a type of convergence has taken place for the rotated genomes, the algorithm has actually maintained several high fitness genomes that, when viewed in the original bit representation, are very different if we choose to compare them using a Hamming metric.

Genome in: Rotated Form	Original Representation	Fitness
0000000000 0000000000 0000010011	1000000000 1000000000 1000000000	78.6432
1010010000 0000000000 0000010011	0111111111 1000000000 1000000000	78.5409
0001101000 0000000000 0000010011	1000000000 1000000000 0111111111	78.5409
0000100000 0000000000 0000010011	1000000000 1000000000 1000000001	78.5409
1011111000 0000000000 0000010011	0111111111 1000000000 0111111111	78.4386
0100100000 0000000000 0000010011	1000000000 1000000001 1000000001	78.4386

Table 1: Highest Ranking genomes for the 1st DeJong Test Function
(Both populations have size 300)

The ability of the population to successfully carry many of the high-fitness genomes to the very end of the run, despite their very different bit patterns, is exactly the type of behaviour that we want. It shows us the Rising Tide Algorithm working as described in section 5.1. However, our current experience with more complex functions demonstrates that isolation of high fitness genomes can be quite difficult but it is not clear whether this is due to an inadequate population size or some inherent inability of the algorithm in evolving high correlation parity strings. Further experiments are being conducted.

12 Discussion and Speculation

Working in GF2 is very convenient. We have the luxury of doing arithmetic operations in a field that provides very useful tools, for example: a linear algebra complete with invertible matrices and Fourier transforms. Nonetheless, the Rising Tide Algorithm is certainly no panacea. Discovery of an optimal rotation matrix is beset with certain difficulties that are related to the mechanisms at work in the learning strategy itself. A key issue underlying the processing of the RTA depends on the fact that the learning algorithm applied to the signum function $f(x)$ will determine a set of parity functions that form a threshold of parity or TOP function. The Boolean output of a TOP is determined by a winning vote of its constituent parity strings. Unfortunately, the subset of the parity strings that win the vote can change from one point to any other in the search space. This reflects the nonlinear behaviour of an objective function. Consequently the derivation of a rotation matrix can be quite demanding. Such a difficulty does not necessarily mean that the strategy is without merit. In fact, the ability to anticipate the "show stopper" carries an advantage not provided by the simple genetic algorithm, which will grind away on any population without any notion of failure. So, a more salutary view would recognize that we should, in fact, expect to meet difficulties and the more clear they are, then the more opportunity we have for meeting the challenge they impose.

A possible approach to handle this problem would be the creation of a tree structure with branching used to designate portions of the search space holding genomes that meet the constraints consistent with particular sets of parity strings (a novel interpretation for speciation studies). A strategy very similar to this has been employed by (Hooker, 1998) in the investigation of constraint satisfaction methods. In this paper, the setting is discrete variable logic instead of parity strings being manipulated in GF2. However, the problems encountered when trying to meet consistency requirements for constraint satisfaction are quite similar to the TOP dilemma. To handle the situation, Hooker describes algorithms that utilize backtracking strategies in so-called k-trees. We intend to carry out further studies to make clearer the interplay between these two problem areas.

As a final speculation, we note that it may be reasonable to see "locality" defined by such a branching process. It meets our demand that the neighbourhood structure be created by the objective function itself and it also carries a similar notion of being trapped within an area that may lead to sub-optimal solutions.

13 Conclusion

We contend that harmonic analysis and especially PAC learning should have significant theoretical and practical benefits for the design of new evolutionary optimization algorithms. The Fourier spectrum of $f(x)$, its distribution of large coefficients and how this relates to the complexity of optimization, should serve to quantitatively characterize functions that are compatible with these algorithms. Although computationally expensive, the DFT does provide a formal strategy to deal with notions such as epistasis and simple (linear) gene linkage expressible as a ring-sum formula. The future value of such a theoretical study would be to see the structure of the search space expressed in terms of the spectral properties of the fitness function. Our view is that this is, in some sense, a more "natural" expression of the intrinsic structure of the search space since it does not rely on a neighborhood structure defined by the search operator chosen by the application programmer.

This paper has presented several novel ideas in a preliminary report on an evolutionary algorithm that involves an explicit use of the DFT. A possible optimization algorithm was described with attention drawn to some of the more theoretical issues that provide a bridge between PAC learning and evolutionary optimization. More extensive empirical results will be the subject of a future report.

We contend that a study of the RTA is beneficial despite the extra computation required by the handling of large matrices that are dependent on the maintenance of two populations each holding two subpopulations. The theoretical ties to learning theory and circuit complexity provide an excellent area for future research related to theoretical analysis and heuristic design. To express this in another way: Unless P = NP, most heuristic approaches when applied to very hard problems, will fail. What should be important to us is why they fail. By categorizing an objective function relative to a complexity class, learning theory will at least give us some indication about what is easy and what is difficult.

References

M. Anthony. Probabilistic analysis of learning in artificial neural networks: The PAC model and its variants. http://www.icsi.berkeley.edu/~jagota/NCS/vol1.html.

D.L. Battle & M.D. Vose. (1991) Isomorphisms of genetic algorithms. In G. Rawlins (ed.), *Foundations of Genetic Algorithms*, 242-251. San Mateo, CA: Morgan Kaufmann.

E. B. Baum. (1991) Neural net algorithms that learn in polynomial time from examples and queries. *IEEE Transactions on Neural Networks*, **2**(1):5-19.

R. K. Belew. (1989) When both individuals and populations search: Adding simple learning to the genetic algorithm. In J. D. Schaffer (ed.), *Proceedings of the International Conference on Genetic Algorithms*, 34-41. San Mateo, CA: Morgan Kaufmann.

N. Bshouty, J. Jackson, & T. Tamon. (1999) More efficient PAC-learning of DNF with membership queries under the uniform distribution. *Proceedings of the 12th Annual Workshop on Computational Learning Theory*, 286-295.

L. Davis. (1989) Adapting operator probabilities in genetic algorithms. In J. D. Schaffer, (ed.), *Proceedings of the International Conference on Genetic Algorithms*, 61-69. San Mateo, CA: Morgan Kaufmann.

L. J. Eshelman, R. A. Caruana, & J. D. Schaffer. (1989) Biases in the crossover landscape. *Proceedings of the Third International Conference on Genetic Algorithms*, 10-19. San Mateo, CA: Morgan Kaufmann.

P. Fischer & H. Ulrich Simon. (1992) On learning ring-sum-expansions. *Siam J. Comput.*, **21**(1):181-192.

S. Forrest & M. Mitchell. (1993) What makes a problem hard for a genetic algorithm? Some anomalous results and their explanation. *Machine Learning*, 13, 285-319.

Y. Freund. (1990) Boosting a weak learning algorithm by majority. *Proceedings of the Third Annual Workshop on Computational Learning*, 202-216.

G. R. Harik. (1997) *Learning Gene Linkage to Efficiently Solve Problems of Bounded Difficulty Using Genetic Algorithms*. Ph. D. dissertation, Computer Science and Engineering, The University of Michigan.

R. Heckendorn & D. Whitley. (1999) Predicting epistasis from mathematical models. *Evolutionary Computation*, **7**(1):69-101. Cambridge, MA: MIT Press.

W. Hoeffding. (1963) Probability inequalities for sums of bounded random variables. *American Statistical Association Journal*, vol. 58, 13-30.

J. N. Hooker. (1998) Constraint Satisfaction Methods for Generating Valid Cuts. In D. L. Woodruff, (ed.), *Advances in Computational and Stochastic Optimization, Logic Programming, and Heuristic Search*, 1-30. Boston, MA: Kluwer Academic.

J. C. Jackson. (1995) *The Harmonic Sieve: A Novel Application of Fourier Analysis to Machine Learning Theory and Practice*. Ph. D. Thesis, Carnegie Mellon University, CMU-CS-95-183.

H. Kargupta & D. E. Goldberg. (1997) SEARCH, blackbox optimization, and sample complexity. In R. K. Belew & M. D. Vose (eds.), *Foundations of Genetic Algorithms 4*, 291-324. San Mateo, CA: Morgan Kaufmann.

M. J. Kearns & U. V. Vazirani. (1994) *An Introduction to Computational Learning Theory*, Cambridge, MA: The MIT Press.

E. Kushilevitz & Y. Mansour. (1993) Learning decision trees using the Fourier spectrum. *SIAM Journal on Computing*, **22**(6):1331-1348.

R. J. Lechner. (1971) Harmonic analysis of switching functions. In A. Mukhopadhyay (ed.), *Recent Developments in Switching Theory*, 121-228. NewYork, NY: Academic Press.

G. E. Liepins & M. D. Vose. (1990) Representational issues in genetic optimization. *J. Expt. Theor. Artif. Intell.*, 2:101-115.

N. Linial, Y. Mansour, & N. Nisan. (1993) Constant Depth Circuits, Fourier Transform, and Learnability. *Journal of the ACM*, **40**(3):607-620.

M. Manela & J. A. Campbell. (1992) Harmonic analysis, epistasis and genetic algorithms. In R. Männer & B. Manderick (eds.), *Parallel Problem Solving from Nature 2*, 57-64. Elsevier.

T. M. Mitchell. (1997) *Machine Learning*, McGraw-Hill.

H. Mühlenbein & T. Mahnig. (1999) The factoring distribution algorithm for additively decomposed functions. *Proc. 1999 Congress on Evolutionary Computation*, 752 - 759.

M. Pelikan, D. E. Goldberg, & F. Lobo. (1999) A survey of optimization by building and using probabilistic models. *Illinois Genetic Algorithms Laboratory Report No. 99018*, University of Illinois at Urbana-Champaign, IL.

N. J. Radcliffe. (1992) Non-linear genetic representations. In R. Männer and B. Manderick (eds.), Parallel *Problem Solving from Nature 2*, 259-268. Elsevier.

J. P. Ros. (1993) Learning Boolean functions with genetic algorithms: A PAC analysis. In L. D. Whitley (ed.), *Foundations of Genetic Algorithms 2*, 257-275. Morgan Kaufmann Publishers, Inc., San Francisco.

M. Sebag & M. Schoenauer. (1994) Controlling crossover through inductive learning. *Parallel Problem Solving from Nature - PPSN III*, 209-218. Jerusalem.

J. E. Smith & T. C. Fogarty. (1996) Recombination strategy adaptation via evolution of gene linkage. *Proceedings of IEEE International Conference on Evolutionary Computing*, 826-831.

L. G. Valiant. (1984) A theory of the learnable. *Communications of the ACM*, **27**(11):1134-1142.

M. D. Vose & G. E. Liepins. (1991) Schema disruption. In R. K. Belew & L. B. Booker (eds.), *Proceedings of the Fourth International Conference on Genetic Algorithms*, pages 237-242. San Mateo, CA: Morgan Kaufmann.

M. D. Vose. (1991) *The Simple Genetic Algorithm*, Boston, MA: Massachusetts Institute of Technology.

Continuous Dynamical System Models of Steady-State Genetic Algorithms

Alden H. Wright
Computer Science Department
University of Montana
Missoula, MT 59812
USA
wright@cs.umt.edu

Jonathan E. Rowe *
School of Computer Science
University of Birmingham
Birmingham B15 2TT
Great Britain
J.E.Rowe@cs.bham.ac.uk

Abstract

This paper constructs discrete-time and continuous-time dynamical system expected value and infinite population models for steady-state genetic and evolutionary search algorithms. Conditions are given under which the discrete-time expected value models converge to the continuous-time models as the population size goes to infinity. Existence and uniqueness theorems are proved for solutions of the continuous-time models. The fixed points of these models and their asymptotic stability are compared.

1 Introduction

There has been considerable development of expected value and infinite population models for genetic algorithms. To date, this work has concentrated on generational genetic algorithms. These models tend to be discrete-time dynamical systems, where each time step corresponds to one generation of the genetic algorithm.

Many practitioners (such as [Dav91]) advocate the use of steady-state genetic algorithms where a single individual is replaced at each step. This paper develops expected value and infinite population models for steady-state genetic algorithms. First, discrete-time expected value models are described, where each time step corresponds to the replacement

* This work was completed while Jonathan E. Rowe was at De Montfort University.

of an individual. It is natural to consider these models in the limit when the population goes to infinity and the time step goes to zero. This paper shows how this limiting process leads in a natural way to a continuous-time dynamical system model. Conditions for the existence and uniqueness of solutions of this model are given.

The steady-state model that uses random deletion has a very close correspondence with the generational model that uses the same crossover, mutation, and selection. The fixed points of the two models are the same, and a fixed point where all of the eigenvalues of the differential of the generational model heuristic function have modulus less than one must be stable under the discrete-time and continuous-time steady-state models. However, a numerical example is given of a fixed point which is asymptotically stable under the continuous-time steady-state model but not asymptotically stable under the generational model.

Let Ω denote the search space for a search problem. We identify Ω with the integers in the range from 0 to $n-1$, where n is the cardinality of Ω. We assume a real-valued nonnegative fitness function f over Ω. We will denote $f(i)$ by f_i. Our objective is to model population-based search algorithms that search for elements of Ω with high fitness. Such algorithms can be *generational*, where a large proportion of the population is replaced at each time step (or generation). Or they can be *steady-state*, where only a single or small number of population members are replaced in a time step.

A population is a multiset (set with repeated elements) with elements drawn from Ω. We will represent populations over Ω by nonnegative vectors indexed over the integers in the interval $[0, n)$ whose sum is 1. If a population of size r is represented by a vector p, then rp_i is the number of copies of i in the population. For example, if $\Omega = \{0, 1, 2, 3\}$, and the population is the multiset $\{0, 0, 1, 2, 2\}$, then the population is represented by the vector $\langle\ 2/5 \quad 1/5 \quad 2/5 \quad 0\ \rangle^T$.

Let $\Lambda = \{x : \sum_i x_i = 1 \text{ and } x_j \geq 0 \text{ for all } j\}$. Then all populations over Ω are elements of Λ. Λ can also be interpreted as the set of probability distributions over Ω. It is natural to think of elements of Λ as *infinite populations*. Geometrically, Λ is the unit simplex in $\Re^n$.

The ith unit vector in $\Re^n$ is denoted by e_i. The Euclidean norm on $\Re^n$ is denoted by $\|\cdot\| = \|\cdot\|_2$, the max norm by $\|\cdot\|_\infty$, and the sum norm by $\|\cdot\|_1$. The Euclidean norm is the default.

Brackets are used to denote an indicatior function. Thus,

$$[expression] = \begin{cases} 1 & \text{if } expression \text{ is true} \\ 0 & \text{if } expression \text{ is false} \end{cases}$$

Vose's random heuristic search algorithm describes a class of generational population-based search algorithms. The model is defined by a *heuristic function* $\mathcal{G} : \Lambda \to \Lambda$. If x is a population of size r, then the next generation population is obtained by taking r independent samples from the probability distribution $\mathcal{G}(x)$. When random heuristic search is used to model the simple genetic algorithm, $\mathcal{G}$ is the composition of a selection heuristic function $\mathcal{F} : \Lambda \to \Lambda$ and a mixing heuristic function $\mathcal{M} : \Lambda \to \Lambda$. The mixing function describes the properties of crossover and mutation. Properties of the $\mathcal{M}$ and $\mathcal{F}$ functions are explored in detail in [Vos99].

Given a population $x \in \Lambda$, it is not hard to show that the expected next generation population is $\mathcal{G}(x)$. As the population size goes to infinity, the next generation population converges in probability to its expectation, so it is natural to use $\mathcal{G}$ to define an infinite population model. Thus, $x \longrightarrow \mathcal{G}(x)$ defines a discrete-time dynamical system on Λ that we will call the *generational model*. Given an initial population x, the trajectory of this population is the sequence $x, \mathcal{G}(x), \mathcal{G}^2(x), \mathcal{G}^3(x), \ldots$.

Note that after the first step, the populations produced by this model do not necessarily correspond to populations of size r.

2 Steady-state evolutionary computation algorithms

Whitley's Genitor algorithm [Whi89] was the first "steady state" genetic algorithm. Genitor selects two parent individuals by ranking selection and applies mixing to them to produce one offspring, which replaces the worst element of the population. Syswerda ([Sys89] and [Sys91]) described variations of the steady-state genetic algorithm and empirically compared various deletion methods. Davis [Dav91] also empirically tested steady-state genetic algorithms and advocates them as being superior to generational GAs when combined with a feature that eliminates duplicate chromosomes.

In this section, we describe two versions of steady-state search algorithms. Both algorithms start with a population η of size r. In most applications, this population would be chosen randomly from the search space, but there is no requirement for a random initial population. At each step of both algorithms, an element j is removed from the population, and an element i of Ω is added to the population, The selection of the element i is described by a heuristic function $\mathcal{G}$. (For a genetic algorithm, $\mathcal{G}$ will describe crossover, mutation, and usually selection.) The selection of element j is described by another heuristic function $\mathcal{D}_r$. (We include the population size r as a subscript since there may be a dependence on population size.)

In the first algorithm, the heuristic functions $\mathcal{G}$ and $\mathcal{D}_r$ both depend on x, the current population. Thus, i is selected from the probability distribution $\mathcal{G}(x)$, and j is selected from the probability distribution $\mathcal{D}_r(x)$.

Steady-state random heuristic search algorithm 1:

1 Choose an initial population η of size r
2 $x \leftarrow \eta$
3 Select i from Ω using the probability distribution $\mathcal{G}(x)$.
4 Select j using the probability distribution $\mathcal{D}_r(x)$.
5 Replace x by $x - e_j/r + e_i/r$.
6 Go to step 3.

The second algorithm differs from the first by allowing for the possibility that the newly added element i might be deleted. Thus, j is selected from the probability distribution $\mathcal{D}_r(\frac{rx+e_i}{r+1})$. This algorithm is an $(r+1)$ algorithm in evolution strategy notation.

Steady-state random heuristic search algorithm 2:

1 Choose an initial population η of size r.

2 $x \leftarrow \eta$
3 Select i from Ω using the probability distribution $\mathcal{G}(x)$.
4′ Select j using the probability distribution $\mathcal{D}_r(\frac{rx+e_i}{r+1})$.
5 Replace x by $x - e_j/r + e_i/r$.
6 Go to step 3.

Some heuristics that have been suggested for for the $\mathcal{D}_r$ function include worst-element deletion, where a population element with the least fitness is chosen for deletion, reverse proportional selection, reverse ranking deletion, and random deletion, where the element to be deleted is chosen randomly from the population. Random deletion was suggested by Syswerda [Sys89]. He points out that random deletion is seldom used in practice. Because of this, one of the reviewers of this paper objected to the use of the term "steady-state genetic algorithm" for an algorithm that used random deletion. However, we feel that the term can be applied to any genetic algorithm that replaces only a few members of the population during a time step of the algorithm.

Random deletion can be modeled by choosing $\mathcal{D}_r(x) = x$.

If the fitness function is injective (the fitnesses of elements of Ω are distinct), then reverse ranking and worst-element deletion can be modeled using the framework developed for ranking selection in [Vos99].

$$\mathcal{D}_r(x)_i = \int_{\sum[f_j < f_i]x_j}^{\sum[f_j \le f_i]x_j} \rho(s)ds$$

The probability density function $\rho(s)$ can be chosen to be $2s$ to model standard ranking selection, and $2 - 2s$ to model reverse ranking deletion. To model worst-element deletion, we define $\rho(s)$ as follows:

$$\rho(s) = \begin{cases} r & \text{if } 0 \le s \le 1/r, \\ 0 & \text{otherwise.} \end{cases}$$

As an example, let $n = 3$, $x = \langle\ \frac{1}{3}\quad \frac{1}{6}\quad \frac{1}{2}\ \rangle^T$, $f = \langle\ 2\quad 1\quad 3\ \rangle^T$, and $r = 4$. Then $\rho(s) = 4$ if $0 \le s \le 1/4$ and $\rho(s) = 0$ if $1/4 < s \le 1$. (The population x does not correspond to a real finite population of size 4. However, this choice leads to a more illustrative example. Also, if $\mathcal{D}_r$ is iterated, after the first iteration the populations produced will not necessarily correspond to finite populations of size r.) Then

$$\mathcal{D}_r(x)_1 = \int_0^{x_1} \rho(s)ds = \int_0^{1/6} 4ds = 2/3,$$

$$\mathcal{D}_r(x)_0 = \int_{x_1}^{x_1+x_0} \rho(s)ds = \int_{1/6}^{1/2} \rho(s)ds = \int_{1/6}^{1/4} 4ds = 1/3.$$

and

$$\mathcal{D}_r(x)_2 = \int_{x_1+x_0}^{x_1+x_0+x_2} \rho(s)ds = \int_{1/2}^{1} \rho(s)ds = 0.$$

For random deletion and reverse ranking deletion, $\mathcal{D}_r(x)$ does not depend on the population size and can be shown to be differentiable as a function of x.

For worst-element deletion, $\mathcal{D}_r(x)$ does depend on the population size, and is continuous but not differentiable.

Lemma 2.1 *If $\mathcal{D}_r$ is defined as above for worst-element deletion, then $\mathcal{D}_r$ satisfies a Lipschitz condition. In other words, there is a constant L_r so that $\|\mathcal{D}_r(x) - \mathcal{D}_r(y)\| \leq L_r\|x - y\|$ for all $x, y \in \Lambda$.*

Proof. Let $x, y \in \Lambda$. Then

$$\begin{aligned}
|\mathcal{D}_r(x)_i - \mathcal{D}_r(y)_i| &= \left| \int_{\sum[f_j<f_i]x_j}^{\sum[f_j\leq f_i]x_j} \rho(s)ds - \int_{\sum[f_j<f_i]y_j}^{\sum[f_j\leq f_i]y_j} \rho(s)ds \right| \\
&= \left| \int_{\sum[f_j<f_i]x_j}^{\sum[f_j<f_i]y_j} \rho(s)ds - \int_{\sum[f_j\leq f_i]x_j}^{\sum[f_j\leq f_i]y_j} \rho(s)ds \right| \\
&\leq r\sum[f_j < f_i]|y_j - x_j| + r\sum[f_j \leq f_i]|y_j - x_j| \\
&\leq 2r\sum|y_j - x_j| \\
&= 2r\|x - y\|_1.
\end{aligned}$$

Thus, $\|\mathcal{D}_r(x) - \mathcal{D}_r(y)\|_\infty \leq 2r\|x - y\|_1$. Since all norms are equivalent up to a constant, $\|\mathcal{D}_r(x) - \mathcal{D}_r(y)\|_2 \leq 2rK\|x - y\|_2$ for some constant K. □

The function

$$\mathcal{H}_r(x) = x + \frac{1}{r}\mathcal{G}(x) - \frac{1}{r}\mathcal{D}_r(x) \tag{1}$$

gives the expected population for Algorithm 1 at the next time step, and the function

$$\mathcal{K}_r(x) = x + \frac{1}{r}\mathcal{G}(x) - \frac{1}{r}\mathcal{D}_{r+1}\left(\frac{rx + \mathcal{G}(x)}{r+1}\right) \tag{2}$$

gives the expected population for Algorithm 2 at the next time step.

Thus, $x \longrightarrow \mathcal{H}_r(x)$ and $x \longrightarrow \mathcal{K}_r(x)$ define discrete-time expected-value models of the above steady-state algorithms. We will call these the *discrete-time steady-state models.*

The following is straightforward.

Lemma 2.2 *If the deletion heuristic $\mathcal{D}_r$ of the discrete-time steady-state models satisfy*

$$\mathcal{D}_r(y) \leq rx + \mathcal{G}(x), \tag{3}$$

where $y = x$ for (1) and $y = \frac{rx+\mathcal{G}(x)}{r+1}$ for (2), then the trajectories of the systems defined by $\mathcal{H}_r$ and $\mathcal{K}_r$ remain in the simplex Λ.

The models for random deletion, reverse ranking deletion, and worst-element deletion all satisfy the hypotheses of lemma 2.2.

3 Convergence of the $\mathcal{K}_r$ heuristic.

In this section we assume that the deletion heuristic is defined by worst element deletion. We give conditions on the fitness function and on $\mathcal{G}$ that assure that $\lim_{t\to\infty} \mathcal{K}_r^t(x)$ exists and is the uniform population consisting of copies of the global optimum.

In evolution strategy terminology, this is an $(r+1)$-ES algorithm which uses an elitist selection method. Rudolph [Rud98] has shown that for this class of algorithms, if there is mutation rate that is greater than zero and less than one, then the finite population algorithm converges completely and in mean. These are statements about the best element in the population rather than the whole population, so these results do not imply our result.

We assume that the fitness function is injective. In other words, we assume that if $i \neq j$, then $f_i \neq f_j$. Since we will not be concerned with the internal structure of Ω, without loss of generality we can assume that $f_0 < f_1 < \ldots < f_{n-1}$. This assumption will simplify notation.

Under this assumption, we can give a simplified definition for the worst-element deletion heuristic $\mathcal{D}_{r+1}$ that is used in the definition of $\mathcal{K}_r$.

$$\mathcal{D}_{r+1}(y)_i = \begin{cases} (r+1)y_i & \text{if } \sum_{j \leq i} y_j \leq \frac{1}{r+1} \\ 1-(r+1)\sum_{j<i} y_j & \text{if } \sum_{j<i} y_j \leq \frac{1}{r+1} < \sum_{j \leq i} y_j \\ 0 & \text{if } \frac{1}{r+1} < \sum_{j<i} y_j \end{cases}$$

Now define $m(x) = \min\{i : x_i > 0\}$, and define $M(x) = 2m(x) + 1 - x_{m(x)}$.

Theorem 3.1 *If $f_0 < f_1 < \ldots < f_{n-1}$ and if there is a $\delta > 0$ such that for all $x \in \Lambda$ such that $x \neq e_{n-1}$,*

$$\sum_{j>m(x)} \mathcal{G}_j(x) \geq \delta,$$

then for any $x \in \Lambda$ there is a $T > 0$ such that $\mathcal{K}_r^t(x) = e_{n-1}$ for all $t \geq T$.

This condition says that $\mathcal{G}(x)$ has a combined weight of at least δ on those points of Ω whose fitness is higher than the worst-fitness element of x. (By "element of x", we mean any $i \in \Omega$ such that $x_i > 0$.) This condition would be satisfied by any $\mathcal{G}$ heuristic that allowed for a positive probability of mutation between any elements of Ω.

To prove this theorem, we need the following results.

Lemma 3.2 *For any $x \in \Lambda$, if $j < m(x)$, then $\mathcal{K}_r(x)_j = 0$.*

Proof. To simplify notation, let m denote $m(x)$.

Let $y = \frac{rx+\mathcal{G}(x)}{r+1}$. Then $\sum_{j<m} \mathcal{G}(x)_j \leq \frac{1}{r+1}$ since $\sum_{j<m} x_j = 0$ and $\sum_{j<m} \mathcal{G}_j \leq 1$. Thus, for $j < m$, $\mathcal{D}_{r+1}(y)_j = y_j$, and $\mathcal{K}_r(x)_j = y_j - \mathcal{D}_{r+1}(y)_j = 0$. □

Lemma 3.3 *For any $x \in \Lambda$, if there is a $\delta > 0$ such that $\sum_{j>m(x)} \mathcal{G}(x)_j \geq \delta$, then*

$$M(\mathcal{K}_r(x)) \geq M(x) + \frac{\delta}{r}.$$

Proof. To simplify notation, again let m denote $m(x)$.

Let $y = \frac{rx+\mathcal{G}(x)}{r+1}$.

Case 1: $\sum_{j \leq m} y_j \leq \frac{1}{r+1}$.

Then

$$\mathcal{D}_{r+1}(y)_m = (r+1)y_m = rx_m + \mathcal{G}(x)_m,$$

and

$$\mathcal{K}_r(x)_m = x_m + \frac{1}{r}\mathcal{G}(x)_m - \frac{1}{r}(rx_m + \mathcal{G}(x)_m) = 0.$$

Thus,

$$M(\mathcal{K}_r(x)) \geq 2(m+1) + 1 - x_{m+1} \geq 2m + 2 \geq M(x) + 1.$$

Case 2: $\sum_{j<m} y_j \leq \frac{1}{r+1} < \sum_{j \leq m} y_j$.

Then

$$\mathcal{D}_{r+1}(y)_m = 1 - (r+1)\sum_{j<m} y_j = 1 - \sum_{j<m} \mathcal{G}(x)_j.$$

Thus

$$\begin{aligned}
\mathcal{K}_r(x)_m &= x_m + \frac{1}{r}\mathcal{G}(x)_m - \frac{1}{r}\mathcal{D}_{r+1}(y)_m \\
&= x_m - \frac{1}{r}\left(1 - \sum_{j \leq m} \mathcal{G}(x)_j\right) \\
&= x_m - \frac{1}{r}\sum_{j>m} \mathcal{G}(x)_j \\
&\leq x_m - \frac{\delta}{r}.
\end{aligned}$$

Also note that

$$\begin{aligned}
\frac{1}{r+1} < \sum_{j \leq m} y_j &\implies 1 < \sum_{j \leq m} (rx_j + \mathcal{G}(x)_j) \\
&\implies x_m - \frac{1}{r}\left(1 - \sum_{j \leq m} \mathcal{G}(x)_j\right) > 0 \\
&\implies \mathcal{K}_r(x)_m > 0.
\end{aligned}$$

Thus,

$$\begin{aligned}
M(\mathcal{K}_r(x)) &= 2m + 1 - x_m + \frac{1}{r}\sum_{j>m} \mathcal{G}(x)_j \\
&= M(x) + \frac{1}{r}\sum_{j>m} \mathcal{G}(x) \\
&\geq M(x) + \frac{\delta}{r}.
\end{aligned}$$

Case 3: $\frac{1}{r+1} < \sum_{j<m} y_j$.
In this case, $1 < \sum_{j<m}(rx_j + \mathcal{G}(x)_j)$, which implies $1 < \sum_{j<m} \mathcal{G}(x)_j$. This is clearly impossible, so this case never happens. □

Proof of theorem 3.1: Let $x \in \Lambda$. Each term of the sequence $M(x), M(\mathcal{K}_r(x)), M(\mathcal{K}_r^2(x)), \ldots$ increases by δ/r from the previous term unless the previous term is $M(e_{n-1})$. Since the terms of the sequence are bounded above by $M(e_{n-1}) = 2(n-1)$, there is a $T > 0$ such that for all $t \geq T$, $M(\mathcal{K}_r^t(x)) = 2(n-1)$ and thus $\mathcal{K}_r^t(x) = e_{n-1}$. □

4 Continuous-time dynamical system models

Our objective in this section is to move from the expected value models of the previous section to an infinite population model. The incremental step in the simplex from one population to the next in the expected value models is either $\frac{1}{r}\mathcal{G}(x) - \frac{1}{r}\mathcal{D}_r(x)$ or $\frac{1}{r}\mathcal{G}(x) - \frac{1}{r}\mathcal{D}_r\left(\frac{rx+\mathcal{G}(x)}{r+1}\right)$. If the population size r is doubled then the size of the incremental step is halved in the first case and is approximately halved in the second case. Thus, in order to make the same progress in moving through the simplex, we need to take twice as many incremental steps of the expected value model. We can think of this as halving the time between incremental steps of the expected value model. We show below that this process corresponds to the well known limiting process of going from the Euler approximation of a differential equation to the differential equation itself.

We define a continuous-time dynamical system model which can be interpreted as the limit of the systems (1) and (2) as the population size goes to infinity and as the time step simultaneously goes to zero. Thus, we are interested in the limits of the functions $\mathcal{D}_r(x)$ for (1) and of $\mathcal{D}_r\left(\frac{rx+\mathcal{G}(x)}{r+1}\right)$ for (2). If this limit defines a continuous function $\mathcal{D}(x)$ that satisfies a Lipschitz condition, then we will show that the continuous-time system defined by the initial value problem

$$y' = \mathcal{E}(y) \qquad y(\tau) = \eta, \qquad \eta \in \Lambda, \tag{4}$$

where $\mathcal{E}(y) = \mathcal{G}(y) - \mathcal{D}(y)$, has a unique solution that exists for all $t \geq \tau$ and lies in the simplex. Further, it can be interpreted as the limit of the solutions of the systems (1) and (2) as the population size goes to infinity and the time step goes to zero.

It is easier to define what we mean by the convergence of the solutions to a family of discrete-time systems if we extend the discrete-time solutions to continuous-time solutions. An obvious way to do this is to connect successive points of the discrete-time trajectory by straight lines. The following makes this more precise.

Define $\mathcal{E}_r(x) = \mathcal{G}(x) - \mathcal{D}_r(x)$ to model the system (1) and define $\mathcal{E}_r(x) = \mathcal{G}(x) - \mathcal{D}_r\left(\frac{rx+\mathcal{G}(x)}{r+1}\right)$ to model the system (2).

Define

$$\begin{aligned} e_r(\tau) &= \eta \\ e_r(t) &= e_r(\tau + k/r) + \mathcal{E}_r(e_r(\tau + k/r))(t - (\tau + k/r)) \quad \text{for } \tau + k/r < t \leq \tau + (k+1)/r \end{aligned}$$

The following Lemma shows the $e_r(t)$ functions interpolate the solutions to the discrete-time systems (1) and (2). The proof is a straightforward induction.

Lemma 4.1 *For* $k = 0, 1, \ldots,$

$$e_r(\tau + k/r) = \mathcal{H}_r^k(\tau) = \mathcal{H}_r(\mathcal{H}_r(\ldots \mathcal{H}_r(\tau)\ldots))$$

or

$$e_r(\tau + k/r) = \mathcal{K}_r^k(\tau) = \mathcal{K}_r(\mathcal{K}_r(\ldots \mathcal{K}_r(\tau)\ldots)).$$

Note that if the solutions to (1) and (2) are in the simplex, then the convexity of the simplex implies that $e_r(t)$ is in the simplex for all $t \geq \tau$.

4.1 Extending the functions $\mathcal{E}$ and $\mathcal{E}_r$ to all of $\Re^n$

The standard existence and uniqueness theorems from the theory of differential equations are stated for a system $y' = F(t, y)$ where y ranges over $\Re^n$. (For example, see theorems 4.3 and 4.5 below.) In many cases, the $\mathcal{E}$ and $\mathcal{E}_r$ functions have natural extensions to all of $\Re^n$. In this case, these theorems can be directly applied. However, we would rather not make this assumption. Thus, to prove existence of solutions, we would like to extend the function $\mathcal{E} : \Lambda \to \Lambda$ to a continuous function defined over all of $\Re^n$. (The same technique can be applied to the $\mathcal{E}_r$ functions.)

Let H denote the hyperplane $\{x : \sum x_i = 1\}$ of $\Re^n$, and let $\mathbf{1}$ denote the vector of all ones. We first define a function R which retracts H onto the simplex Λ. Let $R(x)_i = \max(0, x_i)$. Clearly R is continuous, and

$$||R(x) - R(y)||_\infty \leq ||x - y||_\infty \tag{5}$$

for all x, y.

Then we define a orthogonal projection p from $\Re^n$ onto H. Define p by $p(x) = x + (1 - \sum x_i)\mathbf{1}$. Clearly, p is continuous, and

$$||p(x) - p(y)||_\infty \leq ||x - y||_\infty \tag{6}$$

for all x, y.

If $\mathcal{E} : \Lambda \to \Lambda$ is continuous, then $\mathcal{E}$ can be extended to a continuous function $\widetilde{\mathcal{E}} : \Re^n \to \Lambda$ by defining $\widetilde{\mathcal{E}}(x) = \mathcal{E}(R(p(x)))$. Clearly $\widetilde{\mathcal{E}}$ is bounded.

Lemma 4.2 *If $\mathcal{E}$ satisfies a Lipschitz condition, then so does $\widetilde{\mathcal{E}}$.*

Proof. Let $x, y \in \Re^n$. Then

$$||\widetilde{\mathcal{E}}(x) - \widetilde{\mathcal{E}}(y)||_\infty \leq L||R(p(x)) - R(p(y))||_\infty \leq L||R(x) - R(y)||_\infty \leq L||x - y||_\infty.$$

□

4.2 Existence of solutions in the simplex

The following theorem gives conditions under which a family of approximate solutions to an initial value problem converges to a solution to the problem. We will apply the theorem to show that a subsequence of the $e_r(t)$ functions converge to a solution to (4). If we know that the $e_r(t)$ solutions are contained in the simplex, then this will give us the existence of solutions in the simplex.

Theorem 4.3 *(Theorem 3.1 of [Rei71].) Suppose that the vector function $F(t, y)$ is continuous on the infinite strip $\Delta = [a, b] \times \Re^n$, and (τ, η) is a point of Δ. If ϵ_m, $(m = 1, 2, \dots)$, is a sequence of positive constants converging to zero, and $y^{(m)}$ is a corresponding sequence of approximate solutions satisfying*

$$\|y^{(m)}(t) - \eta - \int_\tau^t F(s, y^{(m)}(s))ds\| < \epsilon_m \tag{7}$$

and for which there are corresponding constants κ, κ_1 such that

$$\|F(t, y^{(m)}(t))\| < \kappa\|y^{(m)}(t)\| + \kappa_1 \quad \text{on } [a, b], \quad (m = 1, 2, \dots) \tag{8}$$

then there is a subsequence $\{y^{(m_k)}\}$, $(m_1 < m_2 < \dots)$, which converges uniformly on $[a, b]$ to a solution $y(t)$ of $y' = F(t, y)$ satisfying $y(\tau) = \eta$.

The following theorem gives conditions under which (4) has solutions in Λ that are limits of the the functions e_r. The uniqueness of these solutions is considered later.

Theorem 4.4 *Suppose that the functions $\mathcal{E}_r$ satisfy the condition of Lemma 2.2 for all r, and that $\lim_{r\to\infty} \mathcal{E}_r = \mathcal{E}$, where $\mathcal{E}$ is continuous on Λ. Let $[a, b]$ be an interval containing τ, and let $\eta \in \Lambda$. Then $y' = \mathcal{E}(y)$, $y(\tau) = \eta$ has a solution $y(t)$ defined on $[a, b]$ which is the limit of a subsequence of the functions $e_r(t)$.*

Proof. Our objective is to apply Theorem 4.3 with $\mathcal{E}(y)$ in place of $F(t, y)$. The hypothesis requires that $\mathcal{E}$ be defined on all of $\Re^n$. The previous subsection shows how to extend $\mathcal{E}$ to $\widetilde{\mathcal{E}}$ which is defined on all of $\Re^n$. To simplify notation, in this proof we use $\mathcal{E}$ in place of $\widetilde{\mathcal{E}}$.

Since any continuous function on a compact set is bounded, $\mathcal{E}$ is bounded by a positive number κ_1 on Λ. This shows that (8) holds for $\mathcal{E}$.

We also need to show that (7) holds. In other words, given $\epsilon > 0$, we need to show that there is an r_1 so that for $r \geq r_1$,

$$\left\| e_r(t) - \eta - \int_\tau^t \mathcal{E}(e_r(s))ds \right\| < \epsilon.$$

Since Λ is compact, the sequence of functions $\mathcal{E}_r$ converges uniformly to $\mathcal{E}$. Thus, there is an r_2 so that if $r \geq r_2$,

$$\|\mathcal{E}_r(x) - \mathcal{E}(x)\| < \frac{\epsilon}{6(b-a)} \quad \text{for all } x \in \Lambda. \tag{9}$$

We claim that given $\epsilon > 0$, there exists an $\delta > 0$ so that for all x,y with $\|x - y\| < \delta$ and $r \geq r_2$,

$$\|\mathcal{E}_r(x) - \mathcal{E}_r(y)\| < \frac{\epsilon}{2(b-a)} \tag{10}$$

To show this, choose δ sufficiently small so that $\|x - y\| < \delta$ implies $\|\mathcal{E}(x) - \mathcal{E}(y)\| < \frac{\epsilon}{6(b-a)}$. Then for $r \geq r_2$ and $\|x - y\| < \delta$,

$$\|\mathcal{E}_r(x) - \mathcal{E}_r(y)\| \leq \|\mathcal{E}_r(x) - \mathcal{E}(x)\| + \|\mathcal{E}(x) - \mathcal{E}(y)\| + \|\mathcal{E}(y) - \mathcal{E}_r(y)\| \leq \frac{\epsilon}{2(b-a)}.$$

Let the step function $g_r(t)$ be defined by

$$g_r(t) \quad = \quad \mathcal{E}_r\left(e_r\left(\tau + k/r\right)\right) \qquad \text{for } \; \tau + k/r \leq t < \tau + (k+1)/r.$$

Then $e_r(t)$ has the integral representation

$$e_r(t) = \eta + \int_\tau^t g_r(s)ds \quad \text{for } t \in [a,b]$$

We claim that that there is an r_1 so that $||g_r(t) - \mathcal{E}_r(e_r(t))|| \leq \frac{\epsilon}{2(b-a)}$ for all $t \in [a,b]$ and $r \geq r_1$.

To show this, consider

$$\begin{aligned}
&|g_r(t) - \mathcal{E}_r(e_r(t))|| \\
&= ||\mathcal{E}_r(e_r(\tau + k/r)) - \mathcal{E}_r(e_r(t))|| \text{ where } k \text{ is chosen so that } |t - (\tau + k/r)| \leq 1/r \\
&= ||\mathcal{E}_r(e_r(\tau + k/r)) - \mathcal{E}_r(e_r(\tau + k/r) + \mathcal{E}_r(e_r(\tau + k/r))(t - (\tau + k/r))|| \\
&= ||\mathcal{E}_r(x) - \mathcal{E}_r(y)||
\end{aligned}$$

where $||x - y|| = ||\mathcal{E}_r(e_r(\tau + k/r))(t - (\tau + k/r))|| \leq \kappa_1/r$. Choose r_1 so that $\kappa_1/r_1 < \delta$ and $r_1 \geq r_2$. Then (10) holds, and $||g_r(t) - \mathcal{E}_r(e_r(t))|| \leq \frac{\epsilon}{2(b-a)}$ for all $t \in [a,b]$ and $r \geq r_1$.

Thus for all $r \geq r_1$,

$$\begin{aligned}
\left\|e_r(t) - \eta - \int_\tau^t \mathcal{E}(e_r(s))ds\right\| &= \left\|\int_\tau^t (g_r(s) - \mathcal{E}(e_r(s)))\, ds\right\| \\
&\leq \left\|\int_\tau^t (g_r(s) - \mathcal{E}_r(e_r(s)))\, ds\right\| + \left\|\int_\tau^t \mathcal{E}_r(e_r(s)) - \mathcal{E}(e_r(s))ds\right\| \\
&\leq \frac{\epsilon}{2(b-a)}(b-a) + \frac{\epsilon}{2(b-a)}(b-a) \\
&\leq \epsilon.
\end{aligned}$$

□

4.3 Uniqueness of solutions

The following is a standard result on uniqueness from the theory of differential equations.

Theorem 4.5 *(Theorem 5.1 of [Rei71].) If on the infinite strip $\Delta = [a,b] \times \Re^n$ the vector function $F(t,y)$ is continuous and satisfies a Lipschitz condition*

$$||F(t,z) - F(t,y)|| \leq \kappa||z - y||,$$

then for each point (τ, η) of Δ there is a unique solution $y(t)$ of $y' = F(t,y)$ on $[a,b]$ satisfying $y(\tau) = \eta$.

Corollary 4.6 *If the $\mathcal{E}_r$ satisfy the hypothesis of Lemma 2.2 and if $\mathcal{E} = \lim_{r\to\infty} \mathcal{E}_r$ satisfies a Lipschitz condition, then the system (4) has a unique solution which is defined for all $t \geq \tau$, and which lies in the simplex Λ.*

Proof. Given any interval $[a, b]$ with $\tau \in [a, b]$ and given $\eta \in \Lambda$, theorem 4.4 shows that (4) has a solution defined on $[a, b]$ which is contained in the simplex. The Lipschitz hypothesis on $\mathcal{E}$ shows that this solution is unique. Since the interval $[a, b]$ is arbitrary, this solution can be defined for all t. □

Let us summarize what we have shown. When the deletion heuristic is independent of population size, as it is for random deletion and inverse ranking deletion, then theorems 4.4 and 4.6 show that the trajectories of the discrete-time systems (1) and (2) approach the solution to the continuous time system (4) as the population size goes to infinity and the time step goes to zero. Thus, (4) is a natural infinite-population model for these discrete-time systems.

Theorems 4.4 and 4.6 do not apply to the case of worst-element deletion since the limit of the $\mathcal{D}_r$ functions as r goes to infinity is not continuous. (However, these theorems can be applied in the interior of the simplex and in the interior of every face of the simplex.) If the fitness is injective, then the function $\mathcal{D} = \lim_{r\to\infty} \mathcal{D}_r$ (where $\mathcal{D}_r$ denotes worst-element deletion) can be defined as follows. Let $k = k(x)$ have the property that $x_k > 0$ and $f_k \le f_j$ for all j such that $x_j > 0$. Then $\mathcal{D}(x)_k = 1$ and $\mathcal{D}(x)_j = 0$ for all $j \ne k$. Figure 1 shows a trajectory of the system $y' = y - \mathcal{D}(y)$ where $\mathcal{D}$ has this definition. In this figure, e_0, e_1, e_2 are the unit vectors in R^3, and the fitnesses are ordered by $f_2 < f_1 < f_0$. The trajectory starts near e_2, and goes in a straight line with constant velocity to the (e_1, e_0) face. In the (e_1, e_0) face, the trajectory goes to e_0 with constant velocity.

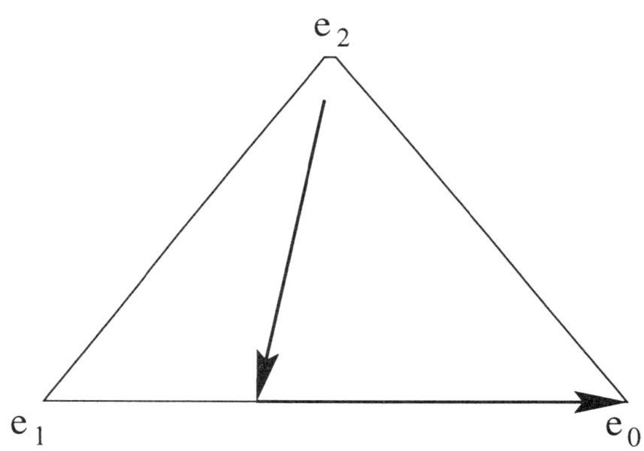

Figure 1 Trajectory of Worst-Element Deletion Continuous-time Model

5 Fixed points for random deletion

Theorem 5.1 *Under random deletion ($\mathcal{D}(x) = x$), all of the following systems:*

$$y' = \mathcal{G}(y) - y, \tag{11}$$

$$x \to x + \frac{1}{r}(\mathcal{G}(x) - x) = \frac{r-1}{r}x + \frac{1}{r}\mathcal{G}(x), \tag{12}$$

$$x \to x + \frac{1}{r}\left(\mathcal{G}(x) - \frac{rx + \mathcal{G}(x)}{r+1}\right) = \frac{r}{r+1}x + \frac{1}{r+1}\mathcal{G}(x) \tag{13}$$

$$x \to \mathcal{G}(x) \tag{14}$$

have the same set of fixed points.

Proof. A necessary and sufficient condition for $\overline{x}$ to be a fixed point of all of these systems is $\mathcal{G}(\overline{x}) = \overline{x}$. □

The results of section 3 and the above results can be used to give conditions under which the fixed points of the steady-state $\mathcal{K}_r$ heuristic of equation (2) using worst-element deletion cannot be the same as the fixed points of the simple GA (or of steady-state with random deletion). We assume injective fitness and positive mutation for both algorithms. (By "positive mutation", we mean a nonzero probability of mutation from any string in the search space to any other.) The results of section 3 show that the only fixed point of the steady-state heuristic of equation (2) is the uniform population consisting of the optimum element in the search space. Any fixed point of the simple GA with positive mutation must be in the interior of the simplex.

6 Stability of fixed points

A fixed point $\overline{x}$ is said to be *stable* if for any $\epsilon > 0$, there is a $\delta > 0$ such that for any solution $y = y(t)$ satisfying $\|\overline{x} - y(\tau)\| < \delta$, then $\|\overline{x} - y(t)\| < \epsilon$ for all $t > \tau$. (For a discrete system, we can take $\tau = 0$, and interpret $t > \tau$ as meaning $t = 1, 2, 3, \ldots$.)

A fixed point $\overline{x}$ is said to be *asymptotically stable* if $\overline{x}$ is stable and if there is an $\epsilon > 0$ so that if $\|y - \overline{x}\| < \epsilon$, then $\lim_{t\to\infty} y(t) = \overline{x}$.

The first-order Taylor approximation around $\overline{x}$ of (11) is given by

$$y' = \mathcal{G}(\overline{x}) - \overline{x} + (d\mathcal{G}_{\overline{x}} - I)(y - \overline{x}) + o(\|y - \overline{x}\|^2).$$

It is not hard to show (see Theorem 1.1.1 of [Wig90] for example) that if all of the eigenvalues of $d\mathcal{G}_{\overline{x}} - I$ have negative real parts, then the fixed point $\overline{x}$ is asymptotically stable.

The first-order Taylor approximation around $\overline{x}$ of (14) is given by

$$\mathcal{G}(y) = \mathcal{G}(\overline{x}) + d\mathcal{G}_{\overline{x}}(y - \overline{x}) + o(\|y - \overline{x}\|^2).$$

It is not hard to show (see Theorem 1.1.1 of [Wig90] for example) that if all of the eigenvalues of $d\mathcal{G}_{\overline{x}}$ have modulus less than 1 (has spectral radius less than 1), then the fixed point $\overline{x}$ is asymptotically stable.

The following lemma is straightforward.

Lemma 6.1 *Let $a \neq 0$ and b be scalars. Then λ is a multiplicity m eigenvalue of an $n \times n$ matrix A if and only if $a\lambda + b$ is a multiplicity m eigenvalue of the matrix $aA + bI$, where I is the $n \times n$ identity matrix.*

Theorem 6.2 *Let $\overline{x}$ be a fixed point of the system (14) where the modulus of all eigenvalues of $d\mathcal{G}_{\overline{x}}$ is less than 1. Then $\overline{x}$ is an asymptotically stable fixed point of (11), (12) and (13).*

Proof. Let λ be an eigenvalue of $d\mathcal{G}_{\overline{x}}$. By assumption $|\lambda| < 1$. Then $\lambda - 1$ is the corresponding eigenvalue for the system (11), and the real part of $\lambda - 1$ is negative.

The corresponding eigenvalue for (12) is $\frac{r-1}{r} + \frac{1}{r}\lambda$, and

$$\left|\frac{r-1}{r} + \frac{1}{r}\lambda\right| \leq \frac{r-1}{r} + \frac{1}{r}|\lambda| < 1$$

The argument for (13) is similar. □

If $d\mathcal{G}_{\overline{x}}$ has all eigenvalues with real parts less than 1 and some eigenvalue whose modulus is greater than 1, then $\overline{x}$ would be a stable fixed point of the continuous system (11) but an unstable fixed point of the generational discrete system (14). For the steady-state discrete system (12), the differential of the linear approximation is $\frac{r-1}{r}I + \frac{1}{r}d\mathcal{G}_{\overline{x}}$. As r goes to infinity, at some point the modulus of all eigenvalues of this differential will become less than 1, and the fixed point will become asymptotically stable.

We give a numerical example that demonstrates that this can happen. (See [WB97] for more details of the methodology used to find this example.) Assume a binary string representation with a string length of 3. The probability distribution over the mutation masks is

$$\langle\ 0.0 \quad 0.0 \quad 0.0 \quad 0.87873415 \quad 0.0 \quad 0.0 \quad 0.12126585 \quad 0.0\ \rangle^T.$$

The probability distribution over the crossover masks is

$$\langle\ 0.26654992 \quad 0.0 \quad 0.73345008 \quad 0.0 \quad 0.0 \quad 0.0 \quad 0.0 \quad 0.0\ \rangle^T.$$

The fitness vector (proportional selection) is

$$\begin{array}{llll}\langle 0.03767273 & 0.40882046 & 3.34011500 & 3.57501693 \\ \ \ 0.00000004 & 3.89672742 & 0.21183468 & 15.55715272\rangle^T.\end{array}$$

The fixed point is

$$\begin{array}{llll}\langle 0.20101565 & 0.21467902 & 0.07547095 & 0.06249578 \\ \ \ 0.26848520 & 0.04502642 & 0.11812778 & 0.01469920\rangle^T.\end{array}$$

This gives a set of eigenvalues:

$$\begin{array}{l}\{\ -1.027821882 + 0.01639853054i, \quad -1.027821882 - 0.01639853054i, \quad 0.5097754068, \\ \quad -0.3498815639, \quad 0.1348641055, \quad -0.01080298133, \\ \quad 0.2146271583 \times 10^{-5}, \quad 0.6960358287 \times 10^{-9}\}\end{array}$$

7 An illustrative experiment

It is a remarkable result that a steady-state genetic algorithm with random deletion has the same fixed-points as a generational genetic algorithm with common heuristic function

$\mathcal{G}$. We can illustrate this result experimentally as follows. Firstly, we choose some selection, crossover and mutation scheme from the wide variety available. It doesn't matter which are chosen as long as the same choice is used for the steady-state and generational GAs. In our experiments we have used binary tournament selection, uniform crossover and bitwise mutation with a rate of 0.01. Together, these constitute our choice of heuristic function $\mathcal{G}$. Secondly, we pick a simple fitness function, for example, the one-max function on 100 bits. Thirdly, we choose two different initial populations, one for each GA. These should be chosen to be far apart; for example, at different vertices of the simplex. In our experiments, the steady-state GA starts with a population of strings containing all ones, whereas the generational GA has an initial population of strings containing only zeros. A population size of 1000 was used.

The two GAs were run with these initial populations. To give a rough idea of what is happening, the average population fitness for each was recorded for each "generation". For the steady-state GA this means every time 1000 offspring have been generated (that is, equivalent to the population size). This was repeated ten times. The average results are plotted in the first graph of figure 2.

To show that the two genetic algorithms are tending towards exactly the same population, the (Euclidean) distance was calculated between the corresponding population vectors at each generation. By "population vector" is here meant a vector whose components give the proportions of the population within each *unitation class*. The results for a typical run are shown in the second graph of figure 2. It can be seen that after around 70 generations, the two GAs have very similar populations. Figure 3 shows the average (over 20 runs) distance between the algorithms where both algorithms are started with the population consisting entirely of the all-zeros string. The error bars are one standard deviation. These figures show that the two algorithms follow very different trajectories, but with the same fixed points.

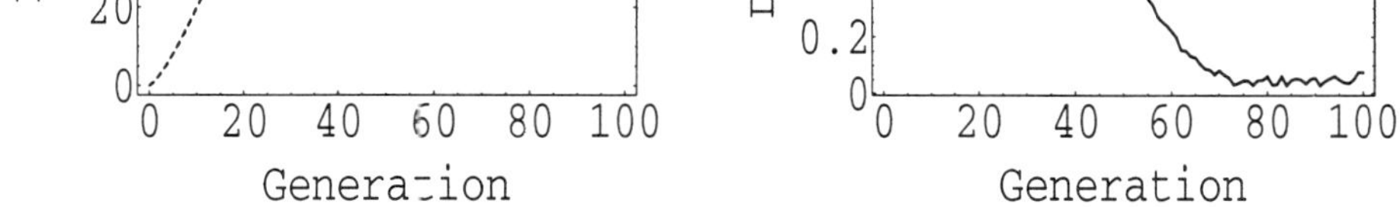

Figure 2 a) average population fitness of steady-state GA (solid line) and generational GA (dashed line), averaged over ten runs. b) Distance between steady-state GA and generational GA for a typical run.

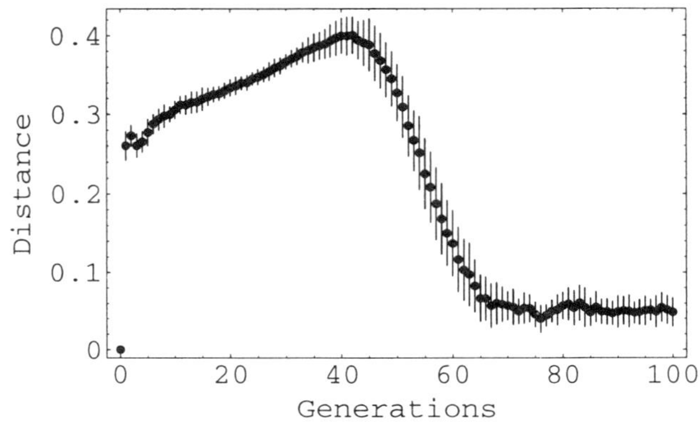

Figure 3 The distance between the steady-state GA and the generational GA averaged over 20 runs. The error bars represent one standard deviation.

8 Conclusion and further work

We have given discrete-time expected-value and continuous-time infinite-population dynamical system models of steady-state genetic algorithms. For one of these models and worst-element deletion, we have given conditions under which convergence to the uniform population consisting of copies of the optimum element is guaranteed.

We have shown the existence of solutions to the continuous-time model by giving conditions under which the discrete-time models converge to the solution of the continuous-time model. And we have given conditions for uniqueness of solutions to the continuous-time model.

We have investigated the fixed points and stability of these fixed points for these models in the case of worst-element and random deletion. Further work is needed to investigate the properties of fixed points for these and other deletion methods.

The relationship of these models to the Markov chain models of steady-state algorithms given in [WZ99] could also be investigated.

Acknowledgments

The first author thanks Alex Agapie for discussions regarding section 3.

References

[Dav91] Lawrence Davis. *Handbook of Genetic Algorithms.* Van Nostrand Reinhold, New York, 1991.

[Rei71] William T. Reid. *Ordinary Differential Equations.* John Wiley & Sons, New York, 1971.

[Rud98] Günter Rudolph. Finite markov chain results in evolutionary computation: A tour d'horizon. *Fundamenta Informaticae*, 35:67–89, 1998.

[Sys89] Gilbert Syswerda. Uniform crossover in genetic algorithms. In *Proceedings of the Third International Conference on Genetic Algorithms*, pages 2–9. Morgan Kaufman, 1989.

[Sys91] Gilbert Syswerda. A study of reproduction in generational and steady state genetic algorithms. In Gregory J. E. Rawlings, editor, *Foundations of genetic algorithms*, pages 94–101, San Mateo, 1991. Morgan Kaufmann.

[Vos99] M. D. Vose. *The Simple Genetic Algorithm: Foundations and Theory.* MIT Press, Cambridge, MA, 1999.

[WB97] A. H. Wright and G. L. Bidwell. A search for counterexamples to two conjectures on the simple genetic algorithm. In *Foundations of genetic algorithms 4*, pages 73–84, San Mateo, 1997. Morgan Kaufmann.

[Whi89] Darrell Whitley. The GENITOR algorithm and selection pressure: Why rank-based allocation of reproductive trials is best. In *Proceedings of the Third International Conference on Genetic Algorithms*, pages 116–123. Morgan Kaufman, 1989.

[Wig90] S. Wiggins. *Introduction to Applied Nonlinear Dynamical Systems and Chaos.* Springer-Verlag, New York, 1990.

[WZ99] A. H. Wright and Y. Zhao. Markov chain models of genetic algorithms. In *Proceedings of the Genetic and Evolutionary Computation (GECCO) conference*, pages 734–742, San Francisco, CA., 1999. Morgan Kaufmann Publishers.

Mutation-Selection Algorithm: a Large Deviation Approach

Paul Albuquerque
Dept. of Computer Science
University of Geneva
24 rue Général-Dufour
CH-1211 Geneva 4, Switzerland

Christian Mazza
Laboratoire de Probabilités
Université Claude Bernard Lyon–I
43 Bd du 11-Novembre-1918
69622 Villeurbanne Cedex, France

Abstract

We consider a two-operator mutation-selection algorithm designed to optimize a fitness function on the space of fixed length binary strings. Mutation acts as in classical genetic algorithms, while the fitness-based selection operates through a Gibbs measure (Boltzmann selection). The selective pressure is controlled by a temperature parameter. We provide a mathematical analysis of the convergence of the algorithm, based on the probabilistic theory of large deviations. In particular, we obtain convergence to optimum fitness by resorting to an annealing process, which makes the algorithm asymptotically equivalent to simulated annealing.

1 INTRODUCTION

Genetic algorithms (GAs) are stochastic optimization algorithms designed to solve hard, typically NP-complete, problems (Goldberg, 1989), (Bäck, 1996), (Vose, 1999). Introduced by Holland (Holland, 1975), these algorithms mimick the genetic mechanisms of natural evolution. An initial random population of potential solutions is evolved by applying genetically inspired operators: mutation, crossover and selection. With time, "better" solutions emerge in the population. The quality of a solution is evaluated in terms of a fitness function. The original optimization problem now translates into finding a global optimum of this function. Note that in general, the convergence of a GA to an optimal solution is not guaranteed. Only few rigorous mathematical results ensuring convergence of GAs are available.

For the past ten years, increasing efforts have been put into providing rigorous mathematical analyses of GAs (Rawlins, 1991), (Whitley, 1993), (Whitley, 1995), (Belew, 1997), (Banzhaf and Reeves, 1999). Towards this end, GAs have been modeled with Markov chains (Nix and Vose, 1992), (Rudolph, 1994). Application of Markov chain techniques has proved very successful in the study of simulated annealing (SA). This approach has produced an extensive mathematical literature describing the dynamics and investigating convergence properties of SA (Aarts and Laarhoven, 1987), (Aarts and Korst, 1988), (Hajek, 1988), (Catoni, 1992), (Deuschel and Mazza, 1994). It was therefore natural to try to carry over SA formalism to GAs. This was to our knowledge initiated by Goldberg (Goldberg, 1990), who borrowed the notions of thermal equilibrium and Boltzmann distribution from SA and adapted them to GA practice. A theoretical basis was later elaborated by Davis for simple GAs (Davis and Principe, 1991). His approach was further developed by Suzuki and led to a convergence result (Suzuki, 1997).

We believe the first mathematically well-founded convergence results for GAs were obtained by Cerf (Cerf, 1996a), (Cerf, 1996b), (Cerf, 1998), who constructed an asymptotic theory for the simple GA comparable in scope to that of SA. The asymptotic dynamics was investigated using the powerful tools developed by Freidlin and Wentzell (Freidlin and Wentzell, 1984) for the study of random perturbations of dynamical systems. Cerf's pioneering work takes place in the wider context of generalized simulated annealing, which was defined by Trouvé (Trouvé, 1992a), (Trouvé, 1992b), extending results of Catoni for SA (Catoni, 1992). The dynamics for simulations in various contexts, like statistical mechanics, image processing, neural computing and optimization, can be described in this setting.

Complementary to the asymptotic approach, novel work has been achieved by Rabinovich and Wigderson in providing an original mathematical analysis of a crossover-selection algorithm (Rabinovich and Wigderson, 1999). Both analyses shed some light on the behavior of GAs. Let us still quote a paper by François in which he proves convergence of an alternate mutation-selection algorithm (François, 1998), also within the framework of generalized simulated annealing.

In this contribution, we address the problem of optimizing a fitness function $F : \Omega \to \mathbb{R}_{>0}$ on the space Ω of binary strings of length l (Ω is the l-dimensional hypercube). We apply to this problem a mutation-selection algorithm, which was introduced in a slightly different form by Davis (Davis and Principe, 1991) and extensively studied in greater generality by Cerf (Cerf, 1996a), (Cerf, 1996b) (the difference resides in the Boltzmann selection to which we add a noise component). We will show that this mutation-selection algorithm is asymptotically equivalent to SA. This emphasizes the importance of the crossover operator for GAs. Our treatment also takes place within the framework defined by the theory of Freidlin-Wentzell for random perturbation of dynamical systems. The main mathematical object consists of irreducible Markov kernels with exponentially vanishing coefficients.

The paper is organized as follows. In section 2 we describe the mutation-selection algorithm and state some convergence results. The proofs of these results are sketched in section 3 where we perform a large deviation analysis of the algorithm. The algorithm is run in three different ways depending on how we let the temperature for the Boltzmann selection and the mutation probability go to zero. We finally draw some conclusions in section 4.

2 MUTATION-SELECTION ALGORITHM

We now describe a two-operator mutation-selection algorithm on the search space Ω^p of populations consisting of p individuals ($\Omega = \{0,1\}^l$).

Mutation acts as in classical GAs. Each bit of an individual in Ω independently flips with probability $0 < \tau < 1$. At the population level, all individuals mutate independently of each other. Mutation is fitness-independent and operates as a blind search over Ω^p.

We consider a modified version of the selection procedure of classical GAs. We begin by adding some noise $g(\xi, .)$ to $\log(F(\xi))$ for technical reasons. It helps lift the degeneracy over the global maxima set of F. The real-valued random variables $g(\xi, .)$, indexed by $\xi \in \Omega$, are defined on a sample space I (e.g. a subinterval of $\mathbb{R}$). They are independent identically distributed (i.i.d.) with mean zero and satisfy

$$|g(\xi,\omega)| < \frac{1}{2}\min\{|\log(\frac{F(\xi_1)}{F(\xi_2)})| : F(\xi_1) \neq F(\xi_2),\ \xi_1,\xi_2 \in \Omega\}, \quad \forall \omega \in I. \tag{1}$$

Hence the random variables $f(\xi, .) = \log(F(\xi)) + g(\xi, .)$ have mean $\log(F(\xi))$ and the function $f(.,\omega)$ has the same optima set as F by assumption (1), but a unique global maximum for almost every sample point $\omega \in I$.

Fix a point ω in the sample space I. Given a population $x = (x_1, \ldots, x_p) \in \Omega^p$ of size p, individual x_i is selected under a Gibbs distribution (Boltzmann selection) with probability

$$\frac{\exp(\beta f(x_i,\omega))}{\sum_{j=1}^{p} \exp(\beta f(x_j,\omega))}, \tag{2}$$

from population x. The parameter $\beta \geq 0$ corresponds to an inverse temperature as in simulated annealing and controls the selective pressure. Note that if we remove the noise and set $\beta = 1$, the above selection procedure reduces to classical GA fitness-proportional selection.

The algorithm is run only after the fitness function has been perturbed by the noise component. For any given sample point ω and τ, β fixed, we get an irreducible Markov chain on the search space Ω^p by successively applying mutation and selection. Denote by $\mu^{\omega}_{\tau,\beta}$ its stationary probability distribution and by $\mu_{\tau,\beta}$ the probability distribution obtained after averaging the $\mu^{\omega}_{\tau,\beta}$'s over the sample space.

Before stating results, we introduce some notations and terminology. We define the set of uniform populations

$$\Omega_{=} = \{(x_1, \ldots, x_p) \in \Omega^p : x_1 = \cdots = x_p\} \tag{3}$$

and the set of populations consisting only of maximal fitness individuals

$$F_{max} = \{(x_1, \ldots, x_p) \in \Omega^p : F(x_i) = \max_{\xi \in \Omega} F(\xi)\}. \tag{4}$$

We also recall that the support of a probability distribution on Ω^p consists of all populations having positive probability.

Each theorem stated below corresponds to a specific way of running the mutation-selection algorithm.

Theorem 1 *Let $\beta > 0$ be fixed. Then, as $\tau \to 0$, the probability distribution $\mu_{\tau,\beta}$ converges to a probability distribution $\mu_{0,\beta}$ with support$(\mu_{0,\beta}) = \Omega_=$. Moreover, the limit probability distribution $\lim_{\beta\to\infty}\mu_{0,\beta}$ concentrates on $\Omega_= \cap\ F_{max}$.*

The first assertion in theorem 1 was already obtained by Davis (Davis and Principe, 1991) and the second by Suzuki (Suzuki, 1997) by directly analyzing the transition probabilities of the Markov chain. However their algorithm did not include the added noise component. We give a different proof in the next section.

Theorem 1 implies that, for β, τ both fixed and $\tau \approx 0$, the mutation-selection algorithm concentrates on a neighboorhood of $\Omega_=$ in Ω^p. Hence a run has a positive probability of ending on any population in $\Omega_=$. The hope remains that the stationary probability distribution has a peak on $\Omega_= \cap\ F_{max}$. This is actually the case, since the probability distribution $\lim_{\beta\to\infty}\mu_{0,\beta}$ concentrates on $\Omega_= \cap F_{max}$. The latter statement can be obtained as a consequence of theorem 3.

Notice that GAs are usually run with $\tau \approx 0$. We believe that the crossover operator improves the convergence speed, but probably not the shape of the stationary probability distribution.

Theorem 2 *Let $0 < \tau < 1$ be fixed. Then, as $\beta \to \infty$, the probability distribution $\mu_{\tau,\beta}$ converges to a probability distribution $\mu_{\tau,\infty}$ with support$(\mu_{\tau,\infty}) = \Omega_=$. Moreover, the limit probability distribution $\lim_{\tau\to 0}\mu_{\tau,\infty}$ concentrates on $\Omega_=$.*

Theorem 2 shows that, in terms of probability distribution support, increasing the selective pressure is equivalent to diminishing the mutation probability. However, $\lim_{\tau\to 0}\mu_{\tau,\infty}$ remains concentrated on $\Omega_=$.

Consequently, it is a natural idea to link the mutation probability τ to the inverse temperature β. The algorithm becomes a simulated annealing process: the intensity of mutation is decreased, while selection becomes stronger. This actually ensures convergence of the algorithm to an optimal solution.

Theorem 3 *Let $\tau = \tau(\epsilon, \kappa, \beta) = \epsilon \exp(-\kappa\beta)$ with $0 < \epsilon < 1$ and $\kappa > 0$. Then, for κ large enough, the probability distribution $\mu_{\tau,\beta}$ converges, as $\beta \to \infty$, to the uniform probability distribution over $\Omega_= \cap\ F_{max}$. Asymptotically, the algorithm behaves like simulated annealing on $\Omega_=$ with energy function $-p\log F$.*

Notice that the initial mutation probability ϵ does not influence the convergence.

The first assertion in theorem 3 was obtained by Cerf (Cerf, 1996a), (Cerf, 1996b), in a much more general setting, but again with a mutation-selection algorithm not including the added noise component. However, we hope that our proof, presented below in the simple case of binary strings, is more intuitive and easier to grasp. Maybe will it illustrate the importance of Cerf's work and the richness of the Freidlin-Wentzell theory.

3 LARGE DEVIATION ANALYSIS

In analogy with the original treatment of simulated annealing, we prefer to deal with $U^\omega = -f(.,\omega)$ the energy function. The optimization problem now amounts to finding the global minima set of U^ω which can be thought as the set of fundamental states of the energy function U^ω. For almost every ω, U^ω has a unique fundamental state.

Denote by $\rho(.,.)$ the Hamming distance on Ω and set

$$d(x,y) = \sum_{i=1}^{p} \rho(x_i, y_i),$$

with $x = (x_1, \ldots, x_p)$ and $y = (y_1, \ldots, y_p)$ populations in Ω^p; $d(.,.)$ is a metric on Ω^p.

Let M_τ be the transition matrix for the mutation process on Ω^p. The probability that a population $x \in \Omega^p$ is transformed into $y \in \Omega^p$ by mutation is

$$M_\tau(x,y) = \tau^{d(x,y)}(1-\tau)^{lp-d(x,y)}. \tag{5}$$

We define the partial order relation $\prec$ on Ω^p by:

$$x \prec y \Leftrightarrow x_i \in \{y_1, \ldots, y_p\},\ \forall i \in \{1, \ldots, p\}.$$

In words, $x \prec y$ if and only if all individuals in population x belong to population y.

Let S_β^ω be the transition matrix for the selection process on Ω^p. The probability that a population $x \in \Omega^p$ is transformed into $y \in \Omega^p$ by selection (see (2)) is given by

$$S_\beta^\omega(x,y) = \begin{cases} \dfrac{\exp\left(-\beta \sum_{i=1}^{p} U^\omega(y_i)\right)}{\left(\sum_{i=1}^{p} \exp(-\beta U^\omega(x_i))\right)^p} & \text{if } x \succ y, \\ 0 & \text{if } x \not\succ y. \end{cases} \tag{6}$$

The transition matrix of the Markov chain corresponding to our mutation-selection algorithm is $S_\beta^\omega \circ M_\tau$. From eqs. (5) and (6), we compute the transition probabilities

$$\begin{aligned} S_\beta^\omega \circ M_\tau(x,y) &= \sum_{z \succ y} M_\tau(x,z) S_\beta^\omega(z,y) \qquad (7) \\ &= \sum_{z \succ y} \tau^{d(x,z)}(1-\tau)^{lp-d(x,z)} \frac{\exp\left(-\beta \sum_{i=1}^{p} U^\omega(y_i)\right)}{\left(\sum_{i=1}^{p} \exp(-\beta U^\omega(z_i))\right)^p}. \end{aligned}$$

The mutation and selection processes are simple to treat on their own. However, their combined effect proves to be more complicated. A way of dealing with this increase in complexity is to consider these processes as asymptotically vanishing perturbations of a simple random process. We study three cases. In the first, mutation acts as the perturbation, while selection plays this role in the second. In the third case, the combination of mutation and selection acts as a perturbation of a simple selection scheme, namely equiprobable selection among the best individuals in the current population.

We will now compute three different communication cost functions corresponding to various ways of running the mutation-selection algorithm. The communication cost reflects the asymptotic difficulty for passing from one population to another under the considered random process.

Write $\tau = \tau(\alpha) = e^{-\alpha}$ with $\alpha > 0$. Asymptotically, for β fixed and $\alpha \to \infty$, eq. (7) yields

$$\lim_{\alpha \to \infty} -\frac{1}{\alpha} \log \left(S_\beta^\omega \circ M_{\tau(\alpha)}(x, y) \right) = \min_{z \succ y} d(x, z).$$

Henceforth, we will use the asymptotic notation

$$S_\beta^\omega \circ M_{\tau(\alpha)}(x, y) \asymp \exp\left(-\alpha \min_{z \succ y} d(x, z) \right).$$

The communication cost for asymptotically vanishing mutation is given by

$$V^M(x \to y) = \min_{z \succ y} d(x, z) . \tag{8}$$

Define the total energy function $\mathcal{U}^\omega : \Omega^p \to \mathbb{R}$ by

$$\mathcal{U}^\omega(y) = \sum_{i=1}^{p} U^\omega(y_i) ,$$

and notice that $\min_{v \prec z} \mathcal{U}^\omega(v) = p \min_{1 \le i \le p} U^\omega(z_i)$. Asymptotically, for τ fixed and $\beta \to \infty$, eq. (7) yields

$$S_\beta^\omega \circ M_\tau(x, y) \asymp \exp\left(-\beta \min_{z \succ y} (\mathcal{U}^\omega(y) - \min_{v \prec z} \mathcal{U}^\omega(v)) \right) .$$

The associated communication cost is given by

$$V^{S,\omega}(x \to y) = \min_{z \succ y} (\mathcal{U}^\omega(y) - \min_{v \prec z} \mathcal{U}^\omega(v)) . \tag{9}$$

Next, let $\tau = \tau(\epsilon, \kappa, \beta) = \epsilon \exp(-\kappa\beta)$ with $0 < \epsilon < 1$ and $\kappa > 0$. Asymptotically, for ϵ, κ fixed and $\beta \to \infty$, eq. (7) yields

$$S_\beta^\omega \circ M_{\tau(\epsilon,\kappa,\beta)}(x, y) \asymp \exp\left(-\beta \min_{z \succ y} (\kappa d(x, z) + \mathcal{U}^\omega(y) - \min_{v \prec z} \mathcal{U}^\omega(v)) \right) .$$

The associated communication cost is given by

$$V_\kappa^{MS,\omega}(x \to y) = \min_{z \succ y} \left(\kappa d(x, z) + \mathcal{U}^\omega(y) - \min_{v \prec z} \mathcal{U}^\omega(v) \right) . \tag{10}$$

3.1 KEY LEMMATA

The lemmata we state below are crucial for the proofs of theorem 1, 2, and 3. We comment on these lemmata in the appendix.

We consider a family of Markov chains on a finite set S, indexed by a real parameter $\alpha > 0$, with irreducible transition matrix $\{q_\alpha(x, y)\}_{x,y \in S}$ satisfying

$$q_\alpha(x, y) \asymp \exp(-\alpha V(x \to y)), \quad x, y \in S,$$

where $0 \leq V(x \to y) \leq \infty$ is the communication cost function.

Let μ_α be the stationary probability distribution on S associated to $\{q_\alpha(x,y)\}_{x,y\in S}$ and define $\mu_\infty = \lim_{\alpha\to\infty} \mu_\alpha$ the limit probability distribution on S.

A function $\psi : S \to \mathbb{R}$ is a potential for the communication cost function $V(x \to y)$, if $V(x \to y) - V(y \to x) = \psi(y) - \psi(x)$ for all $x, y \in S$ such that $V(x \to y) < \infty$.

The following two results are derived from the so-called Freidlin-Wentzell theory (Freidlin and Wentzell, 1984).

Lemma 4 *Assume there is a potential $\psi : S \to \mathbb{R}$ for the communication cost function $V(x \to y)$. Then*

$$support(\mu_\infty) = \{x \in S : \psi(x) = \min_{y\in S} \psi(y)\}.$$

Lemma 5 *Let S_- be a subset of S with the properties:*

1. *for any $x \in S_+ = S \setminus S_-$, there exists $y \in S_-$ such that $V(x \to y) = 0$.*
2. *for any $y \in S_-$, we have $V(x \to y) > 0$ for all $x \in S_+$.*

Then the dynamics can be restricted from S onto S_-.

The sets S_+ and S_- can be respectively thought as repulsive and attractive sets for the dynamics. The dynamics can be restricted from S onto S_-, because in the asymptotic regime the cost for entering S_- is zero, while the cost for leaving S_+ is positive.

3.2 ASYMPTOTICALLY VANISHING MUTATION

In this subsection, we sketch the proof of theorem 1.

Hereafter, we will write (ξ) in place of $(\xi, \ldots, \xi) \in \Omega_=$.

If $x \in \Omega^p \setminus \Omega_=$, there exists $(\xi) \in \Omega_=$ such that $V^M(x \to (\xi)) = 0$. This is readily seen by taking $\xi = x_i$, for any $i \in \{1, \ldots, p\}$, and computing $V^M(x \to (\xi))$ from (8). However, for $(\xi) \in \Omega_=$, the communication cost $V^M((\xi) \to x) > 0$ for all $x \in \Omega^p \setminus \Omega_=$.

Applying lemma 5 to $S = \Omega^p$ and $S_- = \Omega_=$ for the communication cost function $V^M(x \to y)$, we can restrict the dynamics from Ω^p onto $\Omega_=$.

It is easy to check that $V^M((\eta) \to (\xi)) = V^M((\xi) \to (\eta)) = \rho(\eta, \xi)$. Thus, on $\Omega_=$ the cost function is symmetric and is given by the Hamming distance. Therefore,

$$0 = V^M((\eta) \to (\xi)) - V^M((\xi) \to (\eta)),$$

so the function $\psi \equiv 0$ is a potential for $V^M((\eta) \to (\xi))$ on $\Omega_=$. Using lemma 4, we conclude that $support(\mu^\omega_{0,\beta}) = \Omega_=$ for all ω. Finally, theorem 1 follows by averaging out the probability distributions $\mu^\omega_{0,\beta}$ over ω.

3.3 INCREASING THE SELECTIVE PRESSURE

We now take care of theorem 2.

Define the set

$$\Omega_{U^\omega} = \{(x_1, \ldots, x_p) \in \Omega^p : U^\omega(x_1) = \cdots = U^\omega(x_p)\} \tag{11}$$

of equi-fitness populations.

Since $V^{S,\omega}(x \to y) = \min_{z \succ y}(\mathcal{U}^\omega(y) - \min_{v \prec z} \mathcal{U}^\omega(v))$ (see (9)) only depends on y, the function $\psi(y) = V^{S,\omega}(x \to y)$ is itself a potential on Ω^p.

Let $y \in \Omega_{U^\omega}$. Then, taking $z = y$, we have

$$0 \leq \psi(y) \leq \mathcal{U}^\omega(y) - \min_{v \prec y} \mathcal{U}^\omega(v) = 0. \tag{12}$$

Thus $\psi(y) = 0$ for all $y \in \Omega_{U^\omega}$.

If $y \in \Omega^p \setminus \Omega_{U^\omega}$, there exists $i \neq j \in \{1, \ldots, p\}$ such that $U^\omega(y_i) \neq U^\omega(y_j)$ by definition of Ω_{U^ω} in (11). Hence, for any $z \succ y$,

$$\mathcal{U}^\omega(y) - \min_{v \prec z} \mathcal{U}^\omega(v) \geq \mathcal{U}^\omega(y) - \min_{v \prec y} \mathcal{U}^\omega(v) > 0, \tag{13}$$

because $\{v \prec y\} \subset \{v \prec z\}$ by transitivity of $\prec$. Therefore $\psi(y) > 0$ for all $y \in \Omega^p \setminus \Omega_{U^\omega}$. Lemma 4 implies that $support(\mu^\omega_{\tau,\infty}) = \Omega_{U^\omega}$. Notice that the probability that $\Omega_{U^\omega} \setminus \Omega_= \neq \emptyset$ is zero, because the noise component (see (1)) removes the degeneracy from the fitness function and hence, for almost every ω, level sets of U^ω contain at most one element. We get the statement of theorem 2 by averaging out the probability distributions $\mu^\omega_{\tau,\infty}$ over ω.

3.4 AN ANNEALING PROCESS

We go on to sketch the proof of theorem 3.

We begin by defining

$$\Delta = \max_{\xi \in \Omega} U^\omega(\xi) - \min_{\xi \in \Omega} U^\omega(\xi) \tag{14}$$

the energy barrier. Until the end of this subsection, we assume that the exponential decrease rate κ of the mutation probability, is greater than $p\Delta$.

Let $x \succ y$. Taking $z = x$, we get

$$\kappa d(x, z) + \mathcal{U}^\omega(y) - \min_{v \prec z} \mathcal{U}^\omega(v) = \mathcal{U}^\omega(y) - \min_{v \prec x} \mathcal{U}^\omega(v). \tag{15}$$

For $z \neq x$, $d(x, z) \geq 1$ and therefore,

$$\kappa d(x, z) + \mathcal{U}^\omega(y) - \min_{v \prec z} \mathcal{U}^\omega(v) > \mathcal{U}^\omega(y) - \min_{v \prec x} \mathcal{U}^\omega(v). \tag{16}$$

Consequently, eqs. (15) and (16) above imply that, in (10), the minimum over all $z \succ y$ is realized by $z = x$. Comparing with (9), we get

$$V^{MS,\omega}_\kappa(x \to y) = V^{S,\omega}(x \to y) \tag{17}$$

for $y \prec x$.

Let $x \in \Omega^p \setminus \Omega_{U^\omega}$. There exists $y \in \Omega_{U^\omega}$, $y \prec x$, such that $V_\kappa^{MS,\omega}(x \to y) = 0$. Just recall that $V^{S,\omega}(x \to y) = 0$ for any $y \in \Omega_{U^\omega}$ (see eq. (12)).

However, for $x \in \Omega_{U^\omega}$, we have $V_\kappa^{MS,\omega}(x \to y) > 0$ for all $y \in \Omega^p \setminus \Omega_{U^\omega}$. This follows from eqs. (13) and (17).

Applying lemma 5 to $S = \Omega^p$ and $S_- = \Omega_{U^\omega}$ for the communication cost function $V_\kappa^{MS,\omega}(x \to y)$, we can restrict the dynamics from Ω^p onto Ω_{U^ω}. Since the probability that $\Omega_{U^\omega} \setminus \Omega_= \neq \emptyset$ is zero, we will assume that $\Omega_= = \Omega_{U^\omega}$.

Let $(\xi), (\eta) \in \Omega_=$ with $\xi \neq \eta$. Naturally $(\xi) \not\prec (\eta)$ and $(\eta) \not\prec (\xi)$. Now let $\hat{z} = (\xi, \dots, \xi, \eta, \xi, \dots, \xi)$. Then, if $z \prec (\eta)$ is not of the form $\hat{z}$,

$$\begin{aligned}\kappa d((\xi), z) \geq & \kappa(\rho(\xi, \eta) + 1) \\ > & \kappa d((\xi), \hat{z}) + \mathcal{U}^\omega((\eta)) - \min_{v \prec \hat{z}} \mathcal{U}^\omega(v),\end{aligned}$$

where we used the assumption $\kappa > p\Delta$ and eq. (14). Hence,

$$\begin{aligned}V_\kappa^{MS,\omega}((\xi) \to (\eta)) = & \kappa d((\xi), \hat{z}) + \mathcal{U}^\omega((\eta)) - \min_{v \prec \hat{z}} \mathcal{U}^\omega(v) \\ = & \kappa\rho(\xi, \eta) + pU^\omega(\eta) - p \min_{1 \leq i \leq p} U^\omega(\hat{z}_i) \\ = & \kappa\rho(\xi, \eta) + pU^\omega(\eta) - p \min(U^\omega(\xi), U^\omega(\eta))\end{aligned}$$

and thus

$$V_\kappa^{MS,\omega}((\xi) \to (\eta)) = \kappa\rho(\xi, \eta) + p(U^\omega(\eta) - U^\omega(\xi))_+.$$

Therefore,

$$\begin{aligned}\mathcal{U}^\omega((\xi)) - \mathcal{U}^\omega((\eta)) = & p(U^\omega(\xi) - U^\omega(\eta)) \\ = & V_\kappa^{MS,\omega}((\eta) \to (\xi)) - V_\kappa^{MS,\omega}((\xi) \to (\eta))\end{aligned}$$

implying that the energy function pU^ω is a potential on $\Omega_=$.

For almost every ω, $\Omega_= = \Omega_{U^\omega}$ and thus U^ω has a unique minimum. As a consequence of lemma 4, the probability distribution $\mu^\omega_{\tau(\epsilon,\kappa,\beta),\beta}$ converges for almost every ω, as $\beta \to \infty$, to a point mass on the unique minimum of U^ω. The latter is a maximum of the fitness function. Finally, since the random variables $g(\xi, .)$'s are i.i.d., the minimum of U^ω can be equiprobably any maximum of the fitness function. Therefore, averaging over ω yields a uniform probability distribution over the set of global maxima of the fitness function (seen as a subset of $\Omega_=$).

4 CONCLUSION

The mutation-selection algorithm considered in this work helps us improve our understanding of GAs. It differs slightly from the algorithm considered by Davis (Davis and Principe, 1991) and Cerf (Cerf, 1996a), (Cerf, 1996b), because we added a noise component in the Boltzmann selection. This difference is however only technical. We studied this two-operator algorithm by resorting to the theory of Freidlin-Wentzell and by making use of the approach developed in (Deuschel and Mazza, 1994).

The first result (theorem 1) explains the behavior of the algorithm for small mutation probability $\tau \approx 0$. Under this condition, the algorithm is forced to narrow its search to a neighborhood in Ω^p of the set of uniform population $\Omega_=$ (defined in (3)). The latter set is 1-dimensional and corresponds to the diagonal of the search space Ω^p. GAs are usually run with $\tau \approx 0$. Setting $\beta = 1$ and removing the noise component, our selection procedure (see (2)) reduces to classical GA fitness-proportional selection. Hence, we can infer how the combined effect of a low mutation probability and a comparatively strong selection, as in classical GAs, removes diversity from the populations in the long-run. The second result (theorem 2) shows that the effect of increasing the selective pressure is similar, in terms of restricting the search, to lowering the mutation probability.

Since gradually decreasing τ to zero and then letting β tend to infinity, actually constrains the search to the set of maximal fitness solutions in $\Omega_=$, it was natural to link mutation probability τ and selective pressure β. Theorem 3 shows that, by exponentially decreasing τ with β, the algorithm behaves like simulated annealing on $\Omega_=$ with energy function pU. This procedure ensures convergence to an optimal solution in the limit $\beta \to \infty$. Therefore, if we fix β large enough and choose τ accordingly (see theorem 3), the algorithm will end up, in the long-run, in a neighborhood of the set of maximal fitness solutions in $\Omega_=$. Of course, the convergence performances of the algorithm will be no better than those of simulated annealing. In practical situations, the annealed version of the mutation-selection algorithm should be implemented using a cooling schedule of the form $\beta \sim \log n$, where n is the generation number, as it is the case for simulated annealing. Of course, parameters like the initial temperature and initial mutation probability ϵ as well as the exponential rate κ for τ must be set empirically. Prior knowledge about the energy barrier Δ (see (14)) would yield the estimate $\kappa \approx p\Delta$, where p is the population size.

The most interesting question arises in the comparison of the mutation-selection algorithm with classical GAs. Crossover is the distinctive feature between this algorithm and GAs. A generation in a GA is the succession of mutation, crossover and selection. From the considerations of the previous paragraph, we understand more clearly the role of crossover. The latter operator is expected to speed up the search, provided it is not fitness-decreasing on average.

More precisely, the search proceeds in successive stages. First it progresses towards the set $\Omega_=$. On $\Omega_=$, it converges towards the optimal set $\Omega_= \cap F_{max}$ (see (4)). For GAs, crossover is expected to speed up the preliminary convergence stage towards $\Omega_=$, if on average the mean fitness of the offsprings is not smaller than for the parents. However, populations in $\Omega_=$ are invariant under its action. Therefore, on $\Omega_=$, the GA performances are similar to those of simulated annealing.

Finally, we did not study the inhomogeneous Markov chain. It would be interesting to investigate finite time convergence and convergence rates.

APPENDIX

In this appendix, we introduce some notions from the theory of Freidlin-Wentzell (Freidlin and Wentzell, 1984).

As in subsection 3.1, consider a family of Markov chains on a finite set S, indexed by a real parameter $\alpha > 0$, with irreducible transition matrix $\{q_\alpha(x,y)\}_{x,y \in S}$ satisfying

$$q_\alpha(x,y) \asymp \exp(-\alpha V(x \to y)), \quad x, y \in S,$$

where $0 \le V(x \to y) \le \infty$ is the communication cost function. Let μ_α denote the stationary probability distribution on S associated to $\{q_\alpha(x,y)\}_{x,y \in S}$ and $\mu_\infty = \lim_{\alpha \to \infty} \mu_\alpha$.

Let us consider the elements of S as the vertices of the complete oriented graph G on $|S|$ vertices. A spanning tree of G pointing at $x \in S$ is a subtree T of G such that

1. S is the vertex set of T,
2. for every $y \in S$, there is a directed path from y to x.

Denote by $G(x)$ the set of all spanning trees of G pointing at $x \in S$ and define

$$\begin{aligned} V(\gamma) &= \sum_{(y \to z) \in \gamma} V(y \to z), \text{ for } \gamma \in G(x), \\ V(x) &= \min_{\gamma \in G(x)} V(\gamma), \\ V_{min} &= \min_{x \in S} V(x). \end{aligned}$$

The stationary probability distribution μ_α can be estimated in terms of the spanning trees defined above. This is formulated in the result of Freidlin and Wentzell (Freidlin and Wentzell, 1984, lemma 3.1, p.177) stated below.

Lemma 6 *We have the following representation formula for μ_α:*

$$\mu_\alpha(x) \equiv \frac{Q_\alpha(x)}{\sum_{x' \in S} Q_\alpha(x')}, \qquad \forall x \in S,$$

where $Q_\alpha(x) = \sum_{\gamma \in G(x)} \prod_{(y \to z) \in \gamma} q_\alpha(y,z)$.

Moreover,

$$\mu_\alpha(x) \asymp \exp(-\alpha(V(x) - V_{min})). \tag{18}$$

As a corollary to this lemma, we get

$$support(\mu_\infty) = \{x \in S : V(x) = V_{min}\} \tag{19}$$

from (18).

The next lemma is lemma 4 of subsection 3.1 and can be found in (Deuschel and Mazza, 1994) We reproduce the proof here for the sake of clarity.

Lemma 7 *Assume there is a potential $\psi : S \to \mathbb{R}$ for the communication cost function $V(x \to y)$. Then*

$$support(\mu_\infty) = \{x \in S : \psi(x) = \min_{y \in S} \psi(y)\}.$$

Proof: Let $x, y \in S$. For an arbitrary spanning tree $\gamma \in G(x)$, let g_{yx} be the unique geodesic of γ starting at y and ending at x. Define a mapping $R : G(x) \to G(y)$ by $R(\gamma) = (\gamma \setminus g_{yx}) \cup g_{xy}$, where g_{xy} is just the reversed geodesic from x to y. This mapping R is well-defined and onto. Moreover,

$$\begin{aligned} V(R(t)) &= V(\gamma) - V(g_{yx}) + V(g_{xy}) \\ &= V(\gamma) + \sum_{(e^- \to e^+) \in g_{xy}} (V(e^- \to e^+) - V(e^+ \to e^-)) \\ &= V(\gamma) + \sum_{(e^- \to e^+) \in g_{xy}} (\psi(e^+) - \psi(e^-)) \end{aligned}$$

which implies $V(R(\gamma)) = V(\gamma) + \psi(y) - \psi(x)$ for any $\gamma \in G(x)$. It follows that

$$\begin{aligned} V(y) &= \min_{\bar{\gamma} \in G(y)} V(\bar{\gamma}) = \min_{\gamma \in G(x)} V(R(\gamma)) \\ &= \min_{\gamma \in G(x)} (V(\gamma) + \psi(y) - \psi(x)) = V(x) + \psi(y) - \psi(x) \end{aligned} \tag{20}$$

Thus $V(y) - V(x) = \psi(y) - \psi(x)$ for any $x, y \in S$, so there is a constant C such that $V(x) = \psi(x) + C$ for any $x \in S$.

□

Notice from (20) that, if the cost function $V(x \to y)$ admits a potential, then the function $V(x)$ is also a potential for $V(x \to y)$. Two potentials differ by a constant.

The lemma below is lemma 5 of section 3.1.

Lemma 8 *Let S_- be a subset of S with the properties:*

1. *for any $x \in S_+ = S \setminus S_-$, there exists $y \in S_-$ such that $V(x \to y) = 0$.*
2. *for any $y \in S_-$, we have $V(x \to y) > 0$ for all $x \in S_+$.*

Then the dynamics can be restricted from S onto S_-.

Proof: It follows from (Freidlin and Wentzell, 1984, lemmata 4.1-3, pp.185-189) that

1. $\forall x \in S_-$, $V(x)$ is computable from graphs over S_-,
2. $\forall y \in S_+$, $V(y) = \min_{x \in S_-} (V(x) + \bar{V}(x \to y))$,

where the path communication cost $\bar{V}(x \to y)$ is defined as

$$\bar{V}(x \to y) = \bigwedge_{k=2}^{|\Omega|^p} \min_{z_2, \ldots, z_{k-1}} \left(\sum_{i=2}^{k} V(z_{i-1} \to z_i)\right),$$

with $x = z_1$ and $y = z_k$.

Since by assumption $V(x \to y) > 0$ for any $x \in S_-$ and $y \in S_+$, assertions 1 and 2 above justify the restriction of the dynamics to S_-.

□

Acknowledgements

This work is supported by the Swiss National Science Foundation and the Région Rhône-Alpes.

References

Aarts E. and Korst, J. (1988) *Simulated annealing and Boltzmann machines.* John Wiley and Sons, New-York.

Aarts E. and Laarhoven P. V. (1987) *Simulated annealing: theory and applications.* Kluwer Academic.

Banzhaf, W. and Reeves, C., editors, (1999) *Foundations of Genetic Algorithms-5*, San Francisco, CA. Morgan Kaufmann.

Bäck, T. (1996) *Evolutionary Algorithms in Theory and Practice.* Oxford University Press.

Belew, R., editor, (1997) *Foundations of Genetic Algorithms-4*, San Francisco, CA. Morgan Kaufmann.

Catoni, O. (1992) Rough large deviations estimates for simulated annealing, application to exponential schedules. *Annals of Probability*, 20(3):1109–1146.

Cerf, R. (1996a) An asymptotic theory of genetic algorithms. In Alliot, J.-M., Lutton, E., Ronald, E., Schoenauer, M., and Snyers, D., editors, *Artificial Evolution*, volume 1063 of *Lecture Notes in Computer Science*, pages 37–53, Heidelberg. Springer-Verlag.

Cerf, R. (1996b) The dynamics of mutation-selection algorithms with large population sizes. *Annales de l'Institut Henri Poincaré*, 32(4):455–508.

Cerf, R. (1998) Asymptotic convergence of genetic algorithms. *Advances in Applied Probability*, 30(2):521–550.

Davis, T. and Principe, J. C. (1991) A simulated annealing like convergence theory for the simple genetic algorithm. In Belew, R. and Bookers, L., editors, *Proc. of the Fourth International Conference on Genetic Algorithm*, pages 174–181, San Mateo, CA. Morgan Kaufmann.

Deuschel, J.-D. and Mazza, C. (1994) L^2 convergence of time nonhomogeneous Markov processes: I. spectral estimates. *Annals of Applied Probability*, 4(4):1012–1056.

François, O. (1998) An evolutionary strategy for global minimization and its Markov chain analysis. *IEEE Transactions on Evolutionary Computation*, 2(3):77–91.

Freidlin, M. and Wentzell, A. (1984) *Random perturbations of dynamical systems.* Springer-Verlag, New-York.

Goldberg, D. E. (1989) *Genetic Algorithms in Search, Optimization, and Machine Learning.* Addison-Wesley, Reading, MA.

Goldberg, D. E. (1990) A note on Boltzmann tournament selection for genetic algorithms and population-oriented simulated annealing. *Complex Systems*, 4(445-460)

Hajek, B. (1988) Cooling schedules for optimal annealing. *Math. Oper. Res*, 13:311–329.

Holland, J. (1975) *Adaptation in Natural and Artificial Systems.* The University of Michigan Press, Ann Arbor, MI.

Nix, A. and Vose, M. (1992) Modeling genetic algorithms with Markov chains. *Ann. Math. Art. Intell*, 5(1):79–88.

Rabinovich, Y. and Wigderson, A. (1999) Techniques for bounding the rate of convergence of genetic algorithms. *Random Structures and Algorithms*, 14:111–138.

Rawlins, G. J. E., editor, (1991) *Foundations of Genetic Algorithms-1*, San Mateo, CA. Morgan Kaufmann.

Rudolph, G. (1994) Convergence analysis of canonical genetic algorithms. *IEEE Trans. on Neural Networks, special issue on Evolutionary Computation*, 5(1):96–101.

Suzuki, J. (1997) A further result on the Markov chain model of genetic algorithms and its application to a simulated annealing-like strategy. In Belew, R. K. and Vose, M. D., editors, *Foundations of Genetic Algorithms-4*, pages 53–72. Morgan Kaufmann.

Trouvé, A. (1992a) Massive parallelization of simulated annealing: a mathematical study. In Azencott, R., editor, *Simulated Annealing: Parallelization Techniques*. Wiley and Sons, New-York.

Trouvé, A. (1992b) Optimal convergence rate for generalized simulated annealing. *C.R. Acad. Sci. Paris, Serie I*, 315:1197–1202.

Vose, M. D. (1999) *The Simple Genetic Algorithm : Foundations and Theory*. Complex Adaptative Systems. Bradford Books.

Whitley, D., editor, (1993) *Foundations of Genetic Algorithms-2*, San Mateo, CA. Morgan Kaufmann.

Whitley, D., editor, (1995) *Foundations of Genetic Algorithms-3*, San Francisco, CA. Morgan Kaufmann.

The Equilibrium and Transient Behavior of Mutation and Recombination

William M. Spears
AI Center - Code 5515
Naval Research Laboratory
Washington, D.C. 20375
spears@aic.nrl.navy.mil

Abstract

This paper investigates the limiting distributions for mutation and recombination. The paper shows a tight link between standard schema theories of recombination and the speed at which recombination operators drive a population to equilibrium. A similar analysis is performed for mutation. Finally the paper characterizes how a population undergoing recombination and mutation evolves.

1 INTRODUCTION

In a previous paper Booker (1992) showed how the theory of "recombination distributions" can be used to analyze evolutionary algorithms (EAs). First, Booker re-examined Geiringer's Theorem (Geiringer 1944), which describes the equilibrium distribution of an arbitrary population that is undergoing recombination. Booker suggested that "the most important difference among recombination operators is the rate at which they converge to equilibrium". Second, Booker used recombination distributions to re-examine analyses of schema dynamics. In this paper we show that the two themes are tightly linked, in that traditional schema analyses such as schema disruption and construction (Spears 2000) yield important information concerning the speed at which recombination operators drive the population to equilibrium. Rather than focus solely on the dynamics near equilibrium, however, we also examine the transient behavior that occurs before equilibrium is reached.

This paper also investigates the equilibrium distribution of a population undergoing only mutation, and demonstrates precisely (with a closed-form solution) how the mutation rate

μ affects the rate at which this distribution is reached. Again, we will focus both on the transient and the equilibrium dynamics. Finally, this paper characterizes how a population of chromosomes evolves under recombination and mutation. We discuss mutation first.

2 THE LIMITING DISTRIBUTION FOR MUTATION

This section will investigate the limiting distribution of a population of chromosomes undergoing mutation, and will quantify how the mutation rate μ affects the rate at which the equilibrium is approached. Mutation will work on alphabets of cardinality C in the following fashion. An allele is picked for mutation with probability μ. Then that allele is changed to one of the other $C - 1$ alleles, uniformly randomly.

Theorem 1 *Let S be any string of L alleles: $(a_1, ..., a_L)$. If a population is mutated repeatedly (without selection or recombination) then:*

$$\lim_{t\to\infty} p_S(t) = \prod_{i=1}^{L} \frac{1}{C}$$

where $p_S(t)$ is the expected proportion of string S in the population at time t and C is the cardinality of the alphabet.

Theorem 1 states that a population undergoing only mutation approaches a "uniform" equilibrium distribution in which all possible alleles are uniformly likely at all loci. Thus all strings will become equally likely in the limit. Clearly, since the mutation rate μ does not appear, it does not affect the equilibrium distribution that is reached. Also, the initial population will not affect the equilibrium distribution. However, both the mutation rate and the initial population may affect the *transient* behavior, namely the *rate* at which the distribution is approached. This will be explored further in the next two subsections.

2.1 A MARKOV CHAIN MODEL OF MUTATION

To explore the (non-)effect that the mutation rate and the initial population have on the equilibrium distribution, the dynamics of a finite population of strings being mutated will be modeled as follows. Consider a population of P individuals of length L, with cardinality C. Since Geiringer's Theorem for recombination (Geiringer 1944) (discussed in the next section) focuses on loci, the emphasis will be on the L loci. However, since each locus will be perturbed independently and identically by mutation, it is sufficient to consider only one locus. Furthermore, since each of the alleles in the alphabet are treated the same way by mutation, it is sufficient to focus on only one allele (all other alleles will behave identically).

Let the alphabet be denoted as $\mathcal{A}$ and $\alpha \in \mathcal{A}$ be one of the particular alleles. Let $\overline{\alpha}$ denote all the other alleles. Then define a state to be the number of α's at some locus and a time step to be one generation in which all individuals have been considered for mutation. More formally, let S_t be a random variable that gives the number of α's at some locus at time t. S_t can take on any of the $P + 1$ integer values from 0 to P at any time step t. Since this process is memory-less, the transitions between states can be modeled with a Markov chain. The probability of transitioning from state i to state j in one time step will be denoted as $P(S_t = j \mid S_{t-1} = i) \equiv p_{i,j}$. Thus, transitioning from i to j means moving from a state with $S_{t-1} = i$ α's and $(P - i)$ $\overline{\alpha}$'s to a state with $S_t = j$ α's and $(P - j)$ $\overline{\alpha}$'s.

When $0.0 < \mu < 1.0$ all $p_{i,j}$ entries are non-zero and the Markov chain is ergodic. Thus there is a steady-state distribution describing the probability of being in each state after a long period of time. By the definition of steady-state distribution, it can not depend on the initial state of the system, hence the initial population will have no effect on the long-term behavior of the system. The steady-state distribution reached by this Markov chain model can be thought of as a sequence of P Bernoulli trials with success probability $1/C$. Thus the steady-state distribution can be described by the binomial distribution, giving the probability π_i of being in state i (i.e., the probability that i α's appear at a locus after a long period of time):

$$\lim_{t \to \infty} P(S_t = i) \equiv \pi_i = \binom{P}{i} \left(\frac{1}{C}\right)^i \left(1 - \frac{1}{C}\right)^{P-i}$$

Note that the steady-state distribution does not depend on the mutation rate μ or the initial population, although it does depend on the cardinality C. Now Theorem 1 states that the equilibrium distribution is one in which all possible alleles are equally likely. This can be proven by showing that the expected number of α's at any locus of the population (at steady state) is:

$$\lim_{t \to \infty} E[S_t] = \sum_{i=0}^{P} \binom{P}{i} i \left(\frac{1}{C}\right)^i \left(1 - \frac{1}{C}\right)^{P-i} = \frac{P}{C}$$

The Markov chain model will also yield the transient behavior of the system, if we fully specify the one-step probability transition values $p_{i,j}$. First, suppose $j \geq i$. This means we are increasing (or not changing) the number of α's. To accomplish the transition requires that $j - i$ more $\overline{\alpha}$'s are mutated to α's than α's are mutated to $\overline{\alpha}$'s. The transition probabilities are:

$$p_{i,j} = \sum_{x=0}^{min\{i,P-j\}} \binom{i}{x} \binom{P-i}{x+j-i} \mu^x \left(\frac{\mu}{C-1}\right)^{x+j-i} (1-\mu)^{i-x} \left(1 - \frac{\mu}{C-1}\right)^{P-j-x}$$

Let x be the number of α's that are mutated to $\overline{\alpha}$'s. Since there are i α's in the current state, this means that $i-x$ α's are *not* mutated to $\overline{\alpha}$'s. This occurs with probability $\mu^x(1-\mu)^{i-x}$. Also, since x α's are mutated to $\overline{\alpha}$'s then $x+j-i$ $\overline{\alpha}$'s must be mutated to α's. Since there are $P-i$ $\overline{\alpha}$'s in the current state, this means that $P-i-x-j+i = P-x-j$ $\overline{\alpha}$'s are *not* mutated to α's. This occurs with probability $(\mu/(C-1))^{x+j-i}(1-\mu/(C-1))^{P-x-j}$. The combinatorials yield the number of ways to choose x α's out of the i α's, and the number of ways to choose $x+j-i$ $\overline{\alpha}$'s out of the $P-i$ $\overline{\alpha}$'s. Clearly, it isn't possible to mutate more than i α's. Thus $x \leq i$. Also, since it isn't possible to mutate more than $P-i$ $\overline{\alpha}$'s, $x+j-i \leq P-i$, which indicates that $x \leq P-j$. The minimum of i and $P-j$ bounds the summation correctly.

Similarly, if $i \geq j$, we are decreasing (or not changing) the number of α's. Thus one needs to mutate $i - j$ more α's to $\overline{\alpha}$'s than $\overline{\alpha}$'s to α's. The transition probabilities $p_{i,j}$ are:

$$\sum_{x=0}^{min\{P-i,j\}} \binom{i}{x+i-j} \binom{P-i}{x} \mu^{x+i-j} \left(\frac{\mu}{C-1}\right)^x (1-\mu)^{j-x} \left(1 - \frac{\mu}{C-1}\right)^{P-i-x}$$

The explanation is almost identical to before. Let x be the number of $\overline{\alpha}$'s that are mutated to α's. Since there are $P - i$ $\overline{\alpha}$'s in the current state, this means that $P - i - x$ $\overline{\alpha}$'s are *not* mutated to α's. This occurs with probability $(\mu/(C-1))^x(1-\mu/(C-1))^{P-i-x}$. Also, since x $\overline{\alpha}$'s are mutated to α's then $x + i - j$ α's must be mutated to $\overline{\alpha}$'s. Since there are i α's in the current state, this means that $i - x - i + j = j - x$ α's are *not* mutated to $\overline{\alpha}$'s. This occurs with probability $\mu^{x+i-j}(1-\mu)^{j-x}$. The combinatorials yield the number of ways to choose x $\overline{\alpha}$'s out of the $P - i$ $\overline{\alpha}$'s, and the number of ways to choose $x + i - j$ α's out of the i α's. Clearly, it isn't possible to mutate more than $P - i$ $\overline{\alpha}$'s. Thus $x \leq P - i$. Also, since it isn't possible to mutate more than i α's, $x + i - j \leq i$, which indicates that $x \leq j$. The minimum of $P - i$ and j bounds the summation correctly.

In general, these equations are not symmetric ($p_{i,j} \neq p_{j,i}$), since there is a distinct tendency to move towards states with a $1/C$ mixture of α's (the limiting distribution). We will not make further use of these equations in this paper, but they are included for completeness.

2.2 THE RATE OF APPROACHING THE LIMITING DISTRIBUTION

The previous subsection showed that the mutation rate μ and the initial population have no effect on the limiting distribution that is reached by a population undergoing only mutation. However, these factors do influence the transient behavior, namely, the *rate* at which that limiting distribution is approached. This issue is investigated in this subsection. Rather than use the Markov chain model, however, an alternative approach will be taken.

In order to model the rate at which the process approaches the limiting distribution, consider an analogy with radioactive decay. In radioactive decay, nuclei disintegrate and thus change state. In the world of binary strings ($C = 2$) this would be analogous to having a sea of 1's mutate to 0's, or with arbitrary C this would be analogous to having a sea of α's mutate to $\overline{\alpha}$'s. In radioactive decay, nuclei can not change state back from $\overline{\alpha}$'s to α's. However, for mutation, states can continually change from α to $\overline{\alpha}$ and vice versa. This can be modeled as follows. Let $p_\alpha(t)$ be the expected proportion of α's at time t. Then the expected time evolution of the system, which is a classic birth-death process (Feller 1968), can be described by a differential equation:[1]

$$\frac{dp_\alpha(t)}{dt} = -\mu\, p_\alpha(t) + \left(\frac{\mu}{C-1}\right)(1 - p_\alpha(t)) = \left(\frac{\mu}{C-1}\right)(1 - C\, p_\alpha(t))$$

The term $\mu\, p_\alpha(t)$ represents a loss (death), which occurs if α is mutated. The other term is a gain (birth), which occurs if an $\overline{\alpha}$ is successfully mutated to an α. At steady state the

[1] Since the system is discrete in time, *difference* equations would seem more appropriate (e.g., for $C = 2$ see Equation (44) of Beyer (1998) with $p_\alpha(t) = P_M$ and $p_\alpha(t-1) = P_R$). However, in this case differential equations are easier to work with and are adequate approximations to the behavior explored in this paper.

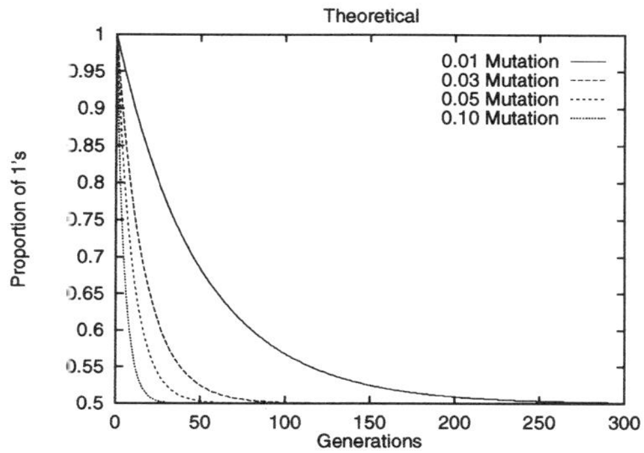

Figure 1 Decay rate for mutation when $C = 2$.

differential equation must be equal to 0, and this is satisfied by $p_\alpha(t) = 1/C$, as would be expected.

The general solution to the differential equation was found to be:

$$p_\alpha(t) = \frac{1}{C} + \left(p_\alpha(0) - \frac{1}{C}\right) e^{\frac{-C\mu t}{C-1}}$$

where $-C\mu/(C-1)$ plays a role analogous to the decay rate in radioactive decay. This solution indicates a number of important points. First, as expected, although μ does not change the limiting distribution, it does affect how fast it is approached. Also, the cardinality C also affects that rate (as well as the limiting distribution itself). Finally, different initial conditions will also affect the rate at which the limiting distribution is approached, but will not affect the limiting distribution itself. For example, if $p_\alpha(0) = 1/C$ then $p_\alpha(t) = 1/C$ for all t, as would be expected.

Assume that binary strings are being used ($C = 2$) and $\alpha = 1$. Also assume the population is initially seeded only with 1's. Then the solution to the differential equation is:

$$p_1(t) = \frac{e^{-2\mu t} + 1}{2} \tag{1}$$

which is very similar to the equation derived from physics for radioactive decay.

Figure 1 shows the decay curves derived via Equation 1 for different mutation rates. Although μ has no effect on the limiting distribution, increasing μ clearly increases the rate at which that distribution is approached. Although this result is quite intuitively obvious, the key point is that we can now make quantitative statements as to how the initial conditions and the mutation rate affect the speed of approaching equilibrium.

3 THE LIMITING DISTRIBUTION FOR RECOMBINATION

Geiringer's Theorem (Geiringer 1944) describes the equilibrium distribution of an arbitrary population that is undergoing recombination, but no selection or mutation. To understand Geiringer's Theorem, consider a population of ten strings of length four. In the initial population, five of the strings are "AAAA" while the other five are "BBBB". If these strings are recombined repeatedly, eventually 2^4 strings will become equally likely in the population. In equilibrium, the probability of a particular string will approach the product of the initial probabilities of the individual alleles – thus asserting a condition of independence between alleles. Geiringer's Theorem can be stated as follows:

Theorem 2 *Let S be any string of L alleles: $(a_1, ..., a_L)$. If a population is recombined repeatedly (without selection or mutation) then:*

$$\lim_{t\to\infty} p_S(t) = \prod_{i=1}^{L} p_{a_i}(0)$$

where $p_S(t)$ is the expected proportion of string S in the population at time t and $p_{a_i}(0)$ is the proportion of allele a at locus (position) i in the initial population.

Thus, the probability of string S is simply the product of the proportions of the individual alleles in the initial ($t = 0$) population. The equilibrium distribution illustrated in Theorem 2 is referred to as "Robbins' equilibrium" (Robbins 1918). Theorem 2 holds for all standard recombination operators, such as n-point recombination and P_0 uniform recombination.[2] It also holds for arbitrary cardinality alphabets. The key point is that recombination operators do not change the distribution of alleles at any locus; they merely shuffle those alleles at each locus.

3.1 OVERVIEW OF MARGINAL RECOMBINATION DISTRIBUTIONS

According to Booker (1992) and Christiansen (1989), the population dynamics of a population undergoing recombination (but no selection or mutation) is governed by *marginal recombination distributions.* To briefly summarize, $\mathcal{R}_A(B)$ is "the marginal probability of the recombination event in which one parent transmits the loci $B \subseteq A$ and the other parent transmits the loci in $A \backslash B$" (Booker 1992). A and B are sets and $A \backslash B$ represents set difference. For example, suppose one parent is xyz and the other is XYZ. Since there are three loci, $A = \{1, 2, 3\}$. Let $B = \{1, 2\}$ and $A \backslash B = \{3\}$. This means that the two alleles xy are transmitted from the first parent, while the third allele Z is transmitted from the second parent, producing an offspring xyZ. The marginal distribution is defined by the probability terms $\mathcal{R}_A(B)$, $B \subseteq A$. Clearly $\sum_{B\subseteq A} \mathcal{R}_A(B) = 1$ and under Mendelian segregation, $\mathcal{R}_A(B) = \mathcal{R}_A(A \backslash B)$. In terms of the more traditional schema analysis, the set A designates the defining loci of a schema. Thus, the terms $\mathcal{R}_A(A) = \mathcal{R}_A(\emptyset)$ refer to the *survival* of the schema at the defining loci specified by A.

[2] P_0 is the probability of swapping alleles. See Stephens et al. (1998) for a recent related proof of Geiringer's Theorem, stemming from exact evolution equations.

3.2 THE RATE AT WHICH ROBBINS' EQUILIBRIUM IS APPROACHED

As stated earlier, Booker (1992) has suggested that the rate at which the population approaches Robbins' equilibrium is the significant distinguishing characterization of different recombination operators. According to Booker, "a useful quantity for studying this property is the coefficient of *linkage disequilibrium*, which measures the deviation of current chromosome frequencies from their equilibrium levels". Such an analysis has been performed by Christiansen (1989), but given its roots in mathematical genetics the analysis is not explicitly tied to more conventional analyses in the EA community. The intuitive hypothesis is that those recombination operators that are more disruptive should drive the population to equilibrium more quickly (see Mühlenbein (1998) for empirical evidence to support this hypothesis). Christiansen (1989) provides theoretical support for this hypothesis by stating that the eigenvalues for convergence are given by the $\mathcal{R}_A(A)$ terms in the marginal distributions. The smaller $\mathcal{R}_A(A)$ is, the more quickly equilibrium is reached, *in the limit*. Since disruption is the opposite of survival, the direct implication is that equilibrium is reached more quickly when a recombination operator is more disruptive.

One very important caveat, however, is that this theoretical analysis holds only in the limit of large time, or when the population is near equilibrium. As GA practitioners we are far more interested in the short-term *transient* behavior of the population dynamics. Although equilibrium behavior can be studied by use of the marginal probabilities $\mathcal{R}_A(A)$, studying the transient behavior requires *all* of the marginals $\mathcal{R}_A(B), B \subseteq A$. The primary goal of this section is to tie the marginal probabilities to the more traditional schema analyses, in order to analyze the *complete* (transient and equilibrium) behavior of a population undergoing recombination. The focus will be on recombination operators that are commonly used in the GA community: n-point recombination and P_0 uniform recombination. Several related questions will be addressed. For example, lowering P_0 from 0.5 makes P_0 uniform recombination less disruptive ($\mathcal{R}_A(A)$ increases). How do the remainder of the marginals change? Can we compare n-point recombination and P_0 uniform recombination in terms of the population dynamics? Finally, what can we say about the transient dynamics? Although these questions can often only be answered in restricted situations the picture that emerges is that traditional schema analyses such as schema disruption *and* construction (Spears and De Jong 1998) do in fact yield important information concerning the dynamics of a population undergoing recombination.

3.3 THE FRAMEWORK

The framework used in this section consists of a set of differential equations that describe the *expected* time evolution of the strings in a population of finite size (equivalently this can be considered to be the evolution of an infinite-size population). The treatment will hold for hyperplanes (schemata) as well, so the term "hyperplane" and "string" can be used interchangeably.

Consider having a population of strings. Each generation, pairs of strings (parents) are repeatedly chosen uniformly randomly for recombination, producing offspring for the next generation. Let S_h, S_i, and S_j be strings of length L (alternatively, they can be considered to be hyperplanes of order L). Let $p_{S_i}(t)$ be the proportion of string S_i at time t. The time evolution of S_i will again involve terms of loss (death) and gain (birth). A loss will occur if parent S_i is recombined with another parent such that neither offspring is S_i. A gain will occur if two parents that are not S_i are recombined to produce S_i. Thus the following differential equation can be written for each string S_i:

$$\frac{dp_{S_i}(t)}{dt} = -\, loss_{S_i}(t) + gain_{S_i}(t)$$

The losses can occur if S_i is recombined with another string S_j such that S_i and S_j differ by $\Delta(S_i, S_j) \equiv k$ alleles, where k ranges from two to L. For example the string "AAAA" can (potentially) be lost if recombined with "AABB" (where $k = 2$). If S_i and S_j differ by one or zero alleles, there will be no change in the proportion of string S_i. In general, the expected loss for string S_i at time t is:

$$loss_{S_i}(t) = \sum_{S_j} p_{S_i}(t)\, p_{S_j}(t) P_d(H_k) \quad where\ 2 \leq \Delta(S_i, S_j) \equiv k \leq L \qquad (2)$$

The product $p_{S_i}(t)\ p_{S_j}(t)$ is the probability that S_i will be recombined with S_j, and $P_d(H_k)$ is the probability that neither offspring will be S_i. Equivalently, $P_d(H_k)$ refers to the probability of disrupting the kth-order hyperplane H_k defined by the k different alleles. This is identical to the probability of disruption as defined by De Jong and Spears (1992).

Gains can occur if two strings S_h and S_j of length L can be recombined to construct S_i. It is assumed that neither S_h or S_j is the same as S_i at all defining positions (because then there would be no gain) and that either S_h or S_j has the correct allele for S_i at every locus. Suppose that S_h and S_j differ at $\Delta(S_h, S_j) \equiv k$ alleles. Once again k must range from two to L. For example, the string "AAAA" can (potentially) be constructed from the two strings "AABB" and "ABAA" (where $k = 3$). If S_h and S_j differ by one or zero alleles, then either S_h or S_j is equivalent to S_i and there is no true construction (or gain).

Of the k differing alleles, m are at string S_h and $n = k - m$ are at string S_j. Thus what is happening is that two non-overlapping, lower-order building blocks H_m and H_n are being constructed to form H_k (and thus the string S_i). In general, the expected gain for string S_i at time t is:

$$gain_{S_i}(t) = \sum_{S_h, S_j} p_{S_h}(t)\ p_{S_j}(t)\ P_c(H_k \mid H_m \wedge H_n) \quad where\ 2 \leq \Delta(S_h, S_j) \equiv k \leq L \quad (3)$$

The product $p_{S_h}(t)\ p_{S_j}(t)$ is the probability that S_h will be recombined with S_j, and $P_c(H_k \mid H_m \wedge H_n)$ is the probability that an offspring will be S_i. Equivalently, $P_c(H_k \mid H_m \wedge H_n)$ is the probability of constructing the kth-order hyperplane H_k (and hence string S_i) from the two strings S_h and S_j that contain the non-overlapping, lower-order building blocks H_m and H_n. This is identical to the probability of construction as defined by Spears and De Jong (1998).

If the cardinality of the alphabet is C then there are C^L different strings. This results in a system of C^L simultaneous first-order differential equations. What is important to note is the explicit connection between Equations 2 – 3 and the more traditional schema theory for recombination, as exemplified by the probability of disruption $P_d(H_k)$ and the probability of construction $P_c(H_k \mid H_m \wedge H_n)$.

3.4 TRADITIONAL SCHEMA THEORY AND THE MARGINALS

We are now in a position to also explain the link between the traditional schema theory and the marginal probabilities. Consider the prior example, where the recombination of the parents xyz and XYZ produced an offspring xyZ. The other offspring produced is XYz. This occurs if $B = \{1,2\}$ and $A \backslash B = \{3\}$ or in the complementary situation where $B = \{3\}$ and $A \backslash B = \{1,2\}$. Hence, as pointed out earlier, $\mathcal{R}_A(B) = \mathcal{R}_A(A \backslash B)$. However, this is identical to the situation in which the third-order hyperplane $H_3 = xyZ$ is constructed from the first-order hyperplane $H_1 = \#\#Z$ and the second-order hyperplane $H_2 = xy\#$.[3] If we use $|\cdot|$ to denote the cardinality of a set, we can explicitly tie the probability of construction with the marginal probabilities:

$$P_c(H_{|A|} \mid H_{|B|} \wedge H_{|A \backslash B|}) \;=\; \mathcal{R}_A(B) \;+\; \mathcal{R}_A(A \backslash B) \;=\; 2\mathcal{R}_A(B) \tag{4}$$

where a hyperplane of order $k = |A|$ is being constructed from lower-order hyperplanes of order $m = |B|$ and order $n = |A \backslash B|$. Interestingly, Equation 4 allows us to correct an error in Booker (1992), where he computes the marginal distribution for P_0 uniform recombination. The marginal distribution should be:

$$\mathcal{R}_A(B) \;=\; [\; P_0{}^{|B|}(1-P_0)^{|A \backslash B|} \;+\; P_0{}^{|A \backslash B|}(1-P_0)^{|B|} \;] \;/\; 2$$

Survival is a special form of construction in which one of the lower-order hyperplanes has zero order. Since disruption is the opposite of survival we can write:

$$P_d(H_{|A|}) \;\equiv\; 1 \;-\; P_c(H_{|A|} \mid H_{|\emptyset|} \wedge H_{|A \backslash \emptyset|}) \;=\; 1 \;-\; 2\mathcal{R}_A(A)$$

As mentioned earlier, according to Christiansen (1989), the smaller $\mathcal{R}_A(A)$ is, the more quickly equilibrium is reached *in the limit*. We can now connect this result to the concepts of disruption and construction in the framework given by Equations 2 – 3. If some hyperplane is above the equilibrium proportion then the loss terms will be more important, as they drive the hyperplane down to equilibrium. A decrease in $\mathcal{R}_A(A)$ indicates that a recombination operator is more disruptive. This increases the loss terms and drives the hyperplane down towards equilibrium more quickly. Likewise, if some hyperplane is below the equilibrium proportion then the gain terms will be more important, as they drive the hyperplane up towards equilibrium. Since marginals must sum to one, if $\mathcal{R}_A(A)$ decreases some (or all) of the other marginals will increase to compensate. Thus, *on the average* a more disruptive recombination operator will increase the $P_c(H_k \mid H_m \wedge H_n)$ terms and hence drive that hyperplane to equilibrium more quickly.

However, as stated before, the caveat lies in the phrase "in the limit". Although a reduction in $\mathcal{R}_A(A)$ increases the other marginals on the average, there are situations where some marginals increase while others decrease. This can cause quite interesting transient behavior. The major contributor to this phenomena appears to be the order of the hyperplane, which we investigate in the following subsections.

---

[3]This assumes that the two lower-order hyperplanes differ at all 3 defining positions. In general, they must differ at all k. Using the notation in Spears (2000), $P_{eq} = 0$.

3.5 SECOND-ORDER HYPERPLANES

We first consider the case of second-order hyperplanes, which are easiest to analyze. Consider the situation where the cardinality of the alphabet $C = 2$. In this situation there are four hyperplanes of interest: (#0#0#, #0#1#, #1#0#, #1#1#).[4] Then the four differential equations describing the expected time evolution of these hyperplanes are:

$$\frac{dp_{00}(t)}{dt} = -p_{00}(t)\,p_{11}(t)\,P_{\rm d}(H_2) \;+\; p_{01}(t)\,p_{10}(t)\,P_{\rm c}(H_2 \mid H_1 \wedge H_1)$$
$$\frac{dp_{01}(t)}{dt} = -p_{01}(t)\,p_{10}(t)\,P_{\rm d}(H_2) \;+\; p_{00}(t)\,p_{11}(t)\,P_{\rm c}(H_2 \mid H_1 \wedge H_1)$$
$$\frac{dp_{10}(t)}{dt} = -p_{01}(t)\,p_{10}(t)\,P_{\rm d}(H_2) \;+\; p_{00}(t)\,p_{11}(t)\,P_{\rm c}(H_2 \mid H_1 \wedge H_1)$$
$$\frac{dp_{11}(t)}{dt} = -p_{00}(t)\,p_{11}(t)\,P_{\rm d}(H_2) \;+\; p_{01}(t)\,p_{10}(t)\,P_{\rm c}(H_2 \mid H_1 \wedge H_1)$$

Thus for this special case the loss and gain terms are controlled fully by one computation of disruption and one computation of construction. If two recombination operators have precisely the same disruption and construction behavior on second-order hyperplanes, the system of differential equations will be the same, and the time evolution of the system will be the same. This is true regardless of the initial conditions of the system.

For example, consider one-point recombination and P_0 uniform recombination. Suppose the defining length of the second-order hyperplane is L_1. Then, $P_{\rm d}(H_2) = L_1/L$ for one-point recombination, and $P_{\rm d}(H_2) = 2P_0(1 - P_0)$ for uniform recombination. The computations for $P_{\rm c}(H_2 \mid H_1 \wedge H_1)$ equal $P_{\rm d}(H_2)$ for one-point and uniform recombination. Thus, one-point recombination should act the same as uniform recombination when the defining length $L_1 = 2LP_0(1 - P_0)$.

To illustrate this, an experiment was performed in which a population of binary strings was initialized so that 50% of the strings were all 1's, while 50% were all 0's. The strings were of length $L = 30$ and were repeatedly recombined, generation by generation, while the percentage of the second-order hyperplane #1#1# was monitored. When Robbins' equilibrium is reached the percentage of any of the four hyperplanes should be 25%. The experiment was run with 0.1 and 0.5 uniform recombination. Under those settings of P_0, the theory indicates that one-point recombination should perform identically when the second-order hyperplanes have defining length 5.4 and 15, respectively. Since an actual defining length must be an integer, the hyperplanes of defining length 5 and 15 were monitored.

Figure 2 graphs the results.[5] As expected, the results show a perfect match when comparing the evolution of H_2 under 0.5 uniform recombination and one-point recombination when $L_1 = 15$ (the two curves coincide almost exactly on the graph). The agreement is almost perfect when comparing 0.1 uniform recombination and one-point recombination

[4] These four hyperplanes have been chosen arbitrarily for illustrative purposes. Also, we assume a binary-string representation, although that isn't necessary.

[5] These results (and all subsequent results) are averaged over 1000 independent runs, with the same starting conditions. The population size was 50 and selection was uniform. 95% confidence intervals are also shown.

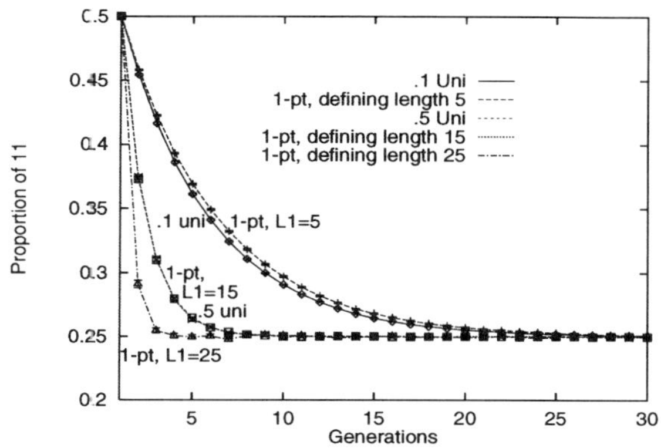

Figure 2 The rate of approaching Robbins' equilibrium for $H_2 = \#1\#1\#$, when $L = 30$.

when $L_1 = 5$, and the small amount of error is due to the fact that the defining length had to be rounded to an integer. As an added comparison, the second-order hyperplanes of defining length 25 were also monitored. In this situation one-point recombination should drive these hyperplanes to equilibrium even faster than 0.5 uniform recombination (because one-point recombination is more disruptive in this situation). The graph confirms this observation.

It is important to note that the above analysis holds even for arbitrary cardinality alphabets C, although it was demonstrated for $C = 2$. The system of differential equations would have more equations and terms as C increases, but the computations would still only involve one computation of $P_d(H_2)$ and $P_c(H_2 \mid H_1 \wedge H_1)$, and those computations would be precisely the same. To see this, consider having $C = 3$, with an alphabet of $\{0, 1, 2\}$. Then $\#0\#0\#$ can be disrupted if recombined with $\#1\#1\#$, $\#1\#2\#$, $\#2\#1\#$, or $\#2\#2\#$. The probability of disruption is the same as it was above. Similarly it can be shown that the probability of construction is the same as it was above.

3.5.1 The Rate of Decay for Second-Order Hyperplanes

It is interesting to note that, as with mutation, the decay of the curves in Figure 2 appears to be exponential in nature. This turns out to be true. To prove this, let us reconsider the differential equation describing the change in the expected proportion of the second-order hyperplane $\#1\#1\#$ at time t:

$$\frac{dp_{11}(t)}{dt} = -p_{00}(t)\, p_{11}(t)\, P_d(H_2) + p_{01}(t)\, p_{10}(t)\, P_c(H_2 \mid H_1 \wedge H_1)$$

In this case we know that $P_d(H_2) = P_c(H_2 \mid H_1 \wedge H_1)$, so the equation can be simplified to:

$$\frac{dp_{11}(t)}{dt} = P_d(H_2)[\, p_{01}(t)\, p_{10}(t) - p_{00}(t)\, p_{11}(t)\,] \tag{5}$$

For the experiment leading to Figure 2 we also know that $p_{01}(t) = p_{10}(t)$ and $p_{00}(t) = p_{11}(t)$:

$$\frac{dp_{11}(t)}{dt} = P_d(H_2)[\ p_{01}(t)\ p_{01}(t)\ -\ p_{11}(t)\ p_{11}(t)\ ]$$

However, since $p_{00}(t)+p_{01}(t)+p_{10}(t)+p_{11}(t) = 1$ it is easy to show that $p_{01}(t) = \frac{1}{2} - p_{11}(t)$. With some simplification this leads to:

$$\frac{dp_{11}(t)}{dt} = P_d(H_2)[\ \frac{1}{4}\ -\ p_{11}(t)\ ]$$

Given the initial condition that $p_{11}(0) = \frac{1}{2}$ the solution to the differential equation is:

$$p_{11}(t) = p_{00}(t) = \frac{1 + e^{-P_d(H_2)t}}{4}$$

Similarly, it is easy to show that the proportions of the #0#1# and #1#0# hyperplanes grow as follows (given the initial conditions that $p_{01}(0) = p_{10}(0) = 0$):

$$p_{01}(t) = p_{10}(t) = \frac{1 - e^{-P_d(H_2)t}}{4}$$

3.5.2 The Rate of Approaching Equilibrium

It is also possible to derive a more general result concerning the rate at which equilibrium is approached. To see this, consider Equation 5 again:

$$\frac{dp_{11}(t)}{dt} = P_d(H_2)[\ p_{01}(t)\ p_{10}(t)\ -\ p_{00}(t)\ p_{11}(t)\ ]$$

Let $\delta(t) = p_{01}(t)\ p_{10}(t) - p_{00}(t)\ p_{11}(t)$. Then it is very clear that:

$$\frac{dp_{11}(t)}{dt} = \frac{dp_{00}(t)}{dt} = -\frac{dp_{01}(t)}{dt} = -\frac{dp_{10}(t)}{dt} = \delta(t)P_d(H_2)$$

Since $\delta(t)$ goes to zero as the proportions of all the second-order hyperplanes approach equilibrium, we can consider $\delta(t)$ to be a measure of *linkage disequilibrium* for second-order hyperplanes. We can now write:

$$\frac{d\delta(t)}{dt} = p_{01}(t)\frac{dp_{10}(t)}{dt} + p_{10}(t)\frac{dp_{01}(t)}{dt} - p_{00}(t)\frac{dp_{11}(t)}{dt} - p_{11}(t)\frac{dp_{00}(t)}{dt}$$

This simplifies to:

$$\frac{d\delta(t)}{dt} = -\frac{dp_{11}(t)}{dt} = -\delta(t)P_d(H_2)$$

The solution to this is simply:

$$\delta(t) = -\delta(0)e^{-P_d(H_2)t} \tag{6}$$

where $\delta(0) = p_{01}(0)\ p_{10}(0) - p_{00}(0)\ p_{11}(0)$.

3.5.3 Summary of Second-Order Hyperplane Results

These results explicitly link traditional schema theory with the rate at which Robbins' equilibrium is approached, for second-order hyperplanes. We have shown that for second-order hyperplanes, the time evolution of two different recombination operators can be compared simply by comparing their disruptive and constructive behavior. Two recombination operators will drive a second-order hyperplane to Robbins' equilibrium at the same rate if their disruptive and constructive behavior are the same. It was also shown that $\delta(t)$, a measure of linkage disequilibrium for second-order hyperplanes, exponentially decays towards zero with the probability of disruption $P_d(H_2)$ being the rate of decay.

Unfortunately, similar results are harder to determine for higher-order hyperplanes, although some interesting results can be shown for P_0 uniform recombination, as shown in the following subsections.

3.6 UNIFORM RECOMBINATION AND LOW-ORDER HYPERPLANES

For P_0 uniform recombination the loss and gain terms of Equations 2 – 3 are especially easy to compute. As stated earlier, losses can occur if an Lth-order hyperplane S_i is recombined with an Lth-order hyperplane S_j such that S_i and S_j differ by k alleles, where k ranges from two to L. But, according to De Jong and Spears (1992) this occurs with probability:

$$P_d(H_k) \;=\; 1 \;-\; {P_0}^k \;-\; (1 - P_0)^k \qquad 2 \le k \le L$$

It can be shown that this is a unimodal function with a maximum at 0.5. Thus, the key point is that when the time evolution of the population undergoing recombination is expressed with C^L differential equations, the effect of increasing or decreasing P_0 from 0.5 reduces *all* of the loss terms in the differential equations, regardless of the order of the hyperplane. This slows the rate at which the equilibrium is approached.

Gains will occur if two hyperplanes S_h and S_j of order L can be recombined to construct S_i. Again, suppose that S_h and S_j differ at k alleles, where k ranges from two to L. Of the k differing alleles, m are at hyperplane S_h and $n = k - m$ are at hyperplane S_j. Then the probability of construction is:

$$P_c(H_k \mid H_m \wedge H_n) \;=\; {P_0}^m (1 - P_0)^n \;+\; {P_0}^n (1 - P_0)^m \qquad 2 \le k \le L,\; 0 < m < k$$

This has zero slope at $P_0 = 0.5$. The question now is under what conditions of n and m will $P_0 = 0.5$ represent a global (and the only) maximum. It is easy to show by counter-example that $P_0 = 0.5$ is not a global maximum for arbitrary m and n (e.g., $m = 1$ and $n = 4$). However, there are various cases where $P_0 = 0.5$ is a global maximum – namely when $m = 1$ and $n = 1$, $m = 1$ and $n = 2$, $m = 1$ and $n = 3$, and when $m = 2$ and $n = 2$ (and the symmetric cases where m and n are interchanged). See Figure 3 for graphs of the probability of construction, as P_0 changes.

Since we are interested in kth-order hyperplanes (where $k = m + n$), we have shown that for low-order hyperplanes ($k < 5$), construction is at a maximum when $P_0 = 0.5$ and construction decreases as P_0 decreases or increases from 0.5.

Thus, consider the time evolution of the hyperplanes in a population that are undergoing recombination, as modeled with the above differential equations. What we have shown is

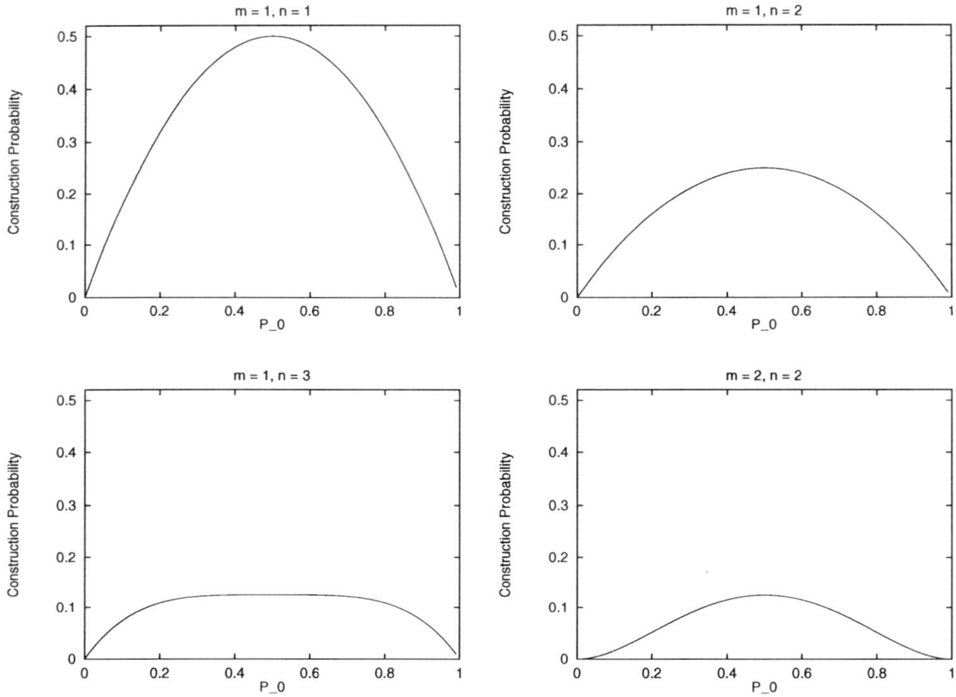

Figure 3 The probability of construction $P_c(H_k \mid H_m \wedge H_n)$ for P_0 uniform recombination on second-order ($m = 1$, $n = 1$), third-order ($m = 1$, $n = 2$), and fourth-order hyperplanes ($m = 1$, $n = 3$ and $m = 2$, $n = 2$). The probability of construction monotonically decreases as P_0 is decreased/increased from 0.5.

that if the hyperplanes have low order ($k < 5$), the effect of increasing or decreasing P_0 from 0.5 reduces *all* of the gain terms in the differential equations. Put in terms of the marginal probabilities we have shown that, for P_0 uniform recombination on low-order hyperplanes ($k < 5$), increasing $\mathcal{R}_A(A)$ (moving P_0 from 0.5) will decrease *all* of the other marginals $\mathcal{R}_A(B)$, $\emptyset \subset B \subset A$. Given this, we can expect that reducing or increasing P_0 from 0.5 should monotonically decrease the rate at which the equilibrium is approached, even during the transient behavior of the system.

To illustrate this, an experiment was performed in which a population of binary strings was initialized so that 50% of the strings were all 1's, while 50% were all 0's. The strings were of length $L = 30$ and were repeatedly recombined, generation by generation, while the percentages of the fourth-order hyperplanes #1#1#1#1# and #0#1#1#1# were monitored. When Robbins' equilibrium is reached the percentage of any of the fourth-order hyperplanes should be 6.25%. The experiment was run with uniform recombination, with P_0 ranging from 0.1 to 0.5 (higher values were ignored due to symmetry).

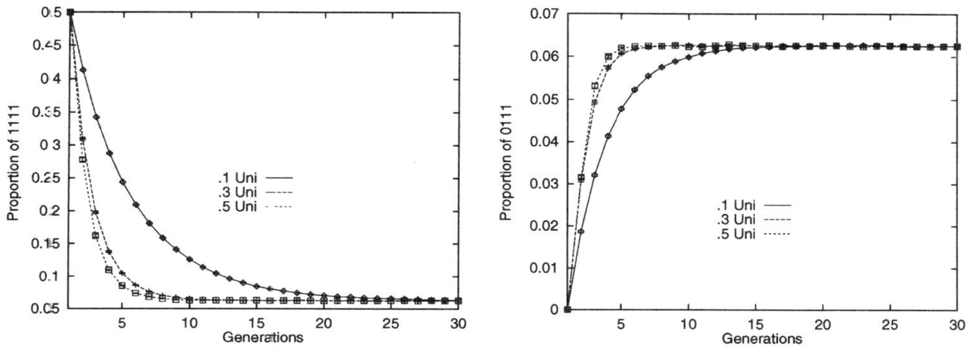

Figure 4 The rate of approaching Robbins' equilibrium for the fourth-order hyperplanes $H_4 = \#1\#1\#1\#1\#$ (left) and $H_4 = \#0\#1\#1\#1\#$ (right).

Figure 4 graphs the results. One can see that as P_0 increases to 0.5, the rate at which Robbins' equilibrium is approached also increases, as expected. This holds even throughout the transient dynamics of the system.

3.7 UNIFORM RECOMBINATION AND HIGH-ORDER HYPERPLANES

It is natural to wonder how this extends to higher-order hyperplanes. Unfortunately, as pointed out above, there will be situations (of m and n) where $P_0 = 0.5$ does not represent a global maximum for construction. However, it is easy to prove that when $m = n$ once again construction decreases as P_0 decreases or increases from 0.5. It appears as if this also holds for those situations where m and n are roughly equal (i.e., both are roughly $k/2$), but eventually fails when m and n are sufficiently different (either m or n is close to 1). Figure 5 illustrates this for eighth-order hyperplanes. Although construction is maximized at $P_0 = 0.5$ when $m = 4$ and $n = 4$, this certainly isn't true when $m = 1$ and $n = 7$. In fact, in that case construction is maximized when P_0 is roughly 0.13.

Put in terms of the marginal probabilities we have shown that, for P_0 uniform recombination on higher-order hyperplanes ($k > 4$), increasing $\mathcal{R}_A(A)$ (moving P_0 from 0.5) will decrease *some* (but not all) of the other marginals $\mathcal{R}_A(B)$, $\emptyset \subset B \subset A$. Given this, we can expect that reducing or increasing P_0 from 0.5 should not necessarily monotonically decrease the rate at which the equilibrium is approached, during the transient behavior of the system.

To illustrate this, an experiment was performed in which a population of binary strings was initialized so that 50% of the strings were all 1's, while 50% were all 0's. The strings were of length $L = 30$ and were repeatedly recombined, generation by generation, while the percentages of the eighth-order hyperplanes $\#1\#1\#1\#1\#1\#1\#1\#1\#$ and $\#0\#1\#1\#1\#1\#1\#1\#1\#$ were monitored. When Robbins' equilibrium is reached the percentage of any of the eighth-order hyperplanes should be approximately 0.39%. The

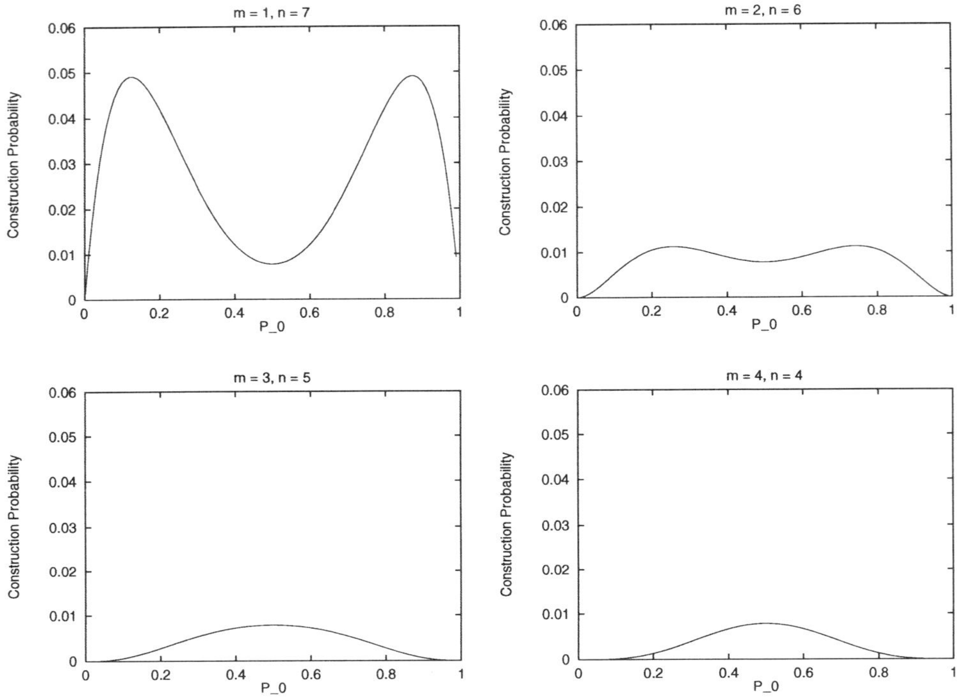

Figure 5 The probability of construction $P_c(H_k \mid H_m \wedge H_n)$ for P_0 uniform recombination, on eighth-order hyperplanes. The probability of construction does not always monotonically decrease as P_0 is decreased/increased from 0.5.

experiment was run with uniform recombination, with P_0 ranging from 0.1 to 0.5 (higher values were ignored due to symmetry).

Figure 6 graphs the results, which are quite striking. Although the proportion of the hyperplane #1#1#1#1#1#1#1#1# decays smoothly towards its equilibrium proportion, this is certainly not true for the hyperplane #0#1#1#1#1#1#1#1#. Although $P_0 = 0.5$ uniform recombination does provide the fastest convergence in the limit of large time, as would be expected, it is also clear that $P_0 = 0.1$ provides much larger changes in the proportions during the early transient behavior. In fact, for all values of P_0 the change in the proportion of this hyperplane is so large that it temporarily overshoots the equilibrium proportion!

In summary, for higher-order hyperplanes, one can see that as P_0 increases to 0.5, the rate at which Robbins' equilibrium is approached also increases, in the limit. However, this does not necessarily hold throughout the transient dynamics of the system. In fact, we have shown an example in which a *less* disruptive recombination operator provides more substantive changes in the early transient behavior.

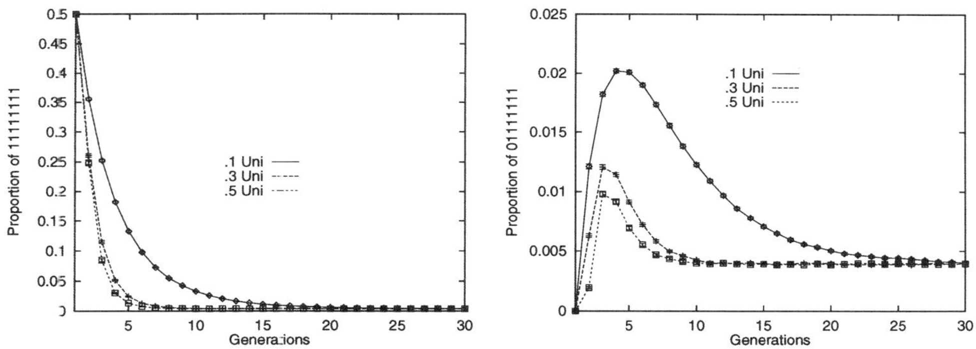

Figure 6 The rate of approaching Robbins' equilibrium for the eighth-order hyperplanes $H_8 = \#1\#1\#1\#1\#1\#1\#1\#1\#$ (left) and $H_8 = \#0\#1\#1\#1\#1\#1\#1\#1\#$ (right).

4 THE LIMITING DISTRIBUTION FOR MUTATION AND RECOMBINATION

The previous sections have considered mutation and recombination in isolation. A population undergoing recombination approaches Robbins' equilibrium, while a population undergoing mutation approaches a uniform equilibrium. What happens when both mutation and recombination act on a population? The answer is very simple. In general, Robbins' equilibrium is not the same as the uniform equilibrium; hence the population can not approach both distributions in the long term. In fact, in the long term, the uniform equilibrium prevails and we can state a similar theorem for mutation and recombination.

Theorem 3 *Let S be any string of L alleles: $(a_1, ..., a_L)$. If a population is mutated and recombined repeatedly (without selection) then:*

$$\lim_{t\to\infty} p_S(t) = \prod_{i=1}^{L} \frac{1}{C}$$

where $p_S(t)$ is the expected proportion of string S in the population at time t and C is the cardinality of the alphabet.

This is intuitively obvious Recombination can not change the distribution of alleles at any locus – it merely shuffles alleles. Mutation, however, actually changes that distribution. Thus, the picture that arises is that a population that undergoes recombination and mutation attempts to approach a Robbins' equilibrium that is itself approaching the uniform equilibrium. Put another way, Robbins' equilibrium depends on the distribution of alleles in the initial population. This distribution is continually changed by mutation, until the uniform equilibrium distribution is reached. In that particular situation Robbins' equilibrium is the same as the uniform equilibrium distribution. Thus the effect of mutation is to move Robbins' equilibrium to the uniform equilibrium distribution. The speed of

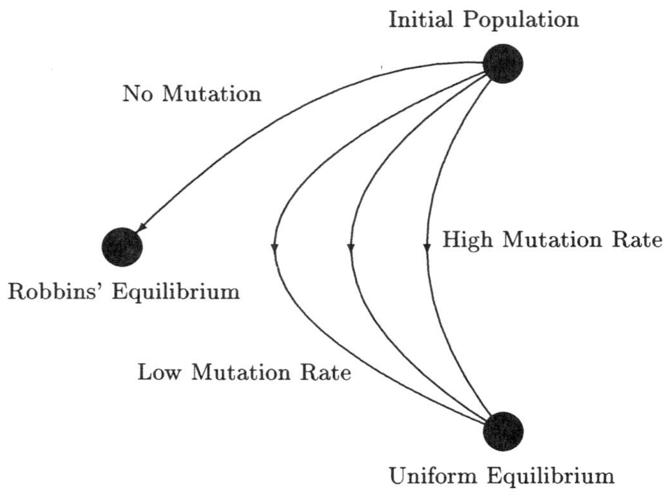

Figure 7 Pictorial representation of the action of mutation and recombination on the initial population

that movement will depend on the mutation rate μ (the greater that μ is the faster the movement). This is displayed pictorially in Figure 7.

5 SUMMARY

This paper investigated the limiting distributions of recombination and mutation, focusing not only on the dynamics near equilibrium, but also on the transient dynamics before equilibrium is reached. A population undergoing mutation approaches a uniform equilibrium in which every string is equally likely. The mutation rate μ and the initial population have no effect on that limiting distribution, but they do affect the transient behavior. The transient behavior was examined via a differential equation model of this process (which is analogous to radioactive decay in physics). This allowed us to make quantitative statements as to how the initial population, the cardinality C of the alphabet, and the mutation rate μ affect the speed at which the equilibrium is approached.

We then investigated recombination. A population undergoing only recombination will approach Robbins' equilibrium. Geiringer's Theorem indicates that this equilibrium distribution depends only on the distribution of alleles in the initial population. The form of recombination and the cardinality are irrelevant. The paper then attempted to characterize the transient behavior of the system, by developing a differential equation model of the population. Using this, it is possible to show that the probability of disruption (P_d) and the probability of construction (P_c) of schemata are crucial to the time evolution of the system. These probabilities can be obtained from traditional schema analyses. We also provide the connection between the traditional schema analyses and an alternative framework based on marginal recombination distributions $\mathcal{R}_A(B)$ (Booker 1992). Survival (the opposite of disruption) is given by $\mathcal{R}_A(A)$ while construction is given by the remaining marginals $\mathcal{R}_A(B)$, $\emptyset \subset B \subset A$.

The analysis supports the theoretical result by Christiansen (1989) that, in the limit, more disruptive recombination operators (higher values of P_d or lower values of $\mathcal{R}_A(A)$) drive the population to equilibrium more quickly. However, we also show that the transient behavior can be subtle and can not be captured this simply. Instead the transient behavior depends on the whole probability distribution $\mathcal{R}_A(B)$, $B \subseteq A$ (and hence on the values of P_c).

The major contributor to interesting transient behavior appears to be the order of the hyperplane. We first examined second-order hyperplanes. By comparing one-point recombination and P_0 uniform recombination directly on second-order hyperplanes, we were able to derive a relationship showing when one-point recombination and uniform recombination both drive hyperplanes towards equilibrium at the same speed. We were also able to show that the linkage disequilibrium for second-order hyperplanes exponentially decays towards zero, with the probability of disruption P_d being the rate of decay. In these situations a more disruptive recombination operator drives hyperplanes towards equilibrium more quickly, even during the transient dynamics.

We then examined P_0 uniform recombination on hyperplanes of order $k > 2$. When $k < 5$ it is possible to show that when recombination becomes less disruptive ($\mathcal{R}_A(A)$ increases), *all* of the remaining marginals $\mathcal{R}_A(B)$ ($\emptyset \subset B \subset A$) decrease. Due to this, once again a more disruptive recombination operator drives hyperplanes towards equilibrium more quickly, even during the transient dynamics. However, when $k > 4$ the situation becomes much more interesting. In these situations some remaining marginals will decrease while others increase. This leads to behavior in which *less* disruptive recombination operators can in fact provide *larger* changes in hyperplane proportions, during the transient phase. These results are important because, due to the action of selection on a real GA population, the transient behavior of a population undergoing recombination is all that really matters.

Finally, we investigated the joint behavior of a population undergoing both mutation and recombination. We showed that, in a sense, the behavior of mutation takes priority, in that mutation actually moves Robbins' equilibrium until it is the same as the uniform equilibrium (i.e., all strings being equally likely).

References

Beyer, H.-G. (1998). On the dynamics of EAs without selection. In W. Banzhaf and C. Reeves (Eds.), *Foundations of Genetic Algorithms*, Volume 5, pp. 5–26. Morgan Kaufmann.

Booker, L. (1992). Recombination distributions for genetic algorithms. In D. Whitley (Ed.), *Foundations of Genetic Algorithms*, Volume 2, pp. 29–44. Morgan Kaufmann.

Christiansen, F. (1989). The effect of population subdivision on multiple loci without selection. In M. Feldman (Ed.), *Math. Evol. Theory*, pp. 71–85. Princeton University Press.

De Jong, K. and W. Spears (1992). A formal analysis of the role of multi-point crossover in genetic algorithms. *Annals of Mathematics and Artificial Intelligence* 5(1), 1–26.

Feller, W. C. (1968). *An Introduction to Probability Theory and its Applications*, Volume 1. Wiley.

Geiringer, H. (1944). On the probability theory of linkage in Mendelian heredity. *Annals of Mathematical Statistics 15*, 25–57.

Mühlenbein, H. (1998). The equation for response to selection and its use for prediction. *Evolutionary Computation 5*(3), 303–346.

Robbins, R. (1918). Some applications of mathematics to breeding problems, III. *Genetics 3*, 375–389.

Spears, W. (2000). *Evolutionary Algorithms: The Role of Mutation and Recombination.* Springer-Verlag.

Spears, W. and K. De Jong (1998). Dining with GAs: Operator lunch theorems. In *Foundations of Genetic Algorithms*, Volume 5. Morgan Kaufmann.

Stephens, C., H. Waelbroeck, and R. Aguirre (1998). Schemata as building blocks: Does size matter? In W. Banzhaf and C. Reeves (Eds.), *Foundations of Genetic Algorithms*, Volume 5, pp. 117–133. Morgan Kaufmann.

The Mixing Rate of Different Crossover Operators

Adam Prügel-Bennett*
Image, Speech and Intelligent Systems Research Group
Department of Electronics and Computer Science
University of Southampton
Highfield, Southampton SO17 1BJ, United Kingdom

Abstract

In order to understand the mixing effect of crossover a simple shuffling problem is considered. The time taken for the strings in a population to become mixed is calculated for different crossover procedures. Uniform crossover is found to mix the population fastest, while single-point crossover causes very slow mixing. Two-point crossover extrapolates between these two limiting cases.

1 INTRODUCTION

One of the benefits of using an evolutionary algorithm is that it opens up the possibility of using a crossover operator. In early Genetic Algorithms single-point or two-point crossover were used to recombine pairs of strings [1–3]. Later multi-point crossover [4] and uniform crossover [5–7] were studied. A short controversy raged over which of these operators was best. Of course, this will depend on the problem being treated. Indeed, for many problems it is necessary to design a problem specific crossover operator [8]. Nevertheless, an important practical issue is to identify characteristics of crossover which allow for a more rational choice of crossover operator.

In this paper we study one such aspect of crossover, namely how efficiently it mixes the solutions. This is a problem independent aspect of crossover, which tells us about how quickly the population will explore the space of solutions. To study this we consider a problem which can be viewed as generalized card shuffle. We start with a pack of cards consisting of N suits with L cards in each suit. The pack is divided into N hands sorted

* email: `apb@ecs.soton.ac.uk`

according to their suit. The hands are then shuffled by pairing them and swapping cards using a uniform, single-point or multi-point crossover strategy. We study how the hands become shuffled over time. In the language of Genetic Algorithms the hands correspond to strings or chromosomes, the cards to genes, while the suits correspond to different alleles.

We define an order parameter to measure the degree of mixing within the population. As the strings become mixed the order parameter decays to the value of a totally mixed population. We define the mixing rate to be the asymptotic rate at which the order parameter decays. The mixing rates for single-point, two-point and uniform crossover are calculated analytically. As one might expect, uniform crossover mixes faster than multi-point crossover which mixes faster than single-point crossover, however, the difference in the rate between uniform and single-point crossover, is more dramatic than one might naively expect. This does not, of course, imply that uniform crossover is always best. Another important factor in choosing a crossover operator is its average cost due to the disruption it causes. A measure of this cost might be the average loss in fitness caused by crossover (this 'interface energy' was computed, for example, in [9, 10] for one particular problem). For problems where the spatial position of the loci have a meaning, uniform crossover may be too disruptive, whereas single-point crossover may produce only a small change in the fitness. However, this cost will depend on the problem being considered. In contrast, mixing of the allele between strings is problem independent.

On completing this paper, a different approach to the same problem was brought to my attention. This approach by Rabani, Rabinovich and Sinclair [11] considered crossover to be a special case of a quadratic dynamical system (QDS)—a generalization of a Markov chain to a process depending on combining two members of a population. In contrast to Markov chains there is no known procedure for solving a QDS. The authors, however, develop tight bounds on the convergence times for the probability distribution of a subclass of QDS to its equilibrium distribution. They use this result to obtain mixing rates for different crossover operators. Rabani *et al.*'s approach is extremely powerful, but has a different character to the approach taken here. In this paper, we consider the evolution of a single statistical property of the population, namely a measure of the degree of shuffling. By concentrating on this simple quantity the problem simplifies considerably. For example, we can quite easily obtain an exact expression for the evolution of this quantity for uniform crossover in a finite population at each generation. This is a more detailed, although less general result than that obtained by Rabani *et al.* The two approaches have different strengths. Rabani *et al.* approach gives a rigorous mathematical framework. Obtaining useful results from such a framework is notoriously hard. The fact that they succeed in finding such a result is very impressive. The tack taken in this paper, which I would not pretend to be of comparable significance to Rabani *et al.*'s general result, is to find a statistical quantity for which we can compute the dynamics. This approach, though often only approximate, allows complex systems to be modelled which are beyond the scope of a rigorous framework—modelling of more complex systems is discussed in the final section of this paper.

2 MODEL

2.1 SHUFFLING

We briefly introduce the shuffling problem together with the notation we shall be using. To denote the individual strings (hands) we use the vector

$$\mathbf{S}^\mu(t) = (S_1^\mu(t), S_2^\mu(t), \ldots, S_L^\mu(t))$$

where the superscript $\mu = 1, \ldots, N$, denotes the different strings and $S_i^\mu(t)$ denotes the alleles (suits) at position i and generation t. We assume that there are L cards in each hand and that the order is always maintained (i.e. at every time step each hand contains cards 1 to L). We denote the allele types (suits) by a Greek letter. Initially $S_i^\mu(0) = \mu$, that is, the genes (cards) of the μth member of the population are initially in allele state μ—the alleles carry information about the ancestors. To form the next generation the strings are paired at random. Each pair, $(\mathbf{S}^\mu(t), \mathbf{S}^\nu(t))$, is shuffled to form a new pair $(\mathbf{S}^\mu(t+1), \mathbf{S}^\nu(t+1))$ according to

$$\begin{aligned} S_i^\mu(t+1) &= \chi_i\, S_i^\mu(t) + (1-\chi_i)\, S_i^\nu(t) \\ S_i^\nu(t+1) &= (1-\chi_i)\, S_i^\mu(t) + \chi_i\, S_i^\nu(t) \end{aligned} \tag{1}$$

where $\chi_i \in \{0, 1\}$ depends on the type of crossover operator. The χ_i's are independently chosen for different pairs

We consider the following types of crossover.

Uniform Crossover. The alleles are chosen randomly from either of the parents,

$$\chi_i = \begin{cases} 1 & \text{with probability } a \\ 0 & \text{with probability } 1-a. \end{cases} \tag{2}$$

The parameter a defines the degree of bias. In the unbiased case $a = 1/2$.

Single-Point Crossover. A locus A $(1 \le A < L)$ is chosen on the string and all alleles up to and including A are taken from one string while all the other alleles are taken from the second string,

$$\chi_i = \begin{cases} 1 & \text{if } i \le A \\ 0 & \text{if } i > A. \end{cases} \tag{3}$$

Two-Point Crossover. The strings are treated as loops, along which we choose two crossing points, A and B. The strings are swapped between these two points,

$$\chi_i = \begin{cases} 1 & \text{if } i \le A \text{ or } i > B \\ 0 & \text{if } A < i \le B. \end{cases} \tag{4}$$

Note that we can either choose A and B independently or we can choose A at random and choose B to be a fixed distance from A. In particular we can choose $0 < A \le N/2$ and $B = A + N/2$ to ensure that a maximum number of alleles are swapped at each 'generation'.

2.2 MIXING RATE

We need to define a measure of shuffling. To do so we first define the 'overlaps', between the strings at time t and the initial strings, to be the number of alleles of type α in $\mathbf{S}^{\mu}(t)$ — that is, the number of alleles that originated in string $\mathbf{S}^{\alpha}(0)$

$$m_{\alpha}^{\mu}(t) = \frac{1}{L}\sum_{i=1}^{L}\left[S_i^{\mu}(t) = \alpha\right] \tag{5}$$

where we have used the notational convention for the indicator function

$$\left[\text{PREDICATE}\right] = \begin{cases} 1 & \text{PREDICATE is true} \\ 0 & \text{PREDICATE is false.} \end{cases} \tag{6}$$

Since every allele ancestor remains in the population and every allele must come from somewhere

$$\sum_{\mu=1}^{N} m_{\alpha}^{\mu}(t) = \sum_{\alpha=1}^{N} m_{\alpha}^{\mu}(t) = 1. \tag{7}$$

We are now ready to define an order parameter, $Q(t)$, measuring the degree of mixing

$$Q(t) = \frac{1}{N}\sum_{\alpha=1}^{N}\sum_{\mu=1}^{N}\left(m_{\alpha}^{\mu}(t)\right)^2. \tag{8}$$

Although this measure is *ad hoc*, it is one of the simplest measures—it depends only on a count of the cards in each hand; a linear measure will not work because of equation (7). Initially $m_{\alpha}^{\mu}(0) = \left[\alpha = \mu\right]$ (the expression in squared brackets is just the Kronecker delta) so $Q(0) = 1$. When the population is totally mixed the order parameter falls to

$$Q(\infty) = \frac{N + L - 1}{N\,L}. \tag{9}$$

(the derivation of this is given in an appendix). We define the mixing rate as the (asymptotic) reduction towards the mixed state produced by a shuffle

$$r = \lim_{t\to\infty}\left(\frac{Q(t+1) - Q(\infty)}{Q(t) - Q(\infty)}\right).$$

3 RESULTS

3.1 UNIFORM CROSSOVER

We can compute the change in the order parameter and consequently the mixing rate exactly for uniform crossover. From equation (1) it follows that

$$\begin{aligned} \left[S_i^{\mu}(t+1) = \alpha\right] &= \chi_i\left[S_i^{\mu}(t) = \alpha\right] + (1-\chi_i)\left[S_i^{\nu}(t) = \alpha\right] \\ \left[S_i^{\nu}(t+1) = \alpha\right] &= (1-\chi_i)\left[S_i^{\mu}(t) = \alpha\right] + \chi_i\left[S_i^{\nu}(t) = \alpha\right] \end{aligned} \tag{10}$$

Since the χ_i's are chosen independently we can average over them. From equation (2) we see that $\langle \chi_i \rangle = a$, where $\langle \cdots \rangle$ denotes the expectation value. To calculate the change in the order parameter we consider

$$\left(m_\alpha^\mu(t+1)\right)^2 = \frac{1}{L^2}\sum_i \left[S_i^\mu(t+1)=\alpha\right] + \frac{1}{L^2}\sum_{i\neq j}\left[S_i^\mu(t+1)=\alpha\right]\left[S_j^\mu(t+1)=\alpha\right]$$

where we have separated out the $i = j$ term and used the property of indicator functions $\left[\cdots\right]^2 = \left[\cdots\right]$. We can now substituting in equation (10) to obtain an expression in terms of variables at time t. Averaging out the χ_i's we obtain after a little algebra

$$\left\langle \left(m_\alpha^\mu(t+1)\right)^2 \right\rangle = \frac{2a(1-a)}{L}\left(m_\alpha^\mu(t) + m_\alpha^\nu(t)\right) + \left(a\, m_\alpha^\mu(t) + (1-a)m_\alpha^\nu(t)\right)^2.$$

This gives the square of the overlaps at time $t+1$ in terms of the overlaps at time t. Putting this into equation (8) we obtain an equation for $Q(t+1)$ in terms of the overlaps at time t. But, using equations (7) and (8) we can simplify this to

$$Q(t+1) = r\,Q(t) + (1-r)Q(\infty) \tag{11}$$

where

$$r = \frac{1-2a(1-a)}{1-1/N}$$

and $Q(\infty)$ is given in equation (9). Equation (11) is a linear recursion relation which has the well known solution

$$Q(t) = Q(\infty) + r^t\left(Q(0) - Q(\infty)\right). \tag{12}$$

Starting from an ordered state we have $Q(0) = 1$. The characteristic mixing time is given by

$$\tau = \frac{-1}{\log(r)} \approx \frac{-1}{\log\left(1-2a(1-a)\right)}. \tag{13}$$

The optimal shuffling is achieved when $a = 1/2$ in which case $\tau \approx 1/\log(2) \approx 1.44$. Every τ generations the distance $Q(t) - Q(\infty)$ is decreased by $1/e$ — for $a = 2$ this distance is halved each generation.

3.2 SINGLE-POINT CROSSOVER

Single-point crossover is more complicated than uniform crossover because the loci are no longer independent of each other—nearby loci are more likely to come from the same ancestor than distant loci. To calculate the effect of single-point crossover we adopt a new approach. We consider the strings to be made up from regions or blocks of genes where the regions are bounded by the points where crossover has occurred. We denote the number of regions in a string $\mathbf{S}^\mu(t)$ by $R^\mu(t)$. We consider, below, how the number of regions grow over time.

We can express the overlaps in terms of block variables. We denote the size of the nth block of $\mathbf{S}^\mu(t)$ by $x_n^\mu(t)$ and the allele type of the nth block by $\beta_n^\mu(t)$. Then the overlap can be written as

$$m_\alpha^\mu(t) = \frac{1}{L}\sum_{n=1}^{R^\mu(t)} x_n^\mu(t)\left[\beta_n^\mu(t) = \alpha\right]. \tag{14}$$

From equation (8) we find the order parameter is given by

$$Q(t) = \frac{1}{N\,L^2} \sum_{\mu=1}^{N} \sum_{n=1}^{R^\mu(t)} \left(\left(x_n^\mu(t)\right)^2 + \sum_{\substack{m=1\\ m\neq n}}^{R^\mu(t)} x_n^\mu(t)\, x_m^\mu(t) \left[\beta_n^\mu(t) = \beta_m^\mu(t)\right] \right) \tag{15}$$

where we have used the identities

$$\sum_{\alpha=1}^{N} \left[\beta_n^\mu(t) = \alpha\right] = 1$$

and

$$\sum_{\alpha=1}^{N} \left[\beta_n^\mu(t) = \alpha\right] \left[\beta_m^\mu(t) = \alpha\right] = \left[\beta_n^\mu(t) = \beta_m^\mu(t)\right].$$

The first term in equation (15) gives the contribution to the order parameter coming from the single blocks while the second term gives the contribution coming from different blocks which, by chance, come from the same ancestors. We do not know the block sizes, x_n^μ. However, as the crossing points are randomly chosen the block sizes will be random except for the constraint

$$\sum_{n=1}^{R^\mu(t)} x_n^\mu(t) = L.$$

Given $R^\mu(t)$ blocks then on average

$$\begin{aligned} \left\langle \left(x_n^\mu(t)\right)^2 \right\rangle &= \frac{L(2L - R^\mu(t) + 1)}{R^\mu(t)(R^\mu(t)+1)} \\ \left\langle x_n^\mu(t)\, x_m^\mu(t) \right\rangle &= \frac{L(L+1)}{R^\mu(t)(R^\mu(t)+1)}. \end{aligned} \tag{16}$$

The calculation of these average values are given in a separate appendix. We are left having to calculate the average number of blocks that come from the same ancestor

$$\sum_{n=1}^{R^\mu(t)} \sum_{\substack{m=1\\ m\neq n}}^{R^\mu(t)} \left[\beta_n^\mu(t) = \beta_m^\mu(t)\right].$$

If each block could come from any ancestor then the probability of two blocks being the same is $1/N$. However, at the first generation the two blocks are guaranteed to come from separate ancestors. To incorporate this fact we assume that the probability of two blocks coming from the same ancestor is $(1 - 1/t)/N$. Using this we find

$$\sum_{n=1}^{R^\mu(t)} \sum_{\substack{m=1\\ m\neq n}}^{R^\mu(t)} \left[\beta_n^\mu(t) = \beta_m^\mu(t)\right] = \frac{\left(R^\mu(t) - 1\right) R^\mu(t) \left(1 - 1/t\right)}{N}. \tag{17}$$

Putting equations (16) and (17) into equation (15) we obtain

$$\langle Q(t)\rangle = \frac{N(2L - R(t) + 1) + (L + 1)(R(t) - 1)(1 - 1/t)}{N\,L\,(R(t) + 1)} \tag{18}$$

where $R(t)$ is the average number of regions per string.

We now consider how the number of regions grow over time. Crossover will produce a new region provided that the cutting point occurs within a block rather than at one of the ends. Since there are $L - 1$ possible cutting points and $R^{\mu}(t) - 1$ region boundaries, there will be a probability of $(L - R^{\mu}(t))/(L - 1)$ that the cutting site occurring within a block. Thus, if at time t there are $R(t)$ regions then the expected number of regions at the next shuffle will be

$$\langle R(t + 1)\rangle = R(t) + \frac{L - R(t)}{L - 1}. \tag{19}$$

This is again a linear recursion, with solution

$$R(t) = L - (L - 1)\left(1 - \frac{1}{L - 1}\right)^{t}. \tag{20}$$

The derivation of $\langle Q(t)\rangle$ is not exact. In particular, we have ignored fluctuations in the number of blocks (equation (18) is not linear in R(t), so fluctuations in R(t) will give rise to systematic corrections). Nevertheless, the corrections are so small that equations (18) and (20) are in almost perfect agreement with simulation results.

The asymptotic behaviour of $Q(t)$ is dominated by the rate of production of new regions. From equation (20) we see that the number of regions increases towards its maximum L at a rate $1 - 1/(L - 1)$. As a consequence the characteristic mixing time is $-1/\log(1 - 1/(L - 1)) \approx L - 1$.

3.3 TWO-POINT CROSSOVER

We consider the case when we choose a crossing point A uniformly between 1 and $L/2$ and set the second crossing point B to be at $A + L/2$. This ensures that exactly half the genes are swapped at each generation. As a consequence at the first generation $Q(1) = 1/2$. Thereafter each half of the string can be treated as a single string (of length $L/2$) which behaves as though they were experiencing single-point crossover. Thus for $t \geq 2$ starting from $R(t)$ *regions in each half of the string* the expected number after shuffling grows as

$$\langle R(t + 1)\rangle = R(t) + \frac{L - 2R(t)}{L}. \tag{21}$$

Using the boundary condition $R(1) = 1$ we find

$$\langle R(t)\rangle = \frac{L}{2} - \left(\frac{L}{2} - 1\right)\left(1 - \frac{2}{L}\right)^{t-1}. \tag{22}$$

Following a similar calculation to that for equation (18) we find

$$\langle Q(t)\rangle = \frac{(N + 1)(L - R(t) + 1) + (L + 2)(R(t) - 1)(1 - 1/(2(t - 1)))}{N\,L\,(R(t) + 1)} \tag{23}$$

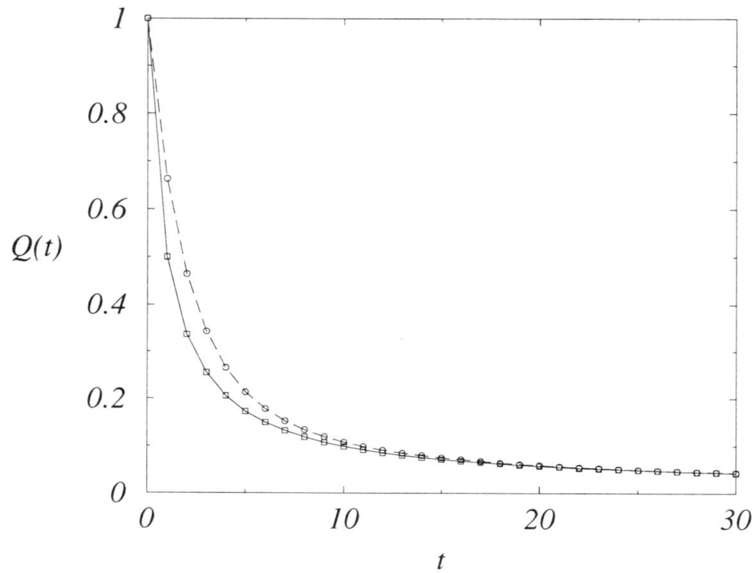

Figure 1 The evolution of the order parameter is shown for two different types of two-point crossover. The solid line shows the case where the separation between the crossing points is set to $L/2$, while the dashed line shows the case when the crossing points are chosen independently. A population size of 100 and string length of 100 was used. The simulations where averaged over 1 000 runs. The errors in the mean are less than the width of the line.

Again the asymptotic decay of $Q(t)$ is dominated by the speed at which new regions are produced. From equation (22) this gives a characteristic shuffling time of $-1/\log(1 - 2/L)) \approx L/2$.

An alternative method for performing two-point crossover would be to choose the two crossing points independently. This complicates the calculations and we have performed simulations only. Figure 1 shows simulation results. Fixing the distance between crossing points to $L/2$ speeds up the initial shuffling. However, the asymptotic mixing rate is the same for both types of crossover.

4 DISCUSSION

We have obtained analytic expressions for the mixing rate for uniform, single-point and two-point crossover. In figure 2 the analytic expressions are plotted for a population size and string length of 100. The curve for uniform crossover is exact. Those for single-point and two-point crossover are approximate, but for these parameters the theory and simulations differ by less than 5×10^{-4}.

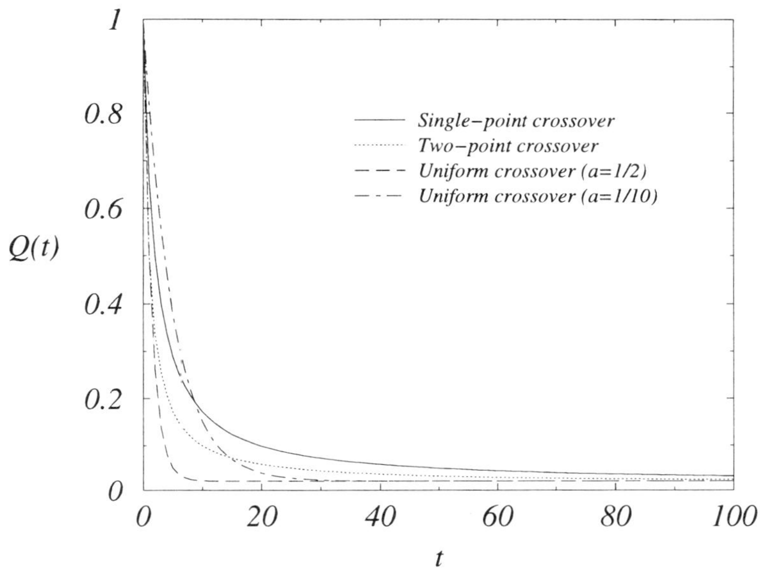

Figure 2 The evolution of the order parameter is shown for uniform, single-point and two-point crossover. In all three cases the population size and string length was set to 100.

Although at the first step, the crossover strategies appear comparable for single-point, two-point and uniform crossover with $a = 1/2$, the shuffling rate continues to reduce rapidly for uniform crossover, but slows down very considerably for single-point and two-point crossover. Two-point crossover shuffles at twice the rate of single-point crossover. In fact, if we rescaled the time so that one generation of two-point crossover equals two generations of single-point crossover the two curves for $Q(t)$ lie almost on top of each other. Multi-point crossover, in which n-points are chosen at random and where every other region is taken from the second parent, will extrapolate between the two-point and uniform crossover curves.

For uniform crossover the mixing rate is $1 - 2a(1 - a)$ (ignoring finite population corrections). This is maximized when the bias, a, is set to $1/2$. For $a \ll 1/2$ the mixing rate will be much reduced and the initially reduction in the order parameter will be much slower than that for single-point or two-point crossover. However, provided $a \gg 1/L$ the asymptotic mixing rate will be much faster for the biased uniform crossover than single or two-point crossover. Thus after a long enough period biased uniform crossover will achieve a better mixing than its rivals. This is illustrated in figure 2 where we have also plotted $Q(t)$ for uniform crossover with $a = 1/10$.

One referee of this paper asked the pertinent question, so what? The answer to this is that modelling has both short and long term objectives. The short term objective is to find an accurate description of the system being studied. The much bolder long term objective is to obtain an understanding of the important features that determine the efficiency of the search performed by a Genetic Algorithm, with the hope of creating a principled approach to designing GAs. This is an accumulative process which can be achieved by understanding the detailed behaviour of simple systems. In this paper we identified a measure of the degree of mixing which allowed us to compute the mixing rates. The result that uniform crossover is faster than two-point crossover which in turn is faster than single-point crossover is, of course, not surprising. A result which was more unexpected (at least, for the author) was that uniform crossover even with a very strong bias towards one parent still has a much faster asymptotic mixing rate than single-point crossover. The mixing rates are important as they provide a measure for how fast crossover causes the population to decorrelate from its initial state. The shorter the decorrelation time the faster the exploration of the search space. Asymptotically single-point crossover is no faster than a mutation of one allele per generation (they both require touching each loci, which takes of order $L\log(L)$ trials), while uniform crossover is dramatically faster, taking $\mathcal{O}(\log(L))$ steps. These results agree with Rabani *et al.*, although we have also calculated how the degree of mixing changes for intermediate times.

To understand what crossover does in a GA, however, necessitates the modelling of the interaction of crossover with the other operators such as selection and mutation. This is part of the long term objective of modelling, of which this paper is only a small contribution. A statistical mechanics analysis of GAs has been carried out for various simple problems (e.g. [9, 10, 12–21]), which use statistical properties of the population to model the system dynamics. However, these studied did not treat the problem of spatial correlations that arise when using single or multi-point crossover. Recently the author has completed a paper treating the dynamics of a GA with two-point crossover [22]. The additional spatial correlations considerably complicate the analysis—not because of the difficulty of modelling crossover (which can be done exactly), but because of the difficulty in estimating the effect of selection on the spatial correlations produced by crossover. This paper uncovers a small part of the story of crossover. It shows how the amount of mixing caused by crossover evolves over generations. How important this is to the larger picture only time will tell.

APPENDIX: TOTALLY MIXED STATE

The overlap parameters $M_\alpha^\mu(t) = L\, m_\alpha^\mu(t)$ define a partitioning of the L alleles in string μ amongst the N initial strings. Total mixing corresponds to a random partitioning so that the probability of the overlaps being $(M_1^\mu, M_2^\mu, \ldots, M_N^\mu)$ is given by the multinomial distribution

$$\frac{1}{N^L}\frac{L!}{M_1^\mu!\, M_2^\mu! \cdots M_N^\mu!}\left[\sum_{\alpha=1}^{N} M_\alpha^\mu = L\right].$$

To find averages over a multinomial probability distribution we note that the multinomial coefficients appear in the following expansion

$$\left(\sum_{\alpha=1}^{N} x_\alpha\right)^L = \sum_{\{M_\alpha\}} L! \left(\prod_{\alpha=1}^{N}\frac{x_\alpha^{M_\alpha}}{M_\alpha!}\right)\left[\sum_{\alpha=1}^{N} M_\alpha = L\right] \tag{24}$$

where the sum is over all integer values of the M_α's. We can use equation (24) to compute averages over the multinomial distribution using the observation

$$\begin{aligned}\langle M_\alpha \rangle &= \frac{1}{N^L}\frac{\partial}{\partial x_\alpha} \sum_{\{M_\alpha\}} L! \left(\prod_{\alpha=1}^{N} \frac{x_\alpha^{M_\alpha}}{M_\alpha !} \right) \left[\sum_{\alpha=1}^{M} M_\alpha = L \right] \Bigg|_{x_\alpha=1} \\ &= \frac{\partial}{\partial x_\alpha} \frac{\left(\sum_{\alpha=1}^N x_\alpha\right)^L}{N^L} = \frac{L\left(\sum_{\alpha=1}^N 1\right)^{L-1}}{N^L} = \frac{L}{N}\end{aligned}$$

similarly

$$\begin{aligned}\langle M_\alpha (M_\alpha - 1)\rangle &= \frac{\partial^2}{\partial x_\alpha^2} \frac{\left(\sum_{\alpha=1}^N x_\alpha\right)^L}{N^L} \Bigg|_{x_\alpha=1} \\ &= \frac{L(L-1)\left(\sum_{\alpha=1}^N 1\right)^{L-2}}{N^L} = \frac{L(L-1)}{N^2}.\end{aligned}$$

From the definition (8) and assuming totally shuffling

$$Q(\infty) = \frac{N}{L^2}\left\langle (M_\alpha^\mu)^2 \right\rangle = \frac{N+L-1}{N\,L}.$$

APPENDIX: STATISTICS OF BLOCK SIZES

We need to calculate $\left\langle (x_n^\mu(t))^2 \right\rangle$ and $\left\langle x_n^\mu(t) x_m^\mu(t) \right\rangle$. We first abstract this problem. We consider a string with L sites which is split into R regions where the position of each region boundary is independently chosen. We then ask what is the probability distribution for the sizes of the regions? For this calculation we can drop the superscript μ and the time index as these are irrelevant. Thus the length of a region we denote by x_n. Our single constraint is

$$\sum_{n=1}^{R} x_n = L.$$

We can write the probability of a partitioning $\mathbf{x} = (x_1, x_2, \ldots, x_R)$ as

$$p(\mathbf{x}) = \frac{1}{Z} \mathrm{e}^{-\sum_n x_n} \left[\sum_{n=1}^R x_n = L \right], \qquad Z = \operatorname*{Tr}_{\{\mathbf{x}\}} \mathrm{e}^{-\sum_n x_n} \left[\sum_{n=1}^R x_n = L \right]$$

where we have used the shorthand

$$\operatorname*{Tr}_{\{\mathbf{x}\}} \equiv \sum_{x_1=1}^{\infty} \sum_{x_2=1}^{\infty} \cdots \sum_{x_R=1}^{\infty}$$

($p(\mathbf{x})$ is not a multinomial distribution as there are no combinatorial factors preferring equi-partitioning.) In the definition of $p(\mathbf{x})$ we have included the term

$$\mathrm{e}^{-\sum_n x_n}$$

which is a constant in light of the Kronecker delta, however, it will act as a regularization term in what follows.

Our aim is to find

$$\langle x_n^2 \rangle = \operatorname*{Tr}_{\{\mathbf{x}\}} x_n^2\, p(\mathbf{x}).$$

We can replace the Kronecker delta with its integral representation

$$\left[\sum_{n=1}^{R} x_n = L\right] = \int_{-\pi}^{\pi} \mathrm{e}^{\mathrm{i}\lambda\left(\sum_{n=1}^{R} x_n - L\right)} \frac{\mathrm{d}\lambda}{2\pi}.$$

Giving

$$\langle x_n^2 \rangle = \frac{1}{Z} \int_{-\pi}^{\pi} \mathrm{e}^{\mathrm{i}\lambda L} \operatorname*{Tr}_{\{\mathbf{x}\}} x_n^2 \mathrm{e}^{-(\mathrm{i}\lambda+1)\sum_{n=1}^{R} x_n} \frac{\mathrm{d}\lambda}{2\pi}.$$

We can perform the sums (notice the regularization term ensures that sums converge) to give

$$\begin{aligned}
\langle x_n^2 \rangle &= \frac{1}{Z} \int_{-\pi}^{\pi} \mathrm{e}^{\mathrm{i}\lambda L} \left(\frac{2\mathrm{e}^{2\mathrm{i}\lambda+2}}{(\mathrm{e}^{\mathrm{i}\lambda+1}-1)^{R+2}} - \frac{\mathrm{e}^{\mathrm{i}\lambda+1}}{(\mathrm{e}^{\mathrm{i}\lambda+1}-1)^{R+1}} \right) \frac{\mathrm{d}\lambda}{2\pi} \\
&= \frac{1}{Z} \int_{-\pi}^{\pi} \mathrm{e}^{\mathrm{i}\lambda L} \left(\frac{2}{R(R+1)}(-D_\lambda^2 + \mathrm{i}D_\lambda) - \frac{\mathrm{i}}{R} D_\lambda \right) \frac{1}{(\mathrm{e}^{\mathrm{i}\lambda+1}-1)^{R}} \frac{\mathrm{d}\lambda}{2\pi}
\end{aligned}$$

where $D_\lambda = \partial/\partial\lambda$. We can integrate by parts so that the remaining integral cancels with the normalization factor Z. We thus obtain

$$\langle x_n^2 \rangle = \frac{L(2L-R+1)}{R(R+1)}.$$

We can calculate $\langle x_n\, x_m \rangle$ in a similar way. However it is easier to observe that

$$L^2 = \left(\sum_n x_n\right)^2 = \sum_n x_n^2 + \sum_{n \neq m} x_n x_m$$

thus

$$\langle x_n\, x_m \rangle = \frac{L - \langle x_n^2 \rangle}{L-1}.$$

References

[1] J. H. Holland. *Adaptation in Natural and Artificial Systems.* University of Michigan Press (Ann Arbor), 1975.

[2] K. A. De Jong. *An Analysis of the Behaviour of a Class of Genetic Adaptive Systems.* PhD thesis, University of Michigan, 1975.

[3] D. E. Goldberg. *Genetic Algorithms in Search, Optimization & Machine Learning.* Addison-Wesley (Reading, Mass), 1989.

[4] W. M. Spears and K. A. De Jong. An analysis of multi-point crossover. In Gregory J. E. Rawlins, editor, *Foundations of Genetic Algorithms*, pages 301–315. Morgan Kaufmann (San Mateo), 1991.

[5] D. H. Achley. *A connectionist machine for genetic hillclimbing.* Kluwer Academic Publishing, 1987.

[6] G. Syswerda. Uniform crossover in genetic algorithms. In *Proceedings of the Third International Conference on Genetic Algorithms*, pages 2–9. Morgan Kaufmann (San Mateo), 1989.

[7] L. J. Eshelman, R. A. Caruana, and J. D. Schaffer. Biases in the crossover landscape. In *Proceedings of the Third International Conference on Genetic Algorithms*, pages 10–19. Morgan Kaufmann (San Mateo), 1989.

[8] P. Galinier and J. K. Hao. Hybrid evolutionary algorithms for graph coloring. *Journal of Combinatorial Optimization*, 3(4):379–397, 1999.

[9] A. Prügel-Bennett and J. L. Shapiro. An analysis of genetic algorithms using statistical mechanics. *Physical Review Letters*, 72(9):1305–1309, 1994.

[10] A. Prügel-Bennett and J. L. Shapiro. The dynamics of a genetic algorithm for simple random Ising systems. *Physica D*, 104:75–114, 1997.

[11] Rabani Y., Rabinovich Y., and Sinclair A. A computational view of population genetics. *Random Structures & Algorithms*, 12(4):313–334, 1998.

[12] M. Rattray. The dynamics of a genetic algorithm under stabilizing selection. *Complex Systems*, 9(3):213–234, 1995.

[13] M. Rattray and J. L. Shapiro. The dynamics of genetic algorithms for a simple learning problem. *Journal of Physics: A.*, 29:7451–7473, 1996.

[14] A. Prügel-Bennett. Modelling evolving populations. *Journal of Theoretical Biology*, 185:81–95, 1997.

[15] J. L. Shapiro and A. Prügel-Bennett. Genetic algorithms dynamics in two-well potentials with basins and barriers. In R. K. Belew and M. D. Vose, editors, *Foundations of Genetic Algorithms 4*, pages 101–116, San Francisco, 1997. Morgan Kaufmann.

[16] M. Rattray and J. L. Shapiro. Noisy fitness evaluations in genetic algorithms and the dynamics of learning. In R. K. Belew and M. D. Vose, editors, *Foundations of Genetic Algorithms 4* pages 117–139, San Francisco, 1997. Morgan Kaufmann.

[17] S. Bornholdt. Probing genetic algorithm performance of fitness landscapes. In R. K. Belew and M. D. Vose, editors, *Foundation of Genetic Algorithms 4*, pages 141–154, San Francisco, 1997. Morgan Kaufmann.

[18] E. van Nimwegen, J. P. Crutchfield, and M. Mitchell. Finite populations induce metastability in evolutionary search. *Physics Letters A*, 229:144–150, 1997.

[19] A. Rogers and A. Prügel-Bennett. Genetic drift in genetic algorithm selection schemes. *IEEE Transactions on Evolutionary Computation*, 3(4):298–303, 1999.

[20] A. Prügel-Bennett. On the long string limit. In W. Banzhaf and C. Reeves, editors, *Foundations of Genetic Algorithms 5*, pages 45–56, San Francisco, 1999. Morgan Kaufmann.

[21] A. Rogers and A. Prügel-Bennett. The dynamics of a genetic algorithm on a model hard optimization problem. *Complex Systems*, 11(6):437–464, 2000.

[22] A. Prügel-Bennett. Modelling crossover induced linkage in genetic algorithms. Preprint, 2000.

Dynamic Parameter Control in Simple Evolutionary Algorithms

Stefan Droste **Thomas Jansen** **Ingo Wegener**
FB Informatik, LS 2, Univ. Dortmund, 44221 Dortmund, Germany
{droste, jansen, wegener}@ls2.cs.uni-dortmund.de

Abstract

Evolutionary algorithms are general, randomized search heuristics that are influenced by many parameters. Though evolutionary algorithms are assumed to be robust, it is well-known that choosing the parameters appropriately is crucial for success and efficiency of the search. It has been shown in many experiments, that non-static parameter settings can be by far superior to static ones but theoretical verifications are hard to find. We investigate a very simple evolutionary algorithm and rigorously prove that employing dynamic parameter control can greatly speed-up optimization.

1 INTRODUCTION

Evolutionary algorithms are a class of general, randomized search heuristics that can be applied to many different tasks. They are controlled by a number of different parameters which are crucial for success and efficiency of the search. Though rough guidelines mainly based on empirical experience exist, it remains a difficult task to find appropriate settings. One way to overcome this problem is to employ non-static parameter control. Bäck (1998) distinguishes three different types of non-static parameter control: dynamic parameter control is the simplest variant. The parameters are set according to some (maybe randomized) scheme that depends on the number of generations. In adaptive parameter control the control scheme can take into account the individuals encountered so far and their function values. Finally, when self-adaptive parameter control is used, the parameters are evolved by application of the same search operators as used by evolutionary algorithms, namely mutation, crossover, and selection. All three variants are used in practice, but there is little theoretically confirmed knowledge about them. This holds especially as far as optimization of discrete objective functions is concerned. In the field of evolution strategies (Schwefel 1995) on continuous domains some theoretical studies are known (Beyer 1996; Rudolph 1999).

Here we concentrate on the exact maximization of fitness functions $f\colon \{0,1\}^n \to \mathbb{R}$ by means of a very simple evolutionary algorithm. In its basic form it uses static parameter control, of course, and is known as (1+1) EA ((1+1) evolutionary algorithm) (Mühlenbein 1992; Rudolph 1997; Droste, Jansen, and Wegener 1998b; Garnier, Kallel, and Schoenauer 1999). In Section 2 we introduce the (1+1) EA. In Section 3 we consider a modified selection scheme that is parameterized and subject to dynamic parameter control. We employ a simplified mutation operator leading to the Metropolis algorithm (Metropolis, Rosenbluth, Rosenbluth, Teller, and Teller 1953) in the static and to simulated annealing (Kirkpatrick, Gelatt, and Vecchi 1983) in the dynamic case. On a given exmaple we prove that appropriate dynamic parameter control schemes can reduce the average time needed for optimization from exponential to polynomial in comparison with an optimal static setting. In Section 4 we employ a very simple dynamic parameter control of the mutation probability and show how this enhances the robustness of the algorithm: in cases where a static setting is already efficient, it typically slows down the optimization only by a factor $\log n$. Furthermore, we prove that an appropriately chosen fitness function can be efficiently optimized. This cannot be achieved using the most recommended static choice for the mutation probability. On the other hand, we present a function where this special dynamic variant of the (1+1) EA is by far outperformed by its static counterpart. In Section 5 we finish with some concluding remarks.

2 THE (1+1) EA

Theoretical results about evolutionary algorithms are in general difficult to obtain. This is mainly due to their stochastic character. In particular, crossover leads to the analysis of quadratical dynamical systems, which is of extreme difficulty (Rabani, Rabinovich, and Sinclair 1998). Therefore, it is a common approach to consider simplified evolutionary algorithms, which (hopefully) still contain interesting, typical, and important features of evolutionary algorithms in general. The simplest and best known such algorithm might be the so-called (1+1) evolutionary algorithm ((1+1) EA). It has been subject to intense research, Mühlenbein (1992), Rudolph (1997), Droste, Jansen, and Wegener (1998b), and Garnier, Kallel, and Schoenauer (1999) are just a few examples. It can be formally defined as follows, where $f\colon \{0,1\}^n \to \mathbb{R}$ is the objective function to be maximized:

Algorithm 1 ((1+1) EA).

1. *Choose* $p(n) \in (0, 1/2]$.
2. *Choose* $x \in \{0,1\}^n$ *uniformly at random.*
3. *Create* y *by flipping each bit in* x *independently with probability* $p(n)$.
4. *If* $f(y) \geq f(x)$, *set* $x := y$.
5. *Continue at line 3.*

The probability $p(n)$ is called the mutation probability. The usual and recommended static choice is $p(n) = 1/n$ (Bäck 1993), which implies that on average one bit is flipped at each generation. All the studies mentioned above investigate the case $p(n) = 1/n$. In the next section we modify the selection step on line 4 such that with some probability strings y

with $f(y) < f(x)$ are accepted too. In Section 4 we modify the (1+1) EA by changing the mutation probability $p(n)$ at each step.

3 DYNAMIC PARAMETER CONTROL IN SELECTION

In this section we compare a variant of the (1+1) EA which uses a simplified mutation operator and a probabilistic selection mechanism. Mutation consists of flipping exactly one randomly chosen bit. While this makes an analysis much easier, the selection is now more complicated: if the new search point is y and the old one x, the new point y is selected with probability $\min(1, \alpha^{f(y)-f(x)})$, where the *selection parameter* α is an element of $[1, \infty)$. So deteriorations are now accepted with some probability, which decreases for large deteriorations, while improvements are always accepted.

The only parameter for which we consider static and non-static settings is the selection parameter α. To avoid misunderstandings we present the algorithm more formally now.

Algorithm 2.

1. *Set* $t := 1$. *Choose* $x \in \{0,1\}^n$ *uniformly at random.*
2. *Create* y *by flipping one randomly (under the uniform distribution) chosen bit of* x.
3. *With probability* $\min\{1, \alpha(t)^{f(y)-f(x)}\}$ *set* $x := y$.
4. *Set* $t := t + 1$. *Continue at line 2.*

The function $\alpha\colon \mathbb{N} \rightarrow [1, \infty)$ is usually denoted as *selection schedule*. If $\alpha(t)$ is constant with respect to t the algorithm is called static, otherwise dynamic. We compare static variants of this algorithm with dynamic ones with respect to the expected run time, i. e., the expected number of steps the algorithms take to reach a maximum of f for the first time.

We note that choosing a fixed value for α yields the Metropolis algorithm (see Metropolis, Rosenbluth, Rosenbluth, Teller, and Teller (1953)), while otherwise we get a simulated annealing algorithm, where the neighborhood of a search point consists of all points at Hamming distance one. Hence, our approach can also be seen as a step towards answering the question raised by Jerrum and Sinclair (1997): Is there a natural cooling schedule (which corresponds to our selection schedule), such that simulated annealing outperforms the Metropolis algorithm on a natural problem? There have been various attempts to answer this question (see Jerrum and Sorkin (1998) and Sorkin (1991)). In particular, Sorkin (1991) proved that simulated annealing is superior to the Metropolis algorithm on a carefully designed fractal function. He proved his results using the method of rapidly mixing Markov chains (see Sinclair (1993) for an introduction). Note that our proof has a much simpler structure and is easier to understand. Furthermore, we derive our results using quite elementary methods. Namely, our proofs mainly use Markov bounds.

In the following we will present some equations for the expected number of steps the static algorithm needs to find a maximum. If we can bound the value of $\alpha(t)$, these equations will also be helpful to bound the expected number of steps in the dynamic case. We assume that our objective functions are symmetric and have their unique global maximum at the all ones bit string $(1, \ldots, 1)$. A symmetric function $f\colon \{0,1\}^n \rightarrow \mathbb{R}$ only depends on the number of ones at the input.

So, when trying to maximize a symmetric function, the expected number of steps the algorithm needs to reach the maximum depends only on the number of ones the actual bit string x contains, but not on their positions. Therefore, we can model the process by a Markov chain with exactly $n+1$ states. Let the random variable T_i (for $i \in \{0,\ldots,n\}$) be the random number of steps Algorithm 2 with constant α needs to reach the maximum for the first time, when starting in a bit string with i ones. As the initial bit string is chosen randomly with equal probability, the expected value of the number T of steps, the whole algorithm needs, is

$$\mathrm{E}(T) = \sum_{i=0}^{n} \frac{\binom{n}{i}}{2^n} \cdot \mathrm{E}(T_i).$$

Hence, by bounding $\mathrm{E}(T_i)$ for all $i \in \{0,\ldots,n\}$ we can bound $\mathrm{E}(T)$. As the algorithm can only change the number of ones in its actual bit string by one, the number T_i of steps to reach the maximum $(1,\ldots,1)$ is the sum of the numbers T_j^+ of steps to reach $j+1$ ones, when starting with j ones, over all $j \in \{i,\ldots,n-1\}$.

Let p_i^+ resp. p_i^- be the transition probability, that the algorithm goes to a state with $i+1$ resp. $i-1$ ones when being in a state with $i \in \{0,\ldots,n\}$ ones. Then the following lemma is an immediate consequence.

Lemma 3. *For the expected number $\mathrm{E}(T_i^+)$ of steps to reach a state with $i+1$ ones for the first time, when starting in a state with $i \in \{1,\ldots,n-1\}$ ones, we have the following.*

a) $\mathrm{E}(T_i^+) = \dfrac{1}{p_i^+} + \dfrac{p_i^-}{p_i^+} \cdot \mathrm{E}(T_{i-1}^+)$

b) For all $j \in \{1,\ldots,i\}$ we have $\mathrm{E}(T_i^+) = \left(\sum_{k=0}^{j-1} \dfrac{\prod_{l=0}^{k-1} p_{i-l}^-}{\prod_{l=0}^{k} p_{i-l}^+}\right) + \dfrac{\prod_{l=0}^{j-1} p_{i-l}^-}{\prod_{l=0}^{j-1} p_{i-l}^+} \cdot \mathrm{E}(T_{i-j}^+)$.

c) $\mathrm{E}(T_i^+) = \left(\sum_{k=0}^{i-1} \dfrac{\prod_{l=0}^{k-1} p_{i-l}^-}{\prod_{l=0}^{k} p_{i-l}^+}\right) + \dfrac{\prod_{l=0}^{i-1} p_{i-l}^-}{\prod_{l=0}^{i-1} p_{i-l}^+} \cdot \dfrac{1}{p_0^+} = \sum_{k=0}^{i} \dfrac{\prod_{l=0}^{k-1} p_{i-l}^-}{\prod_{l=0}^{k} p_{i-l}^+} = \sum_{k=0}^{i} \dfrac{1}{p_k^+} \cdot \prod_{l=k+1}^{i} \dfrac{p_l^-}{p_l^+}$

Proof. a) When being in a state with $i \in \{1,\ldots,n-1\}$ ones, the number of ones can increase, decrease or stay the same. This leads to the following equation:

$$\begin{aligned} E(T_i^+) &= p_i^+ + p_i^- \cdot \left(1 + E(T_{i-1}^+) + E(T_i^+)\right) + \left(1 - p_i^+ - p_i^-\right) \cdot \left(1 + E(T_i^+)\right) \\ \Leftrightarrow \quad E(T_i^+) &= \frac{1}{p_i^+} + \frac{p_i^-}{p_i^+} \cdot E(T_{i-1}^+). \end{aligned}$$

b) Using the recursive equation from a) to determine $\mathrm{E}(T_i^+)$, we can prove b) by induction over j.

c) Since $\mathrm{E}(T_0^+) = 1/p_0^+$, we get c) as a direct consequence.

□

Using these results we now show that there exists a function VALLEY: $\{0,1\}^n \to \mathbb{R}$, such that Algorithm 2 using an appropriate selection schedule with decreasing probability for accepting deteriorations only requires polynomial time while setting α constant implies exponential expected time, independently of the choice of α. We do this by showing that the run time with a special increasing selection schedule is polynomial with very high probability, so that all the remaining cases only occur with exponentially small probability and cannot influence the result by more than a constant.

Intuitively, the function VALLEY should have the following properties: With a probability bounded below by a positive constant, we start with strings for which it is necessary to accept deteriorations. In the late steps towards maximization, the acceptance of deteriorations increases the maximization time. We will show that the following function fulfills these intuitive concepts to a sufficient extent.

Definition 4. *The function* VALLEY : $\{0,1\}^n \to \mathbb{R}$ *is defined by (w. l. o. g. n is chosen even):*

$$\text{VALLEY} := \begin{cases} n/2 - \|x\|_1 & \text{for } \|x\|_1 \le n/2, \\ 7n^2 \ln(n) - n/2 + \|x\|_1 & \text{for } \|x\|_1 > n/2, \end{cases}$$

where $\|x\|_1$ denotes the number of ones in x.

We derive asymptotic results for growing values of n and use the well-established standard notation to characterize the order of growth of functions. For the sake of completeness we give a definition.

Definition 5. *For functions $f\colon \mathbb{N} \to \mathbb{R}_0^+$ and $g\colon \mathbb{N} \to \mathbb{R}_0^+$ we write $f(n) = O(g(n))$ if there exist a constant $n_0 \in \mathbb{N}$ and a constant $c \in \mathbb{R}^+$, such that for all $n > n_0$ we have $f(n) \le c \cdot g(n)$. We write $f(n) = \Omega(g(n))$, if we have $g(n) = O(f(n))$. We write $f(n) = \Theta(g(n))$, if we have $f(n) = O(g(n))$ and $f(n) = \Omega(g(n))$.*

Theorem 6. *The expected number of steps until Algorithm 2 with constant $\alpha(t) = \alpha$ reaches the maximum of* VALLEY *for the first time is*

$$\Omega\left(\left(\sqrt{\frac{\alpha}{4}}\right)^n + \left(\frac{1}{\alpha} + 1\right)^n\right) = \Omega\left(1.179^n\right)$$

for all choices of $\alpha \in [1, \infty)$.

Proof. The idea of the proof is that for large α, i. e., small probability of accepting deteriorations, the expected time to go from state $n/2 - 1$ to state $n/2$ is exponential, while for small α the expected time to come from state $n-1$ to state n is exponential.

When we take a look at the function VALLEY for all x with $\|x\|_1 < n/2$, we see, that it behaves like $-$ONEMAX with respect to Algorithm 2 with a static choice of α. So, if p_j^+ resp. p_j^- is the probability of increasing the number of ones resp. decreasing the number of ones by one, when the actual x contains exactly j ones, we have for all $j \in \{0, \ldots, n/2-1\}$

$$p_j^+ = \frac{n-j}{n} \cdot \frac{1}{\alpha} \text{ and } p_j^- = \frac{j}{n}.$$

Hence, using Lemma 3c), we get for $E(T_i^+)$, the expected number of steps until we reach a bit string with $i+1$ ones, when starting with a bit string with $i < n/2$ ones:

$$\begin{aligned} E(T_i^+) &= \sum_{k=0}^{i} \frac{1}{p_k^+} \cdot \prod_{l=k+1}^{i} \frac{p_l^-}{p_l^+} = \sum_{k=0}^{i} \frac{\alpha \cdot n}{n-k} \cdot \prod_{l=k+1}^{i} \frac{l}{n} \cdot \frac{\alpha \cdot n}{n-l} \\ &= \sum_{k=0}^{i} \alpha^{i-k+1} \cdot \frac{n}{n-k} \cdot \frac{i! \cdot (n-i-1)!}{k! \cdot (n-k-1)!} = \sum_{k=0}^{i} \alpha^{i-k+1} \cdot \frac{\binom{n}{k}}{\binom{n-1}{i}}. \qquad (1) \end{aligned}$$

So $E(T^+_{n/2-1})$ can be bounded below in the following way

$$E(T^+_{n/2-1}) = \sum_{k=0}^{n/2-1} \alpha^{n/2-k} \cdot \frac{\binom{n}{k}}{\binom{n-1}{n/2-1}} \geq \frac{\alpha^{n/2}}{\binom{n-1}{n/2-1}} \geq \frac{\alpha^{n/2}}{2^n}. \tag{2}$$

Hence, $E(T^+_{n/2-1})$ is $\Omega\left(\left(\sqrt{\alpha/4}\right)^n\right)$. So for $\alpha \geq 4 + \varepsilon$ (where $\varepsilon > 0$) this results in an exponential lower bound on $E(T^+_{n/2-1})$, implying this bound for $E(T_i)$ for all $i \in \{0, \ldots, n/2-1\}$. Because this is at least a constant fraction of all bit strings, we have an exponential lower bound on the expected number of steps for any static choice of α with $\alpha \geq 4 + \varepsilon$.

In the following we want to show an exponential lower bound on the expected number of steps $E(T_{n-1})$ for $\alpha < 4 + \varepsilon$. When α is small, deteriorations are accepted with large probability, so that we can expect $E(T_{n-1})$ to be large. To obtain a lower bound on $E(T_{n-1})$ we use Lemma 3b). Since for all $i \in \{n/2+2, \ldots, n-1\}$:

$$p_i^+ = \frac{n-i}{n} \text{ and } p_i^- = \frac{i}{n} \cdot \frac{1}{\alpha},$$

we can bound $E(T^+_{n-1})$ from below by:

$$\begin{aligned} E(T^+_{n-1}) &\geq \sum_{k=0}^{n/2-3} \frac{\prod_{l=0}^{k-1} p^-_{n-1-l}}{\prod_{l=0}^{k} p^+_{n-1-l}} = \sum_{k=0}^{n/2-3} \frac{\prod_{l=n-k}^{n-1} p^-_l}{\prod_{l=n-k-1}^{n-1} p^+_l} = \sum_{k=0}^{n/2-3} \frac{\prod_{l=n-k}^{n-1} \frac{l}{n \cdot \alpha}}{\prod_{l=n-k-1}^{n-1} \frac{n-l}{n}} \\ &= \sum_{k=0}^{n/2-3} \frac{n}{\alpha^k} \cdot \frac{(n-1)!}{(n-k-1)! \cdot (k+1)!} = \sum_{k=0}^{n/2-3} \frac{\binom{n}{k+1}}{\alpha^k} = \alpha \cdot \sum_{k=1}^{n/2-2} \frac{\binom{n}{k}}{\alpha^k} \\ &\geq \alpha \cdot \left(\frac{\left(\frac{1}{\alpha}+1\right)^{n-4}}{2} - 1 \right) = \Omega\left(\left(\frac{1}{\alpha} + 1 \right)^{n-4} \right). \end{aligned}$$

Hence, for all $i \in \{0, \ldots, n/2-1\}$ the expected value of T_i is

$$E(T_i) = \Omega\left(\left(\sqrt{\frac{\alpha}{4}} \right)^n + \left(\frac{1}{\alpha} + 1 \right)^{n-4} \right),$$

which is exponential for all choices of $\alpha \in [1, \infty)$.

As the fraction of bit strings with at most $n/2 - 1$ ones is bounded below by a positive constant, the expected run time is exponential for all α. Numerical analysis leads to the result that this is $\Omega(1.179^n)$. □

Intuitively, one can perform better on VALLEY, if the selection schedule works as follows: in the beginning, deteriorations are accepted with probability almost one, so that the actual point x is almost making a random walk, until its number of ones increases to $n/2+1$. As the difference between the function values for $n/2+1$ and $n/2$ ones is so large, it is very unlikely that the number of ones of the actual x will fall below $n/2+1$, assuming $\alpha(t) > 1$ at this point of time. Hence, if the probability of accepting deteriorations decreases after some carefully chosen number of steps, the maximum $(1, \ldots, 1)$ should be reached quickly:

Theorem 7. *With probability $1 - O(n^{-n})$ the number of steps until Algorithm 2, with the selection schedule*

$$\alpha(t) := 1 + \frac{t}{s(n)},$$

reaches the maximum of VALLEY *for the first time is $O(n \cdot s(n))$ for any polynomial s with $s(n) \geq 2en^4 \log n$. Furthermore, the expected number of steps until this happens is $O(n \cdot s(n))$, if we set $\alpha(t) := 1$ for $t > 2^n$.*

Proof. The basic idea of the proof is to split the run of Algorithm 2 into two phases of predefined length. We show that with very high probability a state with at least $n/2 + 1$ ones is reached within the first phase, and all succeeding states have at least $n/2 + 1$ ones, too. Furthermore, with very high probability the optimum is reached within the second phase. Finally, we bound the expected number of steps from above in the case where any of these events do not happen.

The first phase has length $s(n)/n + 2en^3 \log n$. We want to bound the expected number of steps from above in the first phase Algorithm 2 takes to reach a state with at least $n/2+1$ ones. For that purpose we bound $\mathrm{E}\left(T_i^+\right)$ from above for all $i \in \{0, \ldots, n/2\}$. We do not care what happens during the first $s(n)/n$ steps. After that, we have $\alpha(t) \geq 1 + 1/n$. Pessimistically we assume that the current state at step $t = s(n)/n$ contains at most $n/2$ ones.

We use equation (1) of Theorem 6, which is valid for $i \in \{0, \ldots, n/2 - 1\}$.

$$\begin{aligned}
\mathrm{E}\left(T_i^+\right) &= \sum_{j=0}^{i} \alpha^{i-j+1} \cdot \frac{\binom{n}{j}}{\binom{n-1}{i}} = \sum_{j=0}^{i} \alpha^{j+1} \cdot \frac{\binom{n}{i-j}}{\binom{n-1}{i}} \\
&= \sum_{j=0}^{i} \alpha^{j+1} \cdot \frac{n!}{(i-j)!(n-i+j)!} \cdot \frac{i!(n-1-i)!}{(n-1)!} = \sum_{j=0}^{i} \alpha^{j+1} \cdot \frac{\binom{i}{j}}{\binom{n-i+j}{j}} \cdot \frac{n}{n-i}
\end{aligned}$$

As the last expression decreases with decreasing i, it follows that $\mathrm{E}\left(T_i^+\right) \leq \mathrm{E}\left(T_{i+1}^+\right)$ for all $i \in \{0, \ldots, n/2 - 1\}$. Since the length of the first phase is $s(n)/n + 2en^3 \log n$, we have $\alpha(t) \leq 1 + 2/n$ during the first phase. Using this and setting $i = n/2 - 1$, we get

$$\mathrm{E}\left(T_{n/2-1}^+\right) \leq \sum_{j=0}^{n/2-1} \left(1 + \frac{2}{n}\right)^{j+1} \frac{\binom{n/2-1}{j}}{\binom{n/2+1+j}{j}} \cdot \frac{n}{n/2+1} \leq 2 \sum_{j=0}^{n/2-1} e = en.$$

Hence, by using Lemma 3a) we can bound $\mathrm{E}\left(T_{n/2}^+\right)$ from above by

$$\mathrm{E}\left(T_{n/2}^+\right) = \frac{1}{(n/2)/n} + \frac{(n/2)/n}{(n/2)/n} \cdot \mathrm{E}\left(T_{n/2-1}^+\right) \leq 2 + en.$$

So the expected number of steps until a bit string with more than $n/2$ ones is reached is bounded above by

$$(n/2) \cdot en + 2 + en \leq en^2.$$

We use the Markov inequality and see, that the probability of not reaching a state with more than $n/2$ ones within $2en^2$ steps is at most $1/2$. Our analysis is independent of the current bit string at the beginning of such a subphase of length $2en^2$. So, we can consider the $2en^3 \log n$ steps in the first phase as $n \log n$ independent subphases of length $2en^2$ each. Hence, the probability of not reaching a state with more than $n/2$ ones within the first phase is $O(n^{-n})$.

Assume that Algorithm 2 reaches a bit string with more than $n/2$ ones at some step t with $t \geq s(n)/n$. This yields $\alpha(t) \geq 1 + 1/n$. Let $p(n)$ be some polynomial. The probability to reach a bit string with at most $n/2$ ones within $p(n)$ steps is bounded above by

$$p(n) \cdot \frac{n/2+1}{n \cdot (1+1/n)^{7n^2 \ln n}} < \frac{p(n)}{e^{4n \ln n}} = O(n^{-n})$$

where the last equality follows since $p(n)$ is a polynomial. We conclude that after once reaching a bit string with more than $n/2$ ones, for polynomially bounded number of steps the number of ones is larger than $n/2$, too, with probability $1 - O(n^{-n})$. Hence, after the first phase the probability of not being in a state with more than $n/2$ ones is $O(n^{-n})$.

Now we consider the succeeding second phase, which ends with $t = n \cdot s(n)$, which is polynomially bounded. Therefore, we neglect the case that during the second phase a bit string with at most $n/2$ ones is reached. We saw above, that this case has probability $O(n^{-n})$.

We want to prove that with very high probability the optimum is reached within the second phase. In order to do so, we derive an upper bound on the expected number of steps Algorithm 2 needs to reach the optimum. We do not care about the beginning of phase 2 and consider only steps with $t \geq (n-1)s(n)$. Then we have $\alpha(t) \geq n$. Due to the length of the second phase, we also have $\alpha(t) \leq n + 1$. Using equation (2) of Theorem 6, we can bound $\mathrm{E}\left(T^+_{n/2-1}\right)$ from above in the following way.

$$\mathrm{E}\left(T^+_{n/2-1}\right) \leq \sum_{j=0}^{n/2-1} (n+1)^{n/2-j} \cdot \frac{\binom{n}{j}}{\binom{n-1}{n/2-1}} \leq \sum_{j=0}^{n/2-1} \binom{n}{j} n^{n-j} \leq (1+n)^n$$

Hence, we get an upper bound on $\mathrm{E}\left(T^+_{n/2}\right)$:

$$\mathrm{E}\left(T^+_{n/2}\right) = \frac{1}{(n/2)/n} + \frac{(n/2)/n}{(n/2)/n} \cdot \mathrm{E}\left(T^+_{n/2-1}\right) \leq 2 + (1+n)^n$$

and on $\mathrm{E}\left(T^+_{n/2+1}\right)$:

$$\begin{aligned} \mathrm{E}\left(T^+_{n/2+1}\right) &\leq \frac{1}{(n/2-1)/n} + \frac{(n/2+1)/(n \cdot n^{7n^2 \ln n})}{(n/2-1)/n} \cdot \mathrm{E}\left(T^+_{n/2}\right) \\ &\leq \frac{2n}{n-2} + \frac{n+2}{2n^{7n^2 \ln(n)+1}} \cdot \frac{2n}{n-2}\left((1+n)^n + 2\right) \leq 7. \end{aligned}$$

Using Lemma 3b) for $j = i - n/2 - 1$, we get for all $i \in \{n/2+2, \ldots, n-1\}$

$$\begin{aligned} \mathrm{E}\left(T_i^+\right) &= \left(\sum_{j=0}^{i-n/2-2} \frac{\prod_{k=0}^{j-1} p_{i-k}^-}{\prod_{k=0}^{j} p_{i-k}^+}\right) + \frac{\prod_{k=0}^{i-n/2-2} p_{i-k}^-}{\prod_{k=0}^{i-n/2-2} p_{i-k}^+} \cdot \mathrm{E}\left(T_{n/2+1}^+\right) \\ &\le \left(\sum_{j=0}^{i-n/2-2} \frac{\prod_{k=i-j+1}^{i} p_k^-}{\prod_{k=i-j}^{i} p_k^+}\right) + \frac{\prod_{k=n/2+2}^{i} p_k^-}{\prod_{k=n/2+2}^{i} p_k^+} \cdot 7. \end{aligned}$$

As VALLEY behaves like ONEMAX for all states with at least $n/2+2$ ones with respect to Algorithm 2, we have $p_k^+ = (n-k)/n$ and $p_k^- = k/(n\alpha/t)$. Hence, we get

$$\begin{aligned} \mathrm{E}\left(T_i^+\right) &\le \left(\sum_{j=0}^{i-n/2-2} \frac{\prod_{k=i-j+1}^{i} k/(n\cdot n)}{\prod_{k=i-j}^{i} (n-k)/n}\right) + \frac{\prod_{k=n/2+2}^{i} k/(n\cdot n)}{\prod_{k=n/2+2}^{i} (n-k)/n} \cdot 7 \\ &= \left(\sum_{j=0}^{i-n/2-2} \frac{n^{-2j}\cdot i!/(i-j)!}{n^{-j-1}\cdot (n-i+j)!/(n-i-1)!}\right) + \\ &\qquad \frac{n^{-2i+n+2}\cdot i!/(n/2+1)!}{n^{-i+n/2+1}\cdot (n/2-2)!/(n-i-1)!} \cdot 7 \\ &= \left(\sum_{j=0}^{i-n/2-2} n^{1-j} \cdot \frac{\binom{i}{j}}{(n-i)\cdot \binom{n-i+j}{j}}\right) + \frac{(n/2-1)\cdot \binom{n}{n/2+1}\cdot n^{n/2+1}}{(n-i)\cdot \binom{n}{i}\cdot n^i} \cdot 7. \end{aligned}$$

To obtain an upper bound on the second term, we derive the following for all $i \in \{0, \ldots, n-2\}$.

$$\begin{aligned} & (n-i)\cdot \binom{n}{i}\cdot n^i \le (n-(i+1))\cdot \binom{n}{i+1}\cdot n^{i+1} \\ \iff\quad & \frac{n-i}{n-i-1}\cdot \frac{n!}{i!\cdot (n-i)!}\cdot \frac{(i+1)!\cdot (n-i-1)!}{n!} \le n \\ \iff\quad & \frac{i+1}{n-i-1} \le n, \text{ which is valid for all } i \in \{0,\ldots,n-2\}. \end{aligned}$$

Hence, we get the following upper bound on $\mathrm{E}\left(T_i^+\right)$, as i is at least $n/2+2$:

$$\mathrm{E}\left(T_i^+\right) \le \left(\sum_{j=0}^{i-n/2-2} n^{1-j} \cdot \frac{\binom{i}{j}}{(n-i)\cdot \binom{n-i+j}{j}}\right) + 7.$$

So, by bounding $\mathrm{E}\left(T_{n-1}^+\right)$ from above, we get an upper bound on $\mathrm{E}\left(T_i^+\right)$ for all $i \in \{n/2+2, \ldots, n-1\}$:

$$\begin{aligned} \mathrm{E}\left(T_{n-1}^+\right) &\le n\cdot \left(\sum_{j=0}^{n/2-3} \left(\frac{1}{n}\right)^j \cdot \frac{\binom{n-1}{j}}{\binom{j+1}{j}}\right) + 7 \le n\cdot \left(\sum_{j=0}^{n/2-3} \left(\frac{1}{n}\right)^j \binom{n}{j}\right) + 7 \\ &\le n\cdot (1+1/n)^n + 7 \le en + 7 \le 2en \end{aligned}$$

Hence, for all $i \in \{n/2+1, \ldots, n-1\}$ the value of $\mathrm{E}\left(T_i\right)$ can be bounded above by en^2. Using the Markov inequality, this implies that after $2en^2$ steps the probability that the optimum is not reached is bounded above by $1/2$. Considering the $s(n) \geq 2en^4 \log n$ steps as at least $n^2 \log n$ independent subphases of length $2en^2$ each, implies that the optimum is reached with probability $1 - O(n^{-n})$. Altogether we proved that the optimum is reached within the first $n \cdot s(n)$ steps with probability $1 - O(n^{-n})$.

In order to derive the upper bound on the expected number of steps we consider the case that the optimum is not reached. This has probability $O(n^{-n})$. We use the additional assumption that $\alpha(t) = 1$ holds for $t > 2^n$. We do not care what else happens until $t > 2^n$ holds. Then we have $\alpha(t) = 1$. This implies that the algorithm performs a pure random walks, so the expected number of steps in this case is upper bounded by $O(2^n)$ (Garnier, Kallel, and Schoenauer 1999). This yields that the contribution in case of a failure to the expected number of steps is

$$O(2^n) \cdot O(n^{-n}) = O(1)$$

to the expected run time. Altogether, we see that the expected run time is bounded above by $O(n \cdot s(n))$. □

4 DYNAMIC PARAMETER CONTROL IN MUTATION

In this section we present a variant of the (1+1) EA that uses a very simple dynamic variation scheme for the mutation probability $p(n)$. The key idea is to try all possible mutation probabilities. Since we do not want to have too many steps without any bit flipping, we consider $1/n$ to be a reasonable lower bound: using $p(n) = 1/n$ implies that on average one bit flips per mutation. As for the (1+1) EA we use $1/2$ as an upper bound on the choice of $p(n)$. Furthermore, we do not want to try too many different mutation probabilities, since each try is a potential waste of time. Therefore, we double the mutation probability at each step, which yields a range of $\lfloor \log n \rfloor$ different mutation probabilities.

Algorithm 8.

1. *Choose* $x \in \{0,1\}^n$ *uniformly at random.*
2. $p(n) := 1/n$.
3. *Create* y *by flipping each bit in* x *independently with probability* $p(n)$.
4. *If* $f(y) \geq f(x)$, *set* $x := y$.
5. $p(n) := 2p(n)$. *If* $p(n) > 1/2$, *set* $p(n) := 1/n$.
6. *Continue at line 3.*

First of all, we demonstrate that the dynamic version has a much better worst case performance than the (1+1) EA with fixed mutation probability $p(n) = 1/n$. It is known (Droste, Jansen, and Wegener 1998a) that for some functions the (1+1) EA with $p(n) = 1/n$ needs $\Theta(n^n)$ steps for optimization.

Theorem 9. *For any function* $f\colon \{0,1\}^n \to \mathbb{R}$ *the expected number of steps Algorithm 8 needs to optimize* f *is bounded above by* $4^n \log n$.

Proof. Algorithm 8 uses $\lfloor \log n \rfloor$ different values for the mutation probability $p(n)$, all from the interval $[1/n, 1/2]$. In particular, for each $d \in [1/n, 1/4]$ we have that some mutation probability $p(n) \in [d, 2d]$ is used every $\lfloor \log n \rfloor$-th step. Using $d = 1/4$ yields that in each $\lfloor \log n \rfloor$-th step we have $p(n) \geq 1/4$. In these steps, the probability to create a global maximum as child y in mutation is lower bounded by $(1/4)^n$. Thus, each $\lfloor \log n \rfloor$-th step, a global maximum is reached with probability at least 4^{-n}. Therefore, the expected number of steps needed for optimization is bounded above by $4^n \log n$. □

Note that, depending on the value of n, better upper bounds are possible. If n is a power of 2, $p(n) = 1/2$ is one of the values used and we have $2^n \log n$ as an upper bound. This is a general property of Algorithm 8: depending on the value of n different values for $p(n)$ are used which can yield different expected run times.

Of course, using the (1+1) EA with the static choice $p(n) = 1/2$ achieves an expected run time $O(2^n)$ for all functions. But, for each function with a unique global optimum, the expected run time equals 2^n. For Algorithm 8 such dramatic run times are usually not the case for simple functions. We consider examples, namely the functions ONEMAX and LEADINGONES and the class of all linear functions.

Definition 10. *The function* ONEMAX: $\{0,1\}^n \to \mathbb{R}$ *is defined by* $\text{ONEMAX}(x) := \|x\|_1$ *for all* $x \in \{0,1\}^n$. *The function* LEADINGONES: $\{0,1\}^n \to \mathbb{R}$ *is defined by*

$$\text{LEADINGONES}(x) := \sum_{i=1}^{n} \prod_{j=1}^{i} x_j$$

for all $x \in \{0,1\}^n$.

The expected run time of the (1+1) EA with $p(n) = 1/n$ is $\Theta(n \log n)$ for ONEMAX and $\Theta(n^2)$ for LEADINGONES (Droste, Jansen, and Wegener 1998a).

Theorem 11. *The expected run time of Algorithm 8 on the function* LEADINGONES *is* $\Theta(n^2 \log n)$. *Furthermore, there are two constants* $0 < c_1 < c_2$ *such that with probability* $1 - e^{-\Omega(n)}$ *Algorithm 8 optimizes the function* LEADINGONES *within* T *steps where* $c_1 n^2 \log n \le T \le c_2 n^2 \log n$ *holds.*

Proof. Assume that the current string x of Algorithm 8 contains exactly i leading ones, i. e., $\text{LEADINGONES}(x) = i$. Then, there is at least one mutation that flips the $(i+1)$-th bit in x and increases the function value by at least 1. This mutation has probability at least $(1/n)(1 - 1/n)^{n-1} > 1/(en)$ for $p(n) = 1/n$. This is the case each $\lfloor \log n \rfloor$-th step. In all other steps the number of leading ones cannot decrease. We can therefore ignore all those steps. This can only increase the number of generations before the global optimum is reached. Thus, we have $en \log n$ as an upper bound on the expected waiting time for one improvement. After at most n improvements the global maximum is reached. This leads to $O(n^2 \log n)$ as an upper bound on the expected run time. The probability that after $2en$ steps with mutation probability $p(n) = 1/n$ the number of leading ones is not increased by at least one is bounded above by 1/2. To optimize LEADINGONES at most n such increments can be necessary. We apply Chernoff bounds (Hagerup and Rüb 1989) and get that with probability $1 - e^{-\Omega(n)}$ all necessary increments occur within $3en^2$ steps with mutation probability $p(n) = 1/n$. Therefore, with probability $1 - e^{-\Omega(n)}$, after $3en^2 \log n$ generations the unique global optimum is reached.

The lower bound can be proved in a similar way as for the (static) (1+1) EA with $p(n) = 1/n$ (Droste, Jansen, and Wegener 1998a). The main extra ideas are that the varying mutation probabilities do not substantially enlarge the probability to enlarge the function value and that the number of enlargements in one phase can be controlled.

Assume that the current string x contains exactly i leading ones, i. e., $\text{LEADINGONES}(x) = i$ and that $i < n - 1$ holds. We have $x_{i+1} = 0$ in this case. It is obvious that the $n - i - 1$ bits $x_{i+2}, x_{i+3}, \ldots, x_n$ are all totally random, i. e., for all $y \in \{0,1\}^{n-i-1}$ we have $\text{Prob}\,(x_{i+1}x_{i+2}\cdots x_n = y) = 2^{-n+i+1}$. We consider a run of Algorithm 8 and start our considerations at the first point of time where $\text{LEADINGONES}(x) \geq n/2$ holds. We know that for each constant $\delta > 0$, the probability that $\text{LEADINGONES}(x) > (1+\delta)n/2$ holds at this point of time, is bounded above by $e^{-\Omega(n)}$. The probability to increase the function value in one generation is bounded above by

$$(1 - p(n))^{\text{LEADINGONES}(x)} \cdot p(n) \leq (1 - p(n))^{n/2} \cdot p(n).$$

We consider a subphase of length $\lfloor \log n \rfloor$, such that all $\lfloor \log n \rfloor$ different mutation probabilities are used within this phase. The probability for increasing the function value in one such subphase is bounded above by

$$\sum_{i=0}^{\lfloor \log n \rfloor - 1} \frac{2^i}{n} \cdot \left(1 - \frac{2^i}{n}\right)^{n/2} < \frac{1}{n} \sum_{i=0}^{\infty} 2^i \cdot e^{-2^{i-1}} \leq \frac{\beta}{n},$$

where β is a positive constant.

We say that a generation is successful, if the function value is increased. The probability to increase the function value by at least $k > 0$ in a successful generation equals 2^{-k+1}. Therefore, the probability to increase the function value by at least $2t$ in t successful generations is bounded above by 2^{-t}. We conclude that with probability at least $1 - e^{-\Omega(n)}$ there have to be at least $((1-\delta)/4)\,n$ successful generations before the global optimum is reached.

We consider a slightly modified random process. In this new process after a successful generation the next $\lfloor \log n \rfloor$ generations are guaranteed not to be successful. By this modification it follows that in each subphase there is at most one successful generation. We note that this modified process may take longer to reach the global optimum. But the number of additional generations needed is upper bounded by $n \lfloor \log n \rfloor$, since after at most n successful generations, the global optimum is surely reached. Obviously, the probability to increase the function value in one subphase is bounded above by β/n for the modified process, too. Using Chernoff bounds we conclude that with probability $1 - e^{-\Omega(n)}$ within $((1-\delta)/(8\beta))n^2$ subphases there are at most $((1-\delta)/4)n$ successful generations.

Therefore, with probability $1 - e^{-\Omega(n)}$ Algorithm 8 does not reach the global optimum within

$$\frac{1-\delta}{8\beta} n^2 \lfloor \log n \rfloor - n \lfloor \log n \rfloor$$

generations. Since δ and β are constants with $0 < \delta < 1$ and $\beta > 0$ we see that $\Omega\left(n^2 \log n\right)$ generations are needed with probability $1 - e^{-\Omega(n)}$. □

Theorem 12. *The expected run time of Algorithm 8 on the function* ONEMAX *is bounded above by* $O(n \log^2 n)$. *The expected run time of Algorithm 8 on an arbitrary linear function is bounded by* $O(n^2 \log n)$.

Sketch of Proof:. For ONEMAX we partition $\{0,1\}^n$ into the sets

$$F_i := \{x \in \{0,1\}^n \mid \text{ONEMAX}(x) = i\}.$$

For a linear function f with $f(x) = w_0 + w_1x_1 + w_2x_2 + \cdots + w_nx_n$ (we can assume without loss of generality $w_0 = 0$, $w_1 \geq w_2 \geq \cdots \geq w_n$) we use the partition

$$F_i^* := \{x \in \{0,1\}^n \mid w_1 + \cdots + w_i \leq f(x) < w_1 + \cdots + w_{i+1}\}.$$

Note that for all $i > j$ we have $\text{ONEMAX}(x_i) > \text{ONEMAX}(x_j)$ ($f(y_i) > f(y_j)$) for all $x_i \in F_i, x_j \in F_j$ ($y_i \in F_i^*, y_j \in F_j^*$). For ONEMAX there are $n - i$ mutations of a single bit to leave F_i. For f, there is 1 mutation of a single bit to leave F_i^*. Therefore, in steps with $p(n) = 1/n$ we have at least probability $\binom{n-i}{1}(1/n)(1-1/n)^{n-1} \geq (n-i)/(en)$ to leave F_i and at least probability $(1/n)(1-1/n)^{n-1} \geq 1/(en)$ to leave F_i^*. This is the case each $\lfloor \log n \rfloor$-th step. Again, all other steps cannot do any harm, so by ignoring them we can only increase the number of steps needed for optimization. This leads to an upper bound on the expected run time of $\log n \left(\sum_{i=1}^{n} en/i\right) = O(n \log^2 n)$ for ONEMAX and $\log n \left(\sum_{i=1}^{n} en\right) = O(n^2 \log n)$ for f. □

The exact asymptotic run time of Algorithm 8 on ONEMAX and on arbitrary linear functions is still unknown. For linear functions one may conjecture an upper bound of $O(n \log^2 n)$. We see that Algorithm 8 is by far faster than the (1+1) EA with $p(n) = 1/n$ in the worst case and only slower by a factor $\log n$ in typical cases, where already the (1+1) EA with the static choice $p(n) = 1/n$ is efficient. Of course, these are insufficient reasons to support Algorithm 8 as a "better" general optimization heuristic than the (1+1) EA with $p(n) = 1/n$ fixed. Now, we present an example where the dynamic variant by far outperforms the static choice $p(n) = 1/n$ and finds a global optimum with high probability in a polynomial number of generations.

We construct a function that serves as an example with the following properties. There is a kind of path to a local optimum, such that the path is easy to find and to follow with mutation probability $1/n$. Hence, a local maximum is quickly found. Then, there is a kind of gap to all points with maximal function value, that can only be reached via a direct mutation. For such a direct mutation many bits (of the order of $\log n$) have to flip simultaneously. This is unlikely to happen with $p(n) = 1/n$. But raising the mutation probability to a value of the order of $(\log n)/n$ gives a good probability for this final step towards a global optimum. Since Algorithm 8 uses both probabilities each $\lfloor \log n \rfloor$-th step, it has a good chance to quickly follow the path to the local maximum and jump over the gap to a global one.

Definition 13. *Let $n = 2^k$ be large enough, such that $n/\log n > 8$. First, we define a partition of $\{0,1\}^n$ into five sets, namely*

$$\begin{aligned} L_1 &:= \{x \in \{0,1\}^n \mid n/4 < \|x\|_1 < 3n/4\}, \\ L_2 &:= \{x \in \{0,1\}^n \mid \|x\|_1 = n/4\}, \\ L_3 &:= \left\{x \in \{0,1\}^n \mid \exists i \in \{0,1,\ldots,(n/4)-1\} : x = 1^i 0^{n-i}\right\}, \\ L_4 &:= \left\{x \in \{0,1\}^n \mid (\|x\|_1 = \log n) \wedge \left(\sum_{i=1}^{2\log n} x_i = 0\right)\right\}, \text{ and} \\ L_0 &:= \{0,1\}^n \setminus (L_1 \cup L_2 \cup L_3 \cup L_4), \end{aligned}$$

where $1^i 0^{n-i}$ denotes the string with i consecutive ones followed by $n-i$ consecutive zeros. The function PathToJump: $\{0,1\}^n \to \mathbb{R}$ *is defined by*

$$\text{PathToJump}(x) := \begin{cases} n - \|x\|_1 & \text{if } x \in L_1, \\ (3/4)n + \sum_{i=1}^{n/4} x_i & \text{if } x \in L_2, \\ 2n - i & \text{if } x \in L_3 \text{ and } x = 1^i 0^{n-i}, \\ 2n+1 & \text{if } x \in L_4, \\ \min\{\|x\|_1, n - \|x\|_1\} & \text{if } x \in L_0. \end{cases}$$

Theorem 14. *The probability that the (1 + 1) EA with $p(n) = 1/n$ needs a superpolynomial number of steps to optimize* PathToJump *converges to 1 as $n \to \infty$.*

Proof. With probability exponentially close to 1 the initial string belongs to $L_1 \cup L_2 \cup L_3$. Thus, L_0 is never entered. All global maxima belong to L_4 and are at Hamming distance at least $\log n$ from any point in $L_1 \cup L_2 \cup L_3$. The probability for a mutation of at least $\log n$ bits simultaneously is bounded above by

$$\binom{n}{\log n}\left(\frac{1}{n}\right)^{\log n} \le \frac{1}{(\log n)!}.$$

Therefore, the probability that such a mutation occurs in $n^{O(1)}$ steps is bounded above by $n^{O(1)}/((\log n)!)$ and converges to 0. □

We remark that Theorem 14 can be generalized to all mutation probabilities substantially different from $(\log n)/n$.

Theorem 15. *The expected number of steps until Algorithm 8 finds a global optimum of the function* PathToJump *is bounded above by $O(n^2 \log n)$.*

Proof. We define levels F_i of points with the same function value by

$$F_i := \{x \in \{0,1\}^n \mid \text{PathToJump}(x) = i\}.$$

Note that there are less than $2n+2$ different levels F_i with $F_i \neq \emptyset$. Algorithm 8 can enter these levels only in order of increasing function values. For each level F_i we derive a lower bound on the probability of reaching some $x' \in F_j$ with $j > i$ in one subphase, i. e., a lower bound on the probability

$$q_i := \max\left\{ \min\left\{ \sum_{x' \in \bigcup\limits_{j>i} F_j} \left(\frac{2^k}{n}\right)^{H(x,x')} \left(1 - \frac{2^k}{n}\right)^{n-H(x,x')} \mid x \in F_i \right\} \mid 0 \leq k \leq \lfloor \log n \rfloor \right\},$$

where $H(x, x')$ denotes the Hamming distance between x and x'. Clearly, a lower bound $q_i' \leq q_i$ yields an upper bound of $1/q_i'$ on the expected number of subphases until Algorithm 8 leaves F_i and reaches another level. Summing the upper bounds for all F_i, $i \leq 2n$, we get an upper bound on the expected run time. We distinguish four different cases with respect to i.

Case 1: $i \in \{0, 1, \ldots, (3/4)n - 1\}$
We have $x \in L_0 \cup L_1$, so it is sufficient to mutate exactly one of at least $n/4$ different bits to increase the function value. This implies

$$q_i \geq \binom{n/4}{1} \frac{1}{n} \left(1 - \frac{1}{n}\right)^{n-1} = \Omega(1)$$

for this case. So we have $O(n)$ as an upper bound on the expected number of subphases the algorithm spends in this part of the search space.

Case 2: $i \in \{(3/4)n, \ldots, n - 1\}$
We have $x \in L_2$, that is $\|x\|_1 = n/4$. Among the bits $x_1, x_2, \ldots, x_{n/4}$ there are $i - (3/4)n$ bits with value 1. Among the other bits there are $n - i$ bits with value 1. In order to increase the function value it is sufficient to mutate exactly one of the $(n/4) - (i - (3/4)n) = n - i$ bits with value 0 in the first part of x and exactly one of the $n - i$ bits with value 1 in the second part of x simultaneously. Therefore, we have

$$q_i \geq (n - i)^2 \left(\frac{1}{n}\right)^2 \left(1 - \frac{1}{n}\right)^{n-2} = \Omega\left(\left(\frac{n-i}{n}\right)^2\right)$$

as a lower bound and

$$\sum_{i=(3/4)n}^{n-1} \left(\frac{n}{n-i}\right)^2 = O\left(n^2\right)$$

as an upper bound on the expected number of subphases Algorithm 8 spends in L_2.

Case 3: $i \in \{n, \ldots, 2n - 1\}$
We have $x = 1^{2n-i}0^{i-n} \in L_3$. Obviously, it is sufficient to mutate exactly the right most bit with value 1 to increase the function value. This yields

$$q_i \geq \frac{1}{n} \left(1 - \frac{1}{n}\right)^{n-1} = \Omega\left(\frac{1}{n}\right)$$

as a lower bound on the probability and $O\left(n^2\right)$ as an upper bound on the expected number of subphases until Algorithm 8 leaves this part of the search space.

Case 4: $i = 2n$
In order to increase the function value it is necessary and sufficient that exactly $\log n$ bits, which all do not belong to the first $2 \log n$ positions in x mutate simultaneously. This yields

$$q_i \geq \binom{n - 2\log n}{\log n} p(n)^{\log n} (1 - p(n))^{n - \log n}$$

where we can choose $p(n) \in \left\{1/n, 2/n, \ldots, 2^{\lfloor \log n \rfloor}/n\right\}$ to maximize this lower bound. It is easy to see, that one should choose $p(n) = \Theta((\log n)/n)$ in order to maximize the bound. Therefore, we set $p(n) := (c \log n)/n$ for some positive constant c and discuss the value of c later. This yields

$$\begin{aligned} q_i &\geq \binom{n - 2\log n}{\log n} \left(\frac{c \log n}{n}\right)^{\log n} \left(1 - \frac{c \log n}{n}\right)^{n - \log n} \\ &\geq \left(\frac{n - 2\log n}{\log n}\right)^{\log n} \left(\frac{c \log n}{n}\right)^{\log n} \left(1 - \frac{c \log n}{n}\right)^{n} \left(1 - \frac{c \log n}{n}\right)^{-\log n} \\ &= \left(1 - \frac{2 \log n}{n}\right)^{\log n} c^{\log n} \cdot \Omega\left(\left(\frac{1}{n}\right)^{c/\ln 2}\right) \cdot \Omega(1) \\ &= \Omega\left(n^{(\log c) - c/\ln 2}\right) \end{aligned}$$

as a lower bound on the probability and $n^{(c/\ln 2) - \log c}$ as an upper bound on the number of subphases for this final mutation to a global optimum. Obviously, $(c/\ln 2) - \log c$ is minimal for $c = 1$. Unfortunately, it is not guaranteed that the value $(\log n)/n$ is used as mutation probability. Nevertheless, it is clear that for each d with $0 < d < n/(2 \log n)$ every $\lfloor \log n \rfloor$-th generation a value from the interval $[(d \log n)/n, (2d \log n)/n]$ is used as mutation probability $p(n)$. We choose $d = \ln 2$ and get $O\left(n^{1 - \log \ln 2}\right) = O\left(n^{1.53}\right)$ as an upper bound on the expected number of subphases needed for the final step.

Altogether, we have $O\left(n^2\right)$ as an upper bound on the expected number of subphases before Algorithm 8 reaches the global optimum. As each subphase contains $\lfloor \log n \rfloor$ generations, we have $O\left(n^2 \log n\right)$ as upper bound on the expected run time. □

Note that the probability of not reaching the optimum within $O(n^3 \log n)$ steps is exponentially small.

One may speculate that this dynamic variant of the (1+1) EA is always by at most a factor $\log n$ slower than its static counterpart given that the fixed value $p(n)$ is used by Algorithm 8, i. e., we have $p(n) = 2^t/n$ for some $t \in \{1, \ldots, \lfloor (\log n) - 1 \rfloor\}$. The reason for this speculation is clear: the fixed value of $p(n)$ for the (static) (1+1) EA is used by Algorithm 8 in each $\lfloor \log n \rfloor$-th step. But this speculation is wrong. Our proof rests on the following idea. In principle, Algorithm 8 can follow the same paths as the (1+1) EA with $p(n) = 1/n$ fixed. But if within some distance of the followed path there are so-called traps that, once entered, are difficult to leave, Algorithm 8 may be inferior. Due to the fact that it often uses mutation probabilities much larger than $1/n$, it has a much larger chance of reaching traps not too distant from the path. In the following, we define as an example a function PATHWITHTRAP and prove that the (1+1) EA with $p(n) = 1/n$ is with high probability by far superior to Algorithm 8. One important ingredient of the definition of PATHWITHTRAP are long paths introduced by Horn, Goldberg, and Deb (1994).

Definition 16. *For $n \in \mathbb{N}$ and $k \in \mathbb{N}$ with $k > 1$ and $(n-1)/k \in \mathbb{N}$, we define the long k-path P_k^n of dimension n as a sequence of $l = |P_k^n|$ strings inductively. For $n = 1$ we set $P_k^1 := (0,1)$. Assume the long k-path of dimension $n-k$ $P_p^{n-k} = (v_1, \dots, v_l)$ is well-defined. Then we define $S_0 := (0^k v_1, \dots, 0^k v_l)$, $S_1 := (1^k v_l, \dots, 1^k v_1)$, $B_k^n := (0^{k-1}1 v_l, 0^{k-2}1^2 v_l, \dots, 01^{k-1} v_l)$. We obtain P_k^n as concatenation of S_0, B_k^n, S_1.*

Long k-paths have some structural properties that make them a helpful tool. A proof for the following lemma can be found in (Rudolph 1997).

Lemma 17. *Let $n, k \in \mathbb{N}$ be given such that the long k-path of dimension n is well-defined. All $|P_k^n| = (k+1)2^{(n-1)/k} - k + 1$ points in P_k^n are different. For all $i \in \{1, 2, \dots, k-1\}$ we have, that if $x \in P_k^n$ has at least i successors on the path, then the i-th successor has Hamming distance i to x and all other successors of x have Hamming distances different from i.*

Definition 18. *For $k \in \mathbb{N}$ ($k > 20$) we define the function PATHWITHTRAP: $\{0,1\}^n \to \mathbb{R}$ as follows. Let $n := 2^k$, $j := 3k^2 + 1$. Let p_i denote the i-th point of the long k-path of dimension j. We define a partition of $\{0,1\}^n$ into seven sets $P_0, \dots, P_6$.*

$$
\begin{aligned}
P_1 &:= \{x \in \{0,1\}^n \mid 7n/16 < \|x\|_1 \leq 9n/16\} \\
P_2 &:= \{x \in \{0,1\}^n \mid \|x\|_1 = 7n/16\} \\
P_3 &:= \left\{ x \in \{0,1\}^n \mid (\sqrt{n} < \|x\|_1 < 7n/16) \wedge \left(\sum_{i=j+1}^{j+\sqrt{n}} x_i = \sqrt{n} \right) \right\} \\
P_4 &:= \left\{ x \in \{0,1\}^n \mid \exists i \in \{1, 2, \dots, \sqrt{n}\} : x = 0^j 1^i 0^{n-i-j} \right\} \\
P_5 &:= \left\{ x \in \{0,1\}^n \mid \left(x_1 x_2 \cdots x_j \in P_k^j \right) \wedge \left(\sum_{i=j+1}^{n} x_i = 0 \right) \right\} \\
P_6 &:= \left\{ x \in \{0,1\}^n \mid \left(x_1 x_2 \cdots x_j \in P_k^j \right) \wedge \left(\sum_{i=j+1}^{j+k} x_i = 0 \right) \wedge \left(\sum_{i=j+1}^{n} x_i = k \right) \right\} \\
P_0 &:= \{0,1\}^n \setminus (P_1 \cup P_2 \cup P_3 \cup P_4 \cup P_5 \cup P_6)
\end{aligned}
$$

Given this partition we define

$$
\text{PATHWITHTRAP}(x) := \begin{cases}
n - \|x\|_1 & \text{if } x \in P_1, \\
n - \|x\|_1 + \sum_{i=j+1}^{j+\sqrt{n}} x_i & \text{if } x \in P_2, \\
2n - \|x\|_1 & \text{if } x \in P_3, \\
4n - i & \text{if } (x \in P_4) \wedge (x = 0^j 1^i 0^{n-i-j}), \\
4n + 2i & \text{if } (x \in P_5) \wedge (x_1 \cdots x_j = p_i \in P_k^j), \\
4n + 2\left|P_k^j\right| - 1 & \text{if } x \in P_6, \\
\min\{\|x\|_1, n - \|x\|_1\}/3 & \text{if } x \in P_0,
\end{cases}
$$

for all $x \in \{0,1\}^n$.

Obviously, there is a unique string with maximal function value under PATHWITHTRAP: This string x_{opt} is equal to the very last point of P_k^j on the first j bits and is all zero on the other bits. Moreover, for all $x_0 \in P_0$, $x_1 \in P_1$, $x_2 \in P_2$, $x_3 \in P_3$, $x_4 \in P_4$, $x_5 \in P_5 \setminus \{x_{\text{opt}}\}$, $x_6 \in P_6$ and $x_7 = x_{\text{opt}}$ we have PATHWITHTRAP$(x_i) <$ PATHWITHTRAP(x_j) for all $0 \le i < j \le 7$. The main idea behind the definition of the function PATHWITHTRAP is the following. There is a more or less easy path to follow leading to the global optimum x_{opt}. The length of the path is $\Theta(n^3 \log n)$, so that both algorithms follow the path for quite a long time. In some sense, parallel to this path there is an area of points, P_6, that all have second best function value. The Hamming distance between these points and the path is about $\log n$. Therefore, it is very unlikely that this area is reached using a mutation probability of $1/n$. On the other hand, with varying mutation probabilities "jumps" of length $\log n$ do occur and this area can be reached. Then, only a direct jump to x_{opt} is accepted. But, regardless of the mutation probability, the probability for such a mutation is very small. In this sense we call P_6 a trap. Therefore, it is at least intuitively clear, that the (1+1) EA is more likely to be successful on PATHWITHTRAP than Algorithm 8.

Theorem 19. *The* $(1+1)$ *EA with mutation probability* $p(n) = 1/n$ *finds the global optimum of* PATHWITHTRAP *with probability* $1 - e^{-\Omega(\log n \log\log n)}$ *within* $O(n^4 \log^2 n \log\log n)$ *steps.*

Sketch of Proof:. With probability $1 - e^{-\Omega(n)}$ the initial string x belongs to P_1. Then, no string in P_0 can ever be reached. For all $x \in \{0,1\}^n \setminus (P_0 \cup P_6)$ and all $y \in P_6$ we have that the Hamming distance between x and y is bounded below by $\log n$. The probability for a mutation of at least $\log n$ bits simultaneously is bounded above by

$$\binom{n}{\log n}\left(\frac{1}{n}\right)^{\log n} \le \frac{1}{(\log n)!} = e^{-\Omega(\log n \log\log n)}.$$

Therefore, with probability $1 - e^{-\log n \log\log n}$ P_6 is not reached within $n^{O(1)}$ steps. Under the assumption that P_6 is not reached one can in a way similar to the proof of Theorem 15 consider levels of equal fitness values and prove that with high probability the (1+1) EA with $p(n) = 1/n$ reaches the global optimum fairly quickly. □

Theorem 20. *Algorithm 8 does not find the global optimum of* PATHWITHTRAP *within* $n^{O(1)}$ *steps with probability* $1 - e^{-\Omega(\log^2 n)}$.

Sketch of Proof:. The proof of the lower bound for Algorithm 8 is much more involved than the proof of the upper bound for the (1+1) EA.

Again, with probability $1 - e^{-\Omega(n)}$ the initial bit string belongs to P_1 and P_0 will never be entered. For all $x \in P_1 \cup P_2 \cup P_3$ we have that all strings $y \in P_5$ have Hamming distance at least $\sqrt{n}/2$. Therefore, for all mutation probabilities the probability to reach P_5 from somewhere in $P_1 \cup P_2 \cup P_3$ (thereby "skipping" P_4) within $n^{O(1)}$ steps is bounded above by $e^{-\Omega(\sqrt{n}\log n)}$. We conclude that some string in P_4 is reached with high probability before the global optimum.

It is not too hard to see that with probability $1 - e^{-\Omega(\log^2 n)}$ within $n^{O(1)}$ steps no mutation of at least $(\log^2 n)/n$ bits simultaneously occurs. We divide P_5 into two halves according to increasing function values. One can prove that, with probability $1-e^{-\Omega(\log^2 n)}$, the first point $y \in P_5$ reached via a mutation from some point $x \in P_4$, belongs to the first half. Therefore, the length of the rest of the long k-path the algorithm faces is still $\Theta(n^3 \log n)$. We conclude that with probability $1-e^{-\Omega(\log^2 n)}$ Algorithm 8 spends $\Omega(n^3)$ steps on the path. In each of these steps, where the current mutation probability equals $(\log n)/n$, with probability at least

$$\left(\frac{n}{2\log n}\right)^{\log n} \cdot \left(\frac{\log n}{n}\right)^{\log n} \cdot \left(1-\frac{\log n}{n}\right)^{n-\log n} \geq \frac{e^{-\log n}}{n} > n^{-2.45},$$

some point in P_6, the trap, is reached. We have, with high probability, $\Omega\left(n^3/\log n\right)$ steps on the path with this mutation probability. Thus, with probability $1-e^{-\Omega(\sqrt{n})}$ the trap is entered during this time. So, altogether we have that with probability $1-e^{-\Omega(\log^2 n)}$ Algorithm 8 enters the trap. Once this happens, i. e., some $x \in P_6$ becomes the current string of Algorithm 8, a mutation of exactly $\log n$ specific bits is needed to reach the global optimum. The probability that this happens in one step is bounded above by

$$\max\left\{\left(\frac{2^i}{n}\right)^{\log n}\left(1-\frac{2^i}{n}\right)^{n-\log n} \mid i \in \{0,1,\ldots,\lfloor \log n \rfloor - 1\}\right\}$$
$$\leq \left(\frac{\log n}{n}\right)^{\log n}\left(1-\frac{\log n}{n}\right)^{n-\log n} = e^{-\Omega(\log^2 n)}.$$

This yields on the one hand $\Omega(e^{\log^2 n})$ as a lower bound on the expected run time. And on the other hand we have that, with probability $1-e^{-\Omega(\log^2 n)}$, Algorithm 8 does not find the global optimum x_{opt} of PATHWITHTRAP within $n^{O(1)}$ steps. □

5 CONCLUSIONS

We studied two variants of the (1+1) EA with dynamic parameter control.

The first variant used a probabilistic selection mechanism that accepted deteriorations with a probability depending on a parameter α. We proved on a simple example that a dynamic parameter control can tremendously decrease the expected run time compared to optimal static choices. Our example proves the existence and gives an illustration of an exponential gap between the Metropolis algorithm and simulated annealing in a simple and understandable way.

Second, we considered the (1+1) EA with dynamically changing mutation probabilities. This leads to an enhanced robustness while only slowing the algorithm down by the factor $\log n$ for typical functions. On one example we saw that the dynamic variant outperformed the static one for the most recommended static choice $p(n) = 1/n$. It remains open, whether in practical situations the enhanced robustness of the dynamic variant turns out to be an advantage.

Acknowledgments

This work was supported by the Deutsche Forschungsgemeinschaft (DFG) as part of the Collaborative Research Center "Computational Intelligence" (SFB 531).

References

T. Bäck (1993). Optimal mutation rates in genetic search. In S. Forrest (Ed.), *Proc. of the 5th Int. Conf. on Genetic Algorithms (ICGA '93)*, 2–8. Morgan Kaufmann.

T. Bäck (1998). An overview of parameter control methods by self-adaptation in evolutionary algorithms. *Fundamenta Informaticae 35*, 51–66.

H.-G. Beyer (1996). Toward a theory of evolution strategies: Self-adaptation. *Evolutionary Computation 3*(3), 311–347.

S. Droste, T. Jansen, and I. Wegener (1998a). On the analysis of the (1 + 1) evolutionary algorithm. Technical Report CI-21/98, Univ. Dortmund, Collaborative Research Center 531.

S. Droste, T. Jansen, and I. Wegener (1998b). A rigorous complexity analysis of the (1 + 1) evolutionary algorithm for separable functions with Boolean inputs. *Evolutionary Computation 6*(2), 185–196.

J. Garnier, L. Kallel, and M. Schoenauer (1999). Rigorous hitting times for binary mutations. *Evolutionary Computation 7*(2), 173–203.

T. Hagerup and C. Rüb (1989). A guided tour of Chernoff bounds. *Information Processing Letters 33*, 305–308.

J. Horn, D. E. Goldberg, and K. Deb (1994). Long path problems. In Y. Davidor, H.-P. Schwefel, and R. Männer (Eds.), *Proceedings of the 3rd Parallel Problem Solving From Nature (PPSN III)*, Volume 866 of *Lecture Notes in Computer Science*, Berlin, 149–158. Springer.

M. Jerrum and A. Sinclair (1997). The Markov chain Monte Carlo method: an approach to approximate counting and integration. In D. S. Hochbaum (Ed.), *Approximation Algorithms for NP-hard Problems*, 482–520. PWS Publishers.

M. Jerrum and G. B. Sorkin (1998). The Metropolis algorithm for graph bisection. *Discrete Applied Mathematics 82*, 155–175.

S. Kirkpatrick, C. D. Gelatt, and M. P. Vecchi (1983). Optimization by simulated annealing. *Science 220*, 671–680.

N. Metropolis, A. W. Rosenbluth, M. N. Rosenbluth, A. H. Teller, and E. Teller (1953). Equation of state calculation by fast computing machines. *Journal of Chemical Physics 21*, 1087–1092.

H. Mühlenbein (1992). How genetic algorithms really work. Mutation and hillclimbing. In R. Männer and R. Manderick (Eds.), *Proc. of the 2nd Parallel Problem Solving from Nature (PPSN II)*, 15–25. North-Holland.

Y. Rabani, Y. Rabinovich, and A. Sinclair (1998). A computational view of population genetics. *Random Structures and Algorithms 12*(4), 313–334.

G. Rudolph (1997). *Convergence Properties of Evolutionary Algorithms*. Verlag Dr. Kovač.

G. Rudolph (1999). Self-adaptation and global convergence: A counter-example. In *Proc. of the Congress on Evolutionary Computation (CEC '99)*, 646–651. IEEE Press.

H.-P. Schwefel (1995). *Evolution and Optimum Seeking*. Wiley.

A. Sinclair (1993). *Algorithms for Random Generation and Counting: A Markov Chain Approach*. Boston: Birkhäuser.

G. B. Sorkin (1991). Efficient simulated annealing on fractal energy landscapes. *Algorithmica 6*, 367–418.

Local Search and High Precision Gray Codes: Convergence Results and Neighborhoods

Darrell Whitley, Laura Barbulescu, and Jean-Paul Watson
Department of Computer Science, Colorado State University
Fort Collins, Colorado 80523 USA
{whitley,laura,watsonj}@cs.colostate.edu

Abstract

A proof is presented that shows how the neighborhood structure that is induced under a Gray Code representation repeats under shifting. Convergence proofs are also presented for steepest ascent using a local search bit climber and a Gray code representation: for unimodal 1-D functions and multimodal functions that are separable and unimodal in each dimension, the worst case number of steps needed to reach the global optimum is $\mathcal{O}(L)$ with a constant ≤ 2. We also show how changes in precision impact the Gray neighborhood. Finally, we also show how both the Gray and Binary neighborhoods are easily reachable from the Gray coded representation.

1 Introduction

A long-standing debate in the field of evolutionary algorithms involves the use of bit versus real-valued encodings for parameter optimization problems. The genetic algorithm community has largely emphasized bit representations. On the other hand, the *evolution strategies* (ES) community [10] [9] [10] [1] and, more recently, the *evolutionary programming* (EP) community [4] have emphasized the use of real-valued encodings. There are also application-oriented genetic algorithm researchers (e.g., [3]) who have argued for the use of real-valued representations.

Unfortunately, positions on both sides of the encoding debate are based almost entirely on empirical data. The trouble with purely empirical comparisons is that there are too many factors besides representation that can impact the interpretation of experimental results, such as the use of different genetic operators, or differences in experimental methodology.

This work provides a better theoretical foundation for understanding the neighborhoods induced by a commonly used bit representation: Standard Binary Reflected Gray Codes.

One disadvantage of bit representations is that they generally do not offer the same precision as real-valued encodings. Often, genetic algorithms use 10 bits per parameter, while ES/EP approaches use full machine precision. On the one hand, different levels of precision can impact how accurately the global optimum is sampled, and can even change the apparent location of the optimum. Higher precision results in greater accuracy. But higher precision enlarges the search space, and conventional wisdom suggests that a smaller search space is generally an easier search problem. Yet, this intuition may be wrong for parameter optimization problems where the number of variables is fixed but the precision is not. This work examines how the search space changes as precision is increased when using bit encodings. In particular, we focus on how neighborhood connectivity changes and how the number of local optima can change as encoding precision is increased.

While our research is aimed at a very practical representation issue, this paper explores several theoretical questions related to the use of Gray codes, and high precision Gray codes in particular. These results have the potential to dramatically impact the use of evolutionary algorithms and local search methods which utilize bit representations.

We also present proofs which demonstrate that strong symmetries exist in the Hamming distance-1 neighborhood structure for Gray code representations. Given an L-bit encoding, we then prove that the worst-case convergence time (in terms of number of evaluations) to a global optimum is $\mathcal{O}(L)$ for any unimodal 1-dimensional function encoded using a reflected Gray code and a specialized form of steepest ascent local search under a Hamming distance-1 neighborhood. Under standard steepest ascent, the worst-case number of evaluations needed to reach a global optimum is $\mathcal{O}(L^2)$ for any unimodal 1-dimensional function. In both cases, the number of actual steps required to reach a global optimum is at most $2L$. This $\mathcal{O}(L)$ convergence time also holds for multidimensional problems when each dimension is unimodal and the intersection of the optima for each dimension leads to the global optimum. This includes problems such as the sphere function. In addition, we note some limitations of both Gray and Binary neighborhoods; we then prove that the standard Binary neighborhood is easily accessible from Gray space using a special neighborhood (or mutation) operator.

2 Local Optima, Problem Complexity, and Representation

To compare representations, it is essential to have a measure of problem complexity. The complexity measure we propose is the number of local optima in the neighborhood search space. There is evidence that the number of local optima is a relatively useful measure of problem complexity, that it impacts problem complexity, and relates to other measures such as schema fitness and Walsh coefficients [8] for problems using bit representations.

Suppose we have N unique points in our search space, each with k neighbors, and a search operator that evaluates all k neighboring points before selecting its next move; similar results hold for most non-unique sets of values. A point is considered a local optimum from a steepest ascent perspective if its evaluation is better than all of its k-neighbors. We can sort these N points to create an ordinal ranking, $R = r_1, r_2, ..., r_N$, where r_1 is the global optimum of the search space and r_N is the worst point in the space. Using R, we can compute the probability $P(i)$ that a point ranked in the i-th position in R is a local optimum under an arbitrary representation, given a neighborhood of size k:

$$P(i) = \frac{\binom{N-i}{k}}{\binom{N-1}{k}} \qquad [1 \leq i \leq (N-k)] \tag{1}$$

Proof:

For any point in the search space, there are $\binom{N-1}{k}$ possible sets of neighbors for that point. If the point is ranked in position r_1, then there are $\binom{N-1}{k}$ sets of neighbors that do not contain a point of higher evaluation than the point r_1. Therefore, the point ranked in position r_1 will always be a local optimum under all representations of the function. In the general case, a point in position r_i has only $\binom{N-i}{k}$ sets of neighbors that do not contain a point of higher evaluation than the point r_i. Therefore the probability that the point in position r_i remains a local optimum under an arbitrary representation is $\binom{N-i}{k}/\binom{N-1}{k}$. □

This proof also appears in an IMA workshop paper [7]. These probabilities enable us to count the expected number of local optima that should occur in any function of size N. The formula for computing the expected number of times a particular point will be a local optimum is simply $N! \times P(i)$. Therefore the expected number of optima over the set of all representations is:

$$\mathcal{E}(N,k) = \sum_{i=1}^{N-k} P(i) \times N! \tag{2}$$

Rana and Whitley [7] show that to find the expected number of local optima for a single representation instance, we divide $\mathcal{E}(N,k)$ by $N!$, which yields:

$$\mu(N,k) = \sum_{i=1}^{N-k} P(i) = \sum_{i=1}^{N-k} \frac{\binom{N-i}{k}}{\binom{N-1}{k}} = \frac{N}{k+1} \tag{3}$$

This result leads to the following general observation: in expectation, if we increase neighborhood size we decrease the number of local optima in the induced search space. Can we leverage this idea when constructing bit representations? In particular, can we construct bit representations that increase neighborhood size while also bounding or decreasing the number of local optima?

3 Gray and Binary Representations

Another much-debated issue in the evolutionary algorithms community is the relative merit of Gray code versus Standard Binary code bit representations. Generally, "Gray code" refers to Standard Binary Reflected Gray code [2]. In general, a Gray code is any bit encoding where adjacent integers are also Hamming distance-1 neighbors in the bit space. There are exponentially many Gray codes with respect to bit length L. Over all possible discrete functions that can be mapped onto bit strings, the space of all Gray codes and the space of all Binary representations are identical. Therefore, a "No Free Lunch" result must hold [13] [5]. If we apply all possible search algorithms to Gray coded representations of all possible functions and we apply all possible search algorithms to Binary representations of all possible functions, the behavior of the algorithms must be identical for the two sets of representations since the set of all possible Gray coded and the set of all Binary coded functions are identical [11].

The empirical evidence suggests that Gray codes are usually superior to Binary encodings for practical optimization problems. It has long been known that Gray codes remove the Hamming Cliffs induced by the Standard Binary code, where adjacent integers are represented by complementary bit strings: e.g., 7 and 8 encoded as 0111 and 1000. Whitley et al. [12] note that every Gray code must preserve the connectivity of the original real-valued functions (subject to the selected discretization). Further, because of the increased neighborhood size, Gray codes induce additional connectivity which can potentially 'collapse' optima in the real-valued function. Therefore, for *every* parameter optimization problem, the number of optima in the Gray coded space must be less than or equal to the number of optima in the original real-valued function. Binary encodings offer no such guarantees. Binary encodings destroy half of the connectivity of the original real-valued function; thus, given a large basin of attraction with a globally competitive local optimum, most of the (non-locally optimal) points near the optimum of that basin become new local optima under a Binary encoding.

Recently, we proved that Binary encodings work better on average than Gray encodings on "worst case" problems [11]; a "worst case" function is such that when interpreted as a 1-D function, alternating points in the search space are local optima. "Better" means that the representation induces fewer local optima. (There is a definitional error in this proof; it does not impact "wrapping" functions, but does impact the definition of a worst case function for "non-wrapping" functions. See Appendix 1 for details and a correction.) A corollary to this result is that Gray codes on average induce fewer optima than Binary codes for all remaining functions. For small (enumerable) search spaces, it can also be proven that in general Gray codes are superior to Binary for the majority of functions with bounded complexity. A function with "lower complexity" in this case has fewer optima in real space. We use these theoretical results, as well as the empirical evidence to argue for the use of Gray codes.

But to be comparable to real-valued representations, bit representations must use higher precision. Higher precision can allow one to get "closer" to an optimum, and also creates higher connectivity around the optimum. But what happens when we use higher precision Gray codes?

We first establish some basic properties of Gray neighborhoods. We will assume that we are working with a 1-dimensional function, but results generally apply to the decoding of individual parameters.

4 Properties of the Reflected Gray Space

We begin by asking what happens when a function is "shifted." Since we are working with bit representations, we assume that a *decoder* function converts bits to integers, and finally to real space. Shifting occurs after the bits have been converted to integers, but before the integers are mapped to real values. If there are L bits then we may add any integer between 0 and $2^L - 1$ ($mod\ 2^L$). The only effect of this operator is to shift which bit patterns are associated with which real values in the input domain. Also note the resulting representation is still a Gray code under any shift [6].

What happens when one shifts by 2^{L-1}? Under Binary, such a shift just flips the first bit, and the Hamming distance-1 neighborhood is unchanged. A reflected Gray code is a symmetric reflection. Shifting therefore also flips the leading bit of each string, but it also reverses the order of the mapping of the function values to strings in each half of the space. However, since the Gray code is a symmetric reflection, again the Hamming distance-1 neighborhood does not change. This will be proven more formally.

It follows that every shift from $i = 0$ to $2^{L-1} - 1$ is identical to the corresponding shift at $j = 2^{L-1} + i$. We next prove that shifting by 2^{L-2} will not change the neighborhood structure; in general, shifting by 2^{L-k} will change exactly $k - 2$ neighbors.

Theorem 1 *For any Gray encoding, shifting by 2^{L-k} where $2 \leq k \leq L$ will result in a change of exactly $k - 2$ neighbors for any point in the search space.*

Proof: Consider an arbitrary Gray code, and $k \geq 2$. Divide the 2^L points in the search space into 2^k continuous blocks of equal size, starting from the element labeled 0. Each block contains exactly 2^{L-k} elements corresponding to bit strings or integers (see Figure 1a). Consider an arbitrary block X and arbitrary element with label P within X. Exactly $L - k$ neighbors of P are contained in X. The periodicity of both Binary and Gray bit encodings ensures that the $L-k$ neighbors of P in X do not change when shifting by 2^{L-k}. Two of the remaining k neighbors are contained in the blocks preceding and following X, respectively. Since the adjacency between blocks does not change under shifting, the two neighbors in the adjacent blocks must stay the same.

The remaining $k-2$ neighbors are contained in blocks that are not adjacent to X. We prove that the rest of these $k - 2$ neighbors change. Consider a block Y that contains a neighbor of P. For every Reflected Gray code there is a reflection point exactly halfway between any pair of neighbors. For all neighbors outside of block X which are not contained in the adjacent blocks, the reflection points must be separated by more than 2^{L-k} positions. Shifting X by 2^{L-k} will move it closer to the reflection point, while Y is moved exactly 2^{L-k} positions farther away from the reflection point (see Figure 1b). Point P in X must now have a new neighbor (also 2^{L-k} closer to the reflection point) in the block Z. If the reflection point between X and Z is at location R, then for the previous neighbor in Y to still be a neighbor of P in X it must have a reflection point at exactly $R + 2^{L-k}$. This is impossible since for all neighbors outside of block X which are not contained in the adjacent blocks, the reflection points must be separated by more than 2^{L-k} positions. A similar argument goes for the case when shifting by 2^{L-k} moves X farther away from the reflection point (while Y is moved closer). Thus, none of the previous $k - 2$ neighbors are neighbors after shifting by 2^{L-k}. □

Corollary of Theorem 1: In any reflected Gray code representation of a 1-dimensional function, or parameter of a multidimensional function, there are only 2^{L-2} unique shifts. When $k = 2$, $k - 2 = 0$ and 0 neighbors change. When $k = 1$, we can shift twice by 2^{L-2} and 0 neighbors change each time.

4.1 High Precision Gray Code and Longest Path Problems

We know that a Gray code preserves the connectivity of the real-valued space. If we think about search moving along the surface of the real-valued functions, then increased precision could cause a problem. The distance from any point in the search space and

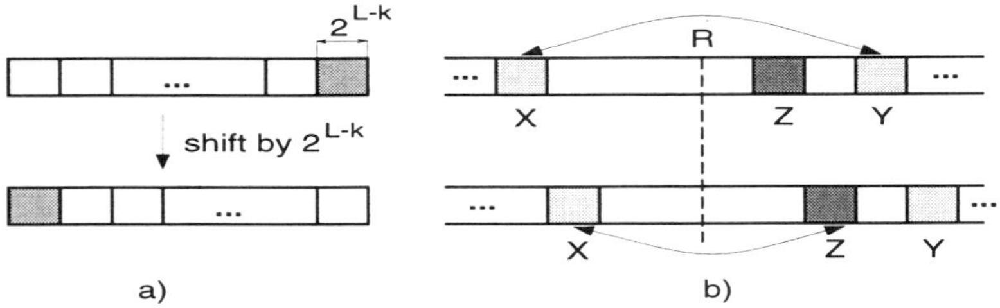

Figure 1 Shifting by 2^{L-k}. **a).** A representation of the Gray codes. **b).** For an arbitrary position in a block X, and an arbitrary neighbor of this position in the block Y, after shifting by 2^{L-k}, the neighbor moves from block Y to block Z.

the global optimum might grow exponentially as precision is increased. If we must step from one neighbor to the next, then as we increase the number of bits, L, used to encode the problem, the distance along this adjacent-neighbor path grows exponentially long as a function of L. On the other hand, we know that connectivity in a hypercube of dimension L is such that no two points are more than L moves away from one another. This lead us to ask what happens when we increase the precision for Gray coded unimodal functions? We prove that the number of steps leading to the optimum is $O(L)$.

4.2 Convergence Analysis for Unimodal and Sphere Functions

Consider any *unimodal real-valued* 1-dimensional function. Steepest ascent local search using the L-bit Hamming distance-1 neighborhood of any Reflected Gray-code representation of any unimodal real-valued function will converge to the global optimum after at most $2L$ steps or moves in the search space.

Lemma 1 *For any 1-dimensional unimodal real-valued function, steepest ascent local search using the L-bit Hamming distance-1 neighborhood of any Reflected Gray-code representation will converge to the global optimum after at most* $2L$ *steps.*

Proof: The proof assumes that all points in the search space have unique evaluations (to prevent search from being stuck on flat spots). We have already shown that for any Gray code representation shifting by 2^{L-2} does not change the structure of the search space. We can thus break the search space into four *quadrants.* This means we can assume the current point, `P` from which we are searching can be located in any quadrant, and the neighborhood structure is identical when `P` is shifted to the same position in any other quadrant of the search space.

Consider the following set of points: { `a, N, b, c, P, c', b', N' a', x, Y, z`}. The points {`N, P, N', Y`} are located in the four quadrants and for any reflected Gray code 2 adjacent points in the sequence `N, P, N', Y, N` are neighbors. Let points `a` and `b` be neighbors in the same quadrant as `N`, with `a` to the left and `b` to the right. The same holds for subsets {`c, P, c'`} {`b', N', a'`} and {`x, Y, z` } as shown in the following figure. The quadrants are labeled Q1, Q2, Q3 and Q4. Neighbors are connected by dashed lines.

Let `P` be the current position of the search. `P` has neighbors `c, c'`, `N`, and `N'`. The neighbors `c` and `c'` are in the same quadrant as `P`, but `N` and `N'` must be in adjacent

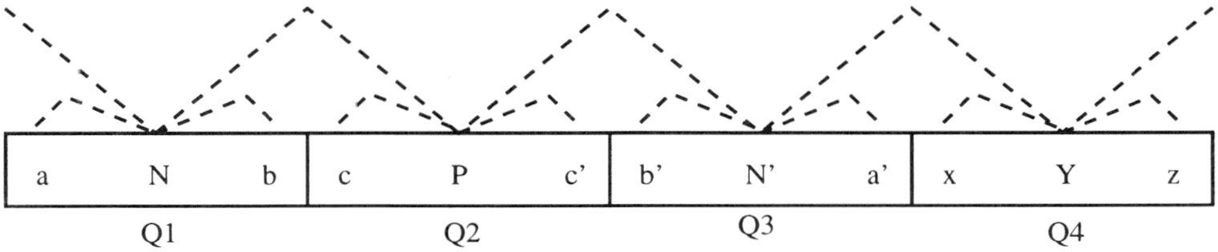

quadrants of the space due to the reflected symmetry of Gray code. `Y` is in a position symmetric to `N` and reachable in 2 moves from `P`.

We now can decompose this problem into a series of cases. For any set of three points $\{w, x\ y\}$, if we know that $w > x < y$ then we know that a minimum, and hence the global minimum, must lie between w and y. (Note we use the same symbol to represent a point and its evaluation.) In this way, each case either eliminates at least half of the search space from further consideration, or leads to at most 2 moves to a neighbor from which it is possible to eliminate at least half of the search space. The only moves that are considered are those that change from one quadrant to another. ("In quadrant" moves can be considered as part of the next move.)

```
POSITION        CASE           MOVE        QUADRANT TO ELIMINATE
========   ==============   ===========   ======================
P               c > P < c'     none            Q1, Q3, Q4
P               N > c < P      none                Q3, Q4
P               P > c'< N'     none                Q1, Q4
P               N'> N < c      goto N
P               c'> N'< N      goto N'
N               a > N < b      none            Q2, Q3, Q4
N               Y > a < N      none            Q2, Q3
N               N > b < c      none            Q3, Q4
N               N > Y < N'     goto Y
Y               x > Y < z      none            Q1, Q2, Q3
Y               N'> x < Y      none            Q1, Q2
Y               Y > z < N      none            Q2, Q3
```

The cases for `N'` are a symmetric reflection of the cases for `N`. There are no other cases. Thus after 2 moves it is always possible to reduce the search space by at least half. Furthermore the remaining quadrants are always adjacent (which is true by inspection).

After discarding half of the search space, we can treat the space as having been reduced by 1 dimension in Hamming Space. This reduction in the dimensionality can be recursively applied until $L = 2$. For $L = 2$ the search space is reduced to four points (one of which is the optimum) and it takes at most two moves to go to the optimum. By summation, it follows that it takes at most $2L$ moves to go from any point in the space to the optimum. □

If the optimum can be reached after at most $2L$ moves, each move normally requires $L - 1$ evaluations under steepest ascent. But if the function is unimodal we only need to evaluate four critical neighbors that are used in the preceding proof. Therefore

Theorem 2 *For any unimodal real-valued function, there exists a special form of steepest ascent local search using the L-bit Hamming distance-1 neighborhood of any Reflected Gray-code representation that will converge to the global optimum after at most $\mathcal{O}(L)$ evaluations.*

Proof: The result follows directly from the proof of Lemma 1. □

4.3 Multi-parameter Problems and Sphere Functions

The proofs only deal with 1 dimensional functions. However, every multi-parameter separable function can be viewed as a composition of real-valued subfunctions. If each real-valued sub-function is unimodal and encoded with at most l bits, a specialized form of steepest ascent Hamming distance-1 local search using any Reflected Gray-code representation will converge to the global optimum after at most $\mathcal{O}(l)$ steps in each dimension. If there are Q dimensions and exactly l bits per dimension, note that $Ql = L$, and the overall convergence is still bounded by $\mathcal{O}(L)$. It also follows that

Theorem 3 *Consider the sphere function, $c_0 + c_1 \sum_i^N (x_i - x_i^*)^2$, where $(x_i^*, ...x_n^*)$ denotes the minimum. For this sphere function, steepest ascent local search using the L-bit Hamming distance-1 neighborhood of any Reflected Gray-code representation will converge to the global optimum after at most $\mathcal{O}(L)$ steps.*

4.4 The Empirical Data

The proof obviously shows that regular steepest ascent, where all L neighbors are checked, will converge in $\mathcal{O}(L)$ steps and $\mathcal{O}(L^2)$ total evaluations. A set of experiments with different unimodal sphere functions encoded using a varying number of bits shows behavior exactly consistent with the proof. The number of *steps* of steepest ascent local search needed to reach the optimum is linear with respect to string length. This is shown in Figure 2. This figure also shows that the number of evaluations used by regular steepest ascent is order $\mathcal{O}(L^2)$ with respect to string length.

But what about next ascent? In the best case, next ascent will pick exactly the same neighbors as those selected under steepest ascent, and the number of steps needed to reach the optimum is $\mathcal{O}(L)$. However, in the worst case an adjacent point in real space is chosen at each move and thus the number of steps needed to reach the optimum is $\mathcal{O}(2^L)$. The linear-time best case and exponential-time worst case makes it a little less obvious what happens on average. The advantage of next ascent of course, is that there can be multiple improving moves found by the time that L neighborhoods have been evaluated. Informally, what are the odds that none of the improving moves which are found are long jumps in the search space? If, for example, one found a best possible move and a worst possible move after evaluating L neighborhoods, the convergence time is still closer to the $\mathcal{O}(L)$ steps and $\mathcal{O}(L^2)$ evaluations associated with blind steepest ascent. The empirical data seems to suggest that the average case is similar to the best case. The rightmost graph in Figure 2 shows that the empirical behavior of Random Bit Climbing appears to be bound by $L \log(L)$ on average. This is in fact better than the L^2 behavior that characterizes the number of *evaluations* required by steepest ascent. The variance is so small in both cases as to be impossible to be seen on the graphs shown here.

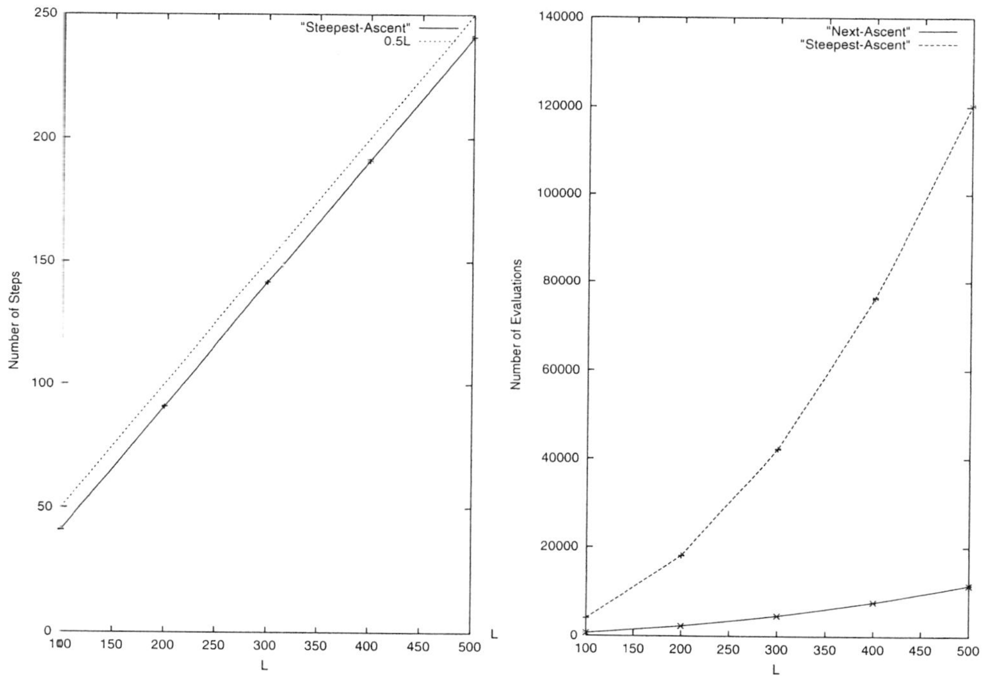

Figure 2 The leftmost graph shows the number of *steps* required by steepest-ascent local search to locate the global optimum for various sphere functions. The rightmost graph shows the number of *evaluations* required to locate the global optimum for sphere functions using both steepest-ascent and the next-ascent algorithm RBC. RBC requires far fewer evaluations. The results are averaged over 1000 initial starting locations. Each graph shows results for a single sphere function; the results for different sphere functions are indistinguishable.

We used Davis's Random Bit Climber (RBC) as our next ascent algorithm. RBC randomized the order in which the bits are checked. After every bit has been tested once, the order in which the bits are tested is again randomized. This randomization may be important in avoiding worst case behavior.

5 High Precision Gray Codes and Local Optima

Our results on the expected number of optima under a neighborhood search operator of size k confirm the intuitive notion that, *in expectation*, larger neighborhood sizes generally result in fewer optima. One way to increase the neighborhood size for bit-encoded parameter optimization problems is to increase the encoding precision of each parameter. This initially seems counter-intuitive, because it also increases the size of the search space. A 10 parameter optimization problem with a 10-bit encoding results in a search space of 2^{100} points, while a 20-bit encoding results in a search space of 2^{200} points. Generally, a smaller search space is assumed to be "easier" than a larger search space. But is this true?

Consider a parameter X with bounds X_{lb} and X_{ub}. From an L-bit representation, an integer y is produced by the standard Binary or Gray decoding process. This integer is then mapped onto an element $x \in X$ by : $x = X_{lb} + y\frac{X_{ub}-X_{lb}}{2^L-1}$. We refer to y as an integer point and x as the corresponding domain point.

We begin with an illustrative example. Let $X_{lb} = 0$ and $X_{ub} = 31$, and consider an L-bit Gray encoding of X, with $5 \leq L \leq 10$. Table 1 shows the L domain neighbors of the domain point *nearest* to 4.0; for reasons discussed below, 4.0 may not be exactly representable under an arbitrary L-bit encoding. Under a 5-bit Gray encoding, the integer neighbors of $y_5 = 4$ are 3, 5, 7, 11, and 27, as shown. And because of the domain bounds, these integers are also the domain neighbors of the point $x = 4.0$.

L	$n \sim 3$	n introduced by increases in precision					$n \sim 5$	$n \sim 7$	$n \sim 11$	$n \sim 27$
5	3.000						5.000	7.000	11.000	27.000
6	3.444					**4.429**	5.413	7.381	11.318	27.064
7	3.661				**4.149**	**4.638**	5.614	7.567	11.472	27.095
8	3.647			**3.890**	**4.133**	**4.619**	5.592	7.527	11.428	26.988
9	3.701		**3.943**	**4.065**	**4.186**	**4.671**	5.642	7.583	11.466	26.996
10	3.727	**3.969**	**4.030**	**4.091**	**4.212**	**4.697**	5.667	7.606	11.485	27.000

Table 1 Neighbors of the point nearest to $x = 4.0$ under a Gray encoding, $5 \leq L \leq 10$.

Table 1 shows that increasing the precision can influence the neighborhood structure under Gray encodings. The point of reference is x and its neighbors are n.

Two things are important about the pattern established in Table 1. First, as precision is increased, the set of neighbors when L = 5 continue to be represented by neighbors near to the original set of neighbors. Thus, all of the original neighbors are **approximately sampled** at higher precision. Second, note that when L = 5, the nearest neighbor of $x = 4.0$ are $n = 3.0$ and $n = 5.0$. All new neighbors of x fall between 3.0 and 5.0.

Observation 1 *Assume that a Gray code adequately samples a real valued function, such that every optimum and saddle in real space is represented in Hamming Space. Further* *assume that the small changes in this original discretization are not sufficient to change the number of local optima over the original set of neighborhood connections. Under these conditions, adding additional precision will not change the number of local optima in Hamming space.*

This observation suggests that we might wish to consider the stability of the original set of neighborhoods as we increase precision. And it also suggests that higher precision does not necessarily change the number of optima, and thus, using higher precision does not hurt or help when "number of local optima" is used as a measure of complexity.

Note our observation makes strong assumptions. Table 1 shows that in fact there is considerable instability in the position of neighbors 3 – 11, there is slight instability in the domain neighbor 27. A contributing cause, albeit minor, to the instability of the domain neighbors is due to the following

Theorem 4 *Let X_{lb} and X_{ub} denote the lower and upper bounds on the domain of a parameter X. Consider bit encodings (Gray or Binary) of X with precisions L and $L+1$. Define $z_L = X_{lb} + y_L \frac{X_{ub}-X_{lb}}{2^L-1}$ for some decoded integer y_L, $0 \leq y_L \leq 2^L - 1$; z_L is a point in the domain of X representable under an L-bit encoding. Then there exists no y_{L+1} (except for 0 and $2^{L+1}-1$) such that $z_L = z_{L+1}$ - i.e., identical points are not representable under bit encoding after changing the precision by one 1.*

Proof: Suppose that there exists y_{L+1} such that $z_L = z_{L+1}$ Using the definition for z_L we obtain:

$$\frac{y_L}{2^L - 1} = \frac{y_{L+1}}{2^{L+1} - 1} \quad \Leftrightarrow \quad (2^L - 1)(y_{L+1} - y_L) = 2^L y_L$$

The equation above implies that $(2^L - 1)$ evenly divides $2^L y_L$, which is a contradiction if $y_{L+1} \neq 0$ and $y_{L+1} \neq 2^{L+1} - 1$! Indeed, $(2^L - 1)$ does not evenly divide 2^L. The only 2 values of y_L which are evenly divided by $(2^L - 1)$ are 0 and $(2^L - 1)$. But if $y_L = 2^L - 1$, then $z_L = z_{L+1} = X_{ub}$, and therefore $y_{L+1} = 2^{L+1} - 1$ (value already accounted for by the theorem). Similarly, if $y_L = 0$ then $y_{L+1} = 0$. □

For example, consider a 10-bit encoding of a parameter X with $X_{lb} = 0$ and $X_{ub} = 16$ The decoded integer 512 maps to the domain value 8.993157. Increasing the precision to 11 bits, the nearest domain values are represented by the integers 1150 (8.988764) and 1151 (8.996580). While the difference is relatively minor (~ 0.004), altering the precision nonetheless changes the representable domain values. Further, this change is independent of the choice of Gray or Binary bit encodings. However note that *this proof does not preclude recycling of point at different precisions.* Table 1 shows that the same points can be resampled when the precision changes by more than 1 bit. Table 1 also shows that the change in distance from some *fixed* reference point *does not* change monotonically as precision is increased.

We can generate examples which prove that it is possible for minor changes in precision to either increase or decrease the number of optima which exists in Hamming Space due to small shifts in the locations of some "original" set of neighbors. Cases exists where two optima with similar evaluation exist at one level of precision in Gray space, and then collapse at higher precision. In addition, two optima in real space that were previously collapsed in Gray space at lower precision can again become separate optima in Gray space at higher precision. Nevertheless, the creation or collapse of an optimum under higher precision appears to be a symmetric process–and we conjecture that in expectation, the creation and collapse of optima will be equal and that no change in the total number of optima would result.

Any remaining instability in the domain neighbors due to increases in precision must be explainable by changes in the neighborhood connectivity patterns. To characterize such changes, we divide the domain of a parameter X into 4 quadrants, denoted $Q1 - Q4$. Under both Gray and Binary encodings, a point in Q1 has a neighbor in Q2. Under a Gray code, the point in Q1 has a neighbor in Q4, and under Binary the same point has a neighbor in Q3. We can also "discard" Q3 and Q4 under both Binary and Gray encodings by discarding the first 1-bit. We can then cut the reduced space into 4 quadrants and the same connectivity pattern holds. (This connectivity pattern is also shown in Figures 3 and 4.)

First, we can show that increases in the precision fail to alter the location of neighbors from the quadrant viewpoint:

Theorem 5 *Consider the decoded integer y_L under an L-bit encoding, $L \geq 2$. Increasing the precision to $L+1$ yields $y_{L+1} = 2 \cdot y_L$. Let $Q^{y_L}_{neighbors}$ represent the set of quadrants in which neighbors of y_L reside. Then $Q^{y_L}_{neighbors} = Q^{y_{L+1}}_{neighbors}$.*

Proof: For the trivial case $y_L = y_{L+1} = 0$, the theorem is obviously true.

Consider $y_l \neq 0$, and z_L the domain point corresponding to y_L. Then, $z_L = X_{lb} + y_L \frac{X_{ub}-X_{lb}}{2^L-1}$. If z_{L+1} is the domain point corresponding to y_{L+1}, then similarly: $z_{L+1} = X_{lb} + y_{L+1} \frac{X_{ub}-X_{lb}}{2^{L+1}-1}$. We will prove that z_L and z_{L+1} reside in the same quadrant, this being equivalent to $Q^{y_L}_{neighbors} = Q^{y_{L+1}}_{neighbors}$.

In the real-valued domain, if z_L resides in the qth quadrant (where $q = 0..3$), then the following inequalities are satisfied:

$$X_{lb} + q\frac{X_{ub} - X_{lb}}{4} < z_L < X_{lb} + (q+1)\frac{X_{ub} - X_{lb}}{4} \tag{4}$$

First, we compute the difference between z_L and z_{L+1}:

$$z_L - z_{L+1} = X_{lb} + y_L\frac{X_{ub} - X_{lb}}{2^L - 1} - (X_{lb} + y_{L+1}\frac{X_{ub} - X_{lb}}{2^{L+1} - 1}) =$$

$$(X_{ub} - X_{lb})(\frac{y_L}{2^L - 1} - \frac{2y_L}{2^{L+1} - 1}) = y_L\frac{X_{ub} - X_{lb}}{(2^L - 1)(2^{L+1} - 1)} \tag{5}$$

Note that the difference is positive; therefore $z_{L+1} < z_L$.

Let z'_L be the domain point corresponding to $y_L - 1$. Then:

$$z_L - z'_L = \frac{X_{ub} - X_{lb}}{2^L - 1} \tag{6}$$

Since $\frac{y_L}{2^{L+1}-1} < 1$, using (5) and (6), we can infer:

$$z'_L < z_{L+1} < z_L$$

If z_L is *not* the first point sampled in the qth quadrant by the L bit encoding, then z'_L must also be in the same quadrant with z_L. Therefore, from the above inequality it results that z_{L+1} must be in the same quadrant with z_L and z'_L.

Consider the case when z_L is the first point sampled in the qth quadrant by the L bit encoding. Since the $y_L = 0$ case was already considered, $q = 1..3$.

Suppose that z_{L+1} is *not* in the same quadrant with z_L. This means that the distance between z_{L+1} and z_L is larger than the distance from z_L to the starting point (in the real domain) of the qth quadrant:

$$z_L - z_{L+1} > z_L - (X_{lb} + q\frac{X_{ub} - X_{lb}}{4}) \quad \Leftrightarrow$$

$$y_L < \frac{(2^{L+1} - 1)q}{8} \quad \Leftrightarrow \quad y_L < \frac{q}{4}(2^L - \frac{1}{2}) \qquad (7)$$

But, from (4):

$$y_L > \frac{q}{4}(2^L - 1) \qquad (8)$$

Using (7) and (8), the difference between the two bounds discovered for y_L is:

$$\frac{q}{4}(2^L - \frac{1}{2}) - \frac{q}{4}(2^L - 1) = \frac{q}{8} \qquad (9)$$

We distinguish 3 cases:

Case 1: $q = 1$

In this case $q(2^L - 1)$ is an odd number. Therefore, there exists an integer number p such that $q(2^L - 1) = 4p + 1$ or $q(2^L - 1) = 4p + 3$. Using (7), (8), and (9), we obtain:

$$p + \frac{1}{4} < y_L < p + \frac{1}{4} + \frac{1}{8} \qquad (10)$$

or

$$p + \frac{3}{4} < y_L < p + \frac{3}{4} + \frac{1}{8} \qquad (11)$$

(10), (11) can not be satisfied for any integer y_L.

Case 2: $q = 2$

In this case $\frac{q(2^L-1)}{2}$ is an odd number. Therefore, there exists an integer number p such that $\frac{q(2^L-1)}{2} = 2p + 1$. This implies:

$$p + \frac{1}{2} < y_L < p + \frac{1}{2} + \frac{2}{8} \qquad (12)$$

Again, Case 2 (12) can not be satisfied for any integer y_L.

Case 3: $q = 3$

As for case 1, $q(2^L - 1)$ is an odd number. However, there exists no integer p such that $q(2^L - 1) = 4p + 3$. Indeed, suppose there exists an integer p such that $3(2^L - 1) = 4p + 3$.

This implies $2^{L-1} = (2/3)p + 1$, where the right hand side of the equality must be integer, and therefore is odd. But 2^{L-1} is an even number. The contradiction obtained confirms that for no integer p, $q(2^L - 1) = 4p + 3$. The only possibility left to express $q(2^L - 1)$ as an odd number is: $q(2^L - 1) = 4p + 1$ where p is integer. For y_L this implies:

$$p + \frac{1}{4} < y_L < p + \frac{1}{4} + \frac{3}{8} \tag{13}$$

It is clear that there exists no integer y_L satisfying (13).

The contradictions obtained for the three possible values of q resulted from the assumption that z_{L+1} is *not* in the same quadrant with z_L. Thus, we proved by contradiction that z_L and z_{L+1} reside in the same quadrant. □

Note that y_L and y_{L+1} are the decoded integers roughly corresponding to the same domain point (Theorem 4 prevents the exact correspondence to the same domain point). Theorem 5 establishes that increasing precision cannot change the quadrants sampled by the neighbors of a y_L, but it says nothing about how the relative densities of those neighbors change in the various quadrants, or how the neighbors can shift positions within quadrants.

To explore the question of neighbor density, we consider an L-bit encoding (Gray or Binary) and an integer y_{L-2} in a quadrant $Q_{y_{L-2}}$. There are $L-2$ neighbors of y_{L-2} in quadrant $Q_{y_{L-2}}$, and exactly one in two of the three remaining quadrants ($Q_{y\_adj\_left}$ and $Q_{y\_adj\_right}$).

Next, we increase the precision by one to $L+1$. Here, $L-2$ neighbors of y_{L-2} are compressed into $\frac{1}{8}$ of the domain, instead of $\frac{1}{4}$ under the L-bit encoding. The remaining 3 neighbors are allocated as follows: exactly one in two of the remaining three new quadrants ($Q_{y\_adj\_left}$ and $Q_{y\_adj\_right}$), and an additional neighbor in the quadrant $Q_{y_{L-2}}$. Because of this compression, we find an increased density of neighbors near x_{L-2} as the precision is increased. In summary:

Observation 2 *For a given integer y, increasing the encoding precision simply increases the density of neighbors near y. Loosely speaking, no new connectivity in introduced by the increased precision except new connectivity which is increasing closer to y.*

This observation is imprecise because the position of y also moves with the increased precision. This is clearly shown in Table 1. In addition to increased density, we see a 'migration' of domain neighbors within quadrants. Examining Table 1, we see that 3.0 under a 5-bit encoding migrates toward 3.7273 under a 10-bit encoding, and the migration is more than can be accounted for by Theorem 4. Consider a 4-bit Gray code and the integer 4, which has neighbors 3, 5, 7, and 11, and a corresponding domain point d_4. Next, increase the precision to 5 bits. Now the domain point nearest to 4.0, subject to Theorem 4, is produced by the integer 8, with neighbors 7, 9, 11, 15, and 23. Since we have roughly doubled the precision, these neighbors correspond roughly to 3.5, 4.5, 5.5, 7.5, and 11.5, respectively, for the integer 4.

6 Combining Gray and Binary Neighborhoods

The "Quadrant" decomposition used previously in this paper also provides a helpful way to visualize connectivity bias in the Gray and Binary neighborhoods. Figure 3 illustrates that

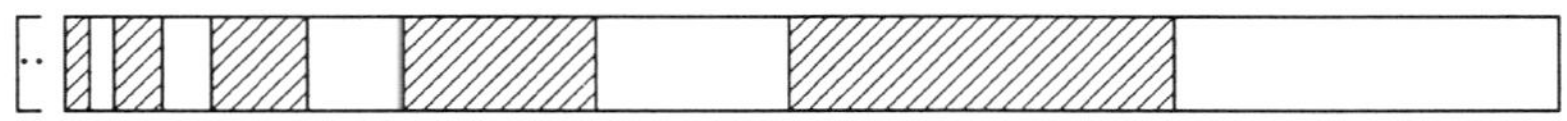

Figure 3 The search space is repeatedly broken into 4 quadrants. Assume the point of interest x is shifted to the first quadrant, discarding the third and fourth quadrants. The space is then reduced by 1 bit and the process is repeated. All Binary neighbors of some point of interest are in the dashed regions, Gray neighbors are in the undashed regions; the two regions are disjoint and complementary.

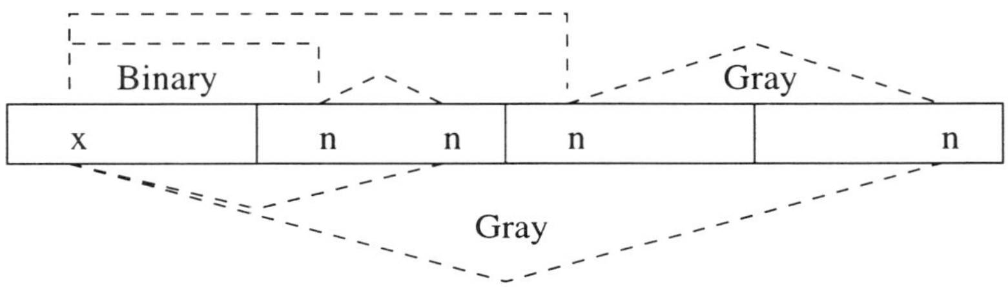

Figure 4 The search space is broken into 4 quadrants. The dashed "rectangular" connectors on the top of the figure locate binary neighbors of x. The dashed "triangular" of the bottom connects to Gray neighbors of x. Note there also the Gray "triangular" connectors on top; Binary neighbors are always two moves away in Gray space.

Binary and Gray neighbors reside in disjunct and complementary portions of the search space. We construct Figure 3 using our prior strategy of shifting any point of interest, x, to the first quadrant. Again, this can be done without changing the neighborhood structure of the space. x has exactly one Binary neighbor in the upper half of the space, in quadrant 3. Also, x has exactly one Gray neighbor in the upper half of the space, in quadrant 4. We recursively identify in the same way the location of the remaining Binary and Gray neighbors of x. First, we can discard quadrants 3 and 4 and consider the lower-dimensional problem. We then repeat the process of shifting the point of interest to the new lower-dimensional first quadrant. The lower dimensional neighborhood is unchanged.

Figure 3 shows how Gray and Binary codes connect x (via a Hamming distance-1 neighborhood) to complementary, disjoint portions of the search space. However, Figure 4 shows that the Hamming distance-1 neighbors under Binary are Hamming distance-2 neighbors in Gray space. Thus it is possible to construct a neighborhood of $2L - 1$ points that include both the Binary and Gray neighbors. The goal of constructing such a neighborhood is to reduce the complementary bias which exists in the Gray and Binary neighborhood structures.

We will show that flipping single bits accesses the Gray neighborhood and that flipping pairs of adjacent bits accesses the Binary neighborhood. Consider the following bit vector B as a binary string. Assume strings are numbered from right to left starting at zero: $B = B_{l-1}, ..., B_1, B_0$. In particular we are interested in the bit B_i. Now convert B to a Gray code using exclusive-or. This results in the following construction.

$$G_{l-1} = B_{l-1}, \quad G_{l-2} = B_{l-2} \oplus B_{l-1}, \quad \cdots, \quad G_i = B_i \oplus B_{i+1},$$

$$G_{i-1} = B_{i-1} \oplus B_i, \quad \cdots, \quad G_0 = B_0 \oplus B_1$$

Now consider what happens when bit B_i is flipped, where $1 \leq i \leq l-1$. G changes at exactly two locations. Thus, we can access the Gray neighborhood by flipping individual bits and the Binary neighborhood by flipping adjacent pairs of bits. By combining Binary and Gray neighborhoods, we can never do worse than the original Gray space in terms of number of local optima which exist. To access these neighbors in a genetic algorithm, we would use a special mutation operator that flips adjacent pairs of bits.

7 Conclusions

We have presented four theoretical results which provide a better understanding of one of the most commonly used bit encodings: the family of Gray code representations. First, we showed that shifting the search space by $2^L - 2$ does not change the Gray code Hamming distance-1 neighborhood. Second, we showed that for any unimodal, 1-dimensional function encoded using a reflected L-bit Gray code, steepest-ascent local search under a Hamming distance-1 neighborhood requires only $\mathcal{O}(L)$ steps for convergence to the global optimum, in the worst case. We showed that this result also holds for multi-dimensional separable functions. Third, we demonstrated how increasing the precision of the encoding impacts on the structure of the search space. Finally, we show that there exists a complementary bias in the Gray and Binary neighborhood structures. To eliminate this bias, a new neighborhood can be constructed by combining Gray and Binary neighborhood structures.

References

[1] T. Bäck. *Evolutionary Algorithms in Theory and Practice.* Oxford University Press, 1996.

[2] James R. Bitner, Gideon Ehrlich, and Edward M. Reingold. Efficient Generation of the Binary Reflected Gray Code and Its Applications. *Communications of the ACM*, 19(9):517–521, 1976.

[3] Lawrence Davis. *Handbook of Genetic Algorithms.* Van Nostrand Reinhold, New York, 1991.

[4] D. B. Fogel. *Evolutionary Computation.* IEEE Press, 1995.

[5] N.J. Radcliffe and P.D. Surry. Fundamental limitations on search algorithms: Evolutionary computing in perspective. In J. van Leeuwen, editor, *Lecture Notes in Computer Science 1000.* Springer-Verlag, 1995.

[6] S. Rana and D. Whitley. Bit Representations with a Twist. In T. Bäck, editor, *Proc. of the 7th Int'l. Conf. on GAs*, pages 188–195. Morgan Kaufmann, 1997.

[7] S. Rana and D. Whitley. Search, representation and counting optima. In L. Davis, K. De Jong, M. Vose, and D. Whitley, editors, *Proc IMA Workshop on Evolutionary Algorithms.* Springer-Verlag, 1998.

[8] Soraya Rana. *Examining the role of Local Optima and Schema Processing in Genetic Search.* PhD thesis, Colorado State University, Department of Computer Science, Fort Collins, Colorado, 1999.

[9] Hans-Paul Schwefel. *Numerical Optimization of Computer Models.* Wiley, 1981.

[10] Hans-Paul Schwefel. *Evolution and Optimum Seeking.* Wiley, 1995.

[11] D. Whitley. A Free Lunch Proof for Gray versus Binary Encodings. In *GECCO-99*, pages 726–733. Morgan Kaufmann, 1999.

[12] Darrell Whitley, Keith Mathias, Soraya Rana, and John Dzubera. Evaluating Evolutionary Algorithms. *Artificial Intelligence Journal*, 85:1–32, August 1996.

[13] David H. Wolpert and William G. Macready. No free lunch theorems for search. Technical Report SFI-TR-95-02-010, Santa Fe Institute, July 1995.

Appendix 1

There is a definitional error in the proof that Binary encodings work better than Gray encodings on "worst case" problems [11].

First, "better" in this case means that over the set of "worst case" problems Binary induces fewer optima that a reflect Gray code. However, a No Free Lunch relationship holds between Gray codes and Binary codes. The total number of optima induced over all functions is the same. Thus, if binary induces fewer optima over the set of "worst case" problems then Gray code must induce fewer optima over the set of "non-worst case" problems

The problem lies in the definition of a "worst case" problems.

In the original proof, two definitions are used of function neighborhoods. For neighborhoods that wrap, adjacent points in real space are neighbors and the first point in the real valued space and the last point in the real valued space are also neighbors. For non-wrapping neighborhoods, adjacent points in real space are neighbors but the first point in the real valued space and the last point in the real valued space are *not* neighbors.

A worst case problem is defined as one where a) every other point in the real space is a local optimum and thus b) the total number of optima is N/2 when there are N points in the search space. For neighborhoods that wrap the two concepts that a) there are N/2 optima and b) every other point in the space is an optimum are identical. However for non-wrapping neighborhoods, these two concepts are not the same. For a non-wrapping neighborhood, there can be N/2 optima and yet there can be one set of optima that are separated by 2 intermediate points instead of one. This can happen when the first and last point in the space are both optima–which can't happen with a wrapping representation.

The proof relies on the fact that every other point in the space is an optimum. Thus, for non-wrapping neighborhoods, the definition of a worst case function must be restricted to the set of functions where every other point in the space is an optimum; with this restriction, the proof then stands. The proof is then unaffected for wrapping representations, since the "worst-case" definitions defines the same subset of functions.

Burden and Benefits of Redundancy

Karsten Weicker*
Institute of Computer Science
University of Stuttgart
Breitwiesenstr. 20–22
70565 Stuttgart, Germany

Nicole Weicker*
Institute of Computer Science
University of Stuttgart
Breitwiesenstr. 20–22
70565 Stuttgart, Germany

Abstract

This work investigates the effects of two techniques introducing redundancy, diploid representations and decoders. The effects of redundancy on mutation, recombination, the structure of the landscape and the interplay between these ingredients are of particular interest. Resulting neutral mutations are found to be the reason for the transformation of local optima into plateau points. Additional neutral recombinations enable a more efficient search on those neutral plateaus. Furthermore, both kinds of neutral operations are shown to have a positive impact on the diversity of the population over time. Lastly, the diploid representation is compared empirically to a macromutation which models the working principles of diploidity. However, this control experiment shows that blind exploring mutations cannote approximate diploidity.

1 INTRODUCTION

When applying evolutionary algorithms for optimization the algorithm has to be tailored to the problem. Besides choosing the operators with their parameters the choice of a suitable representation or encoding function is crucial. Fogel and Ghozeil (1997) have shown that finding a good representation is comparably hard to the choice of good operators. Thus, questions arise regarding the properties of good representations. One possible property is redundancy which is the topic of this examination.

* Email: {Karsten,Nicole}.Weicker@informatik.uni-stuttgart.de

Redundancy occurs whenever the problem is defined on a space that is different from the search space the genetic operators work on and the latter contains more elements. Usually the problem defined space is called the phenotype space and the search space of the genetic operators is called the genotype space.

Following the design principles of Radcliffe (1991) it is desirable to choose the genotype space in a way that there exists a bijection between phenotype and genotype. In contrast, there exist few positive reports on a very beneficial influence of redundant decoders (Hinterding, 1994, 1999). Also in many upcoming more biologically oriented models (e.g. floating representations, Wu & Lindsay, 1997) redundancy is an essential element which cannot be avoided. Therefore, it is important to analyze the advantages and disadvantages of redundancy.

This work discusses the characteristics of different types of redundancy and examines the effects on mutation and recombination operators. Additionally, we discuss the effects of both genetic operators under redundancy with regard to the structure of the landscape and the diversity of populations. This analysis is carried out using the knapsack problem. There are primarily two reasons for choosing this problem: first, the binary encoding is an intuitive and direct representation and, second, many successful reports on redundancy use it either as a stationary (Hinterding, 1994, 1999) or non-stationary problem. The analysis consists of a systematic and complete investigation of small, stationary problem instances and empirical investigations of experiments using medium sized problems.

2 REASONS FOR REDUNDANCY

Redundancy occurs only if the genetic operators are not defined on the phenotype search space S but on a genotype space S'. To evaluate an element of the genotype space, a decoding function $decode : S' \to S$ is used which maps each point of S' to exactly one point in the search space S. Here we assume that *decode* is surjective, i.e. that for each point $s \in S$ there exists a point $s' \in S'$ with $decode(s') = s$. This decoding function is called redundant if S' is bigger than S. If both S and S' are finite this means $|S| < |S'|$. A more formal definition of redundancy is given below by considering that a decoding function is not injective.

Definition 1 (Redundancy) Let $decode : S' \to S$ be the decoding function.

Then *decode* is called *redundant*, $:\iff \; \exists\, s'_1, s'_2 \in S' (s'_1 \neq s'_2) : \; decode(s'_1) = decode(s'_2)$.

There are various reasons for the occurrence of redundant decoding functions. We distinguish four different areas where redundancy is found: coding based, representation based, conceptional, and technical redundancy.

The first two reasons are rather unavoidable and not the topic of this article. Coding based redundancy occurs if the size of the search space S does not match the size of the genotype space which is the cardinality of the alphabet raised to the power of the length of individuals. The second form of unavoidable redundancy is the representation based form which is caused by structural reasons. It is inherent to the considered problem or the optimization method used. An example for problem inherent redundancy is the inversion of permutations for symmetric TSP instances (Whitley, Starkweather, & Fuquay,

1989). This kind of redundancy was investigated by Julstrom (1999). Another example for representation based redundancy is the bloating effect in genetic programming (Blickle & Thiele, 1994; Langdon & Poli, 1997).

Conceptual redundancy exists if redundancy is introduced on purpose by gene interactions. Multiple examples are discussed in detail by Shackleton, Shipman, and Ebner (2000). Special cases of conceptual redundancy are floating representations (e.g. Wu & Lindsay, 1997; Wu & De Jong, 1999) and the introduction of multiploidity. In the latter technique several different mechanisms can be distinguished. On the one hand there are dominance mechanisms on a bit per bit basis (e.g. Goldberg & Smith, 1987; Lewis, Hart, & Ritchie, 1998). On the other hand Dasgupta and McGregor (1992) introduced the structured GA which is a rather high level diploidity, where one (or more) additional bits are used as a switch between two (or more) complete candidate solutions.

In contrast to the three previously discussed kinds of redundancy, the technical redundancy occurs as a side effect of a different concept, e.g. the use of a decoder that improves or repairs the represented solution. The decoder restricts the genotype space to a subset (e.g. those solutions fulfilling certain constraints) which we then call the phenotype space. In the case of knapsack problems the weight constraints must be fulfilled for each valid solution. Often it is possible to design a simple heuristic for the transformation of any candidate solution violating the constraints into a valid solution. Such a heuristic is called a decoder or repair function. Other decoding approaches use a solution builder and code only certain parameters for the builder in the chromosome. Then depending on the setting of the parameters a new valid candidate solution is created by the solution builder (e.g. Paechter et al., 1995). Another possibility for the construction of a restrictive decoder function is the inclusion of an intelligent local optimization in the decoder (e.g. Leonhardi et al. 1998). All three possibilities map a bigger number of solutions to a smaller subset of solutions. Also diploidity may be viewed as technical redundancy since diploid evolutionary algorithms are mostly used as memorizing technique in the context of oscillating non-stationary fitness functions but also for other dynamic problems (e.g. Dasgupta, 1995).

We decided in this work to restrict our attention to technical redundancy which arises as a by-product of techniques introduced for reasons other than redundancy. The two examples we examine are decoder methods and diploidy encoding.

3 INVESTIGATED PROBLEMS AND METHODOLOGY

In the remainder of the work, the analysis of redundancy is divided into four sections and uses various methods and benchmark problems. This section discusses the problems and the methodological approach.

In order to carry out exact and complete investigations of certain landscape characteristics, two small benchmark knapsack problems by Petersen (1967) are used, in particular the problem with 6 items and the problem with 10 items. The 6 items problem is constrained by 7 effective weight constraints and its optimum is $\{2,3,6\}$ with a value of 3800. The 10 items problem is constrained by 10 weight constraints and its optimum is $\{2,4,5,8,10\}$ with value 8706.1. The problem with 6 items is printed in the appendix.

For an empirical investigation of certain hypotheses two additional benchmark problems by Petersen (1967) with 20 and 28 items are used.

As an intuitive representation of the knapsack problem each bit represents inclusion ("1") or exclusion ("0") of an item. The fitness computation is carried out as follows. A fixed base fitness is defined for each problem. If a candidate solution fulfills all constraints the values of the included items are added to the base fitness. If a solution violates a constraint, the values are not considered but a penalty is subtracted for each violated constraint. For the values used in the different problems see the appendix. The fitness function has to be maximized.

In case of the diploidity no complicated dominance mechanisms are considered (e.g. Goldberg & Smith, 1987) but rather the simplified structured GA by Dasgupta and McGregor (1992) is used where each individual contains two complete candidate solutions and an additional bit to determine the currently active solution. The passive candidate solution has no effect on the fitness value. Recall that this is only a very specific kind of diploidity – the results are not valid for more sophisticated dominance mechanisms.

As an example for a decoder, heuristics for the knapsack problem inspired by the work of Hinterding (1994, 1999) are used. In the binary genotype representation a "1" signifies that the item may be considered for inclusion, a "0" that it is definitely omitted. As an inclusion strategy the following heuristics are used as examples.

1. *best fit*: iteratively choose those items that have the highest value and do not violate the weight constraints.
2. *left to right*: iteratively select the items from left to right but only those items are included which do not violate the weight constraints.
3. *right to left*: iteratively select the items from right to left but only those items are included which do not violate the weight constraints.

For the analysis of the two small problems all three strategies are considered. In the empirical examination of experiments only the most promising strategy *best fit* is investigated.

For the exact landscape investigations a one-bit flipping mutation is used. In the empirical investigation a genetic algorithm with mutation rate $p_m = \frac{1}{l}$, where l is the number of knapsack items, and two-point crossover with $p_c = 0.6$ is used. The experiments have been carried out using a genetic algorithm with population size 100 and 3-ary tournament selection. The best fitness in the population is used as a performance measure.

In the empirical analysis, each algorithm has been applied to one problem with 50 different initial random seeds and the respective measures, e.g. best fitness in the population or population diversity, are averaged over those experiments. Additionally, for an analysis of the data the Student's t-test for significantly different means has been used (cf. Cohen, 1995). For each generation the hypothesis is formulated that the mean performance values of two different algorithms do not differ. The t-test has been executed for each generation under the assumption that both algorithms have the same standard deviation with respect to the performance values. F-tests support these assumptions. In the results we consider an error probability of 0.05 as significant. This threshold is displayed in the graphs as lines with t-values 1.96 and -1.96. Values outside the range between these thresholds are significant.

All experiments are conducted for both problems with 20 and 28 items with comparable results. Therefore and because of space restrictions in each case only the results of one problem is shown.

4 ANALYSIS I: DEGREE OF REDUNDANCY

In order to compare different kinds of redundancy, it is necessary to develop measurements for the degree of redundancy. The characteristics and effects of redundancy should be reflected by those measures.

Definition 2 (Redundant points and degree of redundancy) Let $decode : S' \rightarrow S$ be the decoding function. Then the *redundant points to* $s \in S$ are given by the set

$$redundant(s) \quad = \quad \left\{ s' \in S' \;\middle|\; decode(s') = s \right\}.$$

And the *degree of redundancy for* $s \in S$ is defined by $degree_{red}(s) = |redundant(s)|$.

In case of diploidity the initial search space $S = \mathbb{B}^l$ of size 2^l is blown up to the size of 2^{2l+1} since each individual represents two solutions and an additional switching bit. Therefore S' increases by a factor of 2^{l+1}. Nevertheless the mapping is homogeneous and each candidate solution s is represented by 2^{l+1} individuals, i.e. $degree_{red}(s) = 2^{l+1}$.

In case of a decoder the initial search space is reduced to a new phenotype space. But contrary to diploidity it is not obvious which individuals are mapped by the decoder to the same valid candidate solution. Often, it is even not clear whether an arbitrary decoder is surjective, i.e. whether for all valid candidate solutions there exists an individual that is mapped to this solution. Nevertheless, the decoders described above are surjective since each solution fulfilling all constraints is a fixed point of the decoding function.

Table 1 Number of phenotypes classified by their degree of redundancy. The middle section of the table can be read as follows: e.g. 'best fit' has 24 different phenotypes with a redundancy of 1.

	decoder	redundancy degree of each phenotype								valid
problem	technique	1	2	4	8	16	32	64	128	solutions
6 items:	best fit	24	2	1	0	0	1	0		28 of 64
	left to right	4	18	6	0	0	0	0	–	28 of 64
	right to left	8	16	2	2	0	0	0	–	28 of 64
10 items:	best fit	554	59	8	20	2	0	0	1	644 of 1024
	left to right	388	210	38	8	0	0	0	0	644 of 1024
	right to left	384	208	48	4	0	0	0	0	644 of 1024

Table 1 shows how the individuals are mapped to the valid candidate solutions in the two examples. The fact that the numbers of individuals which are mapped onto one valid candidate solution is always a power of two is astonishing at first sight. If we examine the candidate solution of problem 1 which unites 32 individuals, we see that it contains only item 4. Now weight constraint 4 guarantees that each other item cannot be included – i.e. with the best fit strategy all individuals $***1**$ are always mapped to the candidate solution 000100, unaffected by the value of the other bits since item 4 has got the highest value.

We can generalize this effect and find always some patterns or schemata $H \in \{0, 1, *\}^l$ where the weight constraints prevent the inclusion of the starred items and, in case of the best fit heuristic, the value does not conflict with the other included items. Since all instances of such a pattern have the same fitness value they define a search plateau. The size of the plateau is at least 2^k for a schema of order $l - k$, i.e. with k "don't care" symbols. The size of 2^k is due to the greedy repair method where there are often no interdependencies between the selected item and the remaining items. For the 'best fit' heuristic even all excluded items are interchangeable.

5 ANALYSIS II: MUTATION AND THE STRUCTURE OF LANDSCAPE

The usefulness of redundancy in a decoding function is directly affected by the mutation operator. The interplay between both specifies whether neutral mutations are possible or not. If neutral mutations are introduced by the redundancy positive effects take place. A mutation is called neutral if it creates a transition between redundant points.

Definition 3 (Neutral mutation) Let S be the phenotype space with fitness function $\mathit{fit} : S \to \mathbb{R}$ to be minimized. Let S' be the genotype space with a decoding function $\mathit{decode} : S' \to S$, and let $\mathit{mutate} : S' \times \Xi \to S'$ be a genetic operator that maps one point of the genotype space to another depending on some random number of a set Ξ.

Then *mutate* is called a *neutral mutation for* $s' \in S'$ *and* $x \in \Xi$: $\Longleftrightarrow$

$$\mathit{mutate}(s', x) \quad \in \quad \mathit{redundant}(\mathit{decode}(s')).$$

Note, that trivially it holds that $s' \in \mathit{redundant}(\mathit{decode}(s'))$. If the condition above is fulfilled there is a transition between s' and $\mathit{mutate}(s', x)$, both mapping to the same phenotype. The redundant points that are connected through neutral mutations form a *neutral network* (cf. Shackleton et al., 2000). Note that in case of diploidity and decoders all points of the neutral plateaus, discussed in the previous section, are connected by a 1-bit flipping mutation. Thus, those plateaus are transformed into neutral networks and Table 1 reflects their size.

One interesting property of neutral mutations is its possible influence on the structure of the landscape, i.e. local optima can become plateau points which are part of a neutral network. To clarify this statement both local optima and plateau points are formalized.

Definition 4 (Local optimum, plateau point) Supposed the preconditions of Definition 3 are fulfilled. Then a point $s'_1 \in S'$ is called a

- *local optima* : $\Longleftrightarrow$ $\forall\ s'_2 \in S'$ it holds that

$$\left(\exists\ x \in \Xi : \mathit{mutate}(s'_1, x) = s'_2\right) \Rightarrow \left(\mathit{fit}(\mathit{decode}(s'_2)) > \mathit{fit}(\mathit{decode}(s'_1))\right)$$

- *plateau point* : $\Longleftrightarrow$ it holds that

$$\exists\ s'_2 \in S' : \left((\mathit{mutate}(s'_1, x) = s'_2\right) \Rightarrow \left(\mathit{fit}(\mathit{decode}(s'_2)) = \mathit{fit}(\mathit{decode}(s'_1))\right) \text{ and}$$
$$\forall\ s'_2 \in S' : \left((\exists\ x \in \Xi :\ \mathit{mutate}(s'_1, x) = s'_2\right) \Rightarrow \left(\mathit{fit}(\mathit{decode}(s'_2)) \geq \mathit{fit}(\mathit{decode}(s'_1))\right).$$

These definitions imply that for a simple hill climbing algorithm, which does not accept worsening, the local optimum is an end point where the plateau point is not. The plateau point allows further search without deteriorations. However, it is not guaranteed that there exists a better point.

Now, the two kinds of redundancy are investigated with respect to their effect on local optima. It is possible to compute the local optima and plateau points for the 1-bit flipping mutation for the 6 and 10 items problems.

Table 2 This table shows the fractions of local optima and plateau points in the search space for both problems and the considered decoding functions. Furthermore, all possible mutations are classified in improving, worsening, and neutral mutations.

problem	technique	loc. opt.	plateau p.	better	worse	neutral
6 items:	1-bit HC	0.125	0.0	0.5	0.5	0.0
	diploid	0.0	0.115	0.271	0.266	0.463
	decoder (best fit)	0.0	0.344	0.273	0.273	0.453
	decoder (left to right)	0.0	0.281	0.391	0.391	0.219
	decoder (right to left)	0.0	0.156	0.372	0.372	0.255
10 items:	1-bit HC	0.019	0.0	0.5	0.5	0.0
	diploid	0.0	0.016	0.262	0.262	0.476
	decoder (best fit)	0.0	0.109	0.418	0.418	0.164
	decoder (left to right)	0.0	0.020	0.455	0.455	0.089
	decoder (right to left)	0.0	0.014	0.456	0.456	0.088

The neutral mutations of the 1-bit flipping mutation in the case of the diploid representation changes the landscape in such a way that all local optima are eliminated. A neutral mutation occurs with probability at least $\frac{l}{2l+1}$ where only a bit in the passive candidate solution is flipped. That means that each local optima is transformed into a plateau point in the worst case – if the passive solution has a better fitness there is a direct improving mutation by changing the switch bit. This is reflected in Table 2 where the frequency of a local optimum/plateau point decreases with diploidity. In fact, this representation even guarantees that there is always a hill climbing path (with acceptance of equal fitness) from each point in the search space leading to the optimum.

But what are the impeding effects of the diploid representation? First of all a diploid representation results in a huge enlargement of the search space. For the regarded two small problems this means that the size of the search space grows from 64 respectively 1024 up to 8192 respespectively 2097152. Each point in the original search space introduces a plateau of the size of the original search space. Additionally as it is already shown in Table 2 both the probability to improve as well as to worsen have decreased substantially in favor of neutral mutations. But neutral mutations give no clue during optimization whether the mutation is a step towards the right direction. Plateau points being part of huge neutral plateaus approximate pure random walks.

Now, we proceed from the 1-bit hill climber to a genetic algorithm with population size 100 but without recombination. The results for the haploid and the diploid representation

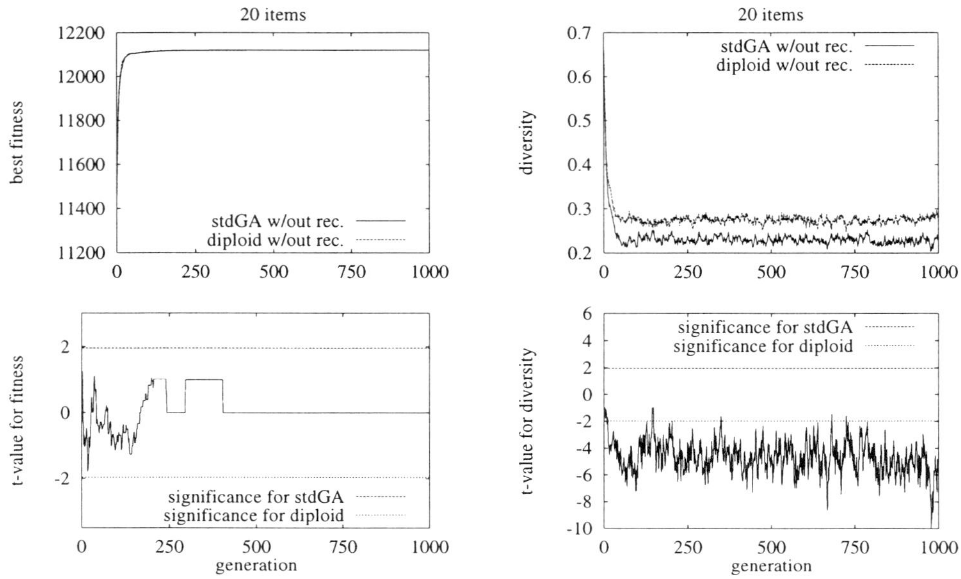

Figure 1 Left: fitness comparison of a GA and a diploid GA, both without recombination. The t-tests show that the difference in performance of the two algorithms is not significant. Right: comparison of the diversity in each population of the same experiments. The t-tests show the higher diversity of the diploid algorithm to be significant.

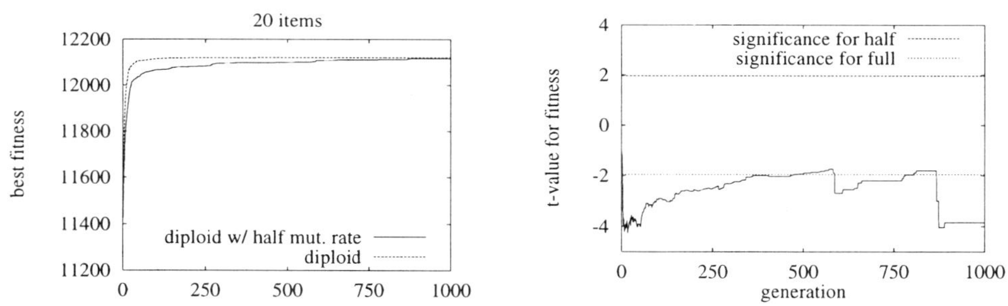

Figure 2 Comparison of best fitness values of the diploid GA without recombination using half and full mutation rate on the problem with 20 items. Most t-tests show the performance of the full mutation rate to be significant.

are shown in Figure 1. In spite of the disadvantages for the diploid representation stated above it performs similar to the standard encoding.

Interestingly the mutation rate for diploid representations should be chosen rather high. Using a normal mutation rate of $p'_m = \frac{1}{l'}$ where l' is the length of the chromosome the

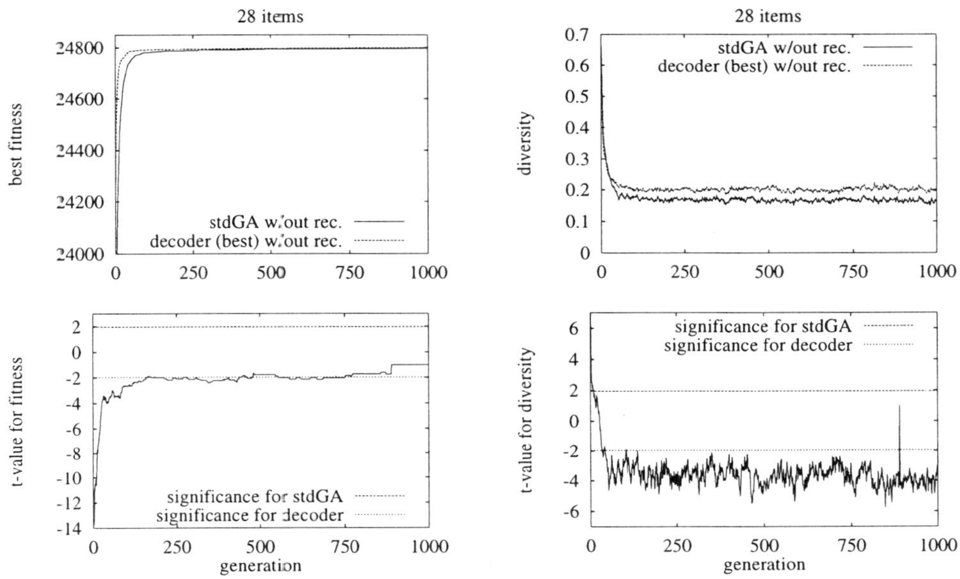

Figure 3 Left: fitness comparison of a GA and a GA using the best fit decoder. The t-tests show that the performance of the decoder is significant at the beginning of the optimization. Right: comparison of the diversity in each population of the same experiments. The t-tests show the higher diversity of the decoder to be significant.

results of a GA without recombination are significantly worse than the same GA with a mutation rate of $p_m = \frac{1}{l}$ where l is the length of the phenotypical representation, i.e. the number of items in the knapsack problem. This is shown in Figure 2 where the full mutation rate corresponds to p_m and the half mutation rate to p'_m.

In the case of the decoder, the introduced neutral networks cause a transformation of each local optimum into a plateau point. Nevertheless this cannot be guaranteed for all local optima and all kinds of decoders. As a consequence there might not be a hill climbing path from each candidate solution to the global optimum.

The analysis of the two exemplary problems in Table 2 shows that for some decoders the number of plateau points is increased considerably, for others only slightly. Especially the best fit strategy seems to have a tendency to rather huge plateaus and, therefore, the number of plateau points increases considerably. The number of neutral mutations in those neutral networks is also reflected in the table. Neutral mutations keep the diversity high but – in the case of bigger problems not considered here – they can also slow down the convergence speed since search is a complete random walk on big plateaus. The left part of Figure 3 shows the comparison of a GA using the normal representation and a GA with best-fit decoder strategy.

It is not clear whether this behavior of the mutation can be generalized for other problems and decoders. Probably it is inherent in the character of the knapsack problem which would be a sufficient reason for most success stories dealing with knapsack problems.

As a next step, we analyze how the size of the basins of attraction changes for the two knapsack problems given. The basin of attraction contains all points of the fitness landscape which are reachable from the local optimum (or plateau point) without encountering a better point. The neutral networks are embedded into the basins. In order to keep the computational cost feasible, only paths consisting of maximally four mutations are considered in order to get to a point with better fitness. All those paths are computed for all local optima and plateau points. Table 3 shows the resulting expected number of mutations until we find a better candidate solution as well as the length of the minimal path leading to such a candidate solution. All results are averaged over all local optima respectively plateau points.

The diploid representation does not affect the existing paths in the standard representation – therefore better paths by neutral mutations and a switch of the activity bit can induce shorter minimal paths. With regard to the expected number of mutations the figures indicate that the basins have been enlarged. This might be the reason for the rather slow convergence.

For the decoders the plateaus also affect the size of the basins of attraction. Table 3 illustrates an increase of the expected number of mutations to get to a better point from a plateau point. Also the minimal path leading to a better point was lengthened. Both measurements indicate a hindering effect on the convergence speed. However the reduction of the search space, the positive effects of neutral mutations, and the structuring of the search space by decoder induced plateaus seem to outweigh those impeding characteristics.

Table 3 Examination of the local optima and plateau points in the fitness landscapes. A neighborhood of up to 4 mutations was computed and used for the assessment of the expected length and the minimal length until an improvement takes place with respect to the starting individual. Column 4 and 6 indicate the percentage of computed paths respectively shortest paths where a better point was found within 4 mutations. The averaged results consider all local optima and plateau points.

problem size ↓	technique	expected length min/avg/max	% < 5 min/avg/max	minimal length min/avg/max	% < 5 avg
6	1-bit HC	2.00/2.53/3.62	6/24/40	2.000/2.28/3.00	100
	diploid	2.92/3.15/3.76	3/10/27	2.00/2.15/3.00	100
	best fit dec.	2.68/3.28/3.63	36/38/42	2.00/2.11/3.00	100
	left to right dec.	2.33/2.65/3.54	10/40/65	2.00/2.13/3.00	100
	right to left dec.	2.80/2.88/3.03	17/33/67	2.00/2.00/2.00	100
10	1-bit HC	–/2.67/3.30	0/16/45	2.00/2.06/3.00	89
	diploid	–/2.97/4.00	0/6/24	2.00/2.12/4.00	92
	best fit dec.	–/2.78/3.68	0/5/7	2.00/2.33/3.00	86
	left to right dec.	–/2.84/4.00	0/9/31	2.00/2.44/4.00	90
	right to left dec.	–/2.07/3.22	0/7/26	2.00/2.00/2.00	71

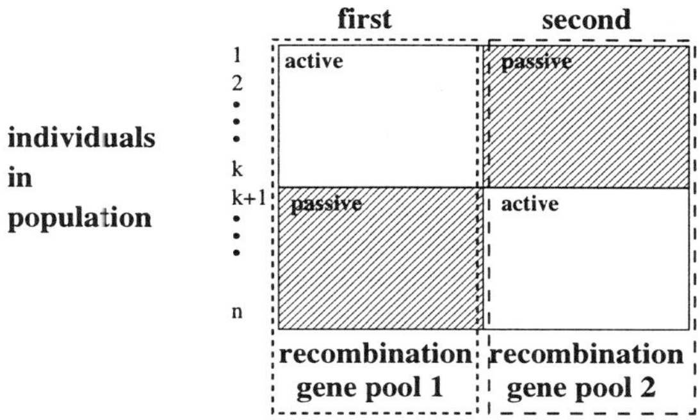

Figure 4 Separation of diploid algorithm into two recombination gene pools.

6 ANALYSIS III: RECOMBINATION

Analogously to the neutral mutation it is possible that redundancy results in neutral recombinations, where a recombination step is called neutral if the first parent and the offspring decode to the same phenotype.

Definition 5 (Neutral recombination) Let S be the phenotype space with fitness function $fit : S \to \mathbb{R}$ to be minimized. Let S' be the genotype space with a decoding function $decode : S' \to S$, and let $recombine : S' \times S' \times \Xi \to S'$ be a genetic operator that maps two points of the genotype space to another genotype depending on some random number of a set Ξ. Let $s_1', s_2' \in S'$ be redundant, i.e. $decode(s_1') = decode(s_2')$.

Then *recombine* is called a *neutral recombination for* s_1' *and* s_2' : $\Longleftrightarrow$

$$\exists x \in \Xi : decode(recombine(s_1', s_2', x)) \quad = \quad decode(s_1').$$

In both investigated techniques plateaus of redundant points arise building neutral networks and in both cases these plateaus allow neutral recombinations within the plateaus. But since the plateaus are expressible through schemata of words over the $\{0, 1, *\}$ (cf. Section 4) in case of the decoder and only through unions of schemata in case of the diploidity, the characteristics of the plateaus are quite different for the different techniques.

The recombination of two instances of a schema results again in an instance of that schema. So for the neutral plateaus that are formed by a single schema each recombination step is a neutral one. This means that the recombination cannot be disruptive within these plateaus. Rather, recombination forms another search operator that works without selection pressure.

In the diploid representation a plateau for a candidate solution $a_1 \ldots a_l$ can be described by $1\, a_1 \ldots a_l * \ldots * \cup 0 * \ldots * a_1 \ldots a_l$. This violates the requirement by Radcliffe's principle of minimal redundancy (Radcliffe, 1991) that redundant points should fall into the same schema (or the more general forma). In case of diploidity both schemata that form one plateau are complementary where the defined positions are disjunctive except the switch bit which is set with complementary values. This effect might be one important reason among others for negative reports on redundant codings. E.g. arbitrary permutations for coding cycles in the symmetric traveling salesperson problem do not support a generalized notion of locus-based formae, since the permutations may be shifted and reversed (Whitley et al., 1989).

Besides this effect a further assessment of the recombination operator in case of diploidity is difficult since the passive and active information form together two distinct gene pools (cf. Figure 4). This may have positive as well as negative effects. The interesting characteristics of the diploidity are the doubling in length of individuals and the separation of each individual in an active and a passive part.

On the one hand, the doubling in length of individuals does not affect the general working principle of the crossover operator. In case of uniform crossover there is no difference between short and long individuals. In case of k-point crossover operators, approximately a $2k$-point crossover was needed to get an equivalent behavior on a diploid candidate solution as in the standard binary case. Otherwise the significance of the crossover decreases.

On the other hand, the existence of active and passive information in one gene pool leads to the effect that premature convergence can be avoided by neutral mutations in passive candidate solutions which do not undergo the selection pressure. This positive effect can become a negative one if too many random passive changes impede a convergence at all and disturb the working principle of the crossover operator.

Summarizing there exist positive and negative effects of diploid representations on the recombination which are not quantifiable. On the problems examined, experiments using GA with and without recombination on diploid representations have shown no significant difference with respect to the performance in Figure 5. This is independent of the mutation rate.

The schemata arising through the use of a decoder have different characteristics. For the knapsack problem each introduced plateau is determined by a definite schema. Therefore, the crossover operator works on the neutral plateau as an additional neutral search operator.

The results of experiments using algorithms with a decoder have shown that there is also no significant performance difference between the algorithm using recombination and the algorithm without recombination (cf. left part of Figure 6).

7 ANALYSIS IV: DIVERSITY

This part of the analysis regards the effects of redundancy on the diversity in the population through neutral mutation and neutral recombination. One hypothesis is that redundancy preserves diversity in the population over the generations. Where a GA on a normal representation converges, i.e. the individuals in the population become identical, even if no global optimum is reached, the inclusion of redundancy causes a basic diversity in the population over time. This avoids early convergence of the algorithm and accordingly continued optimization may be possible.

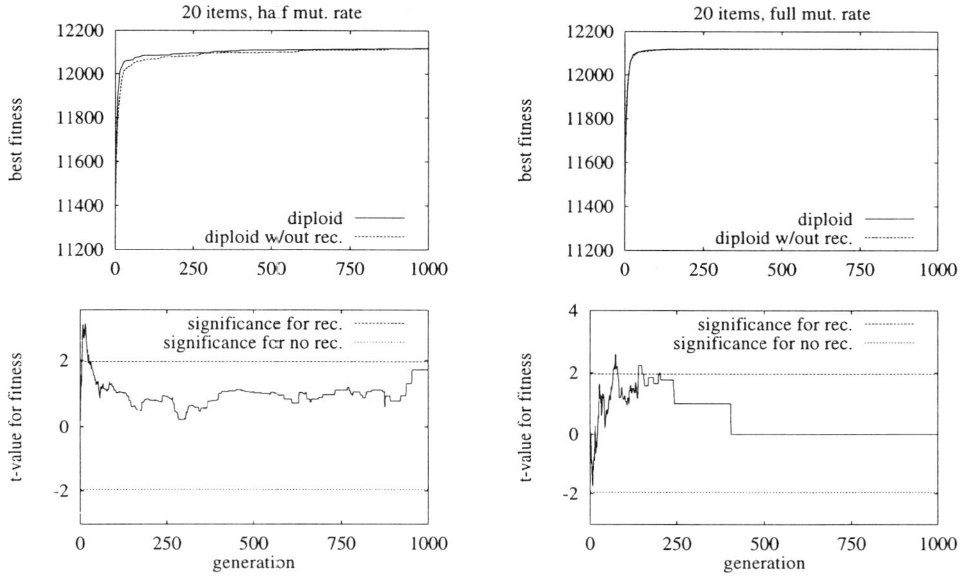

Figure 5 Left: fitness comparison of a diploid GA with recombination and a diploid GA without recombination, both with half mutation rate. The t-tests show that the superior performance of the algorithm with recombination is significant in the first few generations only. Right: fitness comparison of a diploid GA with recombination and a diploid GA without recombination, both with full mutation rate. The t-tests show that the difference in performance of the two algorithms is not significant.

For the assessment of the population's diversity the locus-wise variety in the population is considered which does not take into account the distribution of those values per locus to the individuals in the population. As an empirical measure the Shannon entropy is used.

In order to carry out a fair comparison between the different algorithms concerning the diversity, a phenotypic diversity is considered in case of the diploid algorithms – i.e. only those bits of the currently active solution of all individuals are used for the computation of the diversity.

Definition 6 (Entropy) Let $B = \{b_1, \ldots, b_n\}$ be a multiset of bits with $b_i \in \{0, 1\}$ $(1 \le i \le n)$ and the fractions $P_j(B) = \frac{|\{b \in B \mid b = j\}|}{|B|}$ for $j \in \{0, 1\}$. The B has the *Shannon entropy*

$$H(B) \quad = \quad -\sum_{j \in \{0,1\}} P_j(B) \log P_j(B).$$

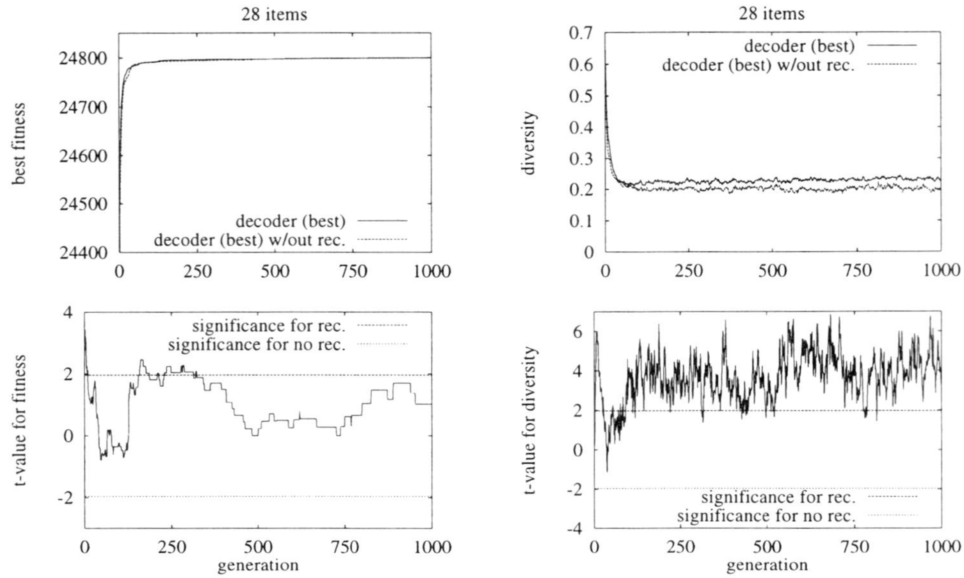

Figure 6 Left: fitness comparison of a GA with recombination and a GA without recombination, both using the best fit decoder. The t-tests show that the difference in performance of the two algorithms is not significant. Right: comparison of the diversity in each population of the same experiments. The t-tests show the higher diversity of the algorithm with recombination to be significant for most generations.

The *average entropy per locus* is defined for the multiset of individuals $P = \{I^{(i)} \in \{0,1\}^l \; |1 \leq i \leq n\}$ with length l as

$$\bar{H}(P) \quad = \quad \frac{1}{l}\sum_{k=1}^{l} H(B_k(P)),$$

where the bits of the different loci are cumulated in the multisets $B_k(P) = \{I_k^{(i)} \mid 1 \leq i \leq n\}$ $(1 \leq k \leq l)$ and I_k is the value in the k-th locus of individual I.

In case of diploidity a comparison to the standard GA shows that, although the performance does not change significantly, the diversity increases for mutation based algorithms (cf. Figure 1). Also Figure 7 shows an additional increase of the diversity by adding recombination to the algorithm using the full mutation rate. Interestingly, with a lower mutation rate there is no significant difference in diversity between recombination based and mutation based algorithms. Since the population average fitness does not change for both mutation rates when adding recombination (not shown in the figures), this indicates that a higher mutation rate enables a more efficient use of neutral recombinations. With a lower mutation rate the neutral recombination does not have an additional diversity increasing effect. The reason for this may be that with a lower mutation rate there exist too

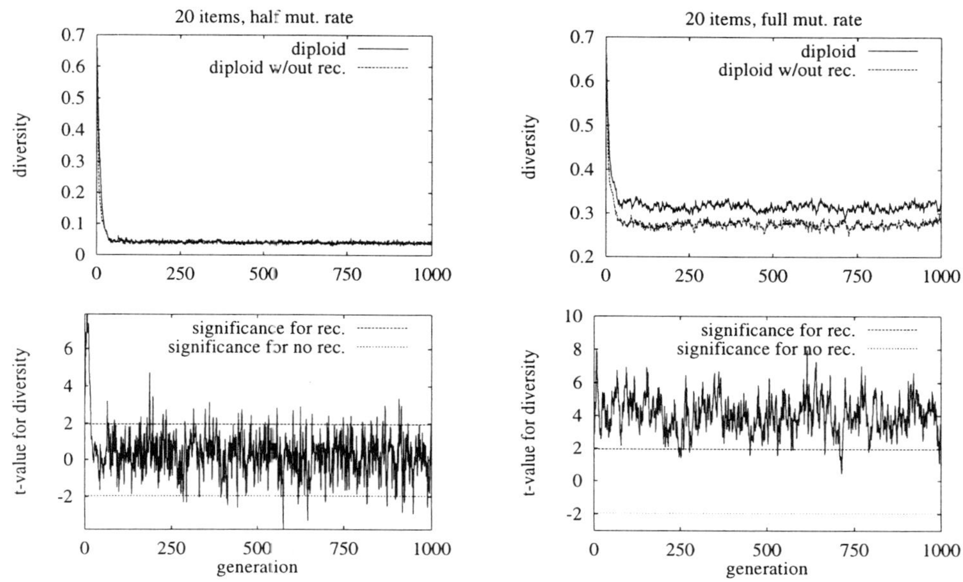

Figure 7 Left: diversity comparison of a diploid GA with recombination and a diploid GA without recombination, both with half mutation rate. The t-tests show the higher diversity of the algorithm with recombination to be significant in the very first few generations only. Right: diversity comparison of a diploid GA with recombination and a diploid GA without recombination, both with full mutation rate. The t-tests show the higher diversity of the algorithm with recombination to be significant.

few instances of one neutral plateau such that the neutral recombination can work. With a higher mutation rate the probability of a recombination of two instances of a neutral plateau is higher.

For the decoder the experiments verify the assumption that the redundancy results in a higher basic diversity in the population. Figure 3 displays the comparison to the standard GA where both algorithms use no recombination. Obviously both the performance as well as the diversity are higher for the decoder algorithm. As Figure 6 shows the addition of a 2-point crossover does increase the diversity which results only in a slight improvement of the performance that cannot shown to be significant.

8 ANALYSIS V: BENEFITS OF DIPLOIDITY – A CONTROL EXPERIMENT

The positive effect of a decoder is clear since on average it restricts the search space on better points (i.e. those that fulfill the constraints or that are local optima). Thus algorithms using a decoder can reach a very good solution very quickly. However this is not the case with diploid representations. Here the average fitness of the search space is

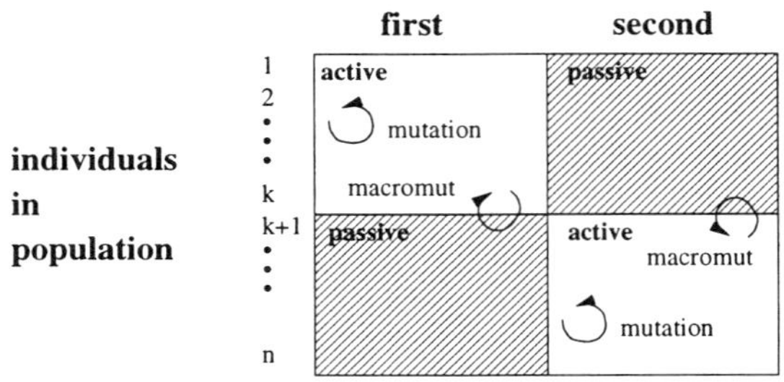

Figure 8 Separation of diploid algorithm into mutation and macromutation.

unaffected. Although the search space is enlarged drastically, a slight performance gain may be observed. Thus, the question arises which effects take place in diploid optimization.

One reason for those benefits might be the fact that half of the genome can explore the search space not being affected by selective pressure while the other half is the visible phenotype. As a consequence a hill climing algorithm cannot get trapped since there are no local optima left in the search space. Thus, in this section we want to examine the hypothesis that the benefitial effects of diploidity rely directly on the blind mutations in the passive part of the genome. To investigate this hypothesis we have designed the following control experiment.

The main idea for this examination is to transform the diploid into a haploid representation and to conserve the effects between active and passive solutions in an additional operator, a macro mutation. Note that this section is restricted to mutation only algorithms.

As it is sketched in Figure 8, all individuals can be classified into two groups depending on the activity status of both candidate solutions in the individual. If each candidate solution has a distinct fitness value, the fitness changes when a mutation takes place in the active candidate solution. In the figure those mutations can only occur in the unhatched set of solutions. In order to assess the impact of the remaining mutations the row of the first or the second candidate solutions in the individuals is considered. With probability $p'_m = \frac{1}{2l+1}$ the activity status changes for an individual and the previously visible candidate solution becomes passive. Now it undergoes approximately l mutations for each locus (each with mutation probability p_m). This behavior can be modeled using a "macromutation": a candidate solution disappears if it becomes passive, undergoes a number of neutral mutations, and re-appears again macromutated.

The standard GA is extended by a macromutation operator which consists of l independent mutations of the individual and is applied with probability p_m. If the macromutation is applied no normal mutation takes place. The macromutation we use is a substitute for diploidity in the same way that the macromutation introduced by Jones (1995) is a substitute for crossover.

The experiments (cf. Figure 9) show that, compared to Figure 1 the macromutation has not significantly worsened the performance of the standard GA. On the other hand the diversity was increased but the diversity of the diploid representation can still be considered to be significant.

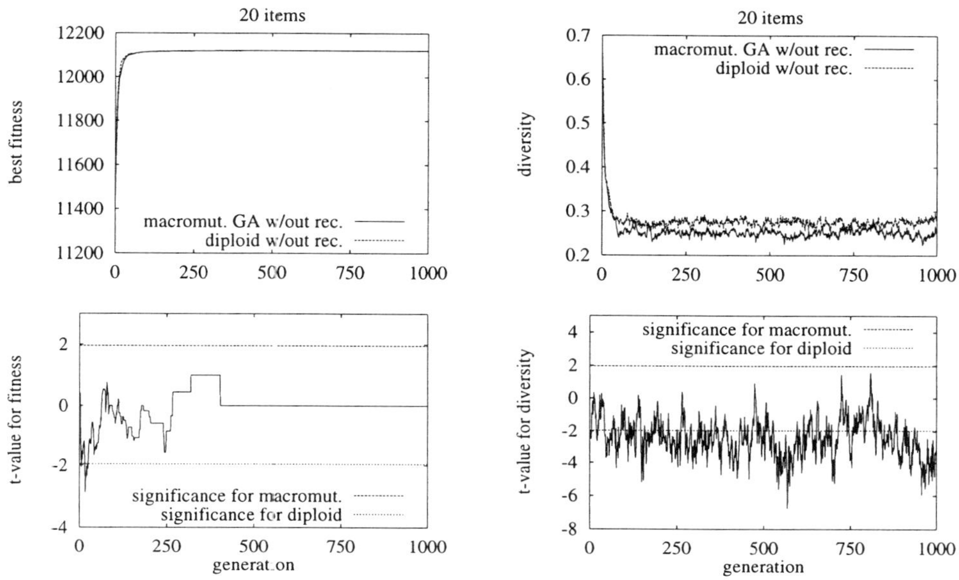

Figure 9 Left: fitness comparison of a GA with macromutation and a GA on a diploid representation. The difference in performance of the two algorithms is not significant. Right: comparison of the diversity in each population of the same experiments. The t-tests show the higher diversity of the diploid algorithm to be significant.

As a consequence we can conclude that a number of blind mutations is not enough to explain the benefitial effects of diploidity. Presumably the doubling of the. genetic information contained in the population as well as the dynamic behavior are at least as important as the passive mutations. Also the substituting macromutation misses the following point. In the diploid population, a candidate solution might deteriorate by switching the control bit, survive for several generations (due to tournament selection), and switch back to a slightly modified good solution. The macromutation cannot be undone in a similar manner.

9 CONCLUSION AND DISCUSSION

In order to conduct a deeper understanding of the effects of redundancy in the context of evolutionary computation two basic techniques introducing redundancy are investigated. These techniques are a simple diploid representation without any dominance mechanism on the one hand and the concept of intelligent decoders on the other. Although diploidity and decoders are completely different mechanisms to introduce redundancy – diploidity increases the search space drastically where decoders reduce the number of relevant candidate solutions – similar effects may be observed.

For both kinds of redundancy several different aspects are focussed on in our analysis and experiments. The interplay of redundancy and mutation results in a change of the number of local optima, plateau points, and the basins of attraction. Neutral mutations have been found to be one reason for this behavior. With respect to the two kinds of redundancy considered the most important difference results from the different sizes of neutral plateaus. Where the neutral mutations in the diploid representation are clearly defined, the effects with decoders depend highly on the concrete decoding function. Surprisingly decoders often produce a higher percentage of plateau points where diploid mechanisms always reduce it (at the expense of a drastic enlargement of the search space).

Besides this effect the influence of redundancy on the recombination operator and the conservation of diversity over the generations are examined. Both redundancy techniques allow neutral recombination to occur. For the diploidity the main effect of the neutral recombination can be seen in a higher diversity when the mutation rate is appropriate but not in the performance. For the decoder the neutral recombination has an effect on the performance in addition to promoting a higher diversity.

If we look at the complete diploid algorithm the positive effects seem to be predominantly with the removal of local optima, exploration by blind mutations, and the higher diversity for the recombination operator. However, this cannot affect search performance in a significant way due to the increased size of the representation, impeding neutral mutations and macromutations, and bigger basins of attraction. The control experiment shows that there are more effects taking place in diploidity which should be extracted and analyzed in future work.

The mechanism of decoders is much harder to analyze formally. One argument for this is, as already mentioned above, that each decoder behaves differently. A second explanation results from the different effects a decoder has on each point of the search space. For these reasons the analysis of the decoder is, at present, only scratching the surface.

However, as is the case with most research, this work provokes more questions than it answers. One of the open problems is the still unexplained working mechanism of the diploidity beyond the macromutation. Also the generalization of those results beyond the knapsack problem and for other techniques like different forms of diploidity with dominance mechanisms (e.g. Goldberg & Smith, 1987; Ng & Wong, 1995), the fitness controlled diploidity by Greene (1996), or the floating representations (Wu & Lindsay, 1997).

Summarizing, redundancy seems to be an interesting aspect which is worth investigation. However redundancy has many facets with various different characteristics. The mapping from those characteristics to the expected performance remains to be done. Future work will reveal more explanations of the effects and working principles of redundancy. In the meantime, our experiments and analyses have begun to explore some of the important issues and concepts that redundancy raises.

Acknowledgements

The authors would like to acknowledge the comments of the anonymous reviewers of this paper and especially the useful remarks of Richard Watson during copyediting.

References

Blickle, T., & Thiele, L. (1994). Genetic programming and redundancy. In J. Hopf (Ed.), *Genetic algorithms within the framework of evolutionary computation* (pp. 33–38). Saarbrücken, Germany.

Cohen, P. R. (1995). *Empirical methods for artificial intelligence*. Cambridge, MA: MIT Press.

Dasgupta, D. (1995). Incorporating redundancy and gene activation mechanisms in genetic search for adapting to non-stationary environments. In L. Chambers (Ed.), *Practical handbook of genetic algorithms, vol.2 – new frontiers* (pp. 303–316). Boca Raton: CRC Press.

Dasgupta, D., & McGregor, D. R. (1992). Nonstationary function optimization using the structured genetic algorithm. In R. Männer & B. Manderick (Eds.), *Parallel Problem Solving from Nature 2 (Proc. 2nd Int. Conf. on Parallel Problem Solving from Nature, Brussels 1992)* (pp. 145–154). Amsterdam: Elsevier.

Fogel, D. B., & Ghozeil, A. (1997). A note on representations and variation operators. *IEEE Trans. on Evolutionary Computation*, *1*(2), 159–161.

Goldberg, D. E., & Smith, R. E. (1987). Nonstationary function optimization using genetic algorithms with dominance and diploidy. In J. J. Grefenstette (Ed.), *Proc. of the Second Int. Conf. on Genetic Algorithms* (pp. 59–68). Hillsdale, NJ: Lawrence Erlbaum Associates.

Greene, F. (1996). A new approach to diploid/dominance and its effects on stationary genetic search. In L. J. Fogel, P. J. Angeline, & T. Bäck (Eds.), *Evolutionary Programming V: Proc. of the Fifth Annual Conf. on Evolutionary Programming* (pp. 171–176). Cambridge, MA: MIT Press.

Hinterding, R. (1994). Mapping order-independent genes and the knapsack problem. In *Proc. of the first IEEE int. conf. on evolutionary computation* (pp. 13–17). IEEE Press.

Hinterding, R. (1999). Representation, constraint satisfaction and the knapsack problem. In *1999 Congress on Evolutionary Computation* (pp. 1286–1292). Piscataway, NJ: IEEE Service Center.

Jones, T. (1995). Crossover, macromutation, and population-based search. In L. J. Eshelman (Ed.), *Proc. of the Sixth Int. Conf. on Genetic Algorithms* (pp. 73–80). San Francisco, CA: Morgan Kaufmann.

Julstrom, B. A. (1999). Redundant genetic encodings may not be harmful. In W. Banzhaf, J. Daida, A. E. Eiben, M. H. Garzon, V. Honavar, M. Jakiela, & R. E. Smith (Eds.), *Proc. of the Genetic and Evolutionary Computation Conf. GECCO-99* (p. 791). San Francisco, CA: Morgan Kaufmann.

Langdon, W. B., & Poli, R. (1997). Fitness causes bloat: Mutation. In J. Koza (Ed.), *Late breaking papers at the GP-97 conference* (pp. 132–140). Stanford, CA: Stanford Bookstore.

Leonhardi, A., Reissenberger, W., Schmelmer, T., Weicker, K., & Weicker, N. (1998). Development of problem-specific evolutionary algorithms. In A. E. Eiben, T. Bäck, M. Schoenauer, & H.-P. Schwefel (Eds.), *Parallel Problem Solving from Nature –*

PPSN V (pp. 388–397). Berlin: Springer. (Lecture Notes in Computer Science 1498)

Lewis, J., Hart, E., & Ritchie, G. (1998). A comparison of dominance mechanisms and simple mutation on non-stationary problems. In A. E. Eiben, T. Bäck, M. Schoenauer, & H.-P. Schwefel (Eds.), *Parallel Problem Solving from Nature – PPSN V* (pp. 139–148). Berlin: Springer. (Lecture Notes in Computer Science 1498)

Ng, K., & Wong, K. C. (1995). A new diploid scheme and dominance change mechanism for non-stationary function optimization. In L. Eshelman (Ed.), *Proc. of the Sixth Int. Conf. on Genetic Algorithms* (pp. 159–166). San Francisco, CA: Morgan Kaufmann.

Paechter, B., Cumming, A., Norman, M. G., & Luchian, H. (1995). Extensions to a memetic timetabling system. In E. K. Burke & P. M. Ross (Eds.), *Proc. of the First Int. Conf. on the Theory and Practice of Automated Timetabling* (pp. 251–263). : Springer.

Petersen, C. C. (1967). Computational experience with variants of the Balas algorithm applied to the selection of R&D projects. *Management Science, 13*(9), 736–750.

Radcliffe, N. J. (1991). Equivalence class analysis of genetic algorithms. *Complex Systems, 5*, 183–205.

Shackleton, M., Shipman, R., & Ebner, M. (2000). An investigation of redundant genotype-phenotype mappings and their role in evolutionary search. In *Proc. of the 2000 Congress on Evolutionary Computation* (pp. 493–500). Piscataway, NJ: IEEE Service Center.

Whitley, D. L., Starkweather, T., & Fuquay, D. (1989). Scheduling problems and travelling salesman: The genetic edge recombination operator. In J. D. Schaffer (Ed.), *Proc. of the Third Int. Conf. on Genetic Algorithms* (pp. 133–140). San Mateo, CA: Morgan Kaufmann.

Wu, A. S., & De Jong, K. A. (1999). An examination of building block dynamics in different representations. In *1999 Congress on Evolutionary Computation* (pp. 715–721). Piscataway, NJ: IEEE Service Center.

Wu, A. S., & Lindsay, R. K. (1997). A comparison of the fixed and floating building block representation in the genetic algorithm. *Evolutionary Computation, 4*(2), 169–193.

Appendix – Fitness computation and problem

The first table shows the exact values of the fitness computation described in the article.

Fitness computation			
problem	base fitness	penalty term	best fitness (inclusive base fitness)
6 items	3800.0	380.0	7600.0
10 items	8000.0	800.0	16706.1
20 items	6000.0	600.0	12120.0
28 items	12400.0	1240.0	24800.0

In the following two tables the problem data of the two small problems is given. In the tables each row corresponds to an item of the problem. Each column corresponds to one weight constraint or the value of the item. The bottom row of each table shows the upper bounds for the weight constraints. The optimal solutions of each problam are indicated by bold face numbers of the contained items.

Problem with 6 items

Item	Weight 1	2	3	4	5	6	7	Value
1	8	8	3	5	5	5	3	100
2	12	12	6	10	13	13	2	600
3	13	13	4	8	8	8	4	1200
4	64	75	18	32	42	48	8	2400
5	22	22	6	6	6	6	8	500
6	41	41	4	12	20	20	4	2000
$\leq$	80	96	20	36	44	48	24	

Problem with 10 items

Item	Weight 1	2	3	4	5	6	7	8	9	10	Value
1	20	20	60	60	60	60	5	45	55	65	600.1
2	5	7	3	8	13	13	2	14	14	14	310.5
3	100	130	50	70	70	70	20	80	80	80	1800
4	200	280	100	200	250	280	100	180	200	220	3850
5	2	2	4	4	4	4	2	6	6	6	18.6
6	4	8	2	6	10	10	5	10	10	10	198.7
7	60	110	20	40	60	70	10	40	50	50	882
8	150	210	40	70	90	105	60	100	140	180	4200
9	80	100	6	16	20	22	0	20	30	30	402.5
10	40	40	12	20	24	28	0	0	40	50	327
$\leq$	450	540	200	360	440	480	200	360	440	480	

Author Index

Key Word Index